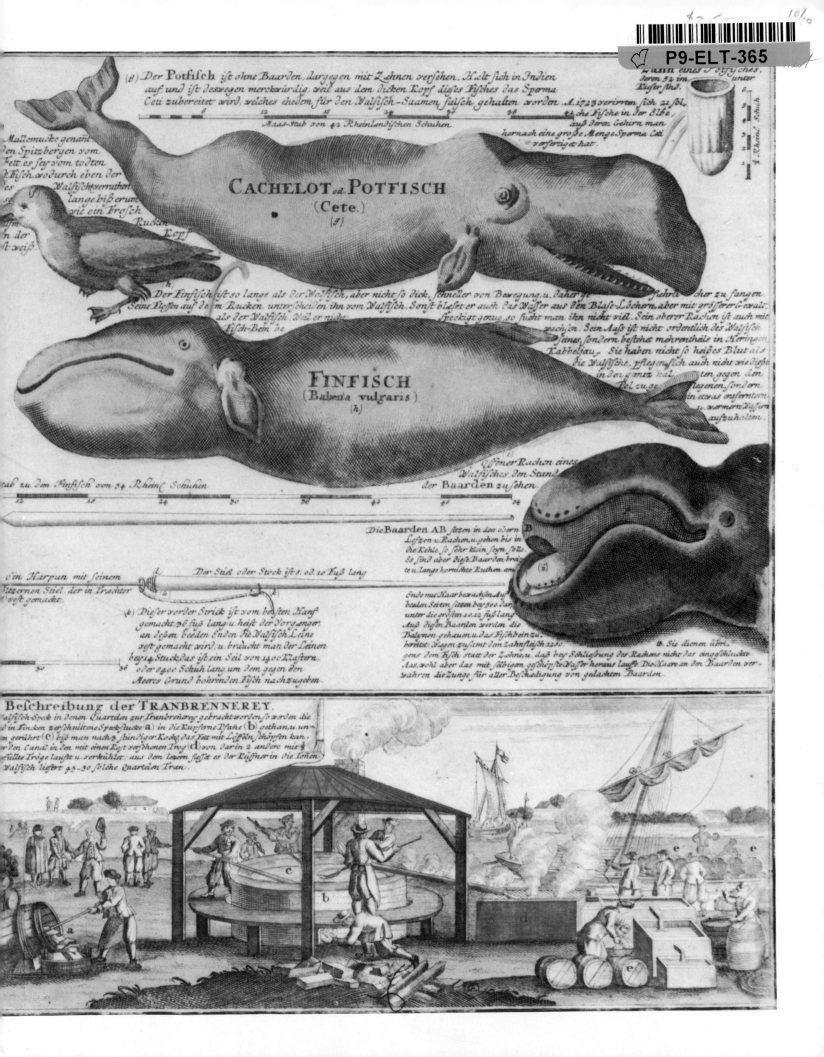

Also by Richard Ellis

THE BOOK OF WHALES

DOLPHINS AND PORPOISES

THE BOOK OF SHARKS

MEN AND WHALES

MEN AND WHALES

RICHARD ELLIS

ALFRED A. KNOPF · NEW YORK 1991

Grateful acknowledgment is made to the following for permission to reprint previously published material:
Alfred A. Knopf, Inc., and *Penguin USA:* Excerpt from *Going to Extremes* by Joe McGinniss. Copyright © 1980 by Joe McGinniss. Rights in the U.K. administered by Penguin USA. Reprinted by permission of Alfred A. Knopf, Inc., and Penguin USA.
Macmillan Publishing Company and *Laurence Pollinger Ltd.:* Excerpt from *Give Me a Ship to Sail* by Alan Villiers. Copyright © 1958, 1959 by Alan Villiers. Copyright renewed. Rights in the U.K. administered by Laurence Pollinger Ltd. Reprinted by permission of Charles Scribner's Sons, an imprint of Macmillan Publishing Company, and of Laurence Pollinger Ltd. on behalf of the Estate of Alan Villiers.
Melanie Jackson Agency: Excerpt from *The Language of Clothes* by Alison Lurie. Copyright © 1981 by Alison Lurie. Reprinted by permission of Melanie Jackson Agency.
Unwin Hyman: Excerpt from *Whales* by E. J. Slipjer. Reprinted by permission of Unwin Hyman, a division of HarperCollins Publishers Limited.

Excerpt from *Warriors of the Rainbow* by Robert Hunter, Henry Holt and Company, Inc.
Excerpt from *Children of the Light* by Everett Allen, Little, Brown and Company.

For illustration credits, see page 537.

Library of Congress Cataloging-in-Publication Data
Ellis, Richard, [*date*]

Men and whales / by Richard Ellis.—1st ed.
    p.   cm.
ISBN 0-394-55839-1
    1. Whaling—History.   2. Whales.   I. Title.
SH383.E36   1991
639.2'8—dc20   90-40616
                                                   CIP

Manufactured in the United States of America
First Edition

Endpapers: Engraving from the Nuremberg (1760) edition of the 1720 Dutch work by C. F. Zorgdrager of the Greenland whale fishery.

Frontispiece: The glory days of Yankee whaling, as portrayed by Clifford Ashley. A gam between the bark *Sunbeam* and the ship *James Arnold.*

Contents

Introduction

The history of whaling is made up of a number of chapters each covering a few centuries and all more or less repeating the same pattern. They resemble the one which has now come to an end in the Antarctic. Each begins with a new discovery and hopeful enterprise, passing through a phase of fierce competition and ruthless exploitation with improving techniques and ended at length in diminishing resources, exhaustion and failure. Man has been both blind and ignorant in the pursuit of the whale, for although whales have been hunted off the coast of Europe certainly since the ninth century it never occurred to anyone to even describe them until the end of the seventeenth. . . .

F. D. OMMANNEY
Lost Leviathan

ALTHOUGH it comes first, the introduction to a book is actually written last. If it were otherwise, the writer would have to set himself a particular task at the outset, and then cleave steadfastly to it from beginning to end. This might be possible in a chronology, where you commence at a given date and pursue the subject to another date, but in something as complex as a *history,* where there are so many extenuating factors at work, the author sometimes feels as if he is completely at the mercy of the events he is writing about, and feels lucky if he finishes at all, let alone finishes what he started to write about.

This has been that sort of project. I wanted to write about the intertwined destinies of whales and men, and since most of that story has concerned the ways in which men killed whales, I knew that the bulk of the story would be about whaling history. It is. But what was supposed to have been a story with a modest beginning (the discovery of the whale by ancient man), a copious middle (the rise of the whaling industry), and a smashing ending (the fall of the whaling industry) somehow became a series of be-

ginnings, where various countries were discovered and settled, if not exclusively by whalers, then in conjunction with them; a plethora of middles, wherein various nations pursued sundry species of whales around the world (or in some cases, in their very front yards); and one ending after another, where a nation abandoned whaling, a species of whale became extinct, or in some cases, where there was no identifiable conclusion at all. The beginnings were all exciting; the middles were richer than I suspected; and the endings regularly surprised me, in their variety, their scope, and their complexities.

I knew that the history of whales preceded the history of mankind, and that therefore the actual beginning of this story was not going to be found. We don't know much about where whales came from, but we do know—perhaps "know" is too strong a word here; we *think* we know—that there were whales on earth long before there were men to see them. There were fossil whalebones found high in the Himalayas, indicating . . . what? That the ancestral whales lived in the mountains? That the Himalayas used to be underwater? The ancestors of whales had legs, fore and aft. This is evident in an examination of the skeletal structure of the whales; they have rudimentary bones where their hind legs should be, and their flippers contain the five-fingered *manus* of all terrestrial mammals. (These X-ray "hands" have led to the egregiously erroneous supposition that whales and dolphins are closely related to people.) And of course, the cetaceans are mammals that give birth to living young that they nurse; they breathe air; and they maintain a constant body temperature despite living from birth to death in a medium that would seem to be totally alien to all these activities.

The evolutionary path that whales took to return

to the sea is a mystery. They (and the unrelated man-atees) seem to be the only living mammals that have made this return journey; seals and sea lions are mammals that feed and travel at sea but breed and give birth on land. If we accept the notion that there has been a sort of "progression" from fish to amphibian to reptile to mammal, we see that it leads out of the water, not back into it. (That is not to say that mammals are descended from reptiles or amphibians from fishes, but only that the earliest vertebrates were aquatic, while some of the more recent developments have been terrestrial.) We believe that whales are descended from terrestrial mammals, but we don't know if the baleen whales are descended from one sort of ancestral kind of mammal and the toothed whales from another. (A similar mystery attends the evolution of our own species, where we are not at all sure what the evolutionary tree looks like. At least we don't have to worry about what happened to the hind legs. . . .)

Once upon a time, however, a whale died and washed up on some shore somewhere, and some sort of man—probably walking on *his* hind legs, although the whale had long since lost his—looked at it and found it big. The reasons that the descendants of that man began to kill the descendants of that whale are complex and varied, but they probably have to do with food. If we accept food and shelter as two of the requirements for the maintenance of the human species, it seems obvious that a dead whale represented tons and tons of food, and therefore fulfilled a basic need, albeit sporadically.

The Egyptians used olive oil for lighting and lubrication, and candles made of other oils such as tallow and beeswax have been in use for thousands of years. If they were lighted at all, medieval houses were lighted with rushes impregnated with animal fats, or they were lighted with wood fires, which were relatively dangerous and difficult to control. Primitive lamps consisted of a vessel that held some sort of oil and a wick that allowed for controlled burning. Certain seeds, such as castor bean, sesame, cottonseed, linseed and rapeseed, yield the so-called vegetable oils when pressed, and when geographical expansion led to the discovery of the coconut palm, its oil was used alongside the others for lubrication and the manufacture of foodstuffs, soaps, varnishes and various other products. Fats and oils are indis-

pensable to domestic life, and the discovery that there was a source of these unguents that did not have to be cultivated, but only harvested, had a salutary effect on the development of European civilization, and a correspondingly devastating effect on the whales.

The oil of the baleen whale is of a type commonly found in a variety of plants and animals, and in fact it is identical in composition to human fat. Whale oil is a true fatty acid, consisting almost entirely of triglycerides, one molecule of glycerine in combination with three of fatty acids. The fatty acids can be combined with an alkali to produce soap, and the glycerol (also known as glycerine) can be used in the manufacture of emollients and explosives. It is also edible, but it was not utilized extensively until the beginning of the twentieth century, when the process known as hydrogenation was developed. By adding two hydrogen atoms to the oleic acid (the commonest fatty acid in whale oil), the oil was changed into a solid fat. Hydrogenated whale oil can be used in the manufacture of margarine, which innovation would have a devastating effect on the world's baleen whale populations in the 1930s.

The "oil" of the toothed whales—particularly that found in the heads of the sperm whale and various species of dolphins—is not technically an oil at all but a wax, a condensation product (ester) of mono-alcohols and fatty acids, that yields the finest candles ever made and would seem to have outlived its usefulness with the discovery of petroleum. Ever innovative, mankind quickly developed more and better uses for sperm oil, incorporating it into steelmaking (for the process known as "quenching"), leather dressing, textile sizing, and again, soapmaking. When treated with sulfur, a process known as sulfurization, sperm oil becomes one of the best lubricants known, and was regularly used as a component in automatic transmission fluids. In a 1977 article on cetacean oils, biochemist Ron Scogin wrote, "This oil has been regarded as so crucial to our national defense that a large stockpile is probably still being maintained for national emergencies."

As soon as he could (women do not figure in the history of whaling until well into the sixteenth century, when they began demanding that their husbands bring home whalebone for corsets) man took to the sea to begin a thousand-year war against the whales. The first skirmishes occurred in the relatively secluded Bay of Biscay, but when the Basques recognized that the killing of whales was good business (a realization that would govern whalers for the rest of their variegated careers), they expanded their killing to another front. They headed across the Atlantic to Newfoundland, where they found more of the "right" whales to kill. On the lookout for oil and the stuff they called "whalebone," which was really a fibrous material that grew from the roof of the mouth of some whale species, whalers from Britain and Holland headed north (originally with Basque harpooners aboard), and threw themselves enthusiastically (albeit coldly) into the business of killing all the Greenland whales they could.

Because whaling has always been attended by tales of heroism, and of killing the great creatures in the face of hostile elements—not to mention the whales' reluctance to be killed, which presented further dangers—it has come down to us as a noble and occasionally even enlightened profession. In the early years of the industry, when men attacked whales with slim iron harpoons, and then held on for dear life, there was a possibility that the whale might triumph. Not that the whales would kill the men and boil them down into fertilizer; rather, for a hunted animal, "triumph" means escape, and many of the whales did indeed escape, a testimony to their determination to stay alive, but also a reflection on the inefficiency of old-time whaling techniques. Hanging on to a wounded, 60-ton animal with a length of rope attached to a bouncing rowboat is nobody's idea of efficient hunting, and the whales so attached occasionally broke the line and escaped, or upended the boat in their flurry. A thrashing whale attached to a boat might easily smash the boat as it tried to escape the searing pain of the harpoon thrust into its vitals. (It was the instinctive response to the pain of a six-foot harpoon in their bodies that caused the whales to flail and react violently, which in turn produced stories—*Moby-Dick* comes to mind first—of savage leviathans that attacked the intrepid whalermen, often for no reason.)

It was a dangerous profession, and many whalemen did not return from voyages to the remote corners of the world. The very nature of the voyages also added to the mystique of whaling; if there were whales to be found in Greenland waters, or off the Galapagos, the Azores, the Marquesas or Tonga; in the Bering, the Sulu or the Tasman Sea; and eventually, in the most remote area in the world, the Antarctic, well, the brave whalers would find them. If it meant three- or four-year voyages with exposure to the great variety of nature's hostilities including cold, heat, rain, snow, scurvy, typhoons, icebergs and cannibals, the whalemen were up to it. They came back with marvelous tales of the South Seas, of Esquimaux, of inscrutable Japanese, of birds that stood upright and others that never set foot on land; of gigantic seals and piebald killer whales—in short, they opened the eyes of the world to the wonders of the sea not only as a road to somewhere else.

IT WAS the nature of some of these whales—called by the whalers the "right" whales because they had thick blubber, they didn't swim too fast for the little boats, and they floated when they were killed—to come close to certain shores to breed. They preferred bays and inlets that were protected from the open sea, a preference that they shared with the settlers who would establish a beachhead for "civilization" in these same protected bays and inlets. Unlike the aborigines whom these settlers sometimes encountered, the whales never disputed the ownership of the land; they innocently required only breeding and calving grounds away from the rough seas and the possible predations of sharks and killer whales.

The settlers looked at the broad backs of the right whales and saw not their grace and beauty, but rather floating oil factories, and more enticingly, floating oil factories that they didn't have to maintain. All they had to do was harvest the limitless bounty, usually for the price of a boat. The right whales died in Siberian waters as soon as these areas were discovered by Russian explorers; in Massachusetts at the hands of the first American settlers; in Table Bay and False Bay in South Africa when the Huguenots arrived there; in Tasmania and Botany Bay when the British transported their first shiploads of convicts; and in the Pacific Northwest when Alaska and Vancouver were settled. (The early Japanese whalers, exhibiting an ecological sensitivity that their descendants did not inherit, were protective of right whale females with calves, and would not kill them.) Only off the barren coast of southern Argentina were the right whales untroubled, because nobody was interested in settling the land. (Even today, there are but a few sheep ranches along the remote South Atlantic coasts of Patagonia, and the sole undisturbed population of right whales in the world still comes to breed in the bays of Golfo San José and Golfo Nuevo.

All these areas also had a smaller population of humpbacks. Humpbacks were far from being the "right" whales to kill; they were usually skinny, had negligible baleen, and sank when they were killed. Nevertheless, the whalers picked them off whenever and wherever they found them. It would not be until 1970—when most of the world's humpbacks had been annihilated—that we would learn that humpback whales were unique in that they sang complex, mysterious songs, but we had virtually eliminated the whales before we could learn what—if anything—the songs meant.

Other species of whales fared just as badly at the hands of the first whalers. After they had reduced the inshore populations of right whales and humpbacks, the whalers discovered that there were whales in the far north that were even *more* right: they had all the attributes of their smaller relatives, but they were bigger, and therefore had more fat that could be boiled into oil and longer baleen plates to satisfy the bottomless maw of Dame Fashion. These whales, known variously as Greenland whales, polar whales or bowheads, are found only in the circumpolar Arctic, and from the sixteenth century to late in the nineteenth, they were killed with such celerity and determination that there are hardly any left.

The story of commercial whaling has been a story of unrelieved greed and insensitivity. In no other activity has our species practiced such a relentless pursuit of wild animals, and if no whale species has become extinct at the hands of the whalers, it has not been for want of trying. They came close with the right whales and the humpbacks; they killed off the bowheads until it was uneconomical to look for any more; they followed the gray whales into their breeding areas in Korea, China, Japan and California, and killed so many of them that by 1930 the species was thought to be gone from the face of the earth. The proud Yankee whalers in their square-rigged ships scoured the Seven Seas so that they could decimate the world's sperm whale populations.

The early whalers achieved these dubious victories with primitive weapons; imagine what they might have done given the ordnance to properly wage the war on the whales. For 850 years of this thousand-year war, the whalers depended upon hand-thrown harpoons. Progress for the early nineteenth-century whaler meant a new toggle design for the harpoon head, or a previously undiscovered stock of whales to throw it at. Of the ten species of "great" whales, five were slaughtered to the brink of extinction in those first eight and a half centuries. The other five—the blue, fin, sei, Bryde's and minke—were designed differently, and although they were seen with disconcerting regularity by the whalers, they swam tantalizingly out of the range and competence of harpooners. These species belong to a group known collectively as the rorquals (from the Norwegian for "grooved whale"), and they are characterized by a series of longitudinal pleats along the throat and belly which enable them to expand their throats as they engulf huge quantities of sea water and small sea creatures. All of these whales are slim and graceful—although one species can weigh as much as 200 tons—and they are capable of speeds that made them completely inaccessible to men in rowing boats.

The rorquals are largely missing from the early history of whaling because the whalers could not catch them, and because, even if they had succeeded, they had no way of handling an animal that weighed 300,000 pounds. To make matters worse for the whalers—but better for the whales—these animals inconveniently sank if and when they were killed, and the only thing worse than trying to handle a 300,000-pound animal at sea is trying to handle a 300,000-pound animal that has sunk. Whaling historians were almost ready to write *finis* to their subject when the populations of right, bowhead, humpback, gray and sperm whales seemed to be at such low levels that there was no point in chasing them any more. Besides, petroleum had been discovered in Pennsylvania in 1859, and it appeared that the need to risk life and limb in chases of dangerous whales had passed. It was almost as if the rorquals had received a pardon.

But of course they hadn't; they received instead a judgment so merciless that it amounted to a generic death sentence. Instead of ignoring the rorquals, the whalers developed a way of chasing and killing them that would bring them to even lower levels than their predecessors in whaling history.

The Norwegian Svend Foyn invented the exploding grenade harpoon.

From 1868 to the present day, virtually every whale killed by the hand of man has been killed by Foyn's inventions. (The only exceptions are the whales that are killed by aborigines who can't afford the heavy artillery.) With the grenade harpoon and the bow-mounted cannon from which to fire it from a steam-powered catcher boat, the heretofore unaccessible rorquals were brought within range.

Now, armed with 200-pound iron shafts that spread foot-long toggles into the body of the whale, and equipped with tubes through which compressed air could be pumped into the body of the dead whale to keep it afloat, powerful catcher-killer boats roamed the oceans seeking out the great blue and fin whales, the smaller sei and Bryde's whales, and the relatively small minke whales. (In fact, the animals are small only by cetacean standards; a full-grown minke can get to be 33 feet long and weigh 10 tons.) The whalers added to their arsenal as technology provided them with more ways to kill and process whales. Once they had found the way to kill the giants, they began to process them in a more modern fashion. The Dutch and British whalers of the seventeenth century had peeled the carcasses at sea, minced the blubber and stuffed it through the bungholes of wooden barrels; then the Nantucket sperm whalers tried-out the whales in iron caldrons on the decks of their sailing ships and fed the fires with the whales' own kindling, when they used the unburned scraps of skin to feed the try-pot fires. Various other whalers did their dirty work on shore, dragging the bloody carcasses up ramps to be reduced to their components in the heat of the Australian or New Zealand sun. When progress came to whale-processing, it came in a swift and deadly form: the invention of the stern slipway, a gaping chute in the rear of a factory ship meant that 100-foot whales could be hauled up on deck and flensed at sea; the whalemen were no longer tied to land stations. Ten-ton pressure cookers received the chopped-up bone and meat and reduced it to meal for use as fertilizer. The oil was stored in steel tanks and transported across the world to be turned into margarine, soap and pharmaceuticals. For the First World War, whale oil was reduced to its glyceride components which in turn were used in the manufacture of nitroglycerine. The second time the industrial nations of the world turned their guns on each other, they concurrently killed whales for oil, meat and margarine.

In war or in peace, whalers always managed to find a way to justify the slaughter. The discovery of petroleum, instead of sparing the whales, provided fuel for the steamers and diesel catchers to get to the far reaches of the globe where the whales could be found. We needed oil for candles or for lighting; corsets and skirts had to be braced with whalebone strips; oil was required to make soap and margarine; hungry people wanted the meat; the livers provided vitamins; men needed work; national pride would be affected if some other country caught more whales. And throughout the history of whaling, as the numbers of whales caught began to decline, the whalers simply escalated their hunting effort. It appeared that everyone knew the whales were being hunted out of existence, but nobody wanted to acknowledge it. Besides, if one nation stopped whaling, or even reduced its effort, the others would obviously move in.

From the day in 1868 when Svend Foyn of Vestfold trained his primitive harpoon cannon on the first blue whale, the numbers of *Balaenoptera musculus* began to decline, and not until it was far too late did anyone recognize that whalers were methodically eliminating the grandest animal that ever lived. They killed them in the North Atlantic and the North Pacific, in the South Atlantic and the Indian Ocean, but the greatest concentration of these magnificent creatures was in the high latitudes of the Antarctic, and the whalers only found their way there after the turn of this century. They then commenced to murder these gentle, 100-foot giants. Because the whalers had ingeniously invented a scheme that concentrated all their efforts on the killing of blue whales, the other species were ignored until the blues became too scarce. Then they turned on the next smallest species, and the next and the next.

Throughout this millennial war on whales, various nations have risen to an uncertain ascendancy. Circumstances allowed the Dutch, the British, the Norwegians or the Japanese to take the lead in the race to eliminate the whales, but other factors usually knocked them from their precarious domination and allowed another nation to pass them in the statistical sweepstakes. Aboriginal whaling was primitive and economical; the numbers of whales were safe because the whalers couldn't have affected the populations even if they had wanted to. When the spectre of commercial greed appeared, however, the stakes were raised. What had been a subsistence activity became a business, and the whales suffered in direct proportion to the prosperity of the whaling communities— the more successful the whaling, the more whales died. It has been said that a rational management scheme (instead of the uncontrolled hunting which allowed the whalers to decide what was best for business) could have provided an almost endless supply of whale meat and oil to the world. Instead, the whaling nations fought amongst themselves for the right to eliminate whale species, and in some cases, came close to achieving this dubious goal. While their economies often suffered—often as a function of bad management—the consequences were nothing compared to the suffering of the whales. If the whaleman was lonely, uncomfortable, cold or hungry, or even if his life was threatened, those were minor inconveniences compared to the massive agony visited upon the whales. Defenseless, trusting creatures, whose size probably precluded a knowledge of fear, the whales were chased until they were exhausted, stabbed and blown up, their babies slaughtered, their numbers reduced to such levels that the very existence of some species was precarious. And still the whalers persisted, convincing themselves that the killing was being done in the name of progress, technology, gross national product, gross national pride, or whatever gods technological man invokes to justify his atrocities against nature.

Are there now or were there ever reasons for this senseless slaughter? Some men died in pursuit of the whale, but a vastly disproportionate number of whales died in this cetacean world war, a war in which one side was heavily armed and the other almost defenseless, obviously because only one side knew there was a war going on. There have been volumes written on the courage of the warriors who risked their lives so that the whales might die for technology and fashion. At one time, whale oil was important for lighting the lamps of Europe and America. But even if we allow for the expediency of whale-killing to avoid darkness, we must still search for the rationale for the prodigious slaughter that followed the discovery of petroleum. Whales were

killed by the hundreds of thousands, in perhaps the most callous demonstration history offers of mankind's self-appointed dominion over animals. We search almost in vain for an expression of sympathy, compassion, understanding or rationality. In their place there was only insensitivity and avarice.

In the long, gory history of whaling, certain fundamental axioms prevail, none of them pleasant. Invariably, the whalers reacted to the depletion of their "resource" when it was too late. If a particular species of whale was in short supply, they simply went after another. Even the conservation community's rally to "save the whales" arrived too late with too little. The grass-roots movement that led to the passage of the whaling moratorium of 1982 was begun only around 1972, when the whalers had already destroyed most of the whales.

In their voluminous logbooks and journals, the whalers have documented the slaughter of the innocents in the name of progress. Was there ever another course? Could the whales have been saved? Yes. It is only when the signals are clear and unequivocal and still we do not act that we can be held accountable. The whaling nations might be excused for not focusing on the whaling problem in 1937; there were other cases before the world court. But when the Second World War was over and the whalers came to Washington to hammer out an agreement to control the whaling industry, they ended up producing a document that virtually guaranteed the elimination of the whales—and the industry, as it turned out. It was one of the most short-sighted exercises in the history of international negotiations. With eight hundred years of history to guide them, the whalers condemned themselves to repeat all the mistakes that had been made before. By 1946, the framers of the International Convention for the Regulation of Whaling knew all about the destruction of the right whales and the disappearance of the Arctic bowheads. They had before them the bitter documentation of the decline of the Pacific gray whale. And yet they persisted: they designed a system to oversee the destruction of the remaining whales of the world.

BECAUSE whaling has been greatly reduced by the 1982 moratorium and by the decimation of whales, this book would not have benefited from extensive research in the field today. Thirty years ago, the case would have been very different. To research a book about whaling then, I might have tried to wangle my way onto an Antarctic whaling voyage, perhaps on the British factory ship *Balaena.* I might have visited the American whaling station at Richmond, California, and watched them work up a couple of humpbacks or gray whales. I could have gone to Sandefjord, Norway, in the spring, and watched the kill statistics come in from the Norwegians, the British, the Japanese and the Dutch. If I had gone to the International Whaling Commission (IWC) meeting, say, in 1959, I would have gone to London, and witnessed the Norwegians and the Dutch walk out. I couldn't have watched the Alaskan Eskimos catch a bowhead, however—they hadn't started this high-tech "aboriginal" hunt yet.

I did manage to do some field research, however, and some of it was in the front lines of the whaling wars. In 1981, at the invitation of the Japanese Whaling Association, I went to Japan and shipped out on a Japanese coastal whaling voyage. I was never really sure why they invited me—I was one of the most vocal critics of their whaling policy—and there were moments when I worried that they had asked me in order to throw me overboard into the North Pacific. I watched the whalers kill a Bryde's whale, and I saw the operations at the whaling stations at Taiji and Wadaura. The Japanese didn't get me to change my mind about whaling, but they did allow me to better understand their point of view. I have seen the whaling village of Lomblen, in Indonesia, and watched the harpooners leap from their *proas.* I have visited the whaling stations at Albany, Western Australia, and Durban, South Africa—both now closed. I have seen the remnants of the whaling station at Tangalooma, Queensland, now transformed into a resort hotel, and the site of the Beacon Island station in Plettenberg Bay, South Africa. I have gone to the whaling station in Horta, in the Azores, and seen piles of sperm whale bones drying on the shingle. I have been in the American whaling towns of Nantucket, New Bedford, Fairhaven, Salem, Mystic, Sag Harbor, San Francisco, Richmond, Honolulu, and Lahaina (Maui). Many of these places have—or even *are*—museums, and in almost all of them I was given access to files, journals, artifacts, photographs, personnel. Since 1980, I have been a member of the United States delegation to the International Whaling Commission, and I have attended meetings in England, Argentina, Sweden, New Zealand and California. I have observed living whales all over the world, from New York to New Zealand. Of the world's "great" whale species, I have seen them all, alive in the ocean, except the bowhead.

With all that travel compressed into a single paragraph, it appears as if I were constantly on the move, visiting whaling stations, sitting in meetings, saving whales. In reality I spent most of my time in my office or in various libraries, tracking down elusive references and trying to absorb and make sense of the deluge of information that exists on the incredibly complex subject I innocently chose to write about.

In the course of all these adventures, at home and abroad, I received help and encouragement from so many sources that it would be impossible to acknowledge them all in this limited space. There are many people whose names I never knew, such as the cook aboard the *Toshi Maru No. 18* who made me a welcome "Western" breakfast of white bread and scrambled eggs when I boarded his ship at four in the morning off Wada, or the man who showed me the squash court where the flensing platform at Tangalooma had once stood.

My earliest professional involvement with whales came through my friendship with David Hill, who kindly invited me to accompany him on freezing street corners in Manhattan and solicit signatures on petitions as we shouted "Save the Whales! Boycott Japanese Goods!" David and I then collaborated on the 1975 *Audubon* magazine article "Vanishing Giants," for which he wrote the text and I did the illustrations. Les Line, the editor of *Audubon,* encouraged us on this project—which indirectly led to the 1980 publication of my *Book of Whales.* At the International Whaling Commission, I was helped and advised (even though my official designation was "adviser") by the four United States commissioners with whom I had the honor to serve: Richard Frank, John Byrne, Anthony Calio and Bill Evans. For the first years of my participation, I represented the National Audubon Society, and I want to thank Glenn Paulsen, Les Line and Marty Hill for their support. Later I represented the Oceanic Society, with the encouragement of its president, Clifton Curtis. It would be impossible for me to list the friends and colleagues whom I met at the various IWC meetings; I can only acknowledge them en masse and hope that I have done their positions justice.

During my visit to Japan, I spent time with Hideo Omura, Seiji Ohsumi and Masaharu Nishiwaki, and afterward I shamelessly badgered them for assistance and clarification on some of the confusing Japanese issues. I went to Western Australia to participate in the opening of the Whaleworld museum at Albany, and there and in Perth I was the guest of Peter Snow, John Bell and John Bannister of the Western Australian Museum. When I went to New South Wales, Tasmania and Queensland, I was aided and abetted by Howard Whelan of *Australian Geographic;* Ron and Valerie Taylor, who provided tactical support; René Davison of Twofold Bay, whose grandfather ran the famous whaling station at Eden; and Peter Ogilvie of Brisbane and points east, who helped me with all things Australian. In South Africa, Graham J. B. Ross of the Port Elizabeth Museum and Peter Best of the South African Museum at Cape Town gave generously of their time and expertise, and my dear friend Beulah Davis of the Natal Sharks Board arranged for me to visit the Union Whaling Company's station at Durban—no easy task, since it is now an active military installation. Ole Lindquist of Iceland helped me with the mysteries of Icelandic history, and Johann Sigurjonsson did likewise with the current state of affairs there. Sven-Olof Lindblad of Special Expeditions made many of my trips possible; it was through his good offices that I managed to visit southeast Alaska, Baja California, Indonesia, Australia, Norway and Iceland.

Not all of my research was done in exotic or historically significant locations; much of it was conducted through the mails, usually with people who *were* in those critical places. For example, I have maintained a long and mutually satisfactory correspondence with Professor M. V. Ivashin of the Research Institute of Marine Fisheries and Oceanography (VNIRO) in Moscow, who sent me the photographs of Soviet whaleships that are included in this book. Dr. Ivashin also supplied me with several articles in Russian, which were translated for me by Valery Gabay, enabling me to understand the often mysterious ways of Soviet historians. Mark Fraker, a biologist who works for British Petroleum in Alaska, was there when the gray whales were rescued and provided me with infor-

mation and photographs of that event. For pictures of contemporary bowhead whaling in Alaska, I am indebted to Dave Withrow of the National Marine Mammal Laboratory in Seattle. Edward Mitchell and Randall Reeves of the Arctic Biological Station in Quebec sent me more useful information than I knew what to do with. Photographic material and advice was received from Patricia Storrar of Plettenberg Bay, South Africa, the author of the definitive book on that fascinating place; and Arthur Credland of the Kingston upon Hull Museum participated eagerly in my search for information on the Hull fishery. When I was in Australia, I had the pleasure of spending time with Bill Dawbin, who doesn't much like the title, but is indeed the "grand old man" of Australian whaling history. He generously provided me with information, anecdotes, and access to his superb photograph collection. I couldn't get back to New Zealand, so when I asked for a little help, my friends Stuart Thompson, Shane Compton and Richard Compton assigned themselves the job of picture researchers and painstakingly reviewed the collections of libraries, museums and newspapers in Auckland and Wellington to find some rare and very special pictures for me. Victor Scheffer, with whom I worked many years ago, was as helpful this time around as he was in the past. I spent a great deal of time at the New Bedford Whaling Museum, where its director—and my loyal friend—Richard Kugler, gave me unstinting support and information and encouraged me to paint the mural of Moby Dick in the museum's Lagoda Room. In the museum's library, Po Adams and Judy Lund helped me solve the mysteries of the museum's enormous collections. Stuart Frank of the Kendall Whaling Museum in Sharon, Massachusetts, has been a friend and supporter throughout this project, and it is through his collections and expertise that many of the illustrations were provided. The Kendall Museum's annual symposia on whaling history were invaluable, exposing me to new interpretations and unexpected revelations, and also putting me into contact with Joost Schokkenbroek, Bjørn Basberg, Thor Arlov, Tetsuo Kawasumi, Uwe Schnall, Klaus Barthelemess, and Bob Webb. Lou Garibaldi and Rick Miller of the New York Aquarium were particularly helpful in my research on belugas in history and in captivity, and Robert Baracz of Sea World provided me with a picture of Gigi, the only large whale ever maintained in an oceanarium. Fred Bruemmer, probably the world's foremost photographer of Arctic wildlife, generously made available his pictures of narwhals and narwhal-hunters. Craig Van Note of the Monitor Consortium in Washington sent me an unending stream of useful information and rare pictures, and on behalf of the entire conservation movement, I want to take this opportunity to thank him.

Through all my travels and investigations, there have been several people whose support has been unwavering. My agent, Carl Brandt, watched over this project from its early stirrings, and my editor, Ashbel Green, watched in horror as again and again I added to an already awkward and cumbersome manuscript. Jenny McPhee at Knopf tolerated my additions, changes, revisions and omissions with remarkable equanimity. The most unwavering and steadfast of all, however, has been Stephanie; without her there would be no book—in fact, without her there would probably be no author.

A Note on the Maps

The maps in this book, all of which were designed and drawn by the author, are included for comparative reference purposes only. Each map was designed for specific geographical objectives, e.g., the relative positions of the Sea of Okhotsk and the Bering Sea, or the location of the Bonin Islands. No attempt was made to have the maps conform to a particular scale, nor are they drawn to the same projection. Thus the size of Greenland varies widely from map to map, depending upon the purpose of the map and the projection employed. In fact, Greenland, which is the largest island in the world, covers an area of some 840,000 square miles, and is almost exactly the same size as Saudi Arabia. (A line drawn from its northernmost to its southernmost point would be 1,700 miles long, the distance from New York to Denver.) On most maps, Greenland appears relatively larger than it is because it is closer to the pole. For example, in the Mercator projection, in which lines of longitude are parallel, Greenland appears to be larger than Africa.

The Whales
They Hunted

WHEN I BEGAN the research that was ultimately to lead to *The Book of Whales* in 1980, my intention was to write only about the natural history of the various whale species; their size, shape, coloration, habits, diet, distribution, parturition and relationships to other whales. I realized almost immediately that men have played an enormous part in the lives of whales, and I therefore included whaling as a prerequisite element in the natural history of whales. I could not possibly have written about any of the great whales without including the historical depredations of the whalers, since in some cases the very existence of the species had been threatened. Although whales are believed to have been on earth for some fifty million years, the last millennium has seen almost incomprehensible changes in their lives, all of which have been brought about directly by men.

The stories about whales could not be told without an introduction to the whales themselves, however. Their biology had a marked effect on the whalers, as well as on the settlement, industry and history of many places where men chose to live. The effect of whales on men has been almost as important as the

effect of men on whales. In many instances, the location of the whales determined the location of the men, and it was biological imperatives that determined the location of the whales.

We cannot view the past through the inverted telescope of the present; whalers in the seventeenth and eighteenth centuries did what they did because, in a sense, they had no choice. Only a few men profited from whaling, but many men died. That it was dirty, dangerous and difficult goes without saying, but it is only through the lens of hindsight that the whaleman's job becomes malicious or cruel. Until the beginning of this century, in fact, it was considered an admirable, romantic profession; one need only read Herman Melville's description of the harpooners Tashtego, Daggoo and Queequeg to see how these noble savages were venerated and how commendable was their work. Oil was needed for light and lubrication; baleen was needed for skirt hoops and corset stays. That whales had to die to provide these things is a fact of seventeenth-, eighteenth- and nineteenth-century life, and if we see the whalers as villains—even though they reduced some populations of whales to dangerously low levels—then we entirely miss the point of their history. The environmental ethic that has pervaded our consciousness is a recent development; we have only just begun to learn the complex nature of the web of all life. In order to understand the sinister alchemy that turned living whales into products, we must first understand the history and biology of the whales.

In *Moby-Dick,* Melville devotes Chapter 32 to "Cetology," and calls it "a matter almost indispensable to a thorough appreciative understanding of the more special leviathanic revelations and allusions of all sorts which are to follow." His chapter, which appears relatively early in the book (there are 135 chapters), elucidates (among other things) the physical characteristics of the various cetacean species known to him and to other whalemen and scientists of his time. Throughout *this* book, I have had occasion to refer to certain species of whales in many different locations and in as many contexts. In order to avoid the repetitious redescription of the right whale, the humpback or the sperm whales as I discuss the history of the interaction of that species with mankind, I have chosen to follow Melville's lead and consolidate the descriptive biological information on each species of "great" whale.

Melville inventoried his whales according to size, but he used *book* size rather than whale size, probably to give his readers a sense of the relative, as opposed to the absolute, differences in size of the animals. Thus the *Folio* whales are the largest; the *Octavo* whales next in descending order of size, and the *Duodecimo* whales the smallest. Although this was a charmingly inventive taxonomic system, it was probably better understood by nineteenth-century Americans than it would be by those of the twentieth, and so this book follows a more conventional plan. Here, the whales are arranged according to phylogenetic associations, those categories that recognize certain anatomical similarities among whales of the same family or genus.

There are some seventy-five species of whales and dolphins, arranged in nine families:
- Balaenidae: The Right Whales
- Balaenopteridae: The Rorquals
- Eschrichtiidae: The Gray Whale
- Physeteridae: The Sperm Whales
- Monodontidae: The Narwhal and the Beluga
- Ziphiidae: The Beaked Whales
- Delphinidae: The Oceanic Dolphins
- Phocoenidae: The True Porpoises
- Platanistidae: The River Dolphins

The first three of these families are the baleen whales, collectively known as *Mysticeti* ("mustache whales"), which feed by trapping food organisms in the keratinous plates that hang from the roof of their mouth. Every other kind of whale has teeth of one sort or another, and they are therefore known as the *Odontoceti.* If another general distinction is needed (the presence of baleen plates would seem to be more than enough), the mysticetes all have paired blowholes on top of their heads, which look something like a giant inverted human nose, while the odontocetes have but a single orifice. (The breathing apparatus of all whales and dolphins is separate from the swallowing mechanism; the animals have to be able to breathe through one set of tubes and swallow through another since they often have to perform these functions simultaneously.) Among the odontocetes are the Delphinidae, which of course are the dolphins, from the Greek word *delphys* for "womb," indicating that the Greeks recognized the mammalian character of this creature even though it looks like a fish. This group includes some forty-three species of toothed cetaceans ranging in size from the 35-foot killer whale to the 6-foot-long black dolphin.

The question of what differentiates a dolphin from a porpoise has been unresolved for centuries and will not be resolved here. There are some obvious differences between the two, particularly as far as teeth are concerned: dolphins have conical teeth not unlike the canine teeth of a dog (although in the case of the killer whale and some of the other large dolphins, they are relatively enormous), while all the porpoises have spade-shaped teeth. The two have been segregated into separate families, the Delphinidae and the Phocoenidae, and for purposes of scientific classification these distinctions are constant. It is only in the vulgate that the problems arise, and particularly in English. There are those who insist on calling some dolphins "porpoises," and vice versa. And despite the irrevocable accuracy of the terms "Delphinidae" and "Phocoenidae," there will apparently always be those who insist on calling the bottle-nosed dolphin—usually the main attraction at a dolphin show—a "porpoise," and others who will argue that all porpoises are dolphins. (The fact is that killer *whales,* pilot *whales,* melon-headed *whales,* false killer *whales* and pygmy killer *whales* are all dolphins.)

The other families of toothed whales are differentiated from the true dolphins by various anatomical variations. The Physeteridae, a family made up of one giant (the sperm whale) and two diminutive variations (the pygmy and dwarf sperm whales), is characterized by a dramatically asymmetrical skull, a single, off-center blowhole, and erupted teeth only in the lower jaw.*

Two smaller toothed whales are grouped together in the family Monodontidae, which means "one-tooth." Of the two, the beluga or white whale has a full set of teeth, but its only relative, the narwhal, has (for purposes of this discussion, although the actuality is somewhat more complicated) only one tooth. But what a tooth it is! Along with the elephants' tusks, the tooth of the narwhal is probably the most celebrated tooth in the world, and one that may have been responsible for the development of the myth of the unicorn.

For a thousand years, and in a thousand locations, men have called whales by different names. This is not surprising, considering the number of available languages, but since whaling was often conducted on a worldwide basis, some sort of mutual language was probably desirable. In whatever the lingua franca, a "big black whale" could be a sperm whale, a fin whale, a right whale or a bowhead. Even if observers were able to differentiate baleen whales from toothed whales, they would still require a common frame of reference to ensure that they were talking about the same creature. Until 1758, when Linnaeus perfected his system of binomial nomenclature, nobody could be sure if the whale referred to in Dutch, English or Eskimo was the same animal. Did it really make any difference? Of course. If everybody called his version of the bowhead something different, then there was no way of knowing whether the species was in danger of being extirpated, which would in turn eliminate the industry. In the case of the bowhead (which Linnaeus called *Balaena mysticetus*), that is almost

---

*"Erupted" teeth are here differentiated from unerupted ones. In many cases, it would be incorrect to say that an animal has no teeth if indeed the teeth are present but never break through the gums. In fact, the sperm whale, which has those mammoth ivory pegs in its lower jaw, also has a full complement of teeth embedded in its upper jaw.

what happened. Under the not totally illogical impression that the number of bowheads was infinite, seventeenth- and eighteenth-century Dutch and British whalers virtually eliminated the species from the eastern Arctic, and in the next century, when a previously unknown population was discovered in the Bering Sea, American whalers came close to repeating the debacle.

The concept of biological extinction existed only in a vague form until people were able to accept the theory of evolution. After all, Noah's Ark carried two of "every living thing of all flesh," and when petrified remnants of various strange creatures were discovered, the only possible explanation was that they had somehow missed the boat. In *The Natural History of the Order Cetacea* (1835), H. W. Dewhurst recounted the discovery of a whale skeleton on a "stupendous high mountain" in Norway. "In all probability," he wrote, "this Zootomical specimen has remained there since the period of the deluge, when it was deposited, which is now more than 4,000 years! No other conjecture can be formed than this. . . ." (Whales, which are the first animals named in the Bible, probably didn't mind a little rain.) Baron Georges Cuvier, the acknowledged father of paleontology and comparative anatomy, identified the possibility of extinction as early as 1796, but it would be another sixty-three years before Darwin's epochal discussion of the origin of species would be published. During those years, which saw the precipitous rise and disastrous decline of open-boat whaling, the whalers would continue their bloody business, with only a passing thought to the possibility that they might run out of whales.

The whalers plied the Seven Seas in search of whales, and as the time between strikes increased and the voyages took longer and longer, surely it must have occurred to some of them that the whales were not an inexhaustible resource. Herman Melville, whalerman and author, was one of the first to raise the possibility of the extinction of whales. He wrote:

But still another inquiry remains, one often agitated by the most recondite Nantucketers. Whether owing to the most omniscient look-outs at the mast-heads of the whale ships, now penetrating even through Behring's straits, and into the remotest secret drawers and lockers of the world; and the thousand harpoons and lances darted all along continental coasts; the moot point is, whether Leviathan can long endure so wide a chase, and so remorseless a havoc; whether he must not at last be exterminated from the waters, and the last whale, like the last man, smoke his last pipe, and then himself evaporate in the final puff.

There is still a great deal we do not know about whales. Most of the accumulated knowledge of the animals has come from those who have killed them, and up to fairly recently the literature on whales has been made up of descriptions of where they might be found so they could be dispatched, and accounts of the adventures attendant upon these activities. That is not to say that there was a complete vacuum; various authors articulated what was known of the biology and natural history of whales for a popular (as opposed to scientific) audience, including William Scoresby (whose book was published in 1820), Henry Dewhurst (1835), Thomas Beale (1835), Herman Melville (1851), Charles Nordhoff (1856), and Charles Scammon (1871). (During the heyday of the whale fishery, dozens—perhaps hundreds—of books were published that described a particular experience or voyage.) In 1900 F. E. Beddard added *A Book of Whales* to "The Progressive Science Series," and thereafter many volumes appeared on the intertwined subjects of whales and whaling. Roy Chapman Andrews wrote an article on worldwide shore-whaling for *National Geographic* in 1911, and followed it with *Whale Hunting with Gun and Camera* in 1916. During the early decades of the twentieth century, British scientists published extensively on the new material they were gathering on the whales of the Antarctic ("The Discovery Reports"), and in 1940 Remington Kellogg wrote an article for *National Geographic* entitled "Whales, Giants of the Sea," in which he described the habits—and the hunting—of the whales and dolphins of the world.

It has been a little less than fifty years since men have been able to remain submerged for any length of time and observe whales; Jacques Cousteau and Emile Gagnan invented the aqualung in 1942. Whales live in remote places, so simply being able to stay underwater was no guarantee of being able to see them, let alone study or photograph them. Some whales lend themselves to field research; others do not. Because they breed and calve in clear tropical waters, humpbacks were the first large whales that were accessible to divers. Killer whales probably spend more time at the surface than any other species of cetaceans, and even though it is not considered advisable to leap into the water with a pod of feeding killer whales, individuals can be identified by their dorsal fin shape and size, so a great deal can be learned about the habits of these large dolphins by following them in a boat. On the other hand, no one had ever been in the water with free-swimming sperm whales until a team of scientist-divers encountered a school in the Indian Ocean off Sri Lanka in 1983. (This crew also made the first underwater footage of blue whales in the same area, much farther north than anyone expected to find them.) The bowhead has probably never been filmed underwater, a circumstance that probably has something to do with the thoroughly inhospitable conditions—to divers, not bowheads—in which it lives. It was not until 1976 that a photographer was able to enter the water and film wild whales of any species. (Prior to that, the only whales filmed underwater had been harpooned or injured.) Off the Hawaiian island of Maui, James Hudnall became the first to photograph living whales underwater, and of course, the whales he photographed were humpbacks.*

*As an indication of how quickly whale photography has come along, consider this: In 1974 I was asked to illustrate the ten species of great whales for *Audubon* magazine, because there were virtually no photographs available of anything but carcasses on the flensing deck, or whales tied alongside a catcher boat. By 1985, when I wrote a ten-year anniversary update of the 1974 article (which was written by David Hill), I solicited—and received—more than six hundred photographs of whales from all over the world. Not all of them were underwater, of course, but their sheer numbers and variety demonstrated the remarkable changes that had taken place in that ten-year period.

The Right Whale
(Balaena glacialis)

THE RIGHT WHALE is a large, black, elongated teardrop of an animal, reaching a maximum length of 60 feet and a weight of 80 tons. It has a huge arched mouth and a proportionately cavernous lower jaw, which is capped by a relatively narrow, spoon-shaped upper jaw, in which are rooted two "sides" of 8- to 10-foot-long baleen plates. In the right whales, the baleen plates play an important role in food-gathering, in contrast to their role in the rorquals,

Right whale (*Eubalaena glacialis*)

whose plates serve only as a strainer after the food has been trapped in the mouth. The lower jaw must also hold these flexible plates—which have been likened to hairy, vertical venetian blinds—when the whale's mouth is closed.

Mostly black, right whales often have an irregular white belly patch. There also have been piebald, spotted, and even all-white individuals. Their flippers are broad, and the leading edge, where the forefinger would be if whales had visible fingers, extends out from the paddle. Whales do indeed have fingers, but they are inside the flippers. This is one of the hereditary characteristics that "proves" that whales and dolphins are descended from land mammals, as there would be no reason for such a development if the whales' ancestors had always been aquatic. They also have vestigial hind legs—small, useless bones embedded in the muscle where the hind legs would be, but so atrophied and reduced over the eons that

they serve no purpose to the whale. To us, however, they clearly point to a terrestrial ancestor.

The horizontal flukes of the right whale are broad in proportion to its body, gracefully tapering to a narrow point at the ends. Others might regard the broadly triangular flukes of the sperm whale, or the multicolored, tattered caudal fins of the humpback as the most striking of whales' tails (Melville devoted an entire chapter to the sperm whale's tail), but there may be no more graceful structure in nature than the flukes of a right whale.

It is the face of the right whale, cavernous lower jaw and all, that immediately differentiates it from its close relative, the bowhead. Where the bowhead is "clean-shaven," that is, it has no "eyebrows," "mustache" or "beard," the right whale has callosities on all those places where a man would grow facial hair, except of course the top of the head. One could make a good case for the statement that a

A gigantic right whale on its back at the whaling station at Sitkalidak Island, Alaska. The curve to the left defines its lower jaw, its right flipper points straight up, and the tips of its flukes have been cut off.

whale's head *has* no top. Where the uppermost portion of the cranium is on most terrestrial mammals (or birds, reptiles, or fish, for that matter), we find the whale's *nose*. It could be argued that this is indeed the top of the whale's head, but during the course of transmogrification from a land mammal to a completely aquatic one, such profound changes have occurred in its physiology that the whale has become a horizontal creature, with more morphological emphasis on front and back than on top and bottom. Because of this horizontality, the brain, which in most other mammals occupies the uppermost portion of the cranium, is behind the jaws rather than above them.

The only concession that the whale has made to the concept of top-and-bottom-ness is, in fact, its nose. The forerunners of today's whales and dolphins had nostrils where one would expect to find them, at the front end of the face. For the whale to be able to exhale and inhale efficiently (assuming, for the sake of this argument, a grand design that directs evolution toward efficiency), it had to be able to perform these respiratory functions smoothly and quickly. Stopping to poke your nose out of the water is neither smooth nor quick, so the nostrils gradually

migrated back to their present location, enabling the whale to expose only a tiny portion of its massive head to exhale (the "spout"), and allowing it to inhale immediately thereafter, all the time moving in its intended direction. (The same anatomy allows a species like the right whale, which often feeds at the surface, to breathe by having its nose exposed while its mouth remains submerged and open.) Among the "reasons" for this migratory nose—and evolution can rarely be shown to move in an uncomplicated or even a single direction—might be that it facilitates escape from predators. Those early whales that had to slow down to breathe while they were being pursued by giant sharks or other fearsome predators probably did not endure to pass along this maladaptive proclivity, while those who had developed a way of catching their breath without slowing down stood a better chance of escaping and thus passing along this useful ability.

The callosities on the faces of right whales are congenital; each individual is born with a pattern that does not change (or if it does, it changes very slowly) during the life of the whale. During their research on the right whales of Patagonia, Roger Payne and his associates have classified these callosities according to their location as "eyebrows," "post-blowhole island," "nostril," "coaming," "lip patch," "rostral island," "mandibular island," "bonnet" and "chin." It is not known what purpose is served for the whales by these keratinous lumps and bumps (some researchers believe that the males use them in battles with other males for breeding dominance), but they are invaluable identifying aids to the researchers.

After scrutinizing some twenty thousand photographs of Patagonian right whales, researchers Roger Payne and Ellie Dorsey noticed a subtle difference in the patterns of callosities between males and females. Before the sexes could be differentiated, however, the scientists used the callosities as a means of identifying individual whales. When we know how to tell one whale from another, a task usually made more difficult by the whale's habit of staying submerged for most of its life, we can then begin to estimate how many whales there are. (For other whale species, other census methods are used, such as counting the number of whales that pass a certain point during their annual migrations. This method works with the bowheads and the gray whales, whose migratory routes are predictable, but for the right whales, whose location is unknown when they are not on their shallow-water breeding grounds, individual identification is the only way of estimating population.)

For purposes of this discussion, all the right whales have been combined into a single group, but researchers are at odds as to how many species there are. Some identify a northern and a southern species (*Balaena glacialis* and *B. australis*), while others choose to lump them together. To further confuse matters, there are cetologists who have decided to divide the genus *Balaena* into two genera: *Eubalaena* for the right whale, and *Balaena* for the bowhead. The southern right whale, whatever its scientific name, was the object of intense fisheries in Australia, New Zealand and South Africa, to the point where the species has been virtually eradicated. Only in southern South America, where there was no beachhead for settlers, could the right whales swim unmolested.

Some time prior to the publication of his famous book on northern whales, William Scoresby inquired of a Captain Day of London as to the location of the right whale fishery conducted in the southern seas. Captain Day replied:

Among many others . . . they occur on the Brazil Banks . . . in the months of November, December and January. In the same months many of these whales are to be found in the Derwent River, New Holland; and also about the Tristian Islands; and in June, July, August and September they occur in Walwick Bay, and other inlets on the coast of Africa. The same animals are likewise met with near the island of St. Catherine, on the coast of Brazil; they also resort to some of the bays to the westward of Cape Horn, and to the northward of Coquimbo on the west coast of South America. The whales resorting to the latter situations are females, which go into shoal water for the purpose of depositing and rearing their young until nature has given them sufficient strength and powers to follow the older animals in all their meanderings in a deeper element than where they are first brought into existence.

From various cold-water locations, where they feed on small crustaceans known as copepods, right whales migrate to warmer, shallower waters to breed and deliver their calves. It is this tendency that made them so appealing to the early whalers; in many locations, the whalers had to do nothing more strenuous than wait for the whales to appear every year. The buoyancy of this fat whale, combined with its plentiful oil and baleen, made it the "right" whale to kill.

Because southern right whales are not seen farther north than their breeding areas, we assume that they head south, toward the lonely, icy reaches of the Antarctic. There, like their sleeker cousins the rorquals, they probably feed on small organisms. Melville described the feeding of the right whale: "As morning mowers, who side by side slowly and seethingly advance their scythes through the long wet grass of marshy meads; even so these monsters swam, making a strange, grassy, cutting sound; and leaving behind them endless swaths of blue upon the yellow sea." In the narrative, Melville has the *Pequod* "steering north-eastward from the Crozetts" in the Indian Ocean south of Madagascar, when it encounters the feeding right whales.

Only in recent years have there been better descriptions of the feeding habits of right whales, and these were made from observations in northern waters. In 1976, Watkins and Schevill published their observations of right whales' feeding behavior in New England waters: "During feeding, the right whale swims with mouth agape, scooping water into this triangular opening and out the sides of the mouth through the plates of baleen. . . . Typically, the whale swims slowly at the surface with its bonnet (of callosities) held well out of the water, and the rest of the body submerged. Sometimes the whale appears to be actually skimming the surface, with much of the baleen above water, the mouth open wide and the tongue visible between the forward portion of the baleen plates." The "strange, grassy, cutting sound" that Melville heard may have been the "baleen rattle" described by these scientists out of Woods Hole, Massachusetts: "Sounds believed to be from the rattle of baleen were heard but only during surface feeding in relatively calm water. This obviously was an adventitious sound, apparently produced by the movement of baleen plates against each other."

Right whales had been reported in the Antarctic— James Clark Ross wrote that in 1840 he had seen whales "of a common black kind—greatly resembling but said to be distinct from, the Greenland whale"—but they had been eliminated from their more northerly breeding areas before the whalers' armada arrived in the Antarctic. By the time the new century saw the beginning of the massive exploitation of the rorqual stocks, the right whales were gone. Only in the protected waters of Golfo Nuevo and Golfo San José, the two bays that define Peninsula Valdés, has anyone been able to study the habits of the southern right whales.

It is necessary to discuss the right whales of southern South America, if for no other reason than that they represent the only population of right whales that was not eradicated. These whales, virtually the last of their kind, living in splendid isolation at the uninhabited bottom of the world off the vast pampas known as Patagonia, have enabled us to learn more about their almost-extinct brethren than we possibly could have from the stragglers that remained in Australia or southern Africa. Of course the *ballenas francas* were known to the Argentines, but their whaling operations in the 1920s were confined to the Antarctic, along with everybody else's. Valdés was the location of several spearfishing championships in the early 1950s, however, and Argentine divers took great pleasure in occasionally diving with the whales. It was not until 1969 that Raymond Gilmore, an American cetologist on board the research vessel *Hero* in

the western South Atlantic, stopped at Valdés and discovered that the right whales were breeding and cavorting there. In the *Antarctic Journal* for November–December 1969, Gilmore wrote, "This is the first time that right whales have been reported from this locality," but he was referring to reports by scientists; Argentines who vacationed or dived in the vicinity of Valdés knew all about the resident right whales. Roger Payne, the man who was to make the right whales famous (as he would also the humpbacks), headed for Patagonia.

Since 1970, Payne has been studying the right whales of Peninsula Valdés. In the process, he has made these gentle giants one of the most intensively studied populations of large whales in the world. From cliff-top lookouts, from the beach, from boats, from airplanes, and even from underwater face-to-face confrontations with the whales, Payne and his associates have photographed and recorded every type of behavior of these heretofore unstudied animals. From a vast catalogue of photographs, in which the callosities of each whale have been shown to be different, Payne has identified more than 600 individuals and has estimated the total population at approximately 750 animals. Of all the southern right whales remaining in the world, this is by far the largest population. In the other areas where these whales were hunted so extensively (Australia, New Zealand, South Africa), there are only relict populations, numbering perhaps in the low hundreds. The total number of right whales left in the Northern and Southern Hemispheres is believed to be no more than 2,000.

Bowhead Whale

(*Balaena mysticetus*)

THE GENERIC NAME *Balaena* is from the Latin for "whale," and *mysticetus* is composed of the Greek components for "mustache" and "whale." (A mustache is not the first thing that comes to mind to describe the elements, no matter how hairy, that are found *inside* the mouth of a whale, but a dead whale's mouth is rarely closed, and the fringed plates often protrude, at least suggesting a mustache.) Although it had many different names throughout its luckless

Bowhead whale (*Balaena mysticetus*)

involvement with the whaling industry (The Whale, The Polar Whale, The Mysticetus, The Greenland Whale, etc.), those local populations of whales to which this variety of names were given are now gone, and only the name "bowhead" is used in English. (Alaskan Eskimos, the last hunters of this whale, call it *Aqvik*.) The derivation of the common name is obvious; the huge mouth, which may occupy a third of the animal's entire length, is arched like a gigantic bow.

Most of the bowheads are gone now, and much of what we know of the bowhead's natural history comes from William Scoresby, whalerman. He is the author of *An Account of the Arctic Regions with History and a Description of the Northern Whale Fishery*, published in 1820, and the most complete account of the bowhead we are ever likely to have.

The size of the largest bowheads is a matter of conjecture, but Scoresby says that the biggest he ever measured was 58 feet long, and he mentions one of 70 feet that he heard was killed off Greenland around 1800. The species is the same in the western Arctic, and records there coincide: Eskimo whalers in recent years have reported whales of 67 feet in length. The rule of thumb for whales is that an adult animal will weigh around a ton per foot, but for a thickset creature like the bowhead the figure is probably considerably higher. Estimates of 120 or more tons appear in responsible accounts, but again, these can only be approximations, given the impossibility of weighing something that large on the ice.

Like its somewhat smaller and slenderer relative the right whale, the bowhead has no dorsal fin. It is black all over, except for a white patch on the chin, which often has a series of black spots in a line. Occasionally, there is a grayish band just forward of the insertion of the 25-foot-wide flukes. Scoresby describes the color as "velvet-black, grey (composed of dots of blackish-brown, on a white ground), and white, with a tinge of yellow.''

As befits an animal of the Arctic, the bowhead has a layer of blubber that may be as much as 20 inches thick. Early whalers hunted the Polar Whale primarily for its baleen, and it was this buoyant layer of fat that kept the whale afloat while the baleen plates were stripped from its cavernous mouth.

In describing the bowhead, Scoresby wrote that its mouth "presents a cavity as large as a room, and capable of containing a merchant ship's jolly-boat full of men.'' Fortunately for the whalers, the bowhead feeds on minute copepods, which it skims from the surface or under it. "When the whale feeds,'' wrote Scoresby, "it swims with considerable velocity below the surface of the sea, with its jaws widely extended. A stream of water consequently enters its capacious mouth, and along with it, large quantities of water insects; the water escapes again at the sides; but the food is entangled and sifted, as it were, by the whalebone, which, from its compact arrangement, and the thick internal covering of hair, does not allow a particle the size of the smallest grain to escape.''

The bowhead has the longest baleen plates of any whale, reaching as much as 14 feet in a large adult. These structures, which may number 600 in the mouth of an individual whale, enabled the whale to successfully trap the copepods as the water ran out, but they also signaled the whale's undoing, since its extravagant baleen made it the prime target for northern whalers from the sixteenth to the nineteenth centuries.

It was not until 1860 that Eschricht and Reinhardt drew a clear distinction between the right whale and the bowhead. Prior to that year, the two species were regularly confused, since few people knew—or cared—that there were two distinct kinds of large black whales with no dorsal fin. The Dutch and the English who hunted whales in the Arctic in the eighteenth century caught bowheads. We know this from William Scoresby's meticulous chronicle of the Greenland Fishery, since he identifies the species as "Balaena Mysticetus: the Common Whale or Greenland Whale,'' and then goes on to give a detailed account of its habits, appearance, size and distribution. In addition, he illustrates the animal more or less accurately, so there is no question of the identity of "this valuable and interesting animal, generally called *The Whale* by way of eminence . . . productive of more oil than any other of the Cetacea. . . .''

Scoresby did not reckon with Herman Melville, who took it as his commission to elevate the sperm whale to the exalted position that had previously been occupied by the bowhead. Melville ardently defended the reputation of the sperm whale, although he depended heavily on Scoresby's *Account of the Arctic Regions* for information on those whales he did not know firsthand. He took every opportunity to satirize Scoresby by referring to him as "Charley Coffin,'' "Captain Sleet,'' and "Doctor Snodhead.'' He wrote that "Scoresby knew nothing of the great sperm whale, compared with which the Greenland whale is almost unworthy mentioning,'' and gloating over poor Scoresby's inability to defend himself or his whale, Melville thundered, "Hear ye! good people all,—the Greenland Whale is deposed,—the great Sperm Whale now reigneth!''

Either because he was too intent upon attacking Scoresby or because he was genuinely confused about the species, Melville managed to get bowheads into the Southern Ocean. In the discussion of feeding included above, the *Pequod* is "steering north-eastward from the Crozetts,'' which puts her somewhere in the Indian Ocean, east of Africa. Melville calls these whales "right whales'' (and in the 1930 edition of *Moby-Dick,* Rockwell Kent has *drawn* right whales), but it is obvious that Melville believes that he is describing "the Great Mysticetus of the English Naturalists; the Greenland Whale of the English Whalemen. . . . It is the whale which for two centuries has been hunted by the Dutch and English in the Arctic seas. . . .'' Later on, he writes that "some pretend to see a difference between the Greenland Whale of the English and the Right Whale of the Americans. But they precisely agree in all their grand features, nor has there yet been presented a single determinate fact upon which to ground a radical distinction.'' Despite Scoresby's careful itemization of the Greenland whale's particulars, the author of *Moby-Dick* chose to ignore the words of "Charley Coffin,'' and distributed his "right whales'' all around the world, from Greenland to the Brazil Banks.

Although information is still scarce, it is believed that the entire bowhead population winters in the southwest Bering Sea, in Soviet waters near the ice

Humpback whale (*Megaptera novaeangliae*)

front. From early April to May, they swim north-eastward past the western end of Saint Lawrence Island, and through the Bering Strait. As the pack ice begins to melt, the bowheads begin to move north, passing along the frozen shores of northern Alaska (the "North Slope"), where the hunters of Gambell and Savoonga (on St. Lawrence Island) and then the mainland villages of Kivalina, Point Hope, Wainwright and Barrow await them. In the fall, the villages of Nuiqsut and Kaktovik on Barter Island join in the hunt that the ice denies them in the spring. Those bowheads that successfully escape the harpoons of the Eskimos cross the Beaufort Sea into Canadian waters, to their summer feeding grounds near the Mackenzie River Delta and Banks Island. Like most migrating species of whales, bowheads eat only during the summer months, when their food supply is abundant. On their wintering grounds, therefore, they probably do not eat at all. Some of the whales may turn westward through the Bering

Strait, and spend the summer in the waters north of Siberia. As the ice begins to thicken in the fall, the whales head south again, although their destination is still a mystery. Like polar bears, these polar whales are international citizens, and show a complete disregard for national boundaries. Of course, this enables anyone to lay claim to them, which is why there are so few of them left today.

Humpback Whale

(*Megaptera novaeangliae*)

MUCH IS CONTAINED in the popular and scientific nomenclature of the humpback. Its hump does not exist (there is only a minimal sort of two-level dorsal fin), but it does arch its back when it dives, which probably accounts for the name. (Never de-

Arching its back as if to show the origin of its common name, a humpback also shows its "two-step" dorsal fin.

terred by lack of firsthand observations, Melville wrote that "he has a great pack on him like a peddler; or you might call him the Elephant and Castle Whale.") There is music, however, in its scientific name. *Megaptera* comes from the Greek for "big wing," and refers to the characteristically elongated flippers that the humpback uses to steer with. *Novaeangliae* is a combination of *novae* (Latin for "new") and the Middle English *angliae* which means "England." Thus the entire name can be translated as "big-winged New Englander," a succinct description of the animal which includes the location from which it was first described.

The humpback is one of the groove-throated whales, but it is not closely related to the other rorquals such as the blue, fin or minke whales. Where the other whales have 60 to 100 neat rows of relatively small throat furrows from the chin to the belly, the humpback averages about 20.

It is a very special creature, now considered the darling of whale-watchers from Massachusetts to the

Great Barrier Reef, and many locations in between. But a very peculiar darling it is. It has a long narrow head terminating in a warty protrusion at the chin and a collection of bumps on its upper and lower jaw that look like stovebolts. Its mouth curves down, giving it a glum countenance. Its elongated flippers, often one-third of its total length, are scalloped and lumpy on their leading edges, and often festooned with barnacles. The flukes are tattered on their trailing edges, and they too often serve as home for clusters of barnacles. If we all didn't love the humpback so much, we might be inclined to describe it as genuinely homely.

At a maximum length of 50 feet (females are usually somewhat larger than males), they can, depending on how much they have eaten, reach a weight of 40 tons. Humpbacks are usually black above and white below, but they display all manner of splotches, spots, streaks and scratches, some of which are the coloration of the whale, while others are scars left by barnacles or other parasites. They are not particularly tidy-looking animals, having protuberances on their snouts, barnacles on their extremities, and a blackish, heavily mottled skin.

Humpbacks breach spectacularly, launching their great bodies almost completely out of the water, and reentering with a prodigious splash. All of the great whales have been known to breach, but some do it more than others, and humpies do it most. "He is the most gamesome and lighthearted of all the whales," wrote Melville, "making more gay foam and white water generally than any of them." Given the power required to launch 40 tons out of the water, and then considering that the humpback is not a particularly fast or powerful whale, this is an astonishing accomplishment. How this ponderous creature can build up the momentum to power that weight out of the water has never been satisfactorily explained. (From underwater viewing locations in oceanarium tanks, we have watched the much lighter, much smaller dolphins leap out of the water, and we know that they must attain a critical speed before they can perform those great leaps. But the humpback is incapable of putting on a burst of speed in the water, let alone out of it; it seems to erupt from a virtual standstill.) Humpbacks often make an additional commotion by slapping their flippers on the surface, or "lobtailing," when they smash the water with their flukes.

Just as we don't know why each right whale has a somewhat different pattern of callosities, or what use it makes of these callosities, we don't know why every humpback has a different pattern of black and white on the underside of its flukes.* Whatever the purpose of these variations to the whales, they have proven extremely valuable to researchers. If it were not for the variation in fluke patterns in the humpbacks, we would not know where they go, nor would we have any idea how many of them there are.

Around 1975 researchers began comparing photographs of fluke patterns in humpbacks, and it

*All animals probably differ slightly in appearance from individual to individual, just as human beings do. Although we can easily differentiate one chestnut horse from another, we have only just begun to recognize individual characteristics in wild animals. Jane Goodall easily differentiated one chimpanzee from another; Diane Fossey knew her gorillas by name, and Cynthia Moss knew every elephant in Amboseli. Every whale may look different from every other one, not to make it easier for us, but to make it easier for them. It is possible that these marks may serve the very basic purpose of providing a means by which whales can tell one another apart.

wasn't long before they realized that these photographs could be coordinated to show the movements of individual whales. If, for example, a whale was photographed off Cape Cod and then in the Caribbean, it was obvious that the whale had migrated from one location to another. In this manner, it was possible for scientists to determine that the Hawaiian breeding population of humpbacks migrated to southeast Alaska to feed. Similarly, the humpbacks seen off the coast of Newfoundland (and occasionally trapped in the fishermen's nets there) winter in the Caribbean, and another population is found off Greenland and migrates south toward the Cape Verde Islands and the northwest coast of Africa. There are at least three discrete North Pacific populations: one that winters around the islands of Japan; one around Hawaii; and a third that occurs off the coast of California. In the South Pacific, separate populations of humpbacks appear in and around Australia, New Zealand and Tonga, and then head south for feeding in the Antarctic.

Because there has been so much concerted observation of humpbacks, we know more about their feeding behavior than that of any other species of large whale. They have been observed in Alaskan waters "lunge feeding," where groups of humpbacks will lunge, huge mouths agape, almost out of the water as they attempt to engulf vast numbers of small fishes. They also practice a weirdly sophisticated feeding strategy commonly known as "bubble-net feeding." In this process, the whales release bursts of bubbles in a helix beneath a school of fish, thereby consolidating the fish and enabling the whales to rise up inside the wall of bubbles and engulf thousands of gallons of living fish soup. They then force the water out through their baleen plates, and swallow the fish that remain. (It is also assumed that humpbacks feed underwater in a more conventional manner, but when they choose to perform these capers at the surface, they attract a lot of attention.) Much of the feeding that has been observed in Alaska seems to be a group effort, which differentiates humpbacks from other large whales whose feeding has been observed to be an individual endeavor.

Humpbacks are the whales that sing. Because these songs have been highly publicized—there are two best-selling recordings available, they have been featured in innumerable television specials, composers

A humpback whale at Akutan in the Pribilofs, showing the mottled coloration of the pleated throat and the characteristically long flippers.

have incorporated the whales' sounds into popular and classical music, and the movie *Star Trek IV* was about the humpback—it has been assumed that all whales sing. In fact, it is only the humpback that produces this intriguing medley of moans, groans, bellows, yawps, wheezes, whines and gurgles. Other baleen whales make low-frequency noises, probably for purposes of communication, but no other cetacean can match the humpback hit parade.* The songs, which consist of discrete phrases, are sung by the whales on their warm-water breeding grounds. We are not sure why the whales sing, but most researchers now believe that the songs are somehow associated with mating and that it is only the males that sing. The songs last about half an hour, and then they are repeated. The whales do not sing in unison; there is no cetacean chorale.

*Recent acoustic studies of the bowhead have shown that these whales also sing. Katy Payne, who with Roger Payne discovered, recorded, and analyzed the songs of the humpback, has written: "Humpback whales are only distantly related to bowheads, but these two species of baleen whales are the only ones that sing complex songs." Their songs are not nearly as intricate or long-lasting as those of the humpback, but their whoops, purrs, and groans are used, according to Christopher W. Clark (1991), "to maintain cohesion in the widely dispersed herd."

Startling as it is to find whales singing, their ability to change the songs annually is surely one of the most remarkable accomplishments in the entire animal kingdom. Researchers began recording the songs around 1970 off Bermuda, and soon realized that there were noticeable modifications from year to year. Certain phrases were dropped, and new ones were added. No one has the faintest idea how the changes are communicated from whale to whale, but every year they all learn the new "words and music," and however it is accomplished, they never repeat a discarded phrase. The humpbacks of different regions have different songs and dialects; their repertoires are completely distinct. Although researchers have been recording and analyzing their songs for almost twenty years, we still don't know how the music of the whales is generated.

It is possible that all species of whales, if studied as closely as the humpbacks, will display a commensurately dazzling catalogue of unique behaviors. When we come to the sperm whale, one of the least known of the large whales, we will certainly encounter some highly unusual activities.

Humpbacks have been studied intensively for close

to twenty years, particularly around the United States. There have been whale-watching boats setting out from Provincetown, Boston, and Gloucester, Massachusetts, since 1975. In addition to the hundreds of thousands who have visited the whales, every voyage has scientists aboard, who have recorded the location, movements, activities and progeny of the Stellwagen Bank population, making them some of the most counted, watched, recorded and photographed whales in history.

In the Hawaiian Islands, the humpbacks are seen on their breeding grounds. Every winter they come from southeast Alaska (by a route that has never been identified) and appear in the warm, clear waters of Maalea Bay, between the islands of Maui and Molokai. From the refurbished whaling port of Lahaina on Maui, thousands of whale-watchers observe these leviathans swimming, sporting, diving, breaching . . . and fighting.

For years the image of the whale has been that of the "gentle giant": a benign, peaceful creature, at one with its environment and ready to teach us all sorts of lessons about peace and love. Imagine the shock when it was seen that male humpbacks battle viciously for dominance, smashing each other with their barnacled flippers, butting and drawing blood. It was clear that many of the scars long observed on humpbacks were not caused by barnacles, but by other whales.

Intensive study has produced some interesting results, many of which simply serve to dispel preconceptions. Because bottle-nosed dolphins that gave birth in aquariums were often accompanied by another female—usually called the "auntie"—it was assumed that the "escort" of a female humpback with a calf was also an auntie. Then Deborah Glockner-Ferrari developed a way of sexing humpbacks underwater (females have what she described as a "hemispherical lobe" posterior to the genital slit; the males lack it), and discovered to everyone's surprise that the escorts were males. (Glockner-Ferrari, like many modern scientists, used photographs as a research tool. Without underwater photographic equipment, her observations would not have been possible.)

After a one-year gestation period, the female gives birth to a single calf which is about 12 feet long. The birth of humpbacks has been observed several times

in their Australian breeding areas in the Great Barrier Reef. The calf nurses for about a year, and then it is weaned to join its population of singing, lobtailing, and endangered brethren. From a total world population that numbered more than 100,000 animals, there are probably no more than 6,000 of these rare and wonderful whales left in the world's oceans.

Gray Whale
(*Eschrichtius robustus*)

IN TIMES PAST, an Atlantic population of gray whales existed, but at some point, perhaps as late as the seventeenth century, the last of these animals was killed. (A discussion of the disappearance of this species will be found when we come to the story of early Atlantic whaling, but we assume that the Atlantic and Pacific populations shared similar characteristics.)

Most other species of large whales are widely distributed: the rorquals and the sperm whale are found throughout the world's oceans, and even the bowhead, which is confined to the Arctic, had a circumpolar distribution. The gray whale, however, is found only in the Pacific, and as of now, only in the eastern Pacific. (There used to be a population that wintered along the Korean and Chinese coasts, but like the Atlantic group, these gray whales were eradicated.)

All gray whales, Atlantic or Pacific, were known as *Eschrichtius robustus*. The generic name refers to D. F. Eschricht, a nineteenth-century German zoologist, and *robustus* is Latin for "strong" or "solid." (They used to be called *Rhachianectes glaucus*, which was not much easier to pronounce.) They are not particularly large as whales go; the largest females have been measured as perhaps 45 feet in length, and they can weigh about 35 tons. They have no dorsal fin; instead a series of crenulations (known to the whalers as "knuckles") run down the back from approximately the place where a dorsal fin would be to the insertion of the flukes. The gray whale is the only large whale in which the upper jaw overhangs the lower, giving it a sort of "parrot-beaked" countenance.

The gestation period for the gray whale is a year;

California gray whale (*Eschrichtius robustus*)

the young are conceived at the lagoons of Baja California and then born there twelve months later. When it is born, a gray whale is black or dark gray, with none of the scratches, splotches, scars or incrustations that characterize the adults. A full-grown adult is so covered with barnacles, whale lice and the remains of these passengers that it acquires a blotchy, mottled appearance. The mother gray whale is fiercely protective of her offspring, probably more than any other species of whale. Whereas whalers would often harpoon a juvenile bowhead knowing that the mother would not leave her injured baby and could thus be easily dispatched, they avoided that practice where gray whales were concerned, since the female "devilfish" would attack anything that seemed to threaten her calf.

Gray whales often poke their heads vertically out of the water, an activity that is known as "spyhopping." They also breach regularly, throwing themselves most of their body length out of the water, then twisting on the reentry, presumably to protect their internal organs from the impact.

Other than man, whose predatory activities will be discussed in greater detail, the primary enemies of the gray whale are sharks and killer whales. There have been reports of great white sharks (notorious attackers of whales) in and around the lagoons, and throughout their range, gray whales are the victims of the killer whales' pack attacks.

It is the most predictably migratory of all whales, journeying every year from the icy waters of the Bering and Chukchi seas to the warm, saline lagoons of Baja California. Early students of the gray whale—such as Charles Scammon, who was responsible for the discovery of its breeding grounds, the introduction of whalers to these heretofore unknown lagoons, and the primary, authoritative discussion of the animals' life and habits—believed that all gray whales made this migration every year, but studies subsequent to the 1874 publication of Scammon's *Marine Mammals of the Northwestern Coast of North America* have shown that there are groups of gray whales that do not make the entire round-trip journey, and may stop off at places like Vancouver Island. However, we can assume that most of the gray whales leave the Arctic in the fall and spend the next couple of months swimming toward Laguna Ojo de Liebre (commonly known as Scammon's Lagoon), San Ignacio Lagoon, and Magdalena Bay.

Baja California is a six-hundred-mile-long, skinny finger of desert and rocks that points southeastward into the Pacific from the bottom of California. The two lagoons and the bay are located on its western coast. Its eastern coast is separated from mainland Mexico by a body of water variously called the Sea of Cortez or the Gulf of California. The whales do not travel to the peninsula in a school; in fact, their passage is orchestrated according to age and gender. First to leave the Arctic are the pregnant females, then the mature males, and finally the immatures of both sexes. (The females that have to deliver their calves are on the strictest timetable; the others can straggle in at their leisure.)

Gray whales are among the few species of migratory whales whose numbers can be calculated by the simplest of all methods: they can be counted. In the northern seas they are spread out all over the place, but as the days begin to shorten, the whales assemble. They begin to move southward, and for reasons that we don't understand but that probably have to do with cetacean practicality and tradition, they all pass through Unimak Pass in the Aleutian Islands. This is one of the places where they can be counted, since the whales pass close to Unimak Island. The whales probably don't mind the weather, but the researchers who station themselves on Unimak in November and December have to put up with what one of them describes as "persistent and heavy winds, clouds, and frequent precipitation." (The United States Coast and Geodetic Survey's *Coast Pilot* simply calls it "the worst weather in the world.")

Less hardy whale-counters have positioned themselves at various spots in southern California (Point Lobos, near San Diego, is a particular favorite), or even at the lagoons themselves. Wherever the counters, they are totaling some 21,000 gray whales, who pass day and night en route to Baja. (In the spring, as they head north, they keep a course much farther offshore, making them more difficult to count on this part of the trip.) For those whales who complete the full round-trip, it is the longest migration made by any mammal: 10,000 miles. Navigation at sea, in storms and at night is not simple, and it is close to

miraculous that these leviathans manage to accomplish this hazardous and difficult journey every year of their lives. It is believed that the whales utilize highly sophisticated skills, including hearing, passive sonar, and even vision, in addition to a magnetic sense that we are only beginning to recognize, and probably many other faculties that is has not occurred to us to study.

When the whales arrive at their breeding lagoons, the pregnant females deliver, and those females not nursing are impregnated. The southward trip has taken its toll; a 30-ton whale might lose 8 tons of blubber on the way down. This is standard operating procedure for baleen whales, however; they are designed to fast for prolonged periods of time, one of the explanations for the thick blubber layer.

By February or March, the whales are ready for their return, as they have not eaten anything since they departed four or five months earlier. (The largest animals that ever lived—this program of gorging and abstaining is not unique to gray whales—can go for months without eating.) In the cold, food-rich waters of the Arctic, gray whales feed twenty-four hours a day. They are bottom-feeders, scooping up huge amounts of tiny copepods, but as might be expected, this procedure allows for a lot of unwanted material to enter the mouth and the stomach. Although no one has witnessed it (because it occurs on the bottom of the Bering Sea, not a particularly popular dive spot), evidence points to a suction method of feeding, where the whale turns on its side and slurps up the copepod-filled mud. It then forces out the mud and water through its short, yellowish baleen plates. "They are known to descend to soft bottoms in search of food," wrote Scammon, "and when returning to the surface, they have been seen with head and lips besmeared with dark ooze from the depths below."

The evidence for the feeding methods of the whales in the Bering Sea consists of photographs and sonar records of shallow, consecutive depressions in the mud, which may have been produced by foraging gray whales. Recent observations have indicated that gray whales also feed at other locations, such as Vancouver Island, where they have been observed (and filmed by Jim Hudnall, who was the first man to photograph humpbacks off Hawaii) to feed on midwater mysid shrimp.

Because of their proximity to shore on the southward leg of their migration, gray whales have been the object of concentrated whale-watching, mostly in southern California. In January and February, they pass San Francisco and Monterey, then Los Angeles, and finally San Diego, their last view of the United States before they enter Mexican waters and the less-populated Baja Peninsula. In the lagoons, they are observed from boats (an activity now carefully regulated by the Mexican government), which has resulted in an enormous number of people being exposed to whales—and vice versa.

Blue Whale

(*Balaenoptera musculus*)

THE BLUE WHALE is the largest animal that has ever lived on earth. The largest ones have been measured at over 100 feet in length, and they may weigh more than 150 tons. (Some of the giant dinosaurs may have been as long or longer, but with their long necks and long tails, they were considerably lighter.) It is obviously impossible to weigh an animal that may total 300,000 pounds, so many of the records are no more than estimates of the sum of the meat, the oil, the blubber, the bones, and the fluids lost in processing. For example, in the *Guinness Book of Animal Facts and Feats,* the following statement appears about a whale killed at Walvis Bay, Southwest Africa, in 1924: "Unfortunately this enormous whale was not weighed piecemeal, but on the basis of its oil yield it must have scaled *at least* 200 tonnes!" This is the whale species about which all those comparisons are made: it weighs more than 40 elephants, 200 cows, 1,600 men, etc. But who can sense the weight of 1,600 men? Putting the size of the blue whale in a contemporary perspective, it is approximately the same length as the 128-passenger Boeing 737,* which, fully fueled, weighs one-fourth as much as an adult blue whale.

From birth, the story of the blue whale is a catalogue of prodigious measurements and accomplish-

---

*According to literature supplied by the Boeing Corporation, the 737-300 is 105 feet 7 inches long. It can be variously modified to take as many as 128 passengers (mixed class), or 149 passengers, all tourist. Empty of fuel, the plane weighs 105,000 pounds, and takes on 5,311 gallons of jet fuel, which adds another 20,000 pounds to its weight before takeoff.

ments. After an eleven-month gestation period a 24-foot-long baby emerges. A blue whale at birth weighs about 4 tons, approximately the weight of a full-grown hippopotamus. (Much of the natal biology of the blue whale is conjecture based on the examination of fetuses on the flensing deck. No one has ever witnessed the birth of one of these giants, and for most of the world's beleaguered blue whales, no one even knows where to look.) The calf is fed on its mother's milk (another activity that has never been witnessed), which is so rich in fat that the neonate puts on some 200 pounds a day—8.33 pounds an hour—for the first six months of its life.

The yearling blue whale is weaned when it is approximately 50 feet long, and then it begins its life-long preoccupation with traveling to where the food is. In the Southern Hemisphere the blues head for the Antarctic, and before the whalers found them, huge herds used to converge for a leviathan banquet that must have been one of the most magnificent sights in the world: amidst the ice floes with gulls and albatrosses wheeling and screeching overhead, hundreds, perhaps thousands of these mottled blue monsters gulped gargantuan mouthfuls of icy water and krill. (*Krill* is simply a Norwegian word for whale food, and refers to a shrimplike crustacean technically known as *Euphausia superba*.) Alas, we will not see this spectacle in our lifetime.

Although the right whales and the rorquals are all baleen whales, their feeding strategies differ substantially. The right and bowhead whales swim through their prey, allowing a stream of plankton and water to pass through their cavernous mouths as they move forward. The rorquals, on the other hand, are much more aggressive in their feeding methods. Upon encountering a school of krill (or fishes or squid), the rorqual drops its lower jaw to form a gigantic scoop, and engulfs as much of the swarm as it can, along with the water. The loosely hinged lower jaw and the numerous ventral pleats allow for an enormous expansion of the throat pouch. (Aerial photographs of feeding blue whales show an incredibly distorted animal that looks for all the world like an eighty-five-foot tadpole.) In his study of the feeding mechanisms of baleen whales, August Pivorunas has estimated that a blue whale can hold seventy tons of water in its mouth when its gular pouch is fully distended.

Southern blue whales feed in the Antarctic because these icy waters are rich enough in oxygen to support

Blue whale (*Balaenoptera musculus*)

immense "rafts" of krill. Once the bouillabaisse of living krill and sea water is engulfed, the whale closes its great maw, and with its fleshy tongue (which is about the size of a small automobile), forces the water out through the sieve of its baleen plates. One scientist estimated that the feeding blue whale requires 1.5 million calories a day. (In human terms, that means that a blue whale consumes as many calories—about 50 million—during a four-month feeding period as the average human being utilizes in his lifetime.)

There are blue whales in all the world's temperate waters, but they appear to belong to separate tribes which do not intermingle. Among those areas in which separate populations of *B. musculus* have been studied are the Gulf of Saint Lawrence, the Sea of Cortez, the Indian Ocean, and the North Atlantic off Iceland and Greenland. There is a record of a blue whale's being trapped in the Panama Canal, and one of the first ones described for science washed ashore at the Firth of Forth in Scotland in 1692.

Although the word "pygmy" hardly seems applicable to an animal that can attain a length of 80 feet,

there is indeed a subspecies of blue whale known as *Balaenoptera musculus brevicauda,** the pygmy blue whale. It is slightly smaller than its relative, and is said to be "silvery-gray" where the blue whale is decidedly bluish in color. It is found only in the Southern Ocean and may not migrate to polar waters to feed. (It was probably a group of these pygmies that filmmaker J. R. Donaldson encountered in the Indian Ocean off Sri Lanka in 1983. It was July when they were filmed underwater—the first time ever—when other Southern Hemisphere blue whales would have been in the Antarctic gobbling up millions of euphausiids.)

At sea, the blue whale can be recognized by its size, its color, the distinctly rearward location of its relatively small dorsal fin, its high, vertical spout, and its habit of raising its flukes out of the water on

*The scientific name of the blue whale can be translated as "muscular winged whale," although there are some who have chosen to translate *musculus* as "little mouse." While that is one of the possibilities, it is more straightforward and logical to assume that "muscular" was the intended translation. *Brevicauda* means "short-tailed." The existence of a pygmy variety creates a problem with the vernacular name of the larger relative: is it the "great" blue whale? The "true" blue whale?

Blue whale model, seen head-on, in the British Museum of Natural History.

every third or fourth dive. There are some individuals that have a diatomaceous film on the belly, which has led to the appellation "sulfur bottom." Melville, whose personal observations of the larger whales was restricted to rights and sperms, regarded this species as one of those whales that was of no particular interest to whalers because its capture would be too difficult: "He is never chased," he wrote, "he would run away with rope walks of line. Prodigies are told of him. Adieu, Sulphur Bottom! I can say nothing more that is true of ye, nor can the oldest Nantucketer."

In 1971, George Small, a professor of geography at Columbia University, wrote a book called *The Blue*

Whale. Although it was scientifically accurate for the most part, it was mainly an emotional paean to the whales and an impassioned cry for their salvation. While the book was written at the height of pelagic whaling, blue whales had been "protected" since 1966. Small estimated the total blue whale population at "something between 0 and 200 individuals," and then cried, "What a monument to man's power of destruction of God's creation!" When calculating the number of blue whale calves that could be born to his hypothetical 0 to 200 population, he contrives to have the females give birth in an area of 9 million square miles, so that there would then be one calf per 1.8 million square miles. Even though we still don't know where blue whales calve, it is unlikely that each one requires a million square miles of ocean, and it is more reasonable to assume that, like other species, they calve in specific, restricted areas.* (Small also wrote that no one knows how blue whales communicate—implying that with so few whales spread out over so much ocean they might never be able to find a mate—but as will be seen, we have now heard the sound of the blue whale, and like everything else about this animal, it is something wondrous to behold.)

Blue whales do not sing; in fact, their phonations, which are the loudest sounds made by a living creature, are below the threshold of human hearing. Only sophisticated recording devices have enabled us to confirm the existence of these powerful, deep-throated murmurs. Just as their source eluded us for so long, the purpose of these low-frequency calls remains a mystery. On the liner notes for *Deep Voices: The Second Whale Record,* Roger Payne wrote,

The problems of cutting records are such that the low sounds cannot be recorded at the same intensity as sounds in more normal human ranges, and as there are no in-

---

*However he arrived at his figures, Small proved to be correct. In my 1980 *Book of Whales,* I took issue with his conclusions about the number of blue whales left in the world, and wrote, "Recent popular works [for which read: Small] have significantly misinformed the public regarding the number of blue whales remaining, offering extremely low numbers and presenting opinions as if they were facts." I thought that his estimates were far too low, and quoted various experts who believed that there were between 10,000 and 30,000 blue whales left in the world. As explained below, Small's figures were much closer than mine to the latest scientific calculations. (As recently as 1984, a study conducted by scientists at the United States Marine Mammal Laboratory in Seattle suggested that the total number of blue whales in the world was around 10,000.)

struments that play such low notes, records are not usually challenged to reproduce sounds as low as these. The origin of these sounds is unknown. They remain a mystery, reflecting how little we really know of the open sea and the sparse, lonely life that wanders through it.

At the International Whaling Commission meetings in San Diego in June 1989, a shocking statistic was made known. Heretofore, the number of living blue whales was believed to be somewhere in the area of 10,000, with most of them concentrated in the Southern Hemisphere. This figure was of course speculative, but scientists felt that the species had made a comeback since its hunting had been outlawed in 1966. For ten years, the whaling and non-whaling nations of the world had been participating in the International Decade of Cetacean Research, usually referred to as the IDCR. (Prior to the annual IWC meeting, the commission's Scientific Committee meets to discuss the various aspects of cetacean biology that will affect the commission's deliberations. Their findings are published in a lengthy *Report,* which is part of the business of the meeting.) The *Report* for 1989 contained the following information: that the IDCR cruises for 1978 to 1986 had sighted only 453 blue whales. (The estimated pre-exploitation population of Antarctic blue whales is 225,000.) Even with generous correction factors for areas and whales missed during the ten-year survey period, the outlook for the blue whale is grim. This figure—not far from the numbers that George Small had hypothesized in 1971—may in fact be too low for recovery. The greatest creature in the history of the planet may become extinct in our lifetime. After slaughtering so many of them, we now find our efforts to protect these magnificent animals have probably come too late.

Fin Whale

(*Balaenoptera physalus*)

IF BEING the second largest animal that has ever lived is not enough to distinguish the fin whale, then consider its coloration: it is the only consistently asymmetrically colored mammal in the world. For reasons that have baffled cetologists for centuries, the finner is black on one side and white on the other. Viewed from its right side, the fin whale can be seen to have a white lower jaw and a collection of light markings that swirl over its back. If we should manage to turn the whale around—no small feat, since a full-grown fin whale can achieve a length of 85 feet—we would see that the left lower jaw is black. In addition, the unusual coloration continues into the mouth, where the baleen plates and the buccal cavity are white toward the front of the right side, while the remainder of the right-side plates and all the left-side plates are striped with alternate bands of cream and gray. There have been many who have speculated on this asymmetry, but the answers elude us. (Some suggest that the peculiar coloration has something to do with feeding, either to present the light or the dark side to its prey, fin whales being opportunistic feeders that eat whatever is available; krill, fishes, squid. Observers, however, have seen the whales feeding either way.)

The fin whale gets its common name from its prominent dorsal fin, which, along with its black and white coloration, easily differentiates it from its larger cousin, the blue whale. It also moves differently, and its habits are not quite the same.

Although it is almost impossible to determine the maximum speed of a wild whale—except when it has been harpooned and is running for its life—the graceful fin whale has long been considered one of the fastest of all marine mammals. In his *Whale Hunting with Gun and Camera,* Roy Chapman Andrews called the finner "the greyhound of the sea," and wrote that "its beautiful slender body is built like a racing yacht and the animal can surpass the speed of the fastest steamship." (Written in 1916, this book is a testimony to the prevailing attitudes toward whales at that time. A scientist like Andrews could admire their lines, and then pay extravagant tribute to the brave men who killed them. Immediately after he sings the praises of the fin whale, he says, "The first one I ever hunted gave us four hours fight, with two harpoons in its body, and furnished abundant proof of what a truly magnificent creature the finback is.")

A 75-foot-long fin whale can weigh approximately 50 tons, considerably less than its bulkier blue cousin. Where the blue whale has a rounded upper jaw (one

Fin whale (*Balaenoptera physalus*)

of its early names was "flathead"), the finback's head is wedge shaped, in keeping with its hydrodynamic capabilities. (Once again we encounter the problem of the "reason" for this difference in design. Neither species has to be able to swim particularly fast to catch its prey, and the enemies of these large whales were, before men took after them in diesel-powered ships, only killer whales, which hunt in packs and can catch the whales anyway. Why then should the fin whale have evolved into a greyhound while the blue whale turned into a lumbering St. Bernard?) Maximum speed for a fin whale has been estimated at 40 kilometers per hour, which effectively put them out of range of the sailing boats and man-powered whaleboats. They swam more or less undisturbed until the late nineteenth century, when the invention of the harpoon cannon allowed the carnage to begin. In a 1976 *National Geographic* article, Victor Scheffer estimated that the "unexploited" population of the world's fin whales was 450,000, and that about 100,000 remained alive at the time he wrote.

Fin whales are probably the most common of the large whales; certainly they are the most widely distributed. They can be found—in greatly reduced numbers—throughout the temperate and subpolar waters of the world, in all oceans and in both hemispheres. They were particularly plentiful in the North Atlantic, and until the population collapsed, they were the mainstay of the Antarctic pelagic whale fishery. It is believed that the migrations of fin whales take them to the high latitudes in summer and toward the Equator in winter for breeding, so that the Northern and Southern Hemisphere populations move generally in the same direction during the year and thus are unlikely to intermingle. Unlike the blues, which are usually seen in pairs or trios, fin whales tend to aggregate in larger numbers, and there are reports of as many as a hundred being seen at one time. Were it not for the blue whale's dominance in the record books, this elegant creature would be a lot better known. Melville, who knew it only by the name "Razor Back," wrote, "he has never yet shown any part of him but his back, which rises in a long sharp ridge. Let him go. I know little of him, nor does anyone else.''

The International Whaling Commission's Scientific Committee *Report* for 1989 gave the results of the International Decade of Cetacean Research assessment of whales sighted in Antarctic waters during the decade. They saw a total of 2,096 fin whales, a figure even more startling than the 453 blue whales because the estimated number of fin whales supposed to be remaining in the Antarctic was in the neighborhood of 85,000 (Mizroch *et al.* 1984).

Sei Whale
(*Balaenoptera borealis*)

THE SEI WHALE acquired its common name from the Norwegian *seje,* which is the name of a fish that appeared off the wild coasts of Norway every spring, along with these roman-nosed rorquals. The name *borealis* simply means ''northern.''

A dark gray animal, the sei is somewhat smaller than the fin whale, reaching a maximum length of 68 feet, although most adults are in the 50–60-foot range. As with all the rorquals, the females of this species are somewhat larger than the males. It is a slim, graceful animal that can reach a weight of 40 tons. The dorsal fin is prominent and sharply falcate, and the rostrum has a single median ridge.

They have very fine, silky baleen fringes, and feed primarily on smaller organisms such as copepods and euphausiids, but they have also been known to consume small schooling fishes. The gestation period is a year, and the calves are weaned when they are five to nine months old.

Like all the rorquals, sei whales are found throughout the world's oceans, in separate populations. They migrate annually, and although the routes are poorly known, their presence in high latitudes in summer indicates that they breed in the warmer waters closer to the Equator. There are populations in the Pacific, the North Atlantic, the Southern Ocean, and off South Africa, Australia and Brazil. It is these Southern Hemisphere seis that head for the Antarctic to feed on the krill that proliferate there.

Sei whale (**Balaenoptera borealis**)

As far as we know, sei whales are the only large whale species that exhibit an often irregular migration pattern. They do adhere to the colder-in-summer, warmer-in-winter cycle, but occasionally large schools of these whales will appear in unexpected numbers in unexpected locations. In the Western Pacific, for example, off Japan and Korea, there have been reported unanticipated "invasions" of sei whales, which are probably responses to unusual environmental conditions. The sei whales were, however, regular enough in their annual visits to the Antarctic for the whalers to base an industry on their appearance there, after the blue and fin whales had been reduced to economic extinction. Scheffer has estimated that the original population of some 200,000 sei whales has now been reduced to 75,000.

Bryde's Whale

(Balaenoptera edeni)

DESPITE EFFORTS to change its awkward common name—which is pronounced, in the Norwegian fashion, *"bru-dah's"*—the name has stuck.* Although the first specimen was described from a stranding in Burma (where the animal "roared like an elephant" before it expired), it became best known—and eventually named in the vernacular—for its appearance in South African waters.

More than any other whaler—except perhaps the (possibly apocryphal) German named Meineke for whom the minke whale is supposed to have been named—Johan Bryde's name is immortalized among the whaling brotherhood because a species of whale was named for him. In 1912, he invited Orjan Olsen, a Norwegian scientist from Christiania (now Oslo) to South Africa to examine some unusual rorquals, and in a newspaper article dated November 12, 1912, Olsen wrote that they were of a species previously unknown. In a 1913 scientific publication, he named the species *Balaenoptera brydei,* but it was subsequently realized that the species was the same one that had been described in 1878 from the specimen

*Lyall Watson, in his *Sea Guide to the Whales of the World,* contended that it should not have been named for Bryde at all, and proposed "Tropical Whale" as its new name, but to no avail.

in Burma, and therefore its correct name was (and is) *Balaenoptera edeni.* Throughout the world, however, its common name is Bryde's whale, and Johan Bryde's name has therefore become an integral part of the cetological literature.

Bryde's whale is not a giant creature, but in the overall scale of things, it is a very large animal indeed. At a maximum length of approximately 45 feet, it is about as long as a trailer truck, and at a known weight of 30 tons, weighs considerably more.

It closely resembles the sei whale, but there are several particulars in which it differs, thus constituting it a distinct species. (For years, the whalers made no such distinction, so the past records—and therefore the status—of the two species are hopelessly confused.) Where the sei has a single ridge running down the center of the upper jaw from blowhole to tip, the Bryde's whale has three such ridges, converging at the forward end of the pointed rostrum. The ventral grooves of the sei whale end before the umbilicus, while those of the Bryde's whale (and those of all the other balaenopterids) run on longer. Where the baleen of the sei whale is fine and silky, that of the Bryde's whale is coarse, which evidently is a function of its feeding habits.

In the early descriptions, Bryde's whale was accused of eating all sorts of unlikely food items, from penguins and gannets to sharks, and although some of these unusual items have been found in the stomachs of captured whales of this species, they probably got there by accident. *B. edeni* eats fishes, such as herring, pilchards, anchovies and mackerel.

The "tropical whale" does not migrate to the Antarctic like its larger cousins. This (along with the confusion between this species and the sei whale) has probably saved the lives of innumerable Bryde's whales. The primary attraction of Antarctic whaling was the availability of the whales; if some of them were going to wander through the Southern Ocean's warmer portions, it would be easier to hunt the ones whose destinations could be more easily predicted. They have been reported from the Gulf of California and both coasts of South America, but they are particularly prevalent off Japan and the Bonin Islands, and of course, South Africa.

The sei and Bryde's whales are poorly known. Although they are large animals by any other standards, they were often not worth hunting because

Bryde's whale (*Balaenoptera edeni*)

they yielded too little meat and oil for the rapacious whalers. The "blue whale unit" (BWU), which was the industry's standard by which the relative values of different species were compared in oil yield, equated 1 blue whale with 2 fin whales, 2½ humpbacks, or 6 sei whales. It was obviously economically advantageous to hunt the larger whales before the smaller ones. Only when the larger species became so hard to find in sufficient numbers did the whalers turn to these poor relations. And when the smaller balaenopterids became worth hunting, the scientists focused their attention on them as well, partially in the interests of pure science (it was important to know about these animals), but also because many of the scientists who studied whales were connected in one way or another with the whaling industry. In 1974, the IWC convened a special meeting at La Jolla, California, to discuss problems of sei and Bryde's whales, and three years later, issued a report that contained more information on these two hitherto obscure species than all the publications that had preceded it in previous centuries.

Minke Whale
(*Balaenoptera acutorostrata*)

ALTHOUGH IT IS the smallest of the rorquals, the minke can reach a length of 33.5 feet, but most specimens have been considerably smaller. Even in the

Minke whale (*Balaenoptera acutorostrata*)

lower ranges, however, this "small" animal can weigh more than 10 tons.

Its scientific name is purely descriptive: *acutus* means "sharp" in Latin, and therefore, *acutorostrata* refers to its pointed rostrum. Its common name (which is pronounced "minky") is anything but descriptive. In early publications, this species is known as the "piked" or "sharp-nosed" whale, or the "lesser rorqual," but somewhere around the turn of the century the new name began to appear. Whalemen tell the story of a German whaler named Meineke (or Meinecke) who worked for Svend Foyn on his pio-

neering whaling voyages in the North Atlantic. To the amusement of his colleagues, Meineke mistook one of these diminutive rorquals for a blue whale, and from then on, they were known to whalers as "Meineke's whale," and thus minke.*

Like all the other rorquals, minkes are worldwide

*Once again, Watson finds "common names based on personal or proper nouns unhelpful," and suggests a return to the descriptive "Piked Whale," but the name minke is likely to stick, since it has been in use for almost a century. In fact, various versions of the name are employed in other languages, such as Japanese, where the whale is known as *minku-kujira*. (*Kujira* means "whale" in Japanese.)

in distribution, but unlike the others, there is a no-ticeable difference between the Northern and Southern Hemisphere varieties. All minkes are dark gray or black above and white below (with much variation in how the two colors come together), but where the northern animals have a pronounced white band on the flipper, the southern ones do not. In addition, where all northern minkes have white ba-leen plates, some of the southern specimens have white baleen only toward the front of the mouth, the remainder being dark. It is therefore likely that a southern subspecies of minke whale will be recog-nized, *Balaenoptera acutorostrata bonaerensis.* Minke whales have a small head, and a gracefully curved dorsal fin. In the North Atlantic, they have been ob-served feeding by lunging with mouths agape through schools of fish. The minke is the only rorqual that can leap completely clear of the water, and it reen-ters head first, like a dolphin. (The other large whales often breach, but they either cannot or don't care to clear the water completely. They usually come about three-quarters of the way out, then twist on their long axis before reentry, presumably to protect their internal organs from the shock of tons of meat and fat hitting the water.)

There are identifiable populations of minke whales in both sides of the North Atlantic, the North and South Pacific, and the Antarctic, where they regu-larly enter the floating ice, farther south than any other species of baleen whale.

As long as there were large whales to be hunted, the whalers did not bother with the diminutive minke. In 1937, as the whalers were gearing up for what would become the greatest whale-slaughter in history, Norman and Fraser wrote, "Lesser Rorquals have no commercial value, but they are sometimes killed by the Eskimos for food and the excellence of the meat has been commented on by more than one author."

As the larger species were progressively eliminated from their Antarctic havens, the minke whales swam undisturbed, except by the occasional killer whale pack. With reduced competition for the food re-sources of the southern ice, the minkes proliferated. In a sort of biological Parkinson's Law, they ex-panded to fill the available space. A minke is only one-third the length of a full-grown blue, so theoret-ically the removal of every adult blue left room for

three minkes. (In the words of the IWC scientists, "The minke whale stocks in the Southern Hemi-sphere do not fit into the Commission's present clas-sification scheme since these stocks have been growing in response to the reduction of other whale stocks.") Since nobody was interested in the minkes, nobody had been counting them, but when it be-came clear that they were the only whales available for hunting, scientists quickly used their increased numbers as an excuse for higher quotas. In 1971–72 the catch was 3,021 minkes; in 72–73, it was 5,745; and in 73–74 it was 7,713. Still, minkes were not included in the IWC's *Schedule** until 1975. From that year onward, the whaling nations (particularly Ja-pan, the USSR, Korea, Brazil and Norway) cam-paigned aggressively for minke quotas, and in 1975, since "the Scientific Committee was unable to reach any conclusion on stock size or maximum sustain-able yield estimates for minke whales," the IWC de-cided that the catch should be "7,000 distributed by areas." The hunt for the minke whale was on. By the next year, the Southern Hemisphere quota had escalated to 8,900 minkes, and the annual reports of the IWC were filled with studies of minke whale biology. By 1977, a special subcommittee had been designated to analyze the minke whale situation, and under the growing pressure of the antiwhaling fac-tion (within and without the IWC), quotas were re-duced annually until 1982, when the moratorium on all commercial whaling was passed.

*The *Schedule* of the IWC is an annual document that incorpo-rates the changing "rules" of whaling, and includes various defi-nitions, classification of whale stocks, last year's amendments, and whatever additional information is required for the conduct of the whaling industry.

Sperm Whale
(*Physeter macrocephalus*)

ASK A CHILD to draw a picture of a whale, and you are likely to get a square-headed, grinning crea-ture with a water fountain spouting out of its head. It is, of course, a version of a sperm whale, the an-imal that comes to mind most often when the word "whale" is mentioned. It is the whale that most Americans think of, since it was the mainstay of one

Sperm whale (*Physeter macrocephalus*)

of our most important nineteenth-century industries and the creature that figures so prominently in *Moby-Dick.* But the sperm whale is not a typical whale; it is not a typical anything. It is one of the most unusual creatures in the world, more easily characterized by its differences from other whales—and from all other animals—than by its similarities.

It is a toothed whale, but it is so much larger than any of the other odontocetes that only its immediate relatives, the pygmy and the dwarf sperm whale, are classified with it, and they have been placed in a separate genus (*Kogia*), because they do not exceed 12 feet in length. *Physeter macrocephalus* virtually defines the Latin term *sui generis,* "of one's own kind." It is a creature of superlatives, contradictions and

anomalies. The only thing on earth that resembles a sperm whale is another sperm whale.

Even its common name misdirects us. When some ancient Europeans first discovered a dead sperm whale on a beach (sperm whales are notorious stranders), they were unable to explain the clear amber liquid in its head, and guessed that it was the animal's seminal fluid. It is not, of course, but hundreds of years later, although we know that the fluid is not the "seed of the whale"—thus *spermaceti*—we do not know what the whale uses it for. (According to South African chemists, the oil in the head of the sperm whale is "a physical mixture of saturated and unsaturated high molecular weight mixed triglycerides and esters.") It has been speculated that the oil in the head of the whale is somehow employed in deep diving, buoyancy, temperature control, or sound production. It may serve all these functions, and perhaps others that we cannot begin to guess at.

Its scientific name is somewhat easier. *Physeter* is a "blower" in Greek, and *macrocephalus* translates as "big head." It looks like an animal with a big head, and it is, but what looks like the animal's head is in fact its nose, the largest nose in the history of the world. (I am calling the organ a nose because it is located above the lower jaw, contains the nasal passages and the single nostril, and is located forward of the brain and the eye. That it might also contain some other structures and a thousand gallons of oil does not make it a head, even though the sperm whale's eternal champion, Herman Melville, wrote that the sperm whale "has no proper nose." He devoted an entire chapter to the whale's head. He sang of its character, its dignity, its power as a battering ram, and in a later chapter reflected on its genius: "Has the Sperm Whale ever written a book, spoken a speech? No, his great genius is declared in his doing nothing to prove it. It is moreover declared in his pyramidical silence.")

Behind this titanic nose is the largest brain in history. The blue whale, a much larger animal, has a much smaller brain. The brain of a full-grown bull sperm whale can weigh 20 pounds, contrasted with the human brain, which weighs about 3 pounds. If we were to believe that the sperm whale's "great genius is declared in his doing nothing to prove it," we would have a difficult time in explaining this massive brain. A brain is a metabolically expensive organ; it requires lots of upkeep. It is not a casual appendage that assists in some everyday function, like the enlarged ears of an elephant. The sperm whale's massive brain would not have developed unless for a reason. The reason may lie in the processing of sound.

Like all odontocetes, the sperm whale relies on echolocation to find its food. It sends out sounds and processes the returning echoes to determine the nature of nearby objects, including its prey. But that only explains part of the problem. The whale still has to catch its food. Contrary to legend, sperm whales do not feed exclusively on giant squid. They probably do not feed on *Architeuthis* at all. Rather, the stomachs of captured sperm whales have re-

vealed much smaller squid, but in much larger numbers. For years, cetologists have wondered how the sperm whale, operating in total darkness, was able to gather enough of the swift cephalopods to sustain itself. It has been speculated—but certainly not proven, since observations would require the diving capabilities of a sperm whale—that the whales (and their smaller cousins, the dolphins) are able to stun their prey with focused bursts of sound, and then gobble them up at leisure. In addition to these echolocating and sound-producing functions, the sperm whale also communicates with its conspecifics by sound, employing a series of clicks, bangs and wheezes.

A whaleman demonstrates the size of a sperm whale's flukes aboard the schooner *Gaspe* in the 1922 film *Down to the Sea in Ships.*

The tooth-studded lower jaw of a sperm whale was wrenched from the skull and brought aboard.

If you examined the lower jaw of an adult sperm whale, the first thing you would notice would be the teeth. Massive ivory pegs, these teeth are familiar because they are the stuff of scrimshaw. During the long idle days between lowerings, whalemen often carved designs on these teeth, which have been called a truly original American art form. Once again, a product from the whale provides a commodity for man, but once again, we are not altogether sure what purpose the structure serves for the whale.

For other creatures, yes, teeth are used for chewing and biting, but for this animal, where hardly anything is what it appears to be, the teeth seem to have a different job. First, sperm whales have no unerupted teeth in the upper jaws, so chewing would seem to be out of the question. If we were to accept the tales of sperm whales battling with giant squid, then we would expect to find the squid marked by puncture wounds from the whale's teeth. Since no such puncture wounds have been found, we now assume that the whale, after stunning the squid with its sonic blasts, gathers them out of the water, using its lower jaw as a pincer. The teeth might be useful in grasping the slippery squid, but this is neither chewing nor biting.

Sperm whales are usually scratched and scarred

all over, occasionally with the sucker marks of squid, but also with what would appear to be tooth marks from other whales. If the males fight with one another, or if there is some other interaction between males and females, it might explain the scars, and consequently explain the teeth. Again, rather than being employed in the usual dental manner, the teeth of sperm whales—like the horns of antelopes*— might be what biologists call a "secondary sexual characteristic," which identifies the dominant males for selective breeding.

The largest male sperm whale (a subject for much conjecture) is about a third again as big as the largest female. Weighing about a ton per foot, a big bull can be 60 feet long, while the females rarely attain 40 feet. They are black in color, but various authors have described them as "grayish-brown," "lead-gray," or "dark brown." Both sexes have white lower jaws, and a mottling of white on the upper lip. There is usually a white patch in the area of the belly, and the older males often have a whitish whorl on the end of the nose, the flattened area that is often referred to as the "forehead." At the end of the nose, on the left side, the sperm whale has a single S-shaped nostril. When it exhales, the whale's spout is directed forward at about a 45-degree angle, which is

*Both male and female antelopes have horns, and they keep them permanently, unlike deer, where only the males have antlers, which are shed annually.

a diagnostic feature at sea. The sperm whale has no dorsal fin, but it has a series of humps running down the midline of its back, the largest of which is located where the dorsal fin would be. On the underside, there is a curious notch which defines the "postanal hump." Aft of the flippers, the whale's body is deeply wrinkled, a characteristic that occurs in no other animal on earth. It is suspected that the hump and the corrugations on the whale's skin are somehow connected with its phenomenal diving ability.

Sperm whales can dive to depths of two miles, which makes them the undisputed deep-diving champions of the mammalian world. In order to do this, they must be able to hold their breath, and keep the functioning muscles supplied with oxygen. This may have something to do with the high content in their muscle tissue of myoglobin, a protein which retains oxygen. It may also have something to do with the vast oil reservoir in their noses—or the oil may have a function completely unexpected.

We have only just begun to understand the sperm whale's world; it was only in 1983 that the first studies were made of the social arrangements of sperm whales, by Dr. Hal Whitehead of Memorial University in Newfoundland. Under the sponsorship of the World Wildlife Fund, Whitehead and his crew spent three seasons in the Indian Ocean off Sri Lanka, watching mothers and calves, and they were the first people ever to witness the birth of a sperm whale.

The hapless whalemen have every reason to be terrified; they are confronting a kind of sperm whale that nobody has ever seen before: one with an extraordinary number of teeth in its upper *and* lower jaws.

(It was during this field study that the first underwater films were made of free-swimming sperm whales.) Prior to Whitehead's important studies, almost everything we knew about the habits of sperm whales came from those who would—or did—kill them.

Sperm whales freely roam the world's oceans from the poles to the tropics, and we still don't know much more about their travels than the nineteenth-century Yankee whaling captains did. We know that the big bulls only associate with the females during the breeding season (which may be eight months long) in the lower latitudes, but at other times of the year they betake themselves to the poles for reasons that have still to be understood. The remainder of the population divides itself into various groups, consisting of nursing females, subadult males or yearlings, but the dynamics of these groupings are not clear. With the exception of the Alaskan and Siberian North Pacific, most of the haunts of sperm whales were known to the New England whalers. In a 1935 study, C. H. Townsend collected records from whaling logbooks and plotted the locations of sperm whale catches from 1792 to 1913. He analyzed the records of 744 vessels which carried out 1,665 voyages and accounted for the death of 36,908 sperm whales. Townsend's charts show the traditional whaling grounds of the Yankee whalers, but not necessarily all the places where the whales aggregate. Evidently, nobody knew there were sperm whales off Sri Lanka until well into the 1980s, and on Townsend's charts there are no records at all of sperm whales having been taken along the great arc from northern Japan past the Aleutian chain and down to northern California, the area that was so heavily worked by the Japanese and Soviet pelagic whalers in the mid-twentieth century.

Only during the time that the breeding-age males isolate themselves in the high latitudes is it possible to find solo sperm whales. At other times this gregarious creature is encountered in groups of fifty or more animals. There have been reports of hundreds, and even thousands of sperm whales sighted at one time, but these may be apocryphal, or exaggerated. (In his *Cruise of the "Cachalot,"* Frank Bullen refers to a school of sperm whales "as far as the eye could reach," but Bullen's narrative is an admixture of fact and fiction, and when he reports such highly unusual occurrences, one is inclined to treat them with an oceanic quantity of grains of salt.)

Whatever it is that causes whales to strand in large numbers, sperm whales have got a large helping of it. Other whales beach themselves in larger numbers (the false killer whale holds the record, with 835), but sperm whales are the largest cetaceans that are subject to mass strandings, and when fifty or sixty—or seventy-two, the record for sperm whales—of these 50-ton creatures arrive on a beach simultaneously, it is a lamentable event of leviathan proportions. More often than not, beached whales die, usually because they were injured or stressed to begin with, but also because they are simply not designed to be out of the water. Without the support of the water, their bodies are too heavy for land, and they suffocate under the weight of their own musculature. Without the benefit of water's cooling conductivity, a whale left in the sun will literally cook in its own blubber. Their skin, which is surprisingly thin (as contrasted with the subdermal blubber layer, which can be a foot thick), dries out and cracks in the heat of the sun, adding to the heat problem. Current research is devoted to returning the unfortunate creatures to the water, but this can only be applied to the smaller cetaceans—you cannot move a beached sperm whale without harming it further.

Also in the realm of unsolved mysteries are the migration tactics of the sperm whales, their fecundity rates, the behavior of males, the breeding ranges, the purpose of their wrinkles and of the vast reservoir of oil in the nose, their maximum diving capabilities, and the reason why they need the largest brain of any animal that has ever lived. Because they are found all over the world, usually underwater, and almost always on the move, sperm whales are probably the hardest of all whales to count. Depending upon who is doing the counting, and whether or not the counter is interested in coming up with a high or a low figure, the estimates of the world's population of sperm whales range from 500,000 to 1.5 million. It is a sobering thought that the quintessential whale is still such an enigma. Men have been killing sperm whales for centuries, and still most of the creatures' habits are unknown to us. We have based an industry on animals about which we knew almost nothing; it has sufficed that we knew how to kill them.

TWO

MAN MEETS WHALE

First Encounters

ONE OF THE EARLIEST RECORDS of man's interactions with whales can be found in the chronicle of the conquests of Alexander the Great, which took place in the fourth century B.C., and was transcribed some three hundred years later by the Greek historian Arrian. Because Alexander's empire included the eastern Mediterranean, the northern shore of the Persian Gulf, and the shore of the Indian Ocean from the Strait of Hormuz to the mouth of the Indus River—and also because many of his campaigns were conducted at sea—we can safely assume that he and his army had many opportunities to see whales. The following passage appears in Arrian's description of the officer Nearchus's encounter in the Indian Ocean:

In this foreign sea there lived great whales and other large fish, much bigger than ours in the Mediterranean. . . . As we set sail we observed that in the sea to the east of us water was blown aloft, as happens with a strong whirlwind. We were terrified and asked our pilots what it was and whence it came. They replied that it was caused by whales, which inhabit this sea. Our sailors were so horrified that the oars fell from their hands. . . . Then I

walked round the fleet and ordered every steersman I met to steer straight at the whales, exactly as if they were going into a naval battle. All the men were to row as hard with as much noise as possible, including yells. . . . The whales, which could be seen just in front of the ships, dived terrified into the depths. Not long after that, they surfaced behind the fleet, blowing water into the air as before. . . . Now and again a few of these whales come ashore, having been stranded on the flat beaches at ebb tide. Often, too, they are flung up on dry land by a violent storm. Then they die and rot. When the flesh has mouldered away, the skeletons are left, which the inhabitants of these shores use for building their houses. The large bones at the side form the beams of their houses, the smaller ones the laths. From the jawbones they make doors.

From this description, it is not possible to identify the whales, for there seem to be two types discussed simultaneously. The schooling behavior (including the mass stranding) suggests sperm whales, but the description of the bones found on the beach would better apply to baleen whales. Whatever the species, it is obvious that stories like these were passed down, modified, embellished, and eventually reconstructed as the stuff of fable and fantasy.

When Jonah fled from Joppa rather than obey the word of the Lord that he go to Nineveh, his ship was caught in a "mighty tempest." To appease the angry God, the mariners cast Jonah into the sea because they knew he had disobeyed the Lord's commands, and immediately "the sea ceased from her raging," a "great fish" swallowed Jonah, and he remained in its belly for three days and three nights. Inside this uncomfortable sanctuary, Jonah repented, and the creature spewed him up again onto dry land.*

In the book of Jonah, there is no mention of a *whale,* but in the book of Job, there are several references to "leviathan," an animal that has been variously interpreted as a crocodile, a shark, and a whale. ("His teeth are terrible round about. His scales are his pride, shut up together as with a close seal. One is so near to another, that no air can come between them. . . . He maketh the deep to boil like a pot: he maketh the sea like a pot of ointment.") Isaiah 27: "The Lord with his sore and great strong sword shall punish leviathan the piercing serpent, even leviathan that crooked serpent; and he shall slay the dragon that is in the sea."† And finally, Psalms 104:25–26: "So is this great and wide sea, wherein are things creeping innumerable, both small and great beasts. There go the ships; there is that leviathan, whom thou hast made to play therein." At best the Bible is ambiguous about the whales; creating them, punishing them, watching them at play, and even feeding Jonah to one of them (maybe). When we really want to know about the whales, the Bible ignores them altogether.

When Noah was commanded to build the ark, he admitted aboard "every beast after his kind, and all the cattle after their kind, and every creeping thing that creepeth upon the earth after his kind, and every fowl after his kind, every bird of every sort," but there is no mention of a fish, a dolphin or a whale. Maybe these creatures were supposed to tag along in the wake of the ark, since they would not be affected by the rains or the "increase in waters." Or perhaps they were not recognized as creatures worth saving, living as they did in an alien environment.

As early as 350 B.C. Aristotle recognized that whales were mammals and not fish. He wrote, "The dolphin, the whale and all the rest of the cetacea, all, that is to say, that are provided with a blow-hole instead of gills, are viviparous . . . just as in the case of mankind and the viviparous quadrupeds." This knowledge, however, was to prove of little use to mankind for a thousand years, because it was based upon random and infrequent examinations of stranded animals. The observation of cetaceans in the wild only occurred when seafarers spotted dolphins at play in the bow waves of their vessels, or when someone like Nearchus encountered and described living whales. Men would not encounter whales until they began to venture out to explore the

---

*This is not the first mention of a whale in the Bible; that distinction is found in Genesis 21: "And God created great whales." It is, however, the first mention anywhere of a man being swallowed by a whale (or a "great fish"). There are very few animals in the sea large enough to swallow a man, and most of them are whales. Of the sharks, only the whale shark, the basking shark, and the great white shark are the requisite size, but the whale shark and the basking shark are plankton-eaters, with the equipment, but not the inclination to swallow a man-sized object. That leaves only the great white, the largest carnivorous shark in the world. This fish has a fully deserved reputation as a man-eater, but it tends to take great bites of its victims, and while there have been survivors of white shark attacks, there is no record of a human victim having been swallowed whole. The largest whales are also plankton-eaters, with gullets barely large enough to pass a good-sized fish. The only cetacean with the anatomical equipment required to swallow a human being is the sperm whale, which usually feeds on squid. A squid weighing over 400 pounds was found in the belly of a sperm whale harpooned off Madeira, so there is no question about the ability of the cachalot to swallow Jonah. Throughout the history of the sperm whale fishery, there have been several tales of whalemen swallowed by the object of their attentions. There are indeed stories of whalemen having been swallowed and recovered alive from the belly of the sperm whale, but under close examination, they begin to resemble the fable of Jonah more than demonstrable fact. An oft-quoted account of a whaler who fell overboard off Newfoundland and was swallowed by a sperm whale is more likely to be true. In this history (published as a letter to the editor of *Natural History* in 1947 by one Edgerton Y. Davis), the man is exhumed from the carcass of the whale, but he is badly crushed, decomposed, and extremely dead. Yes, it is physically possible for a whale to swallow a man, and no, the man would not survive the experience.

†In Isaiah "Leviathan" seems to have become a malevolent marine piercing serpent, so perhaps its designation as a whale is a bit off the mark. Huevelmans (1965) translates "leviathan" as the Hebrew *livyatan,* which he says could be a "snake, crocodile, jackal, whale, dragon and great fish. Quite clearly, all the references cannot apply to the same animal, but they all apply to something big or terrifying. 'Monster' is therefore our best equivalent." In his book, which is called *In the Wake of Sea Serpents,* Huevelmans is attempting to demonstrate the existence of sea serpents, so it is not surprising that he discounts the Biblical whale in favor of a "monster." In *Moby-Dick,* Melville opined that the story of Saint George and the dragon was actually about a whale, "for in many old chronicles whales and dragons are strangely jumbled together, and often stand for each other. . . . Besides, it would much subtract from the glory of the exploit had St. George but encountered a crawling reptile of the land, instead of doing battle with a great monster of the deep."

"And God created great whales, and every living creature that moveth, which the waters brought forth abundantly. . . ." Genesis 1:21. From a 1585 Dutch engraving.

oceans, which would not take place for another fifteen centuries. In the meantime, what observations of cetaceans were to be made would be made from land, or in the inland waterways in which men felt more or less secure.

Undaunted by the absence of real whales to describe, ancient authors described them anyway. Pliny the Elder (who often relied upon Aristotle and other authors) included whales in his *Naturalis Historia,* written shortly before he was killed at Pompeii in the A.D. 79 eruption of Vesuvius. A doctor named Philemon Holland (1552–1637) translated Pliny into Elizabethan English in 1601, and in his discussion of "The Whale," we find the following:

The biggest and most monstrous creature in the Indish Ocean are the whales called Pristis and Balaena. These monstrous Whales named Balaenae, otherwhiles come into our seas also. They say that in the coast of the Spanish Ocean by Gades [Cádiz], they are not seen before midwinter when the daies be shortest: for at their set times they lie close in a certaine calme deepe and large creeke, which they chuse to cast their spawne in, and there delight above all places to breed. The Orcae, other monstrous fishes, know this full well, and deadly enemies they bee unto the foresaid Whales. And verily, if I should portrait them, I can resemble them to nothing els but a mighty masse and lumpe of flesh without all fashion, armed with most terrible, sharpe, and cutting teeth.

When the sixth-century Irish monk known as St. Brendan set out on his North Atlantic voyages, the result was one of the earliest mentions of a whale-human interaction in the European literature. According to Samuel Eliot Morison, "Brendan was a real person . . . and his *Navigatio* is based on a real voyage or voyages, enhanced by the Celtic imagination." Brendan's discovery of Iceland, the Canaries or Madeira, while interesting, does not concern us as much as the delightful tale of his encounter with Jasconius the whale. With his crew of seventeen, Brendan came upon "a bare, treeless black island," but when they built a cooking fire, the island sank beneath them. Jasconius told them they could return, but only if they refrained from lighting fires on his back. The story appears in the *Physiologus,* and again in von Mengenberg's translation of Thomas de Cantimpre's *De natura rerum* ("Of things in nature"):

Some whales are so big that when seen from afar they seem like islands or groves, or resemble great hills. The whale heaps a thick coating of earth upon its back, so that when seamen are driven by the stress of weather upon this earth, they imagine it to be an island and that they have come to land. Rejoiced at this they let down the sails, drop their anchor in the water, build a fire upon the earth and seek to enjoy a little rest. As soon, however, as the whale feels the heat of the fire, it becomes enraged and dives beneath the water, bearing down to the depths both ship and sailors.

A Persian illustration of the fifteenth century that purports to show Jonah and the Whale, although the "whale" has become a large fish.

"And the Lord spake unto the fish, and it vomited out Jonah upon the dry land." Jonah 2:10. A 1566 engraving by Marten-Jacobsz Heemskerk of Haarlem.

It would be another five hundred years before men actually went whaling, but whales would continue to inexplicably cast themselves upon the beaches. In his *Historia Animalium,* Aristotle wrote, "It is not known for what reason they run themselves aground on dry land; at all events it is said that they do so at times, and for no obvious reason." Whales and dolphins have been running themselves aground for as long as men can remember, and probably long before that. In the twenty-two centuries that have elapsed since Aristotle made his prescient comment, we have come no closer to solving the mystery of whale-strandings than the Greeks. Beached whales represented the first important contact between men and whales, one which would set the tone for the inter-action of these two mammals for centuries.*

Not all knowledge of whales came from those that beached, of course; seafarers encountered all sorts of cetaceans as they plied their trade routes or began their hesitant explorations of distant coasts. Men sailed from the ports of Europe, Asia and Africa; for conquest, for trade, or to spread the word of their God, but they did not set sail casually. As the maritime historian J. H. Parry wrote in *The Discovery of the Sea,* "Discovery as an end in itself, exploration in intellectual pursuit of geographical knowledge, or in the romantic pursuit of unusual adventure, is characteristic of a safer, richer, more comfortable society than that of fifteenth-century Europe." There was no such thing as science for the sake of science, and if men found whales, they took them for what they believed them to be: huge, mysterious, threatening creatures. On their early maps, they figured them as large, scaly animals with a frightening array of un-likely appendages: horns, fringes, crests, armor, lumps, bumps, ridges, horrific dentition, and often twin pipes gushing water into the air.

It was not the intention of these mapmakers to

*The question of why whales strand is better treated in a book on whale biology, but because this propensity has been so impor-tant in the introduction of whales to men, a short note is appro-priate here. To this date, no one really knows why cetaceans enter waters so shallow that they cannot float, or throw themselves on the sand so that they die. (As mammals, whales can breathe out of the water, of course, but when they lose the protection of the heat-absorbing water, they can often bake in an envelope of their own blubber.) The theories include failure of the echolocation system, pursuit of prey, pursuit by predators, navigational miscalculations, magnetic anomalies in the land, and even a suicide wish. Because beached whales are often sick and almost always stressed, exami-nations of the living animals or the carcasses are usually less than conclusive.

frighten their fellow men; everyone believed that foreign lands harbored all sorts of mysterious animals and equally strange varieties of men. If this was the case, then surely the ocean, home of the sea serpent and the *kraken* (a giant squid capable of entangling ships in its tentacles and dragging them to the bottom), could be the home of even more terrifying creatures. And for medieval man, these superstitions proved to be true, as the sea spewed forth monsters larger and more terrible than any creature imaginable. There are giant squid, with arms fifty or sixty feet long, and there certainly are leviathans. While they did not have scales, horns or twin blowpipes, they had equally improbable characteristics: giant flattened tails, strange plates where terrestrial mammals had teeth, gigantic reproductive organs (often grotesquely distended in death), and no legs where proper mammals were supposed to have legs. Who could fault the ancients for suspecting that the sea harbored monsters?

We have no way of knowing when or where the first aborigines encountered the first beached whales, but it is obvious that this encounter would eventually lead to whaling. As soon as the inhabitants of what would become Holland, Norway or Vancouver realized that they did not have to depend on the uncertain generosity of the sea to provide a bounty of meat or oil, they would take to the sea themselves, to hunt the whale.

Many of the earliest descriptions of cetaceans were based on beached animals, and for the scientists of the sixteenth and seventeenth centuries, they were a boon. How else could landlocked Robert Sibbald of Scotland have described a blue whale so accurately in his 1692 discussion of the carcass found at Abercorne on the Firth of Forth? At one time or another, every species of whale has come ashore: fin whales, minkes, right whales, humpbacks, gray whales, and dolphins of every sort. But the most celebrated of all stranders is the sperm whale. With its great square head filled with a mysterious waxy substance, its wrinkled hide and peglike ivory teeth, a sperm whale appearing on the beach became a *cause célèbre.* In many of the early descriptions of beached whales, the species is open to question, but once you have seen *Physeter,* there is no possibility of confusing it with any other animal on earth, let alone any other whale. (The veneration of the sperm whale reached

St. Brendan was a real person who lived in sixth-century Ireland. The story about his erecting an altar on the back of a sleeping whale might be slightly fanciful, however.

"On the method of cutting-in sperm and baleen whales." Olaus Magnus, 1555.

its apogee in the nineteenth century, when, during the most productive years of the sperm whale fishery, *Moby-Dick* raised the sperm whale to the soaring heights of hyperbole.)

Almost as soon as methods for reproducing prints were available, illustrations of stranded whales began to appear. In 1551, Conrad Gesner published his *Historia Animalium,* in which he collected and reproduced illustrations of virtually every animal known at his time, including the whale. His pictures of whales (which were based on Olaus Magnus's earlier maps and illustrations) depict fierce-looking tusked sea monsters, larger than the ships that hunt them, and equipped with boarlike tusks and the usual twin-pipe blowholes.

In 1577, the first engraving of a stranded whale appeared in print. By the turn of the seventeenth century, more whales had stranded on European coasts, and with the heightened interest in popular science, more engravings appeared. Either because the whales preferred the coasts of the Netherlands, or because the Dutch had a particular interest in stranded whales, the majority of the early illustrations of whales were the work of Low Country artists. In these elaborately detailed drawings, the good burghers of Holland are often seen perched upon the carcass, standing around in fashionable attire, or occasionally carrying off a bucket of what may very well have been whale oil.

The North Sea coast of Holland would appear to be one of those places (noteworthy others are in New Zealand and Cape Cod) where whales strand with some degree of regularity. From 1531 to around 1690, some 40 whales of assorted species beached themselves on these shingled coasts. Most of them seem to have been sperm whales, and with its huge head, its mouthful of ivory teeth, and—in what appear to be a majority of the cases—its male genitalia prominently exposed, the dead whale must have been a wonder of wonders to the Dutchmen who came to view these monsters. It would be another half-century before the whalers of Rotterdam and Delft would head for the icy seas of Spitsbergen, where they would hunt a totally different creature, the Greenland right whale.

One of the best documented of these aliens from the deep was a 54-foot bull sperm whale (*Potvisch* to the Dutch) that was discovered floundering helplessly in the shallows of Berckhey in February 1598. When the whale expired, its carcass was sold off for the oil, but its fame lies more in its portrayal than in its products. Drawn by the artist Hendrick Goltzius, the Berckhey whale has appeared in countless versions, often accompanied by a descriptive text that marvels at its leviathanic dimensions. In later years, more whales would strand on these beaches and be

immortalized by Dutch engravers, but the Goltzius illustration, repeated and degenerated for two hundred years, has probably been employed more often than any other cetacean depiction, before or since.*

A stranded whale begins to decompose rather quickly, so often the illustration was erroneous in some of its particulars. (In the chapter in *Moby-Dick* on "The Monstrous Pictures of Whales," Melville had the same complaint. He wrote, "Consider! Most of the scientific drawings have been taken from the stranded fish; and these are about as correct as a drawing of a wrecked ship, with broken back, would correctly represent the noble animal itself in all its undashed pride of hull and spars. Though elephants have stood for their full-lengths, the living Leviathan has never yet fairly floated himself for his portrait.") Correct or not, these pictures were the best available, and from them, the civilized world began to learn of gigantic animals that lived in the sea, and occasionally appeared on beaches.

However, long before scientists would examine, dissect, illustrate and classify the whales, people with very little concern for their correct nomenclature would be hunting them in the open seas.

Jenkins (1921) writes, "Although the general opinion is that the Basques were the earliest whalers, Noel de la Moriniere says that this is a misapprehension and that the Northmen were really the first in the field." He says that a man called "Ochther" hunted whales and walruses beyond the North Cape, but then he notes that "there is no evidence that it developed into a regular fishery such as that of the Basques."

His "Ochther" was Othere (or Ottar), a Norseman in the service of King Alfred of Wessex around the year A.D. 890. Alfred (called Alfred the Great) is known for his defense of England against the marauding Danes, and also for the initiation of the *Anglo-Saxon Chronicle,* the first history of England. (Our word "whale" comes from the Anglo-Saxon

---

*An engraving by Goltzius's stepson, Jacob Matham, contains the following verse:

The huge whale, having been tossed on the blue sea,
May the gods prevent its threat,
*   looks upon the shore of Katwijk,*
The terror of the Atlantic, the whale of the deep,
Driven by the wind and its own motion to the shore,
Settled on dry land, stuck on the sand,
We offer it to be recorded, remembered,
*   and spoken about by the people.*

When a sperm whale beached itself at Katwijk in Holland in 1598, Hendrik Goltzius drew it for posterity. This is a contemporaneous engraving by Jacob Matham, based on the Goltzius drawing, one of the first portraits of a stranded cetacean.

hwael, which means "wheel," and probably refers to the shape of the whale's back as it rolls in the water.) Alfred translated many Latin texts, including the one that concerns us here, a description of Europe by one Orosius, who lived four centuries before. To the work of Orosius, Alfred added a description of the northern voyage of Othere, wherein was described the whale- and walrus-hunting of a northern people known as the Biarmians. From the location (the White Sea in northern Russia), and description of the whales hunted ("50 ells" in length, which by one calculation works out to 187 feet), it would appear that the larger ones—whose size was greatly exaggerated—were bowheads, while Othere's "horse-whales" were walruses. In the history of British *Voyages and Discoveries* compiled in the sixteenth century, Richard Hakluyt, a diplomat and scholar, wrote that the principal purpose of Ochther's expedition was "to increase the knowledge and discovery of these coasts and countries, for the more commodity of fishing for horse-whales, which have in their teeth bones of great price and excellency; whereof he brought some at his return unto the King. Their skins are also very good to make cables for ships, and so used."

In medieval Scandinavia, whales were very much a part of the lives of the people, and were therefore incorporated into their literature. A thirteenth-century Icelandic account known as *Konungs skuggsjá* (*Speculum Regale* in Latin; *Konegspiel* in German; "King's Mirror" in English)* describes the whales that are found off Iceland, and includes such mysterious creatures as the horse whale, the red whale,

*The King's Mirror was written in Norwegian, probably as a set of instructions for a king's son. It contains the first description of the ice in the interior of Greenland, a summary of contemporaneous beliefs about the aurora borealis, and the most complete inventory of the sea mammals of Greenland and Iceland up to that time.

and the pig whale, but also discusses recognizable species, such as the killer whale, the narwhal and the sperm whale. The right whale is described thus:

People say it does not eat any food except darkness and the rain which falls on the sea. And when it is caught and its intestines opened, nothing unclean is found in its stomach as would be in other fish that eat food, because its stomach is clean and empty. It cannot open its mouth easily, because the baleen that grows there rise up in the mouth when it is opened, and often causes its death because it cannot shut its mouth. It does no harm to ships: it has no teeth, and is a fat fish and edible.

Long before Christopher Columbus's epic voyage, Norsemen had arrived on the shores of North America. Leading the way was Eric the Red, a Norwegian who had left his homeland for Iceland in the year A.D. 984. The following year he sailed west and discovered Greenland (which he named because he thought the name would entice settlers) and founded a settlement there. In 986 Bjarni Heriulfson, another Icelander, missed Greenland, and came upon the shores of Labrador. Because it was not the Greenland he was looking for (he could see that there were no glaciers), he came about and headed for home. In 1001, the redoubtable Leif Ericsson retraced the voyage of Bjarni, and, according to Norse legend became the first European to set foot upon the North American continent. His initial landing occurred on Baffin Island's desolate, rocky shore, and finding it inhospitable, he set sail again, and this time fetched up on the shore of Labrador. From there he sailed his *knarr* through the Strait of Belle Isle, and landed at a place he called Vinland, which contemporary archaeologists have located at L'Anse aux Meadows, on the northern coast of Newfoundland.

There is an almost complete lack of information on Norse whaling, but the waters in which they sailed were then (and are still) among the whale-richest in the world. There are right whales, humpbacks, fin whales, sperm whales, belugas, narwhals, pilot whales and various species of dolphins in the cold, productive waters of the North Atlantic. The Norse sagas are silent on the subject of whales and whaling, but it would be hard to imagine these hardy seafarers ignoring a plentiful source of food and oil as they plied the otherwise inhospitable seas around Iceland, Greenland and Labrador. There are references, however, to battles royal between various "families" as they dispute the ownership of whale carcasses, which indicates the importance of whales—at least of dead whales—in the lives of the early Norsemen. They left no tryworks, their settlements provide no trace of harpoons or lances, but there are tantalizing hints of Norse whaling in some of the more recent discussions. In his 1928 *History of Whaling,* Sydney Harmer says, "The Icelanders seem to have engaged in whaling . . . and the whale known as 'Slettibaka'* . . . is believed to have been the Biscay whale."

*The modern Icelandic for the right whale is *sletbag,* which means "smooth back."

Early
Icelandic Whaling

ICELAND is a rocky, glacial island of some thirty-nine thousand square miles—approximately the size of the state of Virginia. It is located in what the *World Almanac* calls "the north end of the Atlantic Ocean," between Scotland and Greenland, but it is much closer to Greenland. The capital city of Reyk-javik—the world's northernmost capital—is farther north than Nome, Alaska.

Iceland's early history is to be found in the *sagas,* tales of the exploits of the island's early heroes. The Vikings of Norway evidently brought to Iceland knowledge of the techniques employed in driving whales (probably pilot whales) into the fjords for slaughter. There are occasional mentions of disputes over stranded whales in the sagas, but as far as we know, there was no active whale fishery. An Icelandic bestiary from about 1200 describes some of the whales (but not accurately enough for modern cetologists to identify them as to species), and the *Konungs skuggsjá* lists no fewer than twenty-one sea creatures, some of which can be referred to living whales, dolphins and pinnipeds, and some of which—mermaids and mermen, for example—are clearly mythological.

In a seventeenth-century work by an Icelander named Jon Gudmundsson, there is a list of the various whales that might be found in Icelandic waters, including the sperm whale (*Burhvalur*), the narwhal (*Náhvalur*), the right whale (*Slettbakur*), the fin whale (*Geirreydur*), and the blue whale (*Steypireydur*). With the exception of the right whale, which probably refers to the bowhead and was hunted to extinction after this publication appeared, all these whales can still be seen off Iceland. Also included was something that the author referred to as *Sandloegja,* which has been translated as "sand-lier"—*i.e.,* one that lies in the sand. Each of the above-mentioned whales is illustrated, so there is little doubt as to its identification. The description of the *Sandloegja* is accompanied by a picture of a whale that hasn't been seen in the Atlantic since commercial whaling began, and if the interpretation is correct, it depicts the only whale to have become extinct in recent history.

The California gray whale (*Eschrichtius robustus*) is well known from the North Pacific, where it makes the celebrated round-trip migration from Alaska to Baja California. It was the object of an intense fishery in the nineteenth century which nearly eliminated the species. Fossil remains of a similar—if not identical—species have been found in western Europe (Sweden, England and the Netherlands), and on the east coast of North America from New Jersey to South Carolina. From the evidence, it appears that there was also an *Atlantic* gray whale, which probably maintained similar habits to its Pacific cousin; that is, it fed in cold northern waters (perhaps Iceland and Greenland), and then moved south (Spain, France, England?) to breed and calve. With the exception of the fossil evidence, the only clues to the identity of this whale are found in the work by Gudmundsson and in a debatable reference in a New

England work of 1725, where Paul Dudley describes the "scrag whale" with characteristics that are not applicable to any other species except the gray whale. Whether hunted or occasionally appearing on the beach, the gray whale apparently should be listed in the Icelandic cetacean fauna, even though no living Icelander has ever seen one in his own country. (In his analysis of the whales of the *Konungs skuggsjá,* Ian Whitaker writes that "the gray whale was hunted in the Atlantic between 1100 and 1200, although it has not been found there since the 18th Century." He is unable to correlate this species with any of the thirteenth-century Icelandic names, although he indicates that there are two "unallocated" names, which translate as "hog-whale" and "shield-whale.")

Whales were caught by the Norwegians off the Tromsö coast as early as the ninth or tenth century. The oil was used for lighting and the baleen for jewelry, coopering, and boat-building. "But," as C. B. Hawes wrote in 1924, "with a lamentable lack of foresight, the earliest whaling captains neglected to enlist the services of scholars and historians," so much of the story of early Norse whaling has to be left to conjecture.

One of those who did a lot of conjecturing was Ivan Sanderson. Trained as a zoologist, Sanderson was particularly interested in unusual phenomena, such as the abominable snowman and the Loch Ness monster. He wrote several books on zoological and cryptozoological subjects, but he will probably be best remembered for his *Follow the Whale,* which was published in 1956. In this book, along with some rather good accounts of the biology of whales and some excellent maps, he re-creates the lives of whalers of the past and the present, "corralling the forgotten and more neglected aspects of whaling history and the new discoveries about the whales themselves, and weaving them into a continuous web of narrative." One of these "neglected aspects" is Norse whaling history, but despite the lack of documentation, Sanderson devotes a whole chapter to the subject, fictionalizing what could not otherwise be ascertained. He has the Norsemen under "Thorvald the Long" trapping sei whales in the fjords of Norway at an unspecified time, along with "Bjarni the Yellow standing in the bow holding a trumpet of cow's horn in his hand." He also recounts an Icelandic saga of A.D. 1100, which contains "a delightful passage in which we are told of the stranding of a large rorqual at Rifsker in Iceland and how all the important people who were able went to it." The documentation for this is sparse, but there can be no question that the Norsemen, ranging the North Atlantic from Finnmark to Iceland and from Greenland to North America, had to have encountered whales. Whether they killed the whales in an organized fashion or took them incidentally to their viking and settlement forays may never be known. They did hunt walruses for their skin and ivory tusks, and narwhals for their spiraled ivory tooth, which was passed off as the horn of the fabled unicorn.

Basque Whaling

AS FAR AS we can tell, the first people to hunt large whales in an organized and intentional manner were the Basques. As far back as records go—and even further, perhaps as far back as the Stone Age—these men were hunting whales. In his 1820 *Account of the Arctic Regions,* William Scoresby* suggests that "the Biscayans were the first who ex-

*Scoresby was a scholar as well as a whaleman. In his opening chapter ("Chronological History"), he refers to Oppian, Othere, Hakluyt, and others, and even reproduces the original Anglo-Saxon of Alfred's *Orosius,* correcting some of the errors made in the earlier Daines Barrington translation.

ercised their courage in waging a war of death with the whales," but he attributes their motivation to the protection of their fishing nets, which "would naturally suggest the necessity of driving these intruding monsters from their coasts." Whatever their reasons, the Basques became the paradigms of the whaling industry, establishing the *modus operandi* that would characterize the industry for another thousand years. "Historians have only recently begun to realize," wrote Farley Mowat, "that it was the Basques who lit the flame that was eventually to consume the

Engraved by Hans Bol of Amsterdam and published in 1582, this is the first European print to show commercial whaling. The location is imaginary, but the naked men are probably supposed to represent aborigines, perhaps Newfoundland Indians. Their hats present a problem, and might have something to do with the Basques. The stylized whale probably derives from contemporaneous Dutch drawings of stranded sperm whales.

ICELAND

Norwegian Sea

Varanger Fjord

Faeroe Islands

Shetland Islands

FINLAND

NORWAY

SWEDEN

Gulf of Bothnia

Atlantic Ocean

Helsinki

Leningrad

SCOTLAND

Peterhead
Aberdeen
Dundee

Vestfold

Stockholm

Sandefjord

IRELAND

North Sea

DENMARK

Whitby

Baltic Sea

Hull

ENGLAND

London

•Amsterdam

Ostend

Western Europe, the birthplace of commercial
whaling. The Basque whalers of the Bay of Biscay
were the first, followed by the British and the Dutch,
who sailed north to Spitsbergen and Greenland. In
the late nineteenth century the Norwegians
developed mechanized whaling, first practicing it in
their own waters, and later around the world.

Bay of Biscay

FRANCE

Biarritz
•Bayonne
St.-Jean-de-Luz

SPAIN

mighty hosts of the whale nations." They discovered the "resource," exploited it, and then pursued it so vigorously that it was uneconomical to continue. They probably took their first whales in the shallows, and then, like the bay whalers who were to follow their lead all around the world, realized that it was considerably more expeditious to go after the whales rather than wait for the whales to come to them. The Basques may also have been responsible for the only cetacean extinction in recorded history.

Somewhere around the year A.D. 1000, these intrepid hunters of the Bay of Biscay began the slow but systematic eradication of the whales that came into the protected bays in the shadow of the Pyrenees. Obviously the Basques did not wait for the first millennium to end before beginning their whaling, but most authors cite this as approximately the time they began. (Ommanney writes: "The industry, founded on the Biscay Right whale, was fully developed by the twelfth century but probably dated from much earlier, possibly from the tenth century when the Basques may have learned the craft from Norse whalers.") The Belgian historian W. M. A. De Smet has searched the literature for references to European whaling *before* the Basques, and writes, "Only a few authors are aware of the fact that whaling existed in still earlier days in other European seas, and that it was practiced in the North Sea and the English Channel during the Middle Ages, certainly from the 9th century onward." Although the species of whale in these early instances was rarely recorded, the likelihood is that it was the right whale that was hunted in the North Sea, and perhaps the gray whale, although the precise date of the disappearance of the Atlantic gray is still being debated.

De Smet cites several instances in which whale meat is mentioned in early texts, and suggests that "It is clear from the regularity with which whale meat occurred in these markets that it cannot have come from stranded animals alone and there must have been regular landings." After providing for themselves, the enterprising Basques established markets for the meat and blubber, and even had "consulates" in Holland, Denmark and England to encourage sales. In French, the blubber was known as *lard de carême,* which means "lenten fat," and Europeans were allowed to eat it on designated meatless calendar days. The oil was used for lighting and the manufacture of soap, wool, leather and paint; the

meat was fed to the poor and to the ships' crews, and the baleen was put to all sorts of uses (including being shredded into plumes for the decoration of knights' helmets), the vertebrae were used for seats, and the ribs were employed as fence pickets and beams for cheap housing. The tongue was considered a particular delicacy, and was reserved for the clergy and royalty.

In the unregulated (and largely undocumented) confusion of the Middle Ages, small pockets of Basques lived along the shores of the Bay of Biscay, speaking their own language, about which a contemporaneous cleric wrote, "The Basques speak among themselves in a tongue they say they understand but I frankly do not believe it." In their strongholds in the crook of the elbow of the Iberian peninsula, they were isolated from the turmoil of land wars, fiercely intent upon self-preservation, and coincidentally upon the pursuit of the large black whales (which they called *sarda*) that arrived every autumn in their offshore waters.

It is likely that they also hunted the Atlantic gray whale, although there is no evidence to support this supposition. There is, however, considerable evidence that the Atlantic gray whale (which was called *otta sotta*) was present in the Atlantic during the days of Basque whaling. Remains have been found on both sides of the ocean: in England, Holland and Sweden in the east; and from New York and New Jersey to North Carolina in the west. An account discovered by Fraser suggests that a gray whale (called *sandloegja* by the Icelanders) existed as recently as 1640 in the waters off Iceland. With nothing more than the absence of gray whales to substantiate his claim, Mowat writes "that by as early as the fourteenth century, the otta sotta had been hunted to virtual extinction in European waters." In their 1984 study of the Atlantic gray whale, Mead and Mitchell recognize only Fraser's *sandloegja**; a 1725 description of the "scrag whale" by Paul Dudley, Esq.†; and the 1611 instructions given by the di-

---

*"Sandloegja. Good eating. It has whiter baleen plates, which project from the upper jaw instead of teeth, as in all other baleen whales, which will be discussed later. It is very tenacious of life and can come to land to lie as a seal like to rest the whole day. But in sand it never breaks up."

†"The Scrag whale is near a-kin to the Fin-Back, but instead of a Fin on his Back, the Ridge of ther After-part of his back is scragged with a half Dozen Knobs of Knuckles; he is nearest the right Whale in Figure and for Quantity of Oil; his Bone is white, but won't split."

rectors of the Muscovy Company to Thomas Edge*, as "reliable records of gray whales in the North Atlantic." There are no more gray whales in the Atlantic, and while this unfortunate state of affairs might not be directly attributable to the Basques, it is not unreasonable to assign them some part in the disappearance of these whales.

For many years, the most comprehensive study on the subject of Basque whaling was that written by Sir Clements Markham and published in 1881. While writing a study of William Baffin, he learned "that the first English whaling vessels were in the habit of shipping a boat's crew of Basques to harpoon the whales," so he began to investigate, and ended up in Spain. He found that King Sancho the Wise of Navarre had granted petitions to the city of San Sebastian in the year 1150 for the warehousing of certain commodities, among which were *boquinas-barbas de ballenas,* plates of whalebone. Markham traced the fishery through the records of various cities and towns (he found the "Casa de Ballenas" in Asturias), and acknowledged that it was the Basques who taught the British how to kill whales. He sums up the Basque contribution as follows: "Of course the English, in due time, learnt to strike the whales themselves; but the Basques were their instructors; and it is therefore to this noble race that we owe the foundations of our whaling trade."

More recently, the Spanish cetologist Alex Aguilar has been searching the records for written documentation of Basque whaling and has discovered a reference from Bayona, in the Gulf of Biscay, that dates from the year 1059. From the remains of cetaceans examined at some of the settlements on the shore of the Cantabrian Sea (off the northern coast of Spain), it has been suggested that the Basques occasionally hunted sperm whales, but the predominant object of their fishery was the right whale. Ancient whaling bases have been found along the length of this coastline, which encompasses the provinces of Galicia, Asturias, Santander, and the heart of the Spanish Basque country, Guipuzcoa. From the western tip of northern Spain the sites have Spanish names (Camariñas, Malpica, Antrellusa, Llanes), but as we move eastward, toward the Basque settlements on the Bay of Biscay, the names take on a decidedly Basque flavor: Lequeitio, Ondarroa, Guetaria, Zarauz. Aguilar quotes several sources (including Markham) for the number of whales killed at Lequeitio from 1517 to 1662, and produces a total of some 62 whales, adults and young, from incomplete records, for a provisional average of something less than 2½ whales per year. Occasional records for Guetaria from 1699 to 1789 provide even lower numbers, suggesting that the Biscayan right whales were on the decline by the eighteenth century.

Along the French and Spanish Biscayan coasts, there are several towns and villages whose seals and coats-of-arms depict whale-fishers, including Bermeo, Ondarroa, Motrico, and Fuenterrabia in Spain, and Biarritz, Hendaye, and Guethary in France. Jenkins writes, "In this fishery the Bayonnais took part, and it is one of the most interesting features in the ancient records of the town of Bayonne." For several centuries, the Basques of Biarritz, St.-Jean-de-Luz, Bayonne, San Sebastian and other towns killed the *sarda* in their inshore and offshore waters. This activity did not go unnoticed by the tax-collectors. In 1197, King John of England (acting as the Duke of Guienne) collected a tax on the first two whales taken at Biarritz. In 1261, all whales taken at Bayonne were tithed, a continuation of an earlier, voluntary gift of all whales' tongues to the Church. The kings of Castile and Navarre also extracted taxes from the whalers, often in the form of meat or whalebone. Under a 1324 edict known as *De Praerogativa Regis* (The Royal Prerogative), Edward II of England (1307–27) collected a duty on every whale captured in British waters, and his successors continued to claim the "royal fish" as Crown property.

To this day, we do not know whence the Basques came, or from whom they were descended. (Their blood type distinguishes them from the French and the Spanish, and biologically as well as linguistically they appear to be distinct from any other people now in existence.) As far as we can ascertain from the scanty records and the ruined stone watchtowers (known as *vigías*) that still stand overlooking the bays, they pursued the right whale. (In 1928, Sydney Harmer wrote, "A watchman who tried to use [the towers] for their original purpose would now have an unprofitable occupation, and he would not be likely to see a single whale of this species during his lifetime.")

---

*"The fourth sort of whale is called Otta Sotta, and it is of the same colour as the Trumpa having finnes in his mouth all white but not above a yard long, being thicker than the Trumpa but not so long. He yeeldes the best oyle but not above 30 hogs' heads."

Coats of arms of the medieval French Basque communities of Biarritz (a) and Hendaye (b), and the Spanish Basque villages of Bermeo (c), Fuenterrabia (d), Guetaria (e), and Motrico (f), all showing whales and whaling.

Even more significantly, the Basques are said to have invented the on-board tryworks, where whales could be processed at sea, avoiding the time-consuming and arduous process of towing the carcass to shore and then winching it up on the beach for rendering. According to Jenkins, this distinction belongs to "a captain of Cibourre named François Sopite," but surprisingly, in a book heavily footnoted with obscure references, this important fact goes undocumented. In Sanderson's *Follow the Whale,* however, a whole chapter is devoted to a re-creation of Sopite's accomplishments, including a description of him standing "silently on the poop with his hands behind his back peering out from under his curious floppy black hat." Sanderson seems to have consulted many of the same references listed by Jenkins,

but he doesn't tell us where the hat comes from, or how he knows that Sopite was "smiling wryly" at the success of his experiment. Up to that time, whales were flensed and tried-out on shore, which meant that the whalers could never roam too far from their home ports. As we shall see, however, Sopite's "invention" may have been the invention of some creative authors, since real evidence of the Basque whalers has been uncovered, and there is no indication whatsoever of on-board tryworks.

Even though the hunters never took very many whales in a given season, the right whale (known as the Biscayan whale to distinguish it from the Greenland right whale) disappeared from Biscayan waters, and the Basques had to look farther afield for oil and bone. (Clements Markham, in his study of Basque whaling history, has written that each of the whaling villages may have taken no more than a couple of whales per year. This would not be enough to decimate the population, but it is possible that the disturbance caused by the whalers drove the whales to other, less perilous breeding grounds.)

From Iberia, Basque fishermen crossed the North Atlantic seeking new grounds. Some evidence indicates that they may have fished the Labrador-Newfoundland grounds as early as the fourteenth century, but were driven off by the local Eskimos. The vessels that they used were not known until recently, when a Canadian archaeologist named Selma Barkham followed up some vague hints in the historical records of Labrador and with the help of divers located the wrecks of several Basque ships in the area known as Red Bay. Found sitting on the bottom of the bay were the remains of a three-masted ninety-foot galleon which is believed to have sunk in a storm in 1565, and the complete hull of one of the frail *chalupas.** On two of Red Bay's smaller islands, workers found unmistakable evidence of tryworks, where the blubber of the whales was rendered into oil. Since this endeavor took place between the years 1560 and 1570 (ascertained from documents examined in Spanish archives by Barkham), it would appear that Sopite's "invention" of on-board tryworks was either apocryphal or somehow did not extend to the whaling operation at Red Bay.

*A *chalupa* (in French a *chaloupe* and in the British fishery a *shallop*) was a 25-foot-long whaleboat, rowed by six oarsmen, from which the whale was harpooned and towed to shore.

As the Basques enlarged the scope of their search for whales to the vicinity of Newfoundland and Labrador, they may well have been the first Europeans to fish the Greenland coasts and the Grand Banks, two of the richest cod-fishing grounds in the world. Upon landing, they predated the "official" discoverers of the land known as Terranova, John Cabot and Jacques Cartier. In their pursuit of the sea's bounty, the adventurous Basques visited Ireland, Iceland, Greenland, and evidently sailed as far north as Spitsbergen. They also crossed the Atlantic to find the right whales that inhabited the inshore waters of Newfoundland and Labrador, but it is unlikely that they made these voyages without island-hopping across the perimeter of the Northern Atlantic, much as the Norse had done before them.

Examination of the bones at Red Bay indicate that bowheads were also processed there by the Basques. This location is considerably south of the known range of the bowhead, which inhabits—or inhabited—eastern Arctic waters and the Bering Sea.* (It is likely that the Basques took bowheads farther north, and then brought them back for processing, thereby accounting for bowhead bones in a region where bowheads are not known to have lived.) There are no records of Basques' hunting humpbacks, but these whales are found off the Canadian Maritime coasts and Greenland.

The rich days of Newfoundland and Labrador whaling ended for the Basques as the sixteenth century was ending. The destruction of the Spanish Armada in 1588 meant that Spanish ships of war could no longer protect fishing fleets so far from home, and the Basque whalers ventured across the Atlantic unprotected. They had established shore stations at Tadoussac and Sept-Iles on the St. Lawrence, where they hunted humpbacks and probably belugas. By 1738 the last Basques had left Canada. Why bother with the transatlantic crossings and hostile North Americans when there were fat Greenland whales for the taking in Spitsbergen? The Basques participated in the early Dutch and British expeditions to Spitsbergen, bringing with them five hundred years of whaling experience.

*In a report written in 1904, three-quarters of a century before the Basque *chalupas* were discovered in Labrador, F. W. True wrote, "The records of this industry [sixteenth-century Atlantic whaling] are for the most part buried in obscurity, or have been destroyed, and such as are now known contain no descriptions of whales."

Six Basque harpooners from St.-Jean-de-Luz were part of the crew of the first Muscovy Company expedition to Spitsbergen in 1611. In the early years of the Greenland Fishery (Barendsz had named the Spitsbergen islands "Greenland" when he discovered them in 1596, because he believed they were an extension of the island of that name), the Basques sold their services to whoever was willing to pay, but in addition to their participation in the Dutch/British rivalry, the Spanish Basques also sent their own ships to the northern ice in 1613. No sooner had the Spanish tried to join the fishery on their own than James I of England issued the Muscovy Company an exclusive charter to fish the waters of Spitsbergen, to which the Dutch countered in 1614 by forming their own Noordsche Compagnie with the same objectives.

Although the Spanish Basques had the experience and the expertise, they did not have the naval power to back up their claims, and as the Dutch and the British competed for supremacy in Spitsbergen (the Dutch eventually won the battle because of their more effective management and business practices, but in the end, everybody lost, because they ran out of whales), the Basques faded into whaling oblivion. As time and progress passed them by, their domestic whaling capabilities diminished accordingly. According to J.-P. Proulx, when a whale stranded at St.-Jean-de-Luz in 1764, the hunters could only find old and rusty implements with which to cut it up.

In many respects, the Basques were the advance guard of what would eventually become an all-out war on the whales, but in those relatively uncomplicated times, they were only aware of the nutritional needs that could be fulfilled by the taking of these large, inoffensive animals. They would, however, establish a pattern with regard to the right whale fishery that would serve as an example for virtually every nation that followed their lead: they took the females and calves since they were the most accessible, and by so doing guaranteed the catastrophic degeneration of the breeding population. In a review of the available data, Aguilar estimates that during the period 1530 to 1610, Basque whalers might have taken as many as 40,000 right whales. Medieval Europeans probably didn't have much time to ponder the effects of their actions on future generations, however—certainly not on future generations of whales.

THREE

THE LATER HISTORY OF EARLY WHALING

The Beginning of Industrial Whaling

Like other European powers during the sixteenth century, the British sought the riches of the Indies; their bread and meats were as tasteless as those of the Spanish and the Portuguese, and their merchants were equally interested in gold, silks and spices. Because the routes to the east and west were effectively closed to them, they decided to try to cross to the Indies by the north. The polar ice cap was unknown at that time, so their northerly voyages brought them all sorts of unexpected landfalls. In 1497, after sailing across the Atlantic from Bristol, John Cabot, a Genoese like Columbus, landed at a place in what is now eastern Canada—either Labrador, Newfoundland or Cape Breton Island. He returned to England with nothing of value, but he did bring evidence of human habitation. On another unsuccessful voyage in 1498, John Cabot disappeared at sea, his mission to be taken up by his son Sebastian. In 1508, Sebastian—who may have accompanied his father on one of his voyages as a boy—sailed across the Atlantic, encountering icebergs in the north, and later perhaps sailing as far south as Florida. Nothing on this voyage would convince England that Cabot had found the Spice Islands, but never-

theless the search for a northern passage to India would dominate England's naval activities for another century and a half, and would precipitate an industry that would change the face of western civilization. It would light the lamps of Europe with an oily flame that would burn for three and a half centuries.

The first whalers to explore the coasts of North America were the Basques. Following the trails of the cod-fishermen who reported a plentitude of whales in Newfoundland, the Basques found their way there and encountered previously untapped schools of whales. It may have been as early as 1400 that the Basques discovered the whaling grounds of North America, but the records show very little until their colonization of Red Bay, Labrador, around 1540. (To date, this is the only record of a Basque colony in North America, but it is possible that other, earlier settlements existed.) The Basques hunted whales and walruses north of the Arctic Circle. They were the only people in Europe who had the knowledge and the experience to hunt whales, since they had been doing it for hundreds of years. They were not at all interested in colonization, silks

Franz Josef Land

Novaya Zemlya

Kara Sea

Barents Sea

Spitsbergen

U.S.S.R.

Bear Island

North Cape

Kola
Peninsula

Varanger
Fjord

White Sea

GREENLAND

Davis
Strait

Jan Mayen Island

Norwegian Sea

Leningrad

Reykjavik ICELAND

Cape Farewell

NORWAY

Vestfold

Faeroe Islands

Shetland Islands

SCOTLAND

Atlantic Ocean

Peterhead
Aberdeen

DENMARK

ENGLAND

Whitby
Hull

Amsterdam

Rotterdam

London

N
W   E
S

From England, Scotland and the Netherlands,
seventeenth-century whalers headed north to
the ice in search of the polar whale, the
animal we now know as the bowhead.

or spices, so the North American continent remained unclaimed, except by Columbus, who never
set foot on it; by John Cabot, who believed he had
found India; and by its aboriginal inhabitants, who
were ignored.

Around 1550 the English formed the "Mysterie and
Company of Merchant Adventurers for the Discov-
erie of Regions, Dominions, Islands and Places Un-
knowen," in an attempt to compete with the Spanish
and the Portuguese for trade routes to the Orient.

In 1577, Martin Frobisher sailed north, and although he believed he had discovered the Orient, he found Greenland and Baffin Island, and wrote of "many monstrous fishes and strange fowles," leading the way to the British northern whale fishery.

Sebastian Cabot, then seventy-five years old, was chosen as governor. Since the Iberians had effectively monopolized the southern routes to the Far East around Africa and South America—where they not only found the Spice Islands, but the riches of the Inca, Aztec, and Maya civilizations as well—the English decided to try to find a way to the mysterious east by heading north. They began to search for a Northeast or Northwest Passage to Cathay.

A fleet was assembled in 1553, consisting of the *Bona Esperanza,* the *Bona Confidentia,* and the *Edward Bonaventure* (Edward IV was king at the time), and they sailed north for three weeks after leaving sight of the familiar British coastline. In *Esperanza,* Hugh

Willoughby sighted land and put ashore on northern Norway, which would lead to the erroneous claim that he had discovered Spitsbergen. From there the *Esperanza* and the *Confidentia* took an eastward bearing and headed out into the wild and icy Barents Sea. Completely out of sight of land and sailing in totally unknown waters, they became lost as the winter and the ice closed in upon them. On the desolate shores of the Kola Peninsula in northwestern Russia, the crews and officers of these two ships froze to death.

The surviving ship, *Edward Bonaventure,* under the command of Richard Chancelor, fared better. After rounding the North Cape, the crew spent the winter of 1554 in the town of Archangel. They were taken to Moscow, some fifteen hundred miles away over frozen tundra and ice, where they met with the Emperor, thereby initiating contact with the Russians. Thereafter, the Merchant Adventurers became the Muscovy Company, and while further attempts to find Cathay by sailing east were thwarted by the weather—and the impassable Novaya Zemlya—the whales, who found these otherwise inhospitable waters to their liking, had been found.

Once the company had discovered some regions and dominions to explore, they began to trade with the Russians. They traded cloth and firearms for fish, oil and timber, and in 1576, Queen Elizabeth awarded the company a twenty-year monopoly to hunt whales "within any seas whatsoever." Despite the presence of Basque whalermen on board some of their early voyages, the English were not particularly successful. Some of the ships headed for Vardø in Finnmark (known as "Wardhouse" to the British), to secure fish and whale oil. They also operated around Iceland, where fin whales were abundant, but these swift, powerful rorquals would remain beyond the capabilities of whalers for another three hundred years.

Attempts to discover the Northwest Passage were just as calamitous and futile. In 1585, John Davis in the 50-ton barque *Sunshine,* and John Bruton in the 35-ton *Moonshine* sailed north and discovered the strait between Greenland and Baffin Island that now bears Davis's name, and in 1596 the Dutch navigator Barendsz (subsequently Anglicized to Barents) came upon Bear Island, and then the isolated group of islands known as Spitsbergen. (The question of who found these islands first would remain an issue for many years.) Martin Frobisher and John Davis kept up their unavailing search for the Northwest Passage until 1587, but by the following year, most other seagoing Englishmen were preoccupied with the Spaniards, not the whales, and exploration was suspended while the English fleet was otherwise engaged. Frobisher, of course, was one of the true heroes of the British victory over the Spanish Armada of Philip II, along with Francis Drake and John Hawkins. Drake's innovations in hull and sail design would change not only the manner in which naval battles would be fought in the future, but would also improve the seaworthiness of ocean-going vessels, thus

eventually facilitating the hunting of whales. After 1588, British domination of the northern seas was established, but it would not be long before their Protestant allies, the Dutch, would begin to contest it. In war, the Dutch and the English had to band together against the Catholic majority of Europe, but in commerce, their allegiances were to their exchequers.

The merchants of Hull, whom Scoresby described as "ever remarkable for their assiduous and enterprising spirit," fitted out ships for whaling as early as 1598, despite the monopoly of the Muscovy Company. It was apparent then that there were some huge black whales in the northern ice, and within the next two decades, their breeding grounds were found. Even though the British Crown had granted a monopoly to the Muscovy Company, other nations had heard about the whale-rich waters of the Arctic and were prepared to contest the self-awarded British control of the nascent whale fishery. The "expansion of Europe" was dependent as much upon the fat backs of whales as it was on the search for a new way to India.

Ambroise Paré (1510–90), better known as the founder of modern surgery, visited Biarritz in 1564 and observed the Basque whale fishery there. In his description (*Des Monstres Marins.* 1573), he gave us what is probably the first accurate description of the baleen plates of a whale. He described how "*des lames qui sortent de la bouche. on en fait des vertugales. busques pour les femmes. . . .*"* In 1591 a Bayonne merchant named Peter de Hody returning from Newfoundland with fourteen hogsheads of whale oil aboard, was captured by a British privateer and taken to Bristol. Three years later, the 35-ton *Grace* out of the same British port sailed for Newfoundland, and although they did no whaling, the sailors found the wrecks of two Basque ships, from which they salvaged 700–800 whalebone "finnes."

The whales that were hunted by the Basques in the Bay of Biscay were black right whales, which were, as if to prove this point, known originally as *Balaena biscayensis.* (They are now known as *Balaena glacialis.* and the Northern- and Southern-Hemisphere species are usually considered as one.)

---

* *Vertugal* (or *verdugado*) is the Spanish for "farthingale," a supporting undergarment that held out the skirt. It is said to have been introduced to England by Catherine of Aragon.

Beaufort Sea

Banks Island

Prince of Wales Island

Devon Island

Lancaster Sound

Baffin Bay

GREENLAND

Victoria Island

Somerset Island

Baffin Island

Davis Strait

Cape Farewell

Foxe Basin

Cumberland Sound

Hudson Strait

Labrador Basin

Hudson Bay

LABRADOR

NEWFOUNDLAND

James Bay

Gulf of St. Lawrence

Gaspé Peninsula

St. Lawrence River

NEW BRUNSWICK

NOVA SCOTIA

Bay of Fundy

Northern Canada, showing Greenland and the Davis Strait, where the British and the Dutch eliminated the Greenland whale. The long-sought Northwest Passage runs through Lancaster Sound and then between Banks and Victoria islands.

Because both species of right whale are thoroughly depleted now, it is difficult to determine which was actually hunted and by whom. (There are perhaps 7,000 bowheads alive today, all in the western Arctic; and some 2,000 right whales, dispersed throughout their old breeding and feeding areas—except for the Bay of Biscay, where there are none at all.)* The range of the bowhead in the eastern Arctic was thought to include the circumpolar area north of the Arctic Circle, but the whales roamed from one

*In a recent description of the cetaceans and seals of the coast of France, we find this note: *Sa frequence dans la Golfe de Gascogne, au cours des siècles passés, lui a valu son nom de Baleine de Biscay ou Baleine des Basques mais elle semble en avoir complètement disparu depuis la fin du xixᵉ siècle.*

northerly latitude to another, motivated by food, weather, and ice conditions. It is probable that the whales hunted off Spitsbergen, northern Greenland, the Davis Strait, and Bear Island were bowheads. (We can only determine this by inference, since at approximately the same latitude in the western Arctic—the Beaufort Sea—the last remaining population of bowheads still exists. In his detailed discussion of the zoology of the Arctic, Scoresby mentions only the Mysticete.)

THE FIRST commercial whale-hunting in Canada —in fact, the first commercial whale-hunting in North America—occurred in Labrador. Although the conventional wisdom holds that the Basque whalers had followed the right whales across the Atlantic from the Bay of Biscay, Canadian historian Selma Barkham has called the idea that the Basques followed the whales farther and farther out into the Atlantic until they collided with North America a "ridiculous legend." Rather than chase an ever-diminishing supply of right whales, the Basque whalers intentionally crossed the North Atlantic to harvest the abundant right whales that the cod-fishermen had told them about.

At Red Bay, in Labrador, the first whaling station in North America has been found, dating from approximately 1536—almost a century before the Pilgrims arrived in the *Mayflower* and noticed the right whales in Cape Cod Bay. By the 1540s, the Basques were killing some 300 right whales per year in the Strait of Belle Isle, and casks of oil were being delivered to Bristol, London and Flanders. The fishery declined toward the end of the century, perhaps because the whales were becoming scarce, but perhaps also because many ships were affected by the war between Spain and England in 1588. There are also records of Basque whalers being harassed (and maybe even killed and eaten) by savages they called "Esquimaos." From the waters of Labrador the Basques moved into the St. Lawrence River and fished there until the beginning of the seventeenth century. If the Basques actually took bowheads on some of their earlier voyages to Newfoundland and Labrador (they left no records of the species of whales they hunted), then the credit for discovering a completely new species of whale must go to them.

Unlike the other species—such as the *sarda* which only came into the Bay of Biscay to breed—the bowhead lives its entire life in one region, migrating only with the moving ice. Of course no mammal can live in—or under—solid ice, so when the Arctic seas froze in winter, the whales moved southward.

At the end of the sixteenth century, the Basques of St.-Jean-de-Luz and other villages took whales off Newfoundland, but they represented only a loose confederation, not a particular country. The first official representatives of a European power to hunt whales in the Arctic were the English. In 1604, Captain Jonas Poole of the Muscovy Company fetched up on tiny Bear Island and returned to England with reports of foxes, fowls and walruses. Poole went back

again in 1605, 1606 and 1608, mostly for walrus, but he also brought back reports of plentiful whales. Poole sailed again for the north in 1610 in the *Amitie,* and found himself in Spitsbergen waters, where the whales existed in great abundance. (That the British were still unfamiliar with whale-killing techniques was reflected in Poole's comment that "the Basques were the only people that understood whaling.") In 1611, Poole, in the 60-ton *Elizabeth,* led Thomas Edge, in the *Mary Margaret,* to the newly discovered whaling grounds of Spitsbergen, and one of the six harpooners from St.-Jean-de-Luz killed the first whale there.

The Muscovy Company had given captains Poole and Edge detailed instructions regarding the whales they might encounter. The instructions, which have survived, included the *Bearded whale,* obviously the Greenland whale, which "sort of whale doth yielde usually 400 to 500 finnes and between 100 to 120 hogsheads of oyle"; the *Sarda,* which was the black right whale; the *Trumpa,* which from its description was the sperm whale ("He hath in his mouth teeth of a span long and as thicke as a man's wrist. . . . In the head of this whale is the spermacetti. . . ."); rorquals that are probably the blue, fin and humpback; a little white whale they called *Sewria* (the beluga); and finally the mysterious creature known as *Otta Sotta,* whose description ("of the same color as the Trumpa, having finnes in his mouth all white but not above halfe a yard long, being thicker than the Trumpa but not as long. . . .") might be the minke whale but also might be the now-extinct Atlantic gray whale.

Nowadays it is all too easy to condemn the whalers for their flagrant disregard of conservation principles, for killing virtually all the whales they could find and then scouring the oceans for more. But early whaling must be placed in its historical perspective, and we cannot apply our twentieth-century sensitivity to the whale-hunters of the seventeenth century. The oil that was boiled out of blubber was the primary reason for the hunting of the whales. A clear or amber liquid, it was odorless when fresh, but when it turned rancid from being kept too long in the casks, it began to smell. It was used primarily for lighting, but also for heating and lubrication. Whale oil also provided a base for the manufacture of soap, varnishes and paint, and was used in the

A Whale is ordinarly about 60 foote longe

The whale is cut up as hee lyes floting crosse the stearne of a shipp the blubber is cut from the flesh by peeces 3 or 4 foote long and being rased is rowed on shore towards the coppers

When the whale comes aboue water y̓ shallop rowes towards him and being within reach of him the harpoiner darts his harpingiron at him out of both his hands and being fast they lance him to death

They place 2 or 3 coppers on a roe and y̓ chopping boat on the one side and the cooling boate on the other side to receiue y̓ oyle of y̓ coppers, the chopt blubber being boyled is taken out of the coppers and put in wiker baskets or barowes throw w̓ᶜʰ the oyle is dreaned and runes into y̓ cooler w̓ᶜʰ is ½ fall of water out of w̓ᶜʰ it is convaied by troughs into buts or hogsheads

Whaling in Spitsbergen in 1611. Originally published in Dutch, this series was reengraved and translated into English for *Churchill's Voyages* in 1745.

processing of textiles and rope. The early European whale fisheries made no use of the meat, which must have existed in prodigious quantities. An average bowhead weighs some 60 tons, and subtracting the weight of the bones, viscera and blubber, the remains of these thousands of whales—if there had been either the desire or the means to preserve them—probably could have fed all of Europe. (Scoresby wrote, "The flesh and the bones, excepting the jaw bones occasionally, are rejected.") The jaw bones contained oil—as did all the other bones of the whale—so they were often hoisted aboard and kept, usually by hanging them in the rigging. Holes were drilled in them to allow the oil to seep out (Lubbock wrote that "the oil which dripped from them was considered superior to that from the blubber"), and when these great curving arches were brought home, they were prized as gateposts, fences, or supports for the roofs of sheds. In the Netherlands and Germany, these huge jawbones—the mandibles of the large baleen whales are the largest bones in the animal kingdom—were often hung on the walls of public buildings, either to identify the business that was transpiring within or perhaps to function as a gigantic trophy of the hunt. For seventeenth- and eighteenth-century Europe, oil for illumination and soap-making was evidently more important than protein, and no effort was ever made to preserve the potentially edible portions of the whale. (Across the Arctic ice at about the same time, the Eskimos of Alaska and Siberia were also hunting bowheads, but to them the most important product of the hunt was the meat.) The Basques may have eaten whale meat, but their industry was primarily based on the oil— and to a lesser extent, the whalebone—which they utilized themselves and also sold in England and continental Europe.

The other reason for hunting the whale was for its "finnes." They were, of course, not *fins* at all, but the filtering plates that hang from the roof of the mouths of baleen whales and enable them to sieve their microscopic food out of the sea water. "It is a substance of horny appearance and consistency," wrote Scoresby, "extremely flexible and elastic, generally of a bluish black colour, but not unfrequently striped longitudinally with white, and exhibiting a beautiful play of colour on the surface. Internally it is of a fibrous texture, resembling hair; and the external surface consists of a smooth enamel, capable of receiving a good polish." Wherever a strong, pliable substance was required, this keratinous material was employed. It was used for corset stays, umbrella ribs, ramrods, fishing rods, buggy whips and carriage springs. Cut into thin strips, it was made into sieves, nets and brushes, and further shredded it was used to stuff upholstered furniture. (In later years, as fashions changed, whalebone would be bent into skirt hoops.)

Perhaps the easiest way to recognize the importance of the whale fishery is to compare it to today's petroleum industry. In many places where plastic or oil are employed today, whale products were used then. Of course, there were other oils, such as rape, palm or linseed; and wood and iron were the materials of manufacturing, but whale products were considered superior, and most important, you did not have to cultivate or manufacture them. The stocks of whales swam unharvested in the northern oceans, a ripe source of raw material that was available to those who were willing to outfit the ships and brave the hazards of the hunt.

.   .   .

THE ARCTIC North Atlantic, even now considered one of the most hostile environments in the world, must have been unbearable for the whalemen who were pressed into service. In seas that drenched everything with icy green water, the sailors were packed together in dismal, verminous quarters, where disease was rampant and dampness was perpetual. (The greatest danger to a wooden ship was fire, and therefore heating, drying or cooking fires were painstakingly monitored.) Even today, whaling is one of the most noisome of all occupations, but in the seventeenth century it stank with the combined odors of rancid whale oil, rotten food, unwashed men, filthy bilgewater and human excrement. There were no sewage facilities, and the ships must have reeked so that downwind they could probably be smelled before they were seen.

Provisions varied from ship to ship, but the food ranged from bad to inedible. In the main, victuals aboard the ships of the sixteenth and seventeenth centuries consisted of salt beef (which was more than occasionally horsemeat), pork, fish, cheese and bread or biscuit. Stored in casks, everything—including the water and beer—turned bad, so rather than consume weevil-infested biscuit or drink slimy green water, the whalers often had to eat whatever they could catch: fish, seals, sea birds, or even whale meat. The etiology of scurvy was unknown, and "the plague of the sea" killed off sailors by the thousands.* In addition, food poisoning, typhus, dysentery, and a host of other diseases ran through the ships, incapacitating or killing the crews as well as the officers. It was not uncommon for a ship to lose half its crew on a voyage, and many a vessel was probably lost because there were simply too few hands to handle her or bring her home.

The whaling ships of this period were 250- to 400-tonners, often not longer than 100 feet. They usually carried a crew of thirty to fifty men and an assortment of officers. (The captain was nominally in charge of the ship while she was at sea, but once on the whaling grounds or anchored, command was in the hands of the *spectioneer*—the blubber-cutter.) Hak-

*It was not until 1753 that James Lind, a Scottish physician, recognized that scurvy could be prevented by the ingestion of the juice of oranges, lemons and limes, but the isolation of vitamin C as the specific antiscrobutic did not occur until 1932. Although limes were the preferred preventative—thus the name "limeys" for British sailors—oranges and lemons are actually more effective.

luyt's *English Voyages,* published in 1598, contains a list of the equipment and supplies necessary for a whaling voyage to Spitsbergen:

There must be 55 men who departing from Whardhouse in the moneth of April, must bee furnished with 4 kintals and a halfe of bread for every man. {The list continues:}

250 hogsheds to put the bread in
150 hogsheds of Cidar
6 kintals of oile
8 kintals of bacon
6 hogsheds of beefe
10 quarters of salt
150 pounds of candles
8 quarters of beans and pease
Saltfish & herring, a quantitie convenient
4 tunnes of wine
Half a quarter of mustard seed, and a querne
A grindstone
800 empty shaken hogsheds
350 bundles of hoopes, and 6 quintalines
800 paire of heds for the hogsheds
10 Estachas called roxes for harping irons
10 pieces of Arporieras
3 pieces of Baibens for the Javelines small
2 tackles to turn the Whales
A halser of 27 fadom long to turn ye whales
15 great Javelines
18 small Javelines
50 harping irons
6 machicos to cut the Whale withall
2 dozen of machetos to minch the Whale
2 great hookes to turn the Whale
6 paire of can hooks
6 hooks for staves
3 dozen of staves for harping irons
6 pullies to turne the Whale with
10 great baskets
10 lampes of iron to carie light
5 kettles of 150 li. the piece and 6 ladles
1000 of nailes for the pinnases
500 of nailes of Carabelie for the houses
18 axes and hatchets to cleave wood
12 pieces of line, and 6 dozen of hooks
2 beetles of Rosemarie
4 dozen of oares for the pinnases
6 lanterns

Item, gunpouder & matches for harquebushes as shalbe needed.
Item, there must be carried from hence 5 pinnases, five men to strike with harping irons, two cutters of Whale. 5 coopers & a purser or two.

A NOTE OF CERTAINE OTHER NECESSARIE THINGS BELONGING TO THE WHALEFISHING, RECEIVED OF MASTER W. BURROUGH.

A sufficient number of pullies for tackle for the Whale
A dozen of great baskets
4 furnaces to melt the whale in
6 ladles of copper
A thousand of nailes to mend the pinnases
500 great nailes of spikes to make their house
3 paire of bootes great and strong, for them that shall cut   the Whale
8 calve skins to make aprons or babecans

Upon their arrival in Spitsbergen, the whalers would anchor in one of the island's protected bays and strip the ship for the erection of a shore station. The station included housing for the men, various workshops, and ovens for boiling the blubber. Because the whales traditionally sought refuge in the same bays year after year, hunting them was often a matter of sighting the twin vapor plumes and rolling black backs from shore, and launching one of the shallops. (Later in the fishery, when the whales did not cooperate by making themselves so easily visible, the whalers erected watchtowers.) The whale was harpooned in the Basque fashion by a man standing in the bow, and then lanced repeatedly to kill it. A 1613 journal (quoted in Conway's 1906 *History of Spitsbergen*) indicates that more than one shallop's crew lanced the whale, "as neare his swimming finne and as lowe under water as they can convenientlie, to pierce into his intralls." After a successful hunt, the whale would be towed to the ship or the shallows, and the blubber stripped and boiled down in the furnaces that had been erected. The casks of oil (which floated, of course) were then towed back to the anchored ship, where they would be stowed for the voyage home.

The head of the whale was cut off, and the "finnes" removed. The "white pithie substance" was scraped off the baleen plates, and they were scrubbed with sand because although they remained clean while underwater (a dead Greenland whale floated belly-up), when they were exposed to the water where the blubber was being stripped they became contaminated with the grease from the water "which is alwaies fatty with blubber that floats upon it continuallie." The cleaned "finnes" were sorted according to size, packed in bundles, identified with the company's mark, and stored for shipment.

As if to presage the dismal future of the English fishery, the first Spitsbergen season was a total failure. As Captain Edge's *Mary Margaret* was wrecked in the ice, its crew took to the boats. They were rescued by Captain Thomas Marmaduke, of the *Hopewell,* an "unauthorized" whaler out of Hull. When Marmaduke returned to the wreck of the *Margaret,* he found Poole's *Elizabeth,* from which he loaded the cargo onto the *Hopewell.* In the process, *Elizabeth* was "brought so light that she upset and was lost." Marmaduke took both crews and cargo back to Hull, which resulted in an unmitigated triumph for Hull whaling and an enormous setback for the Muscovy Company.

Marmaduke may even be the missing link between Basque whaling and Spitsbergen whaling. The Basques had built primitive tryworks at Red Bay, Labrador, and the Dutch established their whaling station at Smeerenburg around 1620. Studies by the Dutch whaling historian Louwrens Hacquebord have revealed the existence of similar tryworks and dwellings on Edge Island (southern Spitsbergen) dating from around 1615. Hacquebord believes that these works were erected by Thomas Marmaduke, who was whaling and walrus-hunting there at that time, and that because the English were employing Basque harpooners and crewmen, the structures were similar in nature to those of the Basques at Red Bay.

Undaunted by their losses, the British sent two more vessels to the North in 1612. When the *Whale* (Captain John Russell) and the *Sea-Horse* (Captain Thomas Edge) arrived at Bear Island (originally called Cherie Island), they found two other British ships already there, as well as a German, and a Dutchman commanded by an Englishman named Alan Sallowes, who had been employed by the Muscovy Company but had been forced to leave England because of debt. The British with their Basque harpooners prevailed, and returned home with their holds filled. By 1613, the waters of the northern seas, which for millennia had been the sole province of the seals, walruses and whales, suddenly seemed to fill with sail. Four Dutch and twelve Spanish ships arrived in 1613, but they were all chased off by the British, who had begun to arm their whaling vessels. Nevertheless, 1614 was the last full year of English

supremacy. In that year, the Muscovy Company sent five ships and a pinnace to the whaling grounds. (One of these was the *Thomasine* with a young mariner named William Baffin aboard.) Realizing the tremendous potential of this industry, the Dutch had formed their own enterprise, the Noordsche Compagnie, organized quite differently from the Muscovy Company. Rather than being financed by individuals, the Dutch company was composed of chambers (*kamers*) from various cities such as Amsterdam, Rotterdam, Delft and Hoorn, and obtained an exclusive charter from the Staats-General to hunt whales between Novaya Zemlya and Davis Strait for three years. Obviously, two competing countries could not have exclusive rights to the same resource.

Since Spitsbergen had been found by Willem Barendsz in 1596 (on a voyage dedicated to the discovery of a northern route to China), the Dutch had a fairly good reason to dispute the British claims. However, the British were resolute in their intention to preserve their exclusive rights to the Arctic fishery, and they chased the first Dutch whalers home. From the turn of the century until 1615, Muscovy Company whalers enjoyed almost total control of the fishery. Even so, their whaling was not without dispute, since whalers from York and Hull continued to sail north, and valuable time and energy were expended chasing these interlopers away, not always successfully.

To protect their whalers, the Dutch also sent warships to the Arctic. By 1615, the whaleships and warships of the two nations were in a state of conflict in the bleak fjords of Spitsbergen, and they both realized that whaling conducted as an adjunct to naval warfare would be economically disastrous. To avoid further conflict, the Dutch and the English negotiated a treaty, dividing up the whaling areas. Their agreement allowed the British to fish the waters south of Spitsbergen, while the Dutch took the north. At first this seemed an equitable arrangement, but it soon became apparent that the Dutch got the better deal. On the very northwest corner of the main island (now known as Vest Spitsbergen), on tiny Amsterdam Island, the Dutch established one of the most unusual settlements in the history of human habitation. It was known as *Smeerenburg,* or "blubbertown."

Spitsbergen ("sharp mountains" in Dutch) is a group of three major islands and several smaller ones

58

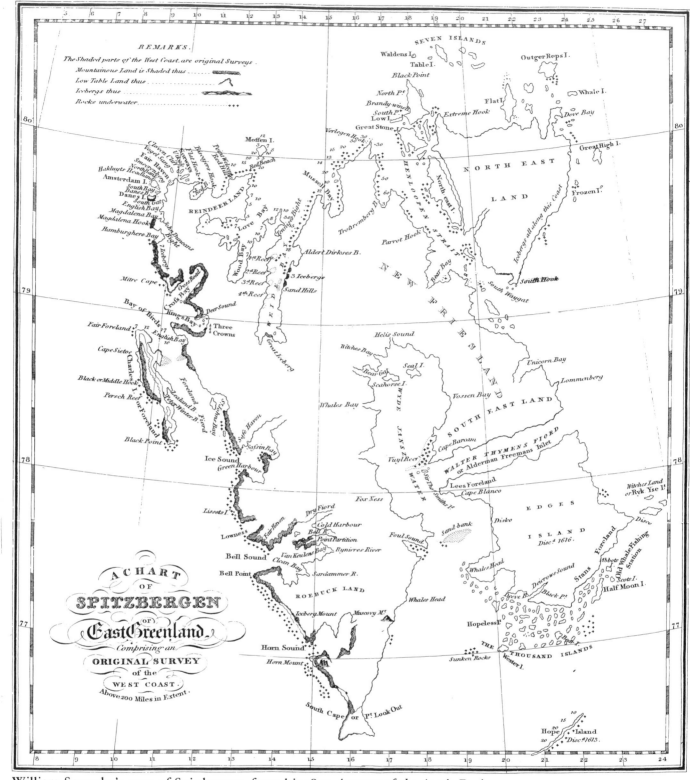

William Scoresby's map of Spitsbergen, from his 1820 *Account of the Arctic Regions.*

in the northern quadrant of the Barents Sea. Seven hundred miles from the North Pole, it is one of the most remote and hostile regions in the world, consisting mostly of barren black mountains, glacial ice fields, snow, rocks, and occasional lichens. Unwelcoming to men in ships, it is the perfect habitat for the Greenland whale. The winter weather may very well be the worst in the world, with snow-laden winds howling across the ice pack from the Pole, dense fogs, treacherous seas, and temperatures that are beyond human endurance. For the well-insulated bowheads, however, the sea around Spitsbergen was a cetacean paradise. Its many secluded bays and inlets provided the calm waters that these behemoths required for their breeding and calving. We have no way of knowing how many of the leviathans existed before the arrival of the whalers, but in his discussion of the early whale fishery, William Scoresby wrote, "At this time, the mysticetus was found in immense numbers throughout the whole extent of the coast, and in different capacious bays in which it abounds. . . . Not only did the coast of Spitsbergen abound with whales, but the shore of Jan Mayen Island, in proportion to its extent, afforded them in like abundance."*

WHILE SPITSBERGEN dominates the geography of early Arctic whaling, other islands also figure in the story. Whales were taken in the waters of Iceland, and also off Greenland, but Iceland is probably too far south for bowheads, and the whales of Greenland would not be exploited for another fifty years, when the Spitsbergen population had run out. Due north of Scotland, and therefore the first possible landfall for ships sailing in that direction, is Jan Mayen Island, discovered in 1611 by the Dutch navigator for whom it was named. Three hundred miles east of Greenland, Jan Mayen is about thirty-five miles long and nine miles wide. It is the peak of a submarine ridge that culminates in the forbidding, 7,000-foot-high Beerenberg volcano. Dense fogs and bitter storms are caused by the convergence of the warm Gulf Stream and the icy Greenland Current. The Hollanders and the Hull whalers utilized Jan Mayen's anchorages for some of the earliest recorded bowhead whaling, but they never set up shop there, because there were no usable harbors.

Even smaller than Jan Mayen is ten-mile-long Bear Island, which was discovered in 1596 by the Dutch navigators Barendsz, Heemskerke and Ryp. Its name—which was later changed to Cherie Island by the British and then back again—derives from the Dutchmen's killing of a polar bear upon their first landing. Jan Mayen and Bear Island are isolated in the extreme, and often locked in the Arctic ice. Because the whales require only a lee shore however—and not always that—these rocky specks of land served as their summer breeding grounds, and therefore the whalers fished their waters as well as the

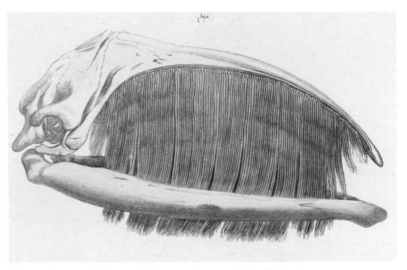

The primary object of the northern whale fisheries was the baleen—also known as "whalebone," although it was not bone at all—that hung from the roof of the mouth of the whale. Shown here is the arched skull of the Polar or Greenland whale, *Balaena mysticetus*.

richer, more productive Spitsbergen. Neither the whalers nor the whales remained in the vicinity of the islands during the winter; the whalers because the weather became intolerable, and the whales because they headed north to where their food supply proliferated. (There were, however, attempts by the Dutch to overwinter crews on Jan Mayen, primarily to protect the boats, casks and other equipment that they left on shore when they returned to their home ports. In 1633 a crew was sent by the Noordsche Compagnie to spend the winter. Although a surviving journal indicates that they were well-enough provisioned, they failed to collect the "lettuce" that might have provided the essential vitamin C to fend off scurvy, and all of them died.)

The Dutch had effectively occupied the Arctic by 1617, and the English fishery, on the wane since its monopoly had been debilitated, was losing ground and money rapidly. In 1626, when the Muscovy Company's fleet arrived in Spitsbergen, they found that whalermen from Hull had gotten there before them, taken their shallops, and burned their casks. The weakness of the company was demonstrated by the aftermath of this event: instead of prosecuting the Hull whalers, the Crown granted them one-fifth of the total tonnage allowed to work the Arctic whaling grounds. A convoluted imbroglio between the

*Using data he does not wholly identify, Farley Mowat postulates a virgin population of 150,000 bowheads. This seems inordinately high, but without a better reference than "my analysis of the records," it is impossible to check his figures.

A French whaler off "Devil's Thumb," Spitsbergen, around 1700. Scoresby described this mountain as "crooked, perfectly naked, being equally destitute of snow and verdure." The whale with the uneven twin spouts is supposed to be a bowhead.

soap-makers of England and the importers of whale oil took place in the 1630s, the result of which was a reduction in the price of oil in England, another factor in the decline of the whale fishery. In 1642, England became embroiled in its Civil War, and for the next few years whaling lost its priority. When the war ended in 1649 with the establishment of the Commonwealth, the Muscovy Company (which by that time had changed its name to the Greenland Company) tried to revive its flagging whaling industry, but with little success.

By this time, of course, Sir Francis Drake had circumnavigated the globe, the Spanish Armada had been soundly defeated, and the routes to the Indies had been plotted. Not surprisingly, the Dutch and the English were bitterly fighting for dominance of the eastern trade in pepper, nutmeg, cinnamon and cloves, just as they were struggling for supremacy in the whale fisheries of the north. The Dutch had formed the Company of Far Lands in 1594, and by 1600 the British responded with the Honourable East India Company. The affairs of the spice trade do not directly concern us here, but the globe-spanning rivalry between the English and the Dutch does. In

1623, on the island of Amboina in the Moluccas, the Dutch governor had executed ten Englishmen, whom he accused of trying to seize his fortress. A settlement was negotiated, whereby the English forswore all intentions in these islands and turned to India. This did not ameliorate the hostilities between the Dutch and English governments, either in the East or in the Arctic, however, and for decades the two nations sparred and skirmished for dominance.

They actually went to war in 1651, over England's Navigation Act, which was enacted to restrict the sale of Dutch whale oil in England. (Prior to this, the Dutch had been able to undercut British prices— even to Englishmen—because their whaling was more efficient and considerably more economical.) The Dutch War ended in 1654, with the Dutch agreeing to pay compensation for the ten men murdered at Amboina and the British agreeing to vacate their claims in the East Indies. Dutch oil continued to flood the English markets, and not even the Hull whalers "with their assiduous and enterprising spirit" could make their business viable. After the war, very few British ships went north, and the last gasp of British Arctic whaling was exhaled in the

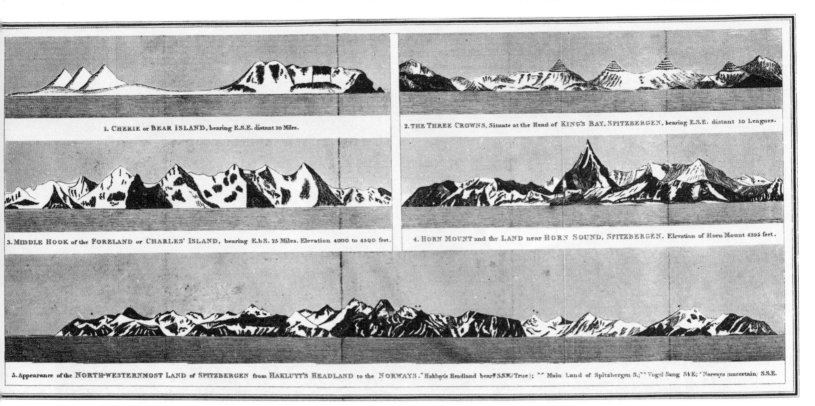

Views of Spitsbergen, from Scoresby's 1820 *Account of the Arctic Regions*.

season of 1682–83, when a combined company of merchants and soap-boilers from Leith invested £1,700 in a whaling voyage which showed a profit of £525.

By the middle of the seventeenth century, other European nations were also participating in this lucrative fishery. Two or three ships were fitted out in Copenhagen every year from 1615 to 1660. *Der Schwartze Adler* ("the Black Eagle") sailed from Ham-

burg in 1648 under the Danish flag with a captain from Bremen. She arrived at Hamburgbukta (a bay named for the German port) in Spitsbergen and found no fewer than five untouched whale carcasses, which had been left to rot by a sister ship that lacked the manpower to process them. Polar bears belligerently prowled the shore, swimming through the melted blubber on the surface of the water. The Hamburgers were still whaling there as late as 1671.

The Dutch Ascendant

As the English whalers were fading, the Dutch were in the ascendant. This was due in no small part to the superiority of their ships. While the British continued to sail in antiquated caravels, the Dutch were developing the *fluit,* an economically produced merchant vessel easily adapted to the mission at hand. The *fluit* ("fly-boat") was a coaster with

a shallow draft and flat bottom, designed to navigate the shallow Flemish banks, and easily armed. While both the Dutch and the British employed Basques as harpooners and blubber-cutters (*specksnyders* in Dutch; *spectioneers* to the British), only the Dutch took the trouble to learn the business from them. The British had experienced some dreadful tribulations

The whale on the white band of the Dutch ensign in the center signifies the trade of the vessel. Almost every element of Dutch whaling is shown here, except the killing of the whale. There are whales close to the ice, men taking a walk, a deer (on top of the crag at right), and a docile polar bear, watching the whole thing from an ice floe. From a grisaille painting by Abram van Salm in 1702.

in their quest for a Northwest Passage and in their whaling exercises: their ships were lost and their crews frozen; they had been defeated in several battles with the Dutch; and their economic policies were a shambles. Upon the death of Queen Elizabeth in 1603, Britain's naval power diminished substantially, and she would not gain dominion over the seas again for a century and a half. The Dutch too suffered losses of ships and men, but despite their setbacks—or perhaps because of them—they persevered. Scoresby (an English whaling captain himself, but of a later period) attributes the failure of the English whale fishery to "a deficiency in the qualifications of the persons commanding the ships, or to the unskilfulness of the crews; to their want of perseverance and confidence; or to their energies being ill applied or imperfectly followed up."

The British effort had consisted almost entirely of

whaling in the waters of Spitsbergen and the other islands, filling their casks with oil that had been boiled out of the blubber by the crew of the ship on shore, and—immediately the holds were filled—heading for home. The Dutch, on the other hand, recognizing the impracticality of such an arrangement, set up a shore station on Jan Mayen Island in 1617. Two years later, a ship of 500 tons was sent to Spitsbergen with timber and other materials for the building of a semipermanent shore facility for the processing of whales. (Many of the first structures were made of oars and sail canvas.) On Amsterdam Island, just offshore, they built tryworks, warehouses, barracks, cooperages, a church and a fortress. The village acquired the name of Smeerenburg, and by 1622 well over a thousand men were spending their three-month summers there. (In 1633–34 and 1635–36, attempts were made to man the station in the winter, but two of the three groups of seven volunteers perished of scurvy in the bitter cold, and the idea was abandoned.)

As practiced at Smeerenburg, whaling was not very different from that pioneered by the Basques, but Dutch innovations greatly improved the efficiency of the industry. When the whale was sighted, whalemen lowered small shallops from the whaleships and pursued it. When they were close enough, a harpoon was thrown to make fast to the whale, and when it had tired—assuming that the iron held and that the whale did not dive under the ice—it was lanced repeatedly until it died. The carcass was then towed to Smeerenburg, where it was flensed.

Virtually every account of this fishery suggests that the processing was performed on shore, with the carcass being winched up some sort of ramp. (Ivan Sanderson, in *Follow the Whale,* even goes so far as to describe in detail the process, with the men pushing great capstans as "the great corpse begins to inch out of the still, dark waters up the great slipway.")

No one seems to have addressed the problem of what became of the vast mountain of meat that would have remained after the flensing, if indeed it took place on shore. Capstans do not operate in reverse, so it would have been impossible to return the bloody heap to the water that way, and towing it would have proven even more problematical. After all, it was the blubber that gave the whale its buoyancy; without it, this mountain of beef and guts would act as a colossal sea anchor for any vessel that tried to move it. Transporting such a steaming, stinking mass on land would strain today's most powerful earth-moving machinery, let alone a gang of tired Dutchmen.*

It is preposterous to consider the whalemen con-

*In his 1984 discussion of the whalers of early Canada, Farley Mowat solves the problem by hypothesizing that the "whalers would trip the capstan brake and allow the naked corpse to slide back into the sea," where it would float away "because the progress of internal decay swiftly produced such quantities of gas as to inflate the carcass into a monstrous, fetid balloon." This presupposes an angle of incline so great as to allow gravity to pull the carcass back into the water, which would have made it difficult—if not impossible—to winch up the dead whale in the first place.

This painting of a sperm whale on the beach at Katwijk by Esaias van den Velde (1587–1630) was probably based on earlier descriptions of stranded whales, but it is a highly original treatment which shows the elaborately costumed gentry, the workers, and even the coastal watercraft.

suming a significant proportion of even one whale, even though it is likely that they ate some of the meat. William Scoresby described the process thus:

The capture of the fish, in which, owing to the particular excellence of the situation, they seldom failed, being accomplished, it was towed to the boats, rowing one before the other "like a team of horses," to the ship's stern, where it lay untouched, from one to two or three days. The fat being then removed, was carried to the shore; where ample conveniences being erected, it was afterwards subjected to heat in a boiler, and the greater part of the oil extracted.

It would appear from Scoresby's account that the whale was stripped of its blubber at sea, altogether eliminating the problem of disposition of the carcass. (In later years, at shore fisheries such as those of Australia and New Zealand, the carcasses of southern right whales would indeed be left on the beach after being towed ashore. Some of the meat was consumed by the whalemen, and some by the aborigines, but for the most part it simply rotted or was eaten by rats, pigs and dogs.)*

When the blubber was flensed from the whale (wherever that occurred), it was chopped into pieces small enough to fit in the "coppers," huge caldrons that were used to render the fat into oil. Once the oil had cooled, it was tapped into waiting casks, which were then stored in warehouses, awaiting transportation to Rotterdam or Delft. (The casks, which held sixty-four English gallons, were known as *quardeels* to the British and *kardeels* to the Dutch.) The baleen, stripped from the mouths of the whales, was cleaned, packed in bales of fifty or sixty blades each, and stored in the warehouses, also awaiting shipment. The long hours of summer in the high Arctic made it possible for these industrious Dutchmen to work in shifts around the clock, and the fat-stoked fires must have been burning almost constantly.

There has been much exaggeration about the size of the settlement at Smeerenburg, including esti-

*Most historians of whaling have assigned the first on-board tryworks to the Yankee sperm whalers of the eighteenth century, but there seems to be some evidence that the Dutch may have preceded them by at least a century. In a note to his 1983 study of "Whaling from the Ecological Angle," Hacquebord writes that he found two references in the Rotterdam archives to whalers' cooking the blubber on board a Dutch ship.

mates of a total population as high as eighteen thousand men and three hundred ships anchored there in a given season. Scoresby wrote of the "yearly visitation of two or three hundred vessels, containing from 12,000 to 18,000 men, being double manned. . . ." The figure of eighteen thousand men would therefore apply to the total number of whalemen that *visited* Smeerenburg during the course of a given summer, but even this seems unjustifiably high. In his history of old Dutch whaling, de Jong suggests that the total population of Smeerenburg in the early years did not exceed a thousand men, and he says that there were only fifteen to twenty ships sent to the North every summer. Hacquebord—who wrote his doctoral dissertation on Smeerenburg—is considerably more conservative, and maintains "that the number of inhabitants . . . fluctuated around two hundred. More often than not, however, this number would not have been reached."

Spitsbergen whaling declined by the middle of the century for a variety of reasons. Hacquebord has identified climatic changes in the region that substantially affected the ice around the islands, and thus the whales. A warm period (identifiable from pollen studies) occurred from 1625 to 1635, and as the Gulf Stream moved farther from the coast of Norway, and the edge of the pack ice moved away from Spitsbergen, the whales remained farther offshore. These conditions led to a shortage of whales in the inshore waters, and the whalers had to venture farther offshore. By the next decade, a cooling trend had occurred, the whales had come back, and there was a corresponding increase in the number taken.

During the most productive years of the Arctic fishery, 300 to 450 whales were captured annually. The Dutch prospered for approximately fifty years, expanding greatly in 1642, when the Noordsche Compagnie relinquished its monopoly, throwing open the industry to all comers. In 1642, 30 to 40 whaleships were outfitted in the Netherlands, and by 1670, 178 ships sailed. In 1675, 83 ships sailed from Hamburg, and the high point of the Dutch fishery came in 1684, when 246 set out for the Arctic. The land stations also proliferated, but this was based on the expectation of an ever-expanding fishery, which was the opposite of what was actually happening. (Using de Jong's lower number of 300 whales per annum for fifty years, an estimated 15,000 whales were taken by the Dutch alone. That figure does not

'tKooken van de Traan
uyt het Walvis spek.
(Boiling the fat out of
the whale.) One of a set
of sixteen prints
showing Dutch whaling
in 1720.

include the British, Danish, French or German fisheries, all of which were operating at various times
between 1600 and 1680.)

Johann Dietz, of Halle, has left a record of his
experiences aboard the Dutch whaler *De Hope,* which
sailed to Spitsbergen between 1685 and 1690. He described the taking of the whales, and the way six or
eight men leapt aboard the carcass to chop away the
blubber, which was sent down to the hold in a canvas chute. The carcass was left for the polar bears,
which the men shot from shipboard. The luxurious
pelts of these white bears were carefully cleaned,
salted and stored for shipment to Holland. (On one
occasion the crew captured a swimming bear a hundred miles from shore and brought it aboard. It ran
wild through the ship, and the men took to the rigging until the captain felled it with his flintlock.
Roast bear was much appreciated, wrote Dietz.) Everyone got scurvy except Dietz (who was later to
become an army surgeon and court barber); he drank
a total of four gallons of French wine with grated
horseradish in it.

Every European country needed oil, and most of
those with access to the northern seas joined the

whale fishery. The Norwegians, who would completely dominate whaling in the later nineteenth and
early twentieth centuries, sent ships to Spitsbergen
and Greenland throughout the eighteenth century,
and the Swedes, who evidently never went whaling
again, fitted out whalers from Gothenburg at the
same time. A man named Jean Vrolicq, who may
have been Flemish, appears in various locations in
the early seventeenth century, from St.-Jean-de-Luz
to Copenhagen. He signed aboard a Dutch ship as
a harpooner for the Noordsche Compagnie, and organized French Arctic whaling from Le Havre,
where, according to Richard Vaughan, "he annoyed
the Dutch by renaming places with French names;
he claimed to have discovered Jan Mayen and called
it Isle de Richelieu." The French did send ships to
the Arctic in the seventeenth century, but their interest and industry waned in later years.

After three decades, the whales of Spitsbergen, Jan
Mayen Island and Bear Island became scarce, and
the whalers were forced to range farther afield; there
were still bowheads in the ice-choked waters of
Greenland. The last Dutch land station on Spitsbergen was shut down in 1670, and from then on, whal-

On February 5, 1691, William III of England entered The Hague for a conference of allies against Louis XIV of France. Over the door of the government building known as the Binnenhof (right) were displayed two jawbones of whales, symbols of the predominant Dutch whaling trade.

ing became a totally different proposition. The British and the Dutch abandoned their bay-whaling enterprises and went whaling in Davis Strait and Baffin Bay. The weather and the ice, so comforting to the polar whales, was anathema to the whalers. In 1777, twelve ships were trapped in the "West Ice" along the northeast coast of Greenland, and drifted south for weeks, being crushed one after another. The last of these ships had 289 men aboard, most of whom had been rescued from other whalers.

During the eighteenth century the fleets declined along with the whales, and they sailed farther and farther to the west. Dutch whaling declined dramatically during the last two decades of the century, and collapsed completely during the French Revolutionary and Napoleonic wars of 1795 to 1804. Not until the southern right whales were discovered in the bays of Australia, New Zealand and South Africa around 1800 would the process of bay-whaling be repeated, up to and including the elimination of the whales.

Britannia Rules the Waves

THE PLACE NAMES on a map of present-day Canada represent a virtual history of its discovery and settlement. There is Hudson Bay and Hudson Strait; Frobisher Bay, Davis Strait, Baffin Island and Baffin Bay, Foxe Basin; and Lancaster, Jones, and Smith sounds. Martin Frobisher sailed from Ratcliffe on the Thames in 1576, in a tiny ship, the 20-ton *Gabriel.* (The other two components of his expedition, the 25-ton *Michael.* and a pinnace whose name has not survived, turned back at the Shetlands.) He rounded Cape Farewell at the southern tip of Greenland and sailed into an enormous inlet that he believed to be a passage to India (the non-existent "Strait of Anian"), which he named for himself because he wanted to be immortalized in the Arctic as Magellan had been in the Antarctic with his own eponymous strait. Although convinced that he had discovered the Northwest Passage, Frobisher never followed the "strait" to the end, and never knew that it was only an inlet. (It is now known as Frobisher Bay.) Along with one Eskimo—who died soon after his arrival—Frobisher brought back samples of a black stone that glistened in the firelight like gold.

It was only iron pyrite—"fool's gold"—but the Elizabethans didn't recognize it, so with his report of the possibility of sailing to Cathay, Frobisher was guaranteed a return voyage. He came back to North America in 1577, in command of the 200-ton *Aid,* and with the blessing and support of Queen Elizabeth. Back at Baffin Island, he mined two hundred tons of the black stones and along the way espied a narwhal "with a horne of two yards long growing out of its snout or nostrels." He returned to England with tons of pyrite, and launched a veritable gold rush. By 1578, fifteen ships were outfitted to return to Baffin Island. Threatening storms threw Frobisher and the fleet off course, and an attempt to sail to the end of "his" strait put him in *Hudson* Strait—which was indeed a strait, one that would have led him into Hudson Bay if he had followed it. Frobisher, however, was under orders to mine gold, and he came about and led his fleet back to England. Upon his return, the products of Frobisher's mining exploits were finally assayed, and their true nature known. Frobisher remained a favorite of the Queen, and was knighted on June 5, 1588, for service in the defense of England against the Spanish Armada.

Davis Strait is a real passage; it separates Greenland from Baffin Island. It was discovered and named by John Davis, a Devonshire man, who sailed in the delightfully named *Sunshine* and *Moonshine* in June of 1585. In thick fogs, he went up the west coast of Greenland until an inlet he named "Gilbert's Sound," but which is now Godthaabsund, the location of Greenland's capital. After entertaining the natives with music, Davis crossed the strait and worked his way back down the coast of Baffin Island, bestowing names on the sounds and inlets that would

become the primary destinations of the Arctic whalemen: Exeter Sound and Cumberland Sound. (Cumberland Sound, which is deeper and longer than Frobisher Bay, was the one that Davis considered must be the Northwest Passage, and he too sailed northwest, believing that he had found the water route to the Orient. Like Frobisher, he thought he had succeeded, so he turned around and sailed back to England to report his success.)

Davis's second voyage, conducted only six months after his return from the first, was again designed to navigate the Northwest Passage and thus secure for England a route to China. In addition to the *Sunshine* and the *Moonshine,* Davis now commanded the 120-ton *Mermaid* and the 10-ton pinnace *North Star.* The navigational aids of the era proved inadequate for Davis's needs, and he became totally lost. In *Moonshine* he missed Cumberland Sound and Frobisher's Strait, and sailed all the way to Labrador searching for them. He returned to England convinced that he had discovered the Northwest Passage. He had not, of course, but he did locate the haunts of the huge herds of polar whales that would eventually draw Englishmen to these desolate regions, and he gave his name not only to a body of water, but to the entire fishery that would operate therein.

At the behest of the Muscovy Company, Henry Hudson attempted to sail to China by way of the North Pole in 1607, but he got only as far as Spitsbergen before the ice stopped him. Two years later, he crossed the Atlantic for the Dutch East India Company, rounded Sandy Hook (in what is now New Jersey), and sailed the *Half Moon* up the great river that bears his name. Again in the employ of the British, he returned to North America and crossed through the strait that was afterward named for him, finally entering the great body of open water in June of 1610. The ship *Discovery* was trapped in the ice, and Hudson was cast adrift, along with his teen-age son and a small crew of sailors. Henry Hudson was never seen again, but his voyages established both the Dutch and the British claims in North America; by 1613, the Dutch had built a fort on a little island that the Indians called Manhattan.

"I doe confidently beleave there to be a passadge," wrote Thomas Button in 1612, "as I doe there is one between Calais and Dover." Like Hudson before him, Button sailed through Hudson Strait and roamed Hudson Bay until he was convinced that there was no exit to the west. The "Company of Merchants of London, Discoverers of the Northwest Passage," was a most optimistically named company that outfitted the next expedition. It retained Robert Bylot as captain (he had sailed with Hudson, and had Bylot Island named for him), and William Baffin as pilot.

Baffin's name will be remembered forever in conjunction with the island and the fishery that carried his name into history, but his skills as a navigator—probably learned during the Spitsbergen whale fishery—enabled Bylot in the *Discovery* to completely circumnavigate the huge body of water that became known as Baffin Bay. They named Smith and Jones sounds after two of their sponsors, and Lancaster Sound after another. (Lancaster Sound, which Baffin did not enter, would prove, two centuries later, to be the entrance to the Northwest Passage.) After an abortive attempt by the Danes in 1619, the British were back in 1631 with two expeditions. One was led by Captain Thomas James, and the other by Luke Foxe. Both men carried letters of introduction from Charles I of England to the Emperor of Japan.

Neither man found what he was looking for, but they both contributed to the knowledge of the Canadian Arctic, and gave their names to places that would be incorporated into the whale fishery that was to occur there during the succeeding centuries. The passage to Cathay might have provided access to the silks, spices, gold and jewels of the Orient, assuming such riches existed. There never was a route over the top, of course; when Roald Amundsen finally made it through the ice of Canada in 1905, he ended up not in the court of an Oriental potentate, but in Nome, Alaska. The value of these voyages—which Samuel Eliot Morison categorized as "glorious failures"—went unrecognized in their own time, but they opened the way for an accumulation of wealth that rivaled the treasure of the Indies, and an orgy of killing that nobody could have imagined.

When the Basques had cleared out of Canada's eastern waters, the whales there received a brief respite. The Dutch and the British were concentrating their efforts to the east, in the grounds of Spitsbergen and Jan Mayen. For almost a century, these whalers prowled the ice of the eastern Arctic, and thoroughly eliminated the Greenland whale, the larger relative of the black right whale, which, because of its early

association with the Basques, was sometimes known as the *Biscayan* right whale. If we accept the eastern North Pacific population of right whales as a discrete stock, then we must confirm the almost total elimination of these whales. In a 1974 study, Dale Rice wrote that the "Kodiak Ground," from Vancouver Island to the Aleutians, "was renowned in the nineteenth century as one of the best areas for hunting right whales during the summer." Today, only a few right whales remain, a testimony to the ruthless efficiency of the whalers, but also a commentary on the inability of some species to recover after being reduced to such low numbers.*

ALTHOUGH the British made sporadic attempts to revive their whaling industry, the fishery was completely dominated by the Dutch in the latter half of the seventeenth century. In 1672 an Act of Parliament removed all duties on whale products brought in by Englishmen, while foreigners had to pay a duty of £9 per ton for oil and twice that per ton of bone. The Company of Merchants for Trading With Greenland was capitalized in 1693 for £40,000, but needed another infusion of capital nine years later. By the turn of the eighteenth century, the British appeared to be completely finished with whaling, and whatever oil and bone they needed had to be imported from Holland.

The South Sea Company had been formed in 1711, primarily to trade in slaves with Spanish America. As a result of wild speculation, the fortunes of the stockholders rose so dramatically that by 1720, the company proposed—and had its proposal accepted by Parliament—to take over a large part of the national debt. From January 1720 to August, the stock rose over 872 points, but by September the market collapsed, in what came to be known as the "South Sea Bubble." In the economic wreckage, the Whig government of Robert Walpole survived, as did the

*Once the species has been drastically reduced, there may be factors that prevent it from ever recovering. Canadian cetologist E. D. Mitchell has written, "of all species, only two, very narrowly-specialized species feed on the same resource and these are the right and sei whales." Right whales are slow feeders, swimming through schools of copepods that become trapped in the fringes of their baleen, while sei whales, feeding on the same invertebrates, take in huge mouthfuls as they feed. Mitchell suggests that the more aggressive feeders will prevail in a competition for a particular resource, and asks, "Does the sei whale compete with the right whale? In the Northwestern Atlantic, has sei whale abundance affected recovery of the right whales?"

A stranded whale, from *Churchill's Voyages,* 1745.

whaling industry. Within the rickety framework of the South Sea Company, Henry Elking proposed to reintroduce a whale fishery to Britain, and his arguments were presented in his 1722 *View of the Greenland Trade and Whale Fishery, with the National and Private Advantages thereof.*

It is a vulgar Error [he wrote], but so riveted in the Minds of ignorant People, that it will be very hard to persuade them to the contrary that the Dutch can fit out their Ships, and go to Greenland, and in a word, carry on the Whale-Fishery cheaper and to more Advantage than the English.

Elking also believed the captains ought to be paid by share instead of a fixed salary; that the blubber and baleen "finnes" ought to be better cleaned; and that the British paid altogether too much to fit out their ships. He reserved special vitriol for the Greenland Company, which, he wrote, "was ill-served by almost all the people they employed, both at home and abroad, pushing them into extravagant and unnecessary expenses, and irregular measures in every

thing. . . ." The Greenland Company had developed a complicated system of command, which had a captain in charge of navigation, a harpooner in charge of whaling operations, and a "General" in charge of the whaling fleet, usually when hostilities were expected. The British had so little experience that even if they arrived successfully on the whaling grounds, they often sailed around in circles, unable to kill a single whale. "For want of right conduct," wrote Elking, "they got no whales, or but few, even when others made a good voyage."

When Elking's proposal was put to the South Sea Company's directors for a vote in 1722, it failed, and it was not until 1724 that the British would send another ship to the Arctic. Henry Elking was named Agent and Superintendent for the Greenland Fishery, at a salary of £100, and 1½ percent of the gross sales. Unfortunately for Elking and for Britain, the South Sea fishery was, according to Gordon Jackson, "the biggest single failure in Britain's long history of involvement with the Arctic." Rather than follow his own suggestions, Elking superintended an extravagant spree of overspending, which totally ignored the existence of serviceable ships, and commissioned a dozen new vessels for 1725 and another dozen for 1726. He built new docks on the Thames—including the Greenland Dock—and new warehouses, boiling houses, and even a new house for himself.

In the first year, the British fleet caught only 25 whales, not enough to pay the wages of the crews and captains, let alone show a profit, and in the following year, they captured 16. The company was forced to request government assistance in 1731, but its record was so dismal that no such help was forthcoming, and the company resolved not to continue with the Greenland trade. In the eight years of its existence, the South Sea Company spent £262,172, and had sales of £84,390, for a loss of £177,782. Elking retired a broken man, in finances and spirit, and the era of joint-stock companies in British whaling was over.

In 1733, the Crown granted a bounty of twenty shillings per ton for privately owned ships outfitted for whaling, in an attempt to revive the industry. By 1750, there were nineteen ships in the Arctic, and three years later, the enterprising merchants of Hull established a whaling company capitalized at £20,000. With two ships, the *Berry* and the *Pool,* they set out to recapture the British predominance in the northern fishery. War and a shortage of whales diminished their dreams, and by 1762 the fishery seemed finished, and Whitby and Hull threw in the towel. Without the support of any company or consortium, however, Samuel Standidge revived the Hull fishery singlehandedly. In 1766 he outfitted a single ship and sent her off on a whaling voyage. Only one whale was killed, but Standidge's captain collected some four hundred seals, which previously had been considered worthless. When he had the skins tanned

In the early days of the Arctic fishery, the whaleships were almost as thickly clustered as the whales. There are five ships in this painting, four whaleboats, and at least four whales, one of which has eight harpoons stuck in him.

(and had a pair of shoes made for himself), he began an entirely new industry for England. Within three years, Standidge was sending three more expeditions to the North, and inspiring the merchants of Whitby, Newcastle and London to follow. (Samuel Standidge was elected sheriff of Hull in 1775, and mayor in 1795. He was knighted by King George III, and died in 1805.)

Perhaps because whaling was not particularly successful during this period, a procession of whales arrived on European shores as if to check on their pursuers. During the winter of 1761–62, four Greenland whales stranded on the coast of Holland, and four more piled up on the beaches of Dover. On February 20, 1762, a 53-foot sperm whale beached himself at Zandevoort, on the North Sea near The Hague. Also in that cetologically curious winter, a whale stranded in the Thames, and the carcass was taken to the Greenland Dock, where thousands of visitors came to see the object of the fishery. Although most of the vessels plying the Thames were Greenlandmen, coming or going from the pursuit of the Greenland whale, this creature was a sperm whale.

From 1761 onward, the British continued to send ships to the Arctic to hunt the Greenland whale, but it was becoming apparent that the Americans were beginning to assert themselves, and furthermore, that they had found a new kind of whale to hunt. While the British and the Dutch were hunting in the cold waters of Greenland, Yankee lookouts in masthead hoops were sighting the forward-angled blows of the spermaceti whale in the tropical waters of the Caribbean and Africa. The Dutch still dominated the fishery, however, sending 124 ships to the Arctic in 1768, compared to the British 50. It was not until 1770 that the British began to catch the flagging Dutch, primarily through the offices of Samuel Standidge, the Hull shipowner. During the "American War" so many ships were needed as troop and supply transports that the whaling industry fell off sharply. Some Nantucket whalemen were captured as prisoners of war, and it was rumored that they were immediately offered employment in the British whale fishery. When the war ended in 1783, British whaling increased enormously, primarily because of an increase in the bounty from twenty shillings per ton to forty. In 1785, William Scoresby Senior made his first voyage as a whaleman, aboard the *Henrietta*.

Interlude: The Sea-Unicorn

NARWHALS probably vie with right whales for the dubious honor of being the first whales hunted by man. The Norsemen patrolling the ice-choked bays of Greenland in the ninth and tenth centuries were probably more than a little surprised to see the slender, twisted tusks of the mottled, 15- to 20-foot-long whales poking out of the water as they swam at the surface. To the Vikings, for whom it did not represent the magical unicorn, the narwhal had a multiplicity of uses. In his *Ivory and the Elephant,* Kunz writes that the Vikings "decorated the prows of their war galleys with these horns, had them carved into sword and dagger hilts, and also set them on staffs and sceptres. Their wives wore hair-pins made out of this material, and curiously wrought charms, which were considered talismans of good luck both in love and war."

The ancient saga of the hunter and the narwhal has changed dramatically throughout the centuries. The first narwhal skulls were probably found on the icy shores of Greenland. The name "narwhal," which is of Icelandic origin, means "corpse whale," and is believed to refer to the pale, spotted coloration of the animal, which was thought to resemble that of a floating corpse. According to another theory, *dentes balaenarum* were found in the "Pool of Corpses," in Iceland where dead sailors were washed ashore.

Unlike whale oil, meat and blubber, however, the

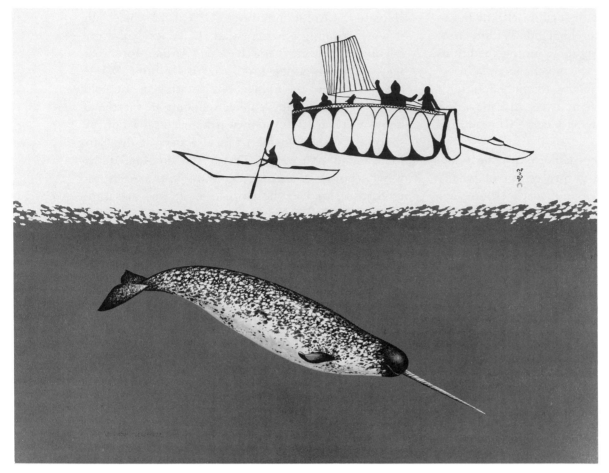

tooth of the narwhal (which occurs only in the males, and can reach a length of 8 feet or more) was *sui generis;* there were no substitutes for it. In fact, it was one of the most desirable objects of the Middle Ages, endowed with magical properties, collected by royalty, and worth more than its weight in gold.

It is difficult to imagine the myth of the unicorn springing up without the narwhal tusk to substantiate it, but there are some other artifacts that might have contributed to its pre-narwhal origins. For example, in Africa and Arabia there are several species of antelopes with straight horns, the oryxes and the gemsbok. An antelope with a pair of straight horns does not look much like a unicorn with a single horn, but the myth did not necessarily have to derive from actual sightings. Antelopes do not shed their horns the way deer do, but it is still possible to imagine a single horn finding its way to a receptive or creative mythologist. There is, however, no other horn that is straight, ivory-white and spiraled like that of the

narwhal. The horns of oryxes are black and prominently ringed at the base. Certainly, all other parts of the unicorn resemble an antelope more than they do a whale.

One of the earliest written records of the unicorn would seem to predate the discovery of the narwhal by almost a thousand years. A Greek physician named Ctesias, in the service of Darius II, King of Persia, returned to his homeland in 398 B.C. and wrote *Indica,* a book containing stories that he had collected during his seventeen years in Persia. One of his tales describes

certain wild asses which are as large as horses, and larger. Their bodies are white, their heads dark red, and their eyes dark blue. They have a horn on the forehead which is about a foot and a half in length. The dust filed from this horn is administered in a potion as a protection against deadly drugs. The base of the horn, for some two hands'-breadth above the brow, is pure white; the upper part is sharp and of a vivid crimson; and the remainder, or middle portion, is black. Those who drink out of these horns, made into drinking vessels, are not subject to the holy disease [epilepsy]. Indeed, they are immune even to poisons if, either before or after swallowing such, they drink wine, water, or anything else from these beakers.*

As far as we can tell, this passage was written some four hundred years before the birth of Christ. Whatever other animals may have been represented here, it seems an unlikely description of a narwhal.

After Ctesius—and probably based to a great extent upon his description—other authors included the unicorn in their studies of natural history. Aristotle, writing about a half-century later, wrote, "There are . . . some animals that have one horn only, for example, the oryx, whose hoof is cloven, and the Indian ass, whose hoof is solid. These creatures have a horn in the middle of their head." Later, Pliny (A.D. 23–79), who is believed to have depended heavily upon the works of Aristotle, described the *monoceros* "with a body like a horse, head like a stag, feet like an elephant, and tail like a boar; it makes a deep bellow, and one black horn two cubits long projects from the middle of its forehead. This animal cannot be taken alive."

Surprisingly, there are several places in the Bible where unicorns are mentioned: Numbers 23:22 says, "God brought them out of Egypt; he hath as it were, the strength of an unicorn." And Job 39:9–11: "Will the unicorn be willing to serve thee, or abide by thy crib? Canst thou bind the unicorn with his band in the furrow? Or will he harrow the valleys after thee? Wilt thou trust him because his strength is great?" "One thing is evident in these passages," writes Shepard, "they refer to some actual animal of which the several writers had vivid if not clear impressions. Although the allusions were made at widely different times, the characterization is consistent, bringing before us a beast remarkable for its strength, ferocity, wildness, and unconquerable spirit. Nothing about it suggests that it was supernatural, a creature of fancy, for it is linked with the lion, the bullock and the calf; yet it was mysterious enough to inspire a sense of awe, and powerful enough to provide a vigorous metaphor." In later years, the absence of the

*This quote—and much of the discussion about the origins of the unicorn myth—comes from Odell Shepard's *The Lore of the Unicorn* and Margaret Freeman's *The Unicorn Tapestries*.

unicorn would be attributed to its missing the ark and drowning in the flood.

Sometime between the second and the fourth centuries, a book of animal legends was produced in Alexandria. It was called the *Physiologus*, and was subsequently translated into Syrian, Arabic, Armenian, Ethiopian, Latin, German, French, Provençal, Icelandic, Italian and Anglo-Saxon. The *Physiologus* (which Willy Ley translates as "somebody who knows nature" and may refer to either the original manuscript or its author) eventually metamorphosed into the medieval bestiary. Since the unicorn was one of the animals prominently featured in this important work, its place in history, mythology and literature was assured.

The tusk of the narwhal is but one of the elements in the myth of the unicorn. The myth predates the Vikings; Ctesius, Aristotle and Pliny wrote about it before anyone had ever seen a narwhal tusk, and their works were well known in medieval Europe. Once the tusks began to appear, it was easy enough to fit the tusk to the fable. It was much easier to believe that this ivory shaft came from a graceful, cloven-hoofed equine that could only be caught by a virgin than from a dumpy, spotted whale. No other animal possesses this tapered ivory shaft (it is actually the upper left canine tooth), but rhinoceroses, antelopes and goats also contributed to the unicorn mythology. By the eleventh century, however, there was a flourishing trade in "unicorn horns" in Europe, and not surprisingly, the animal soon appeared in the literature. In his translation of a twelfth-century bestiary, T. H. White gives this description of "The Monoceros":

A horn sticks out from the middle of its forehead with astonishing splendour to the distance of four feet, so sharp that whatever it charges is easily perforated by it. Not a single one has ever come alive into the hands of man, and, although it is possible to kill them, it is not possible to capture them.

From this account, we can trace the prominent tracks of the unicorn through the natural histories of the Middle Ages. From our contemporary perspective, it is altogether too easy to attribute a naivete or gullibility to those people who believed in unicorns. But as Odell Shepard writes in his superb study of unicorn lore, "The fact that no one ever saw a unicorn did not disturb belief in the slightest degree. No one in mediaeval Europe ever saw a lion or an elephant or a panther, yet these beasts were accepted without question upon evidence in no way better or worse than that which vouched for the unicorn." Besides, there was the incontrovertible evidence of its horn. In his *Historia Animalium,* Conrad Gesner wrote, "one has to trust the words of wanderers and far-going travelers, for the animal must be on earth, or else its horns would not exist. . . ."

Gesner provides an illustration of a distinctly horselike creature with cloven hooves and what looks very much like the tusk of a narwhal sticking out of its forehead. (He also depicts a sea unicorn swimming in the water, a somewhat reptilian creature with a horn coming out of the top of its head.) The equine illustration is used in Edward Topsell's *Historie of Foure-Footed Beastes* (1607), with this description of the properties of the tusk:

The hornes of Unicorns, especially that which is brought from the new Islands, being beaten and drunk in water, doth wonderfully help against poyson: as of late experience doth manifest unto us a man, who having taken poison and beginning to swell was preserved by this remedy. I my selfe have herd of a man worthy to be beleeved, that having eaten a poisond cherry, and perceiving his belly to swell, he cured himself by the marrow of this horne being drunke in wine in a very short space.

By the time Topsell wrote this, however, there was some suspicion that the beast with the alexipharmic horn was not a quadruped. He quotes several authorities, one of whom says that "there be Birds in Ethiopia having one horn on their foreheads, and are therefore called Unicornus: and Albertus saith, there is a fish cald *Monoceros,* and hath also one horn." Topsell dismisses those who believe this nonsense as "vulgar sort of infidell people," but it is evident that the myth of the graceful, blue-eyed animal is threatened. By this time, a proper description of the narwhal had been obtained. In 1577 Martin Frobisher made his second voyage to Baffin Island, and subsequently wrote that he came upon "a great dead fish which, so it seemed, had been embalmed with ice. It was round like a porpoise, being about twelve feet long and having a horn of two yards length growing out of the snout or nostrils. The horn is

wreathed and straight, like in fashion to a taper made of wax, and may truly be thought to be the Sea Unicorn." The news from Britain did not seem to reach the continent. Ulisse Aldrovandi (1522–1605), Gesner's successor as an encyclopedist, produced a multivolume natural history with no less than thirty pages devoted to the unicorn. He places the animal amongst the "split-hoofed" quadrupeds, and includes illustrations of narwhal tusks which he designates *unicornum falsum.* (Apparently, as the true nature of the narwhal was realized, the tusks lost their magical properties. Mammoth ivory, found buried in the snows of Siberia, became *unicornum verum,* however, keeping the myth alive.)

When it became known that there were indeed whales with horns, they began to appear on maps and charts of the sixteenth century. On Abraham Ortelius's 1570 map of Iceland in the first atlas (*Theatrum Orbis Terrarum,* "Theater of the World") we find a sharp-snouted creature which the cartographer-naturalist calls the *Nawhal,* and describes thus:

If any man eat of this fish he dieth presently. It hath a tooth in the forepart of its head standing out seven cubites. This divers have sold for the Unicornes horn. It is thought to be a good antidote and soveraigne medicine against poison. This monster is forty elles in length.

It is unclear who first identified the narwhal as the progenitor of the unicorn. Olaus Magnus (1490–1558), the brother of the archbishop of Uppsala (who is remembered for his insistence upon the existence of sea serpents, drawing them into his map of 1539), said that "the monoceros is a sea-monster that has in its brow a very large horn wherewith it can pierce and wreck vessels and destroy many men." Even after the existence of the narwhal was firmly established, another horned marine creature was believed to inhabit the seas alongside it. In de Rochefort's *Histoire Naturelle* of 1665, we find a plate with an accurate illustration of the *Narwal,* and on the same plate, a picture of a creature captioned *Licorne de Mer,* a fish-shaped animal with prominent scales, a crown on its horselike head, and a long horn protruding from its forehead.

We could, of course, trace the unicorn's path through art and history, noting, for example, its appearance in the coat of arms of England, as the dexter (right) supporter of the royal arms. (Originally, the unicorn appeared as a component of the royal Scots arms, but was incorporated into the arms of England during the reign of James IV of Scotland, 1488–1513, who married the daughter of Henry VII of England, which led to an alliance of Scotland and England. In an article about the unicorn's role in heraldry, quoted in Fox-Davies's *Complete Guide to Heraldry,* a Mr. Beckles Wilson said, "We now know that these so-called unicorn's horns, usually carved, to belong to that marine monster the narwhal or sea-unicorn.")

Probably the most famous pictures in the world of unicorns are contained in two sets of sixteenth-century tapestries. "The Unicorn Tapestries," in the collection of the Cloisters in New York, has seven panels showing the hunt, capture and death of a single unicorn. Everywhere the unicorn appears (he is absent from the first tapestry, which shows the hunters setting out), his horn is a perfect illustration of a narwhal tusk. It is long, white, tapered, and spirally twisted. The second set of unicorn tapestries ("La Dame à La Licorne") is in the Musée de Cluny in Paris. Here there are six panels, five showing the five senses, and one whose subject is unexplained. Every one of the Cluny tapestries also includes a lion, and although the unicorn is decidedly more goatlike than the one shown in the Cloisters tapestries, he too has an unmistakable narwhal tusk for a horn.

THE PATHS of the terrestrial unicorn and the marine unicorn must perforce diverge, for it is not the unicorn that concerns us here; it is the narwhal. Were it not for its anomalous dentition, the narwhal would probably have been ignored by everyone except the Greenland and Canadian Eskimos, who would have—in a hypothetically tuskless world—killed them for their meat, sinews and blubber, all of which they made good use of.

But alas for *Monodon monoceros,* no such tuskless world exists, and this hapless inhabitant of Arctic waters became the object of a concentrated hunt that goes on to this day, even without the attendant mythology of the horn's preventative qualities. Narwhal tusks no longer command a king's ransom, but they are still valuable, perhaps because they are so scarce, but also because they are among the most beautiful of all natural objects. (One was sold in the 1980s at

Detail from the Unicorn Tapestry in the Cloisters, New York. The horn of the unicorn is obviously based on the tusk of a narwhal.

The coronation throne of the kings of Denmark, in Rosenborg Palace, Copenhagen. The vertical elements of this seventeenth-century throne are made from the tusks of narwhals.

1598, and reported "among other things the Horn of a Unicorn, of above eight Spans and a Half in Length, valued at above £10,000." (This may have been the very tusk that Frobisher brought back to Queen Elizabeth I, for her "wardrobe of robes.")

By the seventeenth century, the myth of the unicorn had begun to fade. Its appearance was limited to more decorative contexts, such as the "table carpet with unicorns" in the Metropolitan Museum of Art, or the painting by Domenichino in the Farnese Palace showing a lady cradling a unicorn in her arms. Of this painting, Sir Kenneth Clark wrote that it was "among the latest treatments of the [unicorn] theme to retain some genuine poetry. Trustingly the unicorn, which was also the emblem of the Farnese family, lays its head in the virgin's lap, amid the lush landscape of the Roman Campagna." A beaker of approximately the same period is made from the lower, hollow portion of a tusk; it has a finial on the top in the form of a miniature unicorn, and a bas-relief of a unicorn's head carved into the ivory. By this time, belief in the pharmacological properties of the material may have been replaced by a more prosaic appreciation of its beauty.

Commercial whalers in the Arctic, who were probably uninterested in unicorn mythology, hunted narwhals whenever they encountered them because the horn was (and is) such an exotic item. Scoresby wrote, "When harpooned, the narwal {sic} dives in the same way, and with almost the same velocity as the mysticetus, but not to the same extent. It generally descends about 200 fathoms, then returns to the surface and is dispatched with a lance in a few minutes." When W. G. Burn-Murdoch was a-whaling off Greenland in 1892, he lowered for "unies" but "before we got away, the whales had disappeared." Around 1910, the Hudson's Bay Company established an outpost in the Pond Inlet region of northern Baffin Island, and while prospecting (unsuccessfully) for gold, they also conducted a brisk trade in ivory.

In 1870, the narwhal made a preposterous appearance in a popular work of fiction. In Jules Verne's *Twenty Thousand Leagues Under the Sea*, Professor Aronnax of the Paris Museum of Natural History (and the author of a two-volume work called *Mysteries of the Ocean Depths*) sets out to capture the beast that he believes is responsible for the sightings by all those ships. (This occurs before he is taken aboard Cap-

a New York auction house for $11,000.) The Danish coronation throne (first used in 1671) at Rosenberg Castle in Copenhagen is made of narwhal tusks, and there are tusks and objects carved from tusks in the treasuries of the world. The horn found by Frobisher in 1577 was "reserved as a jewel by the Queen Majesty's Commandment, in her wardrobe of robes," and in the collection of Prince Takamatsu of Japan there are two "unicorn horns." At the Abbey of Saint Denis in Paris there is a 6-foot, 7-inch tusk that was said to have been presented to Charlemagne, and there is another in Strasbourg Cathedral. A German by the name of Hentzner visited Windsor Castle in tain Nemo's submarine *Nautilus*, which, of course, *is* responsible.) Convinced that the perpetrator of the attacks is a gigantic narwhal, Aronnax says,

The ordinary narwhal, or unicorn fish, is a kind of whale which grows to a length of sixty feet. . . . [It] is armed with a kind of ivory sword, or halberd, as some naturalists put it. It is a tusk as hard as steel. Occasionally these tusks are found embedded in the bodies of other kinds of whales, against which the narwhal always wins. Others have been removed, not without difficulty, from the hulls of ships which they had pierced clean through as easily as a drill pierces a barrel. . . . Therefore, until I receive fuller information, I shall be of the opinion that it is a unicorn-fish of colossal proportions, armed not with a halberd but with a real battering ram like a warship, which it could equal in size and strength.

Hardly a word of Aronnax's cetology is correct, so it is not surprising that he is able to postulate an aggressive, ship-sinking narwhal. The maximum length of a narwhal is twenty feet—including the tusk—and it is a completely inoffensive creature. Despite its appearance, the tusk is not used to pierce anything; it is believed to be a secondary sexual characteristic that identifies the dominant males.

Because of its shape, a narwhal tusk lends itself only to certain decorative uses, but it is this very shape that made people believe it was the horn of the unicorn, and therefore, few tusks were carved

A seventeenth-century beaker carved from the tusk of a narwhal, with a finial in the form of a unicorn.

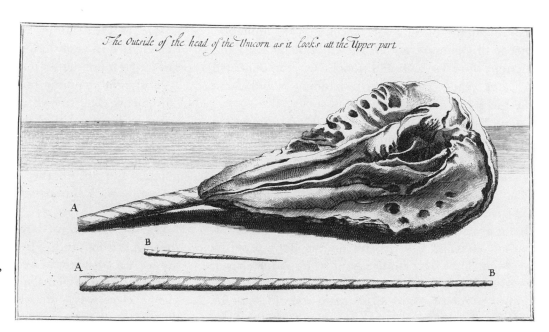

The skull of a narwhal, with the horn cut into three pieces to fit on the original print.

After the kill, Eskimos of northwest Greenland haul a male narwhal to shore.

into anything else. The tusk is solid for about half its length, and hollow for the rest, so you can make out of it only small objects—such as chessmen or napkin rings—or long narrow ones. (The coronation throne of Denmark is constructed of many tusks and sections of tusks, with additional ivory components.) In later years, Yankee scrimshanders would carve the tusks into decorated walking sticks.

The Eskimos of northern Canada and Greenland have always hunted the narwhal. "Progress" has come to the remote Arctic locations where the narwhals live, and, particularly in Canada, animal products have been largely replaced by modern substitutes. Greenland Eskimos, on the other hand, living an even more remote existence than their Canadian cousins, still depend on the bounty of the narwhal. The Greenlanders hunt from paddle-driven kayaks, but by now most Canadian Eskimos have outboard motors, and all of them use rifles. If the carcass of a killed narwhal does not sink, the Eski-

mos tow it to shore and butcher it on the spot, eating the skin as soon as they get the animal onto the beach. Eaten raw, the inch-thick skin, called *muktuk,* is said to taste faintly of hazelnuts, and it is extremely rich in vitamin C. Because a full-grown adult can weigh more than a ton and a half, it can provide a substantial amount of the Eskimos' protein requirements. The sinews are used for sewing, the oil burns with a smokeless flame, and the skin is cured and turned into leather for dog-team traces and boot laces. The ivory tusks were once used for spear points, but now they serve as trade items, providing the Eskimos with an important article of commerce.

On rare occasions, large numbers of narwhals—sometimes thousands—become trapped in the closing ice, an event that Greenland Eskimos refer to as a *savssat.* Finding thousands of prey animals trapped in one place was a signal for an orgy of killing. In the winter of 1914–15, Danish scientist Morten Porsild observed a *savssat* in Greenland where more than 1,000 narwhals were slaughtered; of these more than 200 were adult males with tusks. He described the killing:

Every man placed himself astride a hole with his rifle loaded, awaited calmly the arrival of a school, shot one of the animals—if possible one with a tusk—and harpooned it immediately after the shot; or, if he were exceptionally clever, he simply seized the animal by its nostrils or by one of the flippers. He then enlarged the hole, pulled his prey up, and proceeded with the flensing. By this procedure the cleverest and coolest of the hunters got up to seven animals a day without leaving the spot first chosen.

Because of the remote habitat in which it lives, the narwhal's current numbers are difficult to estimate. Moreover, there are several distinct populations, with a scattered circumpolar distribution. Narwhals are found in the Canadian Arctic, in Greenland waters, around Iceland, and throughout the Soviet Arctic. Total estimates of these popula-

tions range from a pessimistic 10,000 to an optimistic 20,000.

The whale with the horn would probably be one of the most dramatic exhibits ever shown in an aquarium, but unlike its cousin the beluga, the narwhal does not adapt well to captivity. In 1969, during a Canadian Eskimo hunt at Ellesmere Island, a baby was captured when she followed a canoe, apparently mistaking it for her mother, which had been shot. Eskimos and Mountie Al Kirbyson managed to drag the baby narwhal into the canoe—she would have died if abandoned—and transported her overland to the village of Grise Fjord, where they awaited the rescuers. For eight days, the baby was kept in a small pool and fed a mixture of canned milk and sardine oil. Staff members of the New York Aquarium, including marine mammal veterinarian Jay Hyman, superintended the care and feeding of "Umiak" until they could transport her to the Aquarium at Coney Island. For a period of three weeks, Umiak lived in an aquarium tank with a beluga nursemaid. The only narwhal ever kept in captivity died of pneumonia on October 7, 1969.

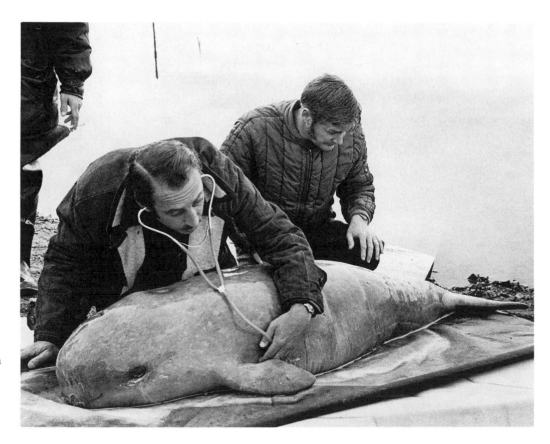

"Umiak" the baby narwhal is examined in northern Canada by veterinarian Jay Hyman before being transported to the New York Aquarium at Coney Island.

FOUR

INSHORE WHALING

Bay Whaling in Japan

As with almost every other country where whaling became important, it was the right whales that were initially responsible for the rise of the Japanese fishery. Wherever there are protected bays and inlets in temperate waters, there are (or rather *were*) right whales. To Australia, South Africa and Patagonia in the south, and western Europe and both coasts of North America, *Balaena glacialis* arrived in the warmer months to breed and deliver its calves. So too in Japan did the whale they know as *semi kujira* ("beautiful-backed whale") appear in the summer months. At first, the whales obliged the people of the coastal villages by occasionally beaching themselves, thus providing a welcome bounty of meat and oil. Later the villagers would recognize the efficacy of searching for the whales rather than waiting for the animals to deliver themselves up.

It was probably from the beached whales that the Japanese developed the habit of consumption of whale meat, a habit that they were to carry forward for a thousand years, until their gustatorial preferences would turn them into pariahs. The road from beached whale to the mechanized war on whales was a long and difficult one.

Whales have figured in Japanese history and literature (the two are often synonymous) since the earliest records. The Ainu, an indigenous Caucasoid people, have lived on the northern island of Hokkaido for at least eight thousand years, and from the Jōmon Period (7000 to 3000 B.C.), their shell mounds contain the bones of whales and dolphins, suggesting that they utilized the remains of whales that beached themselves.

Even though the Japanese have inhabited their islands for thousands of years and undoubtedly benefited from the fortuitous bounty of beached whales, they did no active whaling until somewhere around the end of the sixteenth century, approximately the same time as the Basques, the Dutch and the English were taking bowheads and right whales in the North Atlantic. Even the oceanic conditions are similar: where the North Atlantic has the Gulf Stream bringing warm water up from the south, the western North Pacific has the Kuroshio Current, which flows northward out of the South China Sea, past the Japanese islands and south of the Aleutians until it finally dissipates off northwestern North America.

Gray whales used to migrate down the Pacific

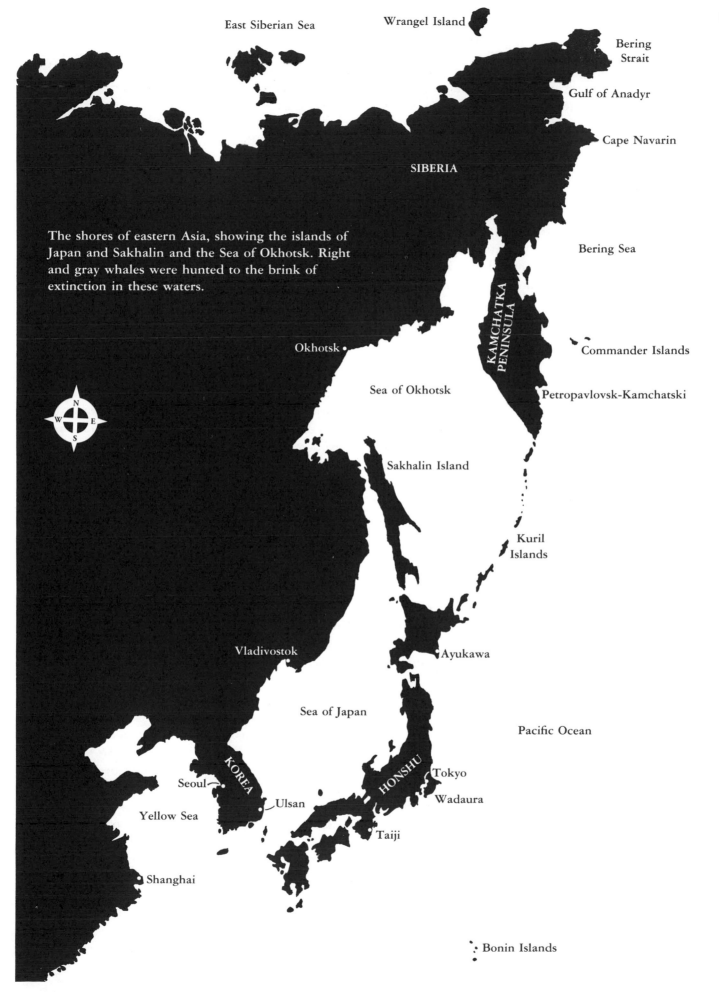

East Siberian Sea

Wrangel Island

Bering Strait

Gulf of Anadyr

Cape Navarin

SIBERIA

Bering Sea

The shores of eastern Asia, showing the islands of
Japan and Sakhalin and the Sea of Okhotsk. Right
and gray whales were hunted to the brink of
extinction in these waters.

Okhotsk

KAMCHATKA PENINSULA

Commander Islands

Sea of Okhotsk

Petropavlovsk-Kamchatski

N
W E
S

Sakhalin Island

Kuril Islands

Vladivostok

Ayukawa

Sea of Japan

Pacific Ocean

KOREA

HONSHU

Tokyo

Seoul

Ulsan

Wadaura

Yellow Sea

Taiji

Shanghai

Bonin Islands

coast of Japan and perhaps deliver their calves in the Seto Inland Sea, the passage that separates the island of Kyushu from the major islands to the north. (Since the gray whale is now extinct in Japanese waters, there can only be suppositions based on early records as to its calving grounds.) Right whales also inhabited the inshore waters all round the islands, but they seemed to favor the protected bays and inlets along the coasts bordering on the Sea of Japan. Both the gray whale and the right whale inhabited the Sea of Japan, the teardrop-shaped, 1,000-mile-long body of water that is contained on the west by Siberia and the Korean peninsula, and on the east by Sakhalin Island and the entire Japanese chain. Protected from the winds and tides of the tempestuous North Pacific, the 400,000-square-mile Sea of Japan is an ideal environment for whales—and for whalers.

In the North Pacific all the rorquals can be found, ranging in descending order of size from the blue whale, the fin whale, the sei whale, Bryde's whale, to the minke. Also included is the humpback, the first whale species to be hunted whenever people realized that these huge beasts could provide them with sustenance. Sperm whales abound off the coasts of Japan—and throughout the North Pacific—and when the other whale species became depleted, the Japanese, like all other whaling nations, turned to the cachalot in order to maintain their industry. Because of its high myoglobin content, the meat of the sperm whale is almost black in color, and not particularly tasty. Only when the stocks of the better-tasting whales were exhausted did the Japanese eat the meat of *makko-kujira.*

One reason that whales do not figure in the social or culinary history of early Japan is that the Buddhist emperors of the sixth and seventh centuries prohibited their subjects from eating meat of any kind. Even so, certain segments of the population managed to circumvent the imperial ordinances by deciding that a whale was not a mammal at all, but rather *isana,* a "large fish" or a "brave fish."

Buddhism waned during the Kamakura Period (1185–1333), to be replaced by the dominance of the warrior class. Japan was invaded by the Mongol hordes in 1274 and again in 1281, and in both instances a typhoon (known as *kamikaze,* the "divine wind") arose and destroyed the invader's ships, encouraging the idea that the Japanese were a divinely

protected nation. The successful defense of their island country also enhanced the Japanese dependence on military strength, and would affect her attitudes toward the Western world for the next six hundred years. It was Kublai Khan (of Coleridge's "pleasure dome," and the grandson of Genghis) who attempted to conquer Japan, the same Khan whom Marco Polo had stayed with for seventeen years. When Marco Polo returned to Venice in 1295 with tales of the riches of the East (including a place called Cipango), these stories inspired the search for the Northwest, the Northeast—any sea passage that would enable Europeans to get to the gold, pearls and spices of Cathay. (Christopher Columbus is known to have read Marco Polo's *Description of the World,* and he too was seeking the gold-roofed palaces of Cipango, even though he fetched up on the goldless islands of the Caribbean.) By 1503 the Portuguese navigator Vasco da Gama had completed his second voyage around Africa to India, and his countrymen were soon trading along the China coast. It was only a matter of time before they would find the exotic and unwelcoming islands of Japan. The first Europeans landed on Japanese soil in 1543, setting off the discord that resulted in the closing of Japan until the arrival of Commodore Perry in 1848.

As used in an evolutionary sense, "convergence" refers to certain traits that develop in unrelated organisms, manifesting themselves somewhat differently, but serving the same function. Cultures also seem to exhibit this tendency, and a particularly evident instance of convergence is seen when one compares the trappings of medieval Japan with those of medieval Europe. With no cross-pollination, both societies sprouted an elaborately layered social hierarchy; they both had an elite warrior class dressed in armor, a complex code of chivalry, a religious establishment marked by numerous monastic orders, a subservient class of workers, and a nascent whaling industry.

During the same period that Elizabeth I was feasting on "porpesse" at Windsor, whale dishes were appearing on the tables of the Tokugawa shoguns. (Again the principle of convergence obtains: beached whales and dolphins were considered "royal fish" by the kings of England, and their highnesses laid claim to the best parts of any whales, dolphins or sturgeon that happened ashore.)

It was during the period of isolation from the rest

of the world that Japan developed her unique style of whaling. With the establishment of the Tokugawa shogunate (also called the Edo Period, since Ieyesu Tokugawa moved the capital from Kyoto to Edo—which became Tokyo—in 1600), whale dishes appeared in the national diet. As the Europeans were perfecting their particular approach to whale-killing (developed by the Basques and modified by the Dutch and the British), the Japanese were busily perfecting a form of whaling that would bear some similarities to the European techniques, but that in one respect would be radically different. Around the middle of the seventeenth century, they began to catch whales with nets.

At first, villagers chased a whale into a bay and closed off the mouth with a net, a technique that is still used in Japan for taking dolphins. Later, it occurred to someone to go after the whales with the nets, rather than waiting for them in a bay or lagoon. Several villages claim this invention, among them Kayoi at the southern end of the island of Honshu on the Sea of Japan, and Taiji, located on the Boso Peninsula, 250 miles southwest of Tokyo. (In the folklore attendant upon this invention, some say it came about because a whaler watched a spider trap its prey in a web; another story has the concept coming to a whaler in a dream.) Taiji's history is an integral element in Japan's whaling history, since even today, the village means "whaling" to the Japanese. It still has a shore station where whales have been brought in for centuries, a whaling museum, and most important, a tradition of supplying men to the industry that goes back to 1606.

Whaling in Japan is said to have been "founded" in that year by Yorimoto Wada, the lord of the manor at Mizuno. (Only a year later, the Jamestown colony was founded in Virginia, the first English settlement on the American mainland.) Like any other coastal village, Taiji probably saw its share of beached whales and dolphins, but Yorimoto had the foresight to organize the boatmen and harpooners into five whaling crews, thus turning what had been a passive, casual operation into a proper fishery. His grandson, Yoriharu Wada (who changed his name

Surrounded by Japanese whaleboats, a right whale is trapped in a net. When it had tired, it would be harpooned.

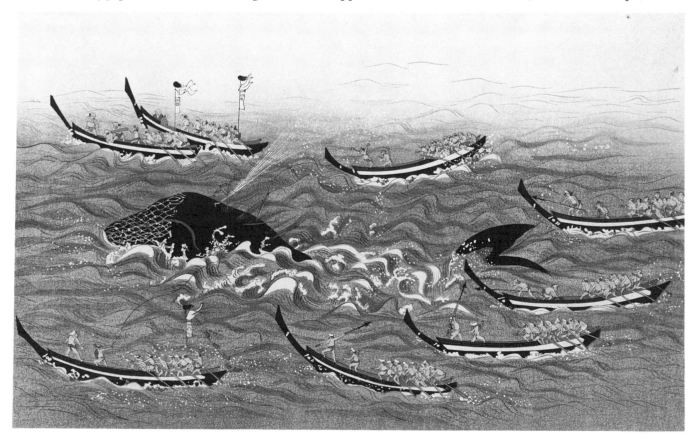

to Kakuemon Taiji), is supposed to have been the man who invented net whaling, some time around 1677.

They primarily hunted four types of whales: the right whale (*Semi kujira*), the humpback (*Zato kujira*), the fin whale (*Nagasu kujira*), and the gray whale (*Ko kujira*). If the opportunity presented itself, however, they took blue whales, sei whales, Bryde's whales, sperm whales and minke whales, but they did not differentiate sei whales from Bryde's, and evidently they didn't identify minkes at all. As was the case with almost all early shore-whaling operations around the world, the humpbacks were the first and hardest hit, probably because they are naturally curious, and innocently approach the boats that contain the men who will kill them. In the first sixty-nine years of the fishery at Kawajiri (1699 to 1768), they took 110 gray whales, 166 rights, 22 fins and 591 humpbacks.

Although the whales of the Japanese fishery were the same as those hunted elsewhere, the methods of whaling were quite different from their analogues in the Western world. European whalers sailed out to where they expected or hoped the whales would be, but the Japanese whalers waited for the whales to come to them. They posted lookouts high on the hills overlooking the sea, and when a whale was spotted, a series of signals were sent to alert the whalers. If the pennant was black with a white stripe down the middle, it meant that a female right whale and calf had been sighted; hunting these was strictly forbidden. Other indicators consisted of variously colored pennants, smoke signals, a stick semaphore, and occasionally the blowing of a conch-shell trumpet. The villagers piled out of their houses and ran to their assigned boats. There were the high-prowed chase boats, the net boats, and the broad-beamed towing boats.

The entire village was involved in the whaling, since the practice required a large labor force. Not only did they have to find and capture the whale, but they had to get it to shore, haul it up on the beach, and process it. A rich individual had to subsidize the whalers, because the number of people to be supported was enormous. In an 1829 publication called *Yogiotoru Eshi* ("Pictures of Whaling"), the author and artist Yamada Yosei lists the following personnel that "used to put to sea during the ten days between the beginning and the middle of January every year":

2 commanders, 3 officers, 50 sailors, 3 clerks, 18 whale slaughterers, 12 tendon scrapers, 2 rice men, 2 boys, 8 managers, 1 bone oil man, 7 watchmen, 3 carpenters, 1 smith, 1 cooper, 1 man in charge of nets, 30 whale catchers, 440 hunters . . . a total of 587 persons who went to Misaki to await putting out to sea.

A right whale and calf, which early Japanese whalers refused to hunt in order to preserve the species.

In this midnineteenth-century woodblock print by Kuniyoshi, the famous samurai swordsman Miyamoto Musashi is shown astride a right whale delivering the *coup de grace*.

When the Japan Whaling Association reproduced the Kuniyoshi print on the cover of a pro-whaling brochure, the swordsman had conveniently disappeared.

Since this type of whaling depended so heavily on nets, they had to be carefully fabricated and strong enough to hold a struggling 60-ton whale. Special hempen ropes were made ("Rope making was the women's task, and men were not employed in it"), and fabricated into nets. At the station at Misaki Island (the one described by Yamada Yosei), each net was 18 fathoms (108 feet) square when spread out, and each net boat carried nineteen of the nets, lashed together. It is said that some of the first nets were made from wisteria vines, and that some of the early rope nets were dipped in pig's blood for strength.

Whaling with nets was not exactly like seining for fish, in that the whalers did not set the nets and hope that a passing whale would blunder into them. It is rather more like the contemporary technique known as "purse-seining," in which a school of fish is surrounded by a net, and then the net is "pursed," or closed, around the prey. When a whale was spotted from shore, the boats were launched, and they gave chase, circling the whale, and hoping to drive it toward the shore and the waiting net boats. Japanese whalers understood that noise is transmitted very well underwater, and they herded the panicked whale by banging on the shafts of their oars with mallets. The net boats, deployed in staggered ranks with their nets suspended vertically in the water, waited for the whale. When the hapless creature had become entangled in the nets, the boats would close in on it, and the harpooner arched his iron upward, so that as it fell it would drive deeply into the back of the whale. Other harpooners would throw their weapons, and soon there was a mortally wounded whale ensnared in the heavy nets. (Only right whales, fin whales and humpbacks were driven into the nets to be harpooned; the gray whale fought savagely enough to destroy the nets, so it was chased down and harpooned.) Yamada Yosei describes the killing of a right whale:

Now some whales come up to the surface of the sea in a short time, but others break surface after about thirty minutes. When the whale comes up it is harpooned by many catchers who are waiting, so that it is weakened and in pain and its moaning is heard like thunder. The surface of the sea becomes bloody all round and the red seas run high. The whale has a gentle nature, even when in pain like that just mentioned, especially the right whale which is the gentlest of all whales. It does not damage the boats even when mad with pain. The harpooners' boats are towed by the whale as it runs away, and follow it so that the whale is harpooned by them as often as it breaks surface. Then comes the scene for which many catchers are waiting—*ken kiri*, the lancing—accomplished by thrusts from lances into the body of the weakened whale. It is terrible enough to make one break out in a cold sweat.

The next act of this drama would cause anyone to break out in a cold sweat. In order to make the still-living whale fast, a whaler would jump onto its back, and as it thrashed and struggled in the foaming, bloody water, he would cut a hole in the septum of the blowholes, through which a heavy rope was passed. Another man leapt on its slippery back, and holding on to one of the implanted harpoons, would cut a hole in the back through which another rope was passed. More men followed into the water, diving beneath the whale's body to encircle it with the ropes that were used to keep it afloat when it was towed to shore. The artist Utagawa Kuniyoshi (1797–1861) illustrated one of the legendary samurai swordsmen of Japan, Miyamoto Musashi, astride the back of a right whale with his sword raised, as if to demonstrate that the *bushi* warrior could subdue even the mightiest creature on earth.

For all this harpooning, stabbing, cutting, and hog-tying, however, the whale was still not dead, and now, with the necessary ropes around it (each of which had a special name), the lancers moved in for the kill:

After that many catchers try to stab the whale to death with their lances and large knives, and some kinds of whale stretch their body as if to die, heave a deep sigh, give a cry, turn round two or three times while fastened to the boats and with the death rattle give up their life. At that moment all the whalers chant three times "May its soul rest in peace," and express their thanks to god and Buddha in a hymn for the capture of the most prized and great right whale.

The carcass of the dead whale was slung between two boats and towed to shore by "more than ten boats in two ranks," where it was winched up onto the beach by means of a great capstan. Yamada Yosei simply says that "the carrying boats are unfastened from the whale and the net is taken off," but surely it must have been difficult to remove a heavy net (which he described as being twenty-eight fathoms long) which had been employed to trap a 60-ton whale. (Ivan Sanderson worried about this too, for in his *Follow the Whale* he wrote, "The resultant mess, as depicted in the illustrations, is so appalling that it becomes an even more acute puzzle trying to fathom how they disentangled the brute after it was killed. If you have ever tried to get a small herring out of a ravelled seine, you will know what I mean.")

Once the whale was on the beach, according to Yamada Yosei, "a great number of factory men, including overseers, each with his own special job," began the process of reducing the whale to its component parts. The bones, blubber, tongue, baleen, entrails and genitals were all removed according to proscribed procedures, and carried off to "a large warehouse, a small warehouse, a bone house, and a tendon house." While the work was going on, there were people who came to the beach to steal the whale meat and would "put it in their bosom, twine it around their waist, or hold it between their legs." (In Plate 16 of his "Pictures of Whaling," the author finds this humorous, but by Plate 18 he writes, "The searcher . . . always tortures the man if he finds he has meat secretly concealed about him.") According to Yamada Yosei, "The flensers and carriers who flock to the scene handle and dispose of a whale as

Plate 20 from the 1829 publication *Yogiotoru Eshi,* by Yomada Yosei, showing the whalers' ritual dance after their return from a successful voyage.

big as a mountain in less than no time because of their well arranged methods and familiarity with the actions they have to perform.''

Whaling was a highly ritualized operation for the early Japanese whalers, and in addition to the specific assignment of different chores, there were also chants and dances that were performed at various times, from the beginning of the whaling season to the catching of the whale. The whalers at Misaki did the "Catchers' Dance" three times "on the night of the moon's ninth day in January," and also when they triumphantly returned with a whale. In *Yogiotoru Eshi,* Plate 20 is devoted to the dancing, and shows the hefty whalers, their hair arranged in a characteristic topknot which allowed them to be pulled from the water in case of trouble, dancing in a wildly uninhibited manner as the drummers beat out the rhythm of the capstans and the women and children huddle together demurely but proudly. One can feel the beat of the drums and the stamping of the dancers' feet, and from their joyful expressions, one knows that they have been successful.

The main object of early Japanese whaling was meat. Franz von Siebold, a German doctor who visited Japan in 1823, wrote that "the right whale's meat is very delicious and is a major part of the diet. . . .

People eat the whale's meat, blubber and internal organs. . . . All over Japan, people eat whale meat.'' It must have seemed very odd indeed to a European to see people eating the stuff that his compatriots fed to sharks.

The Japanese had no way of knowing what was taking place halfway around the world, but they would have been astonished at the wasteful practices of the European whalers, who took the baleen and the blubber and discarded that which the Japanese valued the most, the whale's meat. In fact, the Japanese were much more efficient than any Westerners about utilizing the entire whale. The oil went into soap and lamps, as it did throughout the Western world, but in Japan it was also mixed with vinegar to make a pesticide for rice paddies. The bones were smashed and cooked to produce fertilizer. Sinews were sold to instrument makers for *samisen* strings, and the baleen was used for the ribs of folding fans, lantern handles, fishing rods, plates, and the strings of puppets. Medicines were created from various internal organs, and predictably, the penis was dried and pulverized into a tonic to revitalize the whalers. The entrails were boiled and used for soup, and it is said that the heart membranes were made into drum heads.

The coastal whalers of Taiji, Koyoi, Kochi and Wakayama took some 90 to 100 whales per village per year. They favored the right whale, but unlike their counterparts around the world, who were slaughtering as many right whales as they could find, the Japanese probably didn't cause a significant reduction in the population at this time. In fact, they understood—as the whalers of Australia, South Africa and New Zealand did not—that the right whales were a valuable resource, and they took special care not to kill females with calves. It was perhaps the only instance in the abusive history of whaling where an equilibrium was reached between the whalers and the whales. (Not that the whales benefited from the culling of their numbers, but at least in Japanese waters they were not subject to the wholesale slaughter that was practiced by almost every other "civilized" country.)

Although they preferred the docility and meat of the right whale, Japanese whalers also managed to take any other whales that came within sight of their coastline. From 1698 to 1888, for the Yamaguchi Prefecture alone, the tally is as follows: 294 right whales, 958 humpbacks, 288 gray whales, 709 "other species," and most interestingly, 277 fin whales. Most of the literature of whaling indicates that the fin whale was too strong and too swift to be taken until the development of the harpoon cannon and the steam-powered catcher boat, and yet the Japanese, with their nets and swimming samurais, were able to kill so many of the species they knew as *Nagasu kujira.*

The shoguns could declare their islands off limits to Westerners, but the surrounding oceans were open to anyone with enough men, ships and fortitude. In the early years of the nineteenth century, whalers had discovered the rich whaling grounds of the world's largest ocean, and no Tokugawa isolationist policies were going to keep them away from the abundant harvests. Sailing round the Horn, the whalers entered the previously untapped riches of the Pacific. From the coasts of Peru and Chile, they cruised along the Equator to the Galapagos, the Juan Fernandez Islands, the Marquesas (where a young whaleman named Herman Melville jumped ship), the Tuamotus and New Zealand; and northward to the Hawaiian chain and the vast expanses of the North Pacific, where the sperm whales lived and sported. They sailed from the Marianas northward to the Ryukyus (which the whalers referred to as the "Loo-Choos"), stretching some four hundred miles from Okinawa to Kyushu, the southernmost of Japan's four main islands.

In 1820 the ship *Maro* out of Nantucket sailed for the "Japan Grounds," and Starbuck reports that "in 1821 six or seven ships were cruising in this vicinity, and in the following year, more than thirty visited the field." There are few records of these early days of Pacific whaling, but it is very likely that the insatiable American and European whalers took the oil-rich right whales whenever they encountered them. In C. H. Townsend's 1935 compilation of the whalers' logbook records of the whales they killed, he writes, "during the [summer] months and in about the same latitude, there was much hunting for right whales . . . in the Inland Sea of Japan." (By 1950, however, there were so few right whales in Japanese waters that an eighty-six-page article on "Whales in the Adjacent Waters of Japan" does not mention them once, and by 1977, right whales had become so scarce that the stranding of a single specimen was newsworthy enough for an article in the *Reports* of the Whales Research Institute of Tokyo.)

In 1824, Captain James Josiah Coffin, of the Nantucket whaleship *Transit,* discovered the Bonin Islands. Some five hundred miles southeast of Japan, these tiny specks of land were claimed by Coffin, and then again by the British in 1825. Nobody seemed particularly interested in pressing their claims, and the Bonins were not officially annexed by anybody until Japan did so in 1876. The Bonin Islands (also known as the Ogasawaras) are relatively uninteresting to people, but particularly attractive to whales. From the day of their discovery, they have been the scene of concentrated whaling, first by the Yankees, and then, after a century's respite, by the Japanese.

Three years before Commodore Perry arrived in Japan, Melville had written, "If that double-bolted land, Japan, is ever to become hospitable, it is the whaleship alone to whom credit is due; for already she is on the threshold." She was indeed on the threshold, but Japan's hospitality would be some time in coming. Captain Mercator Cooper, of the Sag Harbor whaler *Manhattan,* had been working the Japan Grounds in March of 1845 when he came upon and rescued twenty-one Japanese fishermen who had

The whaleship *Manhattan* in Japanese waters in 1845, eight years before the arrival of Commodore Perry, as drawn by a Japanese artist.

been shipwrecked on a barren island 350 miles south of Tokyo.* He brought them back to Uraga, but suspicious Japanese government officials refused to let him land. After three weeks of negotiations, Cooper was able to release his passengers, and in the process, the Japanese got their first look at the foreigners who would irrevocably alter their destinies. (Mercator Cooper also has the distinction of being the first whaleman to explore and work the Okhotsk Sea. His voyage led the way for a whaler's invasion of those Siberian waters which would almost bring the indigenous populations of right and bowhead whales to extinction.)

Eight years after the *Manhattan* incident, Commodore Matthew Perry arrived in Japan, and opened the country to the rest of the world. Since European and American whalers had been working the Japan Grounds for thirty years, one of Perry's objectives was to establish bases on Japan's Pacific seaboard where the whalers could replenish their supplies of

*This was the same island on which the Japanese fisherman Manjiro Nakahama had been shipwrecked in 1841, and was rescued from by Captain Whitfield of the New Bedford whaler *John Howland* after 143 days. Nakahama—who became known as John Manjiro—was transported to Fairhaven, Massachusetts, where he lived for five years, learned whaling and navigation, and in 1851 worked his way back to Japan, trying, unsuccessfully, to persuade the Emperor to allow Americans to land on Japanese soil. Manjiro's story is entertainingly told by Tetsuo Kawasami of Keio University in Tokyo, and a fictionalized version appears in C. W. Nicol's 1987 novel *Harpoon*.

food and water. (He was also charged by President Millard Fillmore to attempt to change Japanese policy toward shipwrecked seamen, who previously had been imprisoned or executed.) Perry's official mission was to induce the government to open diplomatic relations with the United States, and he chose to do it with a vengeance. He steamed into Uraga with four ships on July 8, 1853, and sent word that he would deliver the President's letter to the Emperor, by force if necessary. The Japanese stalled for time, and Perry left word that he would return the following year for a response. In February 1854, he arrived in Edo (Tokyo) Bay, this time with nine ships, and realizing that there was no way their feudal society could stand up to the military power of these foreigners, the Japanese agreed to allow United States ships to obtain fuel and supplies and arranged for the first U.S. Consul, Townsend Harris, to be stationed at Shimoda. Four years after his arrival, Harris negotiated a treaty with the Japanese, and as similar arrangements were made with other European countries, the three-hundred-year isolationist reign of the Tokugawa shogunate began to crumble. (An earthquake on November 11, 1855, which destroyed much of the capital city of Edo, added to the sense of a nation no longer in control of its own destiny.) At this time the primacy of the Emperor was revived, and the Meiji Restoration commenced.

Chinese Whaling

ON A SANDSTONE WALL in Ulchu County, southeastern Korea, archaeologists investigating a ruined temple were led to a sandstone wall across a small stream at the head of the Taehwa River. There, some twelve miles from the sea, they were shown a sandstone wall that had long been submerged after the construction of a dam farther downstream. A severe drought in the summer of 1971 exposed the twenty-six-foot-long wall, and it was seen to contain close to two hundred figures of animals; on the right are cattle, deer, dogs, hogs, and cats, and the left side is dominated by remarkably accurate drawings of whales, some free-swimming, and some apparently harpooned. The Korean archaeologist Kim Won-Yong has suggested that the drawings incised in the wall may be as early as the neolithic period, perhaps as early as 6000 B.C. So far, there is no way to date these mysterious drawings, but even if they prove to have been created in the early years of the settlement of Korea—around A.D. 300–600—they would be some of the earliest known illustrations of whaling.

The Chinese have a naval tradition that dates back to the Mongols in the thirteenth century. Chinese naval power reached dramatic heights in the fifteenth century with the exploratory voyages of the legendary eunuch admiral, Cheng Ho, but with the supplanting of the Ming dynasty by the Confucians, the country turned inward and abandoned its maritime inclinations. From 1405 to 1434, the Ming ships visited the Philippines, Indochina, Sumatra, Java, the East Indies, Ceylon, and perhaps even the Red Sea. Of course there are whales in these waters, but references to their capture are few. Writing of the "otherwise undocumented period" before the year 1000, Ivan Sanderson introduces *lung sien hiang,* which he translates as "dragon's saliva perfume," an aromatic

substance collected from large parties of sea dragons. The description of this substance, obviously ambergris, suggests to him "a full-fledged whaling industry in action somewhere off the coast of southern China in those times." Ambergris is a buoyant substance, and its presence might suggest the presence of the sperm whales from which it comes, but it is quite possible to find ambergris without a whaling industry, full-fledged or otherwise.

In search of the spices and silks of the Orient, the ships of the East India Company had been prowling the shores of eastern Asia since 1600. They had been driven out of the East Indies by the Dutch in 1623, but their mariners had discovered tea in China around 1650, and two decades later, tea sales in London had reached an astonishing £94,000. In 1673, John Nieuhoff submitted a report to the East India Company, which detailed *The Cities, Towns, Villages, Ports, Rivers, &c. In Their Passages from Canton to Peking,* and included a description of whaling "near to the Island [of] *Hainan.*" Some of the aspects of his whales are curious, such as, "Instead of Eyes they have two thin Skins which stick out and are three Yards long," which probably refers to the pectoral fins, but the obvious description of baleen suggests a right whale: "The Tongue . . . rests upon eight hundred great and small Pegs or Teeth, which are cover'd with Stuff like Horse-hair, to preserve the Tongue from being hurt as it lies upon them." Nieuhoff's report on whaling concludes, unfortunately, with these words: "The manner of killing them has been sufficiently described by others, and therefore I shall forbear to trouble the Reader with a Relation thereof."

There is no question that whaling was practiced in China, even though the documentation—at least in Western literature—is scarce. In the September

1844 edition of *The Friend,* the whalemen's newspaper published in Honolulu, the following article appeared. It is included here in its entirety:

During the months of January and February, whales and their young resort to the coast of China, to the south of Hailing Shan, in great numbers; and during those months are pursued by the Chinese belonging to Hainan and the neighboring islands with considerable success. The fish generally seem to be in bad condition, and were covered with barnacles and their object in resorting to that part of the coast during that season, is probably to obtain food for themselves and young, from the great quantity of squid, cuttle, and blubber fish which abound, and perhaps also to roll on the numerous sand banks on the coast, in order to clear their skin of barnacles and other animals which torment them. They are often seen leaping more than their whole length out of the water, and coming down perpendicularly so as to strike hard against the bottom.*

It is an exciting scene to see these boats out, in fleets of from 50 to 70, scattered over the bays as far as the eye can reach, under full sail, cruising about in search of their prey. Some steer straight ahead, with the crew facing in different directions, observing the boats in their company, and leaving no chance of a spout escaping unnoticed. Upon others, the harpooner may be seen leaning over the bow ready to strike, and occasionally waving his right or left hand to direct the helmsman after the fish in its various turnings—the strictest silence the while being observed.

The boats are admirably adapted for following up the fish, as they sail well, make little noise in going through the water, and may be turned around in half the time and space that a foreign boat occupies. They are of different sizes; the smallest are about three tons and the largest about twenty-five, carrying two small boats on her

*This description closely parallels Scammon's description of the California gray whale, and it therefore seems very likely that some of the whales hunted by the Chinese were grays. The barnacled condition is normal for gray whales, as is the breaching behavior and the shallow-water habitat. Scammon (p. 24) says: "To our surprise, we saw many of the whales going through the surf where the depth of water was barely sufficient to float them. We could discern in many places, by the white sand that came to the surface, that they must be near or touching the bottom. One in particular, lay for a half-hour in the breakers, playing as seals often do in a heavy surf; turning from side to side with half-extended fins, and moved apparently by the heavy ground swell which was breaking; at times making a playful spring with its bending flukes, throwing its body clear of the water, coming down with a heavy splash. . . ." In a 1984 study, Wang discussed gray whale skeletons found in provinces around the Korean peninsula, and speculated that "a few individuals probably reached as far south as 20°N in the adjacent waters of the east coast of Hainan Island."

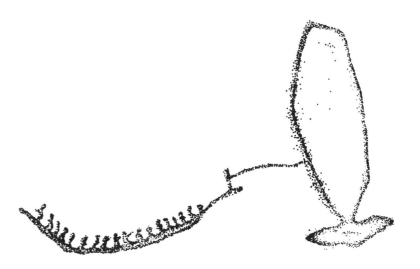

On a sandstone wall at Ulchu in southeastern Korea, a panorama of what may be Neolithic wall drawings was found in 1971. This one appears to show a whale harpooned by a boatload of men, and may be one of the oldest illustrations of whaling in existence.

deck, and a crew of twelve men, of light draft of water and of good length. On the bow is a crooked piece of timber, supported by a stancheon [*sic*], which serves as a rest for the harpoon when not wanted; it enables the harpooner to stretch well out over the bow, and see their fish as they pass below the boat. In this position they are struck, for the weight of the harpoon prevents its being thrown any distance. Abaft the mainmast the deck is rounded so as to form the roof of the cabin; on its top the whale line is coiled.

The harpoon has only one barb, and about fifteen inches from the point of the iron it is made with a socket; above which, an eye is wrought, with a cord attached to the iron, to which the whale line is fastened and stopped slack along the wooden shaft so that when the fish is struck, the iron and the line tightens, the shaft draws out, and leaves less chance of the iron cutting out or loosing its hold on the skin of the fish.

The whale line is made of native hemp, and is about 60 or 70 fathoms long, and from 4 to 6 inches in circumference, according to the size of the boat. Great length of line is not required by them, for there is shoal water along the coast for many miles to seaward. One end of the line is fastened round the mainmast, the remainder is coiled away on the top of the house, and carried forward to the harpoon in the bow, where it is made fast, leaving a few fathoms slack of line.

The boats come out of the different harbors at daylight, and spread themselves soon along the coast. As soon as the fish is seen blowing, away they go in chase. If fortunate enough to get it fast, the sails are lowered, the bight of the line got aft, the rudder unshipped, and the boat allowed to tow stern foremost. The rest of the fleet seeing the sail lowered, come up to assist; and as the fish now keeps pretty much to the surface in its struggle to get away, they soon manage to fasten eight or ten harpoons into it, and in a couple of hours or so it is dead from wounds and loss of blood. They always strike the fish a little behind the blowhole, on the top of the back. When the fish is dead, it is lashed alongside one or two of the boats to float it, and to allow the others to make their lines fast to the tail and tow it on shore. It is surprising that the boats are not stove in, or completely destroyed from their manner of taking the fish, i.e. sailing right over it and then striking it; but from the cool way in which the Chinese manage the whole affair, I have no doubt that personal accidents occur more seldom than with our fishermen. Their greatest danger is when two or three whales are struck together in the same place, and swim round and over each other, so as to foul the lines. The boats are then drawn against each other and over the fish, and run great risk of being soon swamped and stove in pieces. In one instance of this sort that fell under my observation, they had three of their boats swamped, but managed to clear the lines, and kill the fish in a most dexterous manner; after which some of the spare boats returned and towed the damaged boats to shore. They had no lances in their boats, nor in fact any other weapon except the harpoons, which they refused to sell at any price. All the boats had parts of the whale's flesh salted, which they used as provisions. They refused to give any account of what use they made of the fish, and in general, were not disposed to be very civil to strangers, which might arise from jealousy, or a fear of our interfering with their fishery. The fish are, I believe, what whalers call the right whale, and were calculated by those on board to yield on an average of 50 barrels of oil each.

Russian Bay Whaling

THE RUSSIANS, who would have worked the Pacific north of the Japanese and the Chinese, have an exclusive whaling ground of their own, similar to, but much larger than, the Sea of Japan. The northern coast of the USSR is the longest east-west coastline in the world, but it is icebound for most of the year, so most Russian whaling—and foreign whaling in Russian waters—took place in the *Okhotskoye More,* a vast, semienclosed body of water bordered on the west by Siberia, and on the east by the Kamchatka Peninsula and the Kuril Islands. Sakhalin is in the Sea of Okhotsk's southwest quadrant, a 589-mile-long island shaped like a shark that is separated from the Japanese island of Hokkaido by the Strait of La Pérouse. (The whaling difference between the Sea of Japan and the Okhotsk Sea is that the former is bordered on the west by Russia and the Korean peninsula, while the latter is entirely within Russian boundaries.) The Russian inland sea is composed of 611,000 square miles of ice and water. The whalers of the world long knew that this region was particularly attractive to whales, and from the discovery of the Japan Grounds in 1820 to the time the Russians tried to restrict whaling to their own ships, it was a favorite rendezvous for Yankee whalers. In Townsend's compilation of the destinations of American whaleships from 1761 to 1920, he shows a great concentration of right whales and bowheads in the Okhotsk Sea. Starbuck claims that the first bowheads were taken in the Okhotsk in 1843 by the New Bedford whalers *Hercules* and *Janus,* and the French make the same claim for their whaleship *Asia,* which sailed under an American skipper, but the records are ambiguous. By 1848, Thomas Roys had sailed through the Bering Strait east of Kamchatka, and discovered the bowheads there. It is now believed that there were four distinct populations of bowheads: in East Greenland–Spitsbergen; in Hudson Bay; in the eastern and western North Atlantic; and in the western Arctic of the Bering, Chukchi and Beaufort seas. Roys was the first European to encounter the Bering Sea bowheads, but it is still not clear whether these whales shared a range with the bowheads of the Chukchi and Okhotsk seas.

Soviet whaling historian Igor Krupnick contends that whaling among aboriginals of the Chukotka Peninsula (the northernmost peninsula in eastern Siberia) can be dated to the first century B.C. The whales taken were gray whales and bowheads, as evidenced by the excavation of cemeteries on the peninsula. Although we cannot determine what became of the meat, we assume that it was eaten, and the bones of the whales were used for building underground dwellings and meat caches. The preponderance of the bones of smaller whales suggests a fishery based on juveniles.

Certain citizens of northwestern Russia are believed (at least by Russian whaling historians) to have settled Spitsbergen—which they knew as *Grumant*—long before the Dutch and the British got there at the beginning of the seventeenth century. (Even now, although this claim is generally rejected, the Soviets are trying to hold on to Spitsbergen's mineral rights, which are thought to be considerable.) There seems to be no question that some aboriginal Russian whalers knew of Spitsbergen, and may have taken some of the plentiful bowhead whales that wintered in its protected bays as early as the fifteenth century. At the same time, Dutch and British whalers were visiting the barren reaches of northwestern Russia, hunting whales and walruses.

They sailed around what is now known as the North Cape, past the Varanger Fjord, and as far as the Navolok Peninsula, where the Kola River empties into the Barents Sea. Inscriptions on cliff walls there indicate that a Dutch whaler from Flensburg visited some twenty times beginning in 1510. The authorities were levying taxes on Russian whalers even before the end of the sixteenth century. A French traveler named de Martinier visited Kola in 1653 and commented on the houses constructed of the ribs and jawbones of whales.

Thousands of miles to the east, where the cold coast of Russia finally emerges from the ice zone,

aboriginal whalers had been hunting various species of whales since they developed skin boats. They used harpoons, spears, poisoned arrows, and—although the subject is mentioned only in passing in the 1955 study by Nikonorov and Arsen'ev—nets woven of walrus hide. Inhabitants of the Kuril Islands, which stretch from the southern tip of Kamchatka to Hokkaido, hunted whales with poisoned arrows. There is a mention of people becoming sick from consuming the meat of a whale killed with a poisoned arrow, and "whole settlements died after eating a contaminated whale."

In 1648, a cossack officer named Semon Dezhnev, collecting fur tributes for the Tsar, took six small boats down the Kolyma River on the northern coast of Siberia and sailed east. He rounded the Chukchi Peninsula's East Cape (now Cape Dezhnev), and passed through the narrow strait that separates the Eurasian mainland from the North American continent. Dezhnev was therefore the first European to navigate what would later be named the Bering Strait, but his report to Saint Petersburg was barely literate, and remained unnoticed for almost a hundred years.

Tsar Peter the Great (1682–1725) encouraged the Russians in the exploration of the North, and is credited with the establishment of the first government-subsidized whaling company. In 1723 he ordered five ships to be built by the Bajenin family, the premier shipbuilders of Archangel. Each of these ships was over one hundred feet long, with a beam of thirty feet, and was accompanied by six rowing boats. The first three vessels were completed by 1725, and were christened *Grunland Fordur, Valfisch* and *Grono.* Although the crews were Russian, the captains, specksnyders and harpooners were Dutch, since the lowlanders knew more about catching and processing polar whales than anyone in the world, and were hired to teach the trade to the Russians. The Dutchmen could provide everything but good luck, and the *Grunland Fordur* sank with all hands, while the other two ships became lost in the ice between Archangel and Kola.

Peter also sent explorers and topographers to the barren shores of Kamchatka and Okhotsk, and even to the Kuril Islands in 1721. On his deathbed, Peter signed the orders authorizing Bering's first expedition. Ignorant of Dezhnev's discovery, Vitus Jonassen Bering, a Dane in the service of the Tsar, set out from St. Petersburg in 1725, accompanied by his lieutenants Martin Spanberg and Alexei Chirikov. He had been instructed to discover whether or not America and Asia were joined, to facilitate Russian expansion on land. After traveling some forty-six hundred miles overland to Siberia from St. Petersburg, Bering and his extraordinarily hardy crew took three more years before they completed the ships that would carry them into these uncharted, fog-bound, ice-choked waters. With materials they had carried across Siberia by sledge, they built the *Gabriel,* and sailed north, hugging the coastline of Kamchatka. They sighted St. Lawrence Island in 1728, but did not attempt a landing, and made the East Cape, the easternmost point on the Asian mainland. Even though they were aware that the coastline trended sharply westward—and therefore might be the passage between Asia and North America—they were held back by contrary winds and were forced to turn around. They instead sailed around the southern limit of Kamchatka, demonstrating that it was not coterminous with the Japanese island of Hokkaido.

On a subsequent voyage that was a part of Imperial Russia's "Great Northern Expedition" of 1733–43, Bering sailed from Kamchatka in two ships, *St. Peter* and *St. Paul,* on June 4, 1741. (Their point of departure was a harbor that would eventually be named Petropavlovsk after the two ships.) He was searching for "Gamaland," a nonexistent place that Russian cartographers had placed somewhere near the Aleutians, but he found the Alaskan archipelago instead. (Bering, commanding *St. Peter,* got as far east as Kodiak Island, but Chirikov, in the *St. Paul,* reached Prince William Sound before being forced to come about.) Bering's vessel was badly damaged by howling storms that raged incessantly for forty days, and he and his crew were ravaged by scurvy. He struggled back across the North Pacific in November, hoping to make the mainland, but fetched up on a previously uncharted island at the western end of the Aleutian chain, only a hundred miles from Kamchatka. Those who had survived the six-month voyage and the cruel Siberian weather on the Commander Islands (also named for the intrepid Bering) found these barren, rocky outcrops surprisingly rich in animal life. They saw little grayish-blue foxes and sea otters in profusion. The men were starving, and while they could not catch the swift little foxes, they did manage to kill and eat some seven hundred of the thick-furred otters between their stranding in November and their return to Kamchatka in a rebuilt ship in August of 1742. Bering died on this island, but the surviving crew members sailed back to Mother Russia and reported the sea otters and foxes, and also the multitudes of seals and sea lions that hauled out along the rocky shores. They also reported a huge, slow-moving creature, the likes of which had never been seen before—or since.

Browsing on kelp and algae in the inshore shallows of the Commander Islands was a gigantic relative of today's manatees and dugongs, which eventually became known to science as *Hydrodamalis gigas,* and to the layman as Steller's sea cow. Georg Wilhelm Steller was Bering's naturalist, and along with the incredible sea cow, he also identified the sea lion that is named for him. The only contemporaneous illustration ever made of the sea cow was drawn by Sven Waxell, a crew member of the ill-fated *St. Peter.* It shows a ponderous creature with a face like that of a tuskless walrus; short, stubby forelegs, and a horizontal tail like the flukes of a whale. The maximum length of this unlikely creature was thirty feet. Its skin was knobbly and dark brown, thick enough to be made into shoe soles. It had no teeth, but instead there were flat, ridged plates in the upper and lower jaws that it used to grind seaweed into a mush. It was easily killed—but at a maximum weight of eight tons, not so easily hauled ashore for butchering—and it proved to be a godsend for the marooned seamen. They consumed the meat, drank the oil, and used the skin for the repair of their boats.

After Steller and the remaining crew members returned to the mainland, they reported their discoveries to the authorities, and for the next twenty years or so, sealing crews stopped off at *Komandoriskiye Ostrova* to provision with the plentiful meat and oil. We do not have an accurate record of the number of sea cows on the islands during this period, but Leonhard Stejneger, Steller's biographer, has estimated that there were no more than fifteen hundred of them when Bering and his crew arrived. From the sealers' records and logbooks, Stejneger calculated that at least six hundred men wintered there between 1743 and 1763.

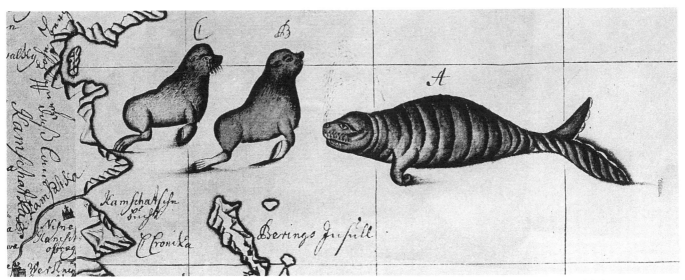

A sea cow (*A*), drawn by Sven Waxell, an officer on Bering's 1742 voyage aboard the *St. Peter,* which was wrecked on the Commander Islands. (*B* is a sea lion and *C* is a fur seal.) This is the only known illustration of a sea cow by someone who actually saw one.

Steller's sea cow is now extinct, and has been since a Russian sealer killed the last one in 1768. It took only twenty-seven years for man to eliminate the sea cow from the face of the earth. In retrospect, however, one cannot hold Bering, Steller, or the sealers responsible for this unprecedented act. They could hardly have known that the population they discovered on these remote islands represented the last of its kind. For all the sealers knew, there would be many more islands to discover, and probably many more strange creatures, including more sea cows.

In addition to describing the sea lion, the jay, and the sea cow that have carried his name into biological immortality, Steller also told of the whaling activities of the aboriginals of the coasts of easternmost Asia:

Whales are taken in the neighborhood of Kamschatka in the number of ways which I shall cite here, however inconceivable such seem, and are astonishing in view of the size of these great sea animals. Around Lapatka and the Kurile Islands the inhabitants travel to the sea in baidars, seek places at which these are accustomed to sleep; as many as they meet, so many do they shoot with poisoned arrows, whereby they suddenly puff out, storm and rage frightfully and go down into the sea, and it happens now and then, that one or more, at times even none of them, are cast upon the shore. When the Kuriles obtain a whale, no one begins to cut it up until all are assembled; first shamanizing takes place, each one puts on his best clothes, and carries home his portion, after this one yurt entertains the other. . . . As soon as the whale comes to the land in Kamschatka, they fasten it with a thin line to a little stick stuck in the sand, and believe certainly on this account, that neither the spirits nor the sea nor *Gamuti*. or spirits of the land, can any longer have any claim to it.

The Russians established the first non-Eskimo settlement in Alaska, at Three Saints Bay, near Kodiak, in 1784. Otto von Kotzebue of the Imperial Russian Navy had discovered the sound that he named for himself in 1816, while searching for the elusive Northwest Passage. Various private citizens tried to form whaling companies for Alaskan waters, such as the Onerskye Company that was established by Count Vorontsov in 1786, but these ventures invariably failed because of the inexperience of the Russian crews. The Russian-American Company had been formed in 1799 to harvest sea otters (nearly driving these animals to extinction as well), and governed the immense expanse of snow, ice, tundra, mountains and islands until 1867, when the entire 589,757 square miles were purchased by the United States for $7.2 million.

After 1850, the Okhotsk Grounds became increasingly popular with American whalers, since other

Kodiak Indians of Alaska hunting a right whale from one-man kayaks.

grounds appeared to be fished out. The ship *Florida,* out of New Bedford, made the Okhotsk Grounds in the summer of 1858. According to the detailed diary kept by Eliza Williams, the wife of the captain, they were surrounded by whales and competing whaleships:

The *Daniel Wood* has come from the head of the Bay and anchored close by us. He got two whales up there, making about 130 bbls. There were not as many up there as here, but about as many ships. . . . We have not got through boiling yet. The cow whale that we first got will stow down 180 bbls. It is the best one that has been taken in the Bay all season.

This afternoon we saw another large one. My Husband is off now to try and get him. Capt. M has gone to steer for him. I can see his boat some ways off. I think they see the whale now. . . . When the whales are molested in one place, they generally leave in droves for another place, and after a while they will be back again. The Bays are full of their feed, so much that the water is dirty in appearance.

It was not until 1853 that the Russians dispatched vessels to protect their shores from foreign invaders in the Okhotsk Sea. Previously, unenforced restric-

tions on foreign vessels hadn't worked, and by 1849 there were 250 vessels in the Sea of Okhotsk, not one of which was Russian. On one memorable day in 1854, some fifty whales were taken in the Okhotsk.

In December 1850, the Russo-Finnish Whaling Company was established, with a total of five whaling ships. The first of these, named *Suomi* for Finland, successfully operated in the Okhotsk Sea, and took 1,500 barrels of blubber and 21,400 pounds of bone, which were sold in Bremen. Another Russo-Finnish ship, called *Turku,* operated in the Yellow Sea and the Sea of Japan, taking bowheads; and the *Ayan* captured several whales in 1854, but they were carried away by winds and currents before they could be processed. The *Graf Berg* and the *Amur* completed the fleet, and because of the plentitude of whales and the government's tax abatements, the Russo-Finnish Company functioned in the black for two years. Then *Ayan* was captured and burned by the English-French fleet that was patrolling the Pacific in conjunction with the war that was going on in the Crimea, and *Amur* was sold. The company wound up in 1863.

A Russo-American Company was set up in that same year with a small factory at Mamga, on Tugursky Bay on the Sea of Okhotsk. At most, there were two of the company's vessels working this region. Russian whalers continued to operate in their protected body of water for the remainder of the nineteenth century, establishing a station on the eastern coast of Aniva Bay; the meat was shipped to Japan, and the baleen was exported to Europe. The Treaty of Saint Petersburg between Russia and Japan in 1875 gave Russia sole control of Sakhalin Island, and Japan all the Kuril Islands.

With whales as with all migratory animals, events that occur in one location can often have far-reaching and often unsuspected ramifications elsewhere. As the American whalers were decimating the gray whale populations of Baja California in the 1860s

and '70s, the aboriginals of the Chukot Peninsula in Siberia were feeling the results of that whaling. The whales that would have returned to the Anadyr Gulf in the summer to feed—and to feed the Eskimos—were being killed off at an alarming rate in the lagoons of Baja. Krupnick writes that the shortage of whales led to "a severe reduction in aboriginal whaling, massive disasters and starvation." When the San Francisco whalers had given up on the Baja gray whales—primarily because they had rendered them too scarce to hunt—the natives of Chukot were able to resume their subsistence hunting. By the time the gray whales had begun their slow recovery, however, the aboriginals faced another threat: "civilized" whaling was coming.

The Origin of American Whaling

THERE IS little doubt that Leif Ericsson was the earliest European to land on North American shores; there is even a stone on the unoccupied No-man's Island off Martha's Vineyard that bears what purports to be his runic signature and the year: 1000. Sailing by way of Iceland and Greenland, he landed on the northern tip of what is now Newfoundland, at a place archaeologists have identified as L'Anse aux Meadows. In a charming display of certitude, F. W. True opens his (1904) *Whalebone Whales of the Western North Atlantic* with the announcement that "the first reference to cetaceans in American waters is in the Saga of Thorfin Karlsefne," and presents the following translation of the document, which is dated A.D. 1008 (the translator is B. F. DeCosta, and "that place" is Buzzards Bay, Massachusetts):

Afterward a whale was cast ashore in that place; and they assembled and cut it up, not knowing what kind of a whale it was. They boiled it with water; and ate it, and were taken sick. Then Thorhall said, "Now you see that Thor is more prompt to give aid than your Christ. This

was cast ashore as a reward for the hymn which I composed to my patron Thor, who rarely forsakes me." When they knew this, they cast all the remains of the whale into the sea and commended their affairs to God.

The exploration of the North American continent was thereafter sporadic, with Columbus's non-landing in 1492; Jacques Cartier's exploration of the St. Lawrence on his three voyages for France from 1531 to 1541, and Walter Raleigh's failed attempts to establish an English foothold at Roanoke Island in 1583 and 1585. Samuel de Champlain, the founder of the first French settlements in North America, was returning to France in 1610 when somewhere in the mid-Atlantic he "encountered a whale, which was asleep. The vessel passing over him awakened him betimes, made a great hole in him near the tail, without damaging our vessel, but he threw out an abundance of blood."

Throughout True's book, which contains the above account of Thorfin, we find references to whales encountered by these intrepid explorers, and many more. In a series of luckless expeditions, Henry Hudson wandered northward and westward before he actually explored the North American continent. He made two unsuccessful voyages for the Muscovy Company of London in 1607 and 1608, sailing as far north as Spitsbergen and to the north of Norway before he was forced to turn back. (His reports of whales and walrus in these icy and inhospitable waters inspired the early Dutch and English whale fisheries.) By 1609, John Smith's stories had filtered back to England, and Hudson—now in the employ of the Dutch East India Company—sailed across the Atlantic in search of a passage that Smith had reported. Failing to find the Northeast Passage, Hudson convinced his crew that they ought to alter their plans and seek the Northwest Passage. When he encountered a navigable river, he sailed north for almost 150 miles before he turned back. (Though Hudson first navigated this *groote rivier,* it was Giovanni da Verrazzano, an Italian in the service of François I of France, who first recorded its existence in 1524.) Hudson's second trans-Atlantic voyage took him from Nova Scotia as far south as the Chesapeake Bay, which he mapped. He returned to England in 1609, and the following year he set out again to seek the fabled Northwest Passage. This time, in the fifty-five-ton *Discovery,* he passed north of Newfoundland, through what later became Hudson Strait, and into the immense inland body of water which he believed would lead to the Pacific Ocean. A mutiny aboard the *Discovery* left Hudson, his son, and several crew members cast adrift in what ironically was to become known as Hudson Bay, and he was never heard of again.

Bartholomew Gosnold was born in Suffolk County, England, in 1571 or 1572. He read law at New Inn, but abandoned this sedentary career for a life of adventure. In 1602 he sailed the bark *Concord* to New England, a voyage that took seventeen weeks. He landed on Cuttyhunk Island and reported that he found "many huge bones and ribbes of whales." Gosnold also discovered that Cape Cod, with its bent elbow enclosing a harbor so commodious that "a thousand sail of ships may ride safely," is an ideal venue for whales. They seek its protected waters for breeding, but there is also something about this protruding, sixty-five-mile-long spit of sand and sea grass that attracts whales to its beaches. The history of

Cape Cod strandings is one that certainly predates the arrival of the British colonists, and the presence of whale carcasses on these beaches was very likely responsible for the initiation of a whaling industry by the Indians. (We assume that the first whales were found on the beach, the locals soon realizing that they could supplement this bounty by chasing the whales instead of waiting for them to die.) Long before any Europeans arrived on American soil, the Indians of the New England littoral were acquainted with the gifts of the sea.

In the journal that he kept on his 1605 voyage to America, Captain George Waymouth described the method by which the Indians hunted the whale:

One especial thing is their method of killing the whale, which they call a *powdawe;* and will describe his form, how he bloweth up the water; and that he is twelve fathoms long; that they go in company of their king with a multitude of their boats; and strike him with a bone made in the fashion of a harping iron fastened to a rope, which they make great and strong from the bark of trees, which they veer out after him; then all their boats come about him as he riseth above the water; with their arrows they shoot him to death; when they have killed him and dragged him to the shore, they call all their chief lords together, and sing a song of joy; and those chief lords which they call sagamores, divide the spoil and give to every man a share, which pieces are so distributed, and they hang up about their houses for provisions; and when they boil them they blow off the fat and put to their pease, maize and other pulse which they eat.

To the south, under the leadership of Captain John Smith, the first recognized European settlers in America landed at Jamestown, Virginia, in 1607. It may also have been John Smith who fitted out the first whaling voyage to New England. In 1614, he arrived at Monhegan Island, off the coast of Maine, with two ships from London: "Our plot was there to take Whales," he wrote, "for which we had one Samuel Cramton and divers other experts in the faculty. . . . We found this Whale-fishing a costly conclusion; we saw many and spent much time in chasing them, but could not kill any."

A small group of dissatisfied Protestants were unhappy with the Reformation introduced by James I of England (the heir of Elizabeth I, who had died in 1603), and tried settling in Holland, which they believed would be more accommodating to their conservative views. The Dutch proved to be no more hospitable to this group of zealots than England had been, however, so they chartered the *Mayflower* (and the *Goodspeed,* which had to turn back) for a voyage to America. Navigational errors and winter storms kept the little ship far to the north of her intended Virginia landfall, and on December 21, 1620, she ended up at the tip of Cape Cod, where the town of Provincetown is now located. As the tiny craft rode at anchor, a party was dispatched to search for a suitable site for a settlement. In a small shallop, they hugged the inner coast of Cape Cod until they came upon a good harbor, which they decided to call Plymouth. The day after Christmas, the *Mayflower* sailed across Cape Cod Bay to the new site, and en route the voyagers found the ship surrounded by large numbers of black whales. They decided to stay.

The difficulties of the early days of the Plymouth Colony are well documented, but less publicized is the part that whales played in the settlement of New England. Among the enticements that kept the first settlers on this bleak, snowblown coast in December of 1620 was the presence of whales. In deciding to stay on the western shore of Cape Cod rather than seek a more propitious site, the colonists recognized that they could probably initiate a fishing industry, since "large numbers of whales of the best kind for oil and bone came daily alongside and played about the ship." Listed among the crew of the *Mayflower* were experienced fishermen—perhaps from the Greenland fishery—who regretted the lack of tackle for capturing the whales that they saw in this new land. One of the *Mayflower*'s passengers wrote:

And every day we saw whales playing hard by us; of which in that place if we had instruments and means to take them we might make a very rich return, which to our grief we wanted. Our master and his mate, and others experienced in fishing, professed we might make three or four thousand pounds worth of oil. They preferred it before Greenland whale-fishing, and propose the next winter to fish for whale here.

The kind of whales that Richard Mather saw "spewing up water into the air, like the smoke of a chimney, and making the sea about them white and hoary," cannot be accurately determined, but they were very likely to have been right whales. We can draw this conclusion from many sources, contem-

poraneous and recent. That they did not identify the species is not surprising, since the right whale was not differentiated from its close relative the bowhead (the object of the Greenland fishery, which was just beginning as the Pilgrims were freezing in Massachusetts) until 1866. Therefore, any large black whale with long baleen plates and a smooth, finless back was considered "the mysticetus." Humpbacks also inhabit (or inhabited) inshore Massachusetts waters, and they were also candidates for the title of "first whale taken in the colonies."

The Royal Charter of Massachusetts (1629) contains these words: "Wee have given and granted . . . all fishes—royal fishes, whales, balan, sturgeons, and other fishes, of what kind and nature soever that shall at any time hereafter be taken in or within the saide seas or waters. . . ." With the Mayflower Compact a reality, the New England settlement began to attract future colonists from all over England, and in 1630 a fleet of seventeen ships carried almost a thousand hardy souls from Olde England to New England. By 1640, there were some twenty thousand people in settlements in and around Boston.

It is now thought that the first organized whale fishery in the American colonies was not in Massachusetts at all, but on Long Island. In the year 1640, on the southern shore of that island, in the town of Southampton, the settlers (who had come from Lynn, in Massachusetts) divided the colony into four wards of eleven persons each, to render drift whales that might be cast ashore. The whales were cut up and the profits shared by "every Inhabitant with his child or servant that is above sixteen years of age. . . ."

As anyone who has ever been downwind of a dead whale knows, the stench can be overpowering. In regard to the trying-out of whales on shore, therefore, Southampton passed a law which read in part, "Where the trying of oyle so near the streets and houses, is so extreme noysome to all passers by, especially to those not accustomed to the sent thereof . . . the cort doth order that noe person after this present yeare shall try any oyle in this towne nearer than 25 poles from Main Street, under penalty of paying five pounds fine." By the end of the seventeenth century, there were established whale fisheries in New England, Long Island and New Jersey, and by the first decades of the next century, the industry had come to North Carolina.

What was it about the whales that caused people to transport themselves across oceans, and once there, devote themselves so enthusiastically to their capture and processing? What substances could be obtained from the whales and what could be got from these substances?

Whale oil (also known as "train oil" at that time) was used for lighting and was an important ingredient in the tanning of leather. Unlike modern housekeepers, who cannot get rid of fat quickly enough, their seventeenth-century counterparts painstakingly preserved all fats to use in the manufacture of soap and candles. The earliest lighting devices consisted of burning brands, which were succeeded by oil lamps with wicks, and eventually by candles, slow-burning cylinders of wax or tallow with a wick at the core. Single candles were replaced by candelabra, later enhanced with prismatic glass adornments. When the first whales were butchered, it was obvious that these blubbery monsters contained enough fat to fuel the lamps and pour the candles of Europe. (And later, when spermaceti was found in the nose of the cachalot, the stuff of the finest smokeless candles was discovered.)

Candles are easy to make: you pour them, insert a wick, let them harden, and light them. There is light where before there was darkness. But what about soap? What ancient figured out that he could mix fats and alkalis in such a way as to loosen dirt from his tunic? The Phoenicians are believed to have used soap made from goat's tallow and wood ashes as early as 600 B.C., and the Celts called their version *saipo,* from which our word is derived. In medieval Europe, soap-making began in Marseilles, moved to Genoa and Venice, and seems to have crossed the English Channel around the twelfth century. The earliest soaps were made of decomposing animal fats boiled with a strong alkali, such as wood or plant ashes. The mixture was then reboiled and more ashes were added until the water evaporated. A slow splitting of the neutral fats causes the fatty acids to react with the alkali carbonates of the plant ash, a process known as "saponification."

In order for soap to work, it has to be dissolved in water, and the material to be washed has to be wetted to loosen the soil molecules from it. As the dissolved soap penetrates the material, it increases the wetting ability of the water by reducing its surface tension; the molecules of the water have a stronger affinity for the molecules of the material to be washed than they do for each other. The soil in the fiber is then dispersed into the wash water, usually accompanied by increased temperatures and some sort of mechanical agitation. The soap suspends the soil in a protective colloid, which prevents it from readhering to the fabric, and in this colloidal solution, it is washed away in the rinse water. In order to perform as detergents (surface-active agents), soaps must have a certain chemical structure: their molecules must contain a hydrophobic element (contained in the animal fats) which attaches itself to the soil making it water-insoluble, and a hydrophilic (water-soluble) element, derived from the alkaline plant ashes, which attaches itself to the water. Soaps made from whale oil cleaned well enough—for the eighteenth century, that is—but they smelled bad.

Whale-oil soap dominated the washtubs of Britain until the beginning of the nineteenth century, when whalers of the Greenland Fishery repeatedly brought back rancid oil, which could only be used to produce foul-smelling soap. The soap was rejected, and it appeared that the whales were going to get a reprieve. Just in time to save the industry, whale oil's potential as an inexpensive street-lighting oil was recognized, however, and the demand for whale products continued.

While the British were arguing over the merits of whale-oil soaps and the American colonists continued to take whales at sea, most whale-harvesting consisted of the equitable division of the dead whales that continued to wash ashore along the Massachusetts coast. (Some of the more resolute whalers ventured as far afield as the Davis Strait in pursuit of the vanishing right whales.) The records are vague, but it is probable that many of these "drift fish" had been harpooned by whalers or fishermen who simply did not have the equipment to haul them to shore. If a carcass came ashore on private property, it belonged to the landowner, but he still had to give one-third to the Crown, in the person of the governor. (It is all too easy to forget that despite the conditions of their departure from England, the Puritans were still loyal subjects of the King, and their descendants would not rid themselves of that yoke until 1776, another hundred years in the future.)

We are assuming that the whales first hunted by

the Puritans were right whales; the limited descriptive material left to us seems to corroborate this, and besides, right whales are known to have occupied Cape Cod Bay. And so, as with early whalers everywhere (except Japan), our illustrious forebears decimated the population of female right whales, making a viable population a virtual impossibility. One study indicates that the high point of the Long Island whale fishery was reached in the year 1707, when III right whales were taken. By 1727, the Boston *News-Letter* could write, "We hear from the towns on the Cape

that the Whale Fishery among them has failed much this Winter, as it has done for several Winters past, but having found a way of going out to Sea Upon that Business, and having made such a Success in it, they are now fitting out such Vessels to sail with all Expedition upon that dangerous Design this Spring, more (its tho't) than have ever been sent out among them." The "dangerous Design" that the Yankees found was the hunting of the sperm whale, and it would take them around the world to places most of them had never heard of.

Bay Whaling in Australia

IN *MOBY-DICK,* Melville wrote:

The great America on the other side of the sphere, Australia, was given to the established world by the whalemen. After its first blunder-born discovery by a Dutchman, all other ships shunned these shores as pestiferously barbarous, but the whale ship touched there. The whale ship is the true mother of that mighty colony. Moreover, in the infancy of the first Australian settlement, the emigrants were several times saved from starvation by the benevolent biscuit of the whale ship luckily dropping anchor in their waters. . . .

There is probably no country on earth whose early history is so intimately involved with whaling. In America, development was certainly affected by whales or whaling—Cape Cod Bay was settled by Pilgrims who decided upon it because of the profusion of whales there—but in Australia, the whaling industry was directly responsible for the first settlements in some areas, and often provided the first European view of the coastal areas of what was then known as New Holland.

Although the Dutch navigator Willem Jansz is generally regarded as the first European to explore these antipodean shores, it was Abel Tasman who brought the news back to Holland. He sailed around

the island that he named Van Diemen's Land in 1642, but it was named for him two centuries later. Jansz landed on the northern coast in 1606, but it was England's greatest explorer and navigator, James Cook, who made the first landing on the east coast in 1770. He made his landfall at Botany Bay (which he wanted to call "Stingray Bay"), and when he came ashore, he allowed Midshipman Isaac Smith to become the first Englishman to set foot on Australia's sandy soil.

Botany Bay is not a particularly good harbor; it was barren and dry then—just as it is now—but it suited Cook's purposes, which were to provide an anchorage after the thousand-mile crossing of the Tasman Sea, and to allow him to ascertain that this was indeed the great southern continent for which he had been searching. The Admiralty had given him secret orders to sail the *Endeavour* as far south as latitude 40° to search for *Terra Australis Incognita.* If he were to find it (and claim it for England), read these orders, it would "redound greatly to the honour of this nation as a maritime power, as well as to the dignity of the Crown of Great Britain, and the advancement and of the trade and the navigation thereof." (The *Endeavour* first encountered the continent at Point Hicks, which was named for Lieutenant Zachary Hicks, who first saw it on April 19, 1770.) The first navigable harbor he found was Botany Bay, as he missed Twofold Bay, which would have made a much better anchorage. (Some eighteen years later, it would have made a better place for the first convicts transported to Australia, since it was much more conducive to settlement, with running water and good soil.)

Having sailed west from New Zealand, Cook had no idea what lay overland; nevertheless, he claimed the entire continent for King George III. He tried to engage the natives in some sort of colloquy, failed, took on fresh water, and continued his journey. He sailed north (naming but not exploring Port Jackson, which would eventually become Sydney Harbour), mapped the previously unexplored east coast of Australia from Point Hicks to Cape York, and threaded through the tortuous barrier reef for almost a thousand miles until he ran onto a coral head which punched a great hole in his flagship's bottom. As the tide began to fall, the gallant *Endeavour* was perched on the coral, with water rushing into her breached hull. To lighten her in hopes of floating her off, as much heavy equipment as could be sacrificed was jettisoned, but still the water poured in. The decision was made to "fother" the ship, whereby a sail filled with oakum and pitch was dragged under the flat-bottomed converted collier, and the pressure of the water on the sail closed the hole. Thus fothered, the *Endeavour* limped into a nearby river mouth (which Cook promptly named the Endeavour River), where she was careened and repaired. After two months of work and exploration—which led to one of the earliest accurate descriptions of a "kanguru"—Cook again set sail for the north, passed through the Torres Strait, which separates Australia from New Guinea, and headed for England.

IN THE eighteenth century, the British penal system was totally different from anything that the modern mind can envision. There were no prisons as we know them—Newgate was a foul place of incarceration, and Tyburn was the site of public hangings—and convicts (whose crimes were often no more serious than the theft of a few pieces of linen or the insulting of a nobleman) were either sentenced to be hung or "transported" to the colonies. This was done both as a means of ridding the country of them and

as a deterrent to others who might be tempted to commit such heinous crimes. There were true criminals among the convicts, of course; not everyone was sentenced for stealing a ha'penny's worth of cheese.

When the American Revolution ended in 1783, the practice of transporting convicts to Maryland and Georgia ended as well, and Britain had to seek elsewhere for a place to put her societal rejects. Thousands of them were housed on "hulks," rotting warships that were permanently anchored in the Thames and served as a repository for the convicted criminals of Georgian England. The conditions aboard these hulks were an abomination. They were disease-ridden, filthy, crowded and, as one might expect, given their location in an English river, so dank that nothing and no one was ever dry. Punishment in those days was *intended* to be as uncomfortable and degrading as possible, and was usually accompanied by heavy shackles, rotting food and merciless flogging. It was not the reformers, of which there were precious few, who wanted the prisoners moved out of their line of sight, but those who realized that there was no more room on the river for these stinking hellships. The government was searching for somewhere else to send its detritus, and various places in Africa were suggested. Nothing was farther from England than her new, unexamined colony on the other side of the world, however, so after the usual bureaucratic boondoggling, New Holland was chosen as the location of the world's first colony of thieves. There were no convicted murderers or rapists among the first shipment (they were usually hung), but among the felons aboard the fleet were a large preponderance of minor thieves, burglars (convicted of "privy theft"), highwaymen, cattle- or sheep-stealers, receivers of stolen goods, swindlers and forgers.

Sir Joseph Banks, who had been Cook's botanist, and whose recollections were probably diffused by time and certainly by distance, suggested the harbor at Botany Bay as a site for a penal settlement, and on May 13, 1787, the "First Fleet" sailed. Under the command of Captain Arthur Phillip, the trip—which was remarkably uneventful, given the nature of the cargo—took eight months, including layovers in Rio de Janeiro and Cape Town. The fleet consisted of eleven ships, which showed on their manifests some

1,500 souls, of whom 736 were convicts. The remainder were companies of soldiers and marines to guard the prisoners, their officers, and the various administrative personnel deemed necessary to start up a penal colony.

Upon landing at their intended location, Phillip realized that Botany Bay, with its sparse vegetation, sandy soil and unprotected harbor, was unsuitable for the permanent settlement his superiors had directed him to establish. Within a week, he moved the whole business, locks, stocks and barrels, twelve miles north to Port Jackson, the harbor that Cook had seen but not investigated. This was, of course, Sydney Harbour, one of the finest natural harbors in the world, and forsaking the already forsaken Botany Bay, Captain Phillip (who had become Governor Phillip upon landing) founded the first permanent settlement on the Australian continent. The date was January 26, 1788.

ALTHOUGH sperm whales figure heavily in the early years of Australian whaling (by 1804 five ships had left New South Wales for England with cargoes of sperm oil), another kind of whale was to dominate Australian whaling for the next fifty years. It was the intention of the British administrators there to establish colonies for transported felons, but a sidebar to the colonization of Australia was the whales. Nobody had to farm or cultivate them; they were just there, swimming offshore as placidly as they had done for

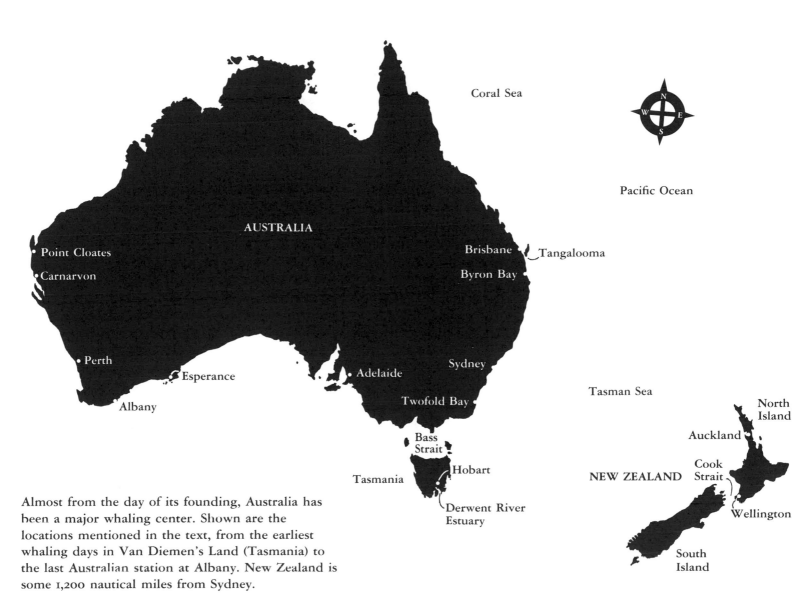

Almost from the day of its founding, Australia has been a major whaling center. Shown are the locations mentioned in the text, from the earliest whaling days in Van Diemen's Land (Tasmania) to the last Australian station at Albany. New Zealand is some 1,200 nautical miles from Sydney.

millennia, ripe and plump for the plucking. Whaling became Australia's first industry. Long before anyone managed to wrest a crop from her stubborn coastal soil, shear one of the millions of sheep that would eventually dominate her balance of trade, or dig a single ounce of gold from her unexpectedly auriferous outback, the whalers were at work in the River Derwent in Tasmania.

The right whales (known to the settlers simply as "black whales") were so thick in the Derwent estuary—fifty or sixty might be seen at one time—that it was considered hazardous for small boats. One observer noted that "it was dangerous to go on the river, unless you kept near the shore." As is their habit, right whales entered enclosed Australian bays and harbors to breed and give birth to their calves. The estuary of the River Derwent is a southward-facing, enclosed complex of islands, peninsulas, channels and bays, perfect for the whales' purposes. It was also perfect for the whalers'.

This was not the hazardous business of pelagic whaling, where a brave lad high in the crosstrees shouts "she blows!" and the boats are lowered for a dangerous pursuit of an uncooperative whale. In Tasmania, the whales were spotted from the shore, and the whaling was like shooting very large fish in a very large barrel. The methods were essentially the same the world over. In a double-ended rowing boat, with five, seven, or sometimes even nine oarsmen pulling, the hunters would approach their hapless quarry. Then the headsman would harpoon the whale, which did not kill the animal but attached the whaleboat to it. When the animal had tired, they would row up on it again, this time with the killing lance, and dispatch it. Between the harpoon and the lance, one can imagine many disputes, and even lost whales. The dead whales—which might weigh as much as 60 tons—then had to be towed to a ramp or slipway so they could be dragged up on shore to the tryworks for the cutting and boiling processes. A single whale might yield 6 tuns* of oil and 300 pounds of bone. Coopers assembled their barrels on shore, and the full casks were then stored in rough-built sheds, awaiting shipment to Hobart Town,

*A tun was an eighteenth-century measurement for liquid that was the equivalent of 252 gallons. Because the volume of oil varies with its temperature, this measurement was abandoned in the twentieth century in favor of the standard *ton,* which was a measure of weight rather than volume.

thence to England. In 1830, the ship *Deveron* sailed for London with 200 tons of oil and 20 tons of bone, a cargo that was worth some £5,000.

"Bay whaling," as it came to be known, required no expensive ships or long ocean voyages; all that was needed was a shore station with a lookout, a crew of stalwart oarsmen, a harpooner, and a means of trying-out the whale on shore. Often the lookouts were abandoned, and the whaling crews simply rowed out into the bays and waited for the whales to arrive. There were so many whalers on the Derwent—and no restrictions or rules whatsoever—that fights broke out regularly between rival crews over who had sighted or harpooned a whale first. On one occasion, no fewer than twenty-one boats took after the same whale. (By 1838, a series of laws had been passed governing the taking of whales; without them, an already chaotic situation would have escalated into bloody warfare.)

Sometime around 1806, a Sydney-born adventurer named James Kelly (who may have been born James Devereaux) circumnavigated Van Diemen's Land (Tasmania) in forty-nine days with four aborigine rowers, and discovered two harbors that would later become the notorious penal colonies of Port Davey and Macquarie Harbour. In 1825, he formed the Derwent Whaling Club, the first organization dedicated to communal whaling, as opposed to the cut-throat competition of the earlier whalers. A prize of eight dollars [*sic*] was given to the first person to sight a whale in the river, and the profits of the club were divided among the five members, "charitable purposes," and the headsman who actually struck the whale.

In 1818, Captain Thomas Raine, of Sydney, established the first whaling station at Twofold Bay, New South Wales, a location that was to play an important part in the discordant history of Australian whaling. Although New South Wales and Tasmania were the first colonized areas and therefore the first places where the Australians went bay whaling, there were whales in other regions as well. The Western Australians, the Victorians, and later, the South Australians went after "their" right whales. Bay whaling was conducted wherever the whales could be found, and whaling enterprises sprang up at Double Corner and Portland Bay in Victoria, and also at Encounter Bay and Port Lincoln, South Australia, before either

The whaling station at Wineglass Bay, on the eastern shore of what was then known as Van Diemen's Land. A whaleship can be seen in the background, and the skull in the foreground is that of a right whale.

of these colonies was officially settled. South Australia was the first "free state" in Australia; that is, it was the first location settled not by convicts but by colonists who came there voluntarily rather than in chains.*

Virtually all inhabited areas in coastal Australia soon witnessed bay whalers chasing the black whales. (Then, as now, there was no settlement along the thousand-mile shore of the Great Australian Bight. This sweeping curve, rudely chopped out of the southern coast of the continent, has no harbors, bays or inlets, and therefore no place for even the most tenacious of Australian settlers to dig in.) The whales, on their annual migrations from the Antarctic, had to swim past the western or eastern coasts of the continent, and at Albany, Perth, Van Diemen's Land,

Encounter Bay, and Sydney Harbour, the whalers waited for their annual bonanza to swim into range. The peak years of bay whaling were 1836 to 1838.

Of course this abundance of cetaceans did not go unnoticed by the American, British or French deep-sea whalers in Australian waters, who had discovered the sperm whale grounds of New Zealand and often came to Hobart Town or Sydney for reprovisioning or refitting. (One day in 1847, there were no less than thirty-seven whaleships in Hobart harbor.) There they would certainly have heard tales of the rich whale harvest, so between seasons they would stand offshore, waiting for the right whales. The bay whalers could not compete with fully stocked ships at sea, and although they occasionally tried to spend two or three days in their cramped longboats in hopes of intercepting the whales before the blue-water whalers got them, they usually returned empty-handed to their stations after a couple of days.

Because right whales are slow-moving and gener-

*In the 1836 report to potential investors in South Australia, the following language was incorporated: "Your Directors are promoting the establishment of off-shore stations for catching the black whales, amidst the bays of the colony, and they hope to be ready for the next season to obtain profitable return."

ally inoffensive (many of the contemporaneous descriptions referred to them as "sleepy"), bay whaling was a relatively easy line of work to get into. The bay stations were rough and primitive—as was almost everything in Van Diemen's Land—but they provided a handsome profit for those entrepreneurs who could stick it out. It didn't take much to be an oarsman, after all, and everyone from farmboys to aborigines could participate. (The only inhabitants of the colony who did not go a-whaling were the convicts. They were obviously untrustworthy; if you put them near a boat, they were likely to try to escape in it.) There was always the danger of a harpooned right whale thrashing in its death-throes and upsetting a boat, but the instances of this happening seem to be rare. While a full-rigged whaleship could cost more than £4,000 to outfit in England (not including the cost of the ship itself), the cost of equipping a whaling station on the Derwent might be £300. And even though sperm oil was more valuable than ordinary whale oil, the time spent traveling back and forth to England often outweighed the profits. Most of the oil went to England, of course; there was hardly any manufacturing in the early years of the new colony. It was considerably more efficient and economical to take the whales in Australia, try-out the oil, and then cask it for its trans-Pacific journey. In *The Tyranny of Distance,* historian Geoffrey Blainey wrote, "For once the long distance from the old world had profited Australia. The clear advantage Australian whaling had over foreign competitors was closeness to the fishing grounds. That proximity was, for more than half a century, one of the nation's few assets."

As long as the whales lasted—and who could imagine that they would not last forever?—the budding capitalists could reap their oily harvest. The Tasmanian industry reached its peak in 1837 when there were thirty-five whaling stations in its bays, and because of the fierce competition, the local government passed the Tasmanian Whaling Act of 1838. From Van Diemen's Land, the enterprising bay whalers, particularly from Launceston, took their industry farther afield, to the Australian mainland. From 1832 to 1841, New South Wales exported £1.7 million worth of whale products. But after that half-century of unbridled progress, things began to go badly for the colony's first industry. Substances that

Ben Boyd (1797–1851) founded a vast empire in New South Wales. When his enterprise failed, he headed off to California to prospect for gold, and was murdered by cannibals on the return voyage.

had heretofore been buried deep in the earth or hidden where no one thought to look for them began to appear. The substances with the most deleterious effects on the whaling industry were two kinds of gold: the yellow kind, which was to disrupt commerce and industry all around the world when it was discovered in California in 1848 and in Australia in 1851, and the black variety, which first gushed out of the earth in Pennsylvania in 1859. As an example of how rapidly a prosperous situation can turn to ashes, let us look at the short, mercurial career of Ben Boyd.

On July 18, 1842, Benjamin Boyd arrived in Sydney. In his *Whaleman Adventurers,* W. J. Dakin describes him thus:

He was a man of about forty-five years of age, full of energy, and with a wide outlook. If he were living to-day, he would be amalgamating match companies! . . . Evidently Australia attracted him, and he was determined to be a "big noise" there. He commenced by floating two concerns in London, the Royal Australian Bank and the Australian Wool Company. Possibly it was the latter which led him actually to descend upon Australia in person. He arrived in Sydney in some style, for he came in his own yacht—the *Wanderer*—with a few friends, who were obviously as keen for adventure as he was.

Amongst his "few friends" were his brother James and a young artist and naval architect named Oswald Brierly. It was said that Boyd had over a million pounds at his disposal, most of it raised from small Scottish investors. Within two years, he had become one of the largest landowners in New South Wales, with aggregate holdings of almost two million acres. For his whaling enterprises, he selected Twofold Bay. Some 240 miles south of Sydney, this embayment had already been chosen as a whaling port by Thomas Raine in 1828, eliciting this comment from the *Sydney Gazette:* "Such an adventure as this we should presume will lead more to open the eyes of the public to the resources of Australia than all the newspaper remarks which might be put forward for a century to come." In 1832 Peter Imlay and his two brothers Alexander and George (all three of whom were surgeons) started a whaling station at Twofold Bay, which was percolating along quite successfully when the flamboyant Mr. Boyd arrived.

Undeterred by the presence of the Imlay brothers' operation, Boyd set up shop across the bay and proceeded to build not only a whaling station, but an entire town, which he modestly named "Boyd Town." He brought carpenters and stonemasons, bricklayers and plasterers, to work on his egregiously self-aggrandizing project. Along with the church, stores, houses, an "Elizabethan-style" hotel, and the various edifices required for a whaling station, Boyd also commissioned a seventy-six-foot-high lighthouse, which dominated the landscape for miles. In February 1844, the *Sydney Record* gave this glowing encomium to the tycoon of Twofold Bay: "Perhaps there is no individual who has done so much and in

Aboard the luxury yacht *Wanderer,* Ben Boyd made a grand entrance into Sydney Harbour on July 18, 1842. He built a whaling station and an entire town at Twofold Bay, but both ventures collapsed.

so short a time as Mr. Benjamin Boyd. . . . [F]or if there is one gentleman more than another who deserves to be amply remunerated for his enterprising speculations, that gentleman is Mr. Boyd. If we had a few more such men in the colony it would soon go ahead."

Oswald Brierly, trained in England as a naval architect, was put in charge of operations of Boyd's whaling station. For reasons that Dakin finds "impossible to explain," Brierly remained at the whaling station for five years. To attract business to the remote outpost, Boyd (or Brierly) ran this ad in the *Hobart Press* every month during 1846:

TO WHALERS

Boyd Town, Twofold Bay, N.S.W.

Ships can refresh or refit at this harbour, free of all port charges, pilotage, etc., and can obtain wood, water, fresh and salt provisions, vegetables, ship chandlery, stores and slops of every kind and description and if required the services of experienced shipwrights and boatbuilders upon the most reasonable terms.

N.B. Oil or bone taken in exchange.

Only five years after this *Aurora australis* scintillated over the desolate scrub of Twofold Bay, his brilliance began to diminish. (The lighthouse, which was to be the blazing symbol of Boyd's enterprise, was never lit.) A combination of factors contributed to the downfall of Ben Boyd, only some of which he could control. He had managed to alienate almost everyone with whom he came into contact, even his staunchest supporter, Oswald Brierly. In his notebook for 1847, Brierly wrote, "The people are disagreeable from the rounds of misunderstandings he has had with everybody." He was seriously overextended with his enormous land-holdings, his baywhaling operations, his ships that were partaking of the sperm whale fishery offshore (at one time he owned no fewer than nine whaleships), his town, and his steamers that transported goods and people between Sydney and Hobart Town. The *Sea Horse,* one of these steamers, hit a rock, and Boyd's insurance claim for £25,000 was refused by the underwriters. Disasters at sea are beyond the control of even the most determined of capitalists, as are fluctuations in the whale-oil and wool markets. From a high in 1840 of over £335,000 in whale exports, sales had fallen

to £16,000 in 1853. In the late 1840s, New South Wales was in the grip of its first depression, and the whaling stations, which had been the major reason for the success of the settlements, were desperately searching for support, and more important, desperately searching for whales.

The Imlays' enterprise had also failed at Twofold Bay, probably for the same reasons: greed, poor management, and a sudden shortage of right whales. Naturally, the Australian bay whalers had assumed that the supply of whales was endless; a bottomless marine oil well that would keep on gushing as long as they could keep tapping it. They slaughtered the mothers and calves with reckless abandon, never realizing that a population that was not allowed to reproduce itself would soon decrease to the point where it was no longer viable. This happened with dramatic suddenness to the right whales of the Southern Hemisphere, as approximately 2,500 of them were killed every year.*

By 1848, Boyd's shareholders in England—even though it took months for news of their investments to reach them—were demanding his replacement. He was succeeded by his cousin, William Sprott Boyd, but Sprott Boyd could not reverse the downward spiral. The shareholders lost all their money, and an additional £80,000 besides. Boyd's empire disintegrated in 1848, and the next year he left Australia aboard his yacht *Wanderer,* headed for the goldfields of California. He was evidently unsuccessful there, for he returned to the South Pacific in 1851. On Guadalcanal in the Solomons, he went ashore among the natives—reputed to be cannibals—and was never seen again. Oswald Brierly returned to England, and after serving in the navy during the Crimean War, he became Sir Oswald Brierly, "Marine Painter to Her Majesty the Queen." He died in 1894.

If Boyd had been able to wait a couple of years,

---

*In a paper published in 1928, Sir Sidney Harmer quotes a study which gives a total of 193,522 southern right whales killed in the period from 1804 to 1817, including catch figures from Australia, New Zealand, Tasmania and South Africa. Although many authors have accepted this figure, it is obviously in error. In Harmer's paper, it is not clear where he got the figure 193,522, because it appears unattributed. As Peter Best points out in his 1970 study of the right whales of South Africa, the *same number* is given by Starbuck (1878), as an estimate of the total number of right whales killed in the Southern Hemisphere and the North Pacific from 1804 to 1877, based on the amount of whale oil landed at U.S. ports during that period. Based on the tables in Starbuck, the average number of right whales killed per year was 2,615.

Right Whaling in the Pacific, a painting by Oswald Brierly, who served as the manager of Ben Boyd's whaling enterprises at Twofold Bay from 1845 to 1850. Brierly returned to England to become court marine painter to Queen Victoria.

he might have saved himself a voyage to California, and if he had done that, he might not have been eaten at Guadalcanal. In 1851, the year of Boyd's demise, Edward Hargraves, himself just back from California, went into the bush west of Sydney and found gold. A gold rush very much like California's ensued, only given the much smaller population of Australia, a much larger proportion of the total populace participated. The discovery of gold also greatly increased the number of free Englishmen who wanted to go to Australia; and the concept of transporting convicts was affected by the gold fever, since many Englishmen were vehemently opposed to their government's sending the dregs of society to Golconda-across-the-sea, especially when they couldn't get there themselves. (In *The Fatal Shore,* his study of the founding of Australia, Robert Hughes wrote, ''With a quarter of Britain, from navvies to viscounts, clamoring for tickets to the southern goldfields, who was to think that a trip to El Dorado at government expense constituted a fearful punishment—especially if, as rumor had it, convicts got a conditional pardon as soon as they stepped ashore at Hobart?'')

The effects of the discovery of gold were far-reaching and momentous. It brought settlers to the colony in droves (close to 100,000 new arrivals landed in Victoria and New South Wales in 1852), and immediately upon landing, they left their ships—as did the crews and sometimes even the captains—to seek their fortunes in the desert. And indeed many of them succeeded. The goldfields of Bendigo and Ballarat were phenomenally productive: weekly production was in the neighborhood of a half-ton a week, and in 1852 the *Dido* arrived in London with 280,000 ounces of gold dust aboard—eight and a half tons.

Since the gold rush coincided with the decline of the whale populations, those who would pull oars or build casks took off *en masse* for the goldfields, and the whaling industry, already in a serious decline, almost ground to a complete standstill. In 1853, exports of whale oil from New South Wales to London totaled £16,000, while in that same year, almost £2 million worth of gold was shipped. Interestingly, a similar situation had prevailed only a couple of years earlier in California, where the 1848 discovery of gold at Sutter's Mill had caused many New England whalemen to desert when their ships reached San

Bay whaling in Twofold Bay, New South Wales. The whales are rights, identifiable by their double spouts, and on the cliffs is Ben Boyd's lighthouse.

Ben Boyd's lighthouse at Twofold Bay, New South Wales, which was never lit. It now stands as part of the national park that celebrates his curious accomplishments.

Francisco, and there too, the whale fishery suffered. (In the United States, in addition to the rush to get to the goldfields, lines were being drawn for a war that would effectively bring an end to the sperm whale fishery, and cripple the country's economy for decades.)

Although Ben Boyd and the Imlays had abandoned Twofold Bay, its immortality was assured by one of the most unusual episodes in all whaling history. Alexander Davidson had come to Australia to work for Boyd as a carpenter, and after Boyd Town had become a ghost town, the Davidson family remained. (Boyd Town no longer appears on the map of Australia, but there is a Ben Boyd National Park, marked by the famous lighthouse.) They lived at the town of Eden on the Kiah River, the site of Imlays' station, and began their own whaling operations in 1866.

Up to this point, humpback whales had not figured noticeably in the story of Australian whaling, but they made a remarkable appearance at Twofold Bay in the latter decades of the nineteenth century. The Davidsons, père et fils, maintained the whaling station at Eden, and they had planned to catch and process whales for the limited market that then existed for oil and bone meal. Whaling methods of the 1870s were not particularly different from those employed forty years earlier; the whalers waited for a shore sighting (in this case, from Ben Boyd's lighthouse), rowed out to harpoon the whale, and if they were successful, towed the carcass back to shore to be tried out. In *Killers of Eden,* a 1961 history of the Davidsons' exploits, Tom Mead describes the fishery in meticulous detail. Mead gives hardly any dates, however, so it is virtually impossible to determine when a particular event occurred. The first whale he mentions is "a black whale," but after that, most of the whales caught appear to have been humpbacks. This is hardly noteworthy, but their method of whaling lifts the Davidsons' story so far out of the ordinary as to render it unique in the annals of whaling, and probably in the entire history of the interactions of men and wild animals—assuming that it is true. According to local legend, the whalers of Eden were assisted by a group of killer whales.

From the beginning of the Davidsons' strange saga, killer whales were a part of it. The whalers would climb to the top of the lighthouse, not looking for the blows of right whales or humpbacks, but rather for the dorsal fins of the school of killer whales that would herd the large whales toward the waiting whalers.

Killer whales are identifiable at the surface by the different configurations of their dorsal fins, and before long, the whalers had come to recognize "Old Tom" (apparently the leader), "Humpy," "Hocky," "Stranger," "Cooper," and some twenty-five other individuals. The killers operated in a distinct pattern, with a part of the school acting as "sentries" at the entrance to the bay, another group in the middle distance, and a third element closer inshore. If the killers did not actually herd the humpies toward the whalers, they certainly kept them from going anywhere else. They also "signaled" the whalers by leaping and splashing noisily when there were humpbacks around, often waking up the whalers in the middle of the night with the crashes of their massive bodies on the surface of the water. (A full-grown bull killer whale can weigh 10 tons.) Only when the whales were close enough to shore would the Davidsons launch their boats. Up to that moment, the killers had not attacked the humpbacks in any way, but they wouldn't have had to. During their attacks, killer whales emit sounds that can best be described as "screams," and these sounds alone would be terrifying enough to the defenseless humpbacks. Killers are the most aggressive of all the toothed whales; they are at the top of the pyramid of the ocean's predators. Their common name comes from their habit of preying on almost anything that swims: seals, dolphins, sharks, fish, penguins and whales. They do not, however, have a taste for humans.

A humpie floats belly-up in the shallow water of the Kiah River station of the Davidson family at Twofold Bay, Australia.

Members of the renowned Davidson family of
Twofold Bay pose with a harpoon gun and bundles
of baleen collected from right whales.

The whalers of Eden would row out to where the
killers had herded their victim, and dispatch it with
lances. As always, this was a difficult process, since
a humpback can weigh as much as 40 tons, and the
killing of an animal of that size is almost always
bloody and dangerous. The story does not end with
the death of the whale, however, since a tithe had to
be paid to the killers who helped in its capture. Before the whale was towed to the station, the whalers
allowed the killers to feed on the tongue and lips. In
Whaleman Adventurers, W. J. Dakin described the
process:

First they press the jaws of the dead whale up and down
until they manage to get the mouth open. Having succeeded, they dive in for that delicacy, the tongue, each
obtaining its mouthful. What a tasty bit and what joy
afterwards! Tis now that the killers appear most human.
Full of fun like a lot of boys, they dive and leap under
the boat and out of the water again and again for half an
hour or more. Meanwhile, the whalemen attach an anchor
to a harpoon line, drop it and go home.

Dakin was skeptical of this unusual symbiosis, and
he admits that he was too late to witness it. But in
his "perusal" of Sir Oswald Brierly's diaries, written
at Twofold Bay some three decades before the Davidsons' enterprise commenced, Dakin finds references to killers' assisting the whalers. "This is a
remarkable confirmation," he writes, "because it is
almost certain that none of the Eden whalemen, during the last eighty years, could have known anything
about the contents of Brierly's diaries, which he had
taken to England with him in 1848."*

"Old Tom" died in 1930. After examining the records and the skeleton, which was mounted and displayed in the museum in Eden, Dakin (a professor
of zoology at the University of Sydney) concluded
that this was the same killer whale that led the hunt
for the Davidsons from 1866 onward. He "unhesi-
tatingly accept[s] the evidence of Old Tom's age being eighty years or more." (Subsequent examination
of the skeleton (Baker 1983) has shown that "this
particular whale, whether 'Old Tom' or not, was only
about 35 years old at his death in 1930.")

ABOUT a thousand miles east of Sydney is tiny Norfolk Island. It had been discovered by Cook on his
second voyage, and its pines, now eponymously famous, were used to make a mast for the *Resolution.*
In 1788, only a week after the first fleet landed at
Port Jackson, Norfolk Island was established as the
second penal colony in England's grand plan to rid
her scepter'd isles of undesirables. Arthur Phillip appointed Philip Gidley King as Superintendent and
Commandant of Norfolk Island, which became the
most notorious of all the penal colonies. Transportation to Norfolk Island was considered "punishment short of death."

There are records of early whalers stopping off at
Norfolk for wood and water, and some of the islanders joined the crews of Yankee whalers. By the
middle of the nineteenth century, the Norfolk Islanders (some of whom had come from Pitcairn Island,
and were the descendants of the *Bounty* mutineers)

*Until I had the opportunity to visit Twofold Bay in 1988, I
was more than willing to accept the story as gospel; in fact, I
repeated it in *Dolphins and Porpoises* in 1982. However, when I talked
to other Davidson historians, I began to wonder whether the story
of the killer whales was true. There is no way to prove it one way
or the other, but the very uniqueness of the event makes it suspect.
If killer whales were given to this sort of behavior, why would they
demonstrate it at Twofold Bay and nowhere else?

As a cure for rheumatism, whalemen sometimes sat inside a decomposing whale to allow the oil to seep into their bodies. Twofold Bay, Australia.

The remains of the Davidson family's whaling station at Twofold Bay. Sixty years after the last whale was killed, vertebrae still litter the yard.

had begun their own whaling industry. As described by Merval Hoare, the island's historian, they have

intermittently, carried on the perilous, laborious, and somewhat unprofitable business of whaling. Right into the mid-twentieth century the old methods of hand-harpooning were used. An ever present danger was the overturning of boats. The chase and harpooning of vic-

tims was often followed by all-day and all-night towings out to sea, and the long pull back to shore was hard work. In view of the frequent accidents, loss of boats, and occasional fatalities that accompanied whaling it is not surprising to learn that sometimes the industry lapsed for several years.

The species of whale that towed the islanders around was not specified, but in the light of future events (a

Whaleships at New Wharf, Hobart, in the 1860s.

century later a humpback fishery would be established on Norfolk Island), we can assume that the whales were humpies.

With the decline of bay whaling in Australia, the whalers who had not completely foundered turned to offshore sperm whaling. Hobart became famous for its whalers, much as New Bedford in Massachusetts had been the heart of the Yankee whale fishery. In the heyday of the Australian whaling industry, Hobart was second only to Sydney as a center of commerce and population. No gold was to be found in Tasmania, however, and the island that was once the epicenter of Australian bay whaling never regained a position of prominence again.

Bay Whaling in New Zealand

THE MAORI knew of the whales, of course; then as now, whales showed an affinity for this place. The islands we know as New Zealand are among the curiously special locations where whales and dolphins frequently beach themselves for unexplained reasons. Although they used whalebone in their crafts and weapons, there is no evidence that the Maori warriors and seafarers ever went whaling themselves. The Maori familiarity with whale meat and whale products was probably a result of the whales that had cast themselves ashore. In some cases, vast amounts of meat and oil appeared as if from the gods, ready to be consumed.

In 1642 Abel Tasman sailed from Amsterdam around southern Africa, searching for Terra Australis. After rounding the Cape of Good Hope, he sailed across the entire Indian Ocean before reaching the first land he had encountered in the South Sea since Mauritius, some five thousand miles in his rear. He claimed this island for the Dutch, and named it for the Governor General of Batavia. From the island he discovered and named Van Diemen's Land, he sailed the *Heemskreck* and the *Zeehaen* across the thousand-mile stretch of open water—which later became known as the Tasman Sea—and found the "large, high-lying land" that he named *Staten Landt.* (It was later named Nieuw Zeeland when it was found to be an island rather than the southern continent that Tasman thought he had discovered.)

The first recorded contact between Europeans and Maoris ended in disaster. At the place that Tasman named "Murderer's Bay" (now Golden Bay) in Cook Strait, four Dutchmen in a rowboat were killed by the aggressive natives. Tasman never set foot on New Zealand's rocky shore. Even though he had hoped to head east in search of a new route to Chile, he could not navigate the treacherous waters of the strait that separates the two islands of New Zealand (or more likely, did not realize it *was* a through passage), and headed north, past Tonga, Java and New Guinea, before returning to Batavia. It was not for another 127 years that the true nature of these islands would be known to Europeans.

Arriving from the east on his first voyage in 1769 (he had come from Tahiti, but then sailed south searching for the southern continent), Captain Cook circumnavigated and mapped both islands with the meticulous precision that was his watchword, and demonstrated that they were definitely not part of any larger landmass. Although he claimed the islands for England, the Crown did not seem particularly interested in these cannibal isles, and another seventy-one years were to pass before New Zealand could properly be said to belong to anyone but the indigenous Maoris. Cook spent six months circumnavigating and provisioning in New Zealand, noting the presence of the straight-boled "spruce pine" (the kauri pine which was important for the cutting of masts and spars); the existence of flax, which was

designated for the manufacture of ropes and cloth; and whales, which he saw off the Otago coast of South Island. At the time of Cook's voyages, the British were expanding their presence in the Arctic—particularly the Davis Strait—and as was always the case with a whaling enterprise, it never occurred to anyone that the supply of whales was not infinite. Therefore, the presence of whales in New Zealand waters was of no great significance to Cook, and he noted it only in passing.

Like their counterparts in Australia, New Zealand bay whalers recognized the efficacy of inshore whaling. It was much less expensive than open-ocean hunting in terms of the initial outlay, much less dangerous, and much easier. There was also very little possibility that a shore station would sink or be lost at sea. They didn't even have to chase the whales. The whales came to them.

There is a distinction, perhaps without a significant difference, between shore whaling and bay whaling. Shore whaling was conducted by whalers whose base of operations was located at a shore station. Their methods were simple and primitive, based on the traditions that had been established more than a thousand years earlier by the Basques. Then and in New Zealand (and at the stations in Australia as well), the whalers spotted the whales from shore—or waited for them to come close inshore—and then rowed out to kill them. In most of the history of shore (and bay) whaling, the object was the right whale, which habitually came close to shore to breed and calve. If any other whales made the mistake of being spotted, they would meet with the same fate.

Bay whaling involved the same techniques (and the same whales), but the base was a ship anchored in a convenient bay. Where the carcass would be towed to the ramp at the shore station, it would be brought to the ship of the bay whalers, or in some cases, when the winds and tides were propitious, the ship would come to the whale. (Sailing ships, unlike motorized vessels, cannot simply go where the captain or crew wants them to. If, for instance, the whale carcass was directly upwind from an anchored whaleship, the hapless crew would have to row their 50- or 60-ton deadweight burden to the waiting whaleship for the trying-out.)

No one is sure how many shore stations there were throughout New Zealand, but it has been estimated that there were as many as a hundred, most of them located on either shore of Cook Strait. The whales also came to the Bay of Islands, a patchwork of some 150 islands on the northeast coast of North Island, the Banks and Otago peninsulas, and Foveaux Strait. Whereas deep-sea whalers were often compulsive cleaners—they often had to remain aboard their vessels for years, and they also had the all-forgiving ocean into which to dump their refuse—no such compulsions energized the shore whalers. Their stations were stinking piles of guts, bones and blubber, attended by pigs, dogs and the ubiquitous rats. (One of the disadvantages of shore whaling lay in the very immobility of the station. Where whaleships could often sail to the location of the dead whale for the trying-out, shore whalers had to tow their prizes to the station, an effort that sometimes took several hours, and was often fueled with rum.) If the whale could not be towed completely out of the water, then it was worked up in shallow water, suspended from "shears," crudely built pulley and scaffold structures that characterized the early New Zealand whaling stations. They served a dual function: when they were not used for suspending whale carcasses for "flinching," they were used to lift boats out of the water so that they could be scraped or repaired.

In 1836, the Nantucket whaler *Mary Mitchell* arrived in Cloudy Bay (South Island) to partake of the right whaling there. Captain Samuel Joy kept a journal, which has proven to be one of the best records of bay whaling in New Zealand waters. He discusses the "toungers"—white men with a crew of Maoris who contracted to tow whales in exchange for the tongue—the whalers' response to the Maori way of life ("I saw with disgust the manner these natives live or rather exist"), but mostly (and lacking any sort of punctuation) the business of bay whaling:

On our first arrival here I found it was the common practice for each Ship to have a house on shore to perform their Coopering in as inpreferred having that duty performed under my own inspection I did not care for having a house but on second thought when I refelected it was also needed for to mend boats under and the time taken for that was generally when the weather was stormy I concluded to have one it was told to me by our toungers that the cost was trifling and altogether at the opinion of the master What and how much be paid I therefore employed 2 chiefs living here to construct me one and they

employed another who was father to one of them and thus I am in a fair way of having a house but to pay 3 people for it (the Principal Chief is absent on one of his marauding traverses like the Ancient band Pirates and his authority delegated to 3 chiefs 1 on the western Shore the other 2 here). . . .

In addition to the British and the Americans, the French also sent a fleet to New Zealand for bay whaling. The first of these seems to have been the *Mississippi* under Captain Rossiter, in Cloudy Bay in 1836, four years before the historic rescue of John Eyre on the south Australian coast.* Within two years, the *Pauline* and the *Adèle* had arrived at Akaroa, and their presence inspired the French government to send the corvette *Heroine*, Captain Cecille, to protect the interests of France. Also present at Akaroa in 1836 was the *Gange*, the ship that had taken the first right whale off Alaska the previous June, along with the *Nil, Gustave, Cosmopolite, Cachalot, Souvenir,* and *Dunkerquoise.*

While the French did not go whaling with the industrious amplitude of the Americans or the British, they formed a substantial part of the Antipodean fishery, especially in New Zealand. Their chronicler was Dr. Felix Maynard (1813–1858), who "had ploughed the Atlantic, the Pacific, and the Indian Oceans, and visited all the straits, from that of Magellan to that of Behring; he had rounded all the capes from Finisterre to Good Hope and the Horn." Although Maynard was no Melville, his collaborator on the book he called *Les Baleiniers* was Alexandre Dumas,† the author of *The Count of Monte Cristo* and *The Three Musketeers,* so his book gives us a more literate and dramatic picture of nineteenth-century French whaling than we might otherwise have expected.

Maynard was ship's doctor aboard the Havre de

---

*In 1840, Edward John Eyre attempted to walk across the continent, along the coast of the Great Australian Bight. With his assistant, John Baxter, and three aborigines, he spent four and a half months in the desert. Baxter was murdered, and two of the aborigines ran away, leaving Eyre and a man named Wylie to stumble into a camp that had been established by the "shore gang" of the French whaler *Mississippi* at Esperance in Western Australia.

†It cannot be determined how much of the book was written by Maynard and how much by Dumas. In the introduction to the 1937 English edition, the translator F. W. Reed wrote, "Call Dumas' share of the work what you prefer, revision, editing, selection, it was done to good purpose. It is not difficult to find in places clear traces of that ability to visualize—and enable his readers to do so—some striking incident or dangerous adventure."

Grace whaler *Asia* on her 1837–38 right-whaling voyage to the South Seas, and his adventures were first published as a serial in a Paris newspaper and then as a book in 1858. *Asia* was right-whaling in Tasmanian waters, later crossing the Tasman Sea to New Zealand, and taking an occasional cachalot in the process. Like Melville, he championed the species he hunted, referring to the right whale simply as "the whale":

The whale has a pointed snout, the cachalot a square one. The lower jaw of the cachalot is garnished with teeth, and their extremities are implanted in hollows in the arch of the palate, each tooth having a corresponding orifice, as a knife has its sheath or a poignard its scabbard. The opening of the throat of the cachalot is large; its double vent-holes are placed in the upper angle of the snout; its tongue is flat like a sole. The tongue of the whale is thick, plump and fat; its double vents open in the nape of the neck; one's little finger would hardly penetrate the opening of the throat; baleen plates from one to ten feet long and bearded on their inner edge are embedded in the palate and enclosed by two immense lips which spring from either side of the immense maxillaries. Briefly, the whale has the shape of a shuttle, seventy or eighty feet long, ending in a nimble tail with two horizontal lobes.

When Maynard visited the Banks Peninsula in 1838, he found the whalers' shore camp "full of animation and strange sights":

Canoes were hauled high and dry upon the beach; huts were built pell-mell, and covered and panelled with yellow leaves; platform larders, raised upon four wooden posts, were laden with sacks of sweet potatoes, bundles of dried fish and cakes of fern; men, swathed in flax mats or in coverings of white wool, sometimes paced gravely, sometimes lay in groups or singly on the lower grounds of the hill; women squatted before the household hearth, alight in the open air; other women were washing or beating between two stones the phormium [flax] soaking in a stream of fresh water; naked children, daubed in red ochre, frisked at the edge of the sea, amid the chaos of whale bones, stripped of their flesh and bleached by the weather, which the ebb tide had abandoned on the shore; dogs howled, wandering about from rock to rock; while, as a background to the picture, showed the sterile mountain upon which the village abuts, and which seems uncultivated and stern, rising to heaven.

Dr. Maynard also provided some revealing insights into nineteenth-century medicine, at least as it

was practiced at sea. In one instance he amputated the right foot of a man named Taillevent who nearly severed it while chopping the baleen out of a right whale's mouth, and in another, he revived a sailor who had been brought aboard unconscious after having been dumped into the sea by a wounded whale. Using "three or four quills from the wing of an albatross" to force his own breath into the bronchial tubes of the drowned man, he then energetically rubbed the length of his spinal column and enveloped him in coverings of well-heated wool. "I also made repeated titillations of the mucous membrane of the nasal cavities," wrote the good doctor, "and after efforts lasting a quarter of an hour and which were crowned with success, my Gascon swallowed a large glass of hot wine in which the cook . . . had flung two or three pinches of pepper." (Perhaps in the interests of medical science, Maynard tasted whale milk, which he collected with a bucket after it had floated from a nursing mother that had been killed. He found that it had an "acrid and nauseating taste; it contracts the tongue and induces an inclination to vomit.")

It was evident even to Maynard that the numbers of available whales were diminishing. He wrote, "The future of the great fisheries, for the encouragement of which the French Government has, for more than twenty years, decreed a number of very important bounties, is seriously threatened by as the result of the destruction of the species known as *right whales,* and formerly regarded as being alone capable of furnishing what is known to commerce as fish oil." He then reviewed the various inventions that might eliminate the dangers of open boat whaling ("the harpoon cannon or the harpoon rifle . . . the harpoon treated with prussic acid," and finally, "the gunsmith Devisme's projectiles and his carbine whale boat"), with the idea that the whalers might then be able to hunt the elusive and dangerous fin backs and humpbacks, "which defend themselves with fury."

The French—and to a lesser extent the Americans—indulged in a unique method of whaling they called *la pêche par association,* which consisted of one of the two "mated" ships remaining at anchor in the bay, while the other tacked around in search of whales, with the crew of both ships aboard. In his description of French bay whaling in New Zealand, Maynard wrote, "Henceforth, therefore, the *Neptune* of Nantes worked with the *Grétry* of Havre, and the *Asia* shared her chances with the *Cousin,* Captain Vasselin." All whales caught were equally divided between the two ships. By 1837, there were fifteen French and thirty-seven American ships in New Zealand waters.

Since the whalers were the descendants of the sealers (in many cases, they were the same people), one might assume that they would have learned a lesson about conservation of resources when the seals ran out. They did not. These ecological freebooters abused their resources shamefully. Not only did they wantonly slaughter as many whales as they could, they did it in a manner that was guaranteed to close out their burgeoning industry almost as soon as they got it going. It was the female right whales that came into the bays and inlets to breed and deliver their 20-foot-long calves, and the whalers often harpooned the calf first, knowing that the mother would not abandon it. Then the mother would be similarly dispatched, and both carcasses would be towed into shallow water for processing. "Any farmer who killed lamb and ewe together would not be in business for very long," wrote one observer, while another said they "have felled the tree to obtain the fruit, and have thus taken the most certain means of destroying an otherwise profitable and important trade."

Although Felix Maynard believed that "the hand accustomed to pulling an oar would be too clumsy for an operation," he still wanted to at least "jostle against a whale" before returning to France. On an oystering, not a whaling, expedition, he got his wish. With the captain and several oarsmen in the launch, they encountered "an enormous whale accompanied by its nursling." Despite their having none of the necessary harpoons or lines aboard, the crew could not let this opportunity pass, and because one of the men brought a lance ("to fling at the wild pigs in Togolabo Bay"), they rowed up to the whales, and the captain stabbed the calf. Maynard continued:

I thought at first that the captain had aimed badly, but soon I comprehended his skill and wisdom. He was aware that the first blow from the lance would not kill the mother, and that she would fly to a distance and be lost to us; but by killing the nursling she would be detained immovable, no matter what might be her fate; as mother she would allow herself to be killed on the spot rather than abandon her calf. . . . Captain Jay was able to strike at his leisure, one, two, three, ten blows. The monster floundered, spouted blood, *flurried,* and died, without moving any farther away than if she had been made fast by the most solid of harpoons. How admirably the power of maternal love dominates the instinct for self-preservation.

An ex-convict named John ("Jacky") Guard is usually considered the first New Zealand bay whaleman. He had been transported to the penal colony at New South Wales in 1815, and after serving out his sentence, he became a sealer. In 1827, at a primitive station at Te Awaiti (on the ragged northeast coast of South Island), Guard eked out a meager living, sometimes reduced to eating turnip tops and collecting the baleen from stranded whales or those he managed to take offshore with his limited equipment and personnel, and selling it to whaleships calling at Cloudy Bay or the Marlborough Sounds. (Guard's son, also called John, was born in 1831, the first white child born on South Island.) Guard's enterprise was plagued by major and minor disasters, ranging from the loss of his ships to the capture and consumption of some of his Maori workers by rival tribesmen. Guard died in 1857, and is buried at Kakapo Bay. His wife, Betty, who bore him nine children, is buried alongside him. The Guard family has acquired historical respectability in the ensuing years; Guards still live at Kakapo, and although the whales and seals are long gone, the family traditionally follows the sea as fishermen.

Several whalers, of whom the best known were John Jones, Dickie Barrett and Phillip Tapsell, married Maori women, prospered at their shore stations, and started families whose descendants proudly claim their origins among New Zealand's founding fathers. But for every legitimate settler, there were dozens of rowdy whalemen, carousing drunkenly in Kororareka and Waikouaiti; chasing women and often fomenting clashes between various Maori groups. In addition to the Maori vs. Maori conflicts, which were pernicious and never-ending, there were also serious ructions between *Pakeha* (European) and Maori. In 1817, for example, at Otago, Maori warriors attacked the brig *Sophia* for reasons that have never been satisfactorily explained but seem to have had something to do with one of the sailors' selling the preserved heads of dead warriors. In retribution, James Kelly, of Sydney, the owner of the *Sophia,* destroyed forty-

The whaling station at Te Awaiti in the 1890s, seventy years after Jacky Guard founded New Zealand's first whaling station. The harpooners in the bows are only posing, since by this time all the right whales had been eliminated from inshore waters.

two Maori canoes and burned a village. Again in 1833, when the *Dragon,* out of Hobart, lowered two boats after whales in the Cook Strait region, the boats were attacked by Maoris, and the crews killed and eaten.

Although not a whaler, the brig *Elizabeth,* out of London, was involved in a horrible massacre, where the ship was taken over by Maori warriors who remained concealed below decks until the ship was sailed by Captain Briggs into the harbor at Banks Peninsula. The Maori chief Te Rauparaha captured and killed these enemies as they came aboard to trade, then stole ashore and murdered the inhabitants of the village. From contemporaneous accounts, Robert McNab describes what happened next:

About eleven o'clock on the day of landing preparations were made for embarking the miscellaneous cargo of live captives and dead human flesh. The prisoners, with the exception of Tamaiharanui, were marched on shore, and seated in rows on the beach, and the preserved flesh was carried off in baskets to the place appointed for the cannibal feast. It was estimated that about one hundred baskets of flesh were landed and that each basket contained the equivalent of one human body.

In full view of the crew of the *Elizabeth,* they then cooked and ate their enemies, accompanied by potatoes, green vegetables and whale blubber.

Never mind that the Maori concept of land ownership differed from that of the Europeans; the Maoris were more than willing to sell their lands, often under ludicrous terms. Settlers would "buy" huge tracts for an axe, a musket or a bolt of cloth. Captain Langlois of the French whaler *Cachalot* acquired the entire Banks Peninsula, all 300,000 acres of it, for 1,000 francs. His first payment consisted of a woolen overcoat, six pairs of linen trousers, a dozen waterproof hats, two pairs of shoes, a pistol, two woolen shirts and a waterproof cloak. When Langlois returned to France in 1839, he founded the Compagnie de Bordeaux et de Nantes pour la colonisation de l'Ile du Sud de la Nouvelle Zélande et ses Dépendances. It was his intention to sell parcels of land to Frenchmen through the Nanto-Bordelaise Company, but before he could get this scheme off the ground, the British had annexed the islands.

The industry did not last long because the whales did not last long. At the Weller Brothers' station at Otago, the history of this fishery can be read in the records of the amount of oil taken over a six-year period. In 1834, they took 310 tuns of black oil; in 1835 they took 260; the following year 210; and by 1839 they were reporting 65. In 1841, they took 10 tuns, and then closed down. In a little more than a decade, the whalemen had come to the islands, eradicated the whales, and established a foothold on the islands which was to set the tone for their colonization for the next century.

From the earliest landings on New Zealand's shores, the European attitude toward the natives was different from that expressed toward the Australian aborigines. At first, it seems to have been based on the European admiration of the Maori ability to kill one another, but it soon metamorphosed into a spirit of mutual respect. (When the English adventurer William Dampier made the first European contact with the aborigines of the west coast of Australia in 1688, he described them as "the miserablest people in the world." Cook's arrival on the east coast in 1770 resulted in a relatively peaceful confrontation; the aborigines threw a couple of spears, then ran away.) The first meeting of the Dutch and the Maoris resulted in the death of four Dutchmen. When Cook himself first confronted the Maoris at the place he called Poverty Bay (because "it afforded us no one thing we wanted"), he too had to fire at the hostile natives, and four of them were killed.

Despite these early conflicts, the whalers and the Maoris were quickly "integrated." The first inter-course took the form of trading, where the whalers would exchange tobacco for much-needed firewood, vegetables and meat. The New Zealand natives were willing to work with the whalers, and some of them became harpooners or even officers. Because there was such a high rate of attrition aboard the whalers from death or desertion, good men were always needed, and they could be recruited from the willing and seaworthy Maori. As soon as they learned the ropes, the Maoris became competent whalemen, and they were in great demand by the captains. Along with the Hawaiians and the natives of other South Sea islands at which the whaleships called, the Maoris joined the ranks of the *kanakas,** the native whalemen. There were some situations where the Maori profited directly from the whales; either they harpooned a whale themselves and sold it to the whalers, or they found stranded whales and sold the bone to the English stations. Contact with the whalers not only "educated" the Maori to the ways of the Europeans, but it also enabled them to obtain the rum and muskets that were to change the primitive way of life of the New Zealand natives forever.

Ashore, the Maori provided the essential agricultural products for the shore-whaling stations and the deep-sea whaleships. For their own consumption, the Maori grew yams, potatoes, fern root and *kumara,* a local sweet potato. For animal protein, they ate shellfish, fish and an occasional rat. (It is true that the Maori were cannibals, but human flesh was not a dietary staple. It was only eaten under ceremonial conditions, when an enemy had been vanquished in battle.) The British settlers introduced all sorts of familiar growing things in their desire to make these islands at the bottom of the world more like Dorsetshire. In 1835, Charles Darwin, stopping at the islands on the *Beagle's* round-the-world journey, noted the following vegetables growing in the garden of the missionary, Mr. Williams: "asparagus, kidney beans, cucumbers, rhubarb, apples, pears, figs, peaches, apricots, grapes, olives, gooseberries, hops, currants, gorse for fences, and English oaks." For the whaleman, conditioned by tradition and appetite, potatoes and pork remained the mainstay of the diet; these were grown and produced accordingly.

*Kanaka, which is the word the Hawaiians use for themselves, became the generic term for any Polynesian or Micronesian native who joined a whaleship.

Rum was another necessity, and more than one observer commented on the state of inebriation (and the overpowering smell of rum) that pervaded the whaling stations. J. C. Crawford, in his 1880 *Recollections of Travel in Australia and New Zealand,* wrote: "One of the horrors of a whaling station was the smell of arrack rum, which infected the air to a great distance. It was simply the most detestable liquid that I have ever met with, and although I tasted it, I could go no further; it must have been poisonous; and as it was the liquor with which the whaling stations were generally supplied, many a death must have resulted from the use of it." Many observers commented on the depraved conditions prevalent at the New Zealand shore stations, but no one was more succinct than the Reverend John Hewgill Bumby, who wrote, "The very sense of decency and propriety seems to be extinct. The very soil is polluted. The very air is tainted." Undoubtedly, there was more rum consumed at these stations than the missionaries would have approved of; this was to be expected where unenlightened men were responsible for their own destinies, and where rum could be gotten cheaply, or even brewed from the local vegetation. (An Irishman who called himself Owen McShane distilled what was locally known as "McShane's Oil," from the sap of cabbage trees. It was reputed to be so potent that it was held responsible for several shipwrecks.) Kororareka* on the Bay of Islands was known to the whalers as the "Hellhole of the Pacific," where fights, brawls, murders, brothels and grog shops characterized the environs. Writing in 1875 in *The Cruise of the "Cachalot,"* Frank Bullen described Kororareka as a place where "orgies of wild debauchery and bloodshed [were] indulged in by the half-savage and utterly lawless crews of the whaleships." The rampant drunkenness and lawlessness were not surprising when one realizes that the nearest policeman was a thousand miles away across the Tasman Sea. As quoted in McNab's *Old Whaling Days,* Lieutenant Chetwode of H.M.S. *Pelorus* referred to the whalers as "a disreputable and lawless set, distrusting each other, and telling innumerable falsehoods to support their villainy."

*Before the Treaty of Waitangi in 1840, Kororareka was the *de facto* capital of New Zealand. Governor Hobson decided to move the capital to Auckland, primarily because of its protected harbor. Yankee whaling captains, firmly ensconced in lawless Kororareka, objected strenuously, but the new government prevailed.

For all their lawlessness and debauchery, whalemen found the Maori women surprisingly receptive to their needs. They married from (or into) the Maori society, more or less according to their respective hierarchies. Captains and officers of rank—who did not have wives or sweethearts in England or America—married the daughters of chiefs, while ordinary seamen married the lower-caste Maoris, sometimes even the slaves taken in the constant tribal skirmishes that characterized the Maori culture. These associations may have occurred because of love, but they were more likely to have been *mariages de convenance.* It was certainly more accommodating for a whaler to have a hut on shore, no matter how wretched, than to live in a swinging hammock in the stinking fo'c's'le of a whaler. Many of these marriages were arranged because the whalemen determined that marriage was a prerequisite of land-ownership, and by marrying into the local establishment, a whaleman could guarantee the safety and protection of his station. The owners of the stations depended upon the local tribesmen for protection against marauders. As H. A. Morton wrote in *The Whale's Wake,* a history of New Zealand whaling, "On the relationship of manager and local chief rested the harmony of the whole district." (There were some, however, like George Weller, who, when he built the station at Otakou, equipped himself with all sorts of ordnance and ammunition, including six cases of muskets, ten barrels of gunpowder, and a case of axes. These may have been intended as trade goods, since nothing was more appealing to the Maoris than weaponry of an advanced sort, but after the station had opened, Weller wrote to Sydney for a howitzer, which was obviously intended for his own defense.)

Maori women were not considered beautiful—certainly not as beautiful as the Tahitians or the Marquesans—but for the intrepid whalemen of New Zealand, they were the best possible helpmeets. They were obedient and trustworthy, but not, as Darwin pointed out, particularly clean. He had written (of all Maoris, not only the women) that they were "filthily dirty and offensive; the idea of washing either their bodies or their clothes never seems to enter their heads." But for whalemen halfway around the world from England—and more than likely to remain there—the Maori women represented stability and domesticity. Many of the early whalers were

A rare photograph of Maori whaling. At the Bay of Plenty station at Te Kawa, members of the Whanau-a-Apanui tribe strip the blubber from a right whale.

from England and Ireland's lower strata; the idea that they could be entrepreneurs or landowners, no matter how small the scale or how rough the conditions, must have been enormously appealing. They married, set up house, had children, and became the first families of New Zealand.

Even the missionaries ventured to New Zealand because of the whales. Samuel Marsden (whom Robert Hughes describes as "a grasping Evangelical missionary with heavy shoulders and the face of a petulant ox") came to the Bay of Islands to reform the Maoris, whom he had first encountered in Sydney, where they were often abandoned by the whalemen. (Marsden had planned to go to New Zealand as early as 1808, but he was deterred by the *Boyd* incident in 1809, where a shore party was killed and eaten by Maoris, who then burned the whaleship *Boyd.*) Before 1814, the year Marsden established the first mission at Kerikeri, all marriages were, by definition, without benefit of clergy. Thereafter, however, a surprising number of whalemen actually married their Maori concubines, and laid the groundwork for the integrated society that was to follow. This was true primarily of the shore whalers

who wanted to put down roots in New Zealand; the deep-sea whalers who put in for provisions at Cloudy Bay or Kororareka could hardly be expected to marry given the duration of their visits. There was, therefore, as at any port of call where whalers stopped, a lively business in prostitution. (In New Zealand, this business seems to have had its roots with the Maori, who used captured slaves for those purposes even before the *Pakehas* arrived.) And, as at all such places, venereal diseases were introduced to people that had known nothing of them previously. In addition, such scourges as measles, consumption, and influenza wreaked havoc in a population that had no immunological defenses against them. But the greatest threats to the culture of the Maori came from guns and rum.

At first, the Maoris disapproved of the consumption of alcohol, but such an attitude could not be expected to last. Before long, rum was being used as a barter item, and the Maoris, who had never distilled anything, were fast on the way to becoming drinkers. But the rum, no matter how much it was consumed or by whom, could not have nearly the effect on the Maoris as the introduction of firearms to an already warlike society whose armament had consisted of spears, clubs and thrown stones. The settlers traded muskets and powder (plus instruction on their use) to the Maoris for water and food, and the Maoris turned the guns on each other. Never slouches at intertribal warfare, the Maoris soon escalated their aggressiveness to the point where they were engaged in real shooting wars. In later years, a famous Maori statesman, Sir Apirana Ngata, would write, "the possession of firearms became the overwhelming motive of the Native mind . . . his control of tribal lands was governed by a new and supreme temptation, so that the new culture appealed to his avarice and desire for vengeance and power." The first tribes to get the guns were the first to assert this vengeance and power. In retaliation, the other tribes also wanted firearms and ammunition, so there was a tremendous increase in the production of goods to trade for weapons. "But it was the trade itself," says Harry Morton, "and not the objects of it, which wrought the most changes in Maori society." A marked increase in pigs, potatoes and flax was needed to ensure the flow of arms to the warlike Maoris, and there were even stories of men offering their wives or children for muskets. Without the trade in firearms, the whalers could get no food, so despite the missionaries' concerns that they were corrupting the natives (as indeed they were), the trade continued. It was to come to a head in 1860, when the Maoris, having been armed for more than three decades, rose up to protest the presence of foreigners on their sacred soil. (By the time of the "Land Wars" of the mid-nineteenth century, shore whaling was over in New Zealand—because the whales had been extirpated. While the Maori uprisings played an important part in the future development of New Zealand, the influence of the whales had substantially diminished.)

SHORE AND BAY whaling were all but finished by 1845. This period also represented the formative years of New Zealand, and was critical in the short, often bloody history of this unusual country. During the fifteen years before 1845, New Zealand's first industry rose and fell; the islands were annexed to England and officially became a colony; and the Maoris, who had remained undisturbed for some five hundred years, were abruptly yanked into the hugger-mugger of the nineteenth century. As the whalers married and produced offspring, the groundwork was being laid for a society the likes of which would be unknown anywhere in the world, a native/European amalgamation that would characterize New Zealand forever, and set her apart from every other colony in the British Empire.

Because they were few in number—one estimate is that there were no more than 300 Europeans in New Zealand in 1830—the whalers had little influence on the actual settlement of the colony. News of the "black whales," however, spread quickly, and within another ten years, this figure had increased tenfold. (Correspondingly, the original Maori population, which may have been as high as 400,000 before the Europeans arrived, was decimated by disease, armed warfare and alcohol, and dropped to 100,000 by 1840.) Since there were no convicts here (except those who had escaped from Australia or the "ticket-of-leave" men, whose sentences had expired or been reduced, but who were not allowed to leave the colony), New Zealand began as a free country.*

Although there were factions that did not desire annexation (the missionaries wanted the Maoris left to them for Christian education, without the negative influences of the Europeans), it was inevitable. Edward Gibbon Wakefield, a self-styled authority on colonization (although he did not actually arrive in New Zealand until 1852), told the House of Commons in 1836 that annexation was not only inevitable, but that it was already taking place "in a most slovenly and scrambling and disgraceful manner." To combat the lawlessness and anarchy that was reported to be rampant in these islands; to protect the Englishmen who were the victims of this disorder; and perhaps most important, once the true description and climate of New Zealand became known, to colonize a territory with a climate remarkably like that of Albion—it was decided in 1840 that New Zealand would be annexed to England. Accordingly, Captain William Hobson, of H.M.S. *Rattlesnake,* out of Sydney, sailed for New Zealand with orders to effect a treaty with the Maori chiefs. The terms of this treaty are somewhat vague, since it is not clear that the document the Maoris read in translation was

---

*Even though it was not officially part of the British Empire, New Zealand was included in the legislative ambit of New South Wales in 1817, to cover the British citizens who had settled or landed there.

Jillett's whaling station at Kapiti Island, off New Zealand's North Island, as it appeared in 1844. Notice the "shears" on the right: they were used to support the carcass during the flensing operation.

the same one the British read in English. Not all of the reigning Maori chiefs signed the agreement, and in fact, South Island, which had a much smaller native population, was annexed without benefit of any treaty at all. In sharp contrast to the situation in Australia, where the "rights" of the aborigines were summarily ignored as the British simply laid claim to the entire continent, there was never any dispute about the original ownership of the land of New Zealand. It had belonged to the Maori, and in exchange for sovereignty—a concept the Maori prob-

ably did not fully understand—they gained "all rights and privileges of British subjects." (To protect them, however, the government had decided that land could only be sold to the Crown, which seemed only to diminish their rights as British citizens.) The Treaty of Waitangi was signed on February 6, 1840, and Captain Hobson became Lieutenant-Governor Hobson, New Zealand's first magistrate. The treaty made New Zealand a dependency of New South Wales, but in 1841, it was declared a Crown Colony in its own right.

Bay Whaling in South Africa

ALL AROUND the southern tip of Africa the southern right whale found itself the focus of the early settlers, who would base a 150-year-long industry on the broad, smooth backs of these leviathans. As was the case in Australia and New Zealand, the whales were hunted until they were too scarce to make the industry profitable.

As usual, the original discoverers of the whales were not looking for them, but rather for a route to somewhere else. In 1488, the Portuguese navigator Bartolomeu Dias became the first European to double the southern tip of Africa, and he was followed a decade later by Vasco da Gama, another Portuguese, who was the first to sail around Africa to

India. (The first European whaler in South African waters was reputed to have been Paulo da Gama, Vasco's brother. In 1497, so the story goes, he harpooned a whale in St. Helena Bay, and was being towed out to sea until the whale stranded on a convenient sandbank.) The Portuguese showed little interest in southern Africa, however, since they had become irrevocably involved in the Guinea coast, and after the Dutch had wrested control of the East Indies from them in 1610, the Hollanders needed a provisioning station for their voyages from Europe, round Cape Esperanza, and thence to the East. The Dutch East India Company dispatched the *Drommedaris,* commanded by Jan van Riebeeck and a complement of about ninety men, who landed at Table Bay in April 1652. His assignment was to establish a refreshment station for the Dutch ships on their way to the East, and by 1659, Dutch vessels were stopping at Table Bay for vegetables, fresh water, and even livestock. Van Riebeeck described "many thousands of whales in Table Bay, Saldanha Bay, and neighboring waters." According to his journals, he encountered a dead whale at the mouth of the Salt River in Saldanha Bay, and called to his trumpeters to play "Wilhelmus van Nassauwen" as he climbed upon it in triumph.

Dutch settlers began to emigrate to this new colony, and to help them work their modest plantations, they began to import slaves from Java and Madagascar. The colony grew apace, and the Dutch established a firm foothold at the bottom of Africa. Then in 1685 Louis XIV of France revoked all the religious freedoms that had been granted to Protestants by the Edict of Nantes in 1598. This led to a mass exodus of Huguenots from France, and some two hundred of them sailed for the Cape in 1688. As early as the turn of the eighteenth century, the seeds of the racial, religious and economic conflicts that were to characterize South African history for the next three hundred years were planted. There was a burgher class (the Dutch and Huguenot farmers who would evolve into the Boers), a slave class that numbered about seventeen thousand by 1700, and the results of the mingling of these two groups, the "coloreds." In the vicinity of the coasts, contrary to the denials by Afrikaaner historians who claim that the area was unoccupied when their forefathers got there, there were Bushmen and Hottentots, and farther inland, Zulus, Pondos, Tembus and Xhosas. The Brit-

ish, who would add another ingredient to this volatile admixture, did not occupy South Africa until 1795, when they annexed the Cape to keep it from falling into French hands and threatening their sea routes to India.

On a small-scale map, the southern tip of Africa looks like the lumpy chin of the skull-shaped continent. On a more detailed map, however, it can be seen that the bottom of Africa is marked by large bays such as Algoa, St. Francis, St. Helena, Plettenberg, and the two bays that define the Cape Peninsula, Table Bay to the north and False Bay (Valsbaai) to the south.

Because right whales were in abundance in the various bays that were sculpted into the southern coast of Africa, it was inevitable that the early settlers would encounter them. As they did throughout the Southern Hemisphere, right whales migrated north from the Antarctic to breed and calve in the warmer waters of various protected bays and inlets.

Seventy miles north of Cape Town is Saldanha Bay, discovered in 1503 by the Portuguese navigator Antonio de Saldanha. The Cape of Good Hope is not the African analogue of Cape Horn—it is not the southernmost point of the African continent. That distinction is held by Cape Agulhas. Cape Town and Saldanha Bay are in the South Atlantic, while everything east of Cape Agulhas (located on the 20-degree line of east longitude) is considered to be in the Indian Ocean. In 1604 Sir Henry Middleton stopped at the Cape en route to India, discovered the seals of Robben Island (in Table Bay) and actually struck a whale in Table Bay.

The whales were recognized as being similar—if not identical—to the North Atlantic *noordkaper,* and since the *noordkapers* were already the basis for the thriving whaling industry in northern Europe and North America, the colonists were eager to start their own whaling industry. There is evidence that the Dutch East India Company was interested in having Van Riebeeck initiate a whaling industry as early as 1654, but he lacked the means to store the oil, and while the company suggested that he store it in holes dug in the ground, the Dutch whaling enterprise in Spitsbergen seems to have supplied Holland with the oil and baleen it needed, much closer to home. The South African right whales were spared for another century, but when the whalers from America, Britain and France heard of the abundance of whales in

South African waters, they arrived in force, and toward the end of the eighteenth century, as the Northern Hemisphere right whale and Greenland whale fisheries were beginning to collapse, the whalers appeared in Walvis, Saldanha and Table bays.

When the American colonists rebelled against King George III, the British reliance on New England as a supplier of whale oil came to an abrupt halt, so the British had to seek elsewhere for oil to light their lamps. Whalers and other ships began to visit the Cape Colony for provisions, and the foreign whalers quickly discovered the right whales in the very bays where they were anchoring. Particular favorites were the bays on the west coast, Saldanha, Angra Pequena and Walvis (which the whalemen referred to as "Woolwich," "Walwich," or its literal translation from the Dutch, "Whale Fish"). Walvis Bay is appealing only to right whales and those who would hunt them; it is hooked into the desolate coast of the barren Namibian Desert, hundreds of miles from anything that even remotely suggests civilization. (It was said that the Yankee captains intentionally chose places like Walvis Bay for inshore whaling to reduce the chances of their crews' jumping ship.) Despite its isolation—or perhaps because of it— Walvis Bay was by far the most popular destination for whalers sailing eastward across the South Atlantic after working the "Brazil Banks" of South America. Walvis Bay was thickly populated with right whales (hence its name) between June and September, and besides, right whaling in protected waters was considerably easier and less dangerous than sperm whaling in the open ocean. By 1795 there were twenty to thirty Yankee whaleships anchoring in Walvis Bay every season.

American whalers also worked their way southward along the coast of southern Africa, finding right whales aplenty at Saint Helena, Saldanha and Table bays, and around the Cape of Good Hope, dangling like a beckoning finger into the South Atlantic. They also entered the sweeping expanse of False Bay, which is so big that it contains several subsidiary bays of its own. In 1788, six American whalers obtained full cargoes from St. Helena Bay, and by 1790 some twenty American whalers took about 400 whales in a three-month period in the same bay. Whaling was so successful in St. Helena Bay that the Yankees were said to take only the heads for the

baleen, and throw the rest of the carcasses—including the blubber—to the sharks. (Occasionally a carcass would drift ashore, where it was eagerly appropriated by the Hottentots.) There was often bad blood between the visiting whalers and the colonists, but the visitors were good customers, and the merchants prevailed over the local whalers; whaleships required fresh water, meat and firewood, even when they were working inshore waters, and merchants can rarely afford to be too selective about their customers. Dutch and British authorities tried to keep the Americans out and restrict whaling to the locals, but they were largely ineffectual, and the Americans continued to whale on the Cape's rich grounds.

The absence of experienced personnel (the colony lacked what one writer called a "purely seafaring class") kept South Africans from starting whaling immediately, and they did not actually begin on their own until 1792. Only one colonial company, Fehrson & Co. (also referred to as Fehrson and Truter), had been set up in Table Bay, where they manufactured a somewhat odoriferous soap. The company was bought by an Englishmen named John Murray, who was "obliged to desist from fishing" after 1803, when the Batavian government annexed the Cape Colony and awarded fishing and whaling rights to Dutch merchants. When the British recaptured the Cape Colony in 1806, Murray began his whaling operations again.

In the early years of the nineteenth century, after the second British occupation of the Cape in 1806, shore-whaling operations were established at Kalk Bay, Gordons Bay, St. Helena, Algoa Bay and Fish Hoek. In response to a request from the British government in 1807, whalers estimated the number of *noordkapers* available annually as 150 for Table Bay and Dassen Island, 300 for Simon's Bay, 500 for Saldanha Bay and St. Helena Bay, and 400 for Algoa and Plettenberg bays—a grand total of 1,350. At first glance, these numbers appear to be wildly inflated, but perhaps van Riebeeck's estimate of "thousands of whales" in Table Bay and Saldanha was not so far off. In St. Helena Bay, for example, there may have been as many as 1,200 whales killed in the years 1791–92.

Round the tip of Africa, on the sperm whale–rich east coast of Natal, the Americans continued to trade with the local merchants, and even the natives, to whom they supplied arms and powder in exchange for food. Threatened with the real or imaginary prospect of the Americans' establishing a colony there, Governor Napier of the Cape Colony annexed Natal in 1841, and two years later, it was added to the British Empire.

In 1803 the African Fishing Society was formed by a group of Dutch merchants for whaling in Table Bay, and in 1806, a shore fishery was established at False Bay by one Pieter Laurens Cloete. The stench of his operation caused the inhabitants of the Cape Colony to insist that he process the whales offshore, in what was known as a "floating fishery." The bays and inlets of the Cape Coast abounded with right whales, and by 1822 the whale fishery was one of the most important industries of the Cape, second only to agriculture.

One name that crops up regularly in the various histories of early Cape whaling is Darby. He was apparently a Malay harpooner, well over six feet tall, who is reputed to have killed over a hundred whales at Algoa Bay, near Port Elizabeth. According to a newspaper account, he was "daring beyond belief, deadly of eye and dynamically powerful." Darby killed the last two whales taken in Algoa Bay, a sperm whale and a right whale, and for years the skeletons hung in the Old Museum at Feather Market Hall in Port Elizabeth, a memorial to the old whaling days.

For approximately seventy years, foreign and South African whalers took the right whales in the bays. Since most of the whales they killed were females, the right whale population took a serious dive, and soon the industry was flagging. The foreigners went elsewhere, and the merchants tried to sell their stations (with the attendant "slave boys"). There were no takers, and the fishery limped along until about 1880 when it collapsed altogether.

Right Whaling in Alaska and Canada

ALTHOUGH RIGHT WHALES were intensively hunted throughout their breeding grounds in the Southern Hemisphere, the northern populations that had not been eliminated by the Basques were soon to become the objects of another, equally destructive fishery. The northwest coast of North America also has secluded bays and inlets, the traditional breeding grounds of *Balaena glacialis,* and when the whalers discovered them, they set about with their usual dispatch to wipe them out.

When Captain Cook left Hawaii (on his third and final voyage) in February of 1778, he headed northwest toward the North American continent. He passed the Strait of Juan de Fuca in the night, and fetched up a week later in a place that he called Nootka Sound, where he needed to repair the *Resolution.* (The sound was actually on the island that would be named for George Vancouver, but Cook believed he had landed on the mainland.) The Nootka Indians were a whaling society, hunting the right whales, gray whales, and humpbacks that frequented the waters of northwestern North America.

Cook and his crews spent almost a month fixing their ships and trading with the natives, and then they weighed anchor and headed north until the coastline trended sharply to the west. The *Resolution* was leaking badly again, so he put into an anchorage he named Sandwich Sound, but which eventually became known as Prince William Sound. From there Cook traced the coast of Alaska until he encountered the Aleutians, and when they found a passage (the Unalaska Pass), they entered the Bering Sea. They crossed the Arctic Circle in mid-August, and although one of Cook's missions was to meet with Lieutenant Richard Pickersgill (who commanded the frigate *Lion* and was supposed to rendezvous with

Cook in an attempt to locate the Northwest Passage), he found himself almost trapped in the ice, and headed back to the Hawaiian Islands, and his rendezvous with death.

Captain George Vancouver was ordered by the Admiralty to sail from England in 1791 to explore the area previously visited by Cook. He sailed around the great island that now bears his name in the spring of 1792, but he failed to find the great river that the American Robert Gray finally located in 1792, and named "Columbia" for his ship. This discovery enabled the Americans to lay claim to Oregon and Washington. (When the east and west coasts of Canada were mapped, it appeared that the elusive Northwest Passage might finally be navigated, but it would be another hundred years before the Norwegian Roald Amundsen, in the *Gjoa,* actually accomplished the journey by ship.)

As Cook and Vancouver were exploring the Pacific for King and Country, other Englishmen were in the same ocean, looking for whales. Samuel Enderby's London whaler *Emelia* had rounded the Horn in 1789, and with that, the vast Pacific was officially opened to whaling. (In the remotest reaches of the South Pacific, British ships were transporting convicts to the penal colonies of Botany Bay, Van Diemen's Land, and Norfolk Island, and finding that this end of the world too had a profusion of heretofore unreported whales.) The War of Independence liberated the thirteen American colonies from British rule, but possession of the remainder of the continent was still in dispute. The Spanish explorers Juan Perez and Francisco Bodega y Quadra said they had been close enough to Vancouver to claim it, and the Frenchman Jean François de la Pérouse had also patrolled the coasts. (The Anglo-Spanish conflict was expanding in the South Pacific as well, where British whaleships were denied access to Spanish ports on the west coast of South America.) Reports of a plentitude of whales off the northwest coast of America attracted the attention of Pitt the Younger, England's prime minister, and he abetted the drafting of the Nootka Convention of 1790, which, among other things, opened Spanish waters in the Pacific Northwest to British whaleships. For complicated political and economic reasons, however, the British never availed themselves of this opportunity, and left the field open to the French and the Americans.

Until about 1835, the whales of the northeastern Pacific were safe from the predations of commercial whalers. Then, when it appeared that the sperm whale fishery was declining, the whalers remembered that there were whales off Vancouver Island. The first documented whaling voyage to the Northwest Coast was made by the French whaleship *Gange,* under Captain Narcisse Chaudière. To the eternal confusion of whaling historians, a ship with almost the same name appears regularly in the Yankee records.* Tradition holds that the first New Englander on the Northwest Grounds was a Nantucketer named Barzillai Folger, in the whaleship *Ganges.* Folger was actually looking for sperm whales, but he found not the cachalots that had so enticed and enriched his fellow islanders, but rather a wholly unexpected population of right whales.

The proud Nantucketer eschewed the lowly right whales, and instead headed south to Baja California, where he hunted sperm whales, the only beasts worthy of the thrust of the Nantucketers' irons. It was therefore Narcisse Chaudière by whose hand the first right whales would die on the Northwest Coast. The crew of Chaudière's *Gange* killed seven right whales in 1835, and according to contemporaneous reports, they were among the largest right whales ever recorded. Webb quotes a report of a whale that was "97 feet long and 84 feet in Surcumferance," but these dimensions are probably as accurate as the spelling.†

No less a whaling historian than Herman Melville wrote about these right whales, but not in *Moby-Dick.* In *Mardi,* the novel he wrote in 1849—two years before the publication of his magnum opus—he wrote this sentence:

But this much let me say: the Right Whale on the Nor'-West Coast, in chill and dismal fogs, the sullen inert monsters rafting the sea all round like Hartz forest logs on the Rhine, and submitting to the harpoon like half-stunned bullocks to the Knife; this horrid and indecent Right whaling, I say, compared to the spirited hunt for

*In the International Whaling Commission's 1986 *Special Report* on right whales, Richard Kugler wrote: "Scammon (1874), citing a Nantucket newspaper, attributes this initial [Alaskan] voyage to an American whaleship *Ganges,* an error repeated by Starbuck (1878), Clark (1887) and most subsequent writers on the subject. . . . What can be said from the present evidence is that the *Gange* of Le Havre was the first known whaleship to take a right whale on the Northwest Coast."

†Randall Reeves, an acknowledged expert on the right whale, believes that "the absolute maximum length is around eighteen meters (fifty-nine feet). . . . They are extremely fat, and may weigh considerably more than fifty tons."

the gentlemanly Cachalot in southern and more genial seas, is the butchery of the white bears upon blank Greenland icebergs to Zebra hunting in Caffraria, where the lively quarry bounds before you through leafy glades.

Melville never saw the Northwest Coast, although he may have spotted right whales south of the Equator. He jumped ship—the New Bedford whaler *Acushnet*—at Nukahiva in the Marquesas in 1842. Without the services of seaman Melville, the *Acushnet* went right whaling off the Northwest Coast in 1843 and 1844.

The whaling that Melville called "horrid and indecent" was considered unpleasantly dangerous by many of his contemporaries. The whale that the New England-

landers had defined as the "right" whale to kill because it was so easy to hunt had somehow mutated into a vicious and uncooperative killer on the Northwest Grounds. In the 1843 log of the *Lucy Ann*, out of Wilmington, Captain John Martin describes one of his many encounters with right whales off Kamchatka:

in the forenoon lowered after Right whales, the Bow boat fastened & set them spouting blood. he was decidedly the most vicious we have encountered since we left the capes of Delaware. while the boat was hauling on to him, he struck Mr. Kendrick on the head & knocked him overboard and he was considered lost forever but one of the boats crew saw him under water & hauled him into the boat where he lay for some time senseless. . . . These Northwest whales are more knowing than the

The ship *Kutusoff* on the northwestern whaling grounds in 1842, cutting-in a right whale. The upper jaw with its baleen attached is being hoisted aboard. Print by Benjamin Russell, the New Bedford painter who (with Caleb Purrington) immortalized the voyage of the *Kutusoff* in a 1,275-foot panorama.

Whales of New Holland they can see a boat at a greater distance & their hearing seems to be more acute. They will let a boat get within almost darting distance & then turn flukes & go down they sometimes keep at a regular distance from the boat & when the crew urge her through the water at their utmost & get too near for his safety off he goes like a flash of lightening to windward & you might as well try to catch old Scratch.

The haunts of the right whales were poorly documented during this period; it would appear that the combination of the Yankee whalers' proprietary interests and Frenchmen's vagueness about recording their voyages has given us only a shadowy idea about where the right whales might have been found. (In his study of the harvest of various whale species from 1785 to 1913, Townsend shows not a single right whale taken south of Queen Charlotte Strait, at the northern tip of Vancouver Island.) The bark *Superior,* out of New London, struck 56 right whales north of Queen Charlotte Sound in 1841, and brought in 26. Captain McLane returned home with 2,000 barrels of oil and 20,000 pounds of baleen. Besides the American and French whalers in the 1850s, there were also Canadian, Dutch, German and Prussian ships working the Northwest Grounds. (The merchants of Bremen handled most of the imports of whale oil into Europe, so it was natural for the Germanic burghers to outfit their own whalers and thus eliminate the middleman.)

In his discussion of the "Right Whale of the Northwestern Coast," Scammon clearly differentiates this species from the bowhead, and writes, "In former years, the Right Whales were found on the coast of Oregon, and occasionally in large numbers; but their chief resort was upon what is termed the 'Kodiak Ground,' the limits of which extended from Vancouver's Island northwestward to the Aleutian Chain. . . . In the southern portion of the Behring Sea, also upon the coast of Kamchatka, and in the Okhotsk Sea, they congregated in large numbers." By the time Scammon wrote his book (1874), the right whales of the Northwest Coast had virtually disappeared. He concludes the chapter with ". . . the whalemen of the North-western Coast made such havoc among these colossal animals (which were regarded as the most vicious of their kind), as to have nearly extirpated them, or driven them to some unknown feeding-ground."

Today there are hardly any right whales left in the North Pacific. Starbuck reports that in 1839 there were 2 whaling ships north of 50°N in the Pacific; by 1843 there were 292. Between 1840 and 1850, there were as many as 400 whaleships working the Kodiak Ground, and while not all of them were successful, they might have taken upward of 2,000 whales per year. American whalers certainly utilized the Okhotsk Sea for their predations on right whales, and Townsend's charts are thick with dots on both sides of the Kamchatka Peninsula, through the Kuril Islands, and into the Sea of Japan. The Japanese were hunting right whales as early as the year 1600. Moreover, Soviet whaling historians now acknowledge that Russian whalers took both right whales and bowheads in the Sea of Okhotsk from 1799 to 1913, and one Soviet cetologist estimates that Russian and American whalers killed as many as 20,000 whales during that period. (A summary of catch figures for the region by the French whaling historian Thierry du Pasquier shows that 8,044 right whales were taken in the North Pacific between 1845 and 1849.) It is not known if the eastern and western North Pacific right whale populations were the same stock. There is the possibility that they were spread out all over the cold coasts of Alaska, Siberia, Kamchatka and Japan—and the open oceans in between—but now that they are gone, we will never know. Like its relatives elsewhere in both hemispheres, the Northwestern right whale was the most available of all species to kill.

In less than ten years, what had seemed an inexhaustible supply of right whales in the Northwest had turned into a scarcity. Whalers had to stretch their seasons into the fall, and by September, the weather threatened to close down the whaling altogether. By 1846, the busiest year in American whaling history, whalers "on the northwest" were in trouble; they were running out of whales. Another twenty years would have to pass before the whalers would find a way to kill the plentiful blue and fin whales which they also spotted from their crow's nests; for now, these leviathans spouted in peace.

The whales were further protected by the discovery of gold in California in 1848. Ships that called at San Francisco were likely to lose their entire crews, as gold fever enticed men to set off into the hills on their own. Hoop skirts came back into fashion, but since there were no more right whales, the whalers sought the bowhead in the Bering Sea for baleen to make the hoops. The United States found itself involved in a major internal war in 1861 (which was responsible for the destruction of many whaleships), and when the war was over, the price of whale oil fell sharply. (That there were still rare right whales to kill off the Northwest Coast was documented by the trying-out of a gigantic specimen taken on the Kodiak Grounds by the *General Pike* in 1861. That whale made 274 barrels.) President Andrew Johnson bought the whale-rich waters of Alaska from Russia in 1867, along with half a million square miles of mountains, ice and trees.

Workmen posing with and on a gigantic right whale, taken at Kodiak, Alaska. Written on the photograph are the following dimensions: "Ht. 15 ft, width 22 ft, length 65 ft, Approx wt. 250 tons."

Interlude: A Short Digression on Fashion

IT IS DIFFICULT to determine if the exigencies of fashion sent men to the Arctic to hunt whales, or if while hunting them already for their oil, they found that the baleen plates were suitable for sale to the manufacturers of corsets and thereby affected the course of fashion. Whatever the sequence of events, whales and women were to be associated for over three hundred years in a manner that would bring death to thousands of whales, and in Dame Fashion's name, pain and suffering to thousands of women. Of course, the whale hunters themselves also suffered and sometimes died in the search for baleen, but not as frequently as the whales. Dr. Felix May-nard, discussing the dangers of whaling in 1837, wrote, "O women! How dearly are the bones of your corsets paid for!"

Animals have always died for mankind; we have killed them for food and for their skins, and for everything else from ritual sacrifices to sport. The death of the whales so that women could cinch in their waistlines, however, has to be one of the few cases in which people killed dumb animals in order to make themselves uncomfortable. "Beautiful," yes—however that term was to be defined at different times and in different places—but undeniably uncomfortable. Besides beauty, women rationalized their discomfort by claiming that it was healthful to be laced into tight, unforgiving cinctures, lest their bodies be unsupported and thus deformed. They strapped themselves in, and they strapped their daughters in, and no matter who complained about the deleterious effects of these crushing, painful undergarments (often it was the women themselves), they persisted in wearing them. A mid-nineteenth-century corset-maker named Roxey Caplin summed it up for all her discomforted sisters-in-bone when she wrote, "Ladies must and will wear stays in spite of all the medical men of Europe. The strong and the perfect feel the benefit of using them, and to the weak and delicate and imperfect, they are absolutely indispensable."

Records left by the Basque whalers are virtually nonexistent, so we have very little idea what became of the baleen from the right whales that they hunted to extinction in European and Canadian waters. Whalebone, which comes from the mouths of whales (and is not really bone, but rather keratin, the stuff of hair and fingernails), was probably first used to make whips and supports for headdresses. It could also be shredded and used for the plumes of helmets and other decorations, but it was not until sometime in the late Middle Ages that its true usefulness was recognized. At the same time that the British and Dutch whalers began their intensive hunt of the Greenland whale in the eastern Arctic, the feeding equipment of these animals would become one of the most valuable commodities in Europe.

Around the beginning of the sixteenth century, whalebone "finnes" were becoming an important part of European commerce, since the silhouette of the female figure was beginning to change. *Corse-tières*—or originally, blacksmiths—made corsets (from the French *cors* or *corps,* which meant "body"; the word "corsets" being derived from the paired, stiffened pieces of linen that were known as a "pair of bodies," subsequently shortened to *bodice*) to enable women to change their outward appearance. First there was the *busk,* a simple strip of wood or bone which was a component of the stomacher on the front of the bodice. Further shaping was accomplished with corsets stiffened by bands of ivory, wood, bone or even iron, but baleen provided an immensely versatile material. It was flexible and strong; it could be heated and molded to any shape; and because of its vertical grain, it could be cut into any width. The unadorned lines of medieval clothing were evolving into molded shapes, specifically those that emphasized the waist in women. (Curiously, this concern for small waists was an echo of already existing men's fashions. According to Nora Waugh, the author of *Corsets and Crinolines,* "from medieval times men had worn {a bodice} under their outer garments; it had been known by various names— cotte, gambeson, doublet, pourpoint, etc." By the sixteenth century, it was called a "waistcoat.")

Fashion was introduced into the Western world, whereby women would compete to display their superiority over one another. In *Seeing Through Clothes,* Anne Hollander defines "fashion" as "constant perceptible fluctuations of visual design, created out of the combined forms of tailored dress and body," and then comments that "true fashion, ongoing in the west since about 1300, demanded reshaping of the body-and-clothes unit, so that some areas of the body are compressed, others padded, some kinds of movement are restricted, others liberated, and later perhaps all these are reversed." The competition in clothing might take the form of richness of fabric, expensive jewels, current designs, or exaggerated shapes. Perhaps the most prevalent of all fashion statements—then as now—is the youthful feminine figure. In the seventeenth century, however, the idealized figure was rather different from what it is today. Nobody saw legs or ankles (they would not be revealed until early in the twentieth century), and the lower body was to be covered by a succession of bulky skirts, crinolines, trains and bustles. The upper torso was the place where women could show

The head of a bowhead whale. The whale is on its back, so the upper jaw is at the bottom of the photograph, and the baleen, usually contained within the huge mouth, is outside the lower jaw.

off. The primary location for this exposition was the waist (and to a much lesser extent, the bosom, as necklines bobbed up and down from throat to cleavage), and for the next four centuries women would attempt to show themselves as having the smallest waist possible. Having been released from the sexlessness of shapeless, rough shifts, women discovered that their bodies could be exaggerated by the employment of artificial devices. By 1650 necklines dropped, exposing more of the bust, the exaggeration of sleeves and hips commenced, and the waist began its ineluctable diminution.

It is believed that the corset was originally introduced from Spain by the English Queen Mary, who married Philip II of Spain in 1554. Mary Tudor, known as "Bloody Mary," was a most unlikely stylesetter. The daughter of Henry VIII and Catherine of Aragon, she was declared a bastard when her father renounced her mother to marry Anne Boleyn. Although she was the first queen to rule England in her own right—from 1553 to 1558—she was better known for her ruthless persecution of Protestants. During her reign, whalebone rods—probably gathered by Basque whalers—were sewn into a garment

of linen and were fastened with ties front and back. Girls of ten often were started on these painful garments, to ensure that their waists would not grow as they did.

Catherine de Médicis (1519–89), the daughter of Lorenzo, married Henry, duc d'Orleans, in 1533, and subsequently became queen of France and the mother of no fewer than three future kings. She was held to be responsible for the infamous St. Bartholomew's Day Massacre in August 1572, where several thousand Huguenots were slaughtered. Despite all the intrigue that surrounded her—or perhaps because of it—Catherine was enormously influential in fashions of food, architecture and dress. Her court was an "earthly paradise," where chivalry reigned and ladies glittered. It was during her reign and regency that the haute cuisine of France first flowered; tables were decorated with the silver and gold of Benvenuto Cellini; and the queen introduced elaborate court ballets. Many of the great chateaus of the Loire Valley were built at this time (although several of them were built for her husband's mistress, Diane de Poitiers), and what one writer called "the most masochistic period in the history of women's undergarments" was ushered in. No beauty herself, Catherine designed her own clothes (rather unusual for a queen), but more significantly, she decreed that the waist should be minuscule. She prescribed the ideal waist at thirteen inches.

Across the Channel, the Puritans had separated Charles I from his head. Under the regime of Oliver Cromwell, the Lord Protector, one would assume that the fripperies associated with the Crown would be condemned, but the "body discipline" associated with corsets was encouraged by the Puritans, and despite the lack of ornament and severity of cut and color of their outer garments, the boned corsets still lingered beneath.

Not everyone approved of the strictures and pressures of fashion. (The critical epithets "straight-laced" and "staid" were introduced at this time.) In his 1653 *Artificial Changeling*, John Bulwer wrote,

Another foolish affectation there is in young Virgins, though grown big enough to be wiser; but they are led blindfold by a custome to a fashion pernitious beyond imagination; who thinking a Slender-Waste a great beauty, strive all they possibly can by streight-lacing themselves, to attain a wand-like smalnesse of Waste, never thinking themselves fine enough until they can span the Waste. By which deadly artifice they reduce their Breasts into such streights, that they soon purchase a stinking breath; and while they ignorantly affect an august or narrow Breast, and to that end by strong compulsion shut up their Wastes in a Whale-bone prison or little-ease, they open the door to Consumptions, and a withering rottenesse.

Throughout Europe—and America, by this time—fashions differed markedly from country to country. It is obviously impossible to talk about "European" styles of dress, since the French, the Dutch, the Germans, the English and the Spanish were all affected by disparate influences and thus looked quite different. The Dutch of the sixteenth century, even though they were the chief suppliers of whalebone, were not much given to the wearing of tightly laced bodices. It is also unlikely that the early American settlers spent much of their time lacing themselves up when they could be praying or working. Nonetheless, to a greater or lesser extent, the styles of Western Europe in the sixteenth and seventeenth centuries were universally marked by the feminine compulsion to maintain a small waist, and "whalebone prisons" would persist until the end of the nineteenth century.

Cromwell died in 1658, and was succeeded by his son, Richard. The younger Cromwell showed none of the aptitude of his father, and was dismissed in 1660. Charles II then returned from his nine-year exile in France, and brought with him all the fashions of France: ribbons, furbelows, silks and velvets again adorned the women of England, and to augment the new fashions, longer corsets were introduced. The foundation was still made of layers of heavy linen, stiffened with paste or glue, with the whalebones inserted in between the layers. It was usually laced up the back, and fully-boned (*baleiné*) or half-boned (*demi-baleiné*). The long narrow lines of furniture and architecture were echoed in the clothes; women tried to lengthen their silhouettes even more by adding more seams and angling the insertion of the whalebone stays to taper the waistline.

By the second half of the seventeenth century, the rounded forms of the Baroque style made way for the finer lines of the style of the court of Louis XIV (1638–1715). Never before had there been such an encompassing influence on fashion throughout Europe, and whatever was worn—or said, or done—at Versailles almost immediately became *de rigueur* throughout the upper classes of other capitals. (As soon as the Sun King began to lose his hair and took to wearing a wig, his whole entourage immediately acquired hairpieces, and shortly thereafter, all of Europe's gentry were bewigged.) The bodice, which had previously been worn beneath the outer garments, suddenly appeared over the blouse and petticoat and, sumptuously decorated, became known as the *corps baleiné*. Whalebone had replaced all other materials as the primary stiffener of corsets, and with a few remissions, would retain that predominance for another two centuries.

Around the turn of the century, the hoop petticoat was introduced (some think from England), which would exaggerate the hips, thus making the waist look smaller by comparison. The great enlargement of skirts defined women's styles for the next hundred years, and of course, the material used to make the skirt hoops was whalebone. It was extremely awkward to wear such a large, cumbersome object, but at least the women were not in pain. It is not a little peculiar that women had to suffer—and whales had to die—in order that the former might be so painfully inconvenienced. Perhaps the phrase "suffer to be beautiful" was coined at this time, since there is no question that the bodices, boned stays, and corsets were brutally uncomfortable. (It is almost impossible to imagine what it must have felt like to wear a corset made completely of iron, or a bodice in which the stays were made of wood. For the practice of squeezing normal-sized waists to a handspan, the word "torture" does not seem inappropriate.)

According to costume historian Aileen Ribeiro, "The eighteenth century produced perhaps the greatest contribution to civilized living in Europe, costume being an equal in terms of style and luxury of materials to the best of the decorative arts." It is not the intention here to chronicle the various permutations of periwigs, mobcaps and mantuas, but the emphasis on fashion, particularly in England, where whalebone corsets were fundamental to the narrow-waisted styles of the times, would be directly responsible for the slaughter of thousands of whales. (During the eighteenth century, the whalers' quarry was changing from right whales and bowheads to sperm whales, which were hunted exclusively for their oil. Unlike whale oil, however, baleen could be stored indefinitely, as long as gnawing rats were kept away from it, and more important, it could be reused.)

With fabrics that were mostly imported from France, the British at court wore a heavily boned bodice, with an elaborately trimmed skirt and train. By the middle of the century (a period described in other disciplines as *rococo*), under the far-reaching influence of Madame de Pompadour, mistress of Louis XV, the bell-shaped hoop skirt gained acceptance, with hoops fashioned of cane or whalebone. (Hoops were apparently introduced into England as early as 1710; in *The Spectator* Sir Roger de Coverly observed that a woman in such a "blown-up petticoat" was obviously pregnant.) Hoops became smaller toward the end of the century, but regardless of what happened below the waistline, above it the bodice was still an integral part of the costume of fashionable women. "The shape of the 1770s and 1780s," writes Ribeiro, "required a tight, firmly waisted bodice, the skirt draped and padded at the back, and the bosom puffed out with a starched muslin handkerchief." (In the latter half of the eighteenth century, publications

such as the *Lady's Magazine* contained "fashion plates," which were illustrations created specifically for the purpose of informing women of the latest styles.)

In England toward the end of the eighteenth century, women's hairstyles became wildly exaggerated, with all manner of decorations, including ostrich feathers affixed to huge hats with sweeping brims and headdresses crowned with the most fantastic decorations: a ship in full sail, a windmill with farm animals, a full garden of flowers. To accompany these excesses the hoop skirts were replaced by an exaggeration of the rump, a style that was eventually to reach fruition in the bustle, and by a puffed-out bodice, which gave the women a sort of pouter-pigeon appearance. By the 1790s, the *Morning Herald* wrote:

The bosom, which nature planted at the bottom of her chest, is pushed up by means of wadding and whalebone to a station so near her chin that in a very full subject that feature is sometimes lost between the invading mounds. The stays—or coat of mail—must be laced as tight as strength can draw the cord. . . .

Georgiana Cavendish, Duchess of Devonshire, wrote the following letter to a friend in 1778:

My dear Louisa, you will laugh when I tell you, that poor Winifred, who was reduced to be my gentlewoman's gentlewoman, broke two laces in endeavoring to draw my new French stays close. You know I am naturally small at bottom but now you might literally span me. You never saw such a doll. Then, they are so intolerably wide across the breast, that my arms are absolutely sore with them; and my sides so pinched!—But it is the "ton"; and pride feels no pain. It is with these sentiments the ladies of the present age heal their wounds; to be admired, is sufficient balsam.

The Duchess of Devonshire was obviously not an ordinary woman; she was regarded as one of the leaders of fashion in England, and was one of the first to adopt the chemise of plain white muslin with a sash belt, a style quickly copied by all ladies after 1785. The poorer classes obviously did not dress in expensive silks and velvets, but they fared little better insofar as corsets were concerned. William Hogarth's drawings of the gin-guzzling trollops of London's streets show the same cinched-in waists as the fashionable portraits of Kneller, Gainsborough and Reynolds.

One of the major disruptions of the corset business was the revolution in France. Prior to 1789, French women of fashion wore the most elaborate silks and satins, but when printed cottons were imported from the East, the richness of fabrics began to decline. During the Terror, it was most inadvisable to wear anything that even remotely suggested royalty, but after the royalist heads rolled, fashions changed to more egalitarian themes, and the brief reversion to classical lines began. The so-called Grecian look was now the ideal, with a soft dress falling from a waistline just below high, rounded breasts. The Directoire period, named for the five *directeurs* who governed France from 1795 to 1799, was characterized by chemises with long sleeves and V neck-

An illustration from an 1838 American publication shows the fashionably compressed waistline of the period.

lines; the waist was not emphasized. The dawn of the nineteenth century saw the rise of Napoleon's influence, which, following his expedition to Egypt, included a new wave of interest in things Oriental. It would appear that the day of the whaleboned body had passed, but the fluctuations of fashion, combined with the steadfast craving for a curvaceous figure, doomed the Empire look and brought back the waist.

Costume historian James Laver has written that by 1822, "The waist, which had been high for a quarter of a century, now resumed its normal position, and when this happens it inevitably becomes tighter and tighter. As a result, the corset once more became an essential element of female dress, even for small girls." By the 1840s, the bright colors, exaggerated hats, and wide hips that blossomed in response to the passing of the Directoire style were passé, and fashions took on a drab look, perhaps because of Queen Victoria, the paradigm of British Empire fashion from 1837 to 1901. As an example of her influence, Victoria's preoccupation with Balmoral, her castle in the Scottish highlands, resulted in a nationwide use of Scotch plaids in dresses. After Prince Albert's death in 1861, she wore various permutations of mourning dress for forty years, which affected British fashion even more substantially.

Petticoats proliferated during the middle of the nineteenth century, and eventually became so plentiful and cumbersome that in 1856 they were replaced by the crinoline. This was a hooped petticoat, worn under the skirt, the whalebone hoops supported by tapes. (It was introduced by the Empress Eugénie, the wife of Napoleon III, on the occasion of their visit to Windsor Castle.) As the skirts continued to grow, it soon became apparent that their wearers were dominating any space—or any piece of furniture—they happened to occupy. One response to this was Mrs. Amelia Bloomer's invention of the full-length pantaloons that bear her name, but the *beau monde* rejected this idea with a passion all out of proportion to its practical purposes, and it would be another fifty years before women would wear bifurcated outer garments on their legs, and then only for cycling. (Until the death of Victoria, women on horseback rode sidesaddle and wore skirts that covered their legs, the saddle, and most of the horse.)

Accept, dear Girl, this busk from me;
Carved by my humble hand.
I took it from a Sperm Whale's Jaw,
One thousand miles from land!
In many a gale,
Has been the Whale,
In which this bone did rest,
His time is past,
His bone at last,
Must now support thy breast.

These verses appear on a piece of carved and inscribed whalebone; a flat piece of ivory about fourteen inches long and an inch and a half wide, it looks rather like a giant tongue-depressor. The reference to the sperm whale is correct. Although most "whalebone" was obtained from the baleen whales, the huge lower jaw of the cachalot provided ivory that could be carved into various items. Embedded in that very lower jaw were the peglike teeth that the scrimshanders decorated—often with pictures of their cinched-in sweethearts—but that is another story.

Although men had been killing the whales on the high seas to provide the whalebone for madame's corsets and hoops, they were very little involved in the design of the clothing that incorporated their hard-won products. Women seemed to choose the fashions of the times—if indeed anyone could be said to "choose" the constantly evolving shape of waistlines, necklines and silhouettes—based superficially on what they regarded as stylish, and more specifically on the pervading ethic of the times. In her *Language of Clothes,* Alison Lurie has written, "These shifts in costume are not arbitrary or whimsical, as some writers on costume have claimed, but the outward and visible sign of profound social and cultural alterations."

Victoria herself was a tiny woman, less than five feet tall, and while certainly no weakling, she chose to appear helpless. Before she grew into the dumpy, unamused caricature that she became in her later years, she had "girlish breasts and a narrow waist, large liquid eyes, no nose or chin to speak of and a tiny rosebud mouth." Attempts by Englishwomen of the 1840s and '50s to emulate their sovereign led an entire nation of otherwise robust women to project an image of frailty. Lurie writes:

Clothes metamorphosed to suit this new ideal. Skirts dropped to the floor again, and the huge puffed sleeves

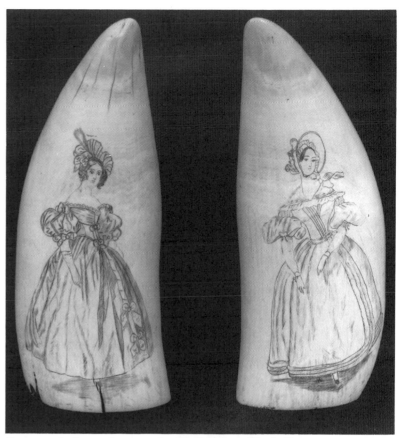

Sperm whale teeth carved with fashionable ladies.

sank weakly towards the wrists and then deflated entirely; neat tucks and braid replaced the flyaway bows and frills of the early 1830s. The look of childish high spirits vanished; instead dresses were cut to accentuate the submissive slope of the dropped shoulders. In these clothes the women walked and moved less vigorously. The longer corsets and heavier skirts weighed them down, while deep collars, tight lace fichus and bulky fringed shawls made it difficult for the fashionable female to raise her arms very far, emphasizing her charming helplessness. . . . The sides of her hat descended and closed in on her face, becoming a poke bonnet that shut out the view on both sides like a horse's blinkers. This inconvenient form of headdress graphically announced that its wearer was too delicate and sensitive to bear the gaze of the multitude. At the same time, it perfectly expressed the idea that a nice woman would naturally have a limited and narrow view of the world, that her glance would not stray aside as she passed through life.

We tend to regard Queen Victoria as a dour, domineering woman, and therefore the childlike in-

In 1871, the year the whaling fleet was lost in the Arctic, *Harper's Bazaar* published this illustration of an "opera toilette," showing the fashions for which the whalers were to have provided the whalebone supports.

nocence that she communicated to her subjects seems contradictory.

Prince Albert opened the Great Exhibition at the Crystal Palace in Hyde Park in 1851. Among the exhibits was one devoted to the "Hygienic" corsets of Roxey Caplin. Mme. Caplin wrote a book to accompany her exhibition of corsets, and it was in the introduction to this book that she wrote that "ladies must and will wear stays. . . ." She recognized that corsets in the past were "always painful and generally injurious," but also that "there must surely be some fascination in this article, or some latent conviction that, after all, it is a good thing, or it would have been banished out of the world long ago." Would that it were so. Mme. Caplin (the wife of a doctor) invented various corsets for little girls, teen-

agers, adults, and even pregnant women. It would be approximately another half-century before women would finally reject the injurious tight-lacing garments, but before the corsets (and the whales) ended, there would be one last campaign, where the waists would be pulled in to absurd proportions once again, and the whales that provided the bone would be driven to the brink of extinction.

In the decade that incorporated the American Civil War, there was an enormous emphasis on tiny waists. In *Gone with the Wind*, Scarlett O'Hara (who had "a seventeen-inch waist, the smallest in three counties") prepares for a ball: "Scarlett obeyed, bracing herself and catching a firm hold of one of the bedposts. Mammy pulled and jerked vigorously and, as the tiny circumference of whalebone-girdled waist grew smaller, a proud, fond look came into her eyes." In an 1867 letter quoted (but not attributed to anyone) by Nora Waugh in *Corsets and Crinolines*, we read of a girl of fifteen who was placed in a fashionable school in London, where "it was the custom for the waists of the pupils to be reduced one inch per month until they were what the lady principal considered small enough. When I left school at seventeen, my waist measured only thirteen inches, it having been formerly twenty-three inches. Every morning one of the maids used to come to assist us to dress, and a governess superintended, to see that the corsets were drawn as tight as possible. After the first few minutes every morning I felt no pain, and the only ill effects apparently were occasional headaches and loss of appetite."

Of course, the medical profession was opposed to this lunacy, but to no avail. In an issue of *The Lancet*, the British medical journal, for 1868, the following plaintive note appears:

Our attention has been directed to a recent number of a popular journal, in which the advocates for Tight-lacing ventilate their erroneous views. It is certainly much to be regretted that any Englishwoman would torture herself or her children by employing tight or unyielding stays or belts. The mischief produced by such a practice can hardly be overestimated. It tends gradually to displace the most important organs of the body, while, by compressing them, it must from the first, interfere with their functions. The grounds upon which Tight-lacing has been recommended are diametrically opposed to the teachings of anatomy and physiology, not to say common sense.

By the 1870s whalebone was becoming scarcer and scarcer—it was in 1871 that New England's entire Arctic whaling fleet was crushed in the ice and had to be abandoned—and corset-makers began to experiment with other materials, such as steel, cane, reeds and fibers. (The English corset-makers of Symington and Co. were reduced to collecting discarded umbrellas for their whalebone ribs.) Two American physicians named Warner developed machinery for shaping plant fibers into cords and then sizing and tempering them to create "an unbreakable exclusive boning material" that they called *coraline.* The son of one of the brothers Warner developed a method of coating flat spring steel so as to render it rustproof; and so, despite the absence of whalebone, women would strap themselves into fiercely restrictive undergarments for another twenty years. The Gay Nineties were to hear the last gasp of the wasp-waisted.

One does not normally associate Oscar Wilde with "Rational Dress," but it was the celebrated velvet jacket, knee breeches and flowing tie that he wore on his visit to America that symbolized this movement. Established in 1881 to protest the tight and deforming corsets worn by women, this group, the Aesthetes, wore clothes influenced by the pre-Raphaelites, and although they were ridiculed for their nonmainstream ideas (as in Gilbert and Sullivan's *Patience*), they were eventually influential in liberating women from their whalebone prisons.

Of the *fin de siècle* shapes, Nora Waugh wrote, "the heavier corset of the end of the century exaggerated this [the narrow waist] still further until the female anatomy was becoming seriously distorted and the women's health affected." Some corsetières, such as Mme. Gaches-Sarraute, of Paris, designed less painful devices, but as always, exaggeration crept back in and the desire to retain the small waist resulted in the famous S-curve, where "the bust billowed out over the low front, and the superfluous abdominal flesh, pressed flat by the heavy front busk, swelled out at the sides on the hips, and on the behind." Charles Dana Gibson gave his name to the girls who exemplified this style, and of them, Alison Lurie wrote, ". . . the ideal female continued to become larger and older. Her size was a sign of increasing public visibility; in growing numbers now women were going to college, working for a living and cam-

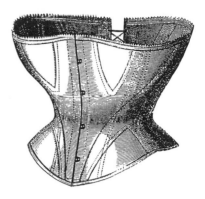

Harper's Bazaar for 1869 showed the "short satin jean corset," which looks not unlike the cuirass from a suit of armor.

High fashion for 1882 demanded a tiny waist, and corsets like this (shown front and back) kept milady cinched in.

paigning for legal and political equality. But even when she remained at home as a showpiece, the late Victorian and Edwardian woman was an impressive creature physically."

Women's fashions continued to develop toward more comfortable and less confining undergarments. It is tempting to follow the evolution of fashion from the beginning of the twentieth century to the present, but by the first decade of this century, there was no market for whalebone, because the whales that had provided it were virtually extinct. Coincident with the disappearance of the bone, so long the mainstay of the stay industry, it appeared that women were beginning to give up the battle, or at least to relax a little. In *The Queen* for January 1901, we find this note:

It is rather curious to find that the crusade against the corset that doctors and physiologists generally have waged for so long should be crowned with success. Not that there is any prospect of the corset being abolished; that is neither possible nor desirable; but the garment has been practically revolutionized so that it supports the figure without compressing it.

As an indication of the magnitude of the whalebone industry, it was recorded that the American whale fisheries of the nineteenth century landed some 90 million pounds of whalebone, worth $450 million. Other materials were developed for the pur-

poses of restraining and reshaping women's bodies, but with these innovations, our interest in the cetological foundations of the foundation industry must conclude.

It is uncustomary to think about whale products being used in a destructive fashion, since we tend to think of whales being killed for oil or meat, which are useful things. If you were a style-conscious woman who lived in Europe from the sixteenth century to the twentieth, or in America from the eighteenth to the twentieth, however, you were painfully aware of the harmful uses to which whale products could be put. By 1913, however, another, even more destructive rationale would be found for killing whales. One of the components of whale oil is glycerine, and glycerine is used in the manufacture of dynamite. Many of the explosions that echoed through the darkened skies of France and Belgium during the First World War were fueled by the fat of whales.

Charles Dana Gibson immortalized the wasp-waisted, hourglass figure of the "Gibson Girls" in his popular drawings of the 1890s.

FIVE

THE SPERM WHALE FISHERY

American Sperm Whaling

TWENTY-FIVE MILES south of Cape Cod is a little island, fifteen miles long and no more than three miles wide. It was discovered in 1602 by Bartholomew Gosnold, a mariner in the service of Walter Raleigh. In 1641 Thomas Mayhew purchased the island from the Plymouth Colony for thirty pounds and two beaver hats. In 1659 Thomas Macy and Edward Starbuck bought the island from Mayhew, and brought over the "Twenty Purchasers," Quakers who needed a foothold in New England, away from the persecution of the mainland Puritans. Families with names like Hussey, Gardner, Swain, Chase and Folger put down roots here, and since the island's soil was too poor to support farming, they recognized the possibilities of starting a whale fishery. (They were encouraged in that endeavor by the early appearance of a right whale that wandered into the harbor and swam around for three days until it died.) In their attempts to learn how to capture whales, they first invited one James Lopar to instruct them in 1672, and later Ichabod Paddock arrived to serve as their tutor. The island, of course, was Nantucket, and it was to become the epicenter of America's whaling industry for more than a century.

The story of Christopher Hussey's accidental encounter with a school of sperm whales has been told so often that it probably no longer matters whether it really happened. In 1712 Captain Hussey was cruising the Massachusetts coast (there were still right whales to be caught at that time), when an unexpected storm blew him out to sea. When the clouds cleared, he saw the spouts of whales, but they were forward-angled blows, not the vertical, paired plumes of the right whales. Hussey managed to capture one of these unusual animals and towed it back to Nantucket. Instead of baleen plates, it had ivory teeth in its underslung lower jaw, and in its head was a great reservoir of clear amber oil, which solidified to wax when exposed to the air.

This was not the first sperm whale the New Englanders had ever seen, but it was probably the first one they had ever intentionally captured. In 1672, according to a report by John Josselyn, Gent., "a *Sperma Ceti Whale* or two were cast upon the shore not far from *Boston* in *Massachusetts Bay* which being cut up into small pieces, and boiled in Cauldrons, yielded plenty of Oyl; the Oyl put up in Hogsheads, and stow'd into Cellars for some time." Although we

Sperm whalers either sailed or rowed up behind their quarry; either way, they tried to be as quiet as possible so as not to "gally" the whale.

have no way of knowing if the voyage was a success—or, indeed, if it ever took place—one Timotheus Vanderuen, captain of the brigantine *Happy Return,* petitioned Governor Andross of the New Plimouth Colony for

License and Permission, with one Equipage Consisting in twelve mariners, twelve whalemen and six Diuers—from this Port, upon a fishing design about the Bohames Islands, and Cap florida, for sperma Coeti whales and Racks . . .

A few years later, however, sperm whales were being hunted with some regularity by New Englanders. The Hon. Paul Dudley, writing in 1724, wrote that a Mr. Atkins, a resident of Boston, "was one of the first that went out a-fishing for the sperma Ceti Whales about the year 1720." (In the same document, Dudley also describes the perils of the sperm whale fishery: "Sometimes the whale is killed by a single stroke, and yet at other times she will hold the whalemen in play for nearly half a day together with

their lances, and sometimes they will get away after they have been lanced, and spouted thick blood, with irons in them and drugs [drogues] fastened to them, which are thick boards about fourteen inches square.")

The first industry practiced by the New England colonists was the export of beaver pelts and furs to England, but these commodities were quickly exhausted, and given the availability of the easily killed right whales close to their shores, they turned their attention from the forests to the sea. The earliest colonial whaling was practiced in the Indian manner; towers were erected along the shore to enable lookouts to watch for whales, and when one was sighted, the whalers took to the boats. As navigation improved, the whalers began to roam farther offshore, occasionally visiting the rich grounds of Georges Bank, and some vessels even ventured south into the vast oceanic river that would become known as the Gulf Stream. (Although the existence of this oceanic current was known to the whalers, it would not be until 1786 that Benjamin Franklin would publish his description of it.) The Yankee whalers also headed north, toward the Gulf of St. Lawrence and the Grand Banks of Newfoundland. By the middle of the eighteenth century, there were some fifty ships bringing oil and bone to England and returning with such things as iron ore, hemp, cloth and other necessities for the burgeoning new colony. By 1775, Nantucket had a fleet of 150 whalers, which ranged in size from 90 to 180 tons.

Nantucket was not the only colonial whaling port, of course; whalers set sail from Sag Harbor and Southampton on Long Island, and other ports in Massachusetts and New York. Early on, however, Nantucket took the lead (it would not be eclipsed until New Bedford asserted itself in the middle of the nineteenth century), and in 1725, some eighty-five whales—all of them rights—were captured off Nantucket. Rather than list the accomplishments of every whaler out of every port, let us track the history of Nantucket, the early paradigm of colonial whaling, and so important in later years that the British actually tried to transport the entire Nantucket whaling operation to Wales. It was, after all, Nantucket where a whaleman stood on Folly House Hill overlooking the ocean, and supposedly told his son, "There is a green pasture where our children's grandchildren will go for bread."

THE BEGINNING of the sperm whale fishery in 1712 did not automatically spare the remaining right whales. Although sperm oil was enormously desirable for lubrication and candle-making, the need for whalebone had not abated. In the middle of the eighteenth century, European women of fashion still required tight-laced corsets, so the New England whalers captured whatever whales they could find, and processed them accordingly. Scammon tells us that "shore-whaling continued for over fifty years, but eventually it was abandoned, for the same reason that the Spitsbergen and Smeerenburg fisheries were—the scarcity of whales near the coast."

Regardless of the species being hunted, the primary product of the whale fishery was oil. (Earlier, however, the Dutch and English whalers of Spitsbergen and Greenland had concentrated on the whalebone, to the extent that they sometimes cut the slabs of baleen from the mouth of the whale and discarded the carcass. Much of the commerce of whaling was

determined by fashion; by the amount of whalebone that would be required to girdle the ladies.) In America, by contrast, there was no court, no royalty, and in the mid-eighteenth century Quaker colony of Nantucket, very little fancy dress.

As practiced in the Greenland fishery (and every other whaling operation until that time), the blubber of the whale was cut off in strips (a process known as "making off"), and packed directly into casks for transport to the home port. Scoresby, writing in 1820, noted that "in the early ages of the fishery [it was] performed on shore; and even so recently as the middle of the last century, it was customary for ships to proceed into a harbor, and there remain so long as this process was going on." By the middle of the eighteenth century, an innovation that would change the nature of the entire industry had been introduced: iron caldrons set in a brick furnace enabled the whalers to render the oil from the blubber aboard the ship instead of on shore. This method seems to have evolved around the year 1750, but there is no individual whose name is associated with the invention. (In Daniel Ricketson's 1858 *History of New Bedford,* there is a record of the 1762 log of the ship *Betsey,* where it is recorded that they "knocked down try-works.") Although it is not possible to identify the father of the on-board tryworks, there were many mothers, all of whom had "necessity" as part of their names. Among the reasons for its introduction were the unpleasant odors associated with the onshore boiling of the blubber into oil, and the energetic protests of the people who lived downwind of a noisome blubber-works. (Even on board ship, blubber stored in casks tended to spoil quickly, and the stench was overpowering to the whalemen.) On the Spitsbergen and Greenland grounds, the cold climate kept the blubber from turning rancid until the ships could get back to a port, but in New England no such natural refrigeration existed, and the heat often "turned" the oil in the blubber before it could be processed. As long as the whales could be caught within sight—or at most, a couple of days' sail—of shore, the blubber could be casked and stowed, but when the whales became scarcer in the home waters, and longer voyages were required, some other method of processing and stowage was called for. Scoresby (who never employed on-board tryworks, even though the idea existed during his whaling days) wrote that it was less efficient to carry home the blubber, since "blubber in bulk, notwithstanding every precaution . . . generally loses much of its oil."

Now that sperm whales were being processed with some regularity, another change was taking place in the whaling industry. Earlier, all whale oil, casked as blubber or tried-out at sea, was considered usable for lighting and lubrication. (It was often referred to as "train oil," from the Dutch *traan* for "tear" or "drop.") It is a true fat, and impregnates every part of the whale, from the bones to the muscles, but most importantly it is found in the blubber. The fat of right whales and bowheads (and the occasional humpback) provided the whale oil that was extensively used from the tenth century until the middle of the nineteenth for heating, lighting, manufacturing of soap and cosmetics, and lubrication of machinery.

Because spermaceti oil is quite different from train oil, its processing and utilization were also different. (The sperm whale has a blubber layer like all other whales, from which oil can be rendered, but the spermaceti oil comes only from the "case," a reservoir in its nose.) Up to the middle of the nineteenth century, candles were the primary source of indoor light. They were usually made out of wax or tallow, and emitted a smelly black smoke as they burned. The head of the sperm whale contained the mysterious fluid which could be used to make a better kind of candle. This wax, which the whale maintains in a liquid form during its lifetime* solidifies when exposed to air, and someone (R. C. Kugler, of the New Bedford Whaling Museum, suggests a Rhode Islander named Jacob Rodriguez Rivera) realized that it might be employed in the manufacture of candles. From sometime around 1750, it was used to manufacture smokeless, odorless candles, the best candles known before or since.

In addition to the liquid oil contained in the case, the sperm whale produced a spongy material also impregnated with oil, known to the whalemen as the "junk." The liquid oil in the case and the oil that was squeezed from the junk were collectively known as "head matter," and were used in the finest lamps and candles. The process of manufacture—which

may or may not have been developed by Rodriguez—was a fairly complicated one. Upon delivery, the sludgelike substance was heated in a large copper vat and the impurities drawn off. It was left to congeal in casks and then bagged in woolen sacks, then to be pressed in a large screw press. The oil squeezed from the head matter was the highest quality, and was used in lamps. Further processing produced lower qualities of sperm oil, used for candles. Sperm-oil candles were particularly popular in Africa and the Caribbean, but as articles of colonial manufacture, they could not be imported into England. Both types of oil were considered superior to the train oil of the right whale, and were priced accordingly. As the market developed for the finer qualities of oil, colonial entrepreneurs appeared. In 1751, one Benjamin Crabb of Rehoboth, Massachusetts, applied to the state house of representatives for a monopoly on the manufacture and sale of sperm-oil candles, which was granted.

A Boston merchant named Thomas Hancock was involved in selling whale oil to the British as early as 1731, and continued as a major supplier through the Seven Years' War (1756–63). Upon his death in 1764, his nephew John continued the business. Young Hancock entered into a trade war with Joseph Rotch & Sons, first of Nantucket and later of New Bedford, and was soundly defeated, going on, as Richard Kugler has said, "to fame in a field better suited to his talents." The Revolution changed the relationship between the colonies and the mother country, and also changed the direction that whaling had taken. Rival merchants recognized the need for consolidation, and what had been a wide-open contest for domination of the industry evolved into the vertically integrated business of the postwar whale fishery, where shipowners controlled much of the sale and manufacture of the whale products.

As the right whales became scarcer, the tempo picked up for the sperm whale fishery. Starbuck has called the period from 1750 to 1784 "the most eventful era to the whale fishery that it has ever passed through." New England whaleships were under constant threat of being captured by privateers (the various wars between France and England for control of the North American colonies were going on at this time), and ships that were not commandeered pursued the fishery as far from home as the Grand

---

*M. R. Clarke, in a comprehensive study of the head of the sperm whale, has suggested that the whale might be able to alter the temperature of the spermaceti, and by changing the material from a solid to a liquid, control its buoyancy.

Banks and the Bahamas. There were also natural disasters attendant upon the nascent whaling industry: ships were lost to storms and occasionally to whales. For reasons of security and increased profitability, the small sloops that had been the mainstay of the fishery were being replaced by larger ships with tryworks aboard; now the whalers could pursue the sperm whale, "the haughty, elusive aristocrat of the high seas." By this time, the method of lowering boats for whales and fastening to them with harpoons attached to the whaleboats had evolved, and would remain the dominant practice for another century. It was this method of whaling—and the great sperm whale—that Melville would immortalize in *Moby-Dick.* At this time, the fluctuations in the price of whale oil made for a most uneasy market. Good catches would overload the market and depress the price, while in a bad year, the scarcity of the oil would make it dearer.

One of the most unusual byproducts of the sperm whale fishery was ambergris. This grayish, waxy, peat-like substance is believed to form as an impaction in the intestine of the whale, but this supposition is almost everything we know about ambergris. We are not even sure how to pronounce it; the French pronunciation is amber-*gree* (it is a French word, after all; *ambre-gris* differentiates it from *ambre-jaune,* the true amber, which is a fossilized resin), but it has also been pronounced amber-*grease* or amber-*griss.* It is associated only with the sperm whale, and some authorities believe that it forms around the beaks of squid. A whale might vomit up a lump of ambergris in its death flurry, or it might be discovered when the whale is cut open, but it has also been found floating in the open ocean, or washed up on shore, far from any visible whales. According to Clifford Ashley, only "sick" whales are likely to contain this substance, but the relationship between ambergris and the health of the whale is not at all clear.

Robert Cushman Murphy, the author of probably the only detailed study of the history, mythology, and uses of this material, wrote, "From time immemorial, ambergris has had a fabulous value and, although its ancient uses have with one exception dropped away, it has not, like the bezoar stone or the alchemist's formula, ceased to be prized by the practical moderns." It was incorporated into cosmetics and love potions, used as a headache remedy and a flavoring for wine, but the "one exception" that Murphy refers to is its use in the fixing of perfume. Even today, when synthetics are available for virtually every commercial chemical function, ambergris is still used—when available—in the manufacture of scents. When gold was selling at less than today's exalted prices, ambergris was often worth its weight in gold. In 1916, R. C. Andrews wrote that "it is exceedingly valuable, the black ambergris being worth at the present time $12.50 an ounce, and the gray, which is of superior quality, $20. As much as $60,000 worth has been taken from the intestines of a single whale."*

The failure of the British whaling industry left the field wide open to the New Englanders, and they were quick to capitalize on it. When the French and Indian War ended in 1763 and France conceded her claims to Canada, the New England whalers moved in. They sailed from Massachusetts and New York to the Gulf of St. Lawrence and the Strait of Belle Isle, and by 1776, they had discovered the whaling grounds off western Africa (Angola and Walvis Bay), the Falkland Islands, and the River Plate grounds of the South Atlantic. In many of these regions, the whalers occasionally encountered a right whale, but the major object of the fishery by this time had become the sperm whale. These explorers in the name of oil were canvasing the world and perfecting their techniques, but instead of flourishing, they fell deeply into debt. The British government, still trying to support its own collapsing whaling industry, placed a duty on all oil and bone carried to England by colonials. Relations were becoming increasingly strained between the Crown and her rambunctious colony; in the years that followed, the infamous Stamp Act would be enacted and repealed; the Townshend Duties ditto, and finally, the Tea Act

---

*In *The Real Story of the Whaler* (1926), A. Hyatt Verill gives a long list of what he describes as an "official" record of ambergris "catches" for a period of seventy-three years. It is too long to reproduce in its entirety, so a few of the more dramatic items from the list are included here:

1858 Schr. *Watchman,* Nantucket 800 lbs.
1866 Bark *Sea Fox,* New Bedford 150 lbs.
1870 Bark *Elizabeth,* Westport 208 lbs.
1883 Bark *Splendid,* Dunedin, N.Z. 983 lbs.

The *Watchman's* good fortune is corroborated in Starbuck (in vol. I, p. 148, he states that the ambergris was sold for $10,000), and the *Splendid* was the ship that Frank Bullen rechristened *Cachalot* in his book. Verill's list may indeed be correct, but it appears with no supporting documentation.

was passed in 1773, leading to the Boston Tea Party in the same year. (The East India Company, planning to sell its tea directly to America without having to first sell it to British merchants, shipped 1,253 chests of tea from London to Boston on four whaleships: *Beaver, Dartmouth, Eleanor* and *William and Anne.* It was this tea that the rebels, led by John Hancock and Samuel Adams, dumped into Boston Harbor.) The next two years saw the first shots fired at Concord Bridge, and for the ensuing decade, most Americans became preoccupied with things other than whaling. (In April 1775, the same time that the "shot heard round the world" was fired, the ship *Amazon,* Captain Uriah Bunker, was discovering the whaling grounds known as the Brazil Banks, some five hundred miles off that country.)

Only the doughty Nantucketers continued their whaling operations during the war; they had no other means of support. Casks of oil and sheaves of bone began to pile up on the wharves of Sherburne-town, but they could not be sold, and much of the material went to waste. At the conclusion of the war, despite the discovery of new and productive grounds, the whaling industry of Nantucket was in ruins. Since their entire economy depended upon trade with Britain, the islanders sided with the British during the war, and many Tories went there to settle. There was even a bizarre plot to circumvent the restrictions on trading with the enemy by establishing a rendezvous in the Falkland Islands, and transshipping Nantucket whale products directly to England without identifying their origins. Samuel Adams caught wind of this treasonous plan, and dispatched John Paul Jones to capture the Nantucket whalers.

Nantucket Goes to England

ON FEBRUARY 3, 1783, the whaleship *Bedford,* out of Nantucket, arrived in London with a cargo of sperm oil. She was flying the rebel colors; it was the first time the Stars and Stripes had been seen in England. After the Revolutionary War the New England whalers had refitted and rebuilt their ships, eager to get back to the business of whaling now that the war was over. The war had given the whales a brief respite, and the whalers captured and processed them with such dispatch that soon there was a glut of oil on the market. To encourage their own industry, the British had attached a duty of £18 per ton to American oil, and in response, the Nantucketers tried to find a way to sell their oil to the British without paying the crippling duty. At first they tried to declare Nantucket an independent country, but this was a little impractical for an island of some five thousand inhabitants. Whaling was their only industry, and without it their economy would fail completely, so they decided to move the mountain to Mohammed. The business was nothing if not mobile—the intrepid whalers were used to spending years at sea—so they would move the whole industry to a place where they could conduct their business in a free and unrestricted fashion.

The Nantucket whalers were the acknowledged world leaders—even though they seemed to be without honor in their own country. They were the masters of the hunt for the spermaceti whale, which provided a much higher quality, clearer oil than that of the "black whale" hunted by the British in the Greenland fishery. The French tried to woo the Nantucketers to pack up and settle in Dunkirk, and at the same time, overtures were being received by the British. When the British government refused to allow Nantucket ships to register as Canadian, forty families moved to Dartmouth in Nova Scotia and established not only a whaling industry, but a proper Quaker colony as well. The Quakers prospered in Nova Scotia, but only until 1791, because at that time the Nantucketers evacuated Canada for Wales. Under the leadership of William Rotch, the Nantucket fishery struggled to keep afloat. By September 1785, he was in England, meeting with the Chancellor of the Exchequer, Pitt the Younger, to discuss a suitable British location for a Nantucket whaling port. Rotch reminded Pitt that Nantucket had remained neutral during the recent war, and was therefore a part of the British kingdom. He said that the Nantucketers "wish to continue the Whale Fishery wherever it can be pursued to advantage. Therefore, my chief business is to ... ascertain if the Fishery is considered an object worth giving encouragement for removal to England."

Four months after his meeting with Pitt, Rotch saw Lord Hawkesbury, of the Committee of Trade. Although the two men were said to despise each other, they managed to enter into some rather complicated negotiations. Rotch requested free entry for one hundred families and twenty whaling vessels with all their equipment and personal effects. He also wanted participation in the British bounty system,* and £20,000 as compensation for losses incurred by moving and fitting out new facilities. When Hawkesbury had agreed to Rotch's requests—except for the bounty arrangement—Rotch promptly took his Nantucketers to France, and settled them at Dunkirk. The Nantucket whalers plied their trade from France for several years, but the British still retained the hope of establishing a major whaling port in England.

About 1790, Charles Francis Greville developed a plan that would lure the Nantucket whalers back

*The bounty system, begun in 1733 and ended in 1824, was devised by the British government to stimulate participation in what by this time had become a colonial—and later, an American—industry. Based on the tonnage of the ship, the government offered financial inducements for shipbuilders to commission whalers, and for owners of existing ships to outfit them for whaling. Later, the government would offer specific bounties per ton of whale oil brought into British ports.

across the Channel. Although there were a hundred families at Dunkirk, Greville proposed moving them, the Nova Scotia community, and the entire population of Nantucket to a place called Milford Haven, in Wales. (Greville owned the property along with his uncle, William Hamilton, whose place in history is illuminated by his marriage to Emma Hamilton, the mistress of Viscount Admiral Nelson, the hero of Trafalgar.) The plan would transfer America's leading whaling port to Milford Haven, which would then make it a worthy competitor to the American whaling ports of New Bedford, Sag Harbor and New London. In a single stroke, America's primary whaling port would become Britain's primary whaling port. The British may have lost the war, but they still had designs on winning the whaling industry.

On August 31, 1792, a fleet of thirteen ships, manned by 182 men, sailed across the Atlantic. They set up shop at Milford Haven, and within five years there were more than 150 Nantucketers commanding British whaling vessels. But Milford Haven was not home for these Nantucket men. The glorious plan of Charles Greville foundered on the rocks of New England loyalty, and because the little island was never really evacuated, its inhabitants remained in the whaling business. The colony at Dunkirk had enabled the Nantucketers to break through the duties on American oil, and the profits from this enterprise went back to Nantucket, not to Milford Haven. The whalers, too, moved back to their island. Since it would not be the Nantucketers who would lead the British whaling industry into the nineteenth century and into previously uncharted waters, it would have to be the British themselves.

British Sperm Whaling

DIFFICULTIES with their overseas colonies inspired the British to concentrate on obtaining their own oil. (Prior to 1770, more than 90 percent of British oil had come from the New England whalers.) To encourage their industry, Parliament offered tax exemptions for ships whaling in the Gulf of St. Lawrence and bonuses to the ships that brought in the five biggest cargoes in a given year. As an added incentive, the government also permitted sealskins caught by British subjects to be admitted duty free.

By 1786, Samuel Enderby was already a name to be reckoned with in British whaling. With his son (also named Samuel Enderby), he had come to England from Boston in 1775, and by that year, he owned several whaleships active in the Greenland fishery. Samuel Enderby, John St. Barbe and Alexander Champion petitioned the Committee of Trade in 1786 for permission to send their ships round the Cape of Good Hope, "where they are credibly informed there are great numbers of whales," and fish for these whales in an area previously reserved for the trade routes of the East India Company. (Enderby, St. Barbe, and Champion had been strongly opposed to the Nantucket colony at Milford Haven because they did not want to encourage competition with their own "Committee of South Whalers from London.") Although there were right whales to be found in the Southern Hemisphere, the South Seas fishery was after richer prizes: the sperm whale, source of the best oil in the world. The *Emelia* (frequently spelled *Amelia*), the first whaleship to take a sperm whale in the Pacific, belonged to the Enderbys. When the *Emelia* returned to Gravesend in 1790, Enderby wrote, "From her account, the whales of the South Pacific are likely to be most profitable; the crew are all returned in good health, only one man was killed by a whale."*

The Enderby family dominated British whaling during this period, enlarging their fleet from seven ships in 1787 to thirty-eight in 1802. They sent ships north to the Arctic and south to the Pacific, where they encountered a multitude of whales—and a multitude of problems. Rounding Cape Horn put you off the Pacific coast of South America, and therefore into territorial waters claimed by Spain. Sperm whales were plentiful off Peru and Chile, but the Spanish, who claimed the entire continent except for Portuguese Brazil, had no intention of allowing foreign vessels to whale in their waters. In April 1789, a Spanish patrol boat captured two British whalers, the *Sappho,* and the *Elizabeth and Margaret,* that had put in for repairs at Porto Deseado on the Patago-

nian coast. Captains Hopper and Middleton were detained and questioned by the Spanish authorities and released only after they had turned over their cargo of seven thousand sealskins. The ensuing discussions with the Spanish (who were more concerned about invasion of their colonial shores than about sealing) resulted in Spain's refusing landing rights for any reason to British vessels.

The United States of America had been established in 1783, but it consisted only of the thirteen colonies clustered on the eastern coast. Ownership of the remainder of the sprawling landmass was asserted variously by Spain, France, Mexico and England. The Spanish claimed sovereignty over all the west coast of North America from latitude 60°N southward (the present-day northern limits of British Columbia), and when a British whaler was captured at Nootka Sound, the stage was set for a confrontation. Pitt was evidently willing to go to war, but the Spanish could not enlist the aid of another power, and agreed to negotiations. The result was the Anglo-Spanish Convention of 1790, which, in part, allowed that British whalers "shall not be disturbed or molested, either in carrying out their fisheries in the Pacific Ocean or in the South Seas, or in landing on the coasts of those seas, in places not already occupied, for the purpose of carrying on their commerce with the natives of the country. . . ." Now only the East India Company, intent upon protecting its trade routes to China and the East Indies, stood between the whalers and the vastness of the Pacific Ocean. After intense negotiations, the South Seas whalers were finally granted the rights to hunt whales as far west as longitude 180°, which incorporated many of the South Pacific island groups but excluded Australia and New Zealand. (Later, with some modifications, this meridian would become the International Date Line.) The southern whalers, led by the familiar trio of Enderby, St. Barbe and Champion (who were rivals, not partners), continued to press for extensions of their fishing rights. It was clear that the whaling industry was perceived as an instrument of the government's policy of trade expansion in the North Pacific, especially insofar as furs from the northwest were concerned.

By 1791, the whalers had license to roam the coastal waters of western South and North America, and all of the islands of the Pacific Ocean not occupied by Spain. New South Wales was sparsely peopled by

---

*The eminent whaling historian Herman Melville has also described this event: "In 1778, a fine ship, the Amelia, fitted out for the express purpose, and in the sole charge of the vigorous Enderbys, boldly rounded Cape Horn, and was the first among the nations to lower a whale-boat of any sort in the great South Sea. The voyage was a skilful and lucky one; and returning to her berth with her hold full of precious sperm, the Amelia's example was soon followed by other ships, English and American, and thus the vast Sperm Whale grounds of the Pacific were thrown open."

A British aquatint showing the "South Sea Whale Fishery," which was the term the British used for fisheries other than the Greenland. By this time (1836), artists were thoroughly familiar with the size, shape and dying habits of the sperm whale. (When a sperm whale was killed, it usually rolled on its back.) This print by Edward Duncan was based on a painting by his father-in-law, W. J. Huggins, and remains one of the best-known images of the sperm whale fishery.

British convicts, but there was a magnificent harbor at Port Jackson (Sydney Cove), where the whaleships might reprovision and refit. (At first, there were very few provisions there, barely enough to feed the settlers, but as the colony grew, the number of ships calling also increased.) Until 1798, British whalers were prohibited from whaling in Australasian waters, but under pressure from Samuel Enderby, Jr., and Benjamin Champion, the restrictions were lifted. When it became possible for British whalers to operate in Australian waters, the ingenious Enderbys hired their vessels to the government for the transportation of convicts to Botany Bay and whaled their way home.

The northern fishery had concentrated on the Greenland whale, but the southern whalers pursued the sperm whale, whose oil was worth two to three times as much as the black oil. For a discussion of the British sperm whale fishery, we have an author whose work is considered as important to the study of whaling history as Herman Melville's. He was Thomas Beale, a London lecturer in anatomy and a surgeon who sailed on two vessels, the *Kent* and the *Sarah and Elizabeth,* from October 1830 to February 1833. Little is known of his life, but in 1835 he published a little booklet of sixty pages called *A Few Observations on the Natural History of the Sperm Whale,* and a couple of years later, he added to it *A Sketch* *of a South Sea Whaling Voyage.* Together, they add up to an important picture of the state of cetological knowledge in the early days of the British sperm whale fishery, and since it is known that Melville owned a copy and referred to it often, Beale's work has come down to us interwoven into the pages of *Moby-Dick.**

Compared to the great body of material about the American sperm whale fishery that has survived, the logbooks and journals of the British fishery are sparse. Of course, the Yankee fishery was far more extensive, with perhaps five voyages for every British one, but that only makes Beale's book that much more important as a record of a whaling voyage. (Also, a doctor on board a whaler had no other duties, and was therefore able to keep extensive notes as Beale did.) The *Kent* sailed around Cape Horn, to the coasts of Chile and Peru, and then via "Owhyhee" (Hawaii) in the Sandwich Islands to the Japan Grounds and the Bonins. She then headed southward to New Ireland and New Britain, and back to the Bonins, where Beale, disgusted at the captain's treatment of the crew, exchanged berths with the surgeon of the *Sarah and Elizabeth,* and headed for home. (Off the coast of California the captain of the *Kent* died, and the dispirited crew, having been out for three and a half years, decided to call it quits, even though they had managed to fill the ship to only half of her capacity.) Of his new shipmates, Beale wrote that "the men were elastic; and merry smiling faces appeared everywhere." The *Sarah and Elizabeth* steered northeast toward the Sandwich Islands, passing through enormous herds of sperm whales and crossing the 180th meridian, halfway around the world from England. From there they headed for the Friendly Islands (Tonga), New Zealand and then the Horn, where following winds and surging waves pushed them eastward across the roaring forties. They rounded the Horn on November 18, 1832, and

pursued a homeward course through the South Atlantic, past Brazil and the Azores, and arrived in England on February 3, 1833. According to his calculations, Beale had traveled over fifty thousand miles in two years and eight months.

Like all good whaling writers, Beale includes a history of the fishery in his book. In the section devoted to the "Rise and Progress of the Sperm Whale Fishery," he identifies 1775 as the first year the British made an attempt to establish a sperm whale fishery. They sent ships of about 100 tons burthen to "South Greenland, coast of Brazil, Falkland Islands, and the Gulf of Guinea . . . but the principal resort of the spermaceti whale not having been discovered, these vessels met with very trifling success." Later, he refers to the "grand mercantile success of sending ships around Cape Horn into the Pacific," when the Enderbys' *Emelia* returned in 1790 with 139 tons of sperm oil. In 1802 the ships "met with considerable success" off New Zealand, and in 1819 the "indefatigable and enterprising Mr. Enderby" sent the good ship *Syren,* Captain Coffin, to the Sea of Japan. Two years and eight months later, they returned with *"three hundred and forty six tons* of sperm oil [Beale's italics], shewing a success unprecedented in the annals of whaling, and which astonished and stimulated to exertion all those engaged in the trade throughout Europe and America."

Beale's description of British whaling shows that it did not differ markedly from the American style. There were the same long cruises, the same sighting of whales from the masthead, the same lowering of boats, and the same bloody death of the whale. He relates some stories that we have not encountered before, however, such as the 1804 attack on the whaleboats of the ship *Adonis,* where a large whale nicknamed "New Zealand Tom" demolished nine boats before breakfast.

Although more and more ships were fitted out in the early years of the new century, the industry was actually in decline. The more vessels there are working a given fishery, the lower the average per-vessel yield, and therefore the lower the profits. The French Revolution and Napoleonic Wars ran raggedly through Europe from 1792 to 1815, involving Britain on the home front, as also did the war that the Americans knew as the War of 1812, which the British called the Anglo-American War. The war began

---

*Howard Vincent calls Beale's book "The primary source book for Melville in composing the cetological section of *Moby-Dick.* . . . He secured his personal copy on 10 July 1850, paying Putnam's $3.38. The care with which he read the book is attested by the many check-marks throughout the book as well as the comments scribbled in the margins." Melville himself wrote, "There are only two books in being which at all pretend to put the living sperm whale before you, and at the same time, in the remotest degree succeed in the attempt. These books are Beale's and Bennett's, both in their time surgeons to English South-Sea whale-ships, and both exact and reliable men."

Yankee whalers put in at New Zealand harbors for provisions, recreation and occasional bay whaling. Ten Yankee whalers are shown at anchor at Wanganui, North Island, in this painting by C. H. Watkins. Shipping records place this scene around 1872.

when American shipping attempted to run the British blockade of France during the Napoleonic Wars; the Americans burned York (Toronto) as part of an attempt to invade Canada; and an equally ineffective attempt by the British to invade America resulted in the burning of the White House. (One of the more unfortunate aspects of this war was the embargo placed on the export of goods to the British; the Nantucket whalers, having only their oil to sell, nearly starved to death.) The Treaty of Ghent in December of 1814 (signed two weeks *before* the Battle of New Orleans) ended the war, confirmed Britain's possession of Canada, and restored all conquered territories.

Sperm Whaling in Australian Waters

SHIPS THAT had carried a cargo of convicts to Australia could not refill their holds there; there was nothing to bring back from that deserted place. Besides, shipping was under the monopolistic control of the powerful East India Company, which required that the ships return by way of Canton, China, to pick up cargoes of tea for transport back to England. The Second Fleet arrived at Sydney Cove in June 1790, but it was of little assistance to the starving colonists. By this time, most of their food was gone, their seed-wheat had failed to germinate, and the colony of convicts and soldiers had proven almost totally incapable of farming the rocky soil of Sydney Cove. Even the second crossing was a disaster, since fully a quarter of the thousand convicts who had left England died en route. Rather than relieving the hardships of the fledgling colony, the Second Fleet only compounded them by adding more mouths to feed.

Ships owned or licensed by the East India Company had been sealing in the Southern Ocean, and were returning to London with full holds and stories of whales in abundance. On August 7, 1788, the whaleship *Emelia* sailed from London, hoping to round Cape Horn and enter the previously untested whaling grounds of the Pacific. Showing remarkable foresight, her owners, the firm of Samuel Enderby & Sons, had written the Board of Trade,

On the success of our ship depends the Establishment of the Fishery in the South Pacific Ocean, as many owners have declared that they shall wait till they hear whether our ship is likely to succeed there. If she is successful a large branch of the Fishery will be carried on in these seas; if unsuccessful we shall pay for the knowledge.

By 1791, when the Third Fleet sailed for Australia, the *Emilia,* under Captain Shields, had rounded the Horn and entered the vast, uncharted Pacific. In the log of the *Emelia,* Shields records the first whales taken in the Pacific:

I fell in with a very large school of Sperma Coeti whales in the Lat. of 31° 20′ South, out of which I killed 5, saved 4; the ground very lively, having blowing, blustery weather. I thought it necessary to go further to the Northward.

Shields's successful whaling took place off Chile, but the existence of plentiful whales in the Pacific was now verified. When the *Emelia* returned to England with a full cargo of sperm oil, it became apparent that another ocean was about to be opened to the whaling industry. Although the waters around Australia were not officially open to whalers, it was obvious that there were whales aplenty there. (A sperm whale had strayed into Sydney Harbour in 1790; it remained there for three weeks before running itself ashore at Manly Cove.) When the Third Fleet was assembled in 1791, it consisted of six ships, five of which were whalers: the *Britannia, William and Ann, Matilda, Mary Ann* and *Salamander.* After depositing his cargo, Thomas Melville, master of the *Britannia,* wrote to her owners in London:

Within three leagues of the shore [Port Jackson] we saw sperm whales in great plenty. We sailed through different shoals of them from 12 o'clock in the day until sunset all round the horizon, as far as I could see from the masthead. In fact, I saw great prospects in making our fishery upon this coast and establishing a fishery here. Our people was in the highest spirits at so great a sight, and I was determined as soon as I got in and got clear of my live lumber to make all possible despatch of the Fishery on this Coast.

So far, no whales had been taken by whalers in the waters of New Holland. (The name Australia was not officially sanctioned until 1829, when the colony of Western Australia was christened.) The honor of taking the first sperm whale in Australian waters was to fall to either Eber Bunker, captain of the *William and Ann,* or Thomas Melville, of the *Britannia,* as they killed several sperm whales after depositing their "live lumber," but only managed to save one apiece because of bad weather. They then departed for the whaling grounds off Peru, which prompted Arthur Phillip, now the governor of the new colony of New South Wales, to write somewhat petulantly:

I believe not one of them gave the coast a fair trial, nor can I suppose that they left it solely on account of bad weather and strong currents. The weather on the coast of Brazil is not better than it is on this coast, nor have the whalers there the advantages of harbours which ships employed on this fishery would have; as to the currents, they are pretty much the same on both coasts.

The East India Company kept a tight hold on trading and shipping in Pacific waters, but the owners of the whaleships—particularly the firms of Samuel Enderby and that of the Champion Brothers—petitioned the government to permit them to fish in the Pacific, and in 1801 the Crown allowed British whaling to take place in Australian waters. By allowing British whalers license to fish the Australian stocks of whales, the British could greatly increase their imports of whale oil, which had diminished substantially with the loss of their American colonies, home of the preeminent whalers in the world.

In 1803, Phillip Gidley King, the governor of New South Wales, sent the initial group of convicts to Van Diemen's Land, the island now known as Tasmania. The first convict ship was H.M.S. *Glatton,* but the whaleship *Albion,* under Nantucketer Eber Bunker, also transported convicts, livestock and supplies to Risdon Cove on the River Derwent, the settlement that eventually became Hobart Town. On his first voyage to Australia with a load of convicts in 1791, Bunker had seen the whales, so he agreed to make the journey to Van Diemen's Land only if he might take a whale or two en route, if the opportunity offered. King agreed, but stipulated that all prisoners on board were to be confined and shackled when the boats were lowered. During the twelve-day voyage from Sydney Cove to the River Derwent, Bunker's *Albion* obviously hugged the shore—except when crossing the Bass Strait—yet the wily Yankee took three sperm whales, the first whales of any kind taken in Tasmanian waters. He later wrote that "the whales were so thick I could take them without looking."

For the British industry, the profits from the southern whale fishery were enormous: For 1784, the value of the fishery was £14,350; for 1785, £23,480; for 1786, £55,753; and for 1787, £107,231.

The repercussions of the southern whale fishery extended far beyond income for the Enderbys and the Champions. Enderby ships were the first to double Cape Horn, and the first (in 1819) to visit Japan. The whalers of London first explored the Mozambique Channel, the Sandwich and Friendly islands, the Moluccas, Fiji and New Zealand. The Enderbys financed an expedition by Captain Colnett to search for non-Spanish bases for the sperm whale fishery, and Colnett fetched up on the Galapagos Islands. It can be said that the British whalers followed closely in the wake of the redoubtable Captain Cook in opening up the vastness that is the Pacific Ocean. In that ocean, thousands of miles from anywhere, were the two islands that their inhabitants knew as *Aotearoa*—"the land of the long white cloud."

New Zealand Waters

WHEN NANTUCKETER Eber Bunker, captain of the whaleship *William and Ann,* had deposited his cargo of convicts at Sydney Harbour in 1791, he killed several sperm whales but saved only one, and then headed east. He may have visited Doubtless Bay, New Zealand, and while he is generally regarded as the first European to hunt whales in New Zealand waters, there is no record of his having been successful. Upon leaving New Zealand, he encountered no more whales until he reached the fertile Peru Grounds, where he successfully filled his holds. By 1801, whalers were fishing the rich grounds off New Zealand, returning the oil to Sydney, and then returning themselves to England for another cargo of convicts. (A variation on this theme involved whalers who intended to fish the rich grounds of the South Pacific: rather than make the outward voyage empty, they sought a cargo—in this case, convicts and supplies—that would help them finance the otherwise unprofitable three- or four-month trip.)

It was not whales that brought the first Europeans to New Zealand—it was seals. Sealers had discovered the populations of fur seals that had lived undisturbed for centuries on the rocky shores of the main and subantarctic island groups, and in what was to become a lamentable pattern throughout the Southern Ocean, they slaughtered the animals by the hundreds of thousands. (Seals were hunted for their fur, which was shipped to China, primarily to be used in the manufacture of felt.) It has been estimated that the endemic population of the New Zealand fur seal (*Arctocephalus forsteri*) was virtually eliminated in the period from 1790 to 1820. Only when the seals had been so depleted that it was not economically advantageous to hunt them did the Australian seal-hunters turn their attention to the whales.

· · ·

NEW ZEALAND'S two thousand miles of coastline are punctuated by all sorts of bays, inlets and channels, as well as Cook Strait (which Cook uncharacteristically named for himself in 1769), and Foveaux Strait, which separates tiny Stewart Island from South Island. Because New Zealand is located in what appears to be a migratory route for sperm whales (very little is known, even to this day, about the habits of these enigmatic creatures), the whalers often found themselves in the vicinity of these islands while hunting the cachalot. In the eighteenth and nineteeth centuries, certain whaling grounds were identified, where the whalers were likely to find their quarry. (Sperm whales feed on bathypelagic squid, and while the whalers of the eighteenth century could not possibly have known it, the whales tended to assemble in the deeper waters of the world's temperate and tropical oceans. To the whalers, any blue water out of sight of land was probably considered deep water.) The Tasman Sea between Australia and New Zealand became known as the "Middle Ground," and the "Solander Grounds" (named for Cook's botanist, Daniel Solander) were located off Stewart Island. Another important sperm whaling center was in the vicinity of Norfolk Island, an iso-

Trypot

lated speck of rock a thousand miles off the coast of New South Wales. In 1790, this became the most dreaded of all the Australian penal colonies, but convicts were of no concern to the whalers. They were only interested in the sperm whales which were likely to pass this desolate, benighted place. The Chatham Islands, to the east of New Zealand, were another popular location for sperm whalers.

Sperm oil was the *sine qua non* of early Pacific whaling; it was the most desirable of all whale products, and the British whaling industry, based in London, was eager for all that could be casked and shipped. During the early years of the nineteenth century, sperm whalers from London and New Bedford, returning from such places as Fiji, Tonga and Samoa, were putting in to the Bay of Islands for provisions in the form of fresh water, firewood, pork, potatoes—and the available favors of Maori women. There was a settlement at Doubtless Bay, and another at Kororareka. In 1809, the whaleship *Boyd* called at Whangaroa harbor for kauri spars. On board was a chief who had been flogged for some misdemeanor en route from Sydney, and this offense caused great anger and anxiety in the Maoris. They demanded vengeance *(utu)*. The *Boyd*'s shore party was killed and eaten by the Maoris, who then dressed themselves in their victims' clothes, rowed back to the ship, murdered the rest of the crew and set fire to the ship. Several months later, the "Boyd Massacre" was avenged by whaling crews in the Bay of Islands, who killed sixty Maoris, including a chieftain whom the whalers thought (incorrectly) had been involved in the burning of the *Boyd*. Thus inflamed, relationships between the *Pakeha* whalers and the natives deteriorated, and throughout the islands, brushfire conflicts flared up. Rapport between *Pakeha* and Maori was not ameliorated by the inclination of the Maori to eat their victims.

Although whalers avoided Whangaroa and the Bay of Islands for some time after that, the two cultures continued to interact; they could not remain segregated for very long. For the whalers the availability of supplies and women was the attraction of the land, while the Maoris benefited from the introduction of weapons that they could use in their continuous tribal conflicts. In addition, the whalers discovered another attraction of the waters of New Zealand: the southern right whales came to the inshore regions of

New Zealand to breed and calve in the austral winter (May through September), just as they did in Australia and Tasmania. Almost instantly, New Zealand's first industry sprang up, almost fully formed, since it had precedents across the Tasman in Van Diemen's Land and Sydney Harbour.

Maoris were a strong, brave, seafaring people, and took naturally to the life aboard the whaleships. Many of the visiting whalers were only too happy to have their crews enhanced by these personable and courageous sailors. In *Omoo,* Melville describes a "Mowree" called Bembo, who

was, if anything, below the ordinary height; but then, he was all compact, and under his swart, tatooed skin, his muscles worked like steel rods. Hair, crisp, and coal-black, curled over shaggy brows, and ambushed small, intense eyes, always on the glare.

Bembo was "a wild one after a fish," and in his capacity as harpooner, he darted one iron which missed, then another, ditto. The whale dove and rose again a mile away, so the whalers took after him with Bembo perched on the gunwales. When Bembo threw another harpoon that also missed, he became so enraged that he leapt onto the back of the whale and stabbed it. When it was apparent that the animal was fast, the intrepid Maori climbed back into the boat.

The shortage of casks was a predominant problem in the early days; one bay whaler stored his oil in pits dug in the ground. On these unexplored shores, the first whalers erected crude huts beside their iron trypots, and in these primitive and squalid conditions, the white settlers established a beachhead in New Zealand.

New Zealand was an accidental colony; there was no policy of settling either free or transported Englishmen there. (In fact, New Zealand was not annexed to Britain until 1840, more than forty years after the first Englishmen arrived.) Even though Cook had spent considerably more time in New Zealand than he had in Australia, the idea of using these isolated islands as a penal colony does not seem to have been considered. Perhaps that was a result of Cook's recognition of the fierce independence of the Maoris, in sharp contrast to what he perceived as the indolent and primitive way of life of the indigenous Australians.

Unlike the Australian aborigines, who had no concept of land ownership, the Maoris had a well-developed agrarian and totemic society. They were a proud and warlike people, and it was no easy task to colonize their islands and appropriate their land. At first, the relationship between the whalers and the Maoris was peaceful, but it was only a matter of time before friction developed. These rough whalers were not the most diplomatic of men, and their tactlessness, combined with the bellicose and proprietary inclinations of the Maoris, would create problems that persist to the present day.

French and Dutch Sperm Whaling

THE FRENCH had visited Spitsbergen in the seventeenth and eighteenth centuries, with what Scoresby describes as "a considerable number of ships." As documented by the French historian Thierry du Pasquier, they sent some 137 whaleships to sea from 1814 to 1868 from the ports of Le Havre, Nantes, Saint-Malo, La Rochelle and Dieppe. In *Les*

Baleiniers Français au XIXème Siècle, du Pasquier (a descendant of one of the Nantucket families that emigrated to Dunkirk in 1786) discusses the decline of French whaling after the Revolution, and its rise after the fall of Napoleon. French whalers roamed the world in ships with names like *Guillaume Tell, Lioncourt, Etoile Polaire, Croix de Sud, Nouvelle Betzy* and

In this early-nineteenth-century print of whaling in the ice after the Frenchman Louis Garneray (which was popular enough to have appeared in British, American and German editions), the head of the whale is visible under water, a most unusual perspective.

Aimable Nanette. It was the French whaler *Gange* that took the first right whales off the northwest coast of North America in 1835, and another with the unlikely name of *Mississippi* that rescued the explorer Edward John Eyre during his historic walk across Australia in June 1841.

In *Moby-Dick* a French whaler appears as the *Bouton de Rose,* which Stubb translates as "Rose Bud." Melville tells us that French whalers were known as "Crappoes," from the not particularly complimentary *crapaud,* or "toad." They are "but poor devils in the Fishery; sometimes lowering their boats for breakers, mistaking them for sperm whale spouts; yes, and sometimes sailing from their port with their hold full of boxes of tallow candles, and cases of

snuffers, foreseeing that the oil they get won't be enough to dip the Captain's wick into." (Stubb talks the French captain into cutting loose his whales because they are rotten, and as one floats away, the *Pequod*'s mate spears a savory lump of ambergris, "worth a gold guinea an ounce to any druggist.") Although they sent ships out until 1868, du Pasquier believes that "French whalers were no longer an important factor in whaling after 1850."

ONE OF the least known—and least successful—entries into the southern whale fishery was the Dutch. Representing a long tradition of northern whaling which stretched back to the early seventeenth century, the burghers of the Netherlands made a feeble attempt to join the sperm whale sweepstakes in the Southern Ocean. The earlier Dutch fishery had collapsed with the arrival on the Greenland grounds of the British ships of Hull and Whitby, and although they sent a couple of ships to the Davis Strait in 1825, their enterprise failed. There was some interest in the numerous whales reported from southern African waters, but when the Cape Colony was lost to Britain in 1815, the interest in whaling went with it.

Encouraged by the endorsement of King Willem I, the Dutch made an attempt to hunt sperm whales in the South Atlantic and the South Pacific, but they met with remarkably little success. Their first vessel was the New England–built *Logan,* under the command of Reuben Coffin, a member of one of the most respected families in Nantucket whaling history. From 1826 to 1830 the *Logan* plied the seas in

search of whales, but evidently they found very few, and those they found they could not catch because of the inexperience of the Dutch crew. In 1832 the *Eersteling* ("Firstling") went to sea under the command of Captain H. F. Horneman, who seems to have had no experience whatsoever in the hunting of whales. The results of this venture were almost a foregone conclusion, exacerbated by the discord between the Dutch sailors and the British who had been brought aboard to advise. The *Prosperina* sailed from Rotterdam in 1836, and in two years found and killed 19 whales. The firm of Reelfs Brothers sent out the *Anna & Louisa* to the South Seas in 1835, and based on the scantiest reports of good fortune, bought the old *Prosperina,* refitted her, and named her *Zuidpool* ("South Pole"). As with every other Dutch sperm whaling voyage, these too failed to re-

". . . the boat is in the act of drawing alongside the barnacled flank of a large running Right Whale, that rolls his weedy bulk in the sea like some mossy rock-slide from the Patagonian cliffs." In *Moby-Dick,* Melville described this print by the French marine painter Louis Garneray (1783–1857).

pay the initial investment. It appeared that whatever whale oil was going to be used in Holland would be delivered there by Yankee whalers.

Sailing through the southern seas, the *Pequod* meets a ship that Melville calls the *Jungfrau.* She is out of Bremen, and commanded by the very un-Germanic sounding "Derick De Deer." "At one time," Melville tells us, "the greatest whaling people in the world, the Dutch and the Germans are now among the least . . . but you occasionally meet with their flag in the Pacific." The *Pequod's* crew takes the sperm whale that both crews had sighted simultaneously, leaving the hapless Dutchmen in pursuit of

a fin back: ". . . the Fin-Back's spout is so similar to the Sperm Whale's, that by unskilful fishermen it is often mistaken for it. And consequently Derick and all his host were in valiant chase of this unnearable brute."*

---

*Not everyone was amused at Melville's mockery of foreign whalers. The Dutch whaling historian Cornelis de Jong comments that "In 17th and 18th century Britain there was a hatred of of the Dutch as maritime and commercial competitors . . . [which] turned into contempt as a result of the decline in Dutch shipping and commerce, fisheries and whaling." According to de Jong, the business of calling Derick de Deer a German occurs because, "Like many Americans, Melville does not always make a distinction between the Dutch and the Germans, sometimes calling both nations *Dutch.*"

Nantucket and New Bedford

THE NANTUCKETERS dominated the American fishery for some fifty years, but then another group rose to challenge their supremacy. A little Massachusetts village on the Acushnet River achieved a primacy that would soon eclipse Nantucket and every other whaling port in the New World. Around 1760, New Bedford began to send whaling ships to the south. By 1770 the New Bedford brigs *Patience* and *No Duty on Tea* had crossed the Atlantic, and later, *Rebecca* became the first of the American whalers to double Cape Horn with a full cargo of sperm oil obtained in the Pacific. "Thus began," wrote Scammon in 1874, "the commercial enterprise at New Bedford . . . which has since become, and still is, the whaling metropolis of the world." In 1774 the entire colonial fleet consisted of 360 vessels employing some 9,000 men, and of this total, Nantucket and New Bedford maintained the lion's share.

They cruised the waters of the world, from the poles to the Equator, slaughtering every whale they could find, until their holds were filled with the thick oil, and their clothes, decks and rigging reeked of the smoky smell of the trypot fires. The ships returned to their home ports, unloaded, and as soon

as they could, made for the whaling grounds again. It appeared that only a war between nations could interrupt the war between man and whales.

In 1812, many Nantucket whalers en route to gain the sanctuary of their home ports fell to British privateers, and the men and booty were impressed into the service of the British. But despite the privations of war, the Nantucketers, knowing no other business, continued to outfit whaleships for their globe-circling voyages. As they worked the grounds off the coasts of western South America—among the most productive sperm whaling grounds in the world— they now found themselves threatened by a new enemy: Peruvian privateers. Many ships were detained in Talcahuano (Chile), where they had stopped to reprovision before sailing home with their cargo of oil. The Honorable Joel R. Poinsett, who had been sent by the American government to see that the ships were protected, somehow got to lead a troop of four hundred Peruvian militiamen against the pirates, and winning the day, gained the release of the ships. Meanwhile, off the Massachusetts coast, British privateers were harassing Nantucket whalers, and they applied for some sort of arrangement whereby

The bark *Lagoda* (left) at the busy New Bedford docks.

their fisheries might be protected. No such protection was forthcoming, and as Starbuck has written, "the people found the history of their sufferings during the Revolution repeating itself with a distressing pertinacity and fidelity, and they bade fair to perish of starvation and cold." By 1815, with the Treaty of Ghent signaling the cessation of hostilities, the Nantucketers hastened to reestablish their only industry, and within a year the wharves were again stacked with greasy casks. The fleet had been reduced to twenty-three vessels by the end of the war; by 1820 there were seventy-two ships, brigs, schooners and sloops flying the flags of Nantucket owners. Although the British tried to assert themselves prior to 1812, their efforts to break their former colony's monopoly on the whale fishery did not survive the War of 1812. During the war, the American whaling industry was seriously damaged by the British practice of impressing crews and capturing ships. In response, the United States frigate *Essex* roamed the South Pacific recapturing ships that had been taken by British privateers, and virtually swept the seas of British whaleships. (This *Essex* was not the whaleship

that became one of the most renowned of all the whaling fleet, distinguished by being stove and sunk by a whale.) By the time the war ended in 1815, the British fleet was in ruins. The beleaguered American whaling industry was resurrected, and entered a period of unmatched prosperity, based partly on the growth of population and economic activity at home, and partly on the needs of the British market for American oils. It was the beginning of the industrial revolution, and the new machinery needed lubricants. By 1833 the American whaling navy numbered 392 ships and more than ten thousand sailors. In another decade, both figures would double.

Despite Britannia's glorious maritime history, she could not compete with the dogged tenacity of the Yankee whalers, and the oceans belonged to the Americans. Under Captain Joseph Allen of Nantucket, the ship *Maro* discovered the rich Japan Grounds in 1820, and in two years' time, there were thirty whalers working there. Fast on their transoms came the whalers who would discover that sperm whales also enjoyed the warm tropical waters of various islands in the South Pacific. The coasts of Zan-

A "camel" floating a whaler over the sandbar that blocked the harbor at Nantucket.

zibar, the islands of the Seychelles, the icy coasts of Kamchatka, and even the mouth of the Red Sea were explored by the far-ranging whalers. It was obvious that the Yankees regarded the whole world as their private whaling preserve. By 1846, the year that is generally held to have been the high point of the New England whale fishery, there were a total of 735 ships, brigs, schooners and barks flying the flags of American owners, with an aggregate weight of 233,189 tons, and a book value of over $21 million.

The desire to participate in the whale-oil bonanza was not restricted to New England, and even though we tend to associate whaling with New Bedford and Nantucket, many other towns sent out whaling ships. In Massachusetts, Salem, Gloucester, Marblehead, Provincetown and Edgartown on Martha's Vineyard; in Connecticut, New London, Stonington and Mystic; and on Long Island (New York), Sag Harbor, Amagansett, East Hampton and Southampton. Even places not normally associated with whaling joined in. In 1834, the whaleship *Ceres* was sold to a Wilmington concern and set out on Delaware's first whaling voyage. The three-year trip was a failure; she

returned home with her holds only 40 percent full. Another ship, the *Lucy Ann,* set out in 1837 for the Pacific, and was successful enough for the Wilmington Company to pay its only dividend in 1840. North Carolina is another state where whales were occasionally taken, but the catch consisted primarily of right whales which once in a while ventured close enough to shore for the whalers to set out after them in small boats. This fishery began around 1667 with the first settlements, but by the Revolution the whales were gone, and the Carolina fishery ended.

Maine is known as a shipbuilding state, but in the 1830s and '40s Maine companies joined in the rush to harvest the floating oil wells of the distant oceans. Whaling was not the get-rich-quick scheme that it appeared to be, however, and within a decade, all the companies had failed. Ships went out from Portland, Wiscasset, Bath and Bucksport, but most did not repay the original investment. The Downeasters returned to what they knew best: the building of ships for others.

The definitive (and probably the only) book on New Jersey whaling begins with these words: "What!

Whaling in New Jersey?" Barbara Lipton then proceeds to document the 150-year history of whaling in that state, from the earliest shore whaling in Delaware Bay to the heyday of New Jersey whaling, when the *Susquehanna,* under Captain David Joy, sailed out of Perth Amboy in 1824, bound for the South Atlantic, and the formation in 1833 of the Newark Whaling, Sealing and Manufacturing Company. The

NWS&M Co. sent out the *Columbia* in 1836 under the Nantucketer Thomas Hussey, and after two years of successful whaling, the ship was driven onto the rocks off Arauco, Chile, and wrecked. No lives were lost, however, and most of the cargo of oil was saved. The last of the New Jersey whalers, the *John Wells* (also owned by the NWS&M Co.), made four voyages between 1834 and 1844, and was sold to a New

A Japanese drawing of Yankee whalers, with a crudely drawn ship in the background. The oarsmen are shown (incorrectly) two abreast in the foreground boat, and somewhat less organized in the background.

A Tough Old Bull. Two boats (lowered from a ship flying the house flag of H. & J. French of Sag Harbor) converge on a bull sperm whale. Painting by W. H. Overend, c. 1850.

Bedford concern in 1850. She continued her career out of New Bedford, and then acquired the dubious honor of being listed among the whaleships that were lost in the great Arctic disaster of 1871.

In their search for oil, the roving whalers opened the world, much as the explorers of the sixteenth century had done in their quest for the wealth of the Indies. In his comprehensive history of the American whaling industry, Starbuck tells us that "So large a portion of our fishing-fleet visited the Pacific that the United States was finally forced, when petition after petition had been sent to Congress, to send an exploring expedition to those seas, the ostensible purpose of which was to render the navigation of that ocean more secure as well in respect to the dangers of the land as in regard to those of the sea." In response to these petitions, the United States Exploring Expedition of 1838–42 was dispatched, under the command of Lieutenant Charles Wilkes.

The six-ship expedition sailed the world for four years, ranging from Tierra del Fuego, where an attempt was made to explore the Antarctic; to the Tuamotus, Samoa and Fiji, where the party confirmed the existence of cannibals. In addition to his crew, Wilkes commanded a coterie of mineralogists, botanists, naturalists and artists (collectively known to the sailors as "the Scientifics"), who had been charged with performing all manner of experiments and investigations, the first time such an expedition had been assembled in peacetime. From Hawaii they sailed to Australia, and then south, where they claimed to have discovered the Antarctic continent on January 16, 1840. (Credit for the discovery has actually been given to the Frenchman Dumont D'Urville.) The results of the expedition were published in nineteen volumes, and the materials collected formed the basis of the Smithsonian Institution.

Whaling and Hawaii

THE DISCOVERY of the rich sperm whale grounds in the Western Pacific had an unexpected consequence: the establishment of the Hawaiian Islands as a provisioning stopover and the subsequent settlement of these previously sleepy tropical islands. Captain Cook had discovered the islands in 1778, and was killed by hostile natives upon his return the following year. Very little activity followed his exploits until the Japan Grounds were discovered, and then a veritable invasion of missionaries, whalers and settlers came ashore on the islands. Hawaii would never be the same. (Although the late twentieth century would see the emergence of whale-watching in Hawaiian waters, there is little evidence that the whalers went there for anything but food, water, refitting and recreation. It is possible that the humpbacks that are the object of this whale-watching were not in evidence in large numbers in the eighteenth and nineteenth centuries, although

there are some records of whalers' hunting humpbacks there.)

King Kamehameha died in 1819, and the first missionaries arrived in Lahaina (then the island kingdom's capital) in 1823. The open roadstead of Lahaina made it particularly attractive for visiting whaleships, and the island's almost unlimited supply of fresh water, fruits, vegetables and hogs made it seem like paradise after months at sea with nothing but salt pork and hardtack. And if that wasn't enough to lure the whalermen to the Sandwich Islands, the presence of agreeable *wahines* was enough to drive the men to mutiny. At first the *wahines* swam out to meet the whaleships, but the missionaries soon put a stop to this wanton behavior, leading to the inevitable establishment of brothels. Men as well as women were in demand; another ramification of the arrival of the whaleships in Hawaii was the profusion of *kanakas* who signed aboard to replace whalemen who had deserted on other islands or had been injured or killed during the voyages. By 1825, one could count no fewer than twenty-three grog shops within a single mile of Lahaina's Front Street, and the brawling became endemic. A prohibition on the sale of alcohol was enacted in 1825, but the seamen's reaction was predictable and violent: they rioted, and in one instance, sailors of the warship U.S.S. *Dolphin* bombarded the house of the Reverend William Richards with cannon shot upon learning that they were to be denied their precious grog.

As early as 1812, traders had reached an agreement with King Kamehameha to harvest the fragrant sandalwood (*iliahi*) trees that grew in profusion on the islands, but within a decade, they had stripped the islands bare of the trees, and the islands were ready for another influx of capital, which was provided by the whalers. The waters are deep enough around these upthrusting volcanic islands to offer a conducive habitat for sperm whales, but it was not the presence of the whales that brought the whalers; it was the location of the islands themselves. A bull sperm whale was killed off the island of Hawaii in 1819, but for the most part, the whalers who stopped at the Sandwich Islands were on their way to or from the Western Pacific, and later, from the Arctic. The chain of islands was about midway between North America and Asia, and close enough to the Equator to make them convenient for winter and summer hunting in the Pacific.

The story of the settlement of the Hawaiian Islands can be told in terms of the conflict between the lawless whalers and the sanctimonious missionaries, who arrived more or less at the same time, and whose objectives were diametrically opposed. The whalers sought a release from the confinement of years at sea in filthy fo'c's'les, while the missionaries wanted to introduce law, order and Christian worship to the very place where the whalers wanted to experience uninhibited drunken debauchery. The whalers had them outnumbered (between 1822 and 1850, hundreds of whaleships anchored at the Hawaiian ports every year, the peak year being 1846, with 596 visits by whaleships), but the missionaries had faith and the printing press. First they codified the Hawaiian language, then they taught the Hawaiians to read. According to one source, the Lahainaluna Seminary on Maui had run off some 113 *million*

pages of proselytizing prose between 1822 and 1842.

Honolulu and Lahaina were also increasingly important as transshipping ports. Instead of sailing across the Pacific with their oil and bone, the whalers offloaded their cargoes in the Hawaiian ports, where they would be transferred to merchant ships and carried back to the mainland. This freed up the whalers to continue their whaling without interruption. (They occasionally took whales in Hawaiian waters, but these were only humpbacks, and did not yield much in the way of oil or bone. Also, the missionaries lobbied strenuously to prohibit the whalers from working on the Sabbath.)

The situation came to a boil in 1852. More than 150 ships anchored in Honolulu harbor had disgorged some two thousand men into the city. A sailor named Henry Burns had been jailed for drunkenness, and when he became too boisterous in his cell, the guards silenced him. Permanently. Word of his demise spread throughout the grog shops and brothels, and before long there was a full-scale, two-day riot in the streets of Honolulu. The police station and several stores were burned to the ground, and only an onshore wind shift prevented the oil-laden ships in the harbor from catching fire.

It is impossible to say how the conflict would have ended if the whalers and the missionaries had continued their confrontations, but the whales disappeared in great numbers, and because of the California Gold Rush, the whalemen did too. Colonel Drake discovered petroleum in Pennsylvania in 1859; the Civil War took its toll on the whalermen and ships; and finally, the Pacific fleet was destroyed in the Arctic in 1871. Just as the Hawaiian economy had shifted from sandalwood to whale oil in the early days of the century, another change would now have to occur, and oil gave way to sugar cane. Honolulu would remain an important port (and eventually replace Lahaina as the capital), but the sleepy Maui village would languish until—of all things—the whales brought it back to life.

In the early 1970s, as whales began to be recognized as the symbol of the burgeoning environmental movement, the humpbacks of Hawaii were discovered. At first, scientists observed the whales of Maalea Bay and the Auau Channel, but soon the inevitable entrepreneurs arrived, in an invasion that made that of the missionaries pale by comparison.

Now little Lahaina is once again the "whaling" capital of Hawaii, but instead of killing the whales, the citizens of Lahaina are dedicated to celebrating them, watching them and exploiting them—in a benign fashion. There are dozens of establishments with whales as their symbols, from frozen yogurt stores to scrimshaw shops. Galleries abound with cheap prints of the romanticized humpbacks, leaping from the water and seductively diving with colorful tropical fishes, and every other person seems to be wearing

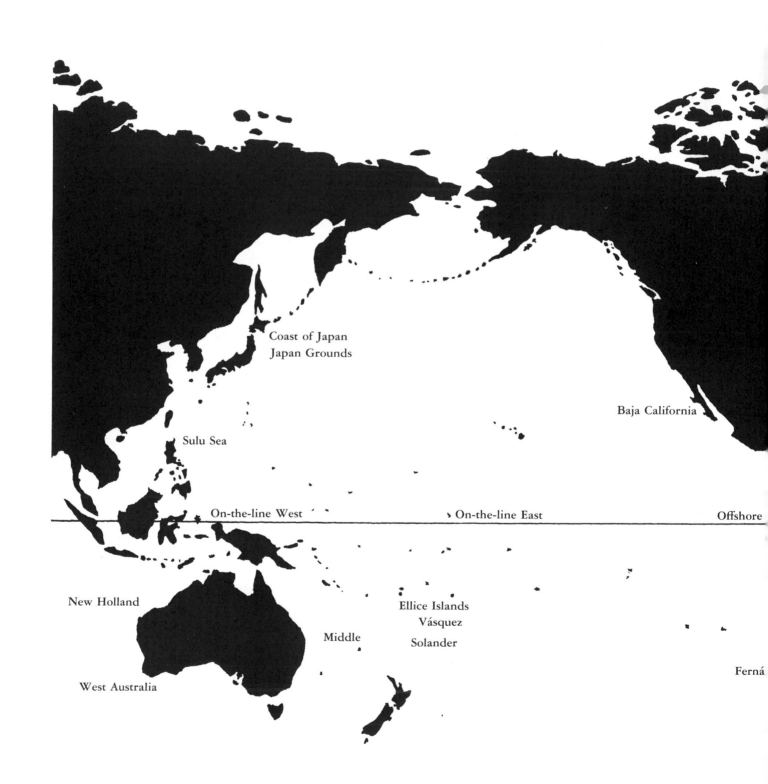

Coast of Japan
Japan Grounds

Baja California

Sulu Sea

On-the-line West

On-the-line East

Offshore

New Holland

Ellice Islands
Vásquez
Middle
Solander

Ferná

West Australia

a T-shirt with a whale on it. During the winter months, as the humpbacks arrive from southeast Alaska to breed and calve in the warm Hawaiian waters, whale-watching boats take hordes of tourists offshore for an hour of two of close-up whale-watching, and although the bitter history of early Hawaiian whaling is not emphasized, the tourist from Minneapolis or Tokyo can come away with the proper sense of wonderment (and a T-shirt) that fulfills his need to pay homage to the whale.

The "grounds" worked by the nineteenth-century sperm whalers. They evidently did not know of the sperm whales' inclination to head for polar waters, nor did they discover the vast numbers of cachalots that inhabited the North Pacific off the Aleutians and Kamchatka.

Decline of the American Fishery

BY THE END of the nineteenth century, almost all the known stocks of right whales and bowheads had been severely depleted. The only whales consistently hunted were the sperm whales, and these were getting harder and harder to find. As with so many aspects of nineteenth-century life, the industrial revolution intervened in the history of whaling, and individual initiative was overtaken by technological advances. Steam whalers replaced the square-riggers, and other oils began to seep into the lighting and lubricating industries.

As early as 1830 an illuminating oil known as "camphene" was being distilled from turpentine. That it was ill-smelling and volatile did not so much militate against its use as it encouraged the search for other substances. Some of the more astute New Bedford merchants had guessed at what was coming with the discovery of petroleum, and in 1859, Messrs. Howland, Taber, Delano, Wood and Hicks (names heretofore indelibly associated with the whaling industry) had erected a factory for the distillation of petroleum. Cottonseed, linseed and palmseed oils

were also being used in soap-making, rope-dressing, and leather-tanning. Whale oil, which had defined the industry and been responsible for the making of history, fortunes and literature—and the unmaking of thousands of whales—was becoming an anachronism. The age of petroleum was about to begin.

After peaking around the middle of the century, the New England whale fishery began a decline from which it never recovered. When gold was discovered at Sutter's Mill in California in 1848, whaleships saw the wholesale defection of their crews—and sometimes their captains as well—as soon as they docked in San Francisco. The Civil War saw the sinking of many whaleships and the scuttling of others. Confederate raiders wreaked havoc on the Yankee whaling fleet, and finally the unforgiving ice of the Arctic crushed thirty-three whalers in the autumn of 1871. In 1857 the powerful New Bedford fleet had consisted of 324 vessels, but fifty years later, it was reduced to 19 ships and barks, 12 schooners and 1 brig. The balance of power had shifted to San Francisco, but there too the handwriting was on the wall, and only feeble attempts were made to revive the prac-

Barrel staves were packed tightly to be stored aboard ship until they were assembled by the cooper.

tically moribund American whaling industry. (Various whale species would be killed from California land stations during the twentieth century, but neither the number of whales killed nor the effects on the local economy were significant.) The cumulative slaughter of various whale species (particularly the sperm whale) obviously contributed to the decline of the industry, as the whalers had to spend more and more time at sea for a steadily declining return.

As collecting the oil became more cost- and time-intensive, the introduction of petroleum as a cheaper substitute for whale oil drove the price even further down. From a high of $1.77 per gallon in 1855, sperm oil had fallen to 40 cents in 1896. Investors were unwilling to spend money on this unremunerative industry. Greasy casks lay rotting on the wharves, and the masts of the whalers rocked in the swell of the harbor, some of them never to sail again. One owner scuttled his vessel in the Acushnet River, and another volunteered a whaleship to be burned as a Fourth-of-July spectacle.

A rise in the price of whalebone revived California whaling, and steam whalers headed for the Arctic to harvest the bowheads, but this industry too was af-

fected by galloping industrial technology, and just as cheaper petroleum substitutes were taking the place of whale oil, spring steel was replacing whalebone for corset stays. The New Bedford whalers stubbornly persevered, and continued to send ships and men to sea, but by the turn of the twentieth century, American pelagic whaling was virtually moribund. The last of the square-rigged Yankee whalers to set out in pursuit of whales was the bark *Wanderer,* which departed from New Bedford on August 25, 1924. She encountered a fierce northeasterly gale, ran aground and was wrecked on the rocks at Cuttyhunk Island on the following day.

The capture of the first sperm whale off Nantucket in 1712 may be apocryphal, but there is no doubt that Nantucketers were in full cry after the cachalot by the middle of the eighteenth century. (By 1748, Boston newspapers were running advertisements for "Sperma Ceti" candles.) The fishery was in decline a little over a century later. Fortunes were made and lost; cities rose and fell; men lived and died . . . all for the magical substance in the head of the whale. In *Moby-Dick,* the Ishmael/Melville narrator says of New Bedford, "Yes, all these brave houses

On August 27, 1924, the day after she sailed from New Bedford, the *Wanderer,* last of the square-rigged whalers to embark on a whaling voyage, was wrecked on the rocks at Cuttyhunk Island.

and flowery gardens came from the Atlantic, Pacific and Indian oceans. One and all, they were harpooned and dragged up hither from the bottom of the sea.'' *Ars longa, vita brevis.* The enduring legacy of the sperm whale fishery will not be the houses of New Bedford and Nantucket; it will not be the salvaged harpoons and the scratched whale teeth that remind us of the whalemen and their victims; it will not be the logbooks and diaries that told of their pleasures and hardships; it will not even be—if an absence can be a monument—the massive destruction of the whales themselves. No, the legacy of the sperm whale fishery will be found only in the pages of Melville's epic narrative, the most powerful parable ever written of the eternal conflict between man and beast.

Interlude:
Life Aboard a Whaler

THE ORIGINAL inhabitants of Nantucket and Martha's Vineyard had been whalers in their own right, and they quickly became assimilated into the New England whaling culture. The harpooner Tashtego in *Moby-Dick* is described as "an unmixed Indian from Gay Head . . . which has long supplied the neighboring island of Nantucket with many of her most daring harpooners,'' and although he was not descended from a whaling people, the African Daggoo, "a gigantic, coal-black negro-savage with a lion-like tread," had "voluntarily shipped on board of a whaler, lying in a lonely bay on his native coast." (It would be a while before "cannibals" or *kanakas* like Queequeg were signed on; first the whalers would have to discover the South Sea islands on which they lived.) The early whalers of the nineteenth century carried a much higher percentage of both Negroes and Indians than in later years.

As the whale fishery was climbing to its position of importance, the profession of whaleman was considered a noble one, and the elite youth of Nantucket, Martha's Vineyard, Long Island and the Massachusetts coastal villages vied for positions aboard the ships. Strapping farm boys traded the plow for the oar in their search for adventure and fortune aboard the whalers bound for exotic ports of call. On Nantucket, the influence of whaling was so strong that eligible maidens would not even consider a suitor unless he had been a-whaling.*

Men from all over America joined the heterogeneous New England whaling navy, and virtually every European country was represented. Not everyone was as noble as the paragons of Nantucket; Hohman lists the following reprobates as also contributing to the whaleships' rosters: "immoral and unprincipled wretches who wanted to get 'off-soundings,' in an attempt to elude the Ten Commandments . . . confirmed drunkards, vagrant ne'er-do-wells, unapprehended criminals, escaped convicts, and dissipated and diseased human derelicts of every description." Because they stopped at ports around the world for food and water, New England whaleships picked up crew members (often to replace those who had died or deserted) from the West Indies, the Cape Verdes, the Azores and numerous islands in the South Pacific. At first only the Hawaiians were known as *kanakas,* but soon the name was applied to any dark-skinned aboriginal, whether he were a Maori, a Samoan or a native of "Kokovoko," as was Queequeg. (Melville wrote that Kokovoko was "an island far away to the West and the South. It is not down on any map; true places never are.")

*Even the oil of the spermaceti whale was nobler than other oils. In a "postscript" to his discussion of the honorable position held by the whaling industry, Melville asks, "what kind of oil is used at coronations? Certainly it cannot be olive oil, not macassar oil, nor castor oil, nor bear's oil, nor train oil, nor cod-liver oil. What can it possibly be, but the sperm oil in its unmanufactured, unpolluted state, the sweetest of all the oils?"

A whaleboat from the *Charles W. Morgan* under sail in 1910.

At approximately the same time that British whalers were depositing their cargoes of convicts and finding themselves in the middle of the rich whaling grounds of Australia and New Zealand, Yankee whalers were cruising almost everywhere in search of sperm whales. It was dangerous work, and sometimes the voyages seemed to last forever, but there were those who saw it as pleasurable and even romantic, the epitome of the wholesome life. So much of whaling depended upon the weather that it is not

Casks of oil line the New Bedford wharf.

surprising to hear the virtues of the industry described in climatological terms, as Scammon did:

A favorite cruising ground was from the Spanish Main westward, to the Galapagos Islands. There a rich harvest rewarded them, where they labored in a genial climate, with an almost uninterrupted succession of fine breezes and genial weather. At certain seasons, north of the equator, the north-east trades blew fresh, and at the south they would frequently increase to a brisk gale; but these periodical breezes, compared with the heavy gales of the Atlantic and the tedious weather around Cape Horn, served only to enliven them into rewarded activity under the heated rays of a tropical sun, when in pursuit of the vast herds of Cachalots which were met with, bounding over or through the crested waves.

In retrospect (Scammon wrote those words in 1874), the voyages were often less than romantic and the weather less than benign. There were indeed fresh breezes, tropical sun, and vast herds of cachalots, but there was also the tedium of years of sailing (the record seems to be the eleven-year voyage made by the ship *Nile,* out of New London: 1858 to 1869), as well as gales, blizzards, typhoons, hurricanes, mountainous seas and howling winds. Conditions aboard these ships were not wholly unlike those aboard the infamous convict ships that took "live lumber" to New Holland. The crew's quarters were stinking holes; their food was cheap, coarse, and maddeningly monotonous; the work itself was dirty and dangerous. A voyage aboard a New England whaler was not a luxury cruise.

In the nineteenth century, the hierarchy of officers and men, so important to the successful operation of a whaling vessel, was rigidly observed, and nowhere was the distinction more evident than in their respective living quarters. The captain lived in relative luxury; the ship's officers had smaller cabins; the boatsteerers, the cooper and the steward occupied the steerage, an irregular compartment fitted with plain bunks. The crew was in the forward section just below the main deck, which followed the shape of the ship: it went from a fairly wide cross section to a narrow, cramped, triangular warren, where the ship's timbers formed the walls, and the pounding of the waves formed the ambience. The lower portion of the foremast often kept the occupants of the fo'c's'le company, reducing even further their limited space, and the only light that entered this literal and figurative rat hole came from the hatchway cut in the deck for the purpose of giving access to the ladder that allowed the men to climb in and out of their quarters. When the weather turned foul, the hatch was closed, and there was no light but stubby candles, and no ventilation whatever. The number of men that occupied this wretched space often exceeded twenty.

No whaleman was ever paid a wage, except in unusual circumstances. If, for instance, a full ship had to take on additional hands on the way home,

their share of the profits would be zero (since they had not participated in the whaling), and they were paid a monthly wage. Ordinarily, each man, from the captain to the cabin boy, received a percentage of the profits—called a lay—at the end of the voyage.

The distribution differed from vessel to vessel—larger ships could carry more oil, and therefore the profits to the crew were likely to be proportionately higher—but while a successful voyage could be better for the captain and the officers, it meant precious little indeed to the foremast hands. (On an unsuccessful voyage, where the profits were low or nonexistent, the crew might receive nothing at all.) The captain might earn $1/8$ or $1/10$ of the net proceeds, while a mate could earn $1/15$ and a harpooner $1/90$. Ordinary seamen could hope at best for $1/150$, and there are instances in the records where a green hand signed aboard for $1/350$. What did this mean in terms of actual money? On board the *Addison*, First Mate Ebenezer Nickerson, whose lay was $1/18$, earned $845. Robert Baxter, the second mate with $1/35$, earned $554.83, and a boatsteerer named Narcisco Manuel, with $1/90$, got $376.56. Compare these figures to those of the crew: John Martin, at $1/175$, earned a total of

The fo'c's'le of a whaler, as shown in the 1922 film *Down to the Sea in Ships.*

PACKING WHALEBONE.

CHARLEY KOTZENBERGER, THE HARPOONER.

$31.85, and Francis Finley, 1/225, got $82.08. During six consecutive voyages totaling 1,218 days at sea from 1845 to 1868, the average lay per voyage on the Salem whaler *James Maury* was $321.21, or about 26 cents a day. This compared unfavorably to wages then being paid to unskilled laborers ashore (an average of 90 cents a day), but landlubbers did not get to visit exotic Pacific islands where they might be eaten by cannibals, or risk their lives fighting gigantic whales.

Infrequently, the men were paid in the specie of whaling; that is, they received casks of oil which they were then able to sell at the prevailing prices in their port of disembarkation. The cooks often received an added benefit: in addition to their lays, they were permitted to save the grease (known as "slush") from their galleys and sell it to soap-makers ashore.

The whaleman's food and bunk space were generously provided without charge, but throughout the voyage he was docked for various items that he had to buy from the ship's stores. Additional items of clothing, tobacco, knives, needles and even thread were charged to each man's account, and if he required spending money in a port of call, this too was deducted from the final reckoning. This was a period where the master's voice was law, and if a man

needed a new shirt or a pair of boots, he could "either pay up or go naked." Although most of the whalemen signed aboard voluntarily, they usually did not know of the dangers and hardships that lay ahead of them, and the "profit-sharing" which at the outset sounded so attractive often deteriorated into an enforced "risk-sharing," which was invariably uncomfortable, inevitably dirty and frequently dangerous.

A document has been preserved in which the price of various items to the seamen has been recorded, as well as the price originally paid for the items by the provisioner. This "list of slops and trade items" (appended to the 1966 publication of the journal of Mary Lawrence, the wife of the captain of the New Bedford whaler *Addison*) indicates that the ship sold goods from the slop chest for approximately twice as much as they paid for them, and sometimes considerably more. A sheath knife that cost 25 cents was sold for 74 cents; for a "wool lined Russia cap" that cost 79 cents the whaleman paid $1.50; a pair of "Vermont pants" originally bought for $1.60 cost $3.00; and a pair of thick boots originally bought for $2.42 were sold for $3.75. Tobacco was a major item of internal and external whaling commerce. The whaler *Canton* shipped 4,329 pounds—over two

THE LAND SHARKS.

THE COOK AND THE PILOT.

tons—of tobacco when she set sail in New Bedford in 1858.

Among the more unusual charges assessed to a whaleman was the cost of desertion. If a man jumped ship, his account included the cost of recapturing him, an expense that was obviously nullified if he remained at large. On the other hand, there were captains who rewarded the lookouts with bonuses for the sighting of whales. This exercise was glorified in *Moby-Dick,* where Ahab nails a gold doubloon to the mainmast and exhorts his crew: "Whosoever of ye raises me a white-headed whale with a wrinkled brow and a crooked jaw; whosoever of ye raises me that white-headed whale, with three holes punctured in his starboard fluke—look ye, whosoever of ye raises me that same white whale, he shall have this gold ounce, my boys!" The "Spanish ounce" that was offered to the crew was a sixteen-dollar gold piece.

On a three- or four-year voyage, a man might earn $100, but the items billed to him often exceeded this amount, so many hands returned to port not only with no spending money, but in debt. The only thing to do to work off this indebtedness was to sign on for another voyage, thus starting the insidious pro-

cess all over again. If and when they made it back to port, the whalemen were set upon by all sorts of "land sharks," eager to assist them in disposing of their wages by enticing them into taverns, brothels and other iniquitous dens where they could make up for the pleasures they had been denied for the past several years. In an 1860 issue of *Harper's* magazine, an observer describes the arrival of the whalemen in New Bedford:

A cart rattles by, loaded with recently discharged whalemen—a motley and a savage-looking crew, unkempt and unshaven, capped with the head-gear of various foreign climes and peoples—under the friendly guidance of a land shark, hastening to the sign of the "Mermaid," the "Whale," or the "Grampus," where, in drunkenness and debauchery, they may soonest get rid of their hard-earned wages, and in the shortest space of time arrive at that condition of poverty and disgust of shore life that must induce them to ship for another four years' cruise.

The system of wages aboard a whaler was obviously not conducive to enthusiasm or hard work. In response to the brutal discipline often administered by the captain, there was bound to be apathy, indifference and suspicion on the part of the foremast hands. There was also a profound class distinction between the officers and the men. Despite the abuses, hardships and low earnings which characterized the industry, however, the labor supply was somehow adequate to meet its needs. As Hohman has written, "The steady stream of men pouring into the forecastles proved sufficient to counteract the continuous labor leakage caused by death, illness, incapacity, discharge and desertion." It was possible (although uncommon) for a dedicated seaman to work his way up through the ranks, and there are instances where a green hand, or even a cabin boy, raised his lay from $1/150$ to $1/15$, and after perhaps twenty years at sea (in four- or five-year increments), a man might command a whaling vessel.

The *Benjamin Tucker,* a New Bedford whaler, brought back 73,707 gallons of whale oil, 5,348 gallons of sperm oil, and 30,012 pounds of whalebone in a voyage that ended in 1851. At the prevailing prices—43 cents a gallon for whale oil, $1.25 a gallon for sperm oil, and 31 cents a pound for bone—the gross value of this cargo was $47,682.73. From this, $2,362.73 was variously deducted, leaving a net of $45,320 to be distributed. But before the profits were divided, the owners took a substantial percentage off the top to compensate for their initial outlay and also because these flinty New Englanders were not in the business for the thrill of the chase. In general, the owners took between 60 and 70 percent of the profits. On the 1805–07 cruise of the *Lion,* the various oils yielded a total of $37,661.02. Of this, $24,252.74 went directly to the owners, leaving $13,045.53 to be divided among the captain and the crew for two years of work.

During its heyday, New Bedford was the richest municipality per capita in America, and Melville described it as "perhaps the dearest place to live in all New England . . . nowhere in America will you find more patrician-like houses, [or] parks and gardens more opulent."

Of course, profits from the whaling industry were not restricted to the owners. They had to repair, refit and reprovision their ships, which provided work and income for the shipwrights, chandlers, coopers, rope-makers, carpenters and blacksmiths, and ready markets for the farmers and greengrocers. The entire township of New Bedford benefited from the outfitting and victualing of the armada of ships that an-nually departed her wharves, loaded with food, clothing and supplies, most of which were bought from local merchants.

In 1858 sixty-five whaleships sailed from New Bedford. To provision these ships for their protracted voyages, the whale fishery contributed $1,950,000 to the coffers of New Bedford merchants to purchase the following articles: 13,650 barrels of flour, 260 barrels of meal, 10,400 barrels of beef, 7,150 barrels of pork, 19,500 bushels of salt, 97,500 gallons of molasses, 39,000 pounds of rice, 1,300 bushels of beans, 39,000 pounds of dried apples, 78,000 pounds of sugar, 78,000 pounds of butter, 19,500 pounds of cheese, 16,300 pounds of ham, 32,500 pounds of codfish, 18,000 pounds of coffee, 14,300 pounds of tea, 13,300 pounds of raisins, 1,950 bushels of corn, 2,600 bushels of potatoes, 1,300 bushels of onions, 400 barrels of vinegar, 2,000 pounds of sperm candles, 32,500 barrels of fresh water, 1,200 cords of wood, 260 cords of pine, 1,000,000 staves, 1,000 tons of iron hoops, 33,000 pounds of iron rivets, 520,000 pounds of sheathing copper and yellow metal, 15,000 pounds of sheathing nails, 52,000 pounds of coopering nails, 400 barrels of tar, 759,000 pounds of cordage, 450 whaleboats, 32,500 boat boards, 65,000 feet of pine boards, 36,000 feet of oars, 8,500 iron poles, 22,500 pounds of flags, 23,000 bricks, 200 casks of lime, 205,000 yards of canvas, 13,000 pounds of cotton twine, 234,000 yards of assorted cotton cloth, 130,000 pounds of tobacco, 39,000 pounds of white lead, 5,200 gallons of linseed oil, 400 gallons of turpentine, 13,000 pounds of paints, 2,600 gallons of new rum, 1,000 gallons of ether liquors, and 120 casks of powder.*

THE CAPTAIN had his own cabin, with a proper bunk, a washstand, a table, and perhaps even a sofa and some extra chairs. The captain's quarters of the whaleship *Florida* "opened off the after cabin on the starboard side and extended nearly to the end of the forward cabin. A small room and a toilet room were aft of the stateroom. A large swinging bed was in the captain's cabin instead of the usual fixed berth." The gimballed bed was a special innovation designed by Captain Thomas Williams, because he was planning to bring Mrs. Williams along.

*From L. B. Ellis, *History of New Bedford,* pp. 421–22.

THE MODEL SKIPPER.

Occasionally the captain took his wife, and even more infrequently, he took his entire family. Captain Williams, of the ship *Florida* out of New Bedford, was accompanied by his wife for a voyage that lasted from September 1858 to October 1861. During the voyage, Eliza Azelia Williams gave birth to two children, who spent the first years of their lives at sea. She also kept a detailed journal of her adventures, which allows us a most unusual perspective of life aboard a whaleship. (The *Florida* was one of the ships that was trapped and destroyed in the Arctic ice in the great disaster of 1871, but by then Eliza Azelia was no longer aboard.) The voyage commenced on September 7, 1858, in New Bedford, and on January 12 of the next year, Mrs. Williams gave birth to a baby boy, whom they named William. (William's arrival might help to explain her seasickness early in the voyage, when she wrote, "It remains rugged and I remain Sea sick. I call it a gale, but my Husband laughs at me and tells me I have not seen a gale yet. If this is not one I know I do not want to see one.") On August 5, 1859, off the rugged coasts of Sakhalin in the Okhotsk Sea, the *Florida* spoke the *Eliza F. Mason,* and Mrs. Williams visited another "lady ship," where the captain had brought his wife and

child, "a Lady Companion, and a little Girl that they brought from the Bay of Islands, New Zealand." On February 27, 1860, Mrs. Williams wrote, "We have had an addition to the Florida's Crew in the form of our little daughter. . . ."

(In his account of his experiences aboard the *Charles W. Morgan* during the years 1849 to 1853, Nelson Haley repeats a story of a woman who shipped in disguise aboard the whaleship *Mitchell.* She kept her secret until she fell ill. When the captain went to visit her in the fo'c's'le, he saw "a young unconscious woman who, in her feverish sleep, had disclosed what she had kept her inviolate secret, surrounded as she was with fifteen or twenty men for eight months." It seems that she had been badly treated by a young man, and had gone to sea in hopes of finding him. The captain put her ashore in Lima, and said, "I have been to sea, man and boy, for over forty years, but never have seen or heard tell of the like of that.")

In 1868, six-year-old Laura Jernegan sailed with her mother, her little brother Prescott, and her father, Jared, master of the New Bedford whaler *Roman.* Her journal has been preserved, and from it we can get glimpses of a whaling voyage from a unique perspective:

Friday 10th [February 1871]
it is quite rough today. But is a fair wind. We have 135 barrels of oil, 60 of hump back and 75 of sperm. We had two birds, there is one now. One died. There names were Dick and Lulu. Dick died. Lulu is going to. . . .
    Good Bye for To Day

Sunday 12th
it is Sunday. it rained last night. Papa made a trap and caught 5 mice, and mama has some hens that have laid 37 eggs.
    Good Bye for To Day

Sunday 19th
. . . I can't think of much to write. We had pancakes for supper. they were real good. it is most night. the Longitude was 117–23. I don't know what the latitude was.
    Good Bye for To Day

Tuesday 21th 1871
It is quite pleasant today. the men are cutting in the whales. they smel dreadfully.
    Good Bye for To Day

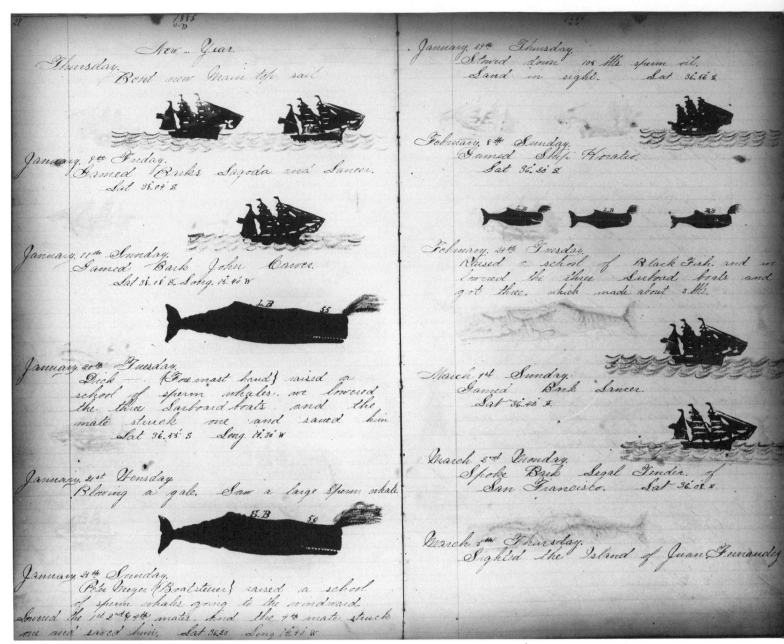

New Year.
Thursday. Bent new Main top sail

January 9th Friday.
Gamed Barks Lagoda and Lancer.
Lat 36.04 S.

January 11th Sunday.
Gamed Bark John Carver.
Lat 36.16 S. Long 76.46 W

January 20th Tuesday.
Dick — {Fore mast hand} raised a
school of sperm whales. we lowered
the three Larboard boats and the
mate struck one and saved him
Lat 36.55 S Long 71.30 W

January 21st Wensday
Blowing a gale. Saw a large sperm whale.

January 24th Sunday.
Peter Breyer {Boatsteerer} raised a school
of sperm whales going to the windward.
Lowered the 1st 2nd & 4th mates. And the 4th mate struck
one and saved him. Lat 36.20 Long 76.46 W

January 29th Thursday.
Stowed down 105 Bbls sperm oil.
Land in sight. Lat 36.46 S.

February 8th Sunday.
Gamed Ship Horatio.
Lat 36.20 S

February 24th Tuesday.
Raised a school of Black Fish. and we
lowered the three Larboard boats and
got three. which made about 3 Bbls.

March 1st Sunday.
Gamed Bark Lancer.
Lat 36.40 S.

March 2nd Monday.
Spoke Bark Legal Tender. of
San Francisco. Lat 36.06 S

March 5th Thursday.
Sighted the Island of Juan Fernandez

A page of the log of the *John P. West,* showing the stamps that illustrate the whales taken (sperm and pilot whales are shown), and also the ships spoken.

It was United States maritime law that a logbook be maintained by the mate or the first officer. (The term "logbook" originated with the practice of casting a log overboard affixed to the ship by a knotted line. The speed at which the line played out—measured in knots—determined the speed of the ship, and the daily records were originally kept in a book reserved for that purpose. Later, the term "logbook" was used to designate the book used for the keeping of all the ship's records.) For the most part, logbooks and journals were kept by the masters. Although rarely educated in the classical sense, most of these men could read and write passably well, and their records have given us an enduring picture of life aboard a whaleship. Even though the maintenance of a logbook was mandatory, it obviously served the whalers particularly well, since the appearance of whales at a known latitude and longitude in one season might enable the whalers to predict their reappearance at the same location the following year and thereby avoid aimless wandering.

The more mundane entries consisted of the ship's position, the number of whales caught, and illness and injury aboard ship, but additional dramatic possibilities were vast. Whaling historian Stuart Sherman, in his introduction to the catalogue of the logbook collection of Paul Nicholson, listed "castaways, mutinies, desertions, floggings, women stowaways, drunkenness, illicit shore leave experiences, scurvy, fever, collisions, fire at sea, stove boats, drownings, hurricanes, earthquakes, tidal waves, shipwrecks, ships struck by lightning, men falling from the masthead, hostile natives, barratry, brutal skippers, escape from Confederate raiders, hard luck voyages and ships crushed by ice." That is not to say that all logbooks read like *Moby-Dick;* dramatic events occurred infrequently, and most of the daily entries—when the ship was not engaged in killing whales—consisted of a remark on the wind direction, the location, and whatever else the keeper of the logbook deemed pertinent. Here is the complete entry for November 18, 1858, from Captain Scammon's log of the bark *Ocean Bird,* heading from San Francisco to Baja California:

At daylight land in sight bearing E. by N. distant 50 miles—wind light—all hands variously employed—ship steering E. by S.—cook still off duty with the venerial.

It is not surprising that few of the foremast hands kept records; their quarters were not conducive to the literary life, and besides, many of them couldn't write. Francis Olmstead could. Of the literary aspirations of his fo'c'sle companions, he wrote

The forecastle of the North America is much larger than those of most ships of her tonnage, and is scrubbed out regularly every morning. There is a table and a lamp, so that the men have conveniences for reading and writing if they choose to avail themselves of them; and many of them are practicing writing every day or learning how to write. . . . When not otherwise occupied, they draw books from the library in the cabin and read; or if they do not know how, get someone to teach them. We have a good library on board, consisting of about two hundred volumes. . . .

Olmstead was a sickly lad who attended Yale University and signed aboard the whaler *North America* in 1839 for his health. There are those who might argue that a whaling voyage was not particularly salubrious, but it suited Olmstead. He cruised for a year throughout the Pacific, and when he completed his cruise, he sat down to record his experiences. His first voyage so strengthened him that he decided to try it again, but after a cruise to the Caribbean in 1844, he weakened and died. He was twenty-five years old.

There were enough literate whalers (and surviving journals) for Pamela Miller to have collected their works in an anthology entitled *And the Whale Is Ours: Creative Writing by American Whalemen.* (Only in recent years has the literary and historical value of these logbooks been recognized. In her introduction, Miller tells of an antiques dealer in New Bedford who remembered seeing stacks of the logbooks for sale as scrap at a nickel a pound.) On the death of a pig, Samuel Braley wrote:

My pet pig fell dowen the forehatchway this morning and broke her back so we had to kill her; I sorry but I don't think that I shall go into mourning for her. I did think at first that I would not eat any of her; but then I thought that it would be like not getting married again in the case of a defunct Wife; or not excepting a legicy, because your Dear aunt or uncle happened to slip their wind, and I leave it to you, so I fell to Eat her because I loved her—better cooked than raw.

Another eulogy for a pig was written by Elizabeth Morey, the young wife of Captain Israel Morey of the Nantucket whaler *Phoenix.*

> *Poor Mr. Hogg is Dead, and Gone,*
> *I never shall see him more,*
> *Or hear him begging me for corn,*
> *His loss I do deplore.*

(Mrs. Morey had the habit of naming the whales that were killed by the crew of the *Phoenix,* and her list includes Jonah, Mercy, The Sea Queen of Russia, Fanny Fern, the Mammoth Cave, Queen Victoria, Prince Albert, Napoleon Boneypart, Josaphene, Queen Caroline, the Russian Ranger and Buster.)

Another literate whaleman was Ben-Ezra Stiles Ely, the son of a Presbyterian minister who briefly attended the Lawrenceville School and the Delaware Academy before running away to sea in 1844. He signed on as green hand on the bark *Emigrant,* out of Bristol, Rhode Island, and spent twenty-seven months as a whaleman, sailing through the South Atlantic, around the tip of Africa to Madagascar, and back to Bristol in February 1847. Ely eventually gave up his wayward career, and like his father, was ordained a minister. There are many journals and diaries that tell of the hardships of whaling, but very few that quote Byron, as Ely does ("The pulse's maddening play/Which thrills the wanderer of the trackless way"), and even fewer that complain of the difficulties inherent in being "a gentleman's son" among ruffians:

One day the mate asked me what I came to sea for, and I replied that it was to see how sailors lived. At this he was offended, and took good care to give me more knowledge than I desired. I saw how sailors lived to my heart's content. I was the smallest person on board the ship, and to gratify his spleen in punishing me, he stationed me in the blubber hold, to pitch up the pieces on deck. Many of them were larger round than my waist, and weighed nearly as much as my whole body. The work was very tiresome, and sometimes I would stagger and fall on the slippery mass, under the weight of my fork, and be nearly immersed in oil.

J. Ross Browne, a journalist who shipped aboard the New Bedford whaler *Bruce* in 1842, kept a journal of his experiences which was published, with major revisions, as *Etchings of a Whaling Cruise* in 1846. Browne wanted to do for whaling what Richard Henry Dana had done for merchant sailing in 1840, that is, exaggerate the problems so that necessary changes would be implemented. Although his account may contain a certain amount of propaganda in the form of negative commentary, he was aboard a whaler for more than a year, and because he is regarded as a reporter and not a writer of fiction, much of the material contained in his book can be taken as fact. (In the introduction to the Harvard University Press edition of his book, the literary historian John Seelye has written, "Browne was a sensitive, accurate reporter. The modern reader who wants to know about life on a whaler . . . must be grateful to him for having painstakingly recorded his experiences.") Here is Browne's description of the place in which he lived:

The forecastle was black and slimy with filth, very small and hot as an oven. It was filled with a compound of foul air, smoke, sea-chests, soap-kegs, greasy pans, tainted meat, Portuguese ruffians and sea-sick Americans. . . . In wet weather, when most of the hands were below, cursing, smoking, singing and spinning yarns, it was a perfect Bedlam. Think of three or four Portuguese, a couple of Irishmen, and five or six rough Americans, in a hole about sixteen feet wide, and as many perhaps, from the bulkheads to the fore-peak; so low that a full-grown person could not stand upright in it, and so wedged with rubbish as to leave scarcely room for a foothold. It contained twelve small berths, and with fourteen chests in the little area around the ladder, seldom admitted of being cleaned. In warm weather it was insufferably close. It would seem like an exaggeration to say, that I have seen Kentucky pig-sties not half so filthy, and in every respect preferable to this miserable hole; such, however, is the fact.

Rats were more numerous on whaleships than on any other vessels, probably because of the profusion of blood and oil that soaked the decks, despite the regular scrubbings. They were more than any ship's cat could cope with, and then as now, there was nothing that could cope with cockroaches. They were endemic aboard the whalers, and for many seamen, the roaches were a more predominant aspect of a whaling voyage than whales. Francis Olmstead wrote that they made "a noise like a flush of quails among the dry leaves of the forest. They are extremely voracious, and destroy almost everything they can find: their teeth are so sharp, the sailors say, that they will eat the edge off a razor."

In *Nimrod of the Sea,* William Davis describes roaches as serving a useful purpose: "His chief recommendation is his insane pursuit of the flea . . . ," but then goes on, "it is a horrible experience to awaken at night, in a climate so warm that a finger-ring is the utmost cover you can endure, with the wretched sensation of an army of cockroaches climbing up both legs in search of some Spanish unfortunate! It reminds me of how many times I have placed my tin plate in the overhead nettings of the forecastle, with a liberal lump of duff reserved from dinner, and on taking it down at supper, have found it scraped clean by the same guerrillas. They leave no food alone, and have a nasty odor, which hot water will scarcely remove. But one becomes philosophical at sea in matters of food."

The crew's rations aboard a whaleship ranged from merely bad to disgusting, but, Browne says, "a good appetite makes almost any kind of food palatable." He describes the usual fare on board the *Bruce* (which he has, for culinary and other reasons, named the *Styx*): "I had seen the time when my fastidious taste revolted at a piece of good wholesome bread without butter, and many a time I had lost a meal by discovering a fly on my plate. I was now glad enough to get a hard biscuit and a piece of greasy pork; and it did not at all affect my appetite to see the mangled bodies of divers well-fed cockroaches in my molasses; indeed, I sometimes thought they gave it a rich flavor." Fresh vegetables were taken on at the outset of a voyage, and often picked up when the vessel put in for provisions, but unless they were used quickly, they rotted. (By Browne's time, the causes of scurvy were known, but if the vegetables were used up and the ship was cruising somewhere off the Aleutian Islands, there was not much anyone could do to prevent the dread disease.) Because of their inability to store much water—and to prevent it from spoiling—the whalers hardly ever drank it. (Scammon tells the story of one captain, who, to preserve the dwindling water supply, had the drinking cup hung from the royal-mast head, requiring any man who wanted a drink to climb all the way up after the cup.) They drank "longlick," a mixture of tea, coffee and molasses, and if the cook was imaginative, he prepared something known as "lob-scouse" (or simply "scouse"), which was a hash made of hard biscuits that had been soaked in the greasy water left over after boiling the salted meat. The mainstay of the whaler's diet was salted meat, which was supposed to be pork or beef, but was occasionally horse. In *Omoo,* Melville described the meat on board a whaleship:

When opened, the barrels of pork looked as if preserved in iron rust, and diffused an odor like a stale ragout. The beef was worse yet; a mahogany-colored fibrous substance, so tough and tasteless, that I almost believed the cook's story of a horse's hoof with the shoe on having been fished up out of the pickle of one of the casks.

In his 1856 book *Whaling and Fishing,* Charles Nordhoff (the grandfather of the Charles Nordhoff who collaborated with James Hall on *Mutiny on the Bounty*) wrote that "ship captains and mates take into serious consideration the fate of certain chickens, ducks and pigs, and enter into long-winded discussions as to the proper time and best method of preparing these animals for the table . . . forecastle

Jack growls at the cook about the ill-prepared bean soup and the raw duff [a flour pudding boiled in a bag], the moldy rice, or half-cooked beef which is set before him."

Because the everyday food was so often inedible (Nordhoff describes the duff made by a certain cook as "that potent breeder of heartburns, indigestion, and dyspepsia . . . the very acme of indigestibility," and Ben-Ezra Ely wrote, ". . . no swine that gleans the gutters ever subsisted on viler meat and bread than did our crew"), the opportunity to eat something fresh was a blessing. The cook prepared sea birds, whatever fish they could catch, turtles, dolphins (off the African coast, Nordhoff describes the harpooning and subsequent eating of a hippopotamus), and since they were engaged in the capture of 50- or 60-ton mammals whose carcasses they would otherwise leave for the sharks, they often ate the meat of the whales. On the eating of various parts of the whale, usually during the trying-out, Browne writes:

About the middle of the watch they get up the bread kid [a kid was a wooden tub], and, after dipping a few biscuits in salt water, heave them into a strainer, and boil them in oil. It is difficult to form any idea of the luxury of this delicious mode of cooking on a long night-watch. Sometimes, when on friendly terms with the steward, they make fritters of the brains of the whale mixed with flour and cook them in the oil. These are considered a most sumptuous delicacy. Certain portions of the whale's flesh are also eaten with relish, though, to my thinking not a very great luxury being coarse and strong. . . .

It was a different world above decks. On December 28, 1856, the crew of the New Bedford whaler *Addison* caught a porpoise, and Mary Chipman Lawrence (the captain's wife) wrote in her journal, "The meat looks very much like beef. The oil is contained in the skin, which they will boil out tomorrow. Had some of the meat fried for dinner and some made into sausage cakes for supper. They are as nice as pork sausages." If a further demonstration of the disparity between the fare of the men and that of the officers is required, here is Mrs. Lawrence's description of Christmas dinner for that same year: "roast chickens, stuffed potatoes, turnips, onions, stewed cranberries, pickled beets and cucumbers, and a plum duff. For tea I had a tin of preserved grape opened and cut a loaf of fruitcake."

Even though they were criticized for their sturdy, utilitarian design, the sight of a whaleship under full sail was enough to stir the heart. The bark *Canton* in 1906.

Unlike their British counterparts, American whalers rarely carried any sort of medical man. It commonly fell to the captain to cope with whatever illness or accident befell his crew, and given the master's experience, it was considerably safer to remain healthy. For internal maladies, whaleships were often equipped with medicine chests, which contained various potions and a manual for their dispensation. (Stories were told of masters who, having run out of medicament Number 12, simply administered equal amounts of Numbers 5 and 7.)

Physical injuries were not uncommon, considering the number of sharp-edged tools, whistling whale lines, and hostile natives—not to mention shipboard arguments between men who were almost always armed with knives. Here again, the master served in the role of surgeon, with the same amount of training as he had as apothecary. In *Nimrod of the Sea*, W. M. Davis tells the gory tale of a whaleman who was yanked from his boat by a kinked line, and dragged some 125 fathoms from the boat. When he was finally picked up, "it was found that a portion of the hand, including four fingers, had been torn away, and the foot sawed through at the ankle, leaving only the great tendon and the heel suspended to the lacerated stump." Equipped with "his carving knife, carpenter's saw and a fish-hook," the captain "amputated the leg and dressed the hand as best he could." And of course there are the two captains in *Moby-Dick* who have had limbs removed by the white whale; Boomer of the *Samuel Enderby* and Ahab of the *Pequod*. Boomer explains how the ship's surgeon amputated his arm and replaced it with "a white arm of Sperm Whale bone, terminating in a wooden head like a mallet," but Ahab, impatient to learn of the whereabouts of the white whale, does not reciprocate by describing the repair job that resulted in his sporting a pegleg of ivory. One assumes that in his combined roles as captain, surgeon and victim, he operated on himself.

AS WHALING VOYAGES increased in distance and duration, it became expedient to enlarge the ships.* In the early days of the fishery (around 1820), the ships averaged around 280 tons burthen, but within two decades, 400-ton vessels were not uncommon. The move toward bigger whaleships contributed to the decline of Nantucket whaling because there was a prominent sandbar across the harbor, and only the smaller, shallower-draft ships could enter. New Bedford, with its excellent harbor facilities, took up the slack.

Whaleships differed from merchantmen of the time in that they usually carried less sail. More canvas meant more men aloft, and the whalers needed as many hands as possible for the boats. One further characteristic of the whaler was the presence of masthead hoops, in which the lookouts stood during the daylight hours to watch for whales.

Square-rigged ships, which gave their name to an era of sailing, ran powerfully before the wind, but were not particularly handy in head- or cross-winds. The whalers did not have to perform any smart sailing maneuvers, nor did they have to sail with great speed. All they had to do was get from one location to another and then lower the boats after the whales.

*All whaling vessels were *ships*—as opposed to *boats,* which were the smaller vessels that the whalers rowed after their quarry. The literature is replete, however, with references to ships, brigs, brigantines, barks, barkentines and schooners. These differentiations have to do with the rigging of the masts, and not with the number of masts, although a three-masted, square-rigged vessel was always known as a *ship.* If the aftermost mast was rigged fore-and-aft, with the sail slung between a gaff and a boom, the vessel was known as a *bark,* the commonest plan, because fewer hands were required to handle the sails, and thus there were more men available for the boats. There were further variations, including the *brig,* where the upper courses of the aftermost mast were rigged with squaresails, but there was also a fore-and-aft sail known as a "spanker." A *barkentine* was square-rigged only on the foremast; the rest fore-and-aft, and a *brigantine* had only two masts, the foremast square-rigged and the mainmast fore-and-aft. A *schooner* had two or more masts, rigged fore-and-aft.

Because of the determined, plodding nature of their craft, the masters rarely sailed at night, preferring instead to furl their sails and wait till dawn before continuing.

It was during the heyday of New England whaling, from 1830 to 1860, that the fabulous clipper ships reached the zenith of sailing-ship design, with their graceful lines, sharply raked bows, and opulence of canvas. In marked contrast to these ocean-going greyhounds, the whalers were sturdy, bluff-bowed, flat-bottomed sailers, designed more for durability and storage than for speed. (The *Lagoda* sailed for

Wharf scene in New Bedford: ship *Eliza Adams* to the left; ship *Horatio* at right.

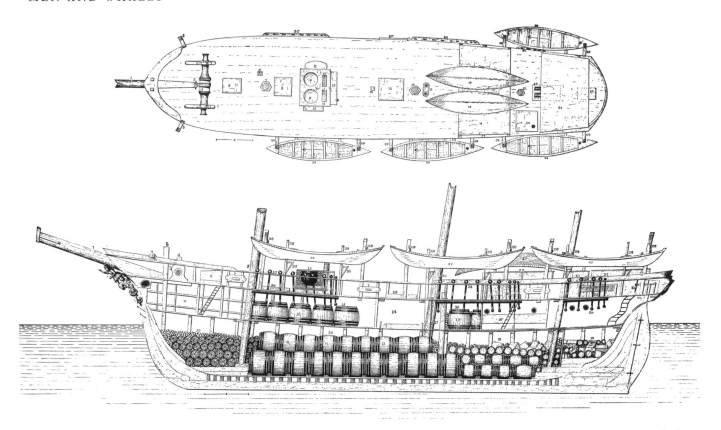

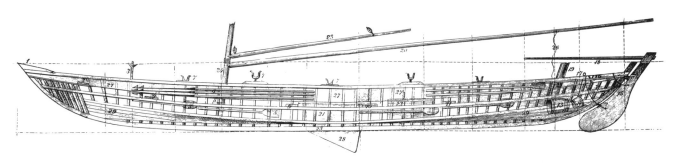

Deck plan of the whaling bark *Alice Knowles,* showing the stowage of casks below decks. Illustration by C. S. Raleigh from *The Fisheries and Fishing Industries of the U.S.*

Construction of a whaleboat. Illustration by C. S. Raleigh from *The Fisheries and Fishing Industries of the U.S.*

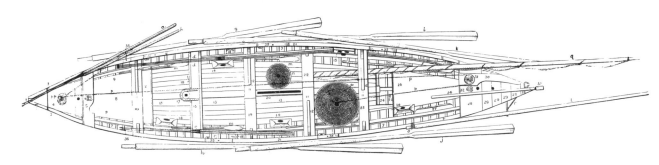

Deck plan of a whaleboat. Illustration by C. S. Raleigh from *The Fisheries and Fishing Industries of the U.S.*

fifty years, and the all-time record-holder, the *Charles W. Morgan,* sailed for more than eighty years, and earned over a million dollars for her owners. The *Lagoda* was copied at half-scale for the New Bedford Whaling Museum, and the *Morgan,* the last of her kind, is now the proud centerpiece of Mystic Seaport in Connecticut.)

A typical whaler was 100 to 150 feet long, and especially broad in the beam to accommodate the fixtures of whaling: heavy brick tryworks on deck, iron caldrons, cooling tanks, davits for the boats, and of course, the space required to perform the trying-out of the whale. Ordinary seamen, whose voyages did not take four or five years, belittled the whaleships as "built by the mile and cut off in lengths as you want 'em." They were usually painted black, and had mock gun ports painted along the sides, supposedly as a deterrent to pirates or hostile savages.

The naval historian Albert Cook Church wrote: "Whaleships differed materially from any other type of merchant ship or clipper in model and equipment, and in fact, both sides of a whaleship differed from each other above the waterline." The larger ships were equipped with four boats, one on the starboard quarter, and three on the port (also known as "larboard") side. This allowed the cutting stages, which were always on the starboard, to be lowered without interference from davits. When a whale or a group of whales was sighted, the lookout shouted "She blows!" or "Blows!" and when the captain had ascertained "where away," the boats were lowered, and the chase began.

All the boats might or might not be lowered, depending upon the number of whales sighted. If only a single whale was seen, the captain might designate one boat to chase it. The starboard boat was reserved for the captain (or the fourth mate, if the captain chose to stay aboard ship during the hunt); the larboard, waist, and bow boats were for the first, second, and third mates, respectively. Each boat contained a regular crew, consisting of five oarsmen, and a boat-steerer/harpooner. Whoever was in command of the whaleboat pulled the steering-oar and gave the orders. The boats were double-enders; in case they got turned around in the frenzy of the hunt, they would be able to maneuver, and they were among the most graceful and utilitarian boats ever designed.

All the requisite equipment would be carefully stowed aboard the whaleboats, from the line, which was carefully coiled in a tub so it could be let out

The graceful lines of a
New England
whaleboat.

rapidly, to the knife that might be required to cut it if a man got his leg entangled. In addition to the six adult men who would be required to man the boat, Scammon lists the contents of a fully equipped whaleboat:

One mast and one yard, one to three sails, five pulling oars, one steering oar, five paddles, three rowlocks, five harpoons, one or two line-tubs, three hand lances, three short-warps, one boat-spade, three lance-warps, one boat-warp, one boat-hatchet, two boat knives, one boat-waif, one boat-compass, one boat-hook, one drag, one grapnel, one boat-anchor, one sweeping-line, lead, buoy, etc., one boat-keg, one boat-bucket, one piggin, one lantern-keg (containing flint, steel, box of tinder, lantern, candles, bread, tobacco, and pipes), one boat-crotch, one tub-oar crotch, half a dozen chock pins, a roll of canvas, a paper of tacks, two

nippers, to which may be added a bomb-gun and four bomb-lances; in all, forty eight articles, and at least eighty-two pieces.

He explains the function of every one of these articles, *e.g.,* "The boat-warp is the painter of the boat; the short-warps are to connect the second harpoon to the main line when the second iron is thrown into the animal. . . . The 'drag' is for 'bending on' to the line to assist in impeding the whale's progress while running. . . . [With] the grapnel, the dead animal's flukes or its head are hauled up, in order to cut and reeve the tow-rope. . . . [The] sweeping-line, lead, and buoy, are used for getting the fin and fluke chains to the whale. . . . The canvas and tacks are to cover holes which may be staved in the boat. . . ."

And the lantern-keg, which contains the homey items of bread, tobacco and pipes, "in the extreme necessity to have a small supply of food, with the luxury of a quid of tobacco or a smoke of a pipe . . . in case the boat should be caught out at night."

The lowering of the boats took place as the ship was underway; the captain did not come about for the comfort or convenience of his crews. Often in high seas, the graceful whaleboats took off after the whales with the men facing the stern; the boatsteerer was the only man who could see the whales. When they had come within range, the harpooner threw the harpoon. It consisted of a wooden shaft, some six feet in length, with a forged iron head. The earliest harpoons had simple fluted arrowhead-shaped heads, but as the fishery developed, more sophisticated designs were introduced. While the two-flued iron pierced the blubber effectively, its razor edges would occasionally pull out as smoothly as they went in. This led to the introduction of the single-flued iron which held much better. Harpooners and blacksmiths had plenty of time, on board the whalers and in port, to work on harpoon design, and all sorts of elaborate heads with toggles, barbs and swivels were tried. The most successful of these designs was the double-barbed "Temple" iron, invented in 1848 by a New Bedford blacksmith named Lewis Temple. A graceful, practical device, the Temple iron consisted of a pointed head that was held in the forward position by a wooden shear-pin that broke off when withdrawal forces were applied. This rotated the head ninety degrees in the flesh of the whale, forming a T-shaped device that would not pull out, because the flattened surfaces were pulling against the meat or blubber. The iron was fastened to the shaft of the harpoon by a line which was bent to the heavy manila line. The line, which Melville calls the "magical, sometimes horrible whale-line," was originally fashioned of hemp, but was later superseded by manila rope, which was stronger and more elastic. "Hemp is a dusky, dark fellow," Melville wrote, "a sort of Indian, but Manilla is as a golden haired Circassian to behold."

Even though tradition demanded that the harpoon and the lance be thrown separately, some creative whalemen tried to design an iron that would fasten to and kill the whale simultaneously. A Scottish toxicologist named Robert Christson invented a poison-headed harpoon, equipped with glass cylinders containing prussic acid, one drop of which is lethal enough to kill a man. There is no evidence that prussic-acid harpoons were used in the American fishery, but they were carried on some vessels. The likelihood is that the American harpooners felt that they had enough problems killing the whale without worrying about killing themselves.

If the iron was well placed—the ideal spot was in the flank, forward of the hump—the boat was fast to the whale, and the injured animal took off. Sometimes the whale sounded, taking out the line at such

Harpoons at the ready, the oarsmen pull toward the whale. Photograph taken by Robert Cushman Murphy on his voyage aboard the New Bedford whaler *Daisy* in 1912.

The lancing. When the whale had tired, the petal-shaped lance was thrust into its vitals. An actual whaling scene from the 1922 film *Down to the Sea in Ships*.

speed that the line smoked as it ran out, and the loggerhead had to be doused with water to keep it from bursting into flame. More often the whale swam at the surface, towing the boat through the waves at a violent clip. Sperm whales are prodigious divers, and no boat could hold enough line for a dive that could be measured in miles. If the whale sounded, another 200-fathom line might be bent to the first, and then another. Eventually, the wounded whale had to surface to breathe.

When this happened, the boatsteerer and the mate went through the unnecessary but inviolate ritual of changing places—no mean feat in a crowded, moving whaleboat in rough seas—where the boatsteerer took on the job of lancing the whale. The lance, also know as the "killing iron," was plunged into the "life" of the whale, a vital artery, the lungs, or the heart. The killing iron consisted of a wooden shaft like that of the harpoon, with a scalpel-sharp head. It was not thrown, but rather stabbed repeatedly into the body of the whale. Melville describes the death-throes of a whale:

The red tide now poured from all sides of the monster like brooks down a hill. His tormented body rolled not in brine but in blood, which bubbled and seethed for furlongs behind in their wake. The slanting sun playing upon this crimson pond in the sea sent back its reflection into every face, so that they all glowed to each other like red men. . . . Stubb slowly churned his long sharp lance into the fish and kept it there, carefully churning and churning, as if cautiously seeking to find some gold watch that the whale might have swallowed, and which he was fearful of breaking ere he could hook it out.

The victory did not always go to the whalers. Sperm whales are immensely powerful creatures, and do not take kindly to being stabbed with spears. The most frequent problem occurred when the whale took it into its 20-pound brain to retaliate. A thirty-foot whaleboat was no match for an enraged, wounded, 60-ton whale, and the harpooned animal might rise up from the depths and grab the boat in its massive jaws, splintering it into so many matchsticks. Both ends of a wounded whale are lethal; the triangular flukes, which might measure 20 feet across, could function as a formidable weapon, crashing down upon the whaleboat and dumping the men into the sea. Other perils faced the whalemen, where the whistling line might take a turn around a leg or an arm, surgically severing it, or yanking the man into

Naturalist Robert Cushman Murphy was aboard the New Bedford whaler *Daisy* from June 1912 to May 1913, and photographed the oarsmen straining to pull the dead weight of the carcass back to the ship for trying-out. (The non-illustrated account of this voyage is Murphy's *Logbook for Grace.*)

the water. Even if the boat was not destroyed, it might be upended and its occupants dumped into the ocean. Many of them could not swim, so such a plunge often spelled death.

An animal that regularly dines on large (although not necessarily giant) squid ought, in theory anyway, to be able to swallow a man. But a whale that consumes 600-pound, ten-armed cephalopods might not be particularly interested in 150-pound bipeds. Sperm whales are accustomed to feeding at great depths, a venue not normally occupied by people. In fact, their occasional feeding on the bottom has resulted in their ingestion of all sorts of curious items, including rocks, shells and sand. Nevertheless, there are records of whales' gobbling up whalemen, leading to the retroactive possibility that it was a sperm whale that swallowed Jonah, a situation that is discussed in some detail in Part Two.

Captain George Wood, sailing on the New Bedford whaler *Ploughboy* on the Offshore Grounds (in the South Pacific west of Peru), had harpooned a whale that turned on his boat and capsized it. The whale grabbed Wood in its mouth, and he wrote that he was "sitting astraddle of his lower jaw under water with his jaw closed holding me tight." With

Wood held in his mouth, the whale brought his flukes down upon the upended whaleboat, killing one man and releasing Wood. Although he was struck several times by the jaw of the whale, the captain gained the safety of the boat, and was taken aboard the *Ploughboy* with his thigh cut to the bone, a wound on his back and another on his head.

A more curious incident occurred in the icy waters of Newfoundland, when a sealer, isolated from his fellows on an ice pan, fell into the water and was swallowed by a sperm whale. Edgerton Davis, a surgeon aboard the sealer, examined the body which had been exhumed from the stomach of the whale after it had been shot, and concluded that there was no way a human could survive in the belly of a whale: "The appearance and the odor were so bad that all save I were forced to turn away, and we were obliged to consign him to the briny deep—the last resting place of many a good sealer—rather than carry him back to his rocky homeland." The most celebrated example, of course, of a whale's attack on a man occurs in *Moby-Dick,* where Ahab has had his leg removed by the white whale: ". . . it was Moby Dick that dismasted me," he says, "Moby Dick that brought me to this dead stump that I stand on now. . . . Aye, aye! It was that accursed white whale that razeed me; made a poor begging lubber of me for ever and a day!"

Although *Moby-Dick* is fiction, the story of an attacking whale is rooted in fact. Melville knew of the true stories of the *Ann Alexander* and the *Kathleen*, two New Bedford whalers that were rammed and sunk by infuriated whales, and he conversed with Owen Chase, the son of the mate of the *Essex*, stove by a whale in the Pacific in 1820. Melville acknowledged this debt when he wrote, "I have seen Owen Chace [*sic*], who was chief mate of the *Essex* at the time of the tragedy; I have read his plain and faithful narrative; I have conversed with his son; and all within a few miles of the scene of the tragedy." (During his brief career as a whaleman on the *Acushnet* in 1841 or '42, Melville had met the son of Owen Chase during a "gam" at sea.) Owen Chase kept a journal of the events of that tragedy and the ensuing voyage which he titled, as per the elaborate custom of the times, *Narrative of the most extraordinary and distressing shipwreck of the Whale-ship Essex, of Nantucket; which was attacked and finally destroyed by a large Spermaceti-whale, in the Pacific Ocean.* The description and the quotes that follow are taken from that journal.

On November 20, 1820, about a year out of Nantucket, the *Essex*, under Captain George Pollard, Jr., was cruising "on the Line" some eighteen hundred miles west of the Galapagos. Chase harpooned a whale which gave his boat a "severe blow with his tail," and stove a hole in it. He cut loose from the whale, stuffed some jackets in the hole, and returned to the ship. He then observed "a very large spermaceti whale, as well as I could judge about eighty-five feet in length," lying quietly a hundred yards off the bow of the *Essex*. The whale charged the ship, smashing into the bow: "The ship brought up as suddenly as if she had struck a rock and trembled for a few seconds like a leaf." The *Essex* began to

The painting commonly known as *All in a Day's Work,* by Charles S. Raleigh in 1878–80. In its death-throes, a harpooned sperm whale might wreck more than one of the comparatively fragile whaleboats.

Capturing a Sperm Whale, an 1835 print by William Page from an original painting by Cornelius Hulsart, is considered the earliest American whaling print. Hulsart was a whaleman who had lost an arm on a whaling voyage, perhaps in an accident like the one shown here.

take in water, and as Chase signaled for the other boats to return, he saw the whale, "apparently in convulsions, on the top of the water about a hundred rods [a rod is 16.5 feet] to leeward. He was enveloped in the foam of the sea that his continual and violent thrashing about in the water had created around him, and I could distinctly see him smite his jaws together, as if distracted with rage and fury." As the ship settled into the water, the whale charged again:

I turned around and saw him, about one hundred rods directly ahead of us, coming down apparently with twice his ordinary speed and, it appeared to me at the moment, with tenfold fury and vengeance in his aspect. The surf flew in all directions about him, and his course towards us was marked by white foam a rod in width, which he made with the continual violent thrashing of his tail. His head was about half out of the water, and in that way he came upon us again and struck the ship.

Later in his narrative, Chase was to reflect on what had transpired, and he concluded that the whale's attack was intentional: "Every fact seemed to warrant me in concluding that it was anything but chance which directed his operations. He made two separate attacks upon the ship within a short interval, both of which, according to their direction, were calculated to do us the most injury. By being made ahead, they thereby combined the speed of the two objects for the shock. To effect this impact, the exact maneuvers which he made were necessary. . . . His aspect was most horrible and such as indicated resentment and fury. He came directly from the shoal which we had just before entered—and in which we had struck three of his companions—as if he were fired with revenge for their sufferings." This was the first recorded instance of a sperm whale's attacking a ship, and because we know he had read Chase's 1821 account, it is not difficult to imagine young Melville's desire to incorporate this incredible story into his whaling novel. In fact, he made it the climax.

As the captain returned to the *Essex,* the ship's decks were awash, and almost dumbstruck, Captain Pollard managed to ask, "My God, Mr. Chase, what is the matter?" Chase replied, "We have been stove by a whale." Chase managed to save a pair of quadrants, two compasses, two books of navigation, the captain's trunk and his own sea chest. The ship sank in ten minutes, but before she disappeared, they cut through the decks and rescued two casks of bread and "as much fresh water as we dared to take in the boats," about sixty-five gallons per boat. They also managed to save "a musket, a small canister of powder, a couple of files, two rasps, about two pounds of boat nails, and a few turtles."

Moby-Dick ends with the sinking of the *Pequod,* but the sinking of the *Essex* is only the beginning of Owen Chase's ordeal. The three whaleboats, with a total complement of twenty men, set out to eastward, trying to make the Pacific coast of South America, some twenty-seven hundred miles away. They sailed south, taking advantage of the prevailing winds, which was the best they could do under the circumstances. (They had oars, of course, but the men were too weak to man them.) On December 20, after a month at sea, suffering blistering sunburn, gut-wrenching hunger and debilitating thirst, they reached what they had identified as Dulcie Island, an uninhabited speck of rock and beach three hundred miles west of Pitcairn Island. If the men had made Pitcairn, at least they would have found people (it was the home of the few remaining descendants of the *Bounty* mutineers), but the landing was so difficult that it probably would have killed them. On Dulcie the desperate survivors of the *Essex* scrounged for food and water, finding only some grasses and some birds, which they consumed ravenously. Three men decided to try their luck on the island rather than endure another indefinite period in the leaking little whaleboats sailing to God knew where. The three boats set off again on December 27, 1820, heading eastward. They hoped to make the Juan Fernández Islands, another two thousand miles away.

With their water almost gone and their bread reduced to an ounce and a half per man per day, the unfortunate wretches began to die. On January 10, after fifty-two days at sea, the second mate succumbed. They "sewed him up in all his clothes, tied a large stone to his feet, and having brought all the boats to, consigned him in a solemn manner to the ocean." During a storm on January 12, 1821, the three boats were separated, and for the duration of his voyage Chase only knew what happened on his own boat. On January 20, Richard Peterson died, and they committed him to the sea, as they had done to Matthew P. Joy. Peterson and Joy would be the last of the crew to receive a burial at sea.

On February 7, after seventy-eight days, Isaac Cole died. This time the survivors did not consign him to the depths, but cut up his body and used it for food. ("In this manner did we dispose of our fellow sufferer, the painful recollection of which brings to mind, at this moment, some of the most disagreeable and revolting ideas that it is capable of receiving.") Of the six men in Chase's boat, three survived, two died and were buried at sea, one was left on Dulcie Island, and one was eaten.

On February 18, after ninety-seven days at sea, Chase and his two companions were spotted by the British brig *Indian,* and they were brought aboard. They had "cadaverous countenances, sunken eyes and bones just starting through the skin," and would not have lasted another three or four days without resorting to the solution used on Captain Pollard's boat. (His boat was picked up off the coast of Chile on February 23 by the Nantucket whaler *Dauphin.* While it was whaling that brought these men to their unfortunate predicament, it was also whaling that saved them. Were it not for the whale-rich grounds of the west coast of South America, there would not have been anybody around to rescue them.) Pollard and Charles Ramsdell were the only survivors of their ninety-six-day ordeal. The captain told his story in Valparaiso: He was in the company of the third boat, and they shared their provisions and their misfortunes until January 28, when the third boat was lost forever. Their provisions had been exhausted by January 14, and on the 25th, Lawson Thomas died and was eaten by his surviving companions. Three more men died of natural causes and were eaten, there being no other thing for the survivors to eat.

On February 1, out of meat, the captain and the three remaining scarecrows drew lots to see which of them would die to save the lives of the others. It fell to young Owen Coffin, the captain's nephew, and "with great fortitude and resignation, he submitted to his fate." When the survivors arrived at Valaparaiso and told their story, a ship was dispatched to rescue the survivors on Dulcie Island. Of the eight men who survived this incredible experience, five went back to whaling, and all five became captains.

In 1851, not far from where the *Essex* had been stove, the *Ann Alexander* was struck by a wounded whale and sunk. The crew put to sea in two boats, and within a fortnight, they were picked up by the whaler *Nantucket.* Five months later, the *Rebecca Simms* harpooned and captured a bull sperm whale, carrying an iron from the *Ann Alexander* and splinters from ship's timbers embedded in his battering-ram head.

In *The Knickerbocker Magazine* for May 1839, Jeremiah N. Reynolds, an officer in the United States Navy, published a piece entitled "Mocha Dick: The White Whale of the Pacific." Reynolds was aboard the whaler *Penguin* as she headed for Santa María for repairs, and he fell into a shipboard conversation with the mate, who believed that "whaling was the most dignified and manly of all sublunary pursuits," and who, "in order to prove that he was not afraid of a whale," had run his boat up against the side of an old bull, leapt to the back of the fish, sheeted his lance home, and returned to the safety of the ship. This same mate, who remains nameless throughout Reynolds' narrative, relates the story of Mocha Dick.

As described by the mate, Mocha Dick was "as white as wool . . . from the effect of age, or more probably from a freak of nature. . . . On the spermaceti whale, barnacles are rarely discovered; but on this *lusus naturae,* they had clustered, until it became absolutely rugged with the shells. In short, regard him as you would, he was a most extraordinary fish; or in the vernacular of Nantucket, 'a genuine old sog' of the first water." The crew utters "in a suppressed tone, the terrible name of MOCHA DICK!" and lowers the boats after the great white whale, his back studded with irons. The mate harpoons him "deep into his thick white side," and they are towed "onward in the wake of the tethered monster," until the whale lessens his impetuous speed. Another boat

closes in—"Good heavens," shouts the mate, "hadn't they sense enough to keep out of the red water!"—and is promptly upended by the whale's flukes. The mate is about to cut the whale loose in order to save the floundering whalemen, but when he sees the captain approaching in another boat, he says, "The captain will pick them up, and Mocha Dick will be ours after all!"

The white whale dives: "By this time two hundred fathoms of line had been carried spinning through the chocks, with an impetus that gave back in steam the water cast upon it. Still the gigantic creature bored his way downward, with undiminished speed. Coil after coil went over, and was swallowed up." Just as they are about to cut the line to keep the boat from being dragged under, the tension lessens, and the whale rises. He tows the boat again, and this time the mate is close enough to plunge a boat-spade into his back, fatally wounding him. "The dying animal was struggling in a whirlpool of bloody foam, and the ocean far around was tinted with crimson. 'Stern all!' I shouted, as he commenced running impetuously in a circle, beating the water alternately with his head and flukes, and smiting his teeth furiously in their sockets, with a crashing sound. . . . [A] stream of black, clotted gore rose in a thick spout above the expiring brute, and fell in a shower around, bedewing, or rather drenching us, with a spray of blood." When they tried-out the carcass— "seventy feet from his noddle to the tips of his flukes"—they found no fewer than twenty harpoons in him, "the rusted mementos of many a desperate recounter." Despite his final flurry, this was not the end of Mocha Dick: "It is of course impossible that Mocha Dick was killed," wrote Howard Vincent in *The Trying-out of Moby Dick,* "for he is deathless. Every reader of *Moby-Dick* knows this."

Reynolds acknowledges that "the particulars of the tale were in some degrees highly colored," but goes on to write that "the facts presented may be a fair specimen of the adventures which constitute so great a portion of the romance of a whaler's life. . . ." White or not, Mocha Dick was a real whale; named not for his color, but for the island of Mocha, off the coast of Chile. Beginning his vendetta some time around 1810, this whale continued to attack ships and boats—not only those associated with whale-killing—throughout the Pacific. In 1840, some two hundred miles off Valparaiso, the British whaler *Desmond* lowered after a huge whale, only to have him turn on the boats and destroy two of them. Two of the whalemen did not make it back to the ship. The whale fit the description of Mocha Dick, a 70-foot behemoth with an 8-foot white scar across his head. Two months later, the Russian whaler *Serepta* was working some five hundred miles to the south when Mocha Dick breached spectacularly between the ship and two boats that were towing a dead whale. He smashed one of the boats, and the other quickly cut the carcass loose and headed for the presumed safety of the ship. The great whale lingered in the vicinity as if standing guard.

The following year, the British whaleship *John Day* was working off the Falklands when the lookout sighted a huge whale. They lowered three boats, two of which were smashed to kindling by the vindictive whale. The migrations of sperm whales were as poorly understood in 1840 as they are today, so when Mocha Dick appeared off the coast of Japan in 1842, no one thought it unusual. He smashed a lumber schooner, but her buoyant cargo kept her afloat long enough for three whalers to come to the scene. The *Yankee, Dudley* and *Crieff* lowered a total of six boats, and in a mad frenzy, Mocha Dick slashed and smashed his way through two of them, swallowed two of the men that were thrown into the water, and destroyed the bowsprit and job boom of the Scottish whaler *Crieff.* Throughout the literature of whaling, the death of Mocha Dick was claimed by many whalers, but his resurrection was the work of Herman Melville.

Frank Bullen was a whaleman who became a writer, like Melville. He sailed on the New Bedford whaler *Splendid* in 1875, but in print he rechristened the ship *Cachalot* and changed the names of all crew members, because he didn't want to "give annoyance or pain to any one, as in many cases strong language has been necessary for the expression of opinions." Many of his stories are so gloriously picturesque that they are regarded as wild exaggerations by whaling historians—for example, the battle Bullen described between a sperm whale and a giant squid has never been witnessed before or since—but he seems indeed to have shipped out aboard the *Splendid,* and despite the skepticism that must accompany his tales, he tells exciting stories, such as

the one he calls "Uncomfortably near being the last." After the author's boat is smashed by the tail of a whale, he is dumped into the water. He turns to see "towering above me . . . the colossal head of the great creature," and muses, "Nor to this day can I understand how I escaped the portals of his gullet, which of course gaped as wide as a church door." He avoids being swallowed, but then finds himself towed along by the whale, and pulls himself "right up along the sloping, slippery bank of blubber until I reached the iron, which, as luck would have it, was planted in that side of the carcass now uppermost." The "carcass" proves not to be dead, however, and takes off with the story-teller attached to a line. Just as the whale is about to breach, it gives a final shudder and dies.

Another standard whaling story concerns the encounter with a sleeping leviathan. Sperm whales, which hunt at such great depths that the water is ink-black, probably depend more on sound than sight. It is possible that they are nocturnal animals, and if this is the case, they may sleep during the day. (How and if sperm whales sleep is completely and unequivocally unknown.) Regardless, a sleeping or dozing whale at the surface might be a serious hazard to navigation. In August 1896, the passenger steamer *Seminole,* en route from New York to Jacksonville, Florida, rammed one whale of a pod (species unknown, but most likely sperm whales), causing it grave injury. As the horrified passengers watched from the railings, the remaining whales turned on the *Seminole* and rammed her no less than four times, causing substantial damage to the steel-hulled ship, but not nearly as much as the havoc that had been wreaked in the same way upon wooden vessels in the past.

IN THE nineteenth century, when so much of the world was still unexplored, the whalemen faced even greater hazards than an occasional sleeping whale. The United States Exploring Expedition under Wilkes had visited many of the island groups in the Central Pacific and found that some of the stories of hostile savages, often cannibals, were true. The Fiji Islands were known—accurately—as The Cannibal Isles, and whenever possible the whalers avoided them. In 1835, the whaler *Awashonks,* out of Falmouth, was attacked by the natives of Namarik in the Marshall Islands, and the captain, the first and second mates, and four crew members were killed before an enterprising whaleman dynamited the deck where the would-be conquerors were standing, and the ship was retaken. The *Syren* was recaptured from Palauan natives only after a box of tacks was scattered on deck, driving the barefoot raiders howling overboard.

The need for fresh vegetables and water often outweighed the threat of being attacked, and even though many of the captains knew or had heard stories of cannibalism and "cutoffs" (a whaleship captured by natives and its crew massacred), they could not resist the temptations of cheap provisioning. Whaleships hardly ever carried money; the very same "slop-chest" that provided the foremast hands with their replacement items of clothing also served as a trading bank. "Recruiting ship" was the term used to describe the acquisition of provisions, and the captain would trade cotton cloth, powder, tobacco, knives and beads for fresh food and water. It was sometimes too much for the parsimonious New Englanders to resist: for a couple of pounds of tobacco or some rusted iron hoops, they could trade for pigs, coconuts, water, wood and women.

The quality of life aboard a whaler was hardly luxurious, but it was often better than life on the farm. Indeed, many whalemen deserted on the islands, not because they were unduly harassed or flogged, but because life on a lush, green island, with free food and even freer women, was an economic and sociological step upward. By the middle of the nineteenth century, there may have been as many as three thousand deserters from whaleships scattered throughout the coral archipelagoes of Micronesia and Polynesia.

Hawaii, Tahiti and the Marquesas are picture-book "South Sea Islands," with tall volcanic mountains, tumbling waterfalls, broad white beaches, and swaying palms. When Herman Melville jumped ship in the Marquesas and subsequently described his experiences in *Typee,* he was responsible for many misinterpretations of life on a tropical island. Not all island groups boasted plentiful paw-paws and willing wahines. Many of these tiny specks in the Pacific were mercilessly unforgiving coral atolls; low rings of sand that had only recently risen out of the Pacific. All along the Equator in the Pacific—the

grounds known as "On the Line"—sperm whales occurred in some profusion. While the vicinity of the Gilbert Islands (then known as the Kingsmill Group) was a good place to kill sperm whales, it was almost as dangerous for the whalers as it was for the whales. The Gilbertese natives were a particularly aggressive and warlike people, but there were also many beachcombers who had been stranded on these islands, men who were eager to lead the natives in attacks on visiting whalers.

Captain Thomas Spencer, of New Bedford, sailed the whaleship *Triton* to Sydenham's Island in January 1848. Even though Spencer knew of the nasty reputation of the islanders of Sydenham's (now known as Nonouti), he put ashore there to trade for food and water, and also for salvage from the ship *Columbia* which had wrecked two years earlier. Unbeknownst to Spencer, a Portuguese sailor named Manuel had also come ashore there. (The records are not clear, but it appears that Manuel was so troublesome that his French captain put him ashore to get rid of him.) Manuel was armed—perhaps with arms that had been salvaged from the *Columbia*—and had already threatened several whalers and merchantmen. It was into this incendiary situation that Thomas Spencer innocently sailed the *Triton.*

Spencer was captured after he had come ashore, and the *Triton* was boarded by Manuel and a band of bloodthirsty Gilbertese. In the ensuing battle, Manuel was killed, and the ship captured by the natives. When Captain Spencer saw his ship's sails disappearing, he gave up all hope and resigned himself to death, perhaps by being eaten. All was not lost. The crew retook the ship, but assuming that Spencer was dead, abandoned him and departed as quickly as possible for the Sandwich Islands. Spencer was rescued by the *Alabama,* another whaleship that had come to Sydenham's for provisions, and he too ended up in Hawaii. Spencer wrote of his adventures immediately he arrived in Hawaii, and since the *Triton* took longer to get there than he did, his report was published before he had learned of the fate of his ship.

In *Whale Hunt,* Nelson Cole Haley tells the rest of the story of the crew of the *Triton* and the death of Manuel ("There was not much life in him for he had been thrust through with a boarding knife two or three times during the first part of the recap-

"Here you are with three or four hundred black-skinned, whooping, roaring ugly devils just ready to board us, and you want me to pull a tooth. Great guns and bags of gold, who would have thought it?" Tooth-pulling illustrated on a pulled tooth.

ture. . . ."), and then leads into the story of his own ship, the renowned *Charles W. Morgan.* At Sydenham's, although they were practically under attack, Haley asks the mate to pull an infected tooth. "I will be damned if I ever heard of such a damn fool thing in all my life," says the mate. "Here you are with three or four hundred black-skinned, whooping, roaring ugly devils just ready to board us . . . and you want me to pull a tooth. Great guns and bags of gold, who would have thought it?" Haley explains that he expects the ship to be captured, and since there is nothing to eat but coconuts on the island, he will starve to death if his tooth is not pulled. "Coconuts be damned," says the mate, "I will pull your head off if you want me to," and with his tooth and a chunk of his jawbone extracted, Haley watches as the *Morgan* drifts closer to Sydenham's amidst a flotilla of Gilbertese canoes manned by caterwauling, gesticulating natives. (It was at this time that Captain John D. Sampson shot a load of buckshot into the bared bottom of one of the chiefs, who had "bowed very low to give it all the effect possible.") A fortuitous breeze saved the *Morgan* as she was about to run aground on Sydenham's Island, leaving behind the natives who "had been dancing up and down with delight" at the prospect of more prisoners.

While an occasional whaler was killed by unfriendly or unreceptive islanders, the effect of the ships' landings on the natives was considerably more severe. Unscrupulous captains would often offer to trade for provisions, and then sail away without giving anything in return, and it is likely that trigger-happy sailors took the lives of many natives without having to worry about punishment so far from any law but the captain's. In *Nimrod of the Sea,* William Davis recounts the story of three kanakas who deserted on a tropical island. After demanding their return from the local natives, "the captain double-shotted his nine-pound guns, sent a round into the crowded grass huts of the village, and carried off three natives." From their home ports and pestilent fo'c'sles, the whalemen brought every conceivable communicable disease to the natives, including yaws, influenza, tuberculosis, cholera, syphilis, and the greatest scourge of the unresistant, measles. Prior to exploration, the population of Tahiti was estimated at some 40,000; by 1830, there were only 9,000 Tahitians left. A single measles epidemic in 1875 killed nearly 30,000 Fijians.

NOT ALL WHALING consisted of hairbreadth interludes with ship-smashing whales or voracious cannibals. In fact, most of the cruises were boring to the point of catatonia. Weeks or months might be spent cruising from one ground to another in search of whales. From the log of the *Acushnet:*

Sunday, Oct. 26, 1845—your humble servant engaged in killing time. . . .

December 16, 1845—Busy doing nothing—nothing to do it with. . . .

Friday, January 23, 1846—Doing nothing special. Dull as you please.

February 4, 1846—Calculated to see whales, made a miscallculation. . . .

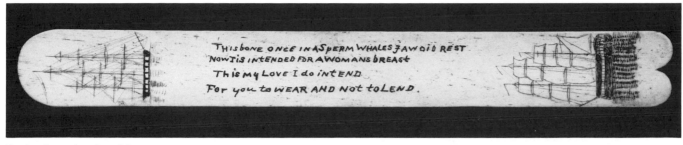

Scrimshaw busk with verse.

July 4, 1846—Employed Eating & Drinking, fretting, Playing Backgammon & Sleeping. . . . Mending a pair of pants. . . .

There was only so much eating, drinking, holystoning of decks, repairing of sails and rigging and yarn-spinning to occupy the sailors on these seemingly endless voyages. To pass the time, some of them created what Clifford Ashley called "the only important indigenous folk art, except for that of the Indians, we have ever had in America; the Art of Scrimshaw."

Although there are very few contemporaneous records of scrimshanders at work—probably because the craft was too insignificant to mention—we assume that the whale teeth were carved during periods of sailing or while waiting in port for provisions or repairs. The teeth were cleaned and polished, then engraved with sail-maker's needles or what Melville referred to as "dentistical implements." The pre-

dominant subjects carved onto the teeth were ships and whaling scenes, and reminders of sweethearts, family and home. The Yankee scrimshanders were best known for their carvings on teeth, but they also fashioned belaying pins, corset stays, canes, knife handles, dominoes, pie-crimpers, and all sorts of tools and boxes. The baleen of the right and bowhead whales was packed into bundles for commerce at home, but occasionally a piece would be shaped into a busk and decorated with contemporary designs. Baleen was colloquially known to the whalers and merchants of the time as whale-*bone,* but it is not bone at all; it is keratin, the substance of human hair and fingernails. Whales have bones like any other mammals, but with the exception of the lower jaw—known as the "pan bone"—and the teeth, whale bones are too porous for carving. (Other cultures recognized the attractive nature of whale ivory. Certain Polynesian natives made necklaces of dolphin teeth, and the pre-missionary Hawaiians crafted the

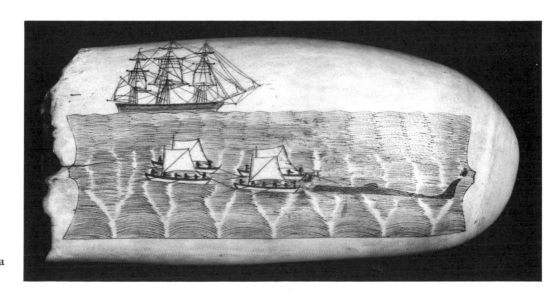

Four boats under sail towing a dead sperm whale, as etched into a tooth.

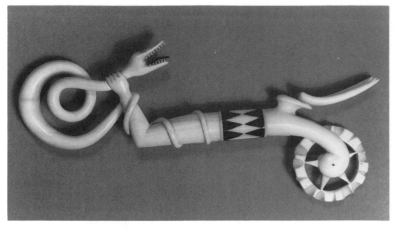

Among the more elaborate scrimshaw items carved from sperm whale teeth were these "jagging wheels." The cogged wheel was used to crimp pie crusts, and the designs on the handles were elaborately frivolous.

beautiful *le niho palaoa,* a gracefully carved sperm whale tooth that was worn by royalty on a necklace of braided human hair.)

Probably the most elaborate project undertaken by the scrimshanders was the *swift,* a complex folding device that was used to hold a skein of wool so that it could be wound. It is difficult to reconcile one of

Only Hawaiian royalty were allowed to wear the *lei niho palaoa,* a gracefully carved sperm whale tooth on a necklace of braided human hair.

these delicate, meticulously engineered contraptions with the stinking conditions of the fo'c'sle, and while there are occasional records of carpenters, coopers, mates, or even captains* working up some of the more elaborate scrimshaw devices, it is more likely that swifts were made on land.

AFTER THE DEATH of the whale, there was still the problem of bringing whale and ship together. If the conquering whaleboat was downwind of the ship, it was a relatively simple matter for Mohammed to sail the ship to the mountain, but if less propitious conditions prevailed, the exhausted whalemen might have to tow the whale back to the ship. And then, after an exhausting chase and a laborious haul with a 50-ton deadweight in tow, the real work began. What had been a free-swimming, powerful sea mammal was effectively reduced to a disparate assortment of its parts, the reduction accomplished by literally tearing it apart.

As in virtually every other aspect of New England whaling, the cutting-in process was described better by Melville than anybody else. (In the Yankee whale fishery, the process of removing the whale from his outer integuments was known as "cutting-in," and the rendering of the blubber into oil was known as "trying-out." In the English fishery, these operations were known respectively as "flensing" and "making off.") In *Moby-Dick* there is one chapter devoted to the actual process, and several more to the by-products, including the "blanket," the "funeral," and the "sphynx"—the last referring to the head of the whale after the body and blubber have been separated from it.

The whale was made fast to the ship by lashing heavy chains through its head and around its flukes. The first part of the whale to be brought aboard was the lower jaw, ripped from the head and laid aside to be dealt with later. Then the whale was decapitated, and if it was a small one, the head was brought aboard. But the head of a large whale, often one-third of its 60-foot, 60-ton body, could not be brought on deck (Melville wrote that "even by the immense tackles of the whaler, this were as vain a

*In the collection of the Mystic Seaport Museum, there are a large number of items carved by Captain Frederick Smith of New Bedford and his wife, Sallie, who seems to have worked alongside him. On the whalers *Ohio* and *John P. West,* Smith reportedly kept a portable lathe in his cabin, and during the 1870s and '80s, the Smiths produced an impressive *oeuvre* of ivory.

The most complicated item made from whale-bone was the swift, a folding reel that was used to hold yarn as it was being wound. It may have required more than a hundred separate pieces, and taken months to make.

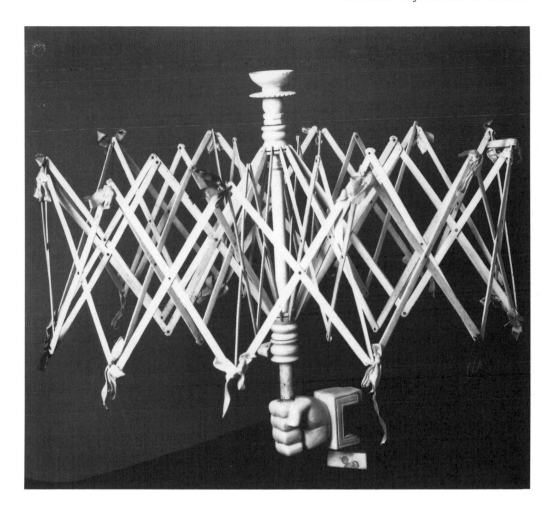

thing as to attempt weighing a Dutch barn in jeweller's scales"), and had to be processed in the water. The "head matter" was saved for last, however, because the carcass of the whale alongside the ship was threatening to the ship by its weight, and the longer it remained unprocessed, the longer the sharks could wreak havoc on the very outer layer of blubber that was of so much interest to the whalers.

By the use of a complicated series of tackles—described by Melville as "ponderous things comprising a cluster of blocks generally painted green, and which no single man can possibly lift"—the cutting stages were lowered, and the process of removing the blubber commenced. Sitting or standing on the lowered cutting stages, men with razor-sharp cutting spades began to slice into the whale's rubbery outer covering. A massive iron hook was inserted in the first piece to come off, and this was hoisted high into the air while the men on the scaffold sliced the blubber. The whale was rotated in the water, and its blubber "stripped off from the body precisely as an orange is sometimes stripped by spiralizing it." The power for this peeling and dismemberment came from the strong backs of the whalemen, who turned the windlass located forward of the foremast.

As the thick spiral of blubber was peeled from the whale, it was cut into sections approximately fifteen feet long and a ton in weight (the "blanket pieces"). These were dropped through a hatch into the blubber room, where they were stored until the carcass of the whale was completely stripped. (With the removal of the blubber and the head, the remainder of the carcass was left for the sharks.) Workers in the dark, bloody blubber room further reduced the blanket pieces to smaller, more manageable "horse pieces," which were then sliced into "Bible leaves," with cuts almost to the skin making them resemble the splayed pages of a thick-leaved book. (It was believed that the opening of the blubber into "pages" made the oil more accessible.) The Bible leaves were then forked back up through the forehatch to the men who would place them in the trypots.

The blubber was minced into "bible leaves" before being placed in the trypots to boil.

Although the trypot fires were usually started with wood, the unmelted skin of the whale made a wonderful fuel, and the whale was therefore cooked in a fire of his own kindling. As the oil was separated from the blubber, it was carefully ladled into a copper cooling tank, where it rested before being casked. Aside from the obvious danger of a fire spreading, the process was—like almost every aspect of whaling—hard, messy and dirty. Oil and blood covered the decks and the people, and the smell was often intolerable. J. Ross Browne called the trying-out process "the most stirring part of the whaling business, and certainly the most disagreeable." He described the nighttime scene aboard the "*Styx*":

Dense clouds of lurid smoke are curling up to the tops, shrouding the rigging from the view. The oil is hissing in the trypots. Half a dozen of the crew are sitting on the windlass, their rough, weather-beaten faces shining in the red glare of the fires, all clothed in greasy duck, and forming about as savage a looking group as ever was sketched by the pencil of Salvator Rosa. The cooper and one of the mates are raking up the fires with long bars of wood or iron. The decks, bulwarks, railing, try-works, and windlass are covered with oil and slime of black-skin, glistering with the red glare of the try-works. Slowly and doggedly the vessel is pitching her way through the rough seas, looking as if enveloped in flames.

At the end of this description, he wrote, "Of the unpleasant effects of the smoke I scarcely know how any idea can be formed, unless the curious inquirer choose to hold his nose over the smoking wick of a sperm oil lamp, and fancy the disagreeable experiment magnified a hundred thousand fold. Such is the romance of life in the whale fishery."

One of the least romantic aspects of the whale fishery was the prospect of fire. Oil-soaked wooden ships upon whose decks fires are being encouraged do not lend themselves to a feeling of security. Care was taken to avoid conflagrations—water was pumped over the decks to keep the planks wet and cool—but occasionally the sails or rigging were ignited by flying sparks, and sometimes the ships burned to the waterline.

When the oil had cooled, it was ladled into the casks that had been made by the cooper. Each barrel held 31½ gallons, and the figures for the fishery were almost always recorded in barrels. Starbuck's 1878 *History of the Whale Fishery,* which contains the records of every American whaling ship, from every American whaling port, "from its earliest inception to 1876" (insofar as these records were known), lists the result of every whaling voyage in sperm oil (barrels), whale oil (barrels), and whalebone (pounds).

A large female sperm whale might yield 35 barrels of oil, while the largest bulls gave up 75 to 90. As with the sometimes questionable lengths of large bulls, where there were reports of 90-footers (Clifford Ashley writes, "If these whalemen's records are accurate, it would appear that the hundred-foot Sperm Whale is not an impossibility"), the yield of these giants was the subject of occasional exaggeration. Because the reports were invariably made by men whose reputation would be enhanced by overstating the yield of individual whales, many of the whales in the 100–150 barrel range must be questioned.*

*If only the whaler's stories remained, we would have no way of verifying the size of the largest whales. There is something that they leave behind, however, and Ashley proposes a novel argument for the existence of gigantic bull sperm whales: he examines a particularly large pair of teeth, over 11 inches long, and suggests that "In the days before the Sperm Whale herds were depleted, there must have been exceptional whales, either larger or older than are found today." Mitchell (1983) finds this argument "well taken, but not conclusive." A look at these teeth, however, which are on display in the New Bedford Whaling Museum, certainly gives one cause to wonder.

When whales were being tried-out, the trypot fires often burned through the night, as shown in this painting by the American marine artist William Edward Norton (1843–1916).

Trypot fires sent billows of oily smoke into the air; the smell carried for miles. Shown here is the bark *Jacob A. Howland* of New Bedford.

The amount of oil that could be taken and stored was enormous, but it didn't necessarily reflect the success of a voyage. The profits of a voyage could only be calculated when the ship reached port and sold the oil and bone at the prevailing prices. A 31-gallon cask was about five feet high and four feet in diameter at its bulging middle. On her maiden whaling voyage, which lasted from October 1841 to September 1843, the *Lagoda* brought home 600 barrels of sperm oil, 2,700 barrels of whale oil and 17,000 pounds of baleen. ("Sperm oil" was the stuff that was ladled out of the whale's "case," and was of a finer quality than "whale-oil," which was rendered out of the blubber. Although they were not averse to taking an occasional right whale or humpback, most

of the whales hunted by the Yankees were sperm whales.) The *Lagoda* was 108 feet long, with a beam of 27 feet. Hunting concluded when there was no more room for the storage of oil, but the whalers sometimes put into port, offloaded some of their greasy cargo, and set out again for the whaling grounds. Some of these sweaty, iron-bound vats were probably stored in the blubber room, but most were stored in the hold.

It was the mysterious "head-matter" of the sperm whale that made it the primary object of this globe-girdling enterprise. Other whales were encased in blubber, and some of them had the long "finnes" that could be converted into milady's bodices. But the spermaceti was the *ne plus ultra* of this business, the pot of liquid gold that attracted the whalers to the Azores and the Galapagos, to Zanzibar and the Japan Grounds, to Kamchatka and the Okhotsk Sea. The stuff is as poorly understood today as it was when some early beachcomber presumed that this vast reservoir in the whale's nose was its seminal fluid. Whatever its purpose to the whale (and it certainly is not its seminal fluid), the amber wax that hardened white as it was exposed to air was worth risking life and limb—and sometimes boat and ship—to the whaler. Kept free from contamination by other oils, sperm oil was worth from three to five times as much as whale oil. In *Nimrod of the Sea*, W. M. Davis records a whale that yielded twenty-seven barrels of spermaceti from the case, and Clifford Ashley's research indicates that the largest bulls gave up something on the order of thirty barrels. At 31.5 gallons per barrel, that works out to 945 gallons of the mysterious liquid wax in the nose of a single whale.

To extract the spermaceti from the head, a much more direct method was employed than the multi-step process of turning blubber into oil. Since the spermaceti already *was* oil, the whalers only had to remove it from the whale and cask it. A hole was cut in the outer fabric of the whale and a man lowered a bucket into it on a long pole, then turned it over to another man on deck who would empty the bucket into a waiting tub—or as Melville put it, "Tashtego downward guides the bucket into the Tun, till it entirely disappears; then giving the word to the seamen at the whip, up comes the bucket again, all bubbling like a dairy-maid's pail of new milk." As with almost every aspect of the fishery, Melville turned this activity into something of dramatic portent, and as Tashtego was ladling the oil out of the whale, he "dropped head-foremost down into this great Tun of Heidelberg, and with a horrible oily gurgling, went clean out of sight!" "Man overboard!" cries Daggoo, and in the ensuing panic, the head breaks loose—with Tashtego still trapped in it—and just as all seems lost ("poor buried-alive Tashtego was sinking utterly down to the bottom of the sea") the redoubtable Queequeg dives in and rescues his fellow harpooner. But the excellence of the spermaceti is such, writes Melville, that "had Tashtego perished in that head, it had been a very precious perishing; smothered in the very whitest and

daintiest of fragrant spermaceti; coffined, hearsed and tombed in the inner chamber and sanctum sanctorum of the whale."

When the oil had all been casked and the casks stowed, the decks were scrubbed down with lye, which had been leached from the cinders and ashes of the tryworks, and the oily, smoky clothes of the whalemen were also scrubbed down, but the pernicious odor of smoked blubber could never really be removed, and until they could exchange their work clothes for new garments, the whalemen usually smelled like disused tryworks.

Despite their discomfort, low wages, and even occasional floggings, the crews of whaleships were remarkably docile. The master's word was law, and when the crew became obstreperous, a "taste of the cat" was not unheard of. Only infrequently did they become so desperate that they rebelled. Since harsh treatment, long hours, uncomfortable quarters and bad food were expected, the whalemen generally endured these indignities in stoic silence. Also, as with any uprising, a leader is required to galvanize men into action, and in the whaleships, these troublemakers were rare. The story of the *Bounty*'s mutiny, which had occurred in 1789—and had nothing whatever to do with whales or whaling—was probably known to every seaman and landlubber on either side of the Atlantic. The fate of Fletcher Christian and the mutineers was not known until 1808, when Captain Mayhew Folger of the Nantucket sealer *Topaz* landed at Pitcairn Island and found the survivors.

On Nantucket Island there lived a young man named Samuel Comstock, who may or may not have heard the tale told by Captain Folger. At the age of nineteen, after three previous cruises, he shipped out aboard the Nantucket whaler *Globe,* departing from Edgartown on the neighboring island of Martha's Vineyard on December 15, 1822. The ship rounded the Horn on March 5, and stopped briefly at Hawaii before heading for the newly discovered Japan Grounds. Despite the reports of plentiful whales off Japan, Captain Worth was unable to locate them, and as they sailed in fruitless circles, the crew became increasingly discontented. Rotten meat was an issue, and conditions were so bad that the captain turned back and headed for Hawaii to reprovision. There several members of the crew deserted, and the *Globe*'s depleted crew was replenished with beachcombers and drunkards. Repeated conflicts between officers and crew increased the tension, and when the captain had one of the men flogged, Comstock decided to initiate a mutiny.

On January 26, 1824, Samuel Comstock led his followers in one of the bloodiest mutinies in American naval history. They murdered Captain Worth with an axe, slaughtered First Mate Beetle with a boarding knife, shot Second Mate Lumbard in the mouth and then bayonetted him, and shot Third Mate Fisher in the back of the head. They heaved the bodies overboard, and with Comstock at the helm, looked for a place where they could land. En route, Comstock decided that one of his crew members was plotting against him, held a "trial" and sentenced him to hang. For two weeks they wandered around, uncertain of their location or destination, until they decided to land at tiny Mili Atoll, in what was then known as the Mulgrave Islands, and is now known as the Ratak chain of the Marshall Islands. It appears that Comstock's original plan was to arrange things so that he was the only survivor, but the natives and his fellow mutineers conspired against his plan for the perfect mutiny. As Comstock began to give the ship's stores to the natives (to ensure their support), the crew members who had signed on in Hawaii realized that they were in for trouble either from their leader or from the natives, and they shot Comstock dead.

Those members of the crew of the *Globe* who had not participated in the mutiny managed to gain control of the ship and sailed away, leaving the mutineers stranded on the island. They would not last long. A bloody conflict between the natives and the whalemen resulted in the death of all the latter but two: William Lay, of Saybrook, Connecticut, and Cyrus Hussey, of Nantucket. The *Globe* was sailed to Valparaiso, where the news of the mutiny was made known, and then returned to Nantucket. Her crew was cleared of complicity in the mutiny, and the *Dolphin,* under the command of Lieutenant John ("Mad Jack") Percival, was dispatched to the Pacific to find and bring back the mutineers. Hussey and Lay had been with the natives for almost a year and a half by the time the *Dolphin* arrived, and they

looked more like natives than American whalemen. After considerable tension—the Marshallese chiefs were prepared to kill the newly arrived Americans and take their ship—and confusion about who they were, the last of the *Globe*'s crew were transported home. Thus ended the story that Starbuck called "the most horrible mutiny that is recounted in the annals of the whale-fishery from any port or nation."*

The savage mutiny aboard the *Globe* was not whaling's only insurrection. When the captain of the New Bedford whaler *Junior* served the crew moldy, weevily bread and stinking, rotten meat, they became progressively more miserable, but had it not been for a harpooner named Cyrus Plummer, they would probably have completed their voyage with only the usual grumbling. Plummer had been flogged for insubordination (he had retaliated when the mate had socked him), and convinced nine of his fellow crew members to mutiny. On Christmas night 1857, off the desolate coast of southeastern Australia, they killed all the officers except the first mate, took to the whaleboats and made for land. They landed at Cape Howe (some 250 miles south of Sydney), and split up into three groups. Six were captured within a couple of days of their landfall, but Plummer and the other three made it to Sydney. They all got drunk, and the other three were captured, but Plummer's luck held until he was trapped because of some gold he had stolen. He was brought back to the United States to stand trial and found guilty of mutiny, a capital crime. Although he was scheduled to hang, the sentence was commuted to life imprisonment by President James Buchanan, and Plummer died in prison.

---

*Not only was this the most horrible mutiny, it was also the best documented. After their return and exoneration, Lay and Hussey wrote a book which they called *A Narrative of the Mutiny on Board the Ship Globe of Nantucket, in the Pacific Ocean, Jan. 1824. And the Journal of a Residence of Two Years on the Mulgrave Islands: With Observations on the Manners and Customs of the Inhabitants.* Samuel Comstock's younger brother George—who was aboard the *Globe* but took no part in the mutiny—also wrote a book about his adventures, and the depositions given by the crew members who sailed the ship to Valparaiso are part of the public record. In addition, whaling historians from Starbuck to Stackpole have discussed the details of the mutiny, and there has been one modern book (*Mutiny on the Globe,* by Edwin Hoyt) devoted entirely to this story.

SIX

RIGHT AND GRAY WHALING

The British Greenland Fishery

Although the Dutch sent the first whalers into the Davis Strait in 1719 when it appeared that the Spitsbergen fishery was over, they were quickly followed by the British. (The Davis Strait was named for John Davis, who discovered it in 1585, eleven years before Barendsz discovered Spitsbergen.) British whalers were encouraged by their government's relaxation of any duties and taxes, as long as the crews were Englishmen. (The high costs of outfitting whaling voyages in the 1730s was a result of having to hire Dutch officers, since the British, according to Scoresby, "were entirely unacquainted with the trade.")

By the end of the eighteenth century, ships from Hull and Whitby in England, and Dundee and Peterhead in Scotland, were dispatched to West Greenland to hunt plentiful Greenland whales. In London the first wet dock (Rotherhithe) was built by the Duke of Bedford on the Thames to accommodate as many as 120 sail. The burgeoning textile industry needed whale oil, primarily for "fulling," the cleaning of wool prior to spinning it, and also to light the interiors of the dark mills where the wool was spun. (By the middle of the century, sperm oil candles were used to light the homes of the gentry because they were odorless and smokeless.) The rise of industrialization called for more and more oil for lubrication, and oil was also used for street-lighting. The northern city of Hull, an early British whaling port, had had street lights since 1713, and by 1750, London was known as the best-lit city in the world, with more than five thousand street lights. At this time too, whalebone was in great demand for skirt hoops and corset stays, so the incentives for the whalers were enormous. To help meet these new requirements, the British government agreed to subsidize the whaling industry. They offered a bounty of thirty shillings per ton (of shipping), but when this did not produce the desired result, they raised it to forty. Two ships were fitted out in 1749; 20 by 1750; and 83 by 1756. By 1788, there were 253 ships engaged.

The city of Hull, which had participated so vigorously in the Spitsbergen fishery, jumped back into the whaling business in 1753, when its magnates raised £20,000 "for carrying on the whale fishery from that port." The following year, they sent the *Pool, Berry, York* and *Leviathan* to the Arctic. During this period, British shipping was being harassed by

William Scoresby, Sr. (1760–1829), Britain's most successful whaling captain.

French privateers, and there were often sea battles that involved ships whose armament consisted mostly of harpoons and flensing knives. By 1758 the whaling fleet was traveling in convoy to resist the predatory French frigates. The other threat to the whale fishery came from within, although it too was inspired by the French: the Royal Navy was on the lookout for able-bodied seamen, and while the Greenland fishery was considered a "protected trade," the whalemen might be press-ganged as they approached their home ports. The Treaty of Paris concluded the Seven Years' War in 1763, but it would not be long before the British were at war again.

While the Yankees ranged the world for sperm whales, the British were hunting the animal known to them as the Greenland or polar whale, to science as *Balaena mysticetus,* and to the American whalers as the bowhead. Scoresby wrote that it

occurs most abundantly in the frozen seas of Greenland and Davis Strait—in the bays of Baffin and Hudson—in the sea to the northward of Behring's Strait, and along some parts of the northern shores of Asia, and probably America. It is never met with in the German Ocean, and rarely within 200 leagues of the British coasts. . . .

The whales of the Davis Strait and Baffin Bay to the north appear to have been a discrete stock that wintered north of Labrador and then moved northward along the west coast of Greenland in April, May and June. By summer the whales had crossed

Baffin Bay and entered the ice-choked waters of Lancaster Sound and other inlets along Baffin Island, then in August they began to make their way southward to their winter habitat in the shifting pack ice of Davis Strait, almost to the open North Atlantic.

When the Dutch whaling industry declined during the early eighteenth century, the British shipowners were ready to rush into the breach. With fewer vessels working the Greenland ice, average catches and prices rose, making the 1740s one of the most lucrative decades for individual owners. More and more owners got into the business, and by 1788, there were more than 250 ships heading for the ice. As with so many aspects of this fishery, it was Scoresby who described it best:

To particularise all the variety in pack-fishing, arising from the winds and weather, size of the fish, state and peculiarities of the ice, &c. would require more space than the interest of the subject, to general readers, would justify. I shall therefore, only remark, that pack-fishing is, on the whole, the most troublesome and dangerous of all others;—that instances have occurred of fish having been entangled during 40 or 50 hours, and escaped after all;—and that other instances are remembered, of ships having lost the greater part of their stock lines, several of their boats, and sometimes, though happily less commonly, some individuals of their crews.

There are many names familiar to historians of the whaling industry, but probably none is more illustrious than that of William Scoresby, Jr. Like Charles Scammon, Thomas Roys, Svend Foyn or Carl Anton Larsen, Scoresby was a whaling captain. Only Herman Melville, whose fame lies equally in a fictional description of a whale and a factual description of the whaling industry, served before the mast.

Born in Cropton, Yorkshire, in 1789, William Scoresby was the son of a whaler, also named William Scoresby. He went to sea on Scoresby senior's *Resolution* in 1799, as a mere lad of ten. Before he made his next recorded voyage to the Arctic, he went back to school, and in 1806 he entered the University of Edinburgh, where he studied chemistry, natural philosophy, and anatomy. Unlike most of his contemporaries in the whaling business, he was remarkably proficient in languages, since he was able to read and translate Latin, French, German, and even Anglo-Saxon in his researches on the early history of

whaling. In 1807, he entered the naval service, but perhaps feeling that his education was incomplete, he returned to Edinburgh after a year at sea. In 1810, he was off again, this time as the captain of the *Resolution,* his father's old ship. He sailed the West Ice for sixteen years, accumulating a truly remarkable record, including a survey of the previously unmapped east coast of Greenland, and the collection of the largest cargo of oil and bone ever brought from Greenland to Liverpool. Upon returning from his last voyage in 1826, he entered Queens' College, Cambridge, where he was ordained a curate, and at the same time, he was elected a Fellow of the Royal

William Scoresby, Jr. (1789–1857), whaleman, clergyman, linguist, scientist, explorer and author of "one of the most remarkable books in the English language," *An Account of the Arctic Regions with a History and a Description of the Northern Whale-Fishery.*

Society. Scoresby junior traveled to Australia in 1857 to gather further data on the magnetism of the earth, and he died on March 21, 1857, in Torquay.

Despite his record as a whaler and a scientist, Scoresby's immortality lies in his written words. In 1820, he published his *Account of the Arctic Regions with a History and Description of the Northern Whale-Fishery,* which is one of the most important books ever written on whaling. In this two-volume work, Scoresby examines the history of the fishery, the ice conditions, the technology of whaling, and the zoology of the Arctic. Volume II includes maps, illustrations of the land formations, snowflake patterns, the tools used in whaling and processing, and the hunted animals—all drawn by "W. Scoresby, Junr."*

Scientist, linguist, historian, clergyman, navigator, cartographer, illustrator, and above all, whalerman, Scoresby is the ideal man to guide us through the labyrinthine history of whaling in the high Arctic. His name has been mentioned before, in the discussions of early European whaling and the Spitsbergen fishery, on which he was as knowledgeable as anyone before his time or since, but it is in the Greenland fishery that Scoresby's monumental contributions become evident. In his 1928 *History of Whaling,* Sir Sidney Harmer wrote, "We are fortunate in having an account of the Greenland Whale written by so talented a man. His temperament was thoroughly scientific, and he touches no subject which he does not illuminate. A large part of our knowledge of whaling is based on the evidence of untrained observers, but in consulting Scoresby we are sure that any account he gives of his own observations is trustworthy, and we are impressed by his scientific acumen and the clarity of judgment with which he handles his material."

Scoresby begins at the beginning (his opening words are "In the early ages of the world . . ."), and

proceeds to "illuminate" Othere (where he corrects the Anglo-Saxon of Orosius), the Basques, the Dutch, the English, the American Colonies and in succinct summaries, the whaling enterprises of the Spaniards, French, Danes, Germans, Norwegians, Prussians and Swedes. There have been subsequent studies of British whaling history, but none has the freshness and the accuracy of Scoresby. Although his publication did not appear until 1820, his history of the early years of the whale fishery is probably the best in existence.*

"Ice whaling," as it was known at the time, was different from any whaling that had preceded it, and because it was without precedent, had to be learned on the job. Even more than the whales, the ice determined the success or failure of a given voyage. (Its importance can be observed in Scoresby's book, where he accords ninety-three pages to descriptions of bergs, fields, floes, drift ice, sludge and hummocks.) All ice affected the whalers, but none more than the drifting ice that came down into Baffin Bay in the spring. The ice that gave the fishery its name comes from the polar ice cap; it drifts south as land ice and sea ice, moved by the gyres and streams of the ever-flexing, living Arctic Ocean, changing into pack and fast ice, always changing, always dangerous, never the same from year to year.†

"The Providence of God," wrote Scoresby, "is manifested in the tameness and timidity of many of the largest inhabitants of the earth and sea, whereby they fall victims to the prowess of man, and are rendered subservient to his convenience in life. . . ." A

---

*In 1851, Scoresby Jr. published an account of his father's "adventurous life." He discussed William Scoresby's "commencement and progress . . . as commander," including such innovations as the replacement of the *steward-surgeon,* previously a combination cook and medical practitioner, with a real doctor; his invention of the enclosed crow's nest (a barrel to replace the lookout's exposed position in the cross-trees); his command of the *Henrietta, Dundee, Resolution, and John of Greenock,* with a total catch of 533 whales, calculated by his son to have brought in almost £200,000. In the "concluding notices" of *My Father,* he wrote, "In character, my Father was patriotic, benevolent and philanthropic; in temper, quick and passionate, but soon composed, and singularly free from animosity against those with whom he had been at variance, and *most foregoing* to those who had injured him."

*In *The Trying-Out of Moby-Dick,* a detailed study of the writing and meaning of Melville's novel, Howard Vincent writes that Scoresby's "two closely-packed volumes are the fullest account ever written by a genuine whaleman gifted with scientific caution and restraint." Even Melville was willing to concede this; he makes many references to a "Charley Coffin," a pseudonym for Scoresby, and then, mentioning Scoresby by name, he says he was "a real professional harpooner and whaleman. . . . On the separate subject of the Greenland or right-whale, he is the best existing authority."

†One of the great disappointments of Scoresby's career was his failure to receive the assignment to search for the Northwest Passage. In 1817 he had written to Sir Joseph Banks, President of the Royal Society, that upon his return from the Arctic, he was able to report that some two thousand square leagues of ice had vanished from the sea between Greenland and Iceland, and that this would be an ideal time to resume the search: "Had I been so fortunate as to have had the command of an expedition for discovery, instead of fishing," wrote Scoresby, "I have little doubt that the mystery attached to the existence of a north-west passage might have been resolved." While Banks agreed that the time was opportune, he sent not Scoresby, but Commanders John Ross and David Buchan, neither of whom came remotely close to succeeding.

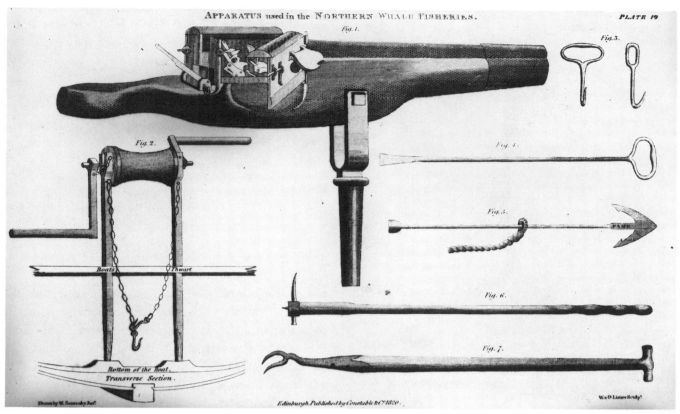

Apparatus used in the northern whale fishery. Drawn by William Scoresby, Jr., from *An Account of the Arctic Regions.*

clear understanding of the purpose for which whales had been placed on earth made it possible for men like Captain Scoresby to kill them with equanimity.

THE GREENLANDMEN were usually ready for departure from their home ports by the end of April, to take advantage of the short Arctic summer. The voyage across the North Atlantic usually took about ten days, and if their origin was Hull or Whitby, they required a circumnavigation of Scotland before heading west. They drifted toward Greenland in search of whales in the pack ice. The other area worked by the British was the Davis Strait, on the west coast of the island, around Cape Farewell. The Farewell passage was particularly dangerous, because the weather was usually bad, and formidable icebergs could appear silently out of the fog. Scoresby described the dangers of encountering icebergs in storms as "one of the most appalling dangers which can be presented to the navigator." It would be hard to imagine anything more terrifying than to be sail-

ing slowly and painstakingly through a dense sea fog, and suddenly see an iceberg towering over your fragile ship. Unlike the *Titanic* (which struck an iceberg and sank far to the south of where this fishery took place), these little wooden windships were eminently sinkable, and it is a testimony to their pilots that so many of them made repeated Arctic voyages in the most inhospitable conditions imaginable. Voyages averaged about four months, but could be shorter if the ships filled their holds in less time—and shorter yet if the ships met with disaster. In 1814 and then again in 1817, British whalers were lost with all hands in the ice of the Davis Strait.

In comparison to the Yankee sperm whale fishery, British whaling was a small-scale enterprise. The Americans had some 635 whalers at sea in 1856, compared to less than 100 from the British ports of Hull, Aberdeen and Peterhead. While the Americans' was a profit-sharing system, the British employed a considerably less democratic arrangement. Each whaling company was composed of partners,

During the course of the struggle, a whale might bend the harpoon shaft like a pretzel.

primarily the merchants, coopers, sail-makers and other businessmen who outfitted the whalers, thereby dividing the profits—and the risk—between a large number of people. The individual hands were paid a monthly wage, often £2, and out of this, like their Yankee counterparts, they had to buy their clothing and supplies from the ships' stores. For each voyage, a man might spend between £5 and £7 on a lamb's wool wig, two or three pairs of mittens, flannel shirts, an underjacket, stockings, drawers, blankets and boots. The captain might receive £8 per month, plus "oil and bone money" dependent upon the success of the voyage, and the harpooners and the spectoneers were also paid a higher wage. The schedule of payments was complicated and awkward; some of the men would be paid upon signing aboard, but the Shetlanders would not be paid until the whalers called again eight months after the voyage had ended.

Because of the location of the fishery, the predominant meteorological condition was cold in all its possible permutations: ice, snow, sleet, spray, biting winds and subfreezing temperatures. Often everything—including the men—was covered with ice. In *Account of the Arctic Regions,* Scoresby wrote that

The hands, if exposed, would have frozen in a few minutes; and even the face would not have resisted the effects of a brisk wind, continued for any length of time. A piece of metal when applied to the tongue, instantly adhered to it, and could not be removed without its retaining a portion of the skin; iron became brittle . . . brandy of English manufacture and wholesale strength was frozen. . . .

When enough ice had formed on the rigging, the ship was in danger of capsizing from the weight, and the rudder, if not freed from accumulated ice, would have quickly become immovable. Fires were lit in the cabins, but if the doors were left open to allow the smoke to escape, the warming effects of the fires were often negated. To survive the bitter cold, the whalemen often wore almost everything they had. In his journal for April 10, 1815—reproduced in part in Tom and Cordelia Stamp's *Greenland Voyager*— Scoresby described the crew's appearance as "the most ridiculous form, and the most tasteless arrangement imaginable." He further described the "large boots, mitts and upper jackets, sashes for the waist, comforters for the neck and immense cow hair wigs for the head and ears, decorated with prodigious tails covering the shoulders and extending halfway down the back. In addition to these some of the crew wear waterproof sealskin jackets, trousers and mitts, forming one of the most grotesque groups that can be readily imagined."

Despite their layers of clothing, the cold severely affected the crews of the Greenland whalers, most frequently manifesting itself in frostbite of the hands, feet and face. During "normal" conditions—that is, when not trapped in the ice—British whalemen were also susceptible to chills, colds (then referred to as *catarrh*), asthmas and scurvy. Scoresby believed that scurvy was caused by the intense cold, and he therefore tried to keep his men as warm as possible. (He also believed that the warmth generated by tea or soup was "preferable to that occasioned by spirits.") On May 11, 1811, Scoresby wrote that the surgeon, "either by love of gain of a 5/ bet or the fear of being called a coward, stripped off most of his clothes and committed his body to the water alongside the *Aim-well,* swam a few yards, and returned amidst the acclamation of the sailors who pronounced him *mad.''*

As with whaling voyages everywhere, food was a matter of great concern. Alexander Trotter, the twenty-year-old doctor aboard the *Enterprise,* wrote in his journal entry for May 25, 1856:

For dinner we had a pie of some sea birds (looms they are called) and they tasted excellent. Perhaps this was owing to our appetites being somewhat sated with beef and pork on board which was all brought from Scotland. A good deal of it is fresh beef however (for hanging it up in legs about the rigging keeps it from spoiling), but for all this as a matter of course it is not half as good as when newly killed. The rest is salted and is nearly as good as the other. But the beef I can easily make myself like, but the bad water tried me most: I have to drink it with lemon juice it tastes so very bad.

Because the captain, surgeon and mate inhabited the cabin, they dined differently from the crew. Indeed, they dined differently from the petty officers (the second mate, spectioneer, harpooners, carpenters and coopers), who occupied cabins below decks, and were known collectively as "half-deck men." Here, according to Basil Lubbock, they enjoyed the "privilege" of hot sea-pie, which is described (in an 1820 sailor's log) as follows:

This savoury dish was made in layers or decks; the first one of bones to keep the paste from burning to the bottom of the pan; then followed a stratum of fresh beef paste and seasonings, deck after deck, until the great kettle was full. Sufficient water was added to enable the mess to be cooked.

(When the *Diana* was trapped in the ice in December 1866, and temporarily abandoned, the crew was reduced to eating a breakfast that consisted of coffee and a scrap of cold beef; a dinner of "the thinnest possible pea soup" and a morsel of salt pork; and tea of "a saucepan of *burgoo*—i.e., thin oatmeal porrige. . . ." By January, scurvy had appeared aboard the ship.)

Each of these small ships—they averaged about three hundred tons—sailed from England with a complement of about twenty men: the master, the mates, a surgeon and specialists such as the carpenter, blacksmith, cooper and cook. There were also harpooners—one to each of the seven whaleboats—and the spectioneer, who was in charge of the flensing operations. When the ship reached the Orkneys or Shetlands, additional crew members would be signed on, primarily as oarsmen.* The full complement of a Hull whaler was about fifty men. On the whaling grounds, the crew was divided up into boat crews, each with a harpooner, a boatsteerer, and oarsmen. The whaleboats, hung from davits, were outfitted with coils of line, harpoons, lances and whatever other furnishings and equipment was necessary for what might be an extended trip in a small, open boat among the icebergs.

The whale was spotted from the crow's nest, and then the boats were lowered. (Often a boat was already lowered to save time; the "bran-boat" was towed along behind the ship.) The lowering of the whaleboats (known as the "fall" from the Dutch word *val,* meaning "jump") was a noisy, frantic routine, since the whalemen were often in such a hurry that they brought their shirts and boots in their hands and dressed in the boats. They rowed after the whale, being careful not to frighten the animal with noise. As in most whaling societies, the role of harpooner was one of high esteem, and in the British ice fishery, the job was reserved for the master or the mates. More practical than the Yankee whalers, the British did not perform the fore-and-aft dance where the harpooner steered the boat and then changed places with the bow oar when the whale was to be struck. Instead, the harpooner manned the bow oar, which put him in position when they were close enough to the whale. The harpoon—an iron shaft with a flat, two-barbed head—was then hurled at the back of the whale. (The whale's head was avoided because it was too bony, and the tail because the harpoon might pass right through it.)

There are few descriptions of the weapons employed during this period; Scoresby discusses and illustrates the throwing harpoons, but he also mentions "an auxiliary weapon, which has, at different

*From the often hazy vantage point of hindsight, it is not clear why such a large proportion of the crews were picked up in the Shetlands or Orkneys. It may have been that the islanders needed paying jobs, or that they had a particular expertise in or enthusiasm for whaling. Whatever the motivation, large numbers of men left the comforts of their homes every year to participate in these cold, dangerous voyages.

When a whale was sighted, "A fall" was shouted, which brought the whalemen rushing on deck, often half-dressed. (This drawing, from the 1862–63 log of the *Tarquin,* of Boston, actually shows sailors being called on deck to reef topsails, but the chaos was similar.)

periods, been of some celebrity. This is the harpoon-gun." There were many experimental weapons, but it was not until the 1800s that guns were being used with any regularity. The Society of Arts of London offered inducements to whalemen who used or improved the weaponry, but "on account of the difficulty and address requisite in the management of it . . . it has not been so generally adopted as might have been expected." Aboard the *Enterprise,* out of Fraserburgh, Alexander Trotter wrote that in the whaleboat's bow was "a loaded harpoon gun like a small cannon with a harpoon in it, and a long line coiled up in the bottom of the boat attached to it." For the most part, cold and ice precluded the priming and loading of weapons in rough seas, and in the centuries-old tradition of the Basques, the harpooners relied on their trusty oarsmen to bring them into range and their strong arms to propel the killing irons.

The moment the whale was struck was the most dangerous in all open-boat whaling. The wounded animal might smash a whaleboat with its flukes, or dive for the bottom threatening to pull the boatload of intrepid whalers with him. Or he might take off for the safety of the ice, taking the line and the boat with him. Often more than one harpoon was needed, as the whale tried to escape under the ice. Weakened by the harpoon, the whale was dispatched with lance thrusts to its vitals: "In dying, it turns on its back or on its side; which joyful circumstance is announced by the capturers with the striking of flags, accompanied by three lively huzzas!" The sea was red with blood, "and the ice, boats and men are often drenched with the same." If there were many whales to be killed at once—there were occasions in the Davis Strait where as many as 10 or 15 whales might be killed at a single fall from one ship—the whalers would kill as many whales as they could, mark them with flags, and then go after the others. In 1823, the whaler *Cumbrian,* of Hull, described ". . . the dead bodies of hundreds of flenched whales, and the air for miles around was tainted with the faetor which arose from such masses of putridity. Towards evening, the numbers come across were even increasing, and the effluvia which then assailed our olfactories became almost intolerable." (Often these large aggregations were composed of young whales or females with calves; age was of no interest to the whalers, and they killed them all. Naturally this accelerated the elimination of the species, since none of these juveniles ever had a chance to breed.)

"Pack fishing" was the term used to describe whaling close to packs of drift ice; this was said to be the favorite haunt of the larger whales. When the pack ice had solidified to become the floating platforms known as "fields," the whalers could indulge in what Scoresby called "the most agreeable, and sometimes the most productive" of all whaling. If the field was extensively frozen, the whales would have to come up to breathe near where they were harpooned; but if it was thin and full of holes, the whales could surface within the field to breathe, and the whalers either lost the whale completely or chased it over the ice, running from hole to hole, trying to spear it. In "crowded ice" or "open packs," the whalers were at a distinct disadvantage, since the ships could barely maneuver among the floes, and they often anchored or fastened to the ice sheet and waited for whales to be spotted so they could take after them in the whaleboats.

To maneuver in the ice-filled or ice-covered waters of Davis Strait, the whalemen devised various tech-

The British northern whale fishery, showing the Hull whaler *Harmony* in the Davis Strait some time before 1829, the year of the print's publication. In the left foreground are narwhals and a walrus; whale jawbones are suspended from the rigging to drain the oil.

Shooting the Harpoon at a Whale, a British print first published in 1813. Although experimental harpoon cannons were used at this time, there would not have been such powerful weapons mounted in a little whaleboat.

niques for moving slowed or trapped ships. "Mill-dolling" consisted of men shifting from side to side in a boat hung under the bowsprit in order to loosen the ice. When the ice thickened even more, the captain would order his company to run forward and aft on the deck, creating a rocking motion and freeing the ship, an aerobic exercise that was known as "overing." To pull the ship forward in even thicker ice, the crew would warp ice anchors ahead of the vessel, then reel themselves along by winching the warps around the capstan. If the ice was too thick to plow through it at all, the saws would be broken out and a path sawn, through which the ship might move. As a last resort, explosives might be used to blast a pathway through the ice to avoid the prospect of being "nipped."

In 1813 the *Esk,* of Whitby, Captain Scoresby, Jr., found herself locked in a large triangular bay formed by massive fields and floes. Also locked in this bay were a number of small whales. The inevitable results obtained for the whales, and Scoresby got to write a section of his book called "Bay Ice Fishing." (To search the hummocks for breathing holes, Scoresby invented what he called "ice-shoes," which seem to have been a primitive form of skis. They

were six feet long, seven inches wide, and fastened to his boots by a loop of leather. "When the ice was smooth," he wrote, "it was easy to move in a straight line; but, in turning, I found a considerable difficulty, and required some practice before I could effect it without falling.") They fished in storms (rarely), and in fog—regularly. Fog was such an important element in the ice fishery that Scoresby devoted an entire section of his chapter "Atmospherology" to it, calling it "one of the greatest annoyances that the arctic whalers have to encounter."

When a whale was killed, it was brought alongside the ship to be flensed—or "flinched," "flenched" or "fleenched," depending upon what part of England the whaleman came from. As with all open-boat whaling, this involved towing the carcass to the ship, but in the ice fishery, this seemed to be an enjoyable activity. Perhaps because there was no longer any danger involved, but only hard work, the whalers "performed with great expressions of joy." The whale was lashed alongside the ship with its head toward the stern, so that even the least forward motion of the ship would not be impeded by the gaping maw of the dead whale. The flensers were lowered down onto the carcass of the whale, with cramponlike "spurs" fastened to their boots to give them some purchase on the slippery belly of the whale. The blubber was cut with flensing knives, peeled off in thick sheets, and hauled on deck, whence it was lowered to the *flens gut,* the center of the ship's hold. There it was reduced to more manageable pieces (sometimes using the gristly flukes as a chopping block), and passed through the bungholes in the storage casks. The two "sides" of baleen were brought aboard in one piece, split into "junks" of five to ten blades each, and stowed away. The British ice whalers saved the blubber, the baleen, and occasionally the jawbones (which were brought home to be used as structural supports for sheds, arches and gateways); tons of meat and viscera were left for the scavenging birds, polar bears and sharks. An average whale produced twenty to thirty tons of blubber and perhaps two tons of baleen. It took about four hours to reduce a whale to its usable components.

Ice whaling enjoyed no facilities for boiling down the blubber at sea; despite the comfort that might have resulted from blubber fires in Greenland waters, on-board tryworks were not part of this fishery. (By this time, they were certainly being employed by the Yankee sperm whalers, but William Scoresby senior—one of the early leaders of British whaling technology—had found it impossible to extract the considerable amount of oil from the spongy "fenks," or unmelted pieces of blubber, and the idea was abandoned.) The Dutch boiled off the oil in Spitsbergen or Greenland, and because the blubber did not have the chance to spoil, their oil was usually purer and cleaner.

En route to the factories of Hull or London, the blubber, which had been in the form of fibrous fat, usually began to liquefy. If not properly cleaned on board ship, it also might begin to spoil, so an arriving whaler quite often stank powerfully, as did its crew.* The casks were emptied into great copper vats, with a capacity of up to ten tons, and boiled to extract the oil out of the blubber. Pieces of blubber that would not melt, known as "fenks" or "fritters," were ladled out of the oil, which was run through a pipe to be cooled in oblong cisterns known

*The process of boiling was also quite malodorous, but "perhaps," wrote Scoresby, "not more so than the vapour arising from any other animal substance submitted to the action of heat when in a putrid state."

To enable him to keep his footing while working on the slippery, rolling carcass of a whale, the whaleman wore a set of "spurs," spiked like a mountaineer's crampons.

as "backs." (The apparatus for preparing the baleen was known as a "steeping-back.") The highest quality whale oil was a pale yellowish color, while the poorer oils were darker. It was sold by the tun, which was the equivalent of 252 gallons. When the oil had cooled, it was casked and stored for distribution throughout the country.

Carrying home tiers of casks of rotting blubber and meat meant that the oil was often seriously contaminated or stale. Originally, the smell of whale-oil lamps was considered unimportant, but as other, sweeter oils came onto the market, whale oil began to lose its popularity. It had been one of the primary ingredients of soap-making, but was being replaced by vegetable oils. (In 1632 the Society of Soapers of Westminster attempted to replace the whale oil being brought in by the Greenland Company with rapeseed oil. In response, the whalers of Hull joined forces with the other soap-makers of northern England to boycott the rapeseed soap. The Greenland fishery, which had been severely threatened by this potential reduction of its sales, was reprieved, at least for the moment. Whale-oil soap dominated the washtubs of Britain until the beginning of the nineteenth century, when whalers of the Greenland fishery repeatedly brought back rancid oil, which could only be used to produce foul-smelling soap. The soap was rejected, and it appeared that the whales were

THE
WHALEBONE
MANUFACTORY,
South street, Kingston-upon-Hull

G. R.

By the King's Letters Patent.

The Public is respectfully informed, that Orders are received and executed with the greatest punctuality and dispatch, for

*SIEVES and RIDDLES of every description.

NETS, with Mashes of various Sizes, for folding Sheep, preventing Hares and Rabbits from passing through Enclosures or Pleasure Grounds, or entering young Plantations.

SLAYS, for Weavers.

TRELICES or GUARDS for Shop-windows, Gratings for Granary, Barn, Warehouse, or Cellar Windows.

Ornamental BLINDS, for House Windows, of various Patterns.

CLOTH of great durability for the preservation of Meat, in Larders, or Safes.

BED BOTTOMS, in place of Sacking.

CARRIAGE BACKS and SIDES; CHAIR and SOFA BACKS, and BOTTOMS, in Black, White, or other Colours, after the manner of Cane in any Pattern.

STUFFING, for Chair and Sofa Bottoms and Backs at a lower Price, and preferable to Curled Hair.

BRUSHES, of different sorts. With a variety of other ARTICLES.

John Bateman,
AND
Robert Bowman.

* Extract from the last address to the Board of Agriculture, by Sir John Sinclair, Bart. on the 7th. June, 1808.—"The Whalebone Sieves, and Nets for confining Sheep, invented by Mr. Bowman, are evidently much more durable, and in other respects greatly to be preferred, to any article of the same sort now in use. It is certainly desirable also, by increasing the consumption of Whalebone, to promote our fisheries, which, like other branches of domestic industry, cannot be too much encouraged."

MYRTON HAMILTON, PRINTER, SILVER STREET, HULL.

going to get a reprieve. Just in time to save the industry, however, whale oil's potential as an inexpensive street-lighting oil was recognized, and the demand for whale products continued.)

Luckily for the whalers, urban Europe began to install street lights around 1720, and the smell of the oil was of no significance. In addition to lighting and soap-making, whale oil was also used in the preparation of leather and woolen cloth, in the manufacture of varnishes and paints, and as a lubricant. (But

by the time Scoresby wrote his book, oil was being replaced in street lamps by coal gas, a distillate of coal. Arguing for the defense, Scoresby demonstrated that "oil-gas" was much sweeter, cleaner and cheaper than "coal-gas," and even showed that "The superiority of the light from oil-gas over other artificial lights, is fully shown by its rendering the delicate shades of yellow and green nearly as distinct as when viewed by solar light.")

The separate baleen plates were scrubbed clean and their hairlike fringes removed. They were then dried in the sun (or at least outdoors; this was England), and packed up in bales for sale and distribution. When softened in hot water, whalebone could be formed to any shape, and as long as it was kept in the new shape as it cooled, it would retain that shape permanently. It had been used almost exclusively in the manufacture of skirt hoops and corset stays, but Scoresby believed (in 1820) that it would be replaced in these functions by plates of steel. (It was not; whalebone was used in corsets and skirts up to the beginning of the twentieth century.) Cut thin along the grain, it was also the material that was used for the ribs of umbrellas and parasols, and was woven into chair seats and backs, like cane. This strong, flexible material was also used for ramrods, fishing rods, carriage springs and buggy whips. The hairy fringes, once removed from the blade, were used like horsehair for the stuffing of mattresses, chairs and sofas.

Whaleships from the Scottish cities of Aberdeen, Dundee, Kirkcaldy and Bo'ness were outfitted after 1750, joining their southern cousins from Newcastle, Whitby, Liverpool and Bristol. Hull, which was to become the leading city in eighteenth-century British whaling, did not enter the trade until 1754. Despite the abundance of whaleships sailing from British ports, the British had not really mastered the art and science of whaling, and required Dutchmen on board to perform the specialized tasks.

Britain had been at war on the high seas with one nation or another all during the period of her whaling expansion; it would be absurd to suggest that the major emphasis of her naval forces was the pursuit of the whale. A century earlier, Britain and Holland had fought over the Navigation Act of 1651, which had resulted in pitched naval battles between the two major European maritime powers. Then followed the

War of the Austrian Succession, where Britain battled her old enemy Spain, and then, in the so-called War of Jenkins' Ear, it was Britain *vs.* France. (Richard Jenkins was the master of the Glasgow brig *Rebecca,* trading with the Spanish in Central America. In an appearance before Parliament in 1739, he showed what he claimed was his own ear in a jar and claimed it had been cut off by the Spaniards, which led to British reprisals.) By 1756, when hostilities erupted in the Seven Years' War, Britain's naval forces were deployed around the world; she was involved in a major dispute with France over dominion of North America and India, and got drawn into what was essentially a continental struggle with France, Austria and Russia. The effect that this prolonged battle had on the whaling industry was critical: British whalemen were press-ganged into the navy on a wholesale basis, leaving many of the whaleships that were not also pressed into service undermanned and ineffectual. Even more important, it brought British naval forces across the Atlantic to engage the French over colonial North America. Later, they would fight the colonials themselves.

The aggressive Nantucket whalers were scouring the seas for sperm whales and shipping the oil to England. They soon came to dominate the industry, and as the price of oil fell, the fishery became less and less remunerative for British whalers. The government under Lord North tried to encourage whaling by offering a special bounty to ships that fished in Canadian waters, and commissioned ten thousand tons of new shipping in anticipation of trouble. Difficulties with her obstreperous colonies led in 1773 to the famous Boston Tea Party. In retaliation for the tea party, the British imposed the infamous "Intolerable Acts" of 1774, one of which was the closure of the port of Boston. The colonists rose up in battle against the redcoats in 1775, and although the Nantucket whalers continued to hunt the sperm whale, they found themselves on the horns of a mighty dilemma: Their primary market had always been England (even at the expense of the British whaling industry), but now, as rebels, they had to swear loyalty to the Americans, and as soon as they did that, their ships were subject to seizure by the British. Some of the Tory whalers felt they had no choice but to transfer their operations to Canada or Newfoundland, while others roamed the globe looking for a neutral home port and ended up in the Falkland Islands.

The American rebellion was a triumph for democracy, but a disaster for whaling. The Nantucket fleet was ruined, and the British, whose whaling industry was none too robust before the war, had no choice but to rebuild, since they had no source of whale oil. Whitby and Hull, the early whaling ports, participated in this expansion, and later, London and

In the early days of the British Greenland fishery, lookouts spotted whales from the rigging. In 1807, William Scoresby, Sr., invented the "barrel" crow's nest, which afforded them greater protection from the elements. In this posed photograph, the man is holding a telescope, and the barrel is on deck.

Liverpool joined in. To encourage the rebuilding of the British fleet, a heavy duty was placed on the import of American oil (the Americans were resuscitating their industry in a hurry), and by 1784, there were 102 whaleships working the Greenland fishery. Many of these ships had been sold off after the war by the British navy, so there was a surplus of shipping, as well as a redundancy of unemployed seamen. By this time, the British had figured out how to conduct a whale fishery without the assistance of the Dutch (who had sided with the Americans during the war), and by the end of the eighteenth century, Britain was the dominant force in the ice fishery.

Because the whales of the Davis Strait and the coasts of Greenland had never been disturbed, the British whale fishery prospered as never before following the American Revolution. As with any industry that depends on fashion, however, whaling fluctuated along with the design of dresses. Bone had been bringing £400 a ton during the 1760s, but by 1799, it was only worth £102. Fashions had changed markedly after the French Revolution as women forsook the wasp waists of the royalists in favor of the Empire Style, in which corsets and petticoats were omitted. Also out was a market for the hundreds of tons of whalebone that the whalers were carrying home, but since the oil was still fetching a high price and the bone came from the same animal, they kept killing the whales and extracting the oil and the bone. In 1812, a Hull newspaper advertised *whale manure,* made from the "grease, finks, the refuse of whale bone, etc.," which "effectively destroys flies in turnips, grubs and other insects, and prevents the wire worm in wheat, and clears the crops from smut and weeds." The corset came back into fashion by 1830 (Queen Victoria ascended the throne in 1837), but by then the whales were in very short supply. Like whalers everywhere, Englishmen looked elsewhere for other whales when one species ran out, and before long, they had discovered that the Southern Ocean, where they were depositing their convicts, was full of sperm whales.

Scoresby's *Arctic Regions* was published in 1820, before the decline in the Greenland Fishery was apparent. Rather than see the industry on the descendant, he wrote that "The British whale fishery of 1814 was uncommonly prosperous, especially at

Greenland; 76 ships on this fishery having procured 1437 whales. . . ." In the five years ending in 1818, Scoresby estimated that the gross value of goods imported into Britain from the Greenland and Davis Strait fisheries was nearly three million pounds sterling. (Some individual records for the fishery include the *Resolution,* Captain Souter, which took 44 whales in 1814, producing 299 tons of oil. Adding in the bounties and the bone, this voyage grossed some £11,000. In 1813, the *John of Greenock,* commanded by William Scoresby, Sr., and the *Esk,* under Scoresby, Jr., produced cargoes valued at approximately the same amount.) The year that Scoresby's book was published was, according to Basil Lubbock, "the most successful in the whole of the Hull fishing records; 60 ships earning £318,880, or over £5000 per ship."

Bounties had been offered to the British whalers since 1733, but after almost a century of government subsidies, the system was not renewed. The loss of the bounty was a blow to the industry, but not nearly as important as the switch from whale oil to rape oil in the manufacture of woolen cloth. (Rape oil is obtained from the crushed seeds of *Brassica napus,* the plant known as rape.) Whale oil was never the first choice for manufacturing textiles, and when seed oils were imported in large quantities, the price of whale oil fell. At the same time, the American government was levying duties on imported seed oils to encourage the New England whaling industry, and when the British refused to maintain the previously high duties on imported whale oil, the American industry prospered as never before and the British fishery began to collapse.

During the 1820s the Arctic fishery peaked—1823 was the best year ever—but the ice was beginning to take its toll on the ships, and their number was falling as the number of whales per ship increased. In the disastrous season of 1826, the *Jean,* of Peterhead, was wrecked in a storm and sunk; her crew sailed and rowed to Iceland. Then the *Lively,* of Whitby, and the *Harpooner,* of Bremen, went down with all hands. The fishing was also a failure; the log of the *Cumbrian,* of Hull, reported, "We have, for the last three weeks, sought diligently for whales, but we have not seen any, neither has there been any whale seen by any of the ships to this period." The "Greenland" fishing, which was to the east of that island, contin-

Sometimes whalers did not return to their home ports at the end of the season, but spent the winter in the ice, snugly buttressed against the weather.

ued to prove unsuccessful, and more and more whalers headed for the Davis Strait.

In the mid-1840s, the coal gas that Scoresby was so worried about also began making inroads into the whale-oil business. Gas works were built throughout England, and the only thing the proponents of whale oil could do was convert their oil to gas too. Sir William Congreve, the inventor of the rocket that was unsuccessfully used against whales in the 1820s, and adviser to the British on gas works, recognized that gas could be made from any oil, and plumped for the use of whale oil as the basis for a gas industry. The fluctuating price of whale oil, however, made it difficult to maintain a steady supply of gas at contract prices, and the prospect of an oil-gas industry faded.

The whales had been fished out of the southern reaches of the Davis Strait, so the whalers had to venture farther and farther north, where the ice and

weather conditions became correspondingly worse. The season of 1830 had been almost a complete disaster, with nineteen of the ninety-one whalers lost, twenty-one returning with no oil at all—what the whalers called "clean"—and the rest of the ships heavily damaged. In the 1831 season the weather again conspired against them, and then again in 1835, they could get into the ice easily enough, but couldn't get out.

In October of that year, long after they should have been back in England, a dozen ships remained locked in the pack ice of the Davis Strait. One of them, the *Alfred,* managed to break out and carry the news home, but even as she was heading for London, the entire crew of the *William Torr,* of Hull, had frozen or starved to death. Among those ships trapped in the ice was the *Viewforth,* of Kirkcaldy. William Elder was an officer aboard the *Viewforth,* and his journal records this harrowing experience:

1 October

These fourteen days we have been in chase every day after day. The mate harpooned another fish but lost her, which now makes four, all averaging as nearly as possible between fifteen and twenty tons each, and had we only got these four we would have had a very safe voyage. We have never heard any news of the rest of the ships, which is remarkable. It was never known to have happened before.

15 October

We have this day seen a ship from the masthead lying beset amongst the loose ice. . . . There were five men left aboard the *Middleton* and three of our men to walk over the ice to her but the distance was too great. They could not reach—and dark night coming on—they returned, but severely frostbitten the most part of them. There was one of our men had fallen in. The frost was so strong that he had not the power to move his limbs. He had to be carried on board.

15 November

This day has been another awful eventful day. The wind did not take off until about 9 A.M. when it moderated a little. What a scene was presented to us when daylight came, in the wreck of the *Middleton*. Oh, I cannot express the feeling that went to our hearts when she was seen. Every one regarded one another in mute despair not knowing and in all likelihood to be our turn next.

18 November

At 10 P.M. the ice drove us in with the land. It was a terrible night, the great towering mountains frowning above you as you saw them dimly through the darkness of the night and expecting every moment that your ship would be dashed upon them. The same time too the ship sustained a heavy pressure (we were afraid she was gone). We got our provisions ashore on the ice immediately. It was an awful night. But thanks be to the Lord for his wonderful mercies, for if he had not been with us and sustained us through so many dangers, long ere now we would have been lost.

The *Viewforth* was trapped in the ice until January 20, 1836. Scurvy was rampant, with all its horrible symptoms of loosening teeth, sores and debilitating weakness. Some of the men had been in their bunks, covered with ice and rime, for two months. Those who did not perish of this sickness, froze to death. Although they had casks of blubber aboard, they did not try to eat it until the end of their ordeal. When the ship finally broke out of the ice—an event caused only by the power of the pack; nothing the weakened men did had any effect—she had to be sailed across the stormy North Atlantic in a howling Arctic blizzard. The 289-ton bark arrived at Stromness, Scotland, on February 14, with seven men able to man the ship, and fourteen corpses. A whaleman's song of the time sums up the feelings they had toward this forbidding endeavor:

> O, Greenland is an awful place,
>   Where the daylight's seldom seen,
> Where there's ice and there's snow,
> And the whale fishes blow,
> Then adieu to cold Greenland, brave boys,
>   Adieu to cold Greenland.

In 1835, seventy-one ships had gone north, but within two years the number had dropped to fifty-one. Hostile conditions, decreasing numbers of whales, and plummeting oil prices offered little encouragement for whalers to continue. Whitby and London had gone out of the whaling business, leaving only Hull and Newcastle to maintain the tradition. By Christmas, there were so many ships unreported from the ice that the Hull merchants outfitted a rescue mission commanded by James Clark Ross. On January 5, 1836, the *Cove* sailed from Hull, but could not continue its mission since she lost her bowsprit in a gale and was forced to return to Stromness. The years 1835 and '36 represent the nadir of British Arctic whaling; only the port of Peterhead prospered, and that because the Peterhead owners encouraged their captains to concentrate on sealing rather than whaling. In 1838, the Peterhead fleet took 80 whales and 28,708 seals.

Just as increased numbers of ships reduced the average yields, decreases in shipping fostered larger yields, and in what would turn out to be its death flurry, the British northern whale fishery flourished during the 1840s, and crashed in the next decade. During the first half of the nineteenth century, more than two thousand voyages had been made to the Davis Strait, and over 90 percent of these were British. The only controls on this fishery were those imposed by nature: the weather was terrible, the ships were crushed or sunk, and the cold was often unbearable. If the whales were scarce, either because they were beyond the reach of the ships or because they had been killed off, the whalers returned home with meager catches. Nobody seems to have realized that the whales represented a finite resource; they all wanted to get in, kill as many whales as they could, make as much money as the market would bear, and then get out.

AT FIRST, marine engines were considered only an auxiliary to sail. In 1850, two steam-equipped vessels, the *Pioneer* and the *Intrepid,* participated in the search for Sir John Franklin* and were held to demonstrate the possibilities of steam for work in the Arctic. In 1857, the Whale and Seal Fishing Company of Hull installed a forty-horsepower auxiliary engine in the *Diana,* which thereby became the world's first steam-powered whaleship. The success of this venture led to the acquisition of two more screw steamers, the *Ann* and the *Truelove.* Both of these vessels were trapped in the ice and lost, and the *Diana* herself figured in one of the most notorious of British whaling tragedies. She was trapped in the ice at Baffin Bay in the winter of 1866 and temporarily abandoned by her crew, who felt they would be safer bivouacking on the ice. They reboarded the ship in the spring as she drifted slowly southward, and with only seven men strong enough to sail her, reached Ronas Voe in the Shetlands on April 2, 1867. (Unlike many other circumstances where the ship's surgeon had little to do but minister to occasional patients or keep a journal, as did Thomas Beale, the chronicler of the British sperm whale fishery, Charles Edward Smith of the *Diana* assumed leadership of the ship during her ice-drift, and since the captain had died on Christmas Day, Dr. Smith was largely responsible for bringing the ship home.)

The period from about 1850 to 1900 saw a major decline in the whaling business in Britain. Ports like London, Peterhead and Whitby began to send out sealing expeditions, while Hull turned to seed-crushing, and became the capital of the industry that helped to put her whalermen out of business. Steam whaling came to Britain around 1860, and marked a brief revival of the industry, since the long trips under sail could now be replaced by (relatively) comfortable voyages under steam power. Unfortunately, the whales and the weather did not cooperate, and steam whaling was not a success in Britain. The iron vessels were terribly uncomfortable, and in the damp cold of the Arctic, their interiors were subject to the most awful condensation. Also, because they employed fuel rather than wind, they had to be able to carry an adequate supply with them, which limited their range. And finally, where wooden hulls were resilient to the pressure of the ice, iron simply gave way. The Peterhead steamer *Empress of India* had heavily reinforced bows and a crew eager to demonstrate that steam whaling represented the profitable wave of the future. An iceberg penetrated her port bow, and she sank in four hours, her crew ignominiously rescued by the crew of a sailing ship. The *River Tay,* a 600-ton steamer with a double-reinforced iron hull and forty-two watertight compartments, sank in minutes after being holed by an iceberg.

In 1880, when he was a twenty-year-old medical student at Edinburgh, Arthur Conan Doyle shipped out as a surgeon on the Peterhead whaler *Hope,* Captain John Gray commanding. For seven months, the future creator of Sherlock Holmes sailed through the northern seas around east Greenland and Jan Mayen Island, observing the seals, walruses, polar bears, and whales. (He was only in his third year of medical school, so he wrote that "it was as well that there was no very serious call upon my services.") Conan Doyle was no more experienced at sailing than he was at doctoring; while sitting on the gunwales he lost his balance and "shot off and vanished into the sea between two ice blocks." The captain told him that as long as he was bound to fall into the ocean, he might as well be on the ice with the sealers. He fell in twice more during the day, and was eventually given the nickname of "Great Northern Diver." Even though the Greenland whaling was in decline by this time, there were still whales to be seen. Captain Gray told Conan Doyle that "there were probably no more than 300 left alive in the whole expanse

*Sir John Franklin sailed in May 1845, in the same *Erebus* and *Terror* that had taken James Clark Ross to the Antarctic in 1840. (Also part of the expedition was Francis Crozier, who had commanded the *Terror.*) At the behest of the British government, he was searching for an eastern passage to the Bering Strait. On July 12, Franklin entertained a whaling captain while his ships were moored to the ice in Baffin Bay, and that was the last that was ever heard of him. His overland journey after his ships were trapped in the ice has been reconstructed from letters, skeletons and other evidence, but the search still goes on for Franklin's ships, with all the equipment and provisions that he had taken for a three-year voyage. Some spoons and other small implements were recovered from the Eskimos in 1857.

A rare photograph of the crew of a Peterhead whaler, taken around 1870. The remainder of the fifty-man crew would be picked up in the Shetlands.

of the Greenland Seas, an area of thousands of square miles.''

The port of Dundee in Scotland saw a revival of her whaling industry when it was discovered around 1850 that no other oil served so well as whale oil for the batching of jute—the process where freshly opened bales were soaked to soften the fibers before spinning. Jute was used for sacking, carpet backing, and the manufacture of linoleum, and Dundee soon had a monopoly on jute-processing in England. Dundee whalers continued to hunt whales in the Davis Strait, and for another twenty years, her ships enjoyed a success that was unequaled anywhere else in Britain.

(There was also a minor fishery for bottlenose whales (not to be confused with bottle-nosed dolphins, which are much smaller) out of Dundee at this time. Captain David Gray, of Peterhead, killed two hundred bottlenoses from the schooner *Eclipse* in 1882. Known to the whalers as ''Chaney Johns'' or ''Botleys,'' these beaked whales (known to science as *Hyperoodon ampullatus*) reach a maximum length of some 30 feet, and yield much less oil than a Greenland whale, but their presence off the Norwegian and Scottish coasts made them easy targets for small-boat whalers. Bottlenoses are gregarious, traveling in groups of five to ten animals, and their inclination to crowd around a wounded comrade made it possible to collect large numbers at one time. A full-grown male might yield 2 tons of oil, and 200 pounds of "spermaceti"—the oil of the head, similar to that of the sperm whale. However productive this whale might be, hunting it was not much fun, according to R. C. Andrews. In *Whale Hunting with Gun and Camera* (1916), he wrote, "The work in bitter cold and freezing water, to say nothing of the ever-present possibility of having one's head, arm, or leg shorn clean off by the whizzing rope, robs bottlenose hunting of its attractiveness.")

As always, the variations in conditions and catch were enormous: in 1867, the Dundee whalers caught 2 whales; the next year they caught 79. For the fishing season of 1869, eight whaleships went to Greenland and succeeded in killing 10 whales—and 28,000 seals. It was only the Gray brothers of Peterhead, with their auxiliary screw whalers *Eclipse* and *Hope,* who kept Britain in the whaling business in the 1870s and '80s. Even though steamers were transporting the whalers to the grounds and carrying the oil back to the boiling yards, the whalers were still lowering the boats and chasing the whales to harpoon them with slender irons. (The steamers were full-rigged because the whalemen believed they had to approach the acoustically sensitive whales as quietly as possible.) The whalers continued to make for the north during the last decades of the nineteenth century, but

with the disappearance of the whales, most of their catch consisted of seals. In *The Arctic Whalers,* Basil Lubbock wrote, "By 1909 it had to be recognized that the Greenland whale was definitely growing scarce, and that the end of the old time Arctic whaling by means of boats was in sight. . . . The last good catches in the Greenland Sea were made by Captain J. Murray of the *Balaena,* who in 1909 caught 4 whales and several narwhals. . . ."

In the ninety years that the British whalers worked the Davis Strait Fishery, they made over two thousand voyages. W. G. Ross has tabulated the results of these voyages, and has concluded that half of them took place during the fishery's first two decades, 1820 to 1840. A slow decline—in the number of voyages and the number of whales—thereafter commenced, but the number of whales killed throughout the ninety years was something on the order of 18,000.

"The tragedy for British whaling," wrote its historian Gordon Jackson, "is that they made the wrong [decisions] and having made them were overcome by the sort of icy paralysis that killed men in Arctic waters. . . . The British phase of whaling, which had begun around 1780, lasted for little more than a century; long before the First World War whaling had entered its Norwegian phase."

The British had steam power, but they did not recognize its potential for the whaling industry. On

An elaborately carved pan bone, showing various stages of the whaling process, including cutting-in and harpooning. The wind appears to be blowing in two different directions.

several occasions, steam whalers rescued sailing ships that had gotten trapped in the ice, but for the most part, the British saw steam only as a means to shorten the long voyages across the North Atlantic to the Arctic. It was the Norwegians who realized that steam could actually be used in the capture of whales, and at the same time eliminate the long voyages altogether. While the remnants of the British whaling fleet were steaming through the schools of whales north of Scotland, Svend Foyn, of Norway, was working on the inventions that would revolutionize the whaling industry—and, by the turn of the century, virtually eliminate British whaling. The huge rorquals had been safe from the whaler's puny hand-thrown harpoons until Foyn's steam catchers, grenade harpoons, and accumulators were perfected. No longer was it necessary to traverse the North Atlantic and flense whales at sea. The Norwegians reinvented shore whaling and brought it to Britain. They moved from their own waters to Iceland in 1889, thence to the Faeroes (1892), and finally to the British Isles.

Of the arrival of the Norwegians, Lubbock wrote:

. . . veterans of the Arctic have had the chagrin, during the past thirty years, of watching the trade fall entirely into the hands of the Norwegians, who, with the aid of modern methods, unlimited enterprise, great business acumen and of a technical skill in which they were without rivals, have made such fortunes at whaling as Hull, Whitby, Peterhead or Dundee never even dreamed of. Indeed, so great has been their success and so enormous their slaughter of every species of whale, that only a close time enforced by International agreement can save the extinction of our greatest mammal in the very near future. [He was writing in 1937, as the seeds of international controls of whaling were being sown.] Where the hand harpoon killed its dozens, the harpoon gun, with its explosive charge, kills its thousands. Yet there is this to be said for modern methods, all waste has been eliminated; for science utilises every part of the whale, bones, blubber and skin.

Christian Salvesen (1827–1911) had come from Norway to Leith, Scotland, in 1851 to establish a base for the Scottish-Norwegian trade in whale oil. He was probably the agent for the sale of Svend Foyn's whale oil in Britain, which totaled some seven thousand barrels, more than the entire British whaling fleet of the period 1880–1900 was able to catch. With capital available to him in England, Salvesen and his son Theodore expanded their British operations, cutting themselves free of their Norwegian connections and purchasing the station at Olna Firth in the Shetlands. It was Theodore Salvesen more than any other individual who was responsible for the twentieth-century revival of British whaling. His catchers roamed the nearby waters of the Shetlands and the Orkneys, killing any and all whales they encountered: fin whales, humpbacks, bottlenoses, sperm whales, right whales, blue whales.

In 1892, an adventurer and artist named W. G. Burn-Murdoch shipped aboard the *Balaena* on the Dundee expedition to the Antarctic. The expedition was unsuccessful in its whaling, but the adventure so stimulated Burn-Murdoch that upon his return to England he signed aboard another whaling voyage out of the Shetlands. While at sea with a Norwegian named Henriksen, he decided to build his own whaling ship. Equipping her with the requisite armaments (a harpoon cannon, sixty-five harpoons of assorted sizes, two small guns for firing the smaller harpoons, and various rifles and boxes of cartridges for hunting polar bears and elephant seals in the Northern and Southern hemispheres, respectively), Burn-Murdoch set off in the 110-foot, diesel-powered *St. Ebba* for a year or so of hunting.

The author/illustrator was a dedicated bear-hunter, but he also provides important details of the prewar whale fishery. (*Whaling and Bear-Hunting* was published in 1917, but although no actual dates are given for the voyage, it appears to have taken place in 1912–13.) Burn-Murdoch's stories about whaling are commonplace, and his stories about cormorant hash and Svend Foyn* are interesting, but his everyday observations are what makes his book valuable:

In the forenoon we fall in with three whalers from Olna Firth, the station of the Salvesens of Leith, and all of his had been scouting in different directions, over hundreds of miles, and not one had seen a spout, and yet where we are, there were numerous whales only a few days ago.

*As told to Burn-Murdoch, Svend Foyn had taken his (first) wife aboard a whaler to show her how his new harpoon worked. He shot a whale too far aft and the ship was towed through a gale for twelve hours with the engines full astern. "Let go, let go," prayed his wife, "I am seek, I am afraid." "No, no," said Foyn, "I vil never let go. I vil show you veech is de strongest, my vill or de vill of de beasts," and he held on and finally got the whale lanced—but it was an awful fight. When they towed the whale ashore in triumph, his wife was nearly dead, and she said: "Now you have shown me your vill is stronger den de beasts—now I vill leave you," and she did.

Like trout, whales seem to be unaccountably on the rise one day, and utterly disappear the next. So we resort to music and painting. Henriksen plays Grieg on the weather-worn melodeon and the artist paints sea turtles.

F. V. Morley, a young journalist (and co-author, with J. S. Hodgson, of *Whaling North and South*), visited the Shetland Islands station of Olna Firth in the early 1920s. He described in great detail the "angular group of red frame buildings with corrugated iron roofs and tall black chimneys"; the flensing deck and the hollow spherical buoy that used to be a life-buoy and was now a death-buoy; it was used to moor the carcasses of whales before they were winched up on the plan (the flensing deck) and their blubber stripped off. Morley writes in a wonderfully baroque style about what he has seen; here is his description of the carcass of a whale:

Marble would not be good enough to lay this corpse upon; for the sight—discard the blemishes—is wonder. This is the sordid remnant, yet the eye may even now replace what has been lost; it may replace, the while the mind stands by, incredulous. Where went that spirit, which played in this magnificence—which made this mountain leap and sport, quickened the eye, retracted that balloon of a tongue, lifted that fallen jaw? This was a lump which solved some wild equation of the elements. This monstrous form and painted shapeliness has burned its way through phosphorescent waves in summer, the black night lighted by luminous clouds of its own breathing; and sinking with an easy silence, it has spiraled to unseen depths, upon unknown desires. . . . It is more lovely and more startling than the Sphinx.

In *The British Whaling Trade,* Gordon Jackson noted that the meat of the whales that were killed by Britons was almost always wasted. Even though Salvesen attempted to market the meat in England, "the failure to do so was one of the tragedies of modern whaling. Not only did it deny to whaling an additional income which would have been of the greatest importance to the trade in its later history; it also denied Europe an immense source of badly needed protein." (Although the meat of whales is eaten in some countries—principally Japan—the British were never able to overcome the attitudes of the early whalers that the carcass was a stinking, often putrid mass which should be as far away as possible from the human nose.) At the same time, however, Theodore Salvesen invented a method for boiling the meat and turning it into a feed for other animals. By 1906, Salvesen had stations in the Faeroes and Iceland, in addition to those in the Shetlands, and the British were on the way to building a rivalry with the Norwegians.

The American Bowhead Fishery

THE SHIPS that sailed from Leeds and Hull, from Rotterdam and Amsterdam knew only of the whales that lived around Spitsbergen, Jan Mayen Land, and Greenland. Since neither the Northwest nor the Northeast Passage had been discovered, nobody had succeeded in navigating the ice-choked regions of northern Canada, and very few European eyes had ever seen the icy reaches of the Bering Sea. The waters that Vitus Bering had discovered in 1728 were virtually an unknown entity. The fifty-five-mile-wide passage that separates the two continents was named for Bering, as was the huge sub-Arctic basin that gyres turbulently between Alaska, the Aleutians, and Siberia. For hundreds of thousands of years, the great whales of the Bering Sea had only been threatened by killer whales and Eskimos, and had managed to achieve an ecological equilibrium that suggested the dawn of the world. It was not to last much longer.

The Spitsbergen fishery collapsed around 1840

with the elimination of the whales, and the whalers moved westward to Greenland and then into the Canadian archipelago. The Dutch retired from the competition, leaving the remaining whales to the British and the Americans. By 1840, even the fishery in Canada was waning, but then it took a remarkable turn, beneficial for the whalers, disastrous for the whales.

Because the bowhead produced such plentiful baleen, and because Dame Fashion decreed a manifold increase in its use for skirt hoops and corset stays, this species quickly eclipsed the sperm whale as the primary object of the global whale fishery. The price of baleen doubled between 1841 and 1846 because fuller skirts had come into fashion and baleen was needed to support their flaring lines. In 1845, the Danish whaler *Neptun,* Captain Thomas Sodring, became the first "foreign" whaler to take a bowhead in the Pacific. By the summer of that year, eleven whaleships called at Petropavlovsk in response to reports of a new kind of whale to be found in the Sea of Okhotsk. By 1847, there were some thirty ships working these remarkably fertile waters. They took 426 whales in that season, 341 right whales and 85 bowheads. (During the first twenty years of the fishery, about 1,391 voyages would be made to the Sea of Okhotsk, mostly by Americans. In this period, the bowheads of the region were almost totally eliminated. In an unpublished study, David Henderson, of the New Bedford Whaling Museum, has estimated that the total kill was on the order of 18,000 bowheads and 3,600 right whales. Bowhead whaling continued sporadically from 1867 to 1896, but today there are no bowheads to be found in the Okhotsk Sea.)

Like so many of his contemporaries, Thomas Welcome Roys was always on the lookout for new whaling grounds. In addition to his own extensive experiences, he maintained a lengthy correspondence with Matthew Fontaine Maury, the oceanographer/ cartographer who was involved in mapping the world's ocean currents. Roys had sailed around the world several times, from the Arctic to the South Pacific, and during his travels, he had begun to hear stories of some unusual whales far to the north. In the summer of 1847, he left Sag Harbor in the 275-ton bark *Superior,* bound, his owners thought, for the traditional whaling grounds of the South Atlan-

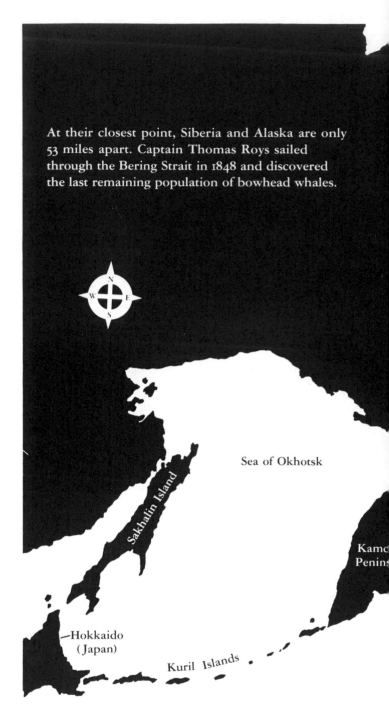

At their closest point, Siberia and Alaska are only 53 miles apart. Captain Thomas Roys sailed through the Bering Strait in 1848 and discovered the last remaining population of bowhead whales.

tic. After achieving poor results off the Crozetts and Desolation Island, he headed for the Pacific. When he arrived at Hobart on March 7, he had only 120 barrels of oil to show for seven months of work. On July 23, 1848, he sailed through the Bering Strait, a thousand miles farther north than any whaleship had ever gone in the Pacific, and came upon a thriving

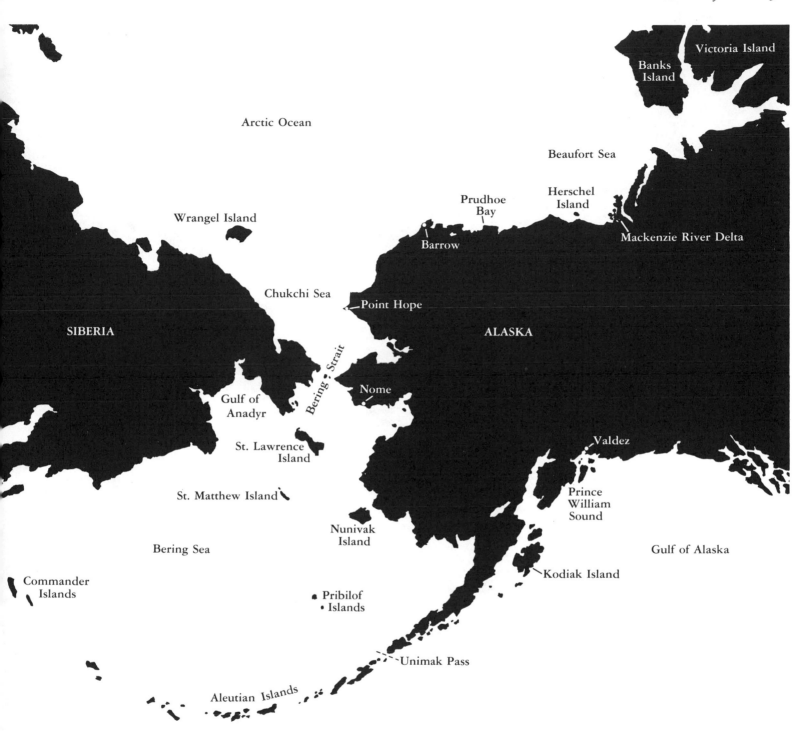

population of bowheads that had previously been known only to the Eskimos.

Upon first lowering the boats in the Bering Sea, Roys's men regarded the giant black whales as "new fangled monsters," since they were familiar only with the smaller humpbacks and right whales of the Southern Ocean. Roys believed that these were the inoffensive—and lucrative—"polar whales" that had been hunted off Greenland, and set about collecting them with dispatch. His crews took 11 bowheads in only thirty-five days during that eventful summer, and sailed for home with eighteen hundred barrels of oil, an accomplishment that normally took two or more seasons.

When the *Superior* reached Honolulu, word of Roys's discovery spread like wildfire. By this time the sperm whale fishery was flagging, so the news revitalized the entire whaling industry. In 1849, 154 ships headed north, and returned to their home ports with 206,850 barrels of oil and 2,481,600 pounds— 12,408 *tons*—of whalebone. The following year, the numbers soared even higher: 243,680 barrels of oil and 3,654,000 pounds of bone.

According to John Bockstoce, the historian of western Arctic whaling, "Roys's cruise was not only the most important whaling discovery of the nineteenth century, it was also one of the most important events in the history of the Pacific. Over the seven decades following his discovery, the richness of the western Arctic whale stocks lured the whaling vessels of the United States, France, Germany, Hawaii, and Australia through the shallow and treacherous waters of the Bering Strait. More than 2,700 whaling voyages were made into Arctic waters at a cost of more than 150 whaleships lost and the near extinction of the bowhead whale, as Roys's whales came to be called."

Just as a gold strike attracts prospectors like a magnet, and a new oilfield draws wildcatters to the area, the discovery of a new whaling ground brings ships from all over the world, eager to cash in on the discovery. The differences between gold and petroleum on the one hand and whales on the other can be found in the nature of the source and the character of the prospectors. Whereas gold-miners were more than a little reluctant to reveal the location of their strike, and oilmen quickly staked out the land on which they had tapped their gushers, whalers eagerly passed the news along to their confederates. Thus, when a new stock of whales was discovered, the grapevine quickly ensured that everyone with an interest would know about it. This led to the phenomenon which occurred in almost every fishery where the habits of the whales were predictable: the whalers quickly arrived on the scene and almost eliminated the whales. (Only the sperm whales, whose migratory habits are still poorly understood, could escape this blitzkrieg; even when the

Opposite: Ice conditions around northern Alaska, the habitat of the bowhead whale.

Clifford Ashley, the painter/whaleman, painted *Hunting the Bowhead,* although his specialty was the sperm whale fishery.

whalers had found their haunts—On the Line, the Japan Grounds, the North Pacific, etc.—the cachalots managed to avoid the savage slaughter that often reduced their toothless cousins to the brink of extinction.) Fifty-seven percent of all western Arctic voyages took place within twenty years of Roys's discovery, and in less than ten years, the whales were so scarce in the Bering Sea that whaling was nearly abandoned there. Only adventurous whalers, rounding Point Barrow and entering the Beaufort Sea, would find the whales' sanctuary, and it would be at a terrible expense: the whaling fleet itself was almost eliminated.

The Eskimos had made at most a minimal impact on the bowhead populations, even though they had been hunting them for millennia. After Roys's discovery, they continued to hunt, but their primitive (and generally ineffectual) methods were quickly modernized, and replaced by the innovations of modern whaling.

The Yankee whaleships usually reached the pack ice by mid-April, just as the whales were beginning their northward migration. Unlike the whales, which powered themselves, the wind-driven ships were at the mercy of the gales, blizzards and williwaws of the Arctic, and were often blown in a direction other than the one in which they intended to go, or worse, trapped in the closing ice. (Occasionally, the whalers took advantage of the moving ice, and hooked themselves to a drifting floe, so as to move with the prevailing currents instead of the contrary winds.) Writing of his experiences in the Arctic, whaleman G. F. Tilton said, "Any Arctic whaleman will tell you that when a man goes into the Arctic he is a total stranger to conditions every year. The land, naturally, is well anchored and don't shift, but that's the one thing that don't vary. In thirty-two years that I spent in the Arctic, I have never seen two summers alike as regards to ice." As with all wind sailors, the whalers were often becalmed and could only watch helplessly as the ice ground and surged around them. Another problem was fog. The dank sea fogs of the Bering Sea are legendary, and whalers were often sailing—or becalmed—blindly in conditions that were comparable to the darkest night.

Despite the abundance and slow swimming speed of the quarry, bowhead whaling was not an easy task. With the water churned by winds and currents and house-sized chunks of ice bobbing at the surface, it was not easy to spot the blow of a whale that only showed its blowhole for a moment. When conditions were deemed propitious, the boats were lowered, and the Yankee whalers took after the bowhead. If the whales were sighted to leeward of the ship, the boats raised their sails, but if they had to chase the whales into the wind, they pulled on their oars. Though whales have no visible ears, their hearing is remarkably acute, and even the Eskimos knew that to approach them, silence was mandatory. The slightest knock would carry through the water, so in order not to "gally" the whale, oarlocks were muffled and talking was forbidden.

If the whale was "gallied," it often headed for the ice and remained below for a surprisingly long time. Scammon wrote that the whale is capable of remaining below for an hour and twenty minutes, but his was a struck whale, not one that was hiding from its pursuers. Toggle harpoons were employed in the early days of Arctic bowhead whaling, but by 1850, the bomb lance had been introduced.

Although it had long been understood that shooting a harpoon was more efficient than throwing it, guns were not successfully employed until William Greener developed his shoulder gun in 1837. Previous experiments had utilized swivel guns mounted on the bows of the whaleboat, which had the distinct disadvantage of being operable only in calm weather. With the shoulder gun—or "Greener's gun," as it came to be known—the whalers could aim and fire from any position, and the whale, which had previously stood a fighting chance of escaping, was now doomed almost from the moment it was sighted. Describing the techniques of ballistic whaling, Scammon wrote, ". . . the time fuse imbedded in the powder contained in the cylinder, causes the bomb to explode, usually killing the whale instantly; and the harpoon being already fastened to the body of the animal, it may be easily secured." (The introduction of explosives to the whale fishery was perhaps the most significant change that occurred in a thousand years of whaling. By the early twentieth century, cannons and grenades would be widely employed, changing the face of whaling forever, from a primitive man-*vs.*-whale hunt to an industry. It was not because of antiquated usage—and certainly not because they believed their quarry was a fish—that the pre-explosive whalers had referred to their business as a "fishery.")

The bomb lance was a metal cylinder fired from a shoulder gun with a recoil that could throw the

Established 1869

FRANK E. BROWN
MANUFACTURER OF   Successor to EBEN PIERCE
Pierce Whaling Guns and Lances
4 SOUTH WATER STREET

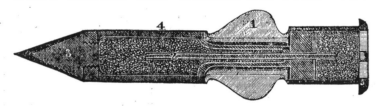
gunner overboard. This same power, however, made it an effective weapon at a range of up to sixty feet. It was particularly effective in the Arctic, since instantaneous killing reduced the possibility of a struck whale's taking refuge under the ice. Occasionally, a wounded whale did run under the ice, so a further improvement was initiated, the darting gun. Captain Ebenezer Pierce invented the darting gun in 1865 (it was Pierce's bomb lance that Scammon described in his 1874 account), and from then on, the hand-thrown harpoon was history.

Where other whales might attack the whaleboat if and when they were harpooned, the bowhead either sounded or ran. Often its response was a combination of both, as the injured animal tried to escape the pain of the harpoon. Bowheads were known to take out a mile of line, "but," wrote Scammon, "it must not be inferred that this was done by the perpendicular course of the whale, for it is found that the line runs out with great swiftness, when the creature begins its return to the surface." (Before the universal acceptance of the darting gun, Yankee whalers would occasionally emulate the Eskimo practice of slashing the tail tendons of the whale to slow down its escape. This was known as "spading flukes," and was considered particularly dangerous, since the thrashing 20-foot flukes could easily upset the whaleboat.)

After the whale had "spouted thick blood," indicating that it was dying, the men in the boats waited until it "finned out," rolling on its side and weakly waving one of its flippers. They then made fast to the whale and towed it to the ship for processing. Cutting stages were lowered, and the cutting-in began. Using complicated tackle, the crew raised the whale's head out of the water, and with razor-sharp spades, the blubber was peeled from the carcass. The "headbone" containing the baleen plates was winched aboard after it was separated from the body, and the upper jaw, which contained some 300 plates on each side, was brought on deck. The plates were then cut from the gums, and carefully cleaned to remove pieces of gum, which, if left to rot, would leave a pernicious stink that could not be removed. Then the individual plates were left on deck to dry, and finally packed in eighty-pound bundles and stored below. (If rats were discovered eating the whalebone, the bundles were brought back on deck, and the ship "smoked," which consisted of sealing all the openings and setting charcoal fires to drive the rats from the hold.)

Unlike their British counterparts, American bowhead whalers tried-out the whales at sea. The blubber was cut into manageable pieces to be boiled down for the oil. The tryworks, great iron caldrons amidships set in brick and fueled first by wood and later with scraps of whale skin, were kept going until the whale had been reduced to its final form, barrels of oil. The boiling-out process could take more than thirty-six hours, during which time acrid black smoke billowed over the ship, and the threat of a ship's fire was always present. The smell of boiling oil pervaded the ship's timbers, rigging and canvas, and it was said that if the wind was right, you could smell a whaler arriving in port long before you could see it.

One year after Captain Roys had completed his epochal voyage into the Bering Sea, forty-six more whaleships were working the bowhead grounds. This was the saving grace of the industry, since it appeared that the whales were disappearing from all their previous haunts. (The abundant Antarctic whale stocks would not be discovered for another fifty years.) "Roys's discovery," wrote Bockstoce, "marked the industry's high point—its final flash of glorious success." Compared to a sperm whale, which yielded perhaps forty-five barrels of oil, a fat bowhead might provide more than three hundred. In addition, where the eating equipment of the cachalot consisted of ivory teeth which might be carved into scrimshaw for decorative objects, the bowheads surrendered bales of precious whalebone. The 1849 season was the most successful in whaling history, and it was followed by another rich harvest in 1850. The 1852 season, however, was a disaster. Where the weather for 1848, '49, and '50 had been comparatively mild, by 1851 the Arctic began to demonstrate its true character. Whales were scarce, and the weather drove many ships into the pack ice. In all, seven ships were lost in that devastating season. By 1854, it appeared that the whales of the Bering Sea had been fished out.

More or less accidentally, the whalers discovered that the whales rounded Point Barrow into the Beaufort Sea. In 1854, five vessels, the *Franklin, Gideon Howland, Hobomok, Rousseau* and *William Thompson*, headed into these comparatively ice-free waters, and although theirs was a less-than-successful whaling expedition, they had found the last refuge of the bowhead. Current estimates give the total bowhead population at some 30,000 animals before whaling began, and records and logbooks of the period indicate a catch of some 7,000 whales by 1854. Where had all the whales gone? Bockstoce suggests that the whales had quickly adapted to the threat: "They learned that there was safety deep in the pack ice where the whaleboats could not go." Until the whal-

ers could discover a way to invade the whales' sanctuary, the whales appeared to be safe.

The seasons of 1859 and 1860 were slow, and the whaling industry, once the proud flag-bearer of New England industrial prowess, seemed to be on the descendant. Besides, in 1860, America was about to be torn asunder by the Civil War. Ships, captains and whalermen who would otherwise have been sailing

To convey a sense of the length of some of the baleen plates of the bowhead, a workman poses with the whalebone stacked vertically.

For industry, bone was cut into short lengths and packed into bundles for shipment.

for oil and bone found themselves conscripted into the navy. The Union had plenty of ships, of course, since New England was the home not only of the whaling fleets, but of most of the country's shipping tonnage as well.

The Confederacy, on the other hand, had virtually no navy at all. Desperate for fighting ships, they began buying whatever they could in Europe. Under James D. Bulloch, an agent for the Confederacy, the raider *Florida* was pressed into service to harass Union shipping. Then followed the *Alabama*, which mounted a successful campaign against Northern shipping, capturing sixty-nine Federal ships before she was sunk by the U.S.S. *Kearsarge* in 1864. The story of the Confederate raider *Shenandoah* (originally commissioned in England as the *Sea King*) is

surely one of the strangest—and most destructive—chapters in the history of American whaling.

A powerful sailing ship with auxiliary steam capability of 850 horsepower, the *Shenandoah*, under Captain James Waddell, headed for the whaling grounds on October 7, 1864. On October 30, she claimed her first prize off Dakar, the bark *Aliana*, out of Searsport, Maine. Waddell took the *Aliana*'s crew prisoner, and then scuttled the bark. Burning and capturing ships as she went, the *Shenandoah* continued her destructive career in the Southern Ocean. Waddell stopped off for repairs in Australia, and then headed for the Arctic. (He would drop off his prisoners at various ports and ransom them to the Union forces.) He arrived in the Okhotsk Sea on May 27, 1865, and a week later captured the bark *Abigail,* out of New Bedford. Thomas Manning of Baltimore, the second mate of the *Abigail,* changed his allegiance from the North to the South on the spot, and signed aboard the *Shenandoah* to help them locate the remainder of the Yankee whaling fleet. Waddell captured or burned the *William Thompson* and the *Euphrates,* both of New Bedford, but when he approached the *Milo* demanding surrender, ship's master Jonathan Hawes told him that the war was over. (The formal surrender at Appomattox had taken place on April 9.) Waddell thought that the report of the surrender was simply a ruse to avoid capture, and he extracted a $40,000 bond from Hawes, payable when the war really *was* over. He then went on to capture the *Sophia Thornton* and the *Jireh Swift,* which he burned to the waterline. On May 23, the *Shenandoah* overtook the trading brig *Susan Abigail,* of San Francisco, and confiscated her cargo of guns, pistols, needles, calico, twine and other Yankee notions. Also aboard the *Susan Abigail,* however, were newspapers reporting Lee's surrender, and the death of President Lincoln on April 15. As a Confederate officer, Captain Waddell had a vested interest in the continuation of the war, so he burned the *Susan Abigail* and continued his rampage. He caught and burned the *Nimrod, William C. Nye* and *Catherine,* and with the crews towed along behind *Shenandoah* in twelve whaleboats, he took off after four more ships, the *Benjamin Cummings, Isabella, Gypsey* and *General Pike.* He captured all but the *Benjamin Cummings,* which he avoided because he had heard that there was smallpox aboard. On May 28, twelve miles southwest of the Diomede Islands, after burning the bark *Waverly,* Waddell spotted no less than ten whaleships clustered together. He burned the *Brunswick, Hillman, Nassau, Isaac Howland, Martha 2nd, Favorite, Covington* and *Congress 2nd,* and bonded the *Nile* and the *James Maury,* sending thcm to San Francisco with 412 prisoners aboard.

Even though he had repeatedly been told that the war was over, Waddell continued his voyage of destruction. In all, he captured or burned twenty-four whaleships before heading south on June 29. There was no way that the remainder of the whaling fleet could know that he was gone, so they stayed in hiding and did very little whaling for the remainder of the 1865 season. The "success" of *Shenandoah* can be directly attributed to her auxiliary power; the whalers could only attempt to sail away from her or hide.

Waddell escaped notice by all the ships who were looking for him and arrived in England on November 5. He and his crew could not be held in neutral Britain, and although they were set free, the United States demanded reparations from England for all damages done by those ships (*Florida, Alabama* and *Shenandoah*) that had been sold to the Confederacy by the British. In 1872, a total of $15.5 million was awarded to the United States by an international tribunal that met in Geneva, to be parceled out to various shipping companies and individuals. The war had affected the whaling industry to a considerable degree: forty-six whaleships were lost to Confederate raiders, and another forty of the older hulks were loaded with granite in 1861 and sunk in the harbors of Charleston and Savannah. The idea was to sink them to blockade the harbors, but the ships sank too deeply in the mud, and the "stone fleet" had little effect on Confederate privateers. Despite the harm visited upon the New England whaling industry by the war, it was minimal compared to what lay in store for the Yankee fleet.

Those whalers that escaped the *Shenandoah* contin-

In June 1865, the Confederate raider *Shenandoah* wreaked havoc among the Yankee whaling fleet, capturing and burning vessels even after the war was over.

ued in business after the war, and ventured farther and farther north in their quest for the elusive bowheads. Petroleum had been discovered in 1859, but its importance to American industry did not become apparent until well into the 1870s. As the price of whale oil dropped compared to the cheaper petroleum, however, the whalers sought to find a way to compensate for falling prices by taking more whales.

In 1867, the *Nile,* under Captain Thomas Long, sailed into the Bering Sea, through the Strait, and into the Chukchi, heading westward into Siberian waters. Here he found a previously unidentified island, which he named Wrangel Island, after Baron Ferdinand Petrovich von Wrangel, a Russian who had explored the Siberian coast on foot in the 1820s. They found no whales here, however, so the whalers came about and headed east, past Cape Lisburne. In 1868 and 1869, despite bitter winds, icy gales and almost intolerable conditions, the whalers persisted and continued the slaughter of the bowheads. The ice, which was to show its true mettle in only a couple of years, stove in hulls, trapped ships, and only reluctantly revealed the whales to those who came to kill them.

FOR THE most part, whaling was a group effort; the captain and the crew worked together to obtain their respective shares of the profits, and concurrently took the risks necessary to ensure a profitable voyage. The whalers competed with each other for whales and profits, however, and a whale captured by one ship was a whale lost by another. It was therefore not a little unusual to see no fewer than thirty-nine ships setting sail together. At Honolulu in April 1871, the New England whaling fleet was refitted and set sail for the Arctic.

They began to arrive at Cape Thaddeus around the first of May, and at Cape Navarin in early June. The first casualty was the bark *Oriole,* which was stove by ice and unrepairable. She was bought by Captain Benjamin Dexter, of the *Emily Morgan,* for $1,350, and her various parts were resold to other ships for $2,541.17, a quick profit for Dexter before he had even sighted a whale. The fleet passed through the Bering Strait between the eighteenth and the thirtieth of June. Very few whales were sighted in July, so the whalers occupied themselves by taking walruses. By early August, most of the fleet was north of Blossom Shoals.

In late August, the entire fleet occupied a strip of water that was no more than half a mile wide. They were strung out over twenty miles in water that was twenty-four feet deep, if that—barely deep enough for them to float. The fleet had encountered ice before, but nothing like the threatening pack that began to close in on them during August of that year. Most of the ships by that time had sailed eastward, and when the great sheet of ice began to grind toward them, there was nowhere for them to go. On September 1, the wind picked up, the ice moved in, and the open water occupied by the whaleships was further reduced. In *Children of the Light,* the history of this disaster, Everett Allen describes the weather that the whalers faced at this time:

When the northwest wind of this place blows seriously, it is in the form of a roaring, undisciplined gale off the roof of the world, a fierce and bitter blast driving needles of thick snow, and there is no standing against it. It is an irresistible force kin to the globe's beginnings; it whistles through the Arctic's half-empty world and threatens to empty it. It drives life out of sight and once unleashed by the deteriorating season, persists unceasing for almost more days than the human spirit can endure.

As the ice closed in around the ships, the captains began to fear the worst—that their ships would not only be trapped, but crushed—and they began to offload their men in hopes of getting them to those ships that were not immediately threatened. The first ship to go was the brig *Comet,* crunched by the inexorably advancing sheet of grinding ice. Then the *Roman,* the northernmost of the fleet, was caught between two floes. She was lifted out of the water by the crushing jaws of ice, splintered like so many tons of kindling, and sank within forty-five minutes. It was an unmistakable demonstration of the awesome destructive power of the ice.

Of the thirty-nine ships in the area, twenty-two were in immediate danger of being trapped, but of those some continued whaling. It was not so much an insensitive or fatalistic attitude that permitted the captain of the *Henry Taber* to lower for whales while ships were being wrecked around him, but rather a firm belief that an offshore wind would eventually drive off the ice pack. No such benign wind arrived.

On September 8, in a driving snowstorm, the ice stove in the *Awashonks* and trapped the *Julian* and the *Eugenia.* By this time, it was obvious that whaling

In September 1871, thirty-nine whaleships had to be abandoned off Icy Cape, Alaska, when the ice began to close in and crush them.

had to be suspended, since all the ships were going to be needed to rescue the men from the damaged vessels. The captains met aboard the *Florida* on September 12, and drew up a document in which they agreed to abandon their ships: "... we the undersigned masters of whaleships now lying off Point Belcher, after holding a meeting concerning our dreadful situation, have all come to the conclusion that our ships cannot be got out this year, and there being no harbor that we can get our vessels into, and not having provisions enough to feed our crews to exceed three months, and being in a barren country, where there is neither food nor fuel to be obtained, we feel ourselves under the painful necessity of abandoning our vessels, and trying to work our way south with our boats. . . ."

The ships could not sail through the narrowing passage, but men could row. Seven ships stood off south of the closing ice, ready to take on the crews of the abandoned ships. On September 14, two hundred whaleboats formed a ragged procession to bring the captains and crews to the waiting ships as the

bulk of the fleet lay abandoned, its spars piercing the lowering skies at strange angles in an icy, moving graveyard. By September 17, the "rescue fleet" had taken aboard 1,129 men. Thirty-two ships had been abandoned, and the estimated loss, including oil and bone in the holds, was approximately $1.5 million in 1871 dollars.

Abandoning their hopes of continuing a profitable whaling season, the seven ships of the rescue fleet began to take on the thousand-plus men who needed a ride home. The motley fleet of overcrowded whaleboats had still to reach the ships, and they did so under the worst possible conditions: terrible weather roiled the waters, and chunks of floating ice threatened the fragile little boats. Sleet and snow roared over them, and freezing spray came over the gunwales. When night fell and the storms continued, they had to come ashore onto the ice and set up camp. With the weather continuing to deteriorate, the rescuers boarded the last of the refugees, and set sail for Honolulu on September 16. The last of the fleet arrived there on November 22. Although only seven of the proud vessels that had left Hawaii six months before had made it back, perhaps the most incredible aspect of this entire catastrophe was that not a single life was lost during the entrapment of the ships or the rescue operation.

Not every man who left Honolulu returned, however. A single boatsteerer, whose name is not recorded, chose to stay behind when everyone else was heading for the boats. Perhaps he thought he could somehow capitalize on the $1.5 million worth of material that was sitting in and on the ice. Enough food for a small army had been left behind, so he would not want for provisions. He spent the next six months alone on a ship, with the wind, the ice and the Eskimos for company. The Eskimos saw the abandoned ships as a rich source of plunder: wood, rope, oil and food—but no liquor. The captains, knowing that the Eskimos would find and drink it, destroyed all their liquor before they left their ships. The Eskimos, however, could not know this, and whatever they found in the medicine chests, they drank. Many of them became sick, and not understanding why, they attributed their illness to evil spirits in the ships. They therefore burned every ship where one of them had gotten sick. The lone white man stayed aboard the *Massachusetts* during the howling winter of 1871–72. Although he was in contact with the Eskimos, they "turned against him," and when he was rescued by returning whalemen the next spring, with nothing but the clothes on his back, he is reported to have said, "A hundred and fifty thousand dollars would not tempt me to try another winter in the Arctic."

In 1872, many whaleships returned to the Arctic to continue whaling, but others went to try to salvage what was left of the 1871 fleet. From '72 to '75, the ships went to the ice and even took whales east of Point Barrow. In 1876, however, another disaster was presaged by the collision of the *Marengo* and the *Illinois* south of the Bering Strait, sending the *Illinois* to the bottom in fifteen minutes. Then the *Arctic,* one of the "rescue fleet" of '71, was crushed in the ice north of Point Franklin. Fourteen of the eighteen ships on the grounds headed for Barrow, unaware that a huge raft of ice was heading north behind them. The ships tried to run south, but could not beat against the current. In a bizarre replication of the 1871 disaster, ten ships were trapped in the clos-

ing ice near Barrow, but this time there was no fleet standing by to rescue them. Most of the whalemen boarded the *Florence* and worked their way out of the ice, but fifty men stayed behind, hoping to be rescued later. This time the survival record was not so good. Only three men came through the bitter Arctic winter, and of the ten ships, only one, the *Clara Bell,* was found in 1877. The following year, three more ships were sunk by ice, and another was lost in a gale.

With the appearance of petroleum and the use of cottonseed- and fish oil in industrial processes, it appeared that whaling was becoming only a marginally profitable business, and the owners were suffering massive losses as well. Why did they persist? Tradition? Hope?

Yet another tragedy awaited the whaling fleet in 1879. Once again the ice began to close in around *Mercury, Helen Mar, Mount Wollaston,* and *Vigilant.* Captains Bauldry and Hickmott, of *Mercury* and *Helen Mar,* rafted together, believing that two ships together had a better chance than one alone. When Bauldry and Hickmott found that they could not get out, they made plans to spend the winter aboard their ships and wait for the ice to break up in the spring. A fortuitous change in wind direction enabled them to get out of the ice, but the *Helen Mar* struck a shoal, badly ripping her bottom. October was no time to be in the Bering Sea, and in a raging snowstorm they threw everything they could overboard. These two damaged ships arrived in San Francisco on November 26, long after they had been given up for lost. The *Mount Wollaston* and the *Vigilant* were never seen again.

MORE THAN forty ships had been lost by 1876, and the North Pacific fleet that once numbered almost three hundred was now reduced to seventeen. The repeated trappings, crushings and sinkings made it clear that sailing ships were ill-suited to cope with the conditions of the western Arctic. The price of whale oil had fallen to an all-time low, and it appeared that the industry was finished. Technology provided a temporary solution. America was then the only major whaling nation that was not using steam power. If foreign successes were not enough, the owners had only to look at their own history to realize that the auxiliary-powered *Shenandoah* which had wreaked such havoc on their sailing ships in 1865 was infinitely better suited to confront the conditions of the Arctic.

It is somewhat difficult to understand, therefore, why it took so long for the Yankee whalers to convert to steam. Perhaps the most parsimonious answer lies in parsimony. Unlike the wind, which was free (and free to drive ships into the ice), steam was relatively expensive. The boilers had to be fueled by coal, and coal cost money. Also, to stow the coal for long voyages, the ships had to provide storage space in the holds, and this space might better be used for casks of oil or sheaves of baleen. Besides, steam had been tried, and it hadn't worked very well. In 1866 a steam boiler had been installed on the bark *Pioneer,* but the steam was inadequate to save the vessel when it was crushed in the ice of Hudson Strait and lost the following year.

More than technology, more than parsimony, the dictates of feminine fashion gave an impetus to the floundering industry. Whereas fashion-conscious Western women of the early Victorian era were content to be seen in high-waisted, tubular dresses that effectively disguised their shapes—Queen Victoria herself was the exemplar—by the 1860s women appeared in tighter bodices and voluminous skirts, supported by hoops of bone. (This time, the Empress Eugénie was the exemplar.) According to Alison Lurie's *The Language of Clothes,* the ideal woman of the 1850s was "supposed to be resourceful, practical, charitable, devout, and above all, strongly maternal." This necessitated a more matronly appearance, where "Curves grew rounder, materials heavier. . . . [I]t was the age of the crinoline and later the bustle, and the increased importance of women in the domestic and social sphere was signaled by their sheer bulk." This increase in overall size, however, was accompanied by a reduction in the waist: "A small waist, created by rigid and painful corseting emphasized the bulk above and below." (Lillian Russell, the music hall star of the 1890s and feminine ideal of her generation, was reputed to have an eighteen-inch waist.) The material used in all this "rigid and painful corseting," of course, was whalebone.

Historically, whaling was very much a man's industry. Men did the hunting, the killing, the flensing, the sailing, the drowning, the dying. But it might be said that much of it was done *for* women. Whoever

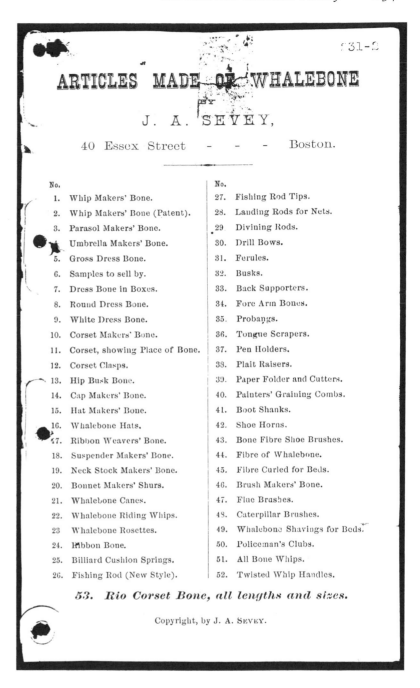

ARTICLES MADE OF WHALEBONE
BY
J. A. SEVEY,
40 Essex Street   -   -   -   Boston.

No.		No.	
1.	Whip Makers' Bone.	27.	Fishing Rod Tips.
2.	Whip Makers' Bone (Patent).	28.	Landing Rods for Nets.
3.	Parasol Makers' Bone.	29	Divining Rods.
4.	Umbrella Makers' Bone.	30.	Drill Bows.
5.	Gross Dress Bone.	31.	Ferules.
6.	Samples to sell by.	32.	Busks.
7.	Dress Bone in Boxes.	33.	Back Supporters.
8.	Round Dress Bone.	34.	Fore Arm Bones.
9.	White Dress Bone.	35.	Probangs.
10.	Corset Makers' Bone.	36.	Tongue Scrapers.
11.	Corset, showing Place of Bone.	37.	Pen Holders.
12.	Corset Clasps.	38.	Plait Raisers.
13.	Hip Busk Bone.	39.	Paper Folder and Cutters.
14.	Cap Makers' Bone.	40.	Painters' Graining Combs.
15.	Hat Makers' Bone.	41.	Boot Shanks.
16.	Whalebone Hats.	42.	Shoe Horns.
17.	Ribbon Weavers' Bone.	43.	Bone Fibre Shoe Brushes.
18.	Suspender Makers' Bone.	44.	Fibre of Whalebone.
19.	Neck Stock Makers' Bone.	45.	Fibre Curled for Beds.
20.	Bonnet Makers' Shurs.	46.	Brush Makers' Bone.
21.	Whalebone Canes.	47.	Flue Brushes.
22.	Whalebone Riding Whips.	48.	Caterpillar Brushes.
23	Whalebone Rosettes.	49.	Whalebone Shavings for Beds.
24.	Ribbon Bone.	50.	Policeman's Clubs.
25.	Billiard Cushion Springs.	51.	All Bone Whips.
26.	Fishing Rod (New Style).	52.	Twisted Whip Handles.

53. *Rio Corset Bone, all lengths and sizes.*

Copyright, by J. A. SEVEY.

it was who decreed that women's waists ought to be cinched in tightly, or that they should wear skirts wide enough to make them look like giant tottering mushrooms, was responsible for the death of thousands of bowhead whales. In defense of women, it must also be said that both sexes required oil, soap, lighting oil and lubricants, so that the decimation of the bowhead cannot be laid at the dainty little feet of nineteenth-century demoiselles. Fashionable women now demanded wasp waists, and wasp waists

The Arctic Oil Works drying yard in San Francisco, with baleen drying. In the background are the bark *J. D. Peters* and the ship *Orca*.

called for more elaborate corsets. More elaborate corsets meant a rise in the demand for whalebone, and this demand sent the whalers north again. The price of whalebone had been $1.12 a pound in 1875, but by 1878 it had soared to an unprecedented $3.25. Suddenly a single bowhead—if one could be found—was worth upward of $5,000.

William Lewis commissioned the first American steam whaler, the *Mary and Helen,* to be built at a shipyard in Bath, Maine. She was launched on July 30, 1879, and went down to New Bedford to be fitted with tryworks. Under Captain Leander Owen, she sailed for the Arctic, and returned with 2,350 barrels of oil and 45,000 pounds of baleen, a total value of more than $100,000. To build the 138-foot bark, Lewis had invested the not inconsiderable sum of

$65,000. On her maiden voyage, the *Mary and Helen* had neatly paid off her owner's entire investment and left him with a considerable profit. It was one of the most spectacularly successful voyages in Arctic whaling history.

Even before the *Mary and Helen* had returned, Lewis was planning to enlarge his fleet of steam whalers. With a group of investors he built the *Belvedere,* the *Lucretia* and then the *North Star.* By 1881 these three ships were ready to sail, but Lewis sold the *Mary and Helen* to the United States government as an Arctic rescue vessel (for $100,000), and then proceeded to build *Mary and Helen II.* The immediate success of the first voyage was not repeated. Only *Belvedere* made a profitable voyage; *Lucretia* could not round Cape Horn and was forced to miss her first

Arctic season, and *North Star* was crushed in the ice at Barrow on her maiden voyage. The simple addition of a boiler was evidently not sufficient to guarantee indestructibility.

On the West Coast, Millen Griffith, Josiah N. Knowles, and George C. Perkins, a former governor of California, commissioned the *Bowhead,* the first of the California steam whalers. With the 1869 completion of the transcontinental railroad, the center of the whaling industry was shifting from the East Coast to the West. As soon as the *Bowhead* had been launched, Griffith & Co. began construction of another steamship, *Orca.* Then came *Narwhal* and *Balaena,* and the California entrepreneurs purchased *Mary and Helen II* from William Lewis. Then they commissioned *Thrasher,* to be built at Bath because the San Francisco shipyards were too busy. With five ships in commission, Griffith, Perkins, Goodall, Knowles and others formed the Pacific Steam Whaling Company. Unlike the New Bedford whalers, which were owned by individual owners, the Pacific Steam Whaling Company, capitalized at $2 million, sold stock to individual investors. Griffith *et al.* also founded the Arctic Oil Works, which processed the oil and bone, another radical departure from Eastern tradition.

Unencumbered by tradition, they could also develop new methods of sailing and fishing. They fitted their whalers with propellers that could be withdrawn, enabling them to sail in otherwise non-navigable waters, and installed the first steam tryworks and iron oil tanks, replacing the antiquated (and dangerous) brick tryworks, the wood and whale-scrap fires, and the wooden casks which often leaked. Under the inspired leadership of Josiah Knowles, they also established the first shore-based whaling stations on the Alaskan coast. The Californians reasoned that the whalers often had to make long and unproductive voyages every spring, so in 1883 they built a permanent facility at Point Barrow, where the whalers could emulate the Eskimo practice of catching the whales as they passed through the narrow leads just offshore. (Sometimes progress entails a backward look.) Already there were shore stations along the California coast for the hunting of gray whales, and Knowles reckoned that they could also trade with the Eskimos for baleen.

The traditionalists objected to steam whalers, claiming that the noise would frighten the sensitive bowheads, and while it probably did to some extent, this drawback was more than compensated for by the maneuverability of the new whalers, which could now enter previously difficult or dangerous waters— and get out again. They usually hunted in the fall season, reached Point Hope around July 10, bunkered with coal from the Corwin Coal Mine (which was owned by the Pacific Steam Whaling Company and was located between Point Hope and Icy Cape), and then headed for Barrow. When the ice began to close, they would follow the whales to their autumn feeding grounds in the open water near Herald Island. In 1879, while the sailing whalers *Vigilant* and *Mount Wollaston* were lost and the *Helen Mar* and *Mercury* were fighting a gale, the Pacific steam whalers were chugging more or less serenely back to San Francisco.

The 1880s saw a rise in the price of baleen, and a concurrent increase in the Pacific fleet. *Grampus* was added in 1886, and *Jesse H. Freeman* two years later. Soon the whalers had pushed east almost to the Canadian border, and in 1888 Captain George Bauldry (master of the *Helen Mar*) reached Barter Island, the easternmost point ever reached by a whaler up to that time. The Mackenzie River delta was the region in which the bowheads congregated to feed—it was, in fact, the destination of their migrations—but sailing ships had regarded the seven hundred miles from Barrow as being too far and too dangerous. A harpooner named Joe Tuckfield was sent east with a group of Eskimos to winter on Herschel Island, and when he returned to the station at Barrow, he reported that the rumors were true: there were whales aplenty around Herschel. More important, he brought the news that the island had a good harbor, which was named Pauline Cove. In August 1889, the *Beluga* and the U.S.S. *Thetis* (sent by the government to establish the position of the 141st meridian, the border between the United States and Canada) hove to at Herschel and surveyed the harbor. The first intentional wintering by whalers high in the western Arctic was about to commence.

Three ships, the *Grampus, Nicoline,* and *Mary D. Hume,* were sent by the Pacific Steam Whaling Company in 1890 with instructions to take no oil, only whalebone, since the price of baleen was skyrocketing. The crews settled in, collecting the abundant driftwood for fires, trading for meat with the Eskimos, and banking their ice-fast ships with snow for insulation against the cold. The winter of 1890–91 passed uneventfully—if living at the top of the world in an unbroken landscape of ice, snow and howling blizzards can be described as uneventful—but they saw no whales, even as spring and summer approached. The *Nicoline* and *Grampus* headed for California in the fall, but the intrepid whalers of the *Hume* decided to remain for another winter.

Although they now had a safe harbor and a base of operations at Pauline Cove, they still conducted their whaling in the old-fashioned way: they put to sea among the ice floes, and searched for the whales. In July of 1891, after the other ships had departed, the *Hume* struck pay dirt. She took 27 whales, and had to return to Herschel in the midst of her bonanza because she was too heavily laden with bone. The *Grampus,* which had returned in the spring of '91, had also found the whalers' El Dorado, and took 21 bowheads off Cape Bathurst.

After two successful seasons at Herschel, the *Mary D. Hume* returned to San Francisco with a $400,000 cargo, harvested from an incredible 37 whales. On the news of this phenomenal success, the Pacific Steam Whaling Company sent four whalers (*Narwhal, Balaena, Newport* and *Grampus*) to the north, along with a supply ship, the 862-ton *Jeanie.*

The *Jeanie* was supposed to transport the accumulated baleen home and bring fresh supplies and men to the base. In fact, this system enabled the *Newport* and the *Hume* to remain in the Arctic for six years. The catches increased (*Narwhal* took 64 whales, and *Balaena* took 62, in 1893–94), and so did the whalers. Other companies soon outfitted steam whalers for the North, and by 1894–95, there were fifteen vessels overwintering.

Houses and storehouses were built, and by 1893 the inevitable missionaries arrived to convert the natives. (The first Anglican mission was established at Herschel in 1897.) The problems attendant upon the close quartering of some five hundred men are well known. Enforced idleness, drinking, deserting, fighting and debauchery of all kinds were reported. Many of the captains had brought their wives or sweethearts, and for men so far from what they knew as civilization, the presence of Eskimo women also caused ructions. All was not fighting and drinking, however. The men passed the time by skiing and tobogganing on the ice, and played various games, including baseball and soccer. They also put on plays and minstrel shows.

Unfortunately, this Arctic idyll was entirely dependent upon the regular appearance of *Balaena mysti-*

The *Mary D. Hume,* the first steam whaler to work the western Arctic.

Pauline Cove, Herschel Island, in the winter of 1893–94. Seven whaleships (*Mary D. Hume, Newport, Grampus, Narwhal, Balanea, Karluck* and *Jeanette*) wintering over.

cetus, and not surprisingly, the whales' interests did not necessarily coincide with those of the whalers. The Pacific Steam Whaling Company began to cut corners in an attempt to stem declining profits, and this caused more disunity. They decided to diversify, and relied more heavily on trading for furs with the Eskimos. By 1908, the fur trade was as important as the whaling business.

Steam power was no guarantee of safety, and again the inexorable ice demonstrated its dominance over the whalers. When the *Navarch* was trapped in August 1897, her crew abandoned her and took to the boats. Captain Whiteside (who had displayed appalling cowardice in the face of the disaster, and abandoned his ship and his crew), Charlie Brower (who was not a member of the crew but had boarded the *Navarch* from the station at Point Barrow and later recorded the ordeal in *Fifty Years Below Zero*), and only twenty-one of the thirty-seven crew members survived. Brower's party had survived for twelve days on the ice with nothing to eat but ice and the soles of their boots. Bockstoce writes that "Brower's

march and drift surely rank with mankind's most punishing tests of survival. . . ."*

*Each of these disasters includes myriad tales of individual heroism and struggle against almost impossible conditions, but there is neither time nor space to incorporate them all. For the reader who would study these fascinating—and terrifying—stories in greater detail, I recommend Charlie Brower's book, and John Bockstoce's definitive study of the entire history of whaling in the western Arctic. One example of this unbelievable fortitude is contained in "Cap'n George Fred" Tilton's eponymous book. He was third mate on the *Belvedere,* which was frozen in the ice at Peard Bay in October 1897. After he watched the *Orca* sink under him—he had gone aboard to salvage some of her supplies—and seen the *Jesse H. Freeman* burn to the waterline after someone had knocked over a lamp inside, he ended up at the whaling station at Point Barrow with the crews of his ship, and those of the *Orca* and the *Freeman.* Provisions were inadequate for the hundred-odd men that were planning to winter there, so Tilton set out to *walk* across Alaska, from Barrow to the United States, a distance of some seventeen hundred miles. (Although Tilton says that he "volunteered to go south to civilization to get help," Bockstoce writes that the captains met and decided that "messengers should be sent south to report that there was no undue cause for worry.") Whatever his motivation, Tilton left Barrow on October 26 (with "two Siberian Indians," who left him at Point Hope), and traveling mostly by dogsled, arrived at Kodiak Island on March 17, 1898. There he rented a schooner and sailed to Prince William Sound, and from there he caught a ride to Portland, Oregon, where he was able to telegraph his owners and tell them the situation. The shipwrecked crews of the steam whalers were rescued by the revenue cutter *Bear* on July 22, 1898.

In 1897, the year *Orca, Belvedere, Jesse H. Freeman* and *Rosario* were lost to the ice, several other vessels had to winter in emergency quarters when they could not make the safety of Pauline Cove on Herschel Island. Josiah Knowles, the inspiration for most of the innovations at Herschel, died in 1896, and the Pacific Steam Whaling Company began to wind down its now unprofitable operations. They shut down the shore stations at Point Hope and Point Barrow, and withdrew their overwintering ships, *Newport* and *Mary D. Hume.* Other companies, still intent upon wringing the last nickel's worth of oil or bone from the Arctic, began to economize by sending smaller, less expensive vessels to the ice. The Eskimos, who had been only too glad to trade baleen for furs, now provided mostly furs to the whalers in exchange for various trade goods, as a further indication of the declining numbers of whales. In 1903, William Lewis, who had been the instigator of steam whaling in the Arctic, introduced the internal-combustion engine in the schooner *Monterey,* but it was to be another twentieth-century innovation that wrote *finis* to the Arctic whaling industry: spring steel was invented in 1909, and as this cheaper and much more accessible commodity replaced baleen in the manufacture of corsets, the price of whalebone plummeted from a high of $5 a pound to 50 cents.

The thirty-year history of steam whaling was all but over. Many innovations which were to affect all future whaling had been introduced, but no inventions could overcome the indisputable shortage of whales. In his detailed studies of the whalers' logbooks and records, John Bockstoce has identified more than twenty-six hundred cruises made from 1848 to 1915. With 98 percent of all these cruises identified, he estimates that approximately 20,000 whales were killed. A further breakdown produces some startling revelations: one-third of the total number of whales killed during the sixty-seven-year period were taken in the first nine years of the fishery, and two-thirds of the total were taken during the first twenty. "These results," writes Bockstoce, "suggest that the bowhead whale population was rapidly depleted during the first 20 years, even though the industry continued to hunt the bowhead in those waters for another 47 years."*

---

*As of 1980, when this study was compiled, the United States government estimate of bowheads alive was 2,200 animals, but since then—with annual catches averaging thirty animals—the scientists' estimates have been raised to around seven thousand.

The California Gray Whale Fishery

CHARLES MELVILLE SCAMMON was born in Pittston, Maine, in 1825, only six years after Herman Melville; there was, as far as we know, no family connection. His family was not a seafaring one, but young Charles decided to go to sea, and by the age of twenty-three, he was in command of a coastal schooner trading in the Carolinas. After a voyage to California in the bark *Sara Moers,* he decided to remain in San Francisco. At the age of twenty-seven, he was in command of the sealing brig *Mary Helen,* harvesting elephant seals for their oil off the coasts of southern California and northern Mexico. In 1853 in the *Lenore,* he was whaling off Panama, and in 1856 he visited Magdalena Bay in search of gray whales. He discovered Laguna Ojo de Liebre in 1858, one of the breeding lagoons of the gray whales. (The northernmost of the major breeding lagoons, it is now known as Scammon's Lagoon.) While he was directly responsible for the initiation of lagoon whaling, which reduced the gray whale population to the point where the species was believed to be extinct by the turn of the century, Scammon's contribution to whaling history was not only in the killing of whales, but in recording the process.

In 1874 he published *The Marine Mammals of the Northwestern Coast of North America; Together with an Account of the American Whale-Fishery,* one of the most important books on whales and whaling ever written. It was issued after he had retired from whaling and had achieved some celebrity as a writer of magazine articles. Not only does the book present detailed accounts of the natural history of the various cetaceans and pinnipeds that were hunted in the West (with illustrations credited to Scammon), it also provides an invaluable history of the American whale fishery recounted by a man who played a significant role in that history.

Although Scammon is indelibly associated with the gray whales, he was not, as is commonly assumed, the originator of the fishery. As early as 1795, Captain John Locke in the British whaler *Resolution* arrived in Baja and began the slaughter that would culminate less than a century later with the virtual elimination of the whales. The decimation of the gray whale population began slowly, since the whalers who came to Baja were not particularly interested in the oil-poor grays. They had come to these protected waters to escape from the winter weather of the North Pacific, and the "scrag" whales that they encountered did not offer the rich oil of the sperms or the easy capture of the docile humpbacks. In the winter of 1845–46 the *United States,* out of Stonington, and the *Hibernia,* out of New London, became the first whalers to exploit Magdalena Bay, and they harvested some forty whales. In the decade between the discovery of Magdalena Bay and the arrival of Captain Scammon, approximately 500 whales were captured. Scammon seems to have been the first whaler to recognize that despite the poor quality of the brownish oil, he could fill his holds in a single season instead of the three or four years that some whaling voyages required.

In the winter of 1855–56, Scammon sailed the brig *Lenore* into Magdalena Bay for his first gray whaling voyage. Two years later he brought the *Boston* over the barrier bar at the lagoon that now bears his name and discovered the heretofore unknown breeding grounds of the gray whales. (There are actually three lagoons in the crook of Vizcaíno Bay, the largest of which is named for a success, and the smaller two— Manuela and Guerrero Negro—are named for ships that foundered there.) Where earlier whalers had

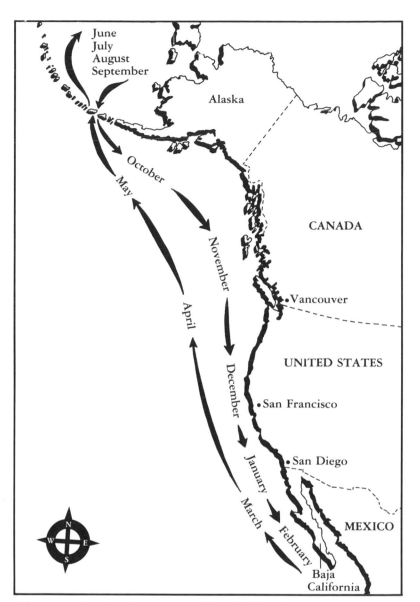

The annual migration route of the California gray whales.

been hunting *Eschrichtius robustus* in the surf, in the kelp, or in the ragged archipelago of Magdalena Bay, Scammon's crew found the whales—especially females and calves—in dense concentrations in the shallow lagoons. He wrote, "As the season approaches for the whales to bring forth their young, which is from December to March, they formerly collected at the most remote extremities of the lagoons, and huddled together so thickly that it was difficult for a boat to cross the waters without coming in contact with them."

The year after Scammon discovered the breeding lagoons, an armada of whaleships headed for Baja California. (Scammon has written that in the 1847–48 season, there were fifty ships there, but David Henderson, who has studied the gray whale fishery in depth, feels that this is "an obvious exaggeration.") In the seasons that followed, the fishery continued in a sporadic fashion, with some successful seasons and some where hardly any whales at all were taken. By 1854–55, however, the whaling picked up dramatically, and there commenced eleven winters that Henderson refers to as the "bonanza period." With Scammon's discovery of Laguna Ojo de Liebre in 1858, a whole new area was opened up, and the following year Scammon performed a similar feat of daring seamanship, and crossed the barrier to the last of the gray whales' sanctuaries, the lagoon known as Ballenas or San Ignacio Lagoon.

The whaleships also anchored outside the mouths of the lagoons and picked off the whales as they entered or left for their migrations. The population of eastern Pacific gray whales, which was at this time only a portion of the total, was never very high. (On the other side of the Pacific, there was no Scammon to record the Japanese and Korean industries.) It has been variously estimated at between 10,000 and 20,000 animals, and Henderson has carefully tabulated the total number killed at all recorded locations at sea and ashore. For the years 1845 through 1874, he estimates that 8,000 whales were killed. Since a substantial proportion of these were females, with or without calves, it is not surprising—although it was probably unexpected by the whalers—that the gray whale population declined so sharply that the whaling was effectively ended by 1874.

Anchoring in the shallow waters of the protected lagoons, the whalers lowered their boats and proceeded to slaughter the grays in unprecedented numbers. Unlike many of the other great whales, gray whales are notoriously reluctant to participate in their own demise, and often the whalers' boats were upset, usually by enraged mothers defending their calves. (In the hunting of other whales, such as the bowhead, it was common practice for the whalers to harpoon the calf, knowing that the mother would stand by her injured offspring and then be harpooned herself. Gray whales, which were known to the whalers as "devilfish," attacked when their calves were threatened, so the whalers harpooned the adults first, and only then the defenseless calves.)

Hardly a day passes [wrote Scammon], but there is upsetting or staving of boats, the crew receiving bruises, cuts, and, in many instances, having limbs broken; and repeated accidents have happened in which men have been instantly killed, or received mortal injury. The reasons of the increased dangers are these: the quick and deviating movements of the animal, its unusual sagacity, and the fact of the sandy bottom being continually stirred by strong currents, making it difficult to see an object at any considerable depth. . . . Should the chase be made with the current, the fugitive sometimes stops suddenly, and the speed of the boat, together with the influence of the running water, shoots it upon the worried animal when it is dashing its flukes in every direction. The whales that are chased have with them their young cubs, and the mother, in her efforts to avoid the pursuit of her and her offspring, may momentarily lose sight of her little one. Instantly she will stop and "sweep" around in search, and if the boat comes into contact with her, it is quite sure to be staved. Another danger is, that in darting the lance at the mother, the young one, in its gambols, will get in the way of the weapon, and receive the wound instead of the intended victim. In such instances, the parent animal in her frenzy, will chase the boats, and, overtaking them, will overturn them with her head, or dash them with a stroke of her ponderous flukes.

Sperm whalers were primarily interested in the larger whales which would yield more barrels of oil, and for hunters of the cachalot, the adult males were the most appropriate animals to kill. Bull sperm whales are a third again as large as females, so the whalers killed them whenever possible. It is conceivable that the removal of the breeding bulls led to a decline in the total population, but it was not nearly as deleterious a practice as the systematic removal of the females with calves, or females that would have become impregnated had they been permitted to survive. Like the southern right whales in Australia, New Zealand and South Africa, the gray whales of California were subjected to the most traumatic whaling policy imaginable, virtually guaranteed to prevent the survival of the species. Although Henderson regards most of Scammon's figures as too high, he quotes the captain as estimating the total remaining population in 1874 at 1,900 animals.

While the New England whalers were still hunting

sperm whales with hand-thrown harpoons, the lagoon whalers were employing the latest advances in whale-killing technology. They were firing their harpoons from guns mounted in the bows of the whaleboats, the predecessors of the harpoon cannons that would shortly be appearing on the steam- and diesel-powered catcher boats used for pelagic whaling. (According to Lytle's detailed study of the evolution of the harpoon, the idea of shooting the whale appeared as early as 1731, but did not take hold until the middle of the nineteenth century.) Of course the development of whale-killing weapons had to parallel the development of people-killing weapons, so the first whaling guns were flintlocks which depended upon a spark that ignited the powder, awkward and impractical in a bouncing whaleboat. With the invention of percussion-ignited guns in the nineteenth century, the stage was set for whaling artillery. Enterprising inventors developed and patented several variations on this theme, but the principle was the same: a swivel gun that could shoot a harpoon into the whale which would remain attached by a line. The first of these innovators was William Greener, who in 1837 invented a gun he described as "protected from damp, or spray from the sea . . . throwing the harpoon with considerable accuracy, to any distance under eighty-four yards." A far cry from the irons that the stalwart harpooners of the Yankee fleet had to throw into the whale as they rowed almost onto its back.

At the same time, the bomb lance was making its appearance. Aimed and fired from the shoulder, this weapon resembled nothing more than a heavy shotgun, and removed the problems of aiming a mounted gun from a bouncing boat. It also eliminated the attachment of the whaleboat to the whale, since this weapon was designed to fire an exploding projectile into the whale, killing it on impact. Both devices were employed in the California fishery, and Scammon wrote that "Each boat is furnished with a Greener's harpoon-gun, mounted at the bow, besides the bomb-gun in general use, which imparts to them more of a military appearance than the usual aspect of a whaling-craft." (Bomb lances are still being used today by the Eskimos of Alaska in their hunt for the bowhead whale.) For the most part, however, the bomb lance replaced the harpoon gun, and in the *Whaleman's Shipping List and Merchant's Transcript* for

A whaleboat with a swivel-mounted "Greener's gun" pursues a gray whale in Baja waters in Scammon's 1874 drawing.

November 13, 1855, we read that "Guns for driving the harpoon have, we believe, been generally abandoned, but we are assured by a manufacturer of fuse, who has lately contracted for making a quality especially adapted to this sub-marine and blubbery location, that the bomb-lance is now being quite extensively employed by many vessels, and some have sent home from the Sandwich islands for further supplies." They shot bomb lances at the whales when they were within what Scammon called "darting distance," sixteen or eighteen feet from the barnacled back of the whale.

AT MORE OR LESS the same time that the whaleships were harvesting the whales in the lagoons of Baja, more enterprising, less traditional, and less expensive operations were being conducted from shore. Humpbacks and fin whales sometimes came close enough to permit sightings, but the primary object of the California shore fishery was the gray whale. Taking advantage of the whales' habit of passing close to land, whalers established shore stations all along the coast of California, sustaining their fishery into the opening years of the twentieth century.

As with any shore fishery, the financial outlay was considerably less than that required to purchase and outfit a ship for a long voyage, and even though the

"Instead of rolling them upon the beach, as is usually done, the cutting-tackles are suspended from an elevated beam, whereby the carcass is rolled over in the water—when undergoing the process of flensing—in a manner similar to that alongside a ship. Nearby are the try-works, sending forth volumes of thick, black smoke from the scrap fires under the cauldrons of boiling oil." Scammon's description (and illustration) of the whaling station at Carmel Bay, California.

gray whales were seriously depleted, the shore-based whalers could make a profit from small annual catches. The crew of a pelagic whaler was thirty or forty men, while it usually took no more than twelve or fourteen men to man a shore station. (At the same time that the fishery was declining in the south, whalers in pursuit of the bowhead whale in the Bering and Okhotsk seas were killing gray whales on their feeding grounds, with the result, as Henderson has written, that "the California herd probably suffered as great a catch and kill as it did during the peak period of gray whaling." Some of these whales comprised what later became known as the "Korean herd," those whales which chose to swim down the coasts of Siberia, China and Japan, where they were subjected to even more pernicious destruction.)

While the lagoon whalers were either Yankees or the descendants of Yankees, the shore whalers of Alta California were almost exclusively Portuguese immigrants from Madeira, the Azores, or the Cape Verde Islands. Many of these men had signed aboard whalers when the ships stopped at their home islands, but undoubtedly some were drawn to California by the Gold Rush. Since gray whaling from shore could only occur during the winter as the whales migrated past the California coasts, the whalers could alternate whaling with the somewhat more stable and traditional practices of herding and farming. Scammon describes the station at Carmel Bay:

Scattered around the foot-hills, which come to the water's edge, are the neatly whitewashed cabins of the whalers. . . . They have their families with them, and keep a pig, sheep, goat, or cow, prowling around the premises; these, with a small garden-patch, yielding principally corn and pumpkins, make up the general picture of the hamlet, which is a paradise to the thrifty clan in comparison with the homes of their childhood.

The methods employed were similar to shore whaling around the world, and not coincidentally, similar to those that the Azoreans were practicing at home. (In the Azores, however, where the primary object of the fishery was the sperm whale, the whales appeared much farther offshore.) As the whales were spotted by shore lookouts, double-ended boats manned by a crew of five or six men were launched from the beach. The shore whalers often used the same bomb lances and harpoon guns as the lagoon whalers, but since their traditions included hand-thrown harpoons, they often killed the whale the old-fashioned way. When the animal had died, it was towed to shore for processing. If practicable, the carcass was winched up onto the beach and as the whale was rolled over, the blubber was peeled off in a continuous spiral. When the necessary equipment was not available, the whale was often processed in ankle-deep water. The blubber was chopped up and triedout in caldrons, casked and shipped by sea to the market, usually in San Francisco.

From Crescent City near the Oregon border and all along the California coast to San Diego, the shore whalers awaited the seasonal arrival of the whales. Historical records indicate that there were no fewer than fifteen stations along this nine-hundred-mile stretch of coast.* Monterey, which operated from 1855 to 1900, was the largest and most successful of these stations. Begun by a Rhode Islander named Davenport, this station changed ownership several times, being owned and operated at one time by the Portuguese Whaling Company. In their forty-five-year history, whalers at the Monterey station recorded a total kill of 655 whales, not including those that were struck and lost, which probably brought the figure closer to 800. For the fifteen stations, the total kill has been estimated in excess of 4,000 whales. (Added to the 8,000 whales killed in Baja and Siberia, this brings the grand total to some 12,000 gray whales killed between 1850 and 1900.)

The Monterey station still stands, in a somewhat altered form. Captain Davenport's house (the "First Brick House") and the Old Whaling Station have been incorporated into Monterey State Historic Park. Artifacts such as a whalebone rocking chair and a pavement fashioned of whale vertebrae provide silent testimony to the short, colorful history of California shore whaling.

*Crescent City, Humboldt Bay, Half Moon Bay, Bolinas Bay, Pigeon Point, Santa Cruz, Monterey, Point Lobos, Point Sur, San Simeon, San Luis Obispo, Point Conception, Goleta, San Pedro, San Diego.

Interlude: Herman Melville and Moby-Dick

HERMAN MELVILLE was not the first author to write fiction about whales and whaling. That honor goes to Sir Walter Scott (1771–1832), the inventor of the historical novel and the author of *Ivanhoe*. In 1821, Scott wrote *The Pirate* (whose authorship, with that of the rest of the *Waverly* novels, was anonymous until 1827), which contains a rousing description of a group of "Zetlanders," who, armed with "Harpoons, swords, pikes, and halberds . . . hayforks, spits, and whatever else could be found that was at once long and sharp," set out to dispatch a whale that had grounded itself. The whale, some 60 feet long, had come in over a sandbar, and was lying still as the hunters approached it by land and by sea. They proceed to stab and harpoon it with their various implements, but instead of killing it they only anger it, so that

he roared aloud, and as he sent to the sky a mingled sheet of brine and blood, and snapping the strong cable like a twig, overset Mertoun's boat with a blow of his tail, shot himself, by a mighty effort, over the bar, upon which the tide had risen considerably, and made out to sea, carrying with him a whole grove of the implements which had been planted in his body, and leaving behind him, on the waters, a dark red trace of his course.

There is little in this account that might be assigned to true whaling history (Scoresby's exhaustive history of the Greenland fishery had been published the year before), but it might be identified as the precursor of things to come: the whale had appeared in the off-shore waters of literature, waiting for its scrivener.

In 1823, a much more formidable whale appears in print; its author is James Fenimore Cooper. In *The Pilot*, the hero is modeled after John Paul Jones in the Revolutionary War, which had concluded in 1783. As if to show that Americans were more competent as whalers than the bumbling Europeans portrayed by Scott, Cooper inserts a somewhat gratuitous scene in which the crew spots a right whale (" 'No sir, 'tis a right whale,' answered Tom, 'I saw his spout; he threw up as pretty a pair of rainbows as a Christian would wish to look at' "), and assembling the necessary equipment (boats, lines, harpoons), they set out after it for sport. They succeed so well at their entertainment that they manage to incapacitate the whale with just a harpoon (" 'I believe you have saved yourself the trouble of using the bayonet you have rigged for a lance,' said his commander, who entered into the sport with all the ardour of one whose youth had been chiefly passed in such pursuits"), and they stand off as the whale goes into its death-throes:

From a state of perfect rest, the terrible monster threw its tail on high as when in sport, but its blows were trebled in rapidity and violence, till all was hid from view by a pyramid of foam, that was deeply dyed with blood. The roarings of the fish were like the bellowings of a herd of bulls, and to one who was ignorant of the fact, it would have appeared as if a thousand monsters were engaged in deadly combat, behind the bloody mist that obstructed the view. Gradually, these effects subsided, and when the discoloured water again settled down to the long and regular swell of the ocean, the fish was seen, exhausted, and yielding passively to its fate. As life departed, the enormous black mass rolled to one side, and when the white and glistening skin of the belly became apparent, the seamen well knew that their victory was achieved.*

In both *The Pirate* and *The Pilot*, the whale bellows and roars—something that whales are not supposed

to do*—and although there are aspects of both novels that ring true, it would be another American who would describe the whale and the whaling profession with what some have described as his own bellowings and roarings.

Another popular work of fiction that incorporates "whaling"—or at least whale-killing—is Jules Verne's *Twenty Thousand Leagues Under the Sea,* published in 1870. In this fantastic novel of another mad captain, the submarine *Nautilus* encounters a school of whales while heading "in the direction of the Antarctic." These are "black whales" which are soon attacked by a school of "cruel and destructive sperm whales" that Captain Nemo decides to kill: "We'll give them no quarter," he says, "these ferocious whales are nothing but mouth and teeth!" Using a steel spur on the prow of the submarine, Nemo destroys the sperm whales by stabbing them and slicing them up: "What carnage! What a noise on the surface! What sharp hissing and strange roars these animals let out!" When he is told that this was nothing but a massacre, Captain Nemo replies, "It was a massacre of harmful animals; the *Nautilus* is not a butcher knife." The narrator of the story, "the honorable Pierre Aronnax, Professor of the Paris Museum," manages to get virtually everything wrong about the whales, which is not unexpected since he regards *Moby-Dick* as a "contradiction of nature" along with "krakens, sea serpents . . . and other reports of delirious sailors."†

---

*Humpback whales "sing"; sperm whales make clicking noises; and various moans, yawps and low-frequency rumbles have been recorded from baleen whales. There are, however, also occasional reports of whales' roaring, such as the right whale in Ben-Ezra Ely's 1849 account, where he writes, "The roar of the right whale, when wounded, is terrific. I have heard it at a distance of four miles." In *The Cruise of the "Cachalot",* Frank Bullen describes "the hoarse bellowings, as of some gigantic bull" of a wounded sperm whale. Unquestionably fictional are the sounds made by the whales trapped in Edgar Allan Poe's maelstrom, where "it is impossible to describe their howlings and bellowings in their fruitless struggles to disengage themselves." The first Bryde's whale described in the scientific literature was a specimen stranded on a Burmese beach that "roared like an elephant and so loud as to be heard a long way off. . . ." And when the Japanese whaling historian Yamada Yosei described the sounds made by a wounded right whale, he said, "its moaning is heard like thunder."

†Even though his descriptions of whales and whaling were bizarre, Verne's prediction for the future of whaling was remarkable. In *Twenty Thousand Leagues Under the Sea,* he also wrote:

The role played by whales in the sailing world and their influence on geographic discoveries has been considerable. It was while following whales that first the Basques, then the Asturians, English and Dutch learned to brave the dangers of the ocean from one pole to the other. Whales like to frequent Arctic and Antarctic waters. Ancient legends even claim that these creatures had led whalers to within only fifteen miles of the North Pole. Even though this statement is false, it is prophetic, for it will probably be through chasing whales into Arctic or Antarctic regions that man will reach one of these unexplored points on the globe.

---

*In his 1858 book *Les Baleiniers,* Felix Maynard wrote, "See Cooper else, that admirable depicter; read *The Pilot,* and you will form an idea of what these last tremors of a whale are like." Neither Maynard nor Dumas seems to have been aware of the 1851 publication of *Moby-Dick.*

Having shipped out as a whaleman aboard the New Bedford whaler *Acushnet* in 1841, Herman Melville spent a hard eighteen months at sea. So hard, in fact, that when the ship put into Nukahiva in the Marquesas, the twenty-three-year-old whaleman deserted. He fictionalized this adventure in *Typee,* but unlike the hero of that book, who lives with cannibals for four months and then escapes, young Melville signed aboard the Australian whaler *Lucy Ann* within a month, and headed for Tahiti. There he was involved in a mutiny of sorts, and after spending some days in a Tahitian jail known as the Calabooza Beretanee, he was released and signed aboard another whaler, the Nantucketer *Charles & Henry.* This ship—his third in less than a year—took him to Lahaina, where he somehow occupied himself for four months before coming home as an ordinary seaman on the frigate *United States.*

Melville's only formal education was the sea; as he has Ishmael say in *Moby-Dick,* "a whale ship was my Yale College and my Harvard." When he returned to New York, he began to write up his adventures, embellishing the facts liberally to produce a quasi-fictional record of his life among the cannibals. His first novel, *Typee,* was published in 1846, and was an immediate sensation. The public couldn't decide if the story of desertion, life among the ferocious Typee, and eventual escape, was fact or fiction. A year after his first success came *Omoo,* to the same enthusiastic reception. His third novel, *Mardi,* published in 1847, was a disaster. A wild allegorical fantasy, it sold so few copies that it practically bankrupted its publishers. To revive his collapsing reputation, Melville wrote *Redburn* in 1849, and *White-Jacket* the following year. It may be difficult to imagine anybody writing so prolifically, but within another year he had completed the manuscript of what he considered his masterpiece, a gigantic tale of good and evil, elaborately articulated through metaphors of the whale fishery. That he knew it would be a difficult work is demonstrated by a letter to Richard Henry Dana dated May 1, 1850, in which he wrote:

It will be a strange sort of book, tho', I fear; blubber is blubber you know; tho' you may get oil out of it, the poetry runs as hard as sap from a frozen maple tree— & to cook the thing up, one must needs throw in a little fancy, which from the nature of the thing, must be ungainly as the gambols of the whales themselves. Yet I mean to give the truth of the thing, spite of this.

Herman Melville (1819–91).

He was struggling to finish the book during the harsh Massachusetts winter of 1851, and wrote to his friend Evert Duyckinck that his room "seems to be a ship's cabin; & at nights when I wake up & hear the wind shrieking, I almost fancy that there is too much sail on the house, & I had better go to the roof & rig in the chimney." In June of 1851, he wrote to Nathaniel Hawthorne (to whom he dedicated the book):

As the fishermen say, "he's in his flurry" when I left him some three weeks ago. I'm going to take him by the jaw, however, before long, and finish him in some fashion or other. What's the use of elaborating what, in its very essence, is so short-lived as a modern book? Though I wrote the Gospels in this century, I should die in the gutter.

Preliminary sketch for the "Moby Dick" murals in the New Bedford Whaling Museum. The white whale is shown with "the harpoons all twisted and wrenched within him."

Melville hoped to enhance his reputation with the whaling book; he was afraid that he would only be remembered as the "man who lived among the cannibals." When *Moby-Dick* was published (first in London in October of 1851, and then in New York in November), his worst fears were realized. He was not even helped by a monstrous coincidence of nature following art; the *Ann Alexander* was stove and sunk by a whale in the Pacific on August 20 of the year he was completing his *magnum opus.* (Melville wondered if "my evil art has raised this monster.") For the most part, the reviews were as savage as the whale himself, and as vindictive as Ahab. Duyckinck wrote (in the *New York Literary World*) that *Moby-Dick* was "an intellectual chowder of romance, philosophy, natural history, fine writing, good feeling, bad sayings. . . ." Other reviewers were less kind. An anonymous writer in the *Southern Quarterly Review* for January 1852 called it "sad stuff, dull and dreary, or ridiculous. Mr. Melville's Quakers are the wretch-

est dolts and drivellers, and his Mad Captain, who pursues his personal revenges against the fish who has taken off his leg, at the expense of ship, crew and owners, is a monstrous bore, whom Mr. Melville has no way helped by enveloping him in a sort of mystery." In London's *New Monthly Magazine* for July 1853, the author was described as "maniacal—Mad as a March hare—mowing, gibbering, screaming, like an incurable Bedlamite, reckless of keeper or strait-waistcoat. . . ." These reviews, along with an 1853 fire at the publishing house that destroyed nearly all his books (most of which were unsold copies of *Moby-Dick*), drove Melville into deeper despair and seclusion. He continued to write (*Pierre* was published in 1852, *Bartleby the Scrivener* in 1853, *Israel Potter* and *Benito Cereno* in 1855, and *Billy Budd* in 1924 [although it was finished in 1891]), but he was forced to take a position as a customs inspector in New York to support himself and his family. He died in 1891, virtually unremembered. (Upon his death, the

New York Times wrote: "There has died and been buried in this city, during the current week, at an advanced age, a man who is so little known, even by name, to the generation now in the vigor of life that only one newspaper contained an obituary account of him, and that of only three or four lines.")

Melville's reputation languished for forty years. In 1893, however, the tide began to turn. An anonymous reviewer (in *The Critic*) called the book a "remarkable romance," and wrote that "the author's extraordinary vocabulary, its wonderful coinages and vivid turnings and twistings of worn-out words, are comparable only to Chapman's translations of Homer. The language fairly shrieks under the intensity of his treatment, and the reader is under an excitement which is hardly controllable. The only wonder is that Melville is so little known and so poorly appreciated." By 1913, he had been promoted to the ranks of "minor fiction writers," and he was hailed as "a great figure in shadow; but the shadow is not of oblivion."

Moby-Dick was on the ascendant; rising from the depths, as it were. In 1917, Carl Van Doren wrote:

Ahab, not Melville, is to blame if the story seems an allegory, which Melville clearly declared it was not; but it contains, nevertheless, the semblance of a conflict between the ancient and scatheless forces of nature and the ineluctable enmity of man. This is the theme, but description can hardly report the extraordinary mixture in *Moby-Dick* of vivid adventure, minute detail, cloudy symbolism, thrilling pictures of the sea in every mood, sly mirth and cosmic ironies, real and incredible characters, wit, speculation, humour, colour. The style is mannered but often felicitous; though the book is long, the end, after every faculty of suspense has been aroused, is swift and final. Too irregular, too bizarre, perhaps, ever to win the widest suffrage, the immense originality of *Moby-Dick* must warrant the claim of its admirers that it belongs with the greatest sea romances in the whole literature of the world.

Two years later, the centennial of Melville's birth was celebrated by Raymond Weaver, who wrote, "If he does not eventually rank as a writer of overshadowing accomplishment, it will be owing not to any lack of genius, but to the perversity of his rare and lofty gifts." Writing in 1923, the British critic Leonard Woolf accused Melville of "execrable English" and an overabundance of semi-colons, which he used "without regard to meaning or convention," but concluded that he "must leave Melville see-sawing between his semi-colons on the one side and greatness on the other." The final apotheosis came from the pen of Lewis Mumford, who published an appreciation of Melville in 1929, assuring his permanent position in American literature. He wrote:

Melville's instrumentation is unsurpassed in the writing of the last century; one must go to a Beethoven or a Wagner for an exhibition of similar powers: one will not find it among the works of literature. Here are Webster's wild violin, Marlowe's cymbals, Browne's sonorous bass viol, Swift's brass, Smollett's castanets, Shelley's flute, brought together in a single orchestra, complementing each other in a grand symphony. Melville achieved a similar synthesis in thought; and that work has proved all the more credible because he achieved it in language, too. Small wonder that those who were used to the elegant pianoforte solos or barrel-organ instrumentation were deafened and surprised and repulsed.

Subsequent critics have further exalted Melville and his masterpiece; there have been comparisons to Homer (the voyage of the *Pequod* as symbolic); Shakespeare (Ahab as Lear); Mark Twain (*Moby-Dick* as the only rival for *Huckleberry Finn* as the greatest work in American literature); Marlowe, Goethe and virtually every other writer in the history of heroic fiction. In their annotated version of *Moby-Dick,* Harrison Hayford and Hershel Parker list some twenty-one scholarly books written on the novel between 1953 and 1969. Perhaps the most useful of these to the amateur is Howard Vincent's *The Trying-Out of Moby-Dick* (1949), in which Melville's debt to earlier authors is discussed in depth, and every cetological, historical and literary element is meticulously examined. There is a Melville Society, whose members publish a journal in which (among notes on scholarship and history) the universities that have published Ph.D. dissertations on Melville are ranked. (Between 1924 and 1980, doctoral candidates at American universities wrote a total of 246 such theses, of which Yale graduate students submitted 56.)

But *Moby-Dick* is not only the scholar's province. "Call me Ishmael" is known to most American schoolchildren, if not through the reading of the novel itself, then through the Classic Comic. The historian M. Thomas Inge has written, "For many of

Joan Bennett, the love interest of Captain Ahab (John Barrymore), in the 1930 Hollywood interpretation of *Moby-Dick*. In this version, the whale loses.

us growing up in the forties, our introduction to Melville came not in the classroom, but by way of the comic book. [*Moby-Dick*] proved to be a best-seller and went through two dozen reprint editions before the firm went out of business in 1971.'' It is impossible to know what Melville would have thought about a comic-book version of his novel—we can guess that he would not have been pleased—but he undoubtedly would have been appalled at the first attempts to make the novel into a movie.

In 1926, *Moby-Dick* was made into a silent film called ''The Sea Beast,'' with John Barrymore as Ahab and Dolores Costello as the woman he loves. (The fact that there are no women in the novel did not seem to bother the movie-makers very much.) With the advent of talking pictures, the moguls at Warner Brothers decided to do it again, with Barrymore as Ahab, but since Costello was married to the star and pregnant with his child, they cast Joan Bennett as Faith, the love interest. By 1930 they had obviously not been informed of the resuscitation of Melville's reputation, and they decided to rewrite the book so drastically that it is barely recognizable. Even the opening sentence, arguably the best-known open-

ing since ''In the beginning,'' has been rewritten, and as the pages turn in the standard Hollywood opening for a movie version of a book, instead of ''Call me Ishmael,'' we see ''There never was, nor will ever be, a braver life than the life of the whaler.'' In this bizarre remake, Ahab acquires a last name (''Ceely''), and a brother named Derek, who misinforms Ahab about Faith's love for him (he wanted her for himself), causing the peglegged John Barrymore to set out after the whale that took his leg. The plot turns in a fashion too complex and ridiculous to detail, with Ahab leaping on the back of the whale—which looks remarkably like a giant potato—and stabbing it repeatedly through a fountain of blood. As we might expect in a version that deviates so wildly from the original, Ahab does not die (only the whale does), the ship does not sink, and the hero returns to New Bedford to be reunited with his lady love in a swirl of ''happily-ever-after'' orchestration.

In 1956, John Huston directed and wrote (in collaboration with Ray Bradbury) a film that was considerably closer to the original. Starring Richard Basehart as Ishmael, Orson Welles as Father Mapple, and Gregory Peck as Ahab, this film might have pleased Melville a little more, since at least it adheres to the basic story, and includes Stubb, Starbuck, Daggoo and Tashtego. (In the John Barrymore version there is no Ishmael, and the only recognizable figure besides Ahab is Queequeg, who is played by a Stepin Fetchit character who beats a conga drum and communes with voodoo spirits.) Much of the language of the film comes from Melville, and although the 135-chapter novel was mightily compressed to make a two-hour film, it is a remarkably faithful interpretation.

Alan Villiers, whose account of shipping out aboard a Norwegian whaler in the Antarctic is discussed later, was hired by Huston to oversee the seafaring aspects of the filming. Of his first meeting with Huston, Villiers wrote (in his 1958 *Give Me a Ship to Sail*) that they were in Claridge's, ''talking quietly about making a masterpiece from Herman Melville's extraordinary, long-winded mixture of mysticism, whaling lore, sea adventure, apocalyptic meanderings, and joy in his ability to get music into the sound of English words.'' There were no whaling ships available, so the film company had to settle for an unseaworthy schooner that Villiers described as "small, strained, decrepit, and useless for any real seafaring." Among the numerous disasters that befell the crew was the disappearance of the first model whale during a storm in the Irish Sea. Described as "a splendid beast for camera angles . . . he was only half a whale, afloat in a complicated system of old oil-drums for buoyancy and steel ribs for support.

But he had no fitting for a towline and that was fatal." (Villiers remembered "a large blubbery balloon of an alleged whale which had ruined an earlier and otherwise passable attempt to film *Moby-Dick.*") Despite all attempts to save it, the model drifted off into the darkness, there to become a serious hazard to shipping—and a sight to shock passengers on any ship that happened upon it.

Poster for the 1956 movie version of *Moby-Dick.* Ahab stands poised in the whaleboat, ready to harpoon the whale.

Under the supervision of whaling expert Robert Clarke, actual sperm whaling was filmed in Madeira in 1955, and three more models of the white whale were fabricated. Of the making of this film, Huston wrote, "*Moby-Dick* was the most difficult picture I ever made. I lost so many battles during it that I even began to suspect that my assistant director was plotting against me. Then I realized it was only God." He went on to write that "Translating a work of this scope into a screenplay was a staggering proposition. Looking back now, I wonder if it is possible to do justice to *Moby-Dick* on film."

The appearance of Moby-Dick—whale and novel—in popular literature has been painstakingly chronicled by M. Thomas Inge in his contribution to the 1986 *Companion to Melville Studies*. Inge not only covers the movies and the comics but also the radio adaptations (of which he lists no fewer than *ten* between 1946 and 1979), television versions (three), recordings, readings, children's books, and even the science fiction works that incorporate Ahab and the white whale. Answering his own question as to why Melville has had such a powerful appeal for the ordinary American, Inge wrote:

Perhaps it has to do with the deep strain of romanticism that persists in American thought and that tends to sympathize with the misunderstood and the alienated, both elements in the mythology about the man and the artist. Perhaps the towering reputation of *Moby-Dick,* a work in the American grain which pushes humanity to the outer limits of the universe, the last frontier indeed, is what grips the imagination of a nation unused to the geographic and economic limitations of modern society.

Indeed, Melville's fictions incorporate a "last frontier," and his tales of life among the cannibals elevated him to the highest ranks of nineteenth-century American "adventure" writers, along with James Fenimore Cooper and Richard Henry Dana. But it might be argued that *Typee, Omoo,* and *Mardi* were more or less typical "shipwreck" tales—albeit wonderfully written—while *Moby-Dick,* generally considered America's greatest novel (it is unquestionably the greatest *whaling* novel ever written), takes us beyond literature, into the world of vindictive whaling masters, folio whales, exotic harpooners, mighty cachalots, danger, excitement, and death—the world of the Yankee whaleman.

SEVEN

THE HEAVY ARTILLERY

Svend Foyn Invents the Grenade Harpoon

THE SCOURING GLACIERS and westward-running rivers of the Scandinavian peninsula have carved the coast of Norway into a spectacular variety of canyons and gorges. These fjords are usually deep and precipitous, not the sort of gently sloping beaches that are particularly conducive to the stranding of whales. We can therefore assume that the first Norwegian whalers did not depend upon random strandings, but pursued their prey from the beginning. Early documents suggest that they employed a drive fishery, where some smaller species of cetaceans, *e.g.,* pilot whales, were herded into fjords and killed. They also exploited the tendency of whales and dolphins to enter the fjords in pursuit of prey, and developed a method of whaling that was particularly suitable for their circumstances. When farmers or fishermen saw a minke or a bottlenose whale enter a fjord, they drew a net across it, trapping the whale. Then they rowed or sailed out to the whale, and either speared it or shot it with poisoned arrows. Later on, the whales were shot with rifles. A country with limited arable land, much of which is forested, Norway has always depended upon food from the sea. Fishing provides sustenance and in-

come for many Norwegians, and to them, the difference between whales and fishes is only a matter of size. From the middle of the nineteenth century to the present day, Norway has led the world in the development and pursuit of whaling.

Given Norway's proximity to the Arctic whaling grounds so intensively worked by the Dutch and the British during the seventeenth and eighteenth centuries, it would have been curious if the Norwegians had not experimented with whaling during that time. Their role in whaling history intensifies several orders of magnitude by the nineteenth century, but in the centuries that preceded that unprecedented expansion, the Norwegians were indeed involved in Arctic whaling.

Thor Arlov, a Norwegian diplomat stationed at Longyearbyen, Svalbard (Spitsbergen), has made a detailed study—perhaps the first of its kind—of the sparse literature on the subject, and searched the customs ledgers of Bergen for records of whalers and sealers that headed to the north. His findings indicate that the Norwegian effort was small and only occasionally profitable, despite substantial government subsidies. Arlov located records of some 258

Arctic voyages originating in Bergen between 1670 and 1810. (In comparison, the South African historian Cornelis De Jong states that during the same period, the Dutch made more than 18,000 Arctic whaling voyages.) Like all the other Arctic whalers of the period, the Norwegians took mostly bowheads, since they were plentiful and yielded great quantities of oil and bone, and they evidently worked the entire eastern Arctic, from Jan Mayen and Spitsbergen as far west as the Davis Strait. Although the hunting of the *Grönlandshval* or *Sletbak* represents only a minor aspect of Norwegian whaling history, from the middle of the nineteenth century to the present day, Norway would lead the world in the development and pursuit of whaling.

Even a Norwegian book about the history of whaling acknowledges that "the Norwegians do not appear to possess any special qualities to mark them out as pioneers of modern whaling; no modern whaling was carried out around the middle of the nineteenth century from the shores of Norway. . . ." But somehow, as the American sperm whale fishery was entering its decline, the Norwegians were assuming the role of the world's predominant whalers. Much of this has to do with a whaleman and inventor named Svend Foyn, but it would be foolishly chauvinistic to assume that modern industrial whaling would not have happened without him. Other men led the way and found pieces of the puzzle; Foyn managed to put them all together in the right place and at the right time.*

One of Foyn's predecessors—in fact, one of the people who might rightly lay claim to the title of father of modern whaling—was Thomas Welcome Roys. (The degree of his recognition can be found in the Norwegian work mentioned above where the authors refer to him as "the Svend Foyn of American whaling.") Roys's discovery of the previously unknown bowhead population of the Bering Sea has been discussed elsewhere in this volume, and while his later exploits in the North Atlantic are less well known, they are no less important in the history of whaling.

After his efforts in the Bering Strait, Roys headed for the North Atlantic to continue his search for "polar whales." He found no more of the mighty bowheads in the eastern Arctic (they had been eliminated a century earlier by the Dutch and the British), but when he encountered blues, fins and humpbacks, he began firing on them with a gun of his own design, in which the harpoon was attached to an exploding shell. Roys shot dozens of rorquals, from the West Indies and West Africa to the Barents Sea, but his weaponry was still developmentally primitive, and more often than not, the harpoon head bounced off the whale or passed through its body without exploding. Then, as Roys was whaling in the Bay of Biscay in 1857, the gun he was firing exploded, severing his left hand. He continued to experiment with various explosive mixtures, head and toggle designs, and rocket devices, but it was not until he linked up with a New York pyrotechnics expert named Gustavus Adolphus Lilliendahl that he

PATENT ROCKET HARPOONS AND GUNS.

FASTEN TO AND KILL INSTANTLY WHALES OF EVERY SPECIES.

WITH PROPER LINES AND BOATS,

SUCH AS WERE USED BY THE OFFICERS OF BARK REINDEER IN 1864,

ALL WHALES ARE SAVED.

N. B.—Two Months' notice required to fill an Order for the Season of 1865.

——FOR SALE BY——

G. A. LILLIENDAHL, - - - - - - - - - **NEW YORK**

*In William Scoresby's *Account of the Arctic Regions,* he gives a capsule summary of the development of the harpoon gun: "The harpoon-gun was invented in the year 1731, and used, it seems, by some individuals with success. Being, however, difficult and somewhat dangerous in its application, it was laid aside for many years. In 1771 or 1772, a new one was produced by the Society of Arts. . . . Since the year 1792, they have generally been in the habit of offering a premium of 10 guineas to the harpooner who would shoot the greatest number of whales in one season. . . . This premium, however, though it has been frequently offered, has been seldom claimed." At the same time, Sir William Congreve (1772–1828), a British artillery officer and inventor, was experimenting with military rocketry. Basing his ideas on Arabic designs, he developed exploding-head rockets that were used against people during the Napoleonic and Crimean wars, and against whales as early as 1821. The principle worked, and a great many whales were killed, but practically all of them sank, and the idea was abandoned.

created a successful "rocket harpoon." (During the course of his experimentation, Roys killed dozens—perhaps hundreds—of whales that he could not retrieve because they sank or escaped mortally wounded.)

With its toggles, pins and flanges, Roys's rocket harpoon was a fairly complicated device, but it worked, and he was granted a patent in 1861. It was fired from the shoulder through a tube, rather like a modern bazooka. With Lilliendahl, Roys began to manufacture rocket harpoons, and began selling them to whalers. During 1864 and 1865, Roys was in Icelandic waters aboard the bark *Reindeer,* successfully employing his own invention. He and Lilliendahl established a whaling station on the east coast of Iceland, and although they had elaborate plans for a steam boiling plant, a hydraulic press and a bone-crushing press, this machinery proved to be impracticable, and Roys and company confined themselves to shooting whales from the shoulder and stripping them of their blubber. Roys had established one of the first shore-based whaling stations, but a shortage of capital and supplies, the harsh Icelandic weather, and the general uncooperativeness of the rorquals conspired in his defeat, and he left Iceland in 1866.*

Svend Foyn visited the station at Seydisfjördur and examined their facility and their weaponry. He had been working on his own invention, which was different in many particulars from Roys's—most significantly in that it was fired from a cannon, not from the shoulder—but there can be little doubt that Foyn was influenced by Roys's and Lilliendahl's design, as well as other contemporaneous inventions. Despite its otherwise insignificant place in the history of industrial development, Norway leapt boldly to the forefront of whaling technology in the 1860s, and kept the lead for almost a century.

The roving Norwegians were always on the lookout for new places to employ their revolutionary devices, and because Norwegian herring fishermen

reported that the heretofore unavailable rorquals could be found in profusion around Iceland, Svend Foyn established a station at Alptafjord in 1883. (Foyn did not remain in Iceland, because the authorities were requiring that whalers there become Icelandic citizens.) The Norsemen set up another station six years later, and the waters around Iceland proved to be so fruitful that by the turn of the century, there were some thirty ships landing more than 1,000 whales a year there. The stocks of blue, fin, sei and humpback whales around western Iceland quickly became depleted (not surprisingly, since the same stocks were being hunted by whalers based in the Faeroes, the Shetlands and the Hebrides), so the whalers moved around to the east. The same thing happened there, and the *Althing,* or Icelandic legislature, declared a ban on all whaling after the 1915 season. The government was obviously concerned about the future of the whaling industry in Iceland; it was estimated that some 17,000 whales were killed in Icelandic waters from 1883 to 1915.

Svend Foyn was born in the town of Tønsberg in 1809, the son of a shipowner. His father was lost at sea when Svend was four, and he was cared for by his mother. Somehow his upbringing translated into a relentless urge to make money, and in a later publication, he identified whaling as the means to his fame and fortune: "God had let the whale inhabit [these waters] for the benefit and blessing of mankind, and consequently I considered it my vocation to promote these fisheries." He seems to have been a man with a great singularity of vision, since virtually everything he did in his early years was dedicated to the profitable and efficient killing of whales. In order to accumulate the necessary capital, he commissioned a sealing vessel and operated between Spitsbergen and Novaya Zemlya. In these frigid waters, Captain Foyn harvested seals and an occasional right whale, but his eye was on the huge rorquals that serenely exhaled into the icy Arctic air and which, up to that time, had been safe from the predation of mankind. From the moment that Svend Foyn fired his first exploding harpoon into the yielding blubber of a blue whale, however, the great balaenopterids began a precipitous decline from which they would never recover.

But Svend Foyn of Vestfold could not have known this; he believed that it was his mission to design a

---

*In 1872, between his adventures in Arabia and Africa, Sir Richard Burton made a visit to Iceland. Since Roys had been there only a few years earlier, Icelandic whalers still talked about him to Burton, and he wrote, "Mr. Tom Roys, an American, accompanied by his four brothers, established himself at Seydisfjord, and used a rocket harpoon patented by himself, and so much 'improved' that it will hardly leave the gun: the shell explodes in the body, kills the animal instantly, and by generating gas, causes the carcass to float. If not, the defunct is buoyed and landed at discretion. . . . I was told, however, that the speculation proved a failure, and Mr. Roys went off to Alaska."

Svend Foyn, the godfather of modern whaling.

better way of chasing and killing whales. In 1863 he contracted for the building of his first whaling ship, the *Spes et Fides* (Hope and Faith), a ninety-four-foot-long schooner-rigged steamship with auxiliary sail. (By an eerie coincidence, the ship was approximately the same length as the blue whales she would be used to hunt.) Unlike her descendants, which have only one cannon on the bows, *Spes et Fides* (nicknamed "Spissa") was armed with no fewer than seven whaling cannons, which would enable her gunners to fire more than one harpoon at a given whale. The thirty-ton ship was powered only by a fifty-horsepower engine, not nearly strong enough to restrain an escaping whale, but she was fitted with "check boards" which could pivot to increase her drag when a whale

was pulling, and what Thomas Roys had called a "compensator," a device that enabled the whale line to take up the shock instead of drawing tight against the immense power of a struggling 80-ton animal. (Although Foyn is usually accorded credit for the invention of the "accumulator"—his term for Roys's compensator—it was actually developed by Roys and incorporated into Foyn's system.) Where Roys tried-out the whales at sea—perhaps a holdover from his experiences in the western Arctic—Foyn first worked up his whales in the shallows near the whaling stations.

His first voyage was a failure. The weather, never particularly good off northern Norway, was terrible; the whales stayed far away from his mini-warship; and when he finally managed to harpoon one, it took off and towed his ship for eight hours. On another occasion, he had harpooned a whale and was standing on the foredeck when his foot became entangled in a coil of rope, and he was yanked into the sea. When he was brought back on board, the taciturn Foyn is reputed to have said, "I lost my cap." For his first voyage, the total catch was 3 whales; the next season yielded no whales at all. In 1865 Foyn sailed for Iceland to see what he could learn from Roys, and the success of the American reassured him that it was indeed possible to kill rorquals with ordnance.

The device that Svend Foyn invented around 1865 and perfected in the ensuing years probably had the most enduring and pernicious effect on the world's whales of any element in the entire history of whaling. From the time of its testing in Norway until the moment of this writing, the harpoon cannon has been in constant use somewhere in the world's oceans. The double explosions of harpoon cannons were heard in Finnmark in 1870; off South Africa in 1920; in the Ross Sea in 1930; off Japan in 1950; off Alaska in 1960; and off California in 1970; and although muted, they are still being heard in Norwegian, Icelandic, Japanese and Antarctic waters today. Wherever whales have been killed in the last hundred years (except by aborigines), they were killed by Foyn's harpoon cannon.

As cannons go, it was not particularly impressive. Its barrel was about four feet long and mounted on a swivel so that it could be swung up and down and right and left to aim at the rolling back of the whale. The first of the cannons was loaded with ordinary

Hunting a Whale from a Steamship in the Norwegian Sea. In this German print published in 1889, the ships and cannons are accurate enough, but it is obvious that the artist never saw a whale.

gunpowder and wadded with gutta percha. The harpoon itself was a lethal-looking object with a heavy pointed head into which was packed an explosive charge designed to explode inside the whale. Immediately behind the head there were four toggles folded back and fastened with a cord. Upon entering the whale's body, the barbs sprang open and crushed a vial of sulfuric acid, detonating an internal explosion and embedding the head of the harpoon in the flesh of the whale, an often lethal blow. In the early days, with multiple cannons on the bow, if the first shot failed to kill the whale, another could be fired, but later, when only one powerful cannon was employed, it had to be reloaded if the first one missed or another shot was needed. Foyn's original cannons were muzzle-loaded, but breech-loading was introduced fairly early, since it was a much safer method on the rolling deck of a ship.

The shaft of the harpoon was fastened below decks with heavy line to a series of rollers and springs, the accumulator, which took up the shock of the strike and enabled the ship (which usually weighed considerably less than the whale) to play the wounded whale like a fish on a line. With the spring-loaded accumulator taking up the shock, the whale could never get the line taut enough to break it. (In later years,

wrought-iron harpoons would be replaced by steel, and the sulfuric-acid device would be replaced by a timer, but for all intents and purposes—which were, of course, the dispatch of large whales—Foyn's invention has remained consistently in use since the day he tried it out on the whales of Finnmark.)

Because of the deadly efficiency of his inventions, Svend Foyn added an entirely new dimension to the whaling industry. In the past, whalers had felt it necessary to make long, difficult voyages to the Arctic (the whales of the Antarctic had not been found yet), but now that the offshore rorquals could be hunted in Norway's front yard, whaling became a local business. In 1868, Foyn killed 30 whales; in 1869, 17, and in 1870, 36. The first shore factory was built at Kirkeö in 1870 for the processing of guano (the residue left after the oil had been extracted), and by 1880 there were twenty whaling companies operating out of Norway, all preying upon the local whale populations. The whale of choice was the blue whale, because it yielded the greatest quantities of meat and oil per unit of effort; then came the finner, the humpback and the sei whale. Because no one had ever bothered these whales, killing them was relatively easy and enormously profitable. By 1896, a total of 2,000 whales per year were being killed.

The death of a whale.

The whales never knew what hit them—figuratively and literally. Very infrequently, one of them fought back, but this was probably a reaction brought about by blind agony rather than malice. In 1890, one of Svend Foyn's catcher boats called the *Gratia* had harpooned a whale off the station of Bøle, and the whale, in its death struggle, charged the steamer and punched right through its hull. The impact finished the dying whale, but the damage to the *Gratia* was so severe that the ship sank in a few minutes. The crew of seven rowed for eight hours before they reached land. In a 1955 recollection of the event, Laurits Larsen of Tønsberg said, "The whale is a peaceable animal. Otherwise no catching boat would be able to withstand it."

"Finnmark" is the name given to that part of Norway located above the Arctic Circle. At 70° north latitude, Hammerfest, its capital, is the northernmost town in the world. Foyn did his earliest whaling in that part of the North Atlantic known as the Norwegian Sea (off the west coast of southern Norway), using the town of Tønsberg as his headquarters, but he later moved his operations around the top of the world to Vadsø on the Varanger Fjord.

The Varanger is a great east-west wedge sliced out of the *eastern* shore of Norway, a country that is almost exclusively a west coast. Here Foyn made one of the very few mistakes in his career: he established his first station well inside the fjord, for protection from the weather. This enabled his rivals to set up much nearer the mouth of the twenty-five-mile-deep fjord, and thus have easier and quicker access to the open Barents Sea. (The Whale Protection Act of 1880 forbade whaling inside the fjord itself.) Although most of the whaling was done off the coasts of Finnmark, the town of Tønsberg, in Vestfold, Svend Foyn's birthplace, was still the whaling capital of Norway.

Since the whales had only to be killed and then towed to shore, large boats were not needed. From about 1880 onward, the whaleships were thirty to forty feet long, twelve to thirteen feet in the beam, and built of iron. They carried a crew of nine: the captain, the gunner, three engineers, three sailors and a steward. Whaling was always dangerous work, and when explosives were a part of the process, it became even more so. During the initial period, the guns often exploded, wounding or even killing the gunners. Despite the accumulators, if a whale managed to pull out the entire length of line, it might tow the ship far from the safety of the fjords and into the open sea. (Another hazard was striking the whale in the tail, where it remained uninjured but attached to the boat.) Foyn also developed another innovation to expedite the process: because these whales had a tendency to sink when they were killed, he began pumping compressed air into the carcasses to keep them afloat.

By 1880 Foyn had perfected his techniques and had successfully launched himself (and Norway) on a new and extremely profitable industry. Within four years, he had set up a processing station at the small town of Vadsø, and the Norwegian government had granted him a ten-year monopoly on whaling. During this period, the shooting and catching were so effective that they outstripped processing capabilities. Foyn needed a way to improve the quality of the oil that he was extracting from the whale carcasses, as he was catching close to 100 whales per year. His monopoly expired in 1882, and other Norwegian entrepreneurs eagerly joined the fray. The whale populations of Finnmark declined in direct proportion to the number of whaleships operating. Because it has always been more numerous than its larger cousin the blue, the fin whale was the major target of the Norse whalers, and for 1885–86, they killed 1,046 fin whales and 148 blues. By the end of the century, the whales of east Finnmark seemed to be fished out, so the whalers moved back around to the west. The inshore whales were gone here too, however, and the operation that had begun as a coastal industry became a pelagic one. The whalers headed north toward Bear Island (*Bjørnøya*), and hunted the blue whales there to virtual extinction, just as the hunters of the polar whale had done a century before.

Soon after the acceptance of Foyn's ordnance in the hunting of large whales, Norwegian small-boat whalers began to use the equipment on the bottlenose whale, which reaches a length of 30 feet and is

A German illustration of early mechanized whaling. The inset shows the harpoon that was employed.

often encountered in small groups in the waters be-tween the Faeroes, Iceland and Spitsbergen. By 1890, there were some seventy Norwegian boats account-ing for about 3,000 whales per year. Bottlenose-whaling was done from rowing boats, which enabled the whalers to approach the skittish bottlenoses more closely than they could have done in noisy steamers. Beaked whales like these bottlenoses are among the rarest and least-known animals in the world, and a cumulative catch that has been estimated at 50,000 animals (Jonsgard 1955) did the total population very little good.

Before he died in 1894 at the age of eighty-five, Svend Foyn had left an indelible and incredible legacy to the whalers who would follow. He had developed most of the technology and techniques now in use in commercial whaling; he had pioneered new whaling grounds throughout the North Atlantic; and the year before he died, he dispatched a sealer, the *Antarctic,* to the southern polar regions to investi-gate the possibility of catching right whales there.

His legacy would be followed first throughout the Northern Hemisphere, and later, throughout the world.

THE DUTCH and British whalers who had so effi-ciently eradicated the bowhead from Arctic waters had been content, because of economic pressures or the abundance of whales, to strip the blubber and the bone from the carcass and leave everything else behind. The nineteenth-century Norwegian whalers were more practical and determined to wring every *krone* from the whale, and when Foyn realized that the bones, meat and viscera contained another 50 percent of the whale's total fat content, he developed methods to extract as much of the oil as possible from the carcass. As with almost every other facet of Norwegian whaling, once Foyn had resolved the problems, other Norwegians followed in his foot-steps, and soon there were guano factories all up and down the coast. In addition to the sacks of guano, the factories produced glue, and although attempts

An 1886 woodblock illustration of Svend Foyn's shore station at Vadsø, Norway. The drawing shows a fin whale, but the bones in the foreground are from a much larger animal, probably a blue.

Early steam whaling in an Iceland fjord. With the invention of the harpoon cannon, whalers were finally able to kill the great blue and fin whales which had eluded them for so long.

were made to market the meat, it wasn't palatable to the Norwegians. The baleen of the rorquals is short compared with that of the right whales, but it was long enough to create a market, especially since there were hardly any right whales left. By the first decade of the twentieth century, whalebone had been replaced for most purposes by spring steel, but by then the fashions had changed, so the whales were spared—or so it seemed.

Norwegian fishermen believed that the whales brought the fish into shore, and if the whales were fished out—as they feared they would be—the fishermen worried that their livelihood would be threatened. When the Norwegian parliament did not enact the protective legislation they wanted, the fishermen of Menhavn destroyed the shore station of the Tanen Whaling Company. After the "Menhavn Riots," of 1904, there was a ban on Norwegian whaling, so the intrepid Norse whalers began to expand their horizons. They took their experience and expertise around the world looking for more whales, and they found them off Iceland, the Faeroes, Spitsbergen, the

Hebrides and the Shetlands. More than their experience, the Norwegians exported their citizens. For decades, the word "whaler" was synonymous with "Norwegian." All over the world, where there were whales to be killed and processed, there would be Norwegians to kill and process them.

In Iceland, for example, blue whales were more numerous than finners. After the Americans Roys and Lilliendahl had attempted to open an Icelandic whaling station, the Danes established a foothold with their Danish Fishing Company (Iceland was at that time a Danish dependency), and in 1875 the Dutch tried and failed to get back into the whaling business there. It took a Christiania (Oslo) man named Thomas Amlie, however, to set up Iceland's whaling industry in 1887 and keep it going until he was lost leading a whaling expedition off the Faeroes in 1897 at the age of eighty-two. Salvesen & Co., of Leith, bought Amlie's operation in 1904, and put it under the capable control of Marcus Bull, another Norwegian, who was trained by Svend Foyn.

For all its newly industrialized efficiency, whaling

was still a dirty, smelly business. Here is a contemporary description of Bull's operation at Hellisfjørd:

As our ship approached the station the bow wave was red with blood. An intolerable stench from the cooker rose to meet us, and everything in the vicinity was covered with a sticky layer of grease. Bull had not yet got the guano factory and the bone mill going, with the result that the flensed carcasses had been tied up in a cove, where about a hundred of these massive beasts lay, polluting the atmosphere. There was slippery, slimy grease everywhere. We inspected the hauling-out slip, which was running with fat and blood. In the cookery, where blubber was boiling in huge vats, we could hardly maintain our footing on the slippery floor. On the beach, bits of baleen plates, vertebrae and debris lay drying in the sun.

Norwegians also pioneered the whaling industry in the Faeroes, that group of islands north of Scotland that are a protectorate of Denmark and are now the scene of a bitter battle over the annual "harvest" of pilot whales. In 1894 Hans Albert Grøn of Sandefjord established the first whaling station in the Faeroes, taking blue and fin whales as they passed by on their migrations to the northern feeding grounds.

Concurrently with the expansion of their whaling activities in the North Atlantic, the Norwegians began to publish a journal that would disseminate information about whales and whaling, advertise various services and materials to the whalers, and eventually, document the history of Norwegian whaling. *Norsk Hvalfangst-Tidende* ("Norwegian Whaling Gazette") was first published in 1912 as the organ of the Norwegian Whaling Association. (Its first editor was Sigurd Risting, who also created the *International Whaling Statistics,* the record of every whale killed and by whom.) In the ensuing years, the *Gazette* was probably the most important journal for the industry, and published many articles that helped to define the business and science of whaling. Its editors closely monitored the whaling business, printing articles on everything from hermaphrodite sperm whales to whaling in Chile. The controversy about the existence of the pygmy blue whale was fought in the pages of this journal, and the complete statistics for every year of commercial whaling were dutifully reproduced. In December 1966, the following notice appeared:

The Norwegian Whaling Gazette will from 1967 be published with six issues per year against the twelve previously. The reason is the reduced Antarctic whaling and as a consequence hereof there is less need of monthly publications.

In fact, there was hardly any need for the publication at all, now that Norway was retiring from the field of whaling. In 1968, after fifty-seven years of continuous operation, the journal closed down altogether. As long as the Norwegians were on top of the whaling business, this publication was a necessity, but when the whaling ceased, the journal did too. (The same thing happened with the Japanese; when Japan quit whaling in 1988, the *Journal of the Whales Research Institute of Tokyo* was indefinitely suspended.)*

Spitsbergen has been part of Norway since 1925, even though it is some four hundred miles north of the North Cape. When the Dutch and English whalers were pursuing the bowhead (or, as it was known then, the Greenland or polar whale), they had sailed up to this forsaken archipelago in the Arctic Ocean, where the Dutch built Smeerenburg, the famous "blubber-town." They systematically slaughtered the whales from 1615 to 1820, but when the whales had run out, the whaling had to cease, and the remaining birds and animals were left in peace—until the whalers returned, that is.

Whalers have the habit of banning whaling after they have taken most of the whales in a given area; perhaps it assuages their consciences. In 1903, after the Norwegians had reduced the rorqual stocks of Finnmark to economic extinction, the *Sorthing* (the Norwegian parliament) prohibited whaling on the northern coasts of Norway. The whalers searched for more whales, and found them far to the north, around Spitsbergen and Bear Island. (Scoresby had noticed the blue and fin whales of Spitsbergen when he sailed up there in the opening years of the nineteenth century, but he realized that they were too much trouble to chase and catch, and had this to say about the blue whale, which he called "the physalis":

---

*The Tokyo *Journal* was devoted primarily to scientific issues, and was published entirely in English, presumably because that is the universal language of science. *Norsk Hvalfangst-Tidende* was published in both Norwegian and English, in columns that ran side by side on the page. This was probably done to allow the Norwegian owners and whalers—who did not necessarily traffic in the language of science—to keep up with changes and events in their industry.

"The great speed and activity of the physalis, render it a difficult and dangerous object of attack; while the small quantity of inferior oil it affords, makes it unworthy of the general attention of the fishers.") With steam-powered vessels and harpoon cannons, however, the physalis was eminently catchable, and the Norwegians were only too eager to exercise their new artillery.

The waters of Spitsbergen saw the first of the Norwegian floating factories in 1903. The *Telegraf* was a 737-ton wooden steamship, fitted out with primitive machinery, but the weather conspired against the success of this expedition, and the crew had to tow the first seven whales they shot all the way to Finnmark. Several months later, the *Telegraf* returned to Spitsbergen waters and was more successful: 57 whales were shot, of which 42 were blues. In the following year, another, larger steamer (the *Admiralen*) was commissioned and collected a respectable 154 whales. Word of the success of this enterprise quickly spread, and by 1905 there were eight companies sending whalers north. A microcosm of the history of all whaling inevitably occurred, and within a couple of years the number of available whales dropped sharply, and many of the companies folded. By the autumn of 1905, the *Admiralen* was dispatched to the Antarctic, and became one of the only floating factories to operate in the Northern and Southern Hemispheres in the same year.

A large proportion of the whales killed in Spitsbergen waters were blues, and despite the cessation of whaling there for economic reasons and the intervention of the First World War, which meant another pause in the killing of whales, the stock of blue whales does not seem to have recovered. (The inability of the blue whale to recover from intensive hunting was to have even more tragic consequences in the Southern Hemisphere; twenty-five years after the end of the hunting of the southern blue whale, the International Whaling Commission's Scientific Committee has concluded that there may be no more than 500 left.) Before they moved on, the Norwegians killed some 50,000 whales on all the grounds of the Norwegian Sea, producing about 1.5 million barrels of oil.

The history of whaling is rife with repeated mistakes; it is an industry where greed has almost always displaced reason, and short-term profit-taking has invariably precluded anything approximating a sensible approach to resource-management. The first practitioners of this benighted approach were the Basques, who, after eliminating the right whales from the eastern North Atlantic, moved across the sea to Newfoundland to complete the job. When the supply of rorquals on their side of the ocean seemed to be running low, the Norwegians crossed the ocean to Newfoundland.

A Tønsberg fisheries inspector named Adolph Nielsen opened the Cabot Steam Whaling Company on Notre Dame Bay on the northeast coast of Newfoundland in 1888. The Norse whalers ranged all around Newfoundland and Labrador, picking off blues, finners and humpbacks. Newfoundlanders (who were not then Canadians, since the island did not join the confederation until 1949) were somewhat less inclined to accept the peremptory arrogance of the Norwegians than the Icelanders or the Faeroese, and after the first season, they began to protest the presence of foreign whalers on their fishing grounds. They maintained that the whales, when pursued, destroyed fishing nets; that the processing of whales gave off an unholy stench; and lastly, given the Norwegian experiences in the other locations where they had so efficiently hunted the whales, that they would destroy Newfoundland's whale populations. Norwegian resourcefulness prevailed, however, and before long, Norwegians were hard at work, catching, killing and processing whales.

Greed knows no international boundaries, and when it appeared that the Norwegians were getting rich by killing Newfoundland's whales, the Newfoundlanders decided that they too wanted to participate. A whaling fever raged through Newfoundland, and in 1903 and 1904, no fewer than twenty-five applications for licenses were filed. Stations popped up like dandelions all around Newfoundland and Labrador. By 1905 the inevitable had happened, and what had begun as a wild speculation in the lives of whales ended up in a crash that ruined whalers and investors alike. There was some perfunctory Canadian whaling in the Gulf of St. Lawrence at Sept-Iles, but with the whales and the Norwegians gone, the whales of the Canadian Maritimes were able to lead relatively peaceful lives, until the 1920s, when the Canadians decided to go back into the whaling business themselves.

Modern Japanese Whaling

IN 1878, while attempting to bring an enormous whale to shore during a storm, 111 men and almost the entire Taiji whaling fleet were destroyed. Whaling out of Japanese villages continued, but the arrival of European technology spelled the end of net whaling. By this time, whaling in other parts of the world was being conducted using catcher boats armed with harpoon cannons. The Japanese were slow to adopt the new technology, however, primarily because they had not developed a seafaring class or a familiarity with large, seagoing ships.

It took a war to enable them to gear up for the war they would conduct on the whales. In their move toward modernization, the Japanese annexed the Ryukyus, and the following year, asserted control of the Bonin Islands. In 1876, using the same bully-boy techniques that had been applied to them some twenty years earlier, the Japanese "opened" Korea. Neither the Russians nor the Chinese were willing to concede their claims there, however, and there followed some intricate jockeying for dominance. The Sino-Japanese War ensued (1894–95), and Japan, much to the surprise of everyone—but especially the Chinese—won easily, and gained control of large areas of eastern China. It was during the latter years of the nineteenth century that the Japanese under the Meiji government began to develop their naval superiority, and were on their way to becoming a world power.

Following the suggestion of Tsar Nicholas II, the Russians formed the Russian Pacific Whaling Company in 1891, and using the new Norwegian methods, they began to hunt the whales that were found off Korea. They sold the meat in Nagasaki, where, according to Tønnessen and Johnsen, "the market for meat for human consumption was inexhaustible."

It was almost immediately apparent to the Japanese that the new methods were far more efficient than their net-whaling techniques, and they began to develop the adaptations necessary to enter the world of modern whaling. (The last nets were used in southwest Honshu in 1909.) In 1898, Joro Oka, the man generally regarded as being the father of modern Japanese whaling, set out on a round-the-world tour to obtain as much material and information as possible in order to move the Japanese into the vanguard. He traveled to Norway for harpoons, cannons and advice; to the Azores to have a look at the sperm whaling there; and to Newfoundland to observe the start-up operations of a new fishery. (Before Oka even finished his tour, T. Takahashi had built the first whaleship in Japan, a wooden vessel he named *Saikai Maru*.) Oka established his company, Nihon Enyo Gyogyo K.K. (later to be known as "Toyo Hogei K.K."), in July 1899, and on February 4, 1900, his Norwegian gunner, Morten Pedersen, shot the first whale, a blue. In 1904, Oka recapitalized his company, and working closely with the Norwegians, from whom he leased and bought whaleships, succeeded in monopolizing the market for whale meat in Japan. Within a few years, there were whaling stations at Ayukawa in Miyagi Prefecture, and Abashiri in Hokkaido, and soon there were five more modern companies hunting, killing and processing whales in Japan.

In 1904, however, the Japanese and the Russians had an altercation over the question of dominance of Manchuria and Korea. Russian whaleships (including the *Mikhail,* the first steam-powered floating factory) had been prowling Korean and Japanese waters, and as soon as hostilities broke out, the Japanese seized the factory ships and the whale-catchers, interning the crews as prisoners of war. Japan went

At the village of Wadaura, a lookout on the roof of the house signals the position of whales to the whalers at sea. They also used smoke signals, flags and trumpets.

on to win the battle of Mukden, destroyed the Russian Baltic squadron at Tsushima, and eventually won the war, thus becoming the first Asian nation to defeat a European power.

One of the results of the Treaty of Portsmouth was the assignment of the Russian warship *Nikolai* to the victorious Japanese. She was quickly refitted with a ninety-millimeter whaling cannon and converted to Japan's first modern whaleship. To teach them the techniques of Norwegian whaling, the Japanese imported three Norwegians who came to live in Taiji. After World War I, Japanese whaling expanded substantially, establishing new companies, working new whaling grounds, building their own ships (instead of leasing them), and processing the oil as well as the meat. In the 1906–07 season, Toyo Hogei's fleet captured and processed 633 whales, up to that time the most ever taken by any company since the implementation of modern whaling methods. Moreover, the company returned a 58-percent dividend to its investors, which inaugurated a boom in the establishment of new whaling companies, all eager to participate in the profits that could be obtained from slaughtering whales.

Many of the companies merged, and by 1916, there were only three large whaling corporations in Japan. They are generally referred to as the Tosa Companies, because their primary operations took place in the Tosa Sea, the large open bay south of the island of Shikoku. Unregulated whaling was obviously destroying the whales, but it was also destroying the companies. Again the indefatigable Juro Oka stepped in, and this time he organized the entire industry. The Japan Whaling and Fishing Association (Nihon Hogeigyo Suisan Kumiai) was established in 1908, with its headquarters in Osaka and Oka as its first president. In a speech given in 1910, Oka defined the future of Japanese whaling:

I am firmly convinced that we shall become one of the greatest whaling nations in the world. The whaling grounds round Korea and Japan offer unlimited possibilities, and should stocks of whales, contrary to expectations, fail in those areas, we have the Sea of Okhotsk and the Bering Sea to the north and we are aware of the great treasure houses to the south. The day will come when we shall hear one morning that whales have been caught in the Arctic and in the evening that whales are being hunted in the Antarctic.

Because Japan was in control of Korea by this time, her whaling activities were widely expanded to both shores of the Sea of Japan. Several species of whale inhabited this body of water, but none was more unusual than the gray whale. Hunted to near-extinction in the eastern Pacific, where it had been the object of a concentrated fishery all along its thirteen-thousand-mile migration route from the Bering Sea to Baja California, the gray whale was believed to be extinct everywhere. American scientist Roy Chapman Andrews visited the Japanese whaling station of Toyo Hogei Kaisha in Ulsan in 1912, and found that the Korean whalers were catching a whale that they referred to as *Koko kujira,* which Andrews translates as "devilfish." In his delightfully titled *Whale Hunting with Gun and Camera,* Andrews describes his first view of a gray whale:

On the next day after my arrival in Ulsan I had started across the bay in a sampan to have a look at the village with Mr. Matsumoto, the station paymaster. We had hardly left the shore, when the siren whistle of a whale ship sounded far down in the bay and soon the vessel swept around the point into view. At the port bow hung the dark flukes of a whale, the sight of which made me breathe hard with excitement, for one of two things must happen—either I was to find that here was an entirely new species, or else was to rediscover one which had been lost to science for thirty years. . . . When the winch began slowly to lift the huge black body out of the water, a very short examination told me that the *koku kujira* really was the long-lost gray whale and not a species new to science.

Sadly, Andrews was seeing some of the last of the western Pacific gray whales. Increased whaling diminished their numbers, and industrial development

A 45-foot-long sei whale on the flensing platform at the whaling station at Ayukawa, Japan.

seems to have driven away the few that were left. (It is possible that the remaining gray whales changed their southern destination, and instead of coming down the coasts of Asia, headed for the coast of North America to breed in the lagoons of Baja California.) From 1910 to 1933, some 1,500 gray whales were taken around Korea, but from then on the numbers dropped so drastically as to suggest that the Korean stock was virtually extinct. There were occasional sightings in Japanese and Korean waters of a straggler coming down the Asian coastline, but after 1966 any sighting at all was considered newsworthy. (When a single gray whale was observed in the spring of 1982, it was only the third seen in Japanese waters since 1937, all the others having been found around Korea.) Like the right, the gray whale had been extirpated from Japanese waters.

Shore whaling in Japan was described by Andrews as "a great industry," and he commended the Japanese for their consumption of whale meat: "Few people realize," he wrote in a 1911 *National Geographic* article, "the great part which whale meat plays in the life of the ordinary Japanese. Too poor to buy beef, their diet would include little but rice, fish, and vegetables were it not for the great supply of flesh and blubber supplied by these huge water mammals. . . ." In the winter whale meat was chopped and eaten raw, but in the summer, when it would spoil quickly, it was cooked and canned. Andrews laments the inevitable disappearance of the large whales (". . . it is probable that long before the slow-moving wheels of government begin to revolve and legislation is enacted for their protection, they will have become commercially extinct"), but he hopes "that the Japanese will get even more than their share while they last." Indeed they did.

The Japanese were too successful in their own backyard. According to Tønnessen and Johnsen, "From the oceans abutting on Japan and Korea larger numbers of whales have in the course of time been caught than have been towed to the shore stations of any other area. Nor has whaling played a

At Ulsan, Korea, young men pose for Roy Chapman Andrews with the pectoral fin of a gray whale.

more important role in the economy of any nation." In the early years of the twentieth century, the Japanese hunted blue whales to the southwest of their islands, humpbacks around Japan and the Bonin Islands, gray whales in the Sea of Japan, and right whales wherever they might appear. The Japanese were slow to hunt sperm whales in any significant numbers until the oil became important. Then, of course, they found their waters teeming with the *makko-kujira* that had enticed the Yankee and British whalers to the Japan Grounds a century earlier.

Modern Russian Whaling

BORN IN FINLAND in 1831, Otto V. Lindholm was Russia's first coastal whaleman—the Svend Foyn of Siberia. In 1861, he and two friends reached the upper reaches of the Amur River, built a boat, and sailed down the river to the Okhotsk Sea at Nikolayevsk. They made a camp there in order to go shore whaling. In the first ten years of Russian whaling in the Far East, they took 65 whales. When Lindholm tried to expand his operation and requested a monopoly on whaling all along the coast as far as the Bering Sea, the government turned him down, and he abandoned the business entirely and returned to Helsinki.

A naval lieutenant named Akim Grigorevitch Dydymov had lobbied strenuously to have Lindholm's application rejected so that he could become the first *Russian* whaler. His original plan involved right whaling and the sale of baleen, but when he heard about Svend Foyn's methods, he made contact with Norway and arranged to have the first modern catcher boat brought to Vladivostok (the *Gennady Nevelsky*), and the first whaling station built at Hajdamak, east of Vladivostok on the Sea of Japan. With the new Norwegian grenade cannon, Dydymov was able to hunt the heretofore uncatchable rorquals. He had retained a Norwegian gunner and captain, but he reserved for himself the honor of shooting the first whale. By 1890, the station had accounted for 73 whales taken off the coast of Korea, which were probably the species the Russians refer to as "Japanese right whales." On the last day of 1890 (probably not the best moment for a Siberian whaling voyage), Dydymov set out with an all-Russian crew (the Norwegians having been dismissed), and his vessel was lost with all hands. Another brief flurry of whaling in the Soviet Arctic was history.

Then came Count Heinrich Kejzerling, who, like Dydymov, had been trained as a naval officer. With a Norwegian adviser named Henry Carlsson, Kejzerling parlayed a government loan of 125,000 rubles into the Pacific Whale Fishing Company, based at the station at Hajdamak which he had bought after Dydymov was lost. In summer, they worked as far north as Sakhalin, then went south to the Sea of Japan in the winter. When the whales were killed, they towed them whole to Nagasaki, where they were prepared for human consumption. In 1900, the company acquired a 3,643-ton steamer which they planned to convert to a floating factory, the first such conversion in the history of whaling. The *Mikhail* received its first whale on July 27, 1903, and within three months had processed 98 more.

The *Mikhail* had been secretly in the employ of the Russian navy all during her maiden whaling voyages, and at the conclusion of the Russo-Japanese War, she was taken as one of the first prizes of the war by the victorious Japanese.

In the dispute between China and Japan over control of Manchuria, the Russians supported China. In 1898, the Russian government acquired the Liaotung Peninsula and agreed to build a railroad across it to their naval base at Port Arthur. (The largest country in the world is mostly landlocked, and a glance at a map will instantly reveal why Russia, and later the Soviet Union, have been sometimes willing to go to war to gain a port that is ice-free all year round.) China's Boxer Rebellion gave the Russians the excuse they needed to bring military units into Manchuria, which greatly antagonized the Japanese. The Russians, under Tsar Nicholas II, believed that the Japanese would back down, and refused to withdraw their troops from Manchuria.

The Russian court apparently believed that a major victory against Japan would head off the growing threat of an internal revolution, so they were prepared to go to war. Without a declaration of war, however, the Japanese attacked Port Arthur and bottled up the Russian fleet. A series of lightning victories by the Japanese resulted in the fall of Port Arthur and the capture of the Russian fleet in the Strait of Tsushima. Peace was negotiated by President Theodore Roosevelt at Portsmouth, New Hampshire, on September 5, 1905. One of the results of the Portsmouth treaty was the "Open Door Policy," insisted upon by America and Britain, which would return Manchuria to the Chinese (along with all the railroads built by the Russians), but it also turned Korea over to the Japanese, and gave the United States freedom of action in the Philippines. More significantly for the Russians, the treaty marked the end of their dominance of the eastern Pacific rim, and signaled the rise of Japan as a major power.

For the next twenty years or so, the Russians tried to start up various whaling companies, but during the period that saw the transformation from Imperial Russia to the Union of Soviet Socialist Republics, whaling was a low-priority subject. (By 1906, American whalers had vacated the Okhotsk Sea and the Anadyr Gulf because the two species of right whales—the right and the bowhead—were commercially extinct.) There was still money to be made from whaling, however, and the Soviet government granted a fifteen-year concession to the Norwegians for whaling along the eighteen-hundred-mile coastline that stretched from Kamchatka to the Bering Sea. In 1923, a Norwegian company sent the *Kommandoren I* to the Okhotsk, but although the rorquals were there, the weather conditions were so miserable, with constant fogs and storms, that even the hardy Norse whalers could not make a go of it, and they departed in 1925.

Undeterred by the failure of the Norwegians, the Soviets decided to try mechanized whaling on their own, but with Norwegian expertise. In 1930 a Soviet trade delegation visited Norway and arranged for the delivery of three whale-catchers, which sailed in 1932 to join the floating factory *Aleut,* an ex-American tanker that had been converted in Leningrad. The crew of the factory ship was Norwegian, as were all the gunners. This contingent killed 199 whales in the Bering Sea in 1933, of which the majority were finners.

In the northwest Pacific, off the Commander Islands and Kamchatka, the flotilla of the converted cargo steamer *Aleut* began taking sperm whales. Up to the 1932–33 season, the catch did not exceed 200 per year, but by 1933–34, the catch increased more than sixfold, and by 1938–39, the Soviet fleet was taking more than 2,500 sperm whales per year. (The *Aleut* also took 645 gray whales from 1935 to 1946.) From 1933 to 1956, Soviet whalers in the "far east" (their eastern coasts) took a total of 23,368 whales of various species, which produced 122,767 tons of oil. During World War II, Soviet whaling was temporarily reduced, and the Soviet flotillas did not go to the Antarctic between 1941 and 1945. Although the *Aleut* worked all during the war to supply meat and oil to the Soviet economy, the Soviet whaling industry expanded only after the war when the USSR annexed the Kuril Islands and occupied the Japanese shore stations that had been there since 1913.

The aboriginal Chukchis, Mechigmen, Kereks, Olyutors and northern Okhotsks continued their sporadic take of gray whales until the 1960s, when their primitive methods were replaced by "state ship" whaling, which provides sustenance to the aboriginals without the risks.

EIGHT

ABORIGINAL WHALING

Indonesia

IN ITS EARLY CHAPTERS, the story of whaling was a simple one: man against whale. Very infrequently, the whale won. (In *Moby-Dick,* despite the rage of Captain Ahab and the skill of the harpooners, the white whale triumphs.) With the passage of time, the hunters changed the nature of the hunt, and turned it into an industry. The hunted whales remained unevenly matched with their opponents; all they had was the hope of escape in the depth and expanse of the ocean. As the industry grew more economically important, technological innovations were introduced that greatly altered the odds. The introduction of diesel catcher boats, exploding harpoons, spotter planes, sonar and asdic greatly changed the nature of the hunt. No longer remotely equitable, it was not even a hunt any more, but a highly mechanized business. The whale had as much of a fighting chance as a tree had against a chain saw.

There are only a few places in the world where people still *hunt* whales. The Caribbean island of Bequia in the Grenadines, for example, has a relic humpback whale fishery that the Bequians learned from Yankee whalers in the nineteenth century. The

Eskimos of Greenland hunt minke whales and humpbacks (they are given a quota by the International Whaling Commission), as well as belugas and narwhals, which are considered "small cetaceans" and are not under the jurisdiction of the IWC. Whalers in the Azores still take an occasional sperm whale, using techniques similar to those of the nineteenth-century Yankee whalers, but this is a dying industry. The European Economic Community has banned the import of whale products into its member nations, and therefore there is no market for the meat, oil and bone meal. (Whale teeth are occasionally smuggled into the United States where they are carved for scrimshaw.) Alaskan Eskimos "hunt" the bowheads that annually pass their North Slope villages, but because of the complexities of politics and other factors, they have upgraded their weaponry to the point where once again, the whale has hardly any chance of escaping. The only place where whaling takes place in a thoroughly primitive manner (and completely unregulated by the IWC) is in Indonesia.

Lomblen, also known as Lembata, is one of a group of islands that make up the Sunda Archipelago (*Nusa Tenggara Timur* to the Indonesians), which includes the large islands of Timor and Flores, as well as the smaller Solor, Adonara, Pantar and Alor. Lomblen/Lembata is only one of the thirteen thousand islands that comprise the three-thousand-mile-long country of Indonesia, but there is something very special about this island. On its southern shore is Lamalarep, one of the few whaling villages in all Indonesia. Lamalarep is the poorest village on the island because it has virtually no industry or agriculture other than whaling, and the success rate of the whalers seems to be rather low. They might capture a whale on three trips out of ten; to put it another way, 70 percent of their trips are unsuccessful. The villagers of Lamalarep do not eat the bulk of the whale meat they take, but dry it in the sun and trade it to other villages for vegetables.

In June of 1979, a research team was sent to La-

malarep by the World Wildlife Fund to investigate the whaling activities there. Unfortunately, on July 17 a giant tidal wave inundated Lomblen, causing over seven hundred casualties and destroying the villages of Wai Teba and Sara Puka. The investigators all survived, however, and remained on Lomblen for three weeks. On July 26, on nearby Rote Island, a "giant shark" (species unidentified) was found with the body of what was thought to be a Lomblen fisherman in its stomach. (It is likely that the shark ate one of the victims of the tidal wave, rather than taking a swimmer or a fisherman.)

At dawn the Lamalarep fleet sets out for a day's hunting. They may roam as far as seventeen miles offshore, but the whales are usually found closer to the islands. The boats (known as *peledang*) are about thirty feet long and brightly painted, often with vigilant eyes on the bows. No nails are used in their construction, only wooden pegs; and the sails are

The whalers of the Indonesian whaling village of Lomblen launch themselves as well as their harpoons.

patchwork rattan, a single gaff-rigged square sail for each boat. A crew of ten to fifteen men rows (or sails, if the winds are favorable) the boat out to the whaling grounds, south of the islands in the Savu Sea. They look for the forward-angled spouts of the largest of the toothed whales, the sperm, which they call *ikan paus* in Bahasa Indonesia. (In the language of the islands that was employed before the introduction of this *lingua franca* by President Sukarno, the sperm whale was known as *kotan klema*.) During the ten weeks that the World Wildlife Fund researchers kept records, the whalers of Lamalarep took sperm whales, killer whales, pilot whales and several species of dolphins. Traditionally, the whalers of Lamalarep do not hunt baleen whales. Although the men of Lamalarep are considered whalers, they will also harpoon any large fish, ray or turtle that they encounter, including sharks, marlin and ocean sunfish.

The whalers of the island are divided into hereditary "corporations," each of which owns a whaling vessel. The vessels—and their names—are passed down from generation to generation, so when a given boat wears out, the next one built by that clan is given the same name.

When a whale is sighted, the *peledang* crews row stealthily upon it, douse the sail, and because they are Christians, they whisper a communal *Pater Noster* for their own protection. The harpooner stands on a narrow platform with his bamboo-shafted harpoon poised. At the critical moment, when he is within striking range of the wrinkled, humped back of the whale, the harpooner launches not only the harpoon, but *himself* through the air, using his strength and his weight to drive the iron deep into the flesh of the whale.

As the whale is slowed or stopped by the pain of the harpoon in its back, another harpooner throws himself on the whale, and if necessary, another. The iron must be planted in exactly the right place to kill the whale; otherwise the fragile *peledang* will be towed for miles as the whale pulls the whalers on the Indonesian equivalent of the "Nantucket sleigh ride." There are stories of boats being towed all the way to Timor by a maddened whale. (In fact, there are many tales about maddened whales in the Timor Sea. One of the most notorious of all these was a bull sperm whale named "Timor Jack," who savaged whaleboats for years until he was taken by setting out a

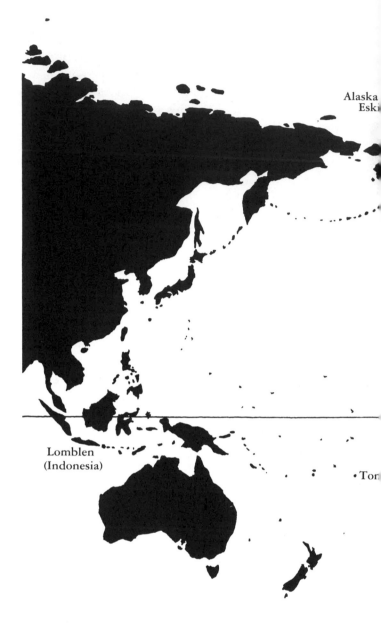

barrel on a line which he attacked, allowing whalers to lance him.) Or the whale will dive—sperm whales are the deepest divers of all the whales—pulling the line out rapidly and unless it is cut, pulling the boat down with it. If the right spot is pierced (the heart or lungs), the whale will spout blood from its blowhole and expire quickly. The dead whale is towed back to the village where it is butchered.

Greenland Eskimos

Azores

Bequia

In scattered locations throughout the world, people still hunt whales in a primitive fashion.

There is a complex system for dividing up the meat of a whale, in which the carcass is portioned out according to rank in the clan and the village. The meat is eaten or bartered to other villages; the oil is used for lamps. The men of the village may carve patterns onto the teeth, like scrimshanders everywhere.

The villagers of Lamalarep kill between 30 and 50 sperm whales every year. They do not take the large bulls, because the big males do not visit these waters. They cannot eat all the meat, so they barter it in neighboring villages. This is in direct contravention of the regulations of the International Whaling Commission, but since Indonesia is not a signatory to the Whaling Convention, the IWC regulations are difficult—if not impossible—to apply.

Tonga

IN HIS journal for August 18, 1699, the British circumnavigator and buccaneer William Dampier* wrote:

We had an abundance of whales about the ship, some ahead, others astern and some on each side making a very dismal noise but when we came out again into deeper water they left us. Indeed the noise they made by blowing and dashing of the sea with their tails, making it all of a breach and foam was dreadful to us, like the breach of the waves in very shoal water or among rocks. The shoal these whales were on had a depth of water sufficient, no less than twenty fathoms, as I said, and it lies in latitude 22 degrees, 22 minutes.

The latitude is equivalent to that of Tonga, and from the description of the whales' antics and the time of year they were observed, they appear to have been humpbacks.

During the heyday of the sperm whale fishery, whalers occasionally put in at the "Friendly Islands," also known as Tonga or Tongatapu, north of New Zealand, and southeast of Fiji. Although Townsend's charts show some catch of sperms around these islands, there was a great concentration of humpbacks to be found there, since the islands probably served as a breeding ground for a population of these whales when they migrated from their Antarctic feeding grounds in the austral winter. (In a 1956 whale-marking program, a whale that was tagged at Tonga

*Dampier (1652–1715) was one of the most fascinating characters in all of British naval history. He crossed the Isthmus of Panama in 1679, plundering the coasts of Mexico, Peru and Chile when he had attained the Pacific. He swashbuckled around the world, marooned himself on the Nicobar Islands in 1688, made his way back to England in 1691, and was then sent by the Admiralty on a circumnavigation of the globe which took him to New Zealand and the west coast of Australia long before Captain Cook. On a privateering expedition he rescued Alexander Selkirk (the prototype of Defoe's Robinson Crusoe) from the Juan Fernández Islands. He published his adventures and retired to London a rich man.

was captured in the Bellingshausen Sea in the Antarctic later that year.)

The island group is composed of three major elements, each of which is made up of many smaller islands and islets. From north to south, they are Vavau (called "Vau Vau" by the whalers); Ha'apai ("Hapai"); and the largest island in the group, Tongatapu. Originally discovered by the Dutch navigator Jakob Lemaire in 1616, the islands were included in Abel Tasman's 1643 itinerary, but Captain Cook claimed them for Britain in 1773, when he bestowed upon them the name of Friendly Islands because of the welcoming reception he got there. (Evidently, the islands were not always friendly. When the sealing brig *Union* stopped there for provisions in 1804, the captain and an agent were killed by the natives.) The Kingdom of Tonga was a British protectorate until 1970, when it was granted complete independence within the British Commonwealth. The approximately 100,000 Tongans are ruled by a king.

When Frank Bullen arrived at Vavau aboard the whaler *Splendid* (which he renamed *Cachalot* in his book), they anchored in the harbor, and then sailed out in the whaleboats to search for humpbacks. They killed a female accompanied by a calf ("If sentiment were ever permitted to interfere with operations such as ours, it might as well have done so now. . . ."), and towed the carcass back to the ship for flensing. Upon their return, "the whole native population seemed to be afloat to make us welcome . . . for our catch represented to them a gorgeous feast. . . . The flesh of the humpback is not at all bad, being but little inferior to that of the porpoise. . . ." Bullen reports that the whale made fifty barrels, a most unusual amount of oil for a humpback, which was usually considered an oil-poor species—but then, Bullen has the reputation for exaggerating almost ev-

Tongan whalers close in on a humpback whale and calf.

erything. As if this fifty-barrel whale were not enough, the next item in his chronicle concerns a "stupendous cliff . . . rising sheer from the water for about a thousand feet," with a cave at its base. The men sail quietly into the dark, cool cave, and are jolted from their reverie by "an awful, inexplicable roar," which has come from a "goodly bull-humpback that found his way in after us, and the sound of his spout, exaggerated a thousand times in the confinement of that mighty cavern, had frightened us all so that we nearly lost our breath." As the whale comes too close to these breathless whalers, they harpoon it, and during its struggles in the dark of the cavern, it "leaped clear of the water like a salmon." Our heroes cannot find their way out of the cavern in the dark, but they do see the phosphorescent trails of many giant sharks feeding on the whale's carcass, and by morning's light, they make their escape. Several wild adventures later, the intrepid chronicler of the cruise of the *Cachalot* bids farewell to Vavau, and leaves us entertained, but not

particularly enlightened about whaling in Tonga.

The islands are mentioned in many discussions of whaling history, but almost always in passing, and invariably in connection with Yankee whalers stopping off there. Somewhere along the line, however, the Tongans began to do a little whaling of their own. Like the Azoreans and some Caribbean islanders, whose grounds had also been visited by Yankees, the natives of Tongatapu slightly modified the techniques and equipment that they had watched others use, and took off after the humpbacks that they saw spouting so close to their shores.

In 1888, a New Zealand whaler based herself on the island of Nukupuli in the Ha'apai group, and filled her holds with humpback oil in a leisurely two years. They left behind a lad named Albert Cook, who decided to stay with a wahine named Liangiangi, and built himself a whaleboat, that being the only trade he knew. Thus, apparently, began whaling by Tongans. Cook crafted harpoons and lances, and sired several sons who followed him in his trade. At

With a harpoon in its side, a humpback cannot escape its Tongan pursuers.

first they sold the oil to passing steamers, but later, as the islanders developed a taste for whale meat, his business prospered. By 1937, the Cook enterprise had acquired a harpoon gun, and that year they took some 29 whales. A New Zealand Maori was the headman in that year, and on one occasion when he fired the gun, it exploded and crippled him, marking the end of mechanized whaling in Tonga. Although guns were eschewed, the Tongan whaleman perfected the art of attaching a stick of gelignite to a harpoon and lighting the fuse just as he launched the iron. If all went according to plan, the gelignite would explode after the harpoon had struck and the whale had dived. (There is a Tongan story about a whaler who harpooned a whale and lit the fuse, expecting the whale to dive. It didn't; it just lay at the surface until the explosive went off, destroying the whaleboat, which was attached to it by a short length of line.)

A New Zealander named Olaf Ruhen decided to spend some time in Tonga (probably in 1965, although he gives no dates in his 1966 book, *Harpoon in My Hand*), and joined the Tongans in their whal-ing. The whalers of Tonga were divided between those who were descended from the Cooks and those who were not, and they could, according to Ruhen, be told apart by their habits: "They [the Cook descendants] are almost the only people in Tonga who consistently hurry about their affairs; they have a consistently energetic gait that singles them out at a distance, and an equally distinctive manner of using their hands."

Ruhen participated in the building of a whaleboat named *Velata*, and also worked on the manufacture of the harpoons and lances, crafted from crankshaft steel that had been rescued from abandoned automobiles. The harpoons were the toggle type, as perfected by the whalemen of New Bedford over a century earlier. It was about this time that one of the Tongan whalemen had acquired a motorboat, which was to change the traditional method of Tongan open-boat whaling. This boat, faster and more maneuverable than a rowing boat, had captured the first whale of the season, and the excitement of the village was high, since the meat represented protein essential to the Tongan economy, and while the oil

The Tongan whale-boat was a graceful craft, obviously based on the New England prototype.

was not saved at all, the meat was eagerly consumed.

Although the equipment and the techniques used on Tonga were borrowed from Yankee whalers, the whale was put to a very different purpose. At first the Tongans tried to sell the oil to passing ships, but eventually they developed such a craving for whale meat that they consumed the red meat, the blubber layer, and even the viscera. At the height of their industry, Tongan whalers were catching as many as twenty humpbacks a year, which were, as W. H. Dawbin has written, "entirely consumed locally." In 1957, Dawbin accompanied Mr. Kuki Cook and his sons on a whaling voyage, where two boats were used, one for the actual hunting, and the other as a standby in case of accident and also to help with the towing. They left at five o'clock in the morning, struck a whale at about noon, and were towed for the next eight hours by a 50-foot humpback which was finally dispatched. When they approached the harbor, a black flag was raised to signal success, and the villagers gathered for their share of the meat. Dawbin wrote, "Even with a whale as large as this one which could have weighed 50 tonnes, nothing

remained except the skeleton by nightfall when it was towed off on the next high tide."

Ruhen was not as lucky. For three weeks, he and the crew of the *Velata* searched for whales, but they did not materialize, perhaps because the pelagic fleets of the Japanese and the Soviets had been busy in New Zealand waters, collecting humpbacks on their way from the Antarctic. (The intensified hunting by the whalers so reduced the humpback populations that even the few whales taken by the Tongans were a threat to the whales' recovery.) Finally, his crew struck a whale. It was a fire drill of a whale-hunt, with people falling overboard, a man getting his leg trapped in the whale line, the *Velata* bouncing along in the waves, and all the time Ruhen's Kiwi friend Roger was filming the exercise. After four thrusts of the lance, which by rights should have killed the whale, the harpoon pulled loose, and the whale escaped.

Other whales were caught that year by other Tongan whalers, and the meat was prepared for eating. "The heart of the whale was not sold," wrote Ruhen. "It never is. It is often given to the royal family or

The harpooner sells the meat of the whale to eager Tongan villagers who wait for their baskets to be filled.

else kept by the whaler himself, for it is the preferred delicacy.'' The Cook family sent Ruhen ten pounds of the heart of a whale, which he grilled, and two hundred pounds of meat for the crew of *Velata*, which meat was baked in coconut cream.

A week before he was scheduled to leave, Ruhen decided to make one last effort to get a whale. He traveled to the volcanic island of Hunga Ha'apai, the most westerly of all the Tongan islands. Again he did not succeed:

That was the end of it. It was not for me in that place in that year to catch a whale, but I tried. And in the total event, I became possessed of something much greater: the friendship of fine men, and a closer understanding. I know what it feels like to hold a whale; it feels strong and fine, and the strength and goodness come from communion of effort. I know what it feels like to lose the game and it is not important.

William Dawbin returned to Tonga at the behest of the government in 1980 to establish a whale-research program. Descendants of the original whalers continued at their trade until that year, when the King of Tonga declared a moratorium on whaling to help preserve the depleted South Pacific humpback stocks.

Poison Whaling

BEFORE THE ADVENT of commercial whaling in Europe, Siberian and Alaskan natives were the most advanced whalers in the world. A thousand years before the Europeans or the Americans had developed such refinements as the toggle harpoon or the whale line, men in skin boats in the northern reaches of the Pacific were harpooning whales. There is a strong possibility that Europeans who first saw these hunters in their kayaks or *baidarkas* adopted the technology that would eventually enable them to fasten onto and kill the larger whales. The whales of the northern Pacific rim include the bowhead, gray, fin, humpback and beluga.

Although the Alaskan coastal Eskimo cultures to the north are much better known for whaling, there were various tribes along the northwestern coast of North America, from Washington to the Aleutians, whose daily lives were influenced by whales. Many of these peoples are now gone, and their cultures, if not eliminated, have been thoroughly integrated into modern society. Whales still appear off their shores, however, as they have done for millennia.

For the most part, assumptions about whales and the Northwest Coast Indians have been based on examination of middens or the occasional nineteenth-century anthropological report, in which whalers or their descendants were described. In other words, not very much is known about the importance of the whale in these societies. Moreover, there were enough differences between the societies that few generalizations are possible, other than that some of the aboriginal peoples of the northwest took whales for food and oil.

In the north, the Aleuts inhabited the inhospitable island chain that stretches from mainland Alaska almost to Kamchatka. These people, who are believed to be descended from Siberian Eskimos, have little in the way of land resources, but their location in the midst of some of the North Pacific's most abundant marine pastures guaranteed them a rich harvest—if they could survive the chase and the weather. The islands form the northern boundary of the "Rim of Fire," the unstable and incendiary zone of earthquakes and volcanoes that encircles the Pacific Ocean. Many of the Aleutian Islands are the exposed tops of submarine volcanoes, and of the 279 islands in the eleven-hundred-mile-long chain, some 46 are active volcanoes.

It is now assumed that the early mammals and the first settlers in North America crossed over from Asia between ten and twenty-five thousand years ago, but geologists do not believe that the Aleutian chain was ever part of the great land bridge known as Beringia. To occupy these islands, therefore, these incredibly hardy folk would have had to gradually move westward in the direction from which their ancestors had come, crossing from island to island, until they arrived at the Komandorskiyes (Commander Islands), which are so far west that they are in Soviet territorial waters.

For the 1741 Second Kamchatka Expedition, Tsar Peter the Great sent Commander Vitus Bering, in the ship *Saint Peter,* and Alexei Chirikov in the *Saint Paul.* Someone on one of these two ships—probably an ordinary seaman—has the unrecorded honor of being the first European to land on the Aleutians. When this unknown sailor set foot on land, there were probably twenty-five thousand Aleuts distrib-

With the disappearance of the right and bowhead whales in the Sea of Okhotsk, the Koryaks, who were accomplished whalers, took only the smaller species, like this beluga.

uted throughout the islands. Because of the abundance of sea lions and sea otters which were killed for their luxurious fur, the Russians were anxious to establish a foothold on these barren islands. But the Aleuts were not willing to relinquish their islands or their seals without a fight, and the history of Russian-Aleut relations was violent and tumultuous. Relations became so strained that a war between the Aleuts and the Russians broke out in 1763, and four Russian ships were destroyed and their crews massacred. The Russians retaliated by sending to the islands a man named Solov'iev, who razed all the villages on Unimak Island, and murdered every single person. Furthermore, he destroyed all the *baidarkas* and weapons he could find, thus eliminating the Aleut means of survival. Solov'iev, whose name is also spelled *Solovey,* has come down in Aleut history as "The Destroyer."

For the next fifty years, the Russians consolidated their power, and by 1804 they were in complete control of the Aleut people, even going so far as to move an entire community to the Pribilofs, north of the Aleutian chain, to establish a sealing community there. (The Russian influence on the Pribilofs is still noticeable, and the killing of the northern fur seals has continued uninterrupted since the middle of the nineteenth century.) While Russia was engaged in a war with England in the Crimea (1854–56), American whalers and traders had reconnoitered the Aleutian Islands, and by 1867, "Seward's Folly" had been completed: the United States, led by Secretary of State William H. Seward, had bought all of Alaska, including the Aleutians.

Before the Europeans arrived, the people called themselves *Unangan,* roughly, "the people," since as with many other northern cultures, they did not know of the existence of any other human beings. The earliest archaeological sites have been dated at some eight thousand years ago, and indicate that the earliest inhabitants of these islands were hunters of sea mammals. In fact, their entire culture was adapted to the utilization of marine resources. They hunted the seals, sea lions, sea otters, fish, dolphins and whales that inhabited or migrated to their inshore waters, and often went to sea in fragile but extraordinarily seaworthy *baidarkas.* They used a hand-thrown, stone-tipped harpoon for whales, and various-sized darts for birds and seals, launched with

a throwing-board. As with many aspects of Amerind society, there was much ceremony attendant upon this hunt. Only men were admitted into the fraternity of whalers, and their knowledge of the secrets and rituals of the process made them an elite subsociety within the tribe.

There is considerable controversy about the methods used by the Aleuts to kill whales. (Most of the whales they hunted are assumed to have been gray whales, but there is some evidence that they occasionally killed a fin whale or a humpback.) In 1834, the Russian explorer Ferdinand Petrovich von Wrangel observed the Aleuts' whaling techniques, and wrote, "if the spear has penetrated through the blubber into the flesh, the wound is mortal; within two or three days the whale dies. . . ." Additional references to whales quickly dying of one-puncture wounds have led to the assumption that the Aleuts anointed their spearheads with aconite, a poison made from the monkshood plant, and that the whales died of poisoning.

A single man (or perhaps two in a double *baidarka*) would paddle out to where the whales were expected to be. When a whale was sighted, the hunter would approach to within fifty or sixty feet, and hurl a slate- or obsidian-tipped spear at the whale. The spearheads were often greased with human fat, had portions of dead bodies attached to them, or were festooned with the garments of widows. Ioann Veniaminov, a Russian priest living in the Aleutians, recorded the preliminary ceremonies and the whaling techniques, and in 1840, he wrote, "The hunter who launched a spear provided with such a charm . . . at once blew on his hands and having sent one spear and struck the whale, he would not throw again." The hunter then returned to his home and waited three days before going to the place where he believed the dead whale would be washed ashore. Aconite is indeed a deadly poison, and was certainly used against people—particularly by the Ainu of northern Japan—but in whaling, it is not clear whether the Aleuts believed that it brought about the death of the whale or if it was employed ritually, along with human fat and widow's garments. Robert Heizer, an anthropologist with a particular interest in whaling, has written, "Indeed, the effectiveness of this whole whaling method depends upon the use of this substance and is not intelligible without its employment." Heizer believes that the Aleuts used poisons to kill whales, although he admits that the evidence for that use is sparse. In fact, he has written that "in the absence of direct archaeological evidence, we have left to us another method of approach—that of inferring cultural transference within the ethnographic time continuum." In other words, we don't really know if the Aleuts used poison-tipped spears, but since some Asian peoples did, and since the Aleuts originated in Asia, the Aleuts must have poisoned their whales.

As further "proof" of this theory, Heizer offers a lengthy discussion of the use of poison in modern whaling, in which he searches the literature and finds such arcana as the Nantucket whalers aboard the *Susan Swain* who carried poisoned harpoons in 1833, and the Scotsman in 1838 who developed a method of injecting whales with hydrocyanic (prussic) acid after they had been harpooned in the normal fashion. A French surgeon named Ackermann developed a method of attaching a vial of prussic acid to a harpoon, and with this *harpon inoculateur* he hoped to poison the whales at the moment of penetration. Heizer quotes at length from an 1866 paper by another Frenchman, one Thiercelin, who actually experimented aboard a whaler with strychnine and curare. Ten whales were shot with his toxic cartridges, and all ten died. Heizer concludes his discussion of poison whaling with these words:

Why poison whaling was not more widely accepted is difficult to say. There is no proof that men were ever killed by handling the whale blubber from the animals killed by poison. The story may have been an excuse on the part of the whaling crews, to avoid implication in this type of whaling which, if accepted, would necessitate smaller crews and would result in fewer jobs. At any rate, our evidence does not indicate that the idea was ever accepted and turned to commercial advantage.

(In later years, the subject of poison whaling would come up again. In Sweden and Norway in the 1950s, curare was tested for whale-killing, but it was found to be useless. It was also realized that the curare dose required to kill a single large whale would have to utilize the entire world production of the poison, and would then render the meat unfit for human consumption.)

"Several hundred years ago," wrote the Norwegian cetologist Åge Jonsgard, "pioneer whaling operations took place entirely within the narrow sounds or fjords during migration periods." When a whale swam unsuspectingly into a narrow fjord, the villagers quickly stretched a net across the mouth of the fjord, and dispatched the whale with poisoned arrows: "The arrows caused blood poisoning," continued Jonsgard, "and after a few days, the whale was so weak that it could easily be dragged ashore. . . . From the inflamed sores of killed animals new poison was obtained for future use." Jonsgard does not identify the type of poison used, but Beth O'Leary, another anthropologist with an interest in aboriginal whaling, does.

Working from primary sources relating to the early Norwegian whale fishery, she describes the techniques used by the peasant farmers of the village of Kvalvag to capture the minke whale. They used "an English-type crossbow from the 13th or 14th century" (whether a facsimile of such a weapon or an actual thirteenth-century crossbow is not clear), armed with an iron-tipped arrow which had been forged by the smiths of Skogsvag "out of an old rusted bolt tempered in animal urine. Before being used, it was stuck in the inflamed sore of a dead whale or in a piece of spoiled meat in order to 'get the poison.' " The arrows, now infected with a toxic bacillus, were known as *dödspiler,* or "death arrows." Because this type of whaling was going on as recently as 1900, Norwegian doctors of that time examined the bacillus in question, and concluded that it could indeed have a weakening effect on the whale by inducing septicemia, or a ptomaine reaction.

O'Leary recognizes that there is very little evidence to back up the theory of poison whaling by the Aleuts, since even under the most ideal circumstances—assuming that poison was used and killed the whale every time—there was always the possibility that the carcass would drift out to sea instead of into shore. (She quotes one 1858 observer who wrote that nine out of ten whales struck will be completely lost.) Finally, O'Leary indicates that "there is evidence that aconite was not used on lances at all," and even if it had been, "it could not have been delivered in sufficient quantities to constitute a lethal dose." (In her 1984 discussion of this conundrum, she questions the pharmacology of the previous arguments, and quotes veterinarian Sam Ridgway, who has written that "A strike to the rete mirabile [a network of small blood vessels] would allow the poison to work more efficiently on respiration and cardiac function.")

Maybe the Aleuts used aconite poison, and maybe they didn't. Perhaps they thought that a small amount of the poison would kill the whale, or that certain prayers and ceremonies would ensure a successful hunt. Whatever they believed, they somehow killed the whales, ate the meat and used the oil.

ON KODIAK ISLAND, south of the Alaska Peninsula, lived a group of Pacific Eskimos known as the Koniag, with a stratified society similar to that of the Aleuts. Also like the Aleuts, they hunted from one- or two-man *baidarkas*. They used slate-tipped spears, and poisoned their arrows with aconite. The senior whalers closely guarded the secrets of the whaling rituals, and may have disguised the use of aconite, a real poison, by claiming that the toxically magic substance was derived from corpses. Regardless of the poison, the success of the venture was greatly dependent upon winds and currents to bring the dead whale to shore.

Charles Melville Scammon not only gave the details of the manner in which the North Pacific whales were located, killed and processed, he also devoted a significant proportion of his study to the history of the industry and the lives of the men who participated in it. His substantial literary skills were employed in his discussion of the California gray whale fishery, but in addition, one of the best accounts of the history of northwest coast whaling is Scammon's, because he seems to have witnessed the events he describes personally. Of the Indians' whaling techniques he wrote:

Like enemies in ambush, these glide in canoes from an island, bluff or bay, rushing upon their prey with a whoop and yell, launching their instruments of torture, and like hounds worrying the last life blood from their vitals. The capture having been effected, trains of canoes tow the prize to shore in triumph. The whalemen among the Indians of the North-west Coast are those who delight in the height of adventure, and who are ambitious of acquiring the greatest reputation among their fellows. Those among them who could boast of killing a whale, formerly had the most exalted mark of honor conferred upon them by a cut across the nose; but this custom is no longer observed.

Although Scammon does not identify these "enemies in ambush" by name, they were probably the Nootka Indians of western Vancouver Island, since they were the most celebrated of the northwest Indian whalers.

Most of the northwest Indian tribes were not whalers, and may not even have utilized drift whales that washed up on their beaches. Among the tribes that did *not* kill whales were the Tlingit, Haida, Tsimshian, Kwakiutl and Coast Salish. Whaling however, is not the only way to incorporate whales into a culture, and cetaceans, especially the killer whale, were very much a part of the lives of the Haida, Tlingit and Kwakiutl people. They revered the killer whale and regarded it as the spiritual lord of the sea. There was a widespread belief that a killer whale could drag a boatload of fishermen to the bottom of the sea and that once there, the people would be transformed into whales. Killer whales appearing in front of villages were believed to be drowned persons returning to communicate with their families. The stylized image of the killer whale, with its high dorsal fin and many-toothed mouth, is one of the most dramatic motifs in all northwestern Indian art. It appears on hats, masks, textiles, carvings, household implements and totem poles throughout the art of the Haida, Tlingit and Kwakiutl. An even more important demonstration of the importance of killer whales in these societies was the selection of the great black and white dolphin as a totemic symbol within the tribe. Along with the bear, raven, eagle and beaver, the killer whale was one of the predominant animal spirits in the pantheon of the Pacific Coast Indians.

That the killer whale should have been an integral part of the lives of the Indians of the Pacific Northwest is not surprising; resident populations of the greatest of the dolphins can be seen immediately offshore throughout the year. Their towering dorsal fins and striking black and white coloration have engendered fear and admiration in less superstitious people than the Haida. Killer whales are strongly familial animals, and recent studies have shown that the pods are led by one or more dominant males, and that the juveniles and females remain in the family group for their entire lives. Although it is not difficult to find these 30-foot dolphins fearsome, it is more appropriate to regard them as the dominant predators of the oceans, and the Indians who saw them in their

On Vancouver Island, this Nootka whaling shrine contained human skulls, wooden statues of whalers, and in the foreground, carved whale figures. The photograph was taken in 1904.

front yards cannot be faulted for assigning mythical powers to them.

When Captain Cook surveyed the Northwest Coast on his third voyage in 1778, he landed in a protected inlet on the western shore of Vancouver Island, which he named King George Sound. (The anchorage had once been called Nootka Sound by either Sir Francis Drake in 1579 or by the Spanish explorer Perez in 1774, and despite Cook's proclivity for nomenclature, the earlier name prevailed.) It was Cook, however, who assigned the name "Nootka" to the Indians, and although they never referred to themselves that way, the name stuck. Upon landing, he encountered a group of some two thousand Indians who lived on Vancouver Island and who moved seasonally to areas of economic importance. The Nootka maintained a stratified society, in which there were chiefs, commoners, and slaves, who were captives of war. (Cook traded for an enormous number of artifacts on his voyages, among which were several carved whalebone clubs, known colloquially as "slave-killers.") These Indians relied almost exclusively on the resources of the sea, particularly fish (herring, halibut, cod, salmon), as well as seals, waterfowl and whales.

Whaling was the core of the Nootka culture, and they had elaborate ceremonies attendant upon this activity. For the most part, they hunted the gray whale on its northern migration, although they may have taken an occasional sperm or fin whale. They carved dugout canoes out of gigantic cedar logs and used harpoons with long lines and sealskin floats attached. The harpooner was a person of high rank, who passed down the magical and practical secrets that made for successful hunting. There was also a whale ritualist who, by appropriate ceremonial procedures, caused whales that had died of natural causes to drift ashore.

The ethnologist Franz Boas had heard of a sacred house near Nootka Sound and was eager to study it. He sent George Hunt to procure it for him, and in the winter of 1903–04, Hunt located the house. After ingratiating himself by performing certain shamanistic acts and curing a sick person, he was allowed to see the house, and over the objections of the tribesmen, the chief sold it to Hunt for $500. It was filled with ninety-five human images, whale sculptures, and human skulls. In his discussion of the Nootka, Philip Drucker described the way this "Whaler's Washing House" was used:

For four nights the owner would bathe, rub his body with branches, and then enter the house to pray. The next four days he wandered around the lake. He would take four steps and then pray. An assistant would follow him to make him return home when he could no longer speak properly due to cold and fatigue. Neither would eat or sleep for these four days. His ritual lasted for four waxing moons. If someone died during this period, he would steal the body or arrange for his assistant to do so. Even though families hid the corpse, they would, through bribes and the like, usually find it. The body was brought to the beach, where it was laid face down over a stone. A stake was driven through the base of the skull and out through the mouth. A hollow tube was placed in the hole, and the chief, standing behind the corpse, shouted through the tube, asking that the whales drift ashore. The chief then eviscerated and dried the corpse and placed it in the shrine.

Prior to a whaling expedition, the hunter abstained from sex, and bathed daily in a freshwater pond, rubbing his skin with hemlock branches until it bled. Then a corpse was attached to the back of the whaler, and he entered the water and "spouted" in imitation of the whale. He put himself into a trance to envision a dream of the whale, and then sang a quiet song to the whale:

Whale, I want you to come near me, so that I will get hold of your heart and deceive it, so that I will have strong legs and not be trembling and excited when you come and I spear you.
Whale, you must not run out to sea when I spear you.
Whale, if I spear you, I want my spear to strike your heart.
Harpoon, when I use you, I want you to go to the heart of the whale.

Whale, when I spear at you and miss you, I want you to take hold of my spear with your hands.
Whale, do not break my canoe, for I am going to do good to you. I am going to put eagle-down and cedar bark on your back.*

When the whale had heard the song, the harpooner and his crew of eight set out in search of him. Sometimes as many as ten canoes participated, so there might be eighty men in pursuit of a single whale. Whaling was still being carried on a century after Cook's landing, and Scammon described the equipment employed:

The Indian whaling canoe is thirty-five feet in length. Eight men make the crew, each wielding a paddle five and a half feet long. The whaling gear consists of harpoons, lines, lances, and seal-skin buoys, all of their own workmanship. The cutting material of both lance and spear was formerly the thick part of a mussell-shell, or of the "abelone;" the line made from cedar withes, twisted into a three-strand rope. The buoys are fancifully painted, but those belonging to each boat have a distinguishing mark. The lance-pole, or harpoon-staff, made of the heavy wood of the yew-tree, is eighteen feet long, weighing as many pounds, and with the lance attached is a truly formidable weapon.

During the hunt, the crew, naked except for basketry hats, sang sacred hunting songs to drive the whale toward shore. The men always tried to approach the whale from the left side in order to thrust the harpoon into the heart. (These eighteen-foot harpoons were too heavy to be thrown, and the whalers had to get close enough to the animal to stab it.) Once the first harpoon had been planted, other harpooners followed suit. When the whale was exhausted or weakened from loss of blood, its tail tendons were severed with a blade on a long pole, and it was killed with an elk-horn lance. To prevent the whale from filling up with water and sinking as they towed it to shore, one of the crew members dived overboard and sewed its mouth shut. While towing the whale to shore, the men sang, "Go into the bay, that is your place," and "Hurry, you are great and swift." (One of the Makah legends involves a thunderbird whose flapping wings bring forth peals of thunder. In concert with the lightning fish, this

*From Swiderski, "The Whale is Listening."

giant bird seizes a whale and carries it off into the mountains to eat it.)

When the whale had been successfully brought to the beach, a festival ensued, with appropriate singing and dancing. The head of the whale was returned to the sea for regeneration, and as much of the meat as could be consumed was eaten on the spot. They had no way of preserving the meat; the blubber was boiled down and the oil stored in skins or bladders. In his study of the art of the Pacific Coast Indians, Boas illustrates four pages of Nootka war clubs made of whalebone, suggesting that the Indians also made opportunistic use of other whale products.

Although they may have been subtribes of the Nootka, the Makah, Quileute, Klallam and Quinault people have been differentiated from them by some anthropologists. They lived south of Vancouver Island, in the area of Cape Flattery on the Olympic Peninsula. The Makah were probably the most intensive whalers of these people, and they might have depended upon whale meat for the majority of their protein. (Examination of middens at Ozette, Washington, has revealed an extraordinary assortment of whale bones, including those of killer whales, gray whales, right whales, sperm whales, fin whales and blue whales.) Their societies were also stratified, and only the highest-ranking men could become whalers. They employed the same ceremonies, materials and

techniques as their northerly relatives, including the cedar dugouts and bark lines with sealskin floats. After the white man arrived, they adopted the sail as an additional means of power, and at the same time replaced mussel-shell spear points with iron. As with almost all whaling prior to the development of exploding grenade harpoons in the late nineteenth century, the coast tribes would repeatedly harpoon the whale until it was exhausted, then kill it with a lance and tow the carcass to shore. By 1850, the Makah had become so proficient at whaling that they were feeding their villages on whale meat and trading surplus oil to visiting European vessels.

Despite the great social emphasis placed on whaling, none of these societies was particularly successful. Only the Makah were able to turn this enterprise into a domestic and commercial success, but they did not flourish. The number of whales killed was never very high, primarily because of the scarcity of the whales and the inefficient method of selecting the harpooner. (The senior whaler was not necessarily the most effective harpooner.) The California gray whales would not be seriously threatened until the mid-nineteenth century, when Captain Scammon discovered their breeding grounds in Baja California, and led an armada of whaleships to slaughter the whales in such numbers that they would become almost extinct.

The Caribbean

WHEN THE EARLY New England whalers headed south and discovered the whales in the Caribbean, they did exactly what whalers were supposed to do: they killed the whales. There are still whalers in the islands, but not many. In fact, as of this writing, there is only one on the island of Bequia, and upon his retirement (or departure from whaling for other reasons), whaling in the Caribbean will come to an end.

Even before the whalers exhausted the supply of

whales in their own New England front yards, they headed south to look for more whales to kill. One of the first records of whales encountered in (or en route to) the Caribbean can be found in the anonymous entry in the London *Philosophical Transactions* for 1665, where "three old females and three cubs" were taken by an unnamed whaler. Three years later, Richard Stafford, the sheriff of the Bermudas, made "the first recorded observations of any person who was familiar with the whales in American waters from actually himself taken part in their capture." Stafford, again writing in *Philosophical Transactions,* said:

We have hereabout very many sorts of Fishes. There is amongst them great store of Whales, which in March, April and May use out Coast. I have myself killed many of them. Their females have an abundance of Milk, which the young ones suck out of the Teats, that grow by their Navell. They have no Teeth, but feed on Mosse, growing on the Rocks at the bottom during these Moneths, and at no other season of the Year. When that is consumed and gone, the Whales go away also. These we kill for their Oyl.

Although Stafford gives no further particulars about the species, we can assume that they were humpbacks because they are still the most common whales to be found in Bermuda waters, and their visits take place during the "Moneths" listed by Stafford. (The Bermuda and Caribbean humpbacks, of course, are the same population that migrates north in the summer to feed off Cape Cod, so the whales sighted in Bermuda were the same individuals that were seen in New England. Until they were killed, that is.)

The Bermuda Fishery was apparently not a particularly popular one, although F. W. True writes that "Mr. J. Matthew Jones of Nova Scotia stated in 1884 that it was prosecuted by the islanders more or less successfully from the earliest times to the present." It was the islands in the Caribbean, known as the West Indies, that proved to be a far richer ground for the whalers. In their formative years, Nantucket whalers sailed south as far as the Bahamas before crossing the Atlantic for the Azores and the west coast of Africa; there were not enough whales to encourage them to remain for any length of time on what later became known as the "Bahama Banks." In those days they probably encountered right whales (only in recent years have they been found to breed off the coasts of Georgia and Florida), and sperm whales have been recorded frequently in the Caribbean, but the preferred prey species in this region is the humpback. It was probably selected because its migrations are predictable, and it doesn't put up much of a struggle when harpooned. On the other hand, its baleen is short and its blubber layer skimpy. (The Honorable Paul Dudley, writing in 1733, said, "The Bone of this Whale is not worth much, tho' somewhat better than the Finback's.") Later, the whalers would find enough reasons to hunt the humpback that the species would almost be eliminated from the face of the earth.

All shore whalers hunted what was available, and if humpbacks were common in West Indian waters, then they would hunt humpbacks. Before the whalers arrived on these islands, stopping off for water and provisions on their way to distant seas, the only whaling that was done was the occasional utilization of beached animals. (Pilot whales, the other object of the Caribbean fishery, are notorious stranders.) By the middle of the nineteenth century, whalers were making scheduled voyages to the Grenadines, specifically for humpbacks and "blackfish," the colloquial name for the 20-foot-long pilot whales. Since various island groups served the whales as breeding grounds, a concentrated fishery in the Caribbean quickly decimated the humpback population. Humpbacks are perhaps the most predictable of all large whales, since their breeding grounds hardly ever vary. In Townsend's 1935 charts of whale-catches, records for the other species—rights, sperms and bowheads—form a spotty pattern with some areas of greater concentration than others, but for the humpback, the plattings look like shot groups: you can cover each of the areas of humpback whaling with your thumb. And one of these areas is the Caribbean, with all the catches recorded from January to May.

Despite allegations to the contrary, whales do not seem to be able to communicate effectively enough to warn future generations of impending danger; the humpbacks returned to their traditional breeding grounds every spring, where the whalers shot them like big fish in a turquoise barrel.

A shortage of whales caused the Yankee whalers to seek more productive grounds, but in exchange for the whales they removed from Caribbean waters, they left a legacy of whale-hunting technology that was to be incorporated into the culture of the Caribbean islands. Whalers continued to provision at the islands well into the twentieth century (the bark *Daisy* aboard which Robert Cushman Murphy kept his "Logbook for Grace" begins her 1912 voyage in Dominica), but from the 1920s to the present, the whales of the Caribbean have been killed by locals.

In the nineteenth century, the island of St. Lucia occasionally served as a headquarters for New England whaling vessels working the Caribbean. The log of the schooner *Franklin,* out of New Bedford, indicates that she anchored off the island nightly during the spring of 1884, and cruised the surrounding waters for humpbacks by day. There are few records of the intervening years, but in 1972, two biologists from the University of Guelph went to St. Lucia to investigate the small whale fishery there. Gaskin and Smith discovered that fishermen armed their boats with harpoons, and took—or tried to take—any dolphin or pilot whale they encountered. They seemed to have very little talent or skill for whaling, and chased many more cetaceans than they caught. A subsequent study by Randall Reeves confirmed their general inefficiency, and he wrote that "they catch mainly animals that bow ride, thus few pilot whales."* St. Lucia joined the International Whaling Commission in 1981, and voted in favor of the moratorium on whaling in 1982. Reeves visited the island in 1987, and reported that the annual catch of small cetaceans is "variously estimated at between 30 and 100." (The jurisdiction of the IWC does not apply to small cetaceans, and thus a country can allow its nationals to kill dolphins and still abide by the moratorium.)

Although the record is unclear, St. Vincent is thought to have been discovered by Columbus on his third voyage in 1498. Now known as St. Vincent and the Grenadines, the country is a chain of islands located about a hundred miles north of Trinidad. It is composed of the islands of St. Vincent (the largest), Mustique, Bequia, Canouan, Union, Grenada and several small islets. Like many other islands in the Lesser Antilles, St. Vincent was probably inhabited by Carib Indians and undisturbed until the eighteenth century, when various European nations attempted settlements on these sunny little islands to grow sugar cane used in the manufacture of rum. The Carib Indians are extinct; the current inhabitants are descended from African slaves that had been imported to work the cane plantations. (In 1675 a slave ship was wrecked off Bequia, and many of the "passengers" fetched up on shore, where they are said to have interbred with the Indians, creating a race of "black Caribs.")

*"Bow-riding" dolphins are those that use the pressure wave generated by a moving ship to ride in front of the vessel. Pilot whales are not bow-riders.

William T. Wallace, a Bequian planter, had signed aboard a whaling ship out of Massachusetts in 1875, and six months later he returned home to set up the first whale fishery in Bequia. Within a few years of the establishment of the Wallace station, the Ollivierre family started another station on their property, which included the island of Petit Nevis, just south of Friendship Bay. By 1910 there were six shore stations in the Grenadines, and the records indicate that the islands exported some 500,000 gallons of whale oil between 1890 and 1925. The meat—which was known locally as "beef"—was a welcome source of protein for the islanders. There had been a whaling station established on Barbados, and another twenty-odd stations throughout the Grenadines, but the best-known—and the only one still in existence—is the one at Friendship Bay on the southern coast of the island of Bequia.

There is not much in the way of industry or agriculture on these volcanic, rocky little islands; they grow bananas, sugar cane and arrowroot, but when Wallace began the whaling station at Friendship Bay in 1875, the island was in the throes of a depression brought about by the collapse of the sugar cane industry. The introduction of whaling brought a much-needed stimulus to the economy: now the islanders had something to sell that other people wanted to buy. (Since whaling was introduced, however, the new and immensely profitable tourism industry has arrived to eclipse everything else.) At the village of Barrouallie on St. Vincent there had been a fishery for pilot whales and dolphins which operated until the mid-1970s, when fuel costs for outboard engines rose drastically, and made expenses greater than income. With the passage of the Marine Mammal Protection Act in 1972, all whale products were prohibited from entering the United States, thereby eliminating the market for the "melon oil" of the blackfish. The meat was eaten, and the oil, mixed with lower-grade body oil, was used as a patent medicine.

Shore lookouts on hilltops would search for the telltale spouts of the whales, and the boats would be launched. The whaleboats are modeled after their Yankee counterparts of the nineteenth century: twenty-six-foot double-enders with five rowing stations and a long steering oar. The boats are crafted of imported spruce, and ballasted with local stone.

When a humpback whale was captured on the Caribbean island of Bequia, the whole village often turned out for the butchering.

A whale is harpooned with a toggle-headed harpoon, and when it has been made fast, lances are thrown at it repeatedly to kill it. The preferred quarry of the Bequian whalers is a female humpback with a calf. While towing the carcass back to the station, men would often have to jump in the water to sew the whale's mouth shut to keep it from filling up with water.

Nineteenth-century Caribbean whalers (like nineteenth-century Caribbean whales) were at the mercy of New England whalers. While the humpbacks were feeding on capelin and sand lances off the Massachusetts coasts, the whalers would harvest them, thus reducing the numbers that migrated south to breed. (In a detailed study of the Caribbean whale fisheries, W. Stephen Price has calculated that Bequian whalers killed over 100 whales per year from 1867 to 1870, and another 500 between 1898 and 1938.) By 1925, all the whaling stations but Bequia had shut down, but an enterprising Norwegian named Otto Sverdrup built a shore station on Glovers Island, south of Grenada, to process the whales he caught with modern catcher boats. From 1924 to 1927, he collected some 200 whales, but within three

years the supply was exhausted and the station was closed down.

From 1930 to 1950, very few whales were caught off Bequia. In 1958, however, either four or six whales were taken (the records are not clear), and with the proceeds a new whaling cooperative was set up on the island. A shore station was erected on Petit Nevis with a concrete slipway and large sheds for the equipment and trying-out.

The whales arrive in January and head north in May, and the entire Caribbean population of humpbacks is thought to number no more than six hundred animals, not many of which come anywhere near Bequia. After a kill, the carcass is towed to the station on Petit Nevis for flensing and trying-out. Few whales are killed in this enterprise; on the infrequent success of one of the voyages, everybody on the island turns out to celebrate. After being salted and dried in the sun, the meat is eaten and the oil used locally for lighting, lubrication and cooking.

St. Vincent and the Grenadines joined the International Whaling Commission in 1982. It was one of the countries brought in by the "conservationist" bloc to stack the commission in favor of the whaling moratorium which indeed was passed at that year's meeting in Brighton, England. After the euphoria of the successful moratorium campaign had died down, however, disturbing rumors began to circulate about this "conservationist" country. Was it possible that a country that had voted to outlaw all commercial whaling was itself a whaling nation? Unfortunately, it was.

In 1982 the Bequian whaling industry received some encouragement with the addition of a power boat to replace the oar-powered whaleboats, and also introduced the use of VHF radios to their otherwise primitive arsenal. (Funds for these technological improvements were raised by a customs official, who solicited Mustique residents and yacht traffic.) It was the results of this modernization that led to the increase in the number of whales taken in 1982, and the reports that began to filter to the IWC. In the spring of 1984, Bequian whalers killed five whales—two cows, two calves and a bull.

By 1985, however, harpooner Athneal Ollivierre was in the hospital, and no whales were taken. He has recovered, but a man born in 1920 probably will not continue in this anachronistic business much longer. At the 1987 IWC meeting, the commissioner for St. Vincent requested a three-whale quota for his country, and under the complex variances occasionally granted to aboriginal or "subsistence" whalers, it passed. The resolution was worded in such a way as to prohibit the Bequians from killing "suckling calves or females accompanied by calves," which pretty much wrote *finis* to Bequian whaling, because those were precisely the animals they were used to killing. They would harpoon the calf first, because it could not swim very fast, and then the mother when she stood by her wounded offspring. The males might not venture into these waters, or the whalers might regard them as too dangerous.

A museum has been established at Point Hilary, the site of the original Wallace cooperative, and the government hopes to be able to keep the memory of the industry alive by encouraging tourists to recognize its importance. The Lesser Antilles are among the least developed of the Caribbean islands, but progress in the form of increased tourism is not far off. Cruising sailors are interested in the natural wonders of their environment, and the long-winged whales of the Caribbean must be placed high on anyone's list of natural wonders.

Greenland

GREENLAND'S COASTS are enormous—as befits the world's largest island—and there is an obvious variation in climatological conditions from the north to the south, as well as on the very different east and west coasts. (The total length of its serrated coastline has been calculated at some 24,430 miles—almost the circumference of the earth at the Equator.) Its northernmost point is the closest land to the North Pole, and Cape Farewell, its southern tip, is at approximately the same latitude as Stockholm. To the west is the Davis Strait and Baffin Bay, separating Greenland from Arctic Canada, and its east coast fronts on the North Atlantic.

European whalers first worked the east coast, since it was closer to England and Holland (and included in the range of the Spitsbergen whale stocks), but by the early nineteenth century, the west coast, known as the "Davis Straits Fishery," became the area of greatest concentration of the whalers. William Scoresby, Jr., traveled to Greenland in conjunction with his whaling enterprises, and later he went back to conduct extensive surveys of the east coast. In 1822 he surveyed some four hundred miles of this desolate coastline, including the most complex of the inlets of the Greenland Sea. Scoresby Sound—which he named for his father and which now appears on

With their kayaks tied in tandem, Eskimos haul a killed narwhal to shore.

maps as *Scoresbysund*—is seventy miles deep, with numerous fjords fed by large glaciers, and a surprising number of hot springs.

Long before the Dutch or British whalers began to kill the plentiful black whales that lived around the coastal fringe of Greenland, there were aboriginals who watched, probably in awe, as these gigantic black mammals rolled by through the icy Arctic waters. The first Greenlanders (the island is believed to have been colonized some forty-five hundred years ago) depended upon the indigenous wildlife for their sustenance. They have been killing whales throughout their history; the local cetacean population con-

sists of an occasional bowhead, fin whales, minkes and humpbacks. In addition, Greenlanders hunt various seals and small cetaceans, including the harbor porpoise, the narwhal and the beluga. Tundra plants like heather, birch, alder, cotton grass and lichens grow along the southern coasts, but elsewhere on this gigantic island, hardly anything grows at all. Of its 840,000 square miles, some 700,000 are completely covered with ice.

The Vikings were the first Europeans to encounter Greenland during their westward voyages well before the year 1000. Two settlements, now known to archaeologists as the Eastern and the Western Settlement, were established on the island's southern tip, its most habitable region. Evidently it was not habitable enough, for the settlements did not last, and within a hundred years they were abandoned. The Portuguese, in the throes of their naval exploration of the known world, petitioned the Norwegians who were more familiar with the conditions of the north to explore the great islands, and around 1472, the king of Norway sent an expedition to Greenland. Two Danes, a Norwegian and a Portuguese named Juano Cortereal landed on the east coast of Greenland, but were driven off by Eskimos. Later the archbishop of Trondheim tried to reach the heathen Eskimos, but his attempts also proved futile. In 1521 King Christian II of Denmark equipped a ship to attempt the colonization of Greenland, but the ship never sailed. Martin Frobisher, in search of the Northwest Passage for Queen Elizabeth, rediscovered Greenland in 1576, but he misidentified it as "Friesland," and it was not until 1585–87 that the indomitable John Davis (also in search of the Northwest Passage) located the island and correctly placed it on the map. By the seventeenth century, Denmark had laid claim to the island, and Greenland Eskimos were kidnapped and exhibited in Copenhagen. When the Norwegian missionary Hans Egede arrived in Greenland in 1721, he found that the natives dressed for whaling as if for a wedding ("the whale likes not un-cleanliness," he wrote in his 1741 *Perlustration*), and when the whale—presumably a bowhead—was harpooned, the hunters were said to jump onto its back, yelling and screaming.

Just as the Eskimos are people of the ice, so too are certain whales creatures of the ice. Found only in the high northern polar latitudes are two small whales (rarely exceeding 15 feet in length): the narwhal (*Monodon monoceros*), and the beluga (*Delphinapterus leucas*). These whales have no dorsal fin, presumably to enable them to swim under the ice without interference. The narwhal is prized for its twisted, spiral "horn" (actually its upper left canine tooth), and the beluga for its flesh. Some 300 narwhals per year are currently being taken, but since this species does not fall under the jurisdiction of the International Whaling Commission, the only records kept are those of the Eskimos themselves.

Less numerous in Greenland waters, the beluga is also caught occasionally by Inuit hunters. In 1918, Porsild wrote that like the narwhal, belugas may become trapped in the ice in groupings called *savssats*, and when this happens, the natives shoot them with rifles or spear them with harpoons. In a 1987 publication of KNAPK (*Kalaallit Nunaanni Aalisartut Piniartullu Kattuffiat*, the Greenland Hunting and Fishing Cooperative), the following statement appears: "In the Thule area, Inuit hunt the Narwhales and Beluga Whales in the traditional hunting methods, which are very delicate and avoid unnecessary exploitation of the stocks. They also utilize all parts of the catch. They dry the meat, set aside the intestines and the rest as dogfood. . . . The meat is stored and even the sinews are kept for sewing the clothing necessary for surviving the Arctic winter."

Like Eskimos elsewhere, the Greenland Inuit originally hunted from kayaks, spearing whales with harpoons and keeping them from sinking with sealskin floats. When European whalers arrived in the eighteenth century, they occasionally shared a catch with the Inuit, but there was no transfer of whaling technology. It was not until 1948 that the Danish government provided the natives with a harpoon cannon, but the take was only in the neighborhood of 18 animals a year. A decade later, more fishing vessels were equipped with harpoon guns, and in addition to the minkes, the Greenlanders took a few humpbacks. On rare occasions, they managed to capture a blue whale, which provided them with an abundance of badly needed protein.

As a subsistence activity, whaling is secondary to fishing, so the fishermen equip their fishing boats with a fifty-millimeter harpoon cannon, which is employed whenever they encounter a passing whale. Greenland fishermen also use a method known as "cooperative hunting," where they surround a minke whale and shoot it with rifles. Earlier, Greenland whalers had to harpoon the whales from a small fishing boat, but now they could chase down and shoot the smaller, much more manageable minkes. It has been estimated that the catch increased from 50 to 300 minkes between 1960 and 1977.

The carcass of a whale provides food for the villages, and an instant snack in the form of *muktuk*, the cubed pieces of fresh blubber with the skin attached. The meat is usually distributed to the inhabitants of the village, but if there is an excess, it goes

After the kill, Eskimos of northwest Greenland eat the *muktuk* from a newly killed male narwhal.

to neighboring settlements. The killing of whales, in addition to providing nourishment for the villagers, also adds to the prestige of the hunter. Almost everyone in Greenland eats whale meat at one time or another during the year. A 1984 study showed that 90 percent of the total population had consumed it during the previous year.

Traditionally, every part of the whale was used, but nowadays, with the availability of plastics and import goods, many of the whale products are discarded. Oil from the blubber was—and still is—used as fuel for lighting, heating and cooking. The meat, blubber and blood are still consumed, but the baleen, which was once used in the manufacture of nets, lashings and utensils, is thrown away. The shoulderblade, which served as a shovel or a scraping board, is also discarded.

THE International Whaling Commission was established in 1949 as a handmaiden of the whaling industry. In the initial convention, gray and right whales were protected "except when the meat and products of such whales are to be used exclusively for local consumption by the aborigines." In other words, what Eskimos and Indonesians did to feed themselves was their own business. When the United States began to lobby for a quota of bowhead whales for their aboriginals, other nations realized that they too needed some sort of a variance from the IWC if their natives were going to be able to hunt whales in the traditional manner. Greenland has been a part of Denmark since 1953, but in 1978, it was given home-rule status. It is still technically a part of Denmark, however, and its causes are pleaded before the IWC tribunal by the Danish commissioner.

Unlike the North Slope Alaskan Eskimos, who control the lucrative petroleum pipeline, the Greenland Inuit have very little bargaining power. Moreover, the isolated nature of some of their settlements makes policing their hunting activities difficult, if not impossible. The workings of the IWC are unknown to the Greenland Inuit. The Danish government is located in Copenhagen, thousands of miles and a couple of oceans from the settlements of Uummannaq or Iginniarfik. They have tried to impose controls on the Inuit, but more often than not, the whales are killed without anyone in Copenhagen knowing it.

When the United States air base was installed at Thule in northwest Greenland in 1951, the natives were moved to the "model Arctic village" of Kanak. The wildlife of this location consists of seals, walrus, and, because it is in the migration path of narwhals, these small whales as well. In a 1976 study of the Inuit and the narwhals, Floyd Durham wrote that "they continue a moderate annual take of narwhals by traditional methods and with maximum utilization of the products. This efficient harvesting is in sharp contrast to that in NE Canada where natives reportedly exploit, for tusks only, the narwhal with small but modern equipment. . . ."

The Inuit now call their country *Kalaallit Nunaat*. There are automobiles in the capital city of Nuuk (formerly Godthaab), and blocks of urban flats are clustered at the harbor. A modern fish-processing plant netted over $1 million in 1982. Although Greenland's is no longer a subsistence economy, large segments of the population—perhaps 25 percent—depend on hunting for existence. Because the pendulum has swung all the way from whale-killing to whale-conservation, some nations believe that no whales at all ought to be killed, by anybody, for any reasons whatsoever. Sidney Holt, one of the most vocal and energetic of the whale-protectors, has written, "The Greenlanders and the Norwegians together have so depleted the minkes in Greenland waters that this species now is officially protected from commercial whaling—which should put it under a double moratorium. . . . As a result of special pleading by the Danish authorities—which other EEC [European Economic Community] countries did not care to challenge—Greenlandic minke whaling is now called 'aboriginal subsistence whaling' by the IWC."

The Alaskan Eskimos did not kill off the bowheads. Rather it was the Yankee whalers, led by Captain Thomas W. Roys, who discovered the dense herds of black whales north of the Bering Strait, and slaughtered them for thirty years. In 1979, when propitious circumstances led to a manifold increase in Eskimo whaling, the bowhead population was already reduced to near-extinction. Those who would save the remaining whales are opposed to any take of bowheads by the Alaskan aborigines, since the bowhead is considered the only species of great whale that has been brought close to biological—as opposed to commercial—extinction. The Eskimos argue that it isn't their fault that there are so few bowheads left and they should not be penalized for the excesses of the white man. All they want is a couple every year to fulfill their traditional, cultural and nutritional needs.

An analogous situation exists with the Greenland Inuit. Their whaling was never significant enough to affect the population of North Atlantic minkes or humpbacks, but the fact remains that these stocks have been substantially reduced. The culprits were the pelagic whalers of Norway and Iceland, who wreaked havoc on the rorquals of the North Atlantic—the stocks that the International Whaling Commission refers to as the "Central North Atlantic Stock," and which used to be known as the "East Greenland–Iceland–Jan Mayen Stock." Norwegian

whalers have been fishing this stock for many years (the Norwegian "small-whale fishery" was dependent upon these minkes), and by 1980 the stock was declared a "protection stock," which means that no commercial whaling is permitted. "Commercial" is the key word, since the Norwegians, although they have agreed to abide by the moratorium, have begun submitting proposals to the IWC that would allow them to take a small number of minke whales (something on the order of 300) every year for the subsistence of their small coastal whalers.

In Seattle, in February 1979, the IWC convened a special meeting "in recognition of the fact that it had become increasingly involved with aboriginal (and in particular, bowhead) whaling." The invited participants included biologists, nutritionists and anthropologists, and while they concentrated on the issue of Eskimo bowhead whaling, they also addressed the comparably complex questions of Greenland Inuit needs. Included in the final report of this meeting was a paper by Danish scientists entitled "Subsistence Hunting: The Greenland Case." In this study, the authors concluded that "subsistence hunting may be interpreted as hunting for one's need, but not necessarily as hunting for one's own (private) consumption. . . . In the traditional Greenlandic hunting a distribution system based on reciprocal relationship was an important factor. Accordingly, subsistence hunting should be regarded as hunting for the household economy, with a distribution system which secures that the community shares the products."

To impress upon the IWC that their needs were legitimate, the Americans began bringing Eskimos—often in modified traditional dress—to the annual meetings. On several occasions, the Eskimos themselves took the microphone to deliver impassioned speeches about their cultural and nutritional needs. At recent meetings, the Danish delegation has featured Greenland Eskimos, also occasionally in costume. Following the lead of the Japanese, who have produced a flood of slick propaganda booklets, the Greenlanders have begun to print glossy, colorful brochures dedicated to pleading their cause. At the 1989 meeting of the IWC in San Diego, the Danes requested and received an allocation of 12 Central Atlantic minkes per year for 1990–92; 190 minkes from the West Greenland stock; and 42 fin whales from West Greenland waters. Since there is no Danish whaling industry, all these allocations are for the Greenlanders under the rubric of "aboriginal subsistence whaling."

The Danes and the Greenlanders are very much aware that their "aboriginal" whaling can be seen as threatening to already endangered stocks, but they also regard the regulations as threatening to their way of life. In the KNAPK booklet quoted above, they write

The great whales are nowadays considered a remarkable and unique endangered species because of exploitation by whaling ships and by pollution damage. That situation has caused a panic reaction. Although we are a small population, and cannot "destroy" the whales through our hunting, we have strict regulations on whaling. In 1950 Denmark became a member of the International Whaling Commission. The Commission decides how many whales may be caught in Greenlandic waters and makes decisions for the coming year. Now, members of the Commission adhering to environmentalists' concerns are saying that it is necessary to introduce regulations for Inuit hunting for smaller whales. *So far, we have been living without interference in our remote country. We have been hunters without disturbing other peoples. But our hunting tradition is now under scrutiny by other peoples.* [Their italics.]

Alaskan Eskimos

THE INUIT called him *aqvik;* the Spitsbergen whalers called him "the whale"; William Scoresby knew him as "the Mysticetus"; and Herman Melville, who rarely got anything wrong in his cetology, got him totally confused with his close relative, the right whale.* The scientists called him *Balaena mysticetus,* and today, we know him as the bowhead. He lives in the most inhospitable environment in the world; an icy jumble of wind-whipped gales, pack ice, freezing water, twenty-four-hour days and twenty-four-hour nights. Of all the great whales, his is the shortest migration. He never leaves the Arctic, but cruises from the Bering Sea through the narrow Bering Strait, then along the ice edge to the North Slope of Alaska and into the Chukchi and Beaufort seas. It is said that there are isolated populations of bowheads in the Soviet Arctic, and a few in the eastern oceans. In 1970 a 21-foot-long juvenile appeared in Osaka Bay, and died a day later. Japanese scientists wrote that this was probably the southern record for the species, since it has "occurred no other place in the world on 33°28'N around San Diego and Casablanca, for example." Bowheads are gone now from the eastern Arctic, having been slaughtered to extinction by the Basque, Dutch and British whalers of three centuries ago. The only known population of bowhead whales in the world is found in the western Arctic Ocean, off the coast of northern Alaska.

For eons, the Eskimos of the western Arctic have hunted the bowhead whale. The unexploited resident population has been estimated at 40,000 animals. Now there are between 5,000 and 7,000 bowheads left in Alaskan and Siberian waters. If it isn't the rarest large animal in the world, at a length of 60 feet and a weight of even more tons, it is certainly the largest rare animal in the world.

Of all the world's aboriginal whale-hunters, the Eskimos are probably the most efficient, not only because they have developed special techniques and equipment, but because they have to be. Theirs is an unforgiving environment, and survival is their primary concern. Eskimos spend more time hunting than any other people in the world.

---

*Melville cannot really be faulted for his misidentification; *Moby-Dick* was published in 1851, and it would not be until 1861 that Eschricht and Reinhardt would publish the definitive differentiation between the two species of balaenid whales.

As the long winters drew to an end, and the watery sun began to rise higher in the Arctic sky, the hunters started to prepare for the arrival of the whales. They sharpened their harpoons and lances, repaired the sealskin floats and walrus-skin boats, and resewed the seams of their clothing. Before the whales arrived, ritual ceremonies were performed in special houses (known as *karigi*) to ensure a successful hunt. The spirit of the whale was honored so as not to offend the other whales and to ensure future success. So much depended upon the success of the spring hunt that a village might be threatened with starvation if no whale was caught. The whaling captains (*umialiks*) assumed almost priestly duties, overseeing all village activities in preparation for the hunt. Special songs and amulets were a part of these rites, and from the earliest preparations to the distribution of the meat, strict codes of conduct were followed. For example, women and children were not allowed on the ice, and back in the village, the *umialik*'s wife had to remain particularly docile because her behavior was believed to influence the behavior of the whale. To the *Inupiat* ("The People"; the way the Eskimos refer to themselves), whaling was a dangerous business, and ritual played an integral part in its execution. Whatever could be done to ensure the safety of the men was critical; if the boat capsized, the water temperature that was ideal for a bowhead whale would kill a man in minutes.

All the necessary equipment was moved onto the ice by dogsled, and lookouts positioned themselves on the ice waiting for the whales to pass by. When one or more of the bowheads were sighted, the Eskimos launched their skin boats (*umiaks*), in pursuit of the whale. Each *umiak* contained seven to ten men, and was approximately twenty feet long. When the whale was sighted, the Eskimo hunters paddled quietly after it, trying whenever possible to approach it from directly ahead or directly behind. The eyes of the bowhead are located on the side of its enormous head, and it can only see to the side. When it was in range, the harpooner hurled an ivory-headed spear that was attached to a sealskin float with a walrus-hide rope. Sometimes the spear was poorly thrown, and the whale dived under the ice. If that happened, it might or might not be retrieved. Often with several harpoons in its back, the whale towed the sealskin floats, which hampered its diving, and also

To ensure a successful hunt, Alaskan Eskimos charmed whales to the umiak with a plaque carved with the image of the whale.

marked its position for the whalers. When the whale tired, the hunters closed in on it, and slashed its tail tendons so it couldn't swim. Then they lanced it repeatedly until it died.

When the hunt was successful, the huge carcass was hauled ashore by the combined efforts of the whalers and the villagers who had come to the edge of the ice to assist and celebrate. A hundred tons of meat, fat and oil nurtured one or more villages for a long time, and that which was not consumed was fed to dogs or used to bait traps. They ate the muscle, liver, brain, heart, kidneys and small intestines, as well as the blubber, which they cut off in small chunks and called *muktuk*. The gut was made into waterproof clothing and translucent windows, and of course the oil was used for heating, cooking and lighting. The baleen was employed in the manufacture of thread, whaling gear, fishing equipment, combs, toys, traps and amulets. The bones were utilized for fences and sled runners, and house-construction occasionally featured the giant ribs and jawbones.

Although no records were kept, it is estimated that the Eskimo whalers may have taken 20 whales a year. Totals varied considerably, and one year the whales might come in close to the ice edge, but the next they might travel too far offshore for the whalers to spot them from their observation posts.

Eskimos have no written history, so the origin of their whaling enterprise is lost. Estimates of the time they have been hunting range from eight hundred to four thousand years. The people we know as Eskimos are believed to have crossed the land bridge that once joined Siberia to Alaska, so a history of these people incorporates both shores of the Bering Strait.

Nowadays, hunting of the bowhead occurs in the offshore waters of northern Alaska, as the whales migrate along the coastline. If the ice forms close to shore, the whales move farther off, making observation—and therefore hunting—correspondingly more difficult. The whale-hunts were an integral part of Eskimo culture for centuries, and if their stocks of whales had not been discovered by Yankee whalers in the middle of the nineteenth century, they might have gone on for centuries more.

Interlude:
Whaling in the Azores

THEY CALLED IT the Western Islands Grounds because it was an island group west of North America, but it was closer to Europe than America. These islands were among the earliest areas visited by the sperm whalers of New England in the eighteenth century. Early in the history of the fishery that was to dominate much of New England's commercial history, it was discovered that the waters around the Azores were among the favorite haunts of sperm whales. It soon became apparent that there were other attractions at these islands: food and water could be obtained there, and more important, men willing to sign aboard could be expeditiously recruited.

From his observatory at Sagres at Cape Saint Vincent in Portugal, the westernmost point in continental Europe, Henry the Navigator (1394–1460) inspired the explorers who would extend the boundaries of the known world. Infante Dom Henrique (as he is known to the Portuguese) was the patron of Gil Eannes, the first man to round the previously untried Cape Bojador on the western hump of Africa, opening the South Atlantic for the voyages of such heroes as Bartolomeo Dias, Vasco da Gama, and Ferdinand Magellan. In 1427 the pilot Diogo de Sevilha, possibly on a return voyage from Madeira, reached the islands that would eventually be named

the Azores, but it was Gonçalo Velho Cabral who is credited with the official discovery of the islands in 1431. Cabral first claimed Santa Maria, then São Miguel, Terceira ("third"), São Jorge, Graciosa, Pico, and Faial. The seven islands were named Ilhas dos Açores ("Isles of Hawks"), and within a year, the Portuguese had settled in. While searching for the nonexistent island of Antilia, Diogo de Tieve discovered the remaining two islands in 1452.

The peaks of submerged volcanoes rising from the Mid-Atlantic Ridge, the nine islands of the Azores archipelago sizzled out of the North Atlantic some nine hundred miles east of Portugal. The water around these islands can be over a mile deep; a perfect locale for the deep-feeding cachalot. After Cabral found the islands, the whales would have only another three centuries—the blink of an eye in cetacean history—to swim unmolested in Azorean waters. The whalers were coming.

As they extended their horizons, the Yankee whalers sailed first to the Bahamas and the West Indies, then out into the Atlantic. The currents of the North Atlantic circulate in a roughly clockwise fashion, but there are enough subcurrents, drifts and gyres to make sailing less than easy. The same surface ocean movements that allowed Columbus to sail in a south-

The harbor at Horta, on the island of Fayal in the Azores, with American sperm whalers picking up provisions.

westerly arc to reach the Caribbean also assisted the whalers as they hitched a ride onto the northerly segment of the Atlantic gyre which pushed them toward Spain and Portugal, and eventually south to Africa. (Although Ponce de León is believed to have been the first to describe the Gulf Stream, during the early sixteenth century, the whalers recognized its benefits early in the eighteenth. These benefits were illustrated and published in 1786 by Benjamin Franklin, the cousin of a Nantucket whaler named Timothy Folger.) Perhaps the whales were not in evidence when they first explored Azorean waters, but the Nantucket whalers first sighted the West African whales in 1773, and five years later, they discovered the Western Islands Grounds.

The usual route for whaling in the Atlantic—only the broadest of generalizations, since the whales rarely appeared where or when they were supposed to—would consist of a southward bearing in the spring, to the Carolinas and the West Indies, thence to the Azores, the Cape Verdes, and the coast of Africa in the summer. Eventually, the whalers would recross the South Atlantic, and work the Brazil Banks or the Falklands. The ships would return to New England in July and after refitting, sail for the Grand Banks to the north. "Plum-pudding" whaling was the way these short, relatively safe Atlantic voyages were described. It would not be until 1789 that the British whaler *Emelia* would round the Horn and initiate the era of round-the-world whaling voyages.

Because the British whaling fleet was active in Greenland waters, the Atlantic was open to the colonists. During the mid-eighteenth century, French and Spanish privateers and pirates roamed the Atlantic, adding yet another threat to an already hazardous pursuit. The dogged Yankee whalers persevered, however, and continued to visit the Western Islands for sperm whales, because the islands had the reputation of being the home of particularly large whales. (In a 1971 account of Azorean whaling, Trevor Housby describes the capture of a 61-footer, one of the largest bull sperm whales ever measured.) Even though there were large whales to be found there, however, the Azores were only a way-station on the way to such places as the Cape Verde Islands and the whaling grounds of southern Africa.

During the height of square-rigged whaling, the whalers would plunder the waters of the Western Islands for whales, and the lands for whalers. Since the days of Vasco da Gama, Portuguese sailors have demonstrated an inordinate desire to go down to the sea in ships. While the Portuguese proved to be brave and competent whalemen, however, early New England chauvinism relegated the Azoreans to the same class as anyone who was not a "full-blooded Yankee"—whatever that was supposed to mean in 1820. In later years, Hohman would write, "as the better type of American forsook the forecastles, their bunks were filled by criminal or lascivious adventurers, by a motley collection of South Sea Islanders known as Kanakas, by cross-bred negroes and Portuguese from the Azores and the Cape Verdes, and by the outcasts and renegades from all the merchant services of both the Old World and the New." When Clifford Ashley, the writer and painter, shipped aboard the *Sunbeam* in 1904, he described the crew in detail, concluding, "The South Sea Islands, East Indies, Cape Verdes, Azores and Canaries, all were liberally represented on our list. Profane, dissolute and ignorant they were, yet, on the whole, as courageous and willing a lot as one could desire."

Most narratives of Atlantic whaling include a visit to the Azores; among the arrivals was the *Bruce,* which J. Ross Browne named *Styx* in his *Narrative of a Whaling Cruise.* Here he describes his first sight of the islands in 1842:

Terceira is a remarkably picturesque island, beautifully laid out in farms, which at this season of the year have a rich golden hue that bespeaks abundant crops. The coast is broken and rugged, and in many places so steep as to preclude the possibility of ascent. Part of the island seems to have been ingulfed by an earthquake, which accounts for the rugged appearance of the coast. It is visited at certain seasons of the year by heavy gales and rains, es-

pecially in October and November, when there is frequently danger in approaching it. While we lay off and on, awaiting a suitable opportunity of running in, we had hard, shifting winds, and it rained almost incessantly. Mount Brazil, and other elevated portions of the island, were covered most of the time with white, misty clouds.

Browne describes the Azorean whalers as wearing "sennet hats with sugar-loaf crowns, striped bedticking pantaloons patched with duck, blue shirts, and knives and belt. They were all barefooted. . . ."

It is impossible to determine when the Azoreans began whaling on their own, but the Portuguese seemed to have maintained a sperm whale fishery, which "they had learned from the New Englanders and carried on upon the coast of Brazil" as early as 1785. The islands sustained an international fishery for perhaps a hundred years, but by 1870, the only whalers operating out of the Azores were the Azoreans themselves.

They fitted out their own whaleships, but they were never particularly successful. Their first attempt was the *Cidade da Horta,* a brig that had been abandoned in the islands by the French as being unseaworthy. They probably never sent out more than ten of their own vessels, because their economy was never strong enough to lay out the considerable sums required to build, pay for and man a full-rigged ship. Instead, the Azoreans would sign aboard foreign vessels. Nevertheless the islands later developed a technique that would not be duplicated anywhere else in the world: shore whaling for sperm whales.

In shore whaling, which involves spotting whales from lookouts, the prey has almost invariably been the relatively placid right whale, and less frequently the humpback. The reasons for these choices are obvious. Both the right and the humpback are inshore creatures; slow-swimming, passive animals that, more often than not, rolled over and died when they had been lanced. The cachalot, on the other hand, is a dangerous threat, given to smashing whaleboats in its death-throes, and less frequently to attacking whaleships and sinking them. It was indeed a courageous whaler who chose to approach the most fearsome of all the great whales in a fragile little cockleshell.

It is possible that the Azoreans learned shore whaling from the Basques, who may have called at the islands as they extended their right-whale fishery to Newfoundland in the sixteenth century. (The Basque term *vigía,* which means a lookout, is still in use in the Azores today, and the word *cachalote* is also of Basque origin.) The village of Horta (also known as Porto Pim) on the island of Faial is believed to have been the site of the first shore station in the Azores, sometime around 1832. The Azorean records are scanty, but it is known that the American consul, a man named Dabney, set up a tryworks at Horta in 1850. From Faial, the industry spread to the other islands, and soon there were stations on São Jorge, Graciosa, Terceira and São Miguel. The Pico islanders began whaling around 1853, following an outbreak of phylloxera that almost totally wiped out the vineyards which had been their main source of revenue. By 1898 there were no less than twenty-nine whaling companies working in the Azores.

Originally, the whaleboats had been imported from New Bedford, but around the turn of the century, a whaleman named Machado built the first boat at Pico. Shortly thereafter, the laborious method of rowing or sailing out to the whaling grounds was abandoned in favor of motorboats, which towed the killing boats out to sea. Although this greatly improved the Azoreans' efficiency by allowing them to go to the whales without the endless hours of backbreaking rowing or time-consuming tacking, the innovation was one of the few attempts at modernization that the Azoreans made. Curiously, at the same time that they adopted motorized launches, the Azoreans abandoned the hand-held harpoon guns which they had been using—somewhat uneasily—since around 1885. They also introduced two-way radios to facilitate communication between the *canoas.* With the exception of the radios and the towing boats, which replaced the whaleship in putting the whalers close to the whales, Azoreans continued to kill and process cachalots in a manner that almost precisely replicated that of the Yankee whalers. Despite the anachronistic nature of the fishery, its economy allowed the technology to be exported. (By 1900, most of the world's whaling was being conducted with exploding harpoons and steam- or diesel-powered catcher boats.) Open-boat whaling was introduced to Madeira in 1941, and although they had only a brief time there, Azorean whalers established a similar fishery in Brazil in 1950.

NOTICE TO WHALEMEN.

The subscriber having lately removed with his family from Edgartown, Mass., to Magdalen, of Pico, opposite Fayal, (Western Islands,) hereby gives notice to all Vessels touching at the Islands, that he is prepared and will furnish at short notice, such

Fruit and Vegetables

for RECRUITS, as the Islands afford, and at the lowest possible prices. All vessels touching at the Islands for supplies will do well to call as above.

FRANCIS J. SYLVIA.

Western Islands, Nov. 1st, 1841.

From the *vigías* on the cliffs, the lookouts stood watch from dawn until dusk, every day of the year. They used powerful binoculars, which they claimed enabled them to spot whales at a distance of thirty miles. When blows were sighted, a rocket was set off to alert all the whalers, who then set out in pursuit. (Another vestige of the Yankee whaling industry was the introduction of English terms into Portuguese. They cried *bloz!* or *baleia!* when a whale was sighted, called the bull whale a *bulo,* the boom a *bûme,* and the junk the *janco.*) The whaleboats, known as *canoas,* were thirty-eight feet long (ten feet longer than the average American whaleboat), and as graceful and seaworthy as the Yankee whaleboats that Clifford Ashley had called "the most perfect water craft that have ever floated." They were smooth-sided, or carvel-built, unlike the Yankee boats, which were clinker-built. (The Azoreans believed that the acute hearing of the sperm whale enabled it to hear the slap of the water on the strakes.) Where their Yankee predecessors employed six-man crews, the Azorean double-enders shipped a crew of seven. The Azorean harpooner and the steersman did not make the dangerous and awkward change of places after the whale had been struck, so that the harpooner both made fast to the whale and lanced it. Like almost everything else in the Azorean fishery, the harpoons employed followed the New England fashions

In the *canoa,* Azorean whalemen pull toward a sperm whale.

As the oarsmen watch expectantly, the Azorean harpooner hurls his heavy lance.

of the mid-nineteenth century, with a "Temple" toggle head that pivoted to a right angle when plunged into the whale. The boats were equipped with a gaff mainsail and a jib, and if possible, the boat was sailed right onto the whale for the harpooning. Often the Azorean whalers would paddle up to the whale under sail, using canoe paddles that Robert Clarke described as "betraying their Red Indian origin by their shape and the way they were used." The rowing oars were sixteen to eighteen feet long, and the steering oar was about twenty-three feet in length. Clarke wrote, "In the history of seafaring trades there can scarcely be a more remarkable survival than the present use in the Azores of hand weapons to take and

kill great whales." The harpoon was not the killing instrument, but was used to make the whale fast to the boat. After the whale towed the boat (which might consume several hours), the whalers threw the lance, a spearlike projectile which was driven deep into the body of the exhausted whale. A towing strap was inserted into the whale's upper jaw so that it could be brought back to shore, sometimes a distance of twenty-five or thirty miles. The toggle was reeved into the head rather than the tail because a whale is designed to move forward through the water.

(When John Huston was filming *Moby Dick* in 1955, he sent a crew to film actual whaling in Madeira.

In the shallows, Azorean whalers section a sperm whale before winching the pieces onto the shore. The small row-boat is used only for this cutting; the *canoas* were more than thirty feet long.

Once the whale has been cut into sections, it is winched ashore for further flensing.

The early scenes of whalers chasing and harpooning sperm whales show better than any text the process and the excitement of the chase. The white whale, unavailable for filming, was represented by several ninety-foot steel, wood and latex models that were eventually lost at sea off Ireland to the bewilderment of cruising sailors. Whaling in Madeira, some five hundred miles southeast of the Azores, is a smaller version of the Azorean fishery and was founded by Azoreans. From 1941 to 1949, almost 1,000 whales were taken by 102 Madeiran whaleboats. The last factory closed in 1981.)

Dead whales were usually brought to the stations in the late afternoon and processed the following day.

Before the steam-powered whaling station was built at Lages do Pico in 1950, the whales were beached on the rocks at the entrance to the harbor and worked up there. First the head was cut off with a razor-edged blubber spade, then the carcass was stripped of its blubber. Formerly, only the teeth and the blubber were saved, but in later years, the meat was used in the manufacture of fertilizer and live-stock feed.

The statistics of the number of whales obtained are not available, but from 1895 to 1897 some 480,000 liters of whale oil were exported from the Azores. Up to the opening years of the twentieth century, the Azorean fishery had flourished, but by the time of World War I, it had begun to flag. Sperm oil had been used in England and the United States primarily for the manufacture of fine candles, but by 1910 paraffin was substituted and candles became cheaper. Sperm oil had only a limited application in the manufacture of cosmetics and medicinal salves, and because the market was diminishing, the catches decreased as well. In 1910, the Azores accounted for some 73 percent of all sperm whales caught in the world, but by 1915, the figure had fallen to a depressing 3.8 percent. World War II saw the return of the factory fleets to the high seas, and their pursuit of sperm whales in the North Atlantic reduced the Azorean catch. In 1949, there were only 125 *canoas* operating out of nineteen stations, and the total catch was some 500 whales. As the whaling industry declined and the economy of the islands plummeted, there was a mass evacuation. Whaling was perceived as a dangerous occupation (in 1974 two men were killed when a whale smashed a *canoa*), and it became increasingly difficult to interest young men in this line of work. Many Azoreans crossed the Atlantic to take up residence in New England, and the large Portuguese-speaking enclaves in Massachusetts and Rhode Island are the results of that emigration.

Sperm whale teeth, stored in the Azores, have been finding their way to New England where they are carved into scrimshaw and sold illegally to unsuspecting collectors. There is still a cottage scrimshaw industry in the Azores, but with the passage of the Marine Mammal Protection Act in 1972, it has become illegal to bring whale products into the United States, and the European Economic Community has also imposed strict prohibitions on the import of whale products. With the disappearance of the Azorean markets, the whaling industry has ground to a halt.

Although Portuguese observers attended the meetings of the International Whaling Commission for many years, the country never applied for membership in the commission, perhaps because the government realized that participation would result in sanctions against her whaling. By 1966 sperm whales had been placed in the "protected" category, which meant that they could not be legally killed anywhere. The Azoreans continued to fish in a sporadic fashion, but like so many other whaling operations, theirs

was an ecological and economic anachronism, doomed to obsolescence.

In a 1976 *National Geographic* article, Don Moser wrote that "whaling is dying out in the Azores," and quoted harpooner Almerindo Lemos as saying he can make more money working on a tuna boat. "But I have a craving," says Lemos, "I have an addiction." In 1976, only 200 whales were killed, and since then the number has dropped. In 1982 the boats were still visible, and there were huge piles of dried-out skulls and bones, but it was obvious that the industry, if not over, was on its last legs.

Although commercial whaling officially ceased in 1984, the Azorean Department of Fisheries issued a permit for five male sperm whales to be taken in 1987 in an attempt to stimulate the Azorean economy. Three whales were harpooned and brought to shore, but since the whaling factories had closed down, there were minimal facilities for processing them. A tractor was used to strip off the blubber, and some of the meat was sold for fish bait and fertilizer. The rest of the carcasses were towed out to sea and discarded, and the teeth were made into scrimshaw trinkets. In their 1988 IWC report, Deimer, Gordon and Arnbom wrote:

The killing of whales led to a debate and protest both inside and outside the Azores. The member of the European Parliament for the Azores, Prof. Vasco Garcia, was prominent amongst those opposing the whaling and proposed that other ways, such as whale-watching, should be found to exploit the region's cetacean resources. The Azores' position as a semi-autonomous part of a new member of the EEC added a further complication to the situation. It appears that whaling is still permitted within the archipelago.

Even though they have to be smuggled in, the teeth still provide souvenirs for tourists on the Azores. The idea of initiating a whale-watching business in the islands as a means of "exploiting the region's cetacean resources" seems doomed to failure; the whales appear too far offshore and too infrequently—and the weather is often too nasty—to encourage tourist interest. Whaling has ended in the Azores, after a century of intensive exploitation. Now only the *Museu dos Baleeiros* in Lages do Pico, with its whaleboats, harpoons and scrimshaw, exists as a reminder of the glory days of Azorean whaling.

NINE

WHALING OUTSIDE THE ANTARCTIC

South Africa: 1880–1975

OFF THE EAST COAST of southern Africa were the sperm whale habitats known as the Delagoa Bay Grounds, the Zanzibar Grounds, and the Mahé Banks, in addition to the productive waters of the Mozambique Channel, which separates the island of Madagascar from the African continent. The first American whaleship to cross the Equator was the Nantucket ship *Amazon,* which reported the discovery of the Brazil Banks in the South Atlantic in 1775. Even when they were whaling in the Indian Ocean, the American whalers overwintered at the Cape; by 1785 several Nantucket whalers were working the Delagoa Bay Grounds and returning to Cape Town for anchorage. (The east coast of southern Africa is one of the most dangerous coasts in the world. The Agulhas Current, moving southward along the coast, often meets a swell moving northeastward, causing what a 1773 mariner's guide referred to as "monstrous seas," that can break the backs of today's supertankers, never mind the comparatively tiny whaleships of the eighteenth and nineteenth centuries.)

As the numbers of right whales declined, so naturally did the South African whalers. When the right

whales had declined to the point where they could no longer be hunted economically, the whalers turned to another species, found farther offshore. Foreign whalers hunted sperm whales in the waters of Delagoa Bay and Madagascar; they even had their own Moby Dick, a bull sperm whale called "Madagascar Jack" that menaced whaleships off southeast Africa. Many species of whales would be killed in South Africa's productive waters, but by the end, it would be the great cachalot whose life and death would define South African whaling.

In 1867, the year diamonds were discovered along the Vaal and Orange rivers, Svend Foyn of Norway invented the harpoon cannon, the device that so dramatically changed the method by which whales were killed. Hungry for profits and finding themselves short of whales in their own waters, the Norsemen fanned out throughout the world's oceans as their Viking forebears had, only in these raids, their victims were whales. As the nineteenth century came to an end, the Norwegians were establishing footholds throughout the whaling countries of the world. In their *History of Modern Whaling,* Tønnessen and Johnsen wrote, "In the oceans on both sides of South

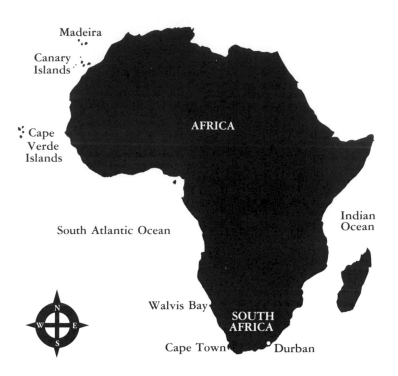

The African continent, showing those locations involved in whaling.

Africa were to be found the richest whaling grounds outside the Antarctic and the North Pacific. . . . In the period 1908 to 1916 a total of some 33,200 whales were caught, processing some 962,000 barrels of oil.''

One of the early outposts was established at Plettenberg Bay, a broad bight carved out of the southern shore of the African continent. The first whale fishery was established there in 1831 by a Scot named John Archibald Sinclair, who supplemented his income by selling provisions to visiting ships and also clubbing some of the numerous seals that inhabited the bay. In the early nineteenth century, the whalers took both humpbacks and right whales, but the humpbacks of Plettenberg Bay were quickly fished out. Sinclair maintained his fishery until he died in 1859. He was succeeded by a man named Jeffries, and then Cornelis Watson took over. Watson ran the fishery until 1899 when he was towed out of sight by a right whale one moonless night; although his boat washed ashore a week later, his body was never found. A week later, a dead right whale with Watson's harpoon still in it washed ashore at Cape Town.

In 1912, the Norwegian whaling company of Harald Haarfage arrived on the scene, and built a most ambitious station on Beacon Island, a small, rocky outcrop just offshore. Huge boilers were installed on the island, and all the other necessary construction for the operation of a major whaling enterprise was put in place. Under the direction of Captain Jacob Odlund, a fleet of whale-catchers and a factory ship arrived from Norway, and whaling began in earnest. Early in the first season (1914) some 21 whales were killed, yielding eighty-eight hundred barrels of oil and four thousand sacks of guano. From then on, however, disaster shadowed the station on Beacon Island. Whaleships sank or ran aground, and in July of that year, the boiling plant, manure dryer, bone crushers, guano factory and electric-lighting plant burned to the ground. Two months after the fire, the whaler *Plesang* was thrown upon the rocks and wrecked, taking five of her ten crew members down with her. Her hulk blocked the entrance to the harbor, but the pounding of the waves destroyed the remains before the detonators for blasting the wreck out of the way could be imported from Europe.

Because of the war in Europe, prices for whale oil were up, and despite the attendant disasters, Odlund reported a profit for 1915. His ships ranged the Cape coast from Mossel Bay to Cape Recife, and took whales that were reported by the lighthouse-keepers at these outposts. A large surplus of oil was built up, but they were unable to sell it, and by 1916, with no outlet for their product, the whalers had to suspend operations. The vessels were converted to other uses, and the processing equipment was sold off to the Union Whaling Company in Durban.

A resort hotel has been built on Beacon Island, now joined to the mainland by landfill. Standing outside the hotel is a white-painted harpoon cannon from a whaler, and a large, rusty iron trypot. It is unlikely that many holidaymakers would recognize these objects, and even though whales may occasionally be seen spouting in Plettenberg Bay, the place of this island in South Africa's whaling history is largely forgotten.

IN AFRICA between 1900 and 1914, the Norwegians established no less than fourteen whaling stations, including one at Durban, which was under the supervision of Johan Bryde, a Sandefjord businessman

The Norwegian whaling station at Beacon Island, Plettenburg Bay, as it appeared in 1914.

and the man for whom Bryde's whale was named. Bryde formed a partnership with Jacob Egeland, the Norwegian consul in Durban, and in 1908 the first whale was taken in African waters using modern methods. (After the first season, the citizens of Durban complained so vociferously about the smell that the factory was forced to move out of the harbor, and around the Bluff to the ocean side. Because of the heavy seas that sometimes attended this location, however, the whales could not be safely dropped there, so the practice began of dropping the carcasses inside the harbor, then trucking them around the Bluff to the processing station by railroad.) Operating as the South African Whaling Company, Bryde then obtained permission to build another land station at Donkergat, Saldanha Bay, and from 1910 to 1913, Norwegian whalers scoured African waters from Angola to Mozambique, killing the thousands of humpbacks that were migrating northward.

In the early days of whaling, Durbanites took a particular interest in the new industry appearing off their shores. Of course there was the smell to contend with—described by one writer as "a particu-

larly penetrating, clinging, fat sort of odour, which makes one anxious to vomit without delay, and hangs around one's nasal membranes for days"—but other aspects of the whale fishery also attracted the attention of the locals. Whale meat was eaten in some of Durban's best restaurants and clubs, where it met with mixed reactions. "Porpoises"—probably bottle-nosed dolphins—were considered a threat to fishing, and one of the duties of the Fisheries Inspector was to shoot them with a rifle, which led to a rumor that there was soon to be a company that would bottle the porpoise oil. (There was also a fishery for bottle-nosed dolphins off Cape Hatteras, North Carolina, and another at Cape May, New Jersey, in the late nineteenth century, specifically for the "jaw oil," which was used as a lubricant for watches and clocks. No such enterprise seems to have been undertaken in South Africa.)

In 1909, Jacob Egeland brought his cousin Abraham Larsen to Durban, and with British financing, started what was to become the most durable whaling enterprise in South Africa, the Union Whaling Company. In July 1908, two whale-catchers were brought over from Sandefjord, and by November, they had taken 106 whales.

By 1914, because of the war in Europe and "difficulties with British authorities" (Bryde had sold whale oil and meal to the Germans, despite a British prohibition on trading with the enemy), the Norwegians were forced to lease the Saldanha Bay station to a South African company, the Southern Whaling and Sealing Co., and with that, and the failure of the station at Plettenberg Bay, Norwegian operations in South Africa ceased.

THE LAND STATION at Walvis Bay, long considered an isolated outpost, suddenly became the focus of a war that was being fought thousands of miles away. The station had been a British enclave in what was otherwise known as German Southwest Africa, and in 1914, German troops landed at the whaling station, although the British factory ship *Pentaur* escaped with all hands. In 1916, the British occupied Southwest Africa, and ended the German presence in southern Africa.

The Durban station closed down until 1922, and when it was reopened, there were two companies operating there, the Union and Premier whaling companies. (The Union Whaling Company was

On the grounds of the Beacon Island Hotel, Plettenburg Bay, South Africa, a harpoon cannon has been painted white and serves as a garden ornament.

The founders of the Durban Whaling Company pose with their first whale in 1908. On the left is Jacob Egeland, manager of the station, and on the right is his cousin, Abraham Larsen.

named in 1908 in honor of the forthcoming Union of South Africa.) The two companies used a common slipway to haul the whales out of the water, and then applied a system that was unique in the history of whaling: they transported the whales from the shore to the factory by railroad.

In 1926, the "Discovery Committee" (a British organization that sought information on whales and whaling, particularly in the Southern Hemisphere) sent the zoologists N. A. Mackintosh and J. F. G. Wheeler to the Donkergat station at Saldanha Bay to study the whales that were being caught there (they were mostly blues and fins), and in 1929 the committee sent A. H. Laurie and F. D. Ommanney to Durban to study the whales caught off the Natal coast. In his *Lost Leviathan* (1971), Ommanney described the process:

The unique feature of the whaling stations at Durban was the manner in which the whales arrived at their last rites. They came by train. A single track railroad of wobbly appearance ran from the harbour mouth round the headland beyond the lighthouse and then along a mile and a half of loose driven sand to the whaling station, both of which had been built along the track like a railway station platform. The catchers dropped their whales at the harbour entrance overnight and a harbor tug hauled them

up a slipway where they were in due course winched up on to specially-built, low-slung bogey trucks. They were then trundled off to their obsequies by tank engines with a cow catcher and a huge square headlamp on the front. The harbour authorities were very strict because of the complaints about the smell, so that no carcass was allowed to lie at the slipway for more than a few hours. If it had not been trundled away within the stipulated time, the harbour tug towed it remorselessly out to sea. Owing to the wobbliness of the track, and the fact that it was often buried by wind-blown sand, the train with its monstrous cargo often got stuck or the trucks came off the rails. It then had to wait, with the engine hissing indignantly, until a breakdown crane was brought.

Once at the station, the whales were processed by natives, whom Ommanney describes as

mainly made up of Zulus, but there was a proportion of boys from further up-country. The Zulus were coal black and shining and had splendid white teeth, but there were several men of paler shades of brown, bronze and dull gold. They danced and pirouetted around the whale carcasses as though round a sacrificial victim, brandishing and twirling their flensing knives into the air so that the sun glinted on the blood-stained blades as on the assegais of Chaka's impis. Above the rattle of the winches and the hiss of steam echoed the wild shrieks and laughter of the

The complex facilities of the Union Whaling Company, Durban. The station was located at the Bluff, away from the city, because the smell was so awful. The carcasses had to be transported by railroad, which can be seen in the foreground above the surf line.

A blue whale carcass at the slip at Durban before it was transported by railroad to the processing station at The Bluff (1930).

blubber boys and the meat haulers wielding their hooks. The flensers chanted as the crackling strips of blubber peeled back and sometimes danced around in bare feet in the muck and slime holding their knives aloft like spears.

Although the colorful nature of the flensers moderated (and presumably, their shrieks and laughter subsided), the methods remained the same from Ommanney's time until the closing of the Union Whaling Company's station in 1975.

While the Norwegians quit South Africa, they persisted off the other coasts of Africa. The number of whaling stations in German Southwest Africa, the French Congo, and Portuguese East Africa expanded from five in 1910 to twenty-five in 1912. For the most part, the whales that were hunted by the Norwegians off the coasts of these countries were humpbacks (a total of 4,430 of these whales were killed off the Congo from 1912 to 1914), but they also took Bryde's whales, sperm whales, and what few right whales were left. In addition, African whalers took blue and fin whales that had migrated up from the Antarctic, and in the peak years of 1926 and 1927, a total of 3,500 blue whales and 2,400 fin whales were killed.

From the early years of the nineteenth century,

South African whaling was characterized by lateral movement among the whaling companies, incorporating one with another, folding one and reopening another, so it is difficult to keep track of the ownership of the stations and companies. The Southern Cross Whaling Company, for instance, was "wound up" in 1914 because of the war-imposed difficulties encountered in shipping the oil to Europe. A firm originally called the Union Whaling and Fishing Company changed its name successively to African Whales, Park Rhynie Whaling Company, and Grinrod Whaling before it shut down in 1922. The new Union Whaling Company was founded in 1921 by Egeland and Larsen, and operated alongside Lever Brothers' Premier Whaling Company at the Bluff at Durban. In 1932, Lever Brothers sold the Premier Whaling Company to the Union Whaling Company, and when the companies amalgamated, operations were moved to the larger, more modern facilities of Premier Whaling. Union Whaling Company Ltd. would remain South Africa's only whaling company from 1953 until 1976.

THE INTRODUCTION of the stern slipway (where the whale carcasses were winched aboard through a whale-sized hole in the stern) in 1925 changed the

Stripping the blubber from a fin whale at The Bluff, Durban, around 1930.

nature of industrial whaling. Prior to that year, the floating factories sailed south and waited in a protected anchorage for their catchers to bring the whales to them, but afterward, along with many other whaling nations, the South Africans headed for the Antarctic to hunt the giant blue and fin whales. They were, after all, among the countries closest to the whaling grounds there. The Kerguelen Sealing and Whaling Company (a subsidiary of Irvin and Johnson of Cape Town) first sent the converted *Radioleine* to the south in 1928–29, and after two seasons, they had commissioned another factory ship, the *Tafelberg*.

In his discussion of whaling in the Antarctic, A. G. Bennett wrote, "South Africa has been well attended by the whaler, and stations have persisted for long periods at certain points. The results are not generally so favourable as in the colder regions; in other words, the whales are not so fat—a fact that has an obvious explanation in the absence of the food they prefer." (This opinion was not actually borne out; in fact, South African whaling—particularly the station at Durban—has been among the world's most productive. And in other locations in Africa, such as Walvis Bay, some of the largest blue whales ever recorded were captured; one that was 91 feet long and produced 305 barrels of oil, and in 1931,

a monster female was captured that was 101 feet long and yielded 354 barrels of oil.) The size and condition of whales depended upon the time of year they were taken. If they had just arrived in South African waters after feeding in the South for four months, they were as fat as they would ever be; but if they were captured after they had delivered and nursed their calves, they were likely to be almost emaciated, since they had not eaten for months.

One of the peculiarities of whale biology can be seen here. The largest animals in the world migrate annually to their feeding grounds, where they gorge themselves round the clock on minute crustaceans. During those periods when they are on the move or on their breeding grounds, however, they do not eat at all. Thus the gigantic blue and fin whales of the Southern Hemisphere feed only in the Antarctic, which they visit from October to March. For the rest of the year, they subsist on the stored fat which constitutes their blubber. It was this layer of fat which was rendered into oil, and encouraged the whalers to seek them out and kill them.

Because of the conflicts between the Norwegians and the other Europeans who administered colonies in southern Africa, a novel idea sprang up around 1913 concerning the disappearing stocks of whales.

The French, whose colonies in Central Africa included Gabon, Moyen-Congo, and Oubangi-Chad (later federated into Afrique Equatoriale Française), suggested that there be an international agreement for the regulation of whaling. Obviously, it was an idea whose time had not come, for as the Norwegian whaling historians Tønnessen and Johnsen have written, "The world was still living in the age of liberalism, paying homage to free competition on the high seas. Marine biological scientific research was as yet still in its infancy."

Still, it was clear to even the most rapacious of whalers that some controls had to be exercised. As early as 1914, the provincial governments of Natal and the Cape Province posted restrictions on the catching of undersized whales and females with calves. There were also limits set on the number of whaling vessels that any company could employ, but there were many violations of these restrictions, and in general South African whaling was unfettered by local laws.

The idea of international control of whaling was postponed by World War I, and would not be addressed again until the 1920s—and even then it would not become a reality until 1931. In that year, the League of Nations brought forth a Convention for the Regulation of Whaling, which among other things forbade the killing of right whales, suckling calves, and females of other species. All data on size, oil yield and other pertinent information were to be sent to the Bureau of Whaling Statistics in Sandefjord, Norway. The convention came into force in 1935, and although South Africa was a signatory, neither Natal nor the Cape Province incorporated the convention's language into its provincial regulations concerning whaling. Irvin and Johnson reopened the station at Donkergat in 1936, but the whales did not appear in sufficient numbers, and in 1938 the station was shut down. It was obvious that pelagic whaling had replaced shore-based whaling, and in 1937 the Durban-based Union Whaling Company purchased the *Fraternitas* (which, as the *Sir James Clark Ross,* had been the first factory ship in the Antarctic), renamed her *Uniwaleco,* and sent her off to Madagascar and then to the Antarctic.

The South African government had ratified the 1937 London amendments to the 1931 Geneva Convention on whaling which called for minimum size limits for blue, fin and humpback whales, a three-month season, and inspectors aboard each factory ship. The two whaling companies objected strenuously to the London agreements, but eventually South Africa passed the Sea Fisheries Act, which put control of all living marine resources into the hands of the central government. The days of uncontrolled buccaneer whaling were over in South Africa.

WITH GERMANY and Japan entering the Antarctic fracas, more whales were killed than ever before (a total of 46,039 in 1937–38), but when the world went to war again, the issue of whale conservation was rendered moot. For the duration, the whales were saved. Both South African factory ships were casualties; the *Uniwaleco* was torpedoed by the Germans in 1941, and the *Tafelberg* was sunk off Ireland while carrying fuel oil and Sherman tanks. Although neither of the factory ships survived, those whale-catchers that were not turned into minesweepers by the South African navy continued their shore-whaling activities, and the station at the Bluff in Durban was kept open. South Africa was the only country in the world to continue whaling on a large scale during the war.

After 1945, Union Whaling operated only one factory ship. The British had appropriated the German factory ship *Unitas*—at 22,300 tons, the largest and best-equipped factory ship in the world—and renamed her *Empire Victory.* She was leased to Union Whaling, where she was rechristened *Abraham Larsen* in honor of the founder of the company. The *Abraham Larsen* ex-*Empire Victory* was sent to the ice after the war, and she turned an enormous profit in those early years. For the 1946–47 season, her take was 206,000 barrels of oil, and the books of Union Whaling showed a profit of £1.5 million. To produce such profits, the whalers of the *Larsen* killed 1,195 blue whales, 983 fin whales and 388 sperm whales. In the next season, as blue whales became scarcer, UWC whalers could only find 740 blues, but they more than made up for it by shooting 1,725 fins and 493 sperms. Blue whales became so scarce that by 1957, South Africa's last year in the ice, the *Larsen*'s gunners could find only nine to kill.

Following Antarctic voyages, individual seamen got bonuses of £400, and the gunners, who were rewarded for each whale they shot, received "film

First known as the *Unitas* when she was built by the Germans in 1937, this factory ship was turned over to the British after the war and became *Empire Victory*. In 1945, the South Africans leased her and changed her name to *Abraham Larsen*.

star incomes." (When the ships returned from months in the Antarctic, the crews were often paid by check rather than cash. According to a 1952 newspaper article, "The Union Whaling Company does this deliberately so that the men will find it more difficult to be parted from their hard-earned money by good-time girls, confidence men and thieves who swarm around the docks when the whalermen return.")

Durban's position as a whaling port was essential to its burgeoning economy. Not only were its seamen able to earn considerably more money than their local counterparts for "going to the ice," but they—and the whaling company—got to spend all their money in Durban. Local merchants vied with each other to provision the factory ship and its fleet of catchers with fuel, equipment, clothing, food, liquor and other matériel required for months in the Antarctic. In November 1955, as the *Larsen* prepared to head south for a four-and-a-half-month season on the

ice, her chief steward reported that her stores carried 267,000 pounds of butter, 75,000 pounds of cheese, and 12,500 tins of canned fish—in addition to 1.9 million cigarettes, 2,000 pounds of tobacco, 2,000 pints of beer, 1,015 bottles of "spirits" and 80 bottles of rum.

For ten years, the whaling nations of the world visited "the great whale refrigerator" in the South, and systematically slaughtered the whales there. It was conceivably the most short-sighted exercise in the entire myopic history of whaling, since even when it was obvious that there were too many ships hunting too few whales, the whaling nations persisted in their relentless slaughter.

Since the rorquals of the Antarctic had been spared while the nations of the world were busy annihilating each other, the first seasons for the *Larsen* in the Antarctic were enormously successful. The catcher boats, which had been converted to gunboats, were returned to the whaling company, and

Sperm whales, shown here awaiting processing, were the primary object of the fishery at Durban.

some swift corvettes were converted to catchers. From 1952, however, catches and prices dropped drastically. When the baleen whales of the South had been so decimated that even the International Whaling Commission began to worry about them, the South Africans turned their attention to the sperm whales. (The right whale has been protected by international agreement since 1937, but the South Africans apparently didn't get the message until well into the 1950s.) In 1957, Union Whaling sold the *Abraham Larsen* ex-*Empire Victory* ex-*Unitas* to the Japanese (who named her *Nisshin Maru*), and the company retired permanently from Antarctic whaling.

In the eighteenth and nineteenth centuries, whalers hunted sperm whales for the oil in their noses, but when the great stocks of baleen whales were discovered in the Antarctic—along with the means to catch and process them—the whaling fraternity focused their attention and their harpoon cannons on the rorquals. The liquid wax found in the nose of the cachalot was inedible, and could only be used industrially, but the oil of the baleen whales, an edible, liquid fat, could be used in the production of margarine, shortening and toilet soaps. As the num-

bers of rorquals declined, catchers out of Durban and Donkergat increased their taking of sperm whales. Of all the species of "great" whales, only the sperm existed in sufficient numbers to support a continuous fishery. (Even now, after centuries of whaling, estimates of the world sperm whale population number well over a million, probably more than all the other great whales combined.) The popularity of this whale, however, and its use as a symbol in the massive "Save the Whales" campaign, made it impossible—despite the assertions of scientists that it was not an endangered species—for any Western country to continue to kill these creatures. (The Japanese, bound by no such sentimental strictures, withstood all pressures to cease and desist in their slaughter of sperm whales, and even after the passage of the 1982 moratorium, they continued to do so.)

Advanced technology in the form of spotter aircraft was introduced to South African whaling in 1954. Ken Pinkerton, an ex-Royal Air Force pilot, flew the first missions for Union, spotting sperm whales from an altitude of five hundred feet and radioing their position to the catcher boats. Soon

Pinkerton and fellow pilots Bob Matthews and Sid Rowe were using two spotter planes flying eight to ten hours a day to report the location of whales to catcher boats. A far cry from lookouts in the crow's nest, these pilots reduced the whale's chances of escaping to near zero. They would drop a dye marker where they had sighted the whale, then call in its location to the nearest catcher boat. As of 1960 (according to an article in the Natal *Mercury*), Pinkerton's crews had flown 367,310 miles on whale-spotting operations, and had been credited with the kill of 2,545 whales. In 1961, while Natal whaling was still in its ascendancy, Pinkerton (with L. C. Surmon) wrote a paper on whale migrations, growth, habits and diseases. Surmon, who began his career as a laboratory assistant and rose through the ranks to become joint managing director of Union Whaling, was not particularly well qualified to talk about whale diseases, eyesight and sound production, but no one was better suited to discuss migration patterns, ocean currents and whale movements than Pinkerton, who had watched them from the air for seven years.

During World War II, Union Whaling was bought by a Johannesburg company, Unit Securities Trust. Abraham Larsen and his son Ernest were eased out of the company, and R. K. Fraay was brought in as chairman. He hired a chemist named C. G. Scully to run the company, and Scully picked young Hans Knudsen to run the Durban station. Knudsen, a Norwegian-trained chemist, oversaw the change from the processing of baleen whales to the processing of sperm whales. The collapse of the fin whale population meant that the meat of these whales, previously the basis for a meat-extract market, was no longer available, so the company had to invest some R300,000 in the installation of a freezing and packing facility for the processing of sperm whale meat. Previously considered inedible, sperm whale meat was now turned into meat meal, which, along with the valuable oil, turned the company's profit picture around. Knudsen also initiated the extraction of vitamin A from the gigantic livers of the whales, which continued until 1965, when synthetic vitamin oils were developed. In 1967, a freezing plant was built to process the meat of fin whales for sale to Japan, but by the following year (according to the chairman's report), "The meat freezing plant operated satisfactorily, but suffered from a shortage of baleen whales. The demand for our frozen meat in Japan and in South Africa is such that we should have no difficulty in disposing of much larger quan-

A South African whaler at sea. A whale has just been shot, and another is lashed alongside.

tities if we could catch more baleen whales." Unfortunately, there was a worldwide shortage of baleen whales, brought about directly by the whaling industry that now bemoaned their absence. In the ten-year period from 1950 to 1959, South African fin whale catches averaged 565 per year. In the 1968 season, the Durban whalers could only find 62 fin whales to shoot. With the disappearance of fin whales off the Natal coast, the Union Whaling Company began to suffer serious financial losses, and by 1968 the decision was made to direct its efforts toward the capture and processing of sperm whales.

Sperm oil was an enormously versatile product; according to a study by L. C. Surmon and Peter Best, it could be used "for cosmetics, pharmaceuticals, biodegradable detergents, candles, additives for heavy-duty lubricating oils, greases, precision-instrument lubricating oils, printing inks, wetting agents, fatty alcohols, fatty acids, and as a general chemical intermediate." Cold-filtered and "sulfurized," it was a superb lubricant, and was considered the finest oil available for the lubrication of delicate machinery. When "sulfated" (combined with sulfuric acid and then neutralized with ammonia), it was used for tanning leather. Meat and bone-meal products were supplied for protein additives to animal feeds, whale-meat extract served as a food-flavoring ingredient, and frozen whale meat was used for human and animal consumption. (Much of it ended up in pet food.) The teeth were exported by the ton to the Orient for ivory-carving.

In 1968, the UWC had to cut back again. The fleet of catchers was reduced from twelve to six, and the total staff, once as high as a thousand, was halved.

Public pressure was being brought to bear on whaling nations, and even the South Africans, congenitally impervious to public opinion, felt the pressure. (In 1971, the United Nations Stockholm Conference on the Environment recommended that there be a ten-year moratorium on whaling, and although this recommendation was passed unanimously, it was not enacted by the International Whaling Commission until 1982.) Fuel oil was one of the major expenses in running a whaling fleet, and the Arab oil embargo of 1974 made it increasingly uneconomical to bunker large ships for extended voyages. By 1975 the Union Whaling Company, once the largest shore-based whaling station in the world, shut down. The catcher boats were sold, some for scrap, and one, the *F. H. Hughes,* was towed out to sea and scuttled because she was in danger of sinking on her moorings.

When the whaling station closed, historian Cornelis de Jong proposed preserving "a set of harpoons, flensing knives, hooks and other tools, the furnace of the blacksmith who straightened harpoons bent by struggling whales, and above all, one of the six fast, storm-battered, dapper whaleboats." His suggestions were ignored, and although two of the whale-catchers, the *Pieter Molenaar* and the *C. G. Hovelmeier,* were actually purchased by the Van der Stel Foundation, the Durban City Council did not recognize their importance, and the moment was lost. Although there was some talk about turning the whaling station into a museum or a maritime center, it sat untended at the foot of the Bluff until the South African Army claimed it for a military base and practice range.

Australia: 1950–1978

BECAUSE OF THE importance of whale oil in international trade, the Australian Commonwealth Government brought over Captain Alf Melsom from Norway to advise them in launching a modern whaling industry. He toured the country, looking for suitable sites for whaling operations, and in 1949 the Australian government, acting on his recommendations, established a large shore factory at Carnarvon, in Western Australia north of Shark Bay. Australia was one of the original signatories to

At Tangalooma, Queensland, a worker examines the flipper of a humpback that has been hauled up on the flensing platform. The station was active from 1952 to 1962.

the International Whaling Convention, and although she had set up the Australian Whaling Commission in 1949, Australian whaling was essentially under the control of the international organization. Catches were regulated according to IWC quotas, and also according to various Australian acts which governed whaling within Australia's coastal waters.

By 1956, there were five land stations in Australia: Tangalooma and Byron Bay on the east coast, and Carnarvon, Point Cloates and Albany on the west.

Tangalooma is located on Moreton Island off Brisbane in Queensland. Moreton Island—one of the world's largest sand islands—lies on the northward migration route of the humpbacks coming from their Antarctic feeding grounds. It was an ideal location for humpbacking. In the early years of the fishery at Tangalooma, the whalers rarely had to venture out of sight of the island. The station was constructed in 1951, and was in full operation by the following year. The whalers had been imported from Norway, as had the catcher boats, *Kos I, II,* and *III.* In their first full season, the Tangalooma whalers killed 600 humpbacks, including a 51-footer that was, up to that time, the largest humpback ever taken in Australian waters. (In 1908, a 97-foot-long blue whale was killed at Twofold Bay and was long believed to be the larg-

est whale ever killed.) Business was so good that another station was opened at Byron Bay in 1954. For approximately a decade, the Queensland stations flourished, but after 1961, the whales became scarce, and business began to flounder.

Early on, the only "population studies" on the humpbacks were done by the whalers themselves, and they—perhaps like fishermen everywhere—were given to enthusiastic exaggeration. They carried on as if the supply was inexhaustible, and while they assumed that they were fishing on a population of some 60,000 whales, later studies proved that the population was never larger than 10,000. Furthermore, in the Antarctic, factory ships were harvesting humpbacks fervently. Because of the tremendous pressure on the offshore whale stocks by Soviet and Japanese factory ships, the whales never made it close enough to shore to allow the waiting Aussies to catch them.

The Australians had to travel much farther afield to find the whales, and began taking them on the whales' way south to the feeding grounds, when their blubber layer—and therefore their oil yield—was much reduced. Although they replaced the catcher boats with newer models and even took to searching the seas with spotter planes, the whales were simply not there, and Tangalooma and Byron Bay closed down in 1962.

Tangalooma is now a holiday resort, and the visitor is hard-pressed to find reminders of its whaling history. There are a couple of harpoons on display, but these mean no more to visitors than pictures of full-rigged ships under sail. The flensing deck was converted to a tennis court, and then a convention center. Silver gulls and shags perch on the half-submerged stumps of the landing ramp, and the last of the Tangalooma whalers have been sunk offshore in shallow water to provide a protected harbor for visiting yachtsmen.

In 1956, a station opened on Norfolk Island, a thousand miles east of the Australian mainland. (There had been whaling on Norfolk Island before: in 1894, whaling was the island's primary industry, and in 1949, a New Zealand company tried to establish a company there, but it failed after two seasons.) The Norfolk Island Whaling Company, a subsidiary of the Byron Bay Company in New South Wales, opened the station at Cascade Bay, and with two catchers, the *Norfolk Whaler* and the *Byrond I,* they hunted humpbacks and towed them to shore to

be hauled up a steep concrete ramp for processing. (As the Pitcairners discovered when they settled at Norfolk Island in 1856, two years after its penal colony had been closed down, there are no protected landing areas on the island.) The oil was transported to Sydney by an oil tanker and exchanged for furnace oil and petrol to be used on the island. It appeared as if the isolated island had found an industry; in a 1958 magazine article, Captain Brett Hilder wrote, "A prosperous era seems at last to have arrived for their idyllic Norfolk Island." Basing an industry on the exploitation of a finite supply of animals is always chancy, however, and although the whalers met their quotas for the first years of the Cascade Bay station, within a couple of years they had fished out the surrounding waters, and the station was shut down in 1962.

Like the right whales before them, the humpbacks could not possibly survive the concentrated attack on their numbers, and by 1962 the humpback fisheries had completely collapsed. Although it could never be proven, there was a strong suspicion that the Antarctic whalers were catching more humpbacks than they were reporting to the International

The whaleship *Tangalooma* tows a whale carcass to the station on Moreton Island (Queensland) for processing.

Whaling Commission, and of course, this period coincided with the operations of the *Olympic Challenger,* Aristotle Onassis's pirate whaler, which was bound by no restrictions whatever, killing any and all whales it encountered, and responsible to no one but Mammon.

The following year, when it was obvious that the species was economically extinct, all humpback whaling was forbidden south of the Equator, but again it was a case of too little, too late. The only whales left for Australian whalers were the sperm whales, and the last whaling station in the country was the one at Albany, Western Australia.

IN 1947, the Albany Whaling Company was formed by a group of local businessmen, who used old air force rescue boats as chasers. As the Norwegians had predicted, this venture failed, as did the next attempt to start up a whaling operation at Cheyne's Beach in 1949. The Norwegians returned in 1952, and with their advice and equipment, whaling resumed at Albany. They used proper catcher boats (the *Cheynes II, III* and *IV*), and until the 1963 ban on humpback whaling, they took an average of 86 whales a year. In 1955, however, they had begun to take sperm whales farther offshore, and as the humpback catch declined and eventually disappeared altogether, sperm whale catches rose accordingly. According to company records, a total of 14,695 sperm whales were taken during the period 1955 to 1978. During this same period, sperm whaling was coming under tighter scrutiny by the IWC, and various restrictions on size and gender were imposed. Despite the size of the sperm whale catches compared to the humpback numbers, the same era saw enormous catches in the North Pacific by Russian and Japanese whalers. For example, in the decade 1961–71, the total number of sperm whales killed outside the Antarctic (which figure included the Western Australian catch) was 211,650.

The handwriting was on the wall by this time, and the days of Australian whaling were numbered. Curiously, the calligraphers were the Australians themselves. In 1977, in response to what he called "a natural community disquiet about any activity that threatens the extinction of any animal species . . . particularly when it is directed against a species as special and intelligent as the whale," Prime Minister Malcolm Fraser ordered an inquiry to examine "whether Australian whaling should continue or cease [and] the consequences for international whaling of Australia's decision." Under the chairmanship of Sir Sidney Frost, this board of inquiry held public hearings at Albany, Perth, Sydney and Melbourne, and heard testimony from everyone from the Cheynes Beach Whaling Company and the Western Australian government to Project Jonah and Friends of the Earth. There was to have been a hearing at Albany to discuss the results of the inquiry, but as Sir Sidney wrote in the Preface to the 1978 report, ". . . this hearing was deprived of much of its substance by the announcement on the first day of the proceedings that the whaling company would cease operations in the near future." (The Cheynes Beach Whaling Company took its last sperm whale on November 20, 1978, and quietly closed down.) Notwithstanding the closure of the Cheynes Beach station, the board of inquiry concluded "that Australian whaling should end, and that, internationally, Australia should pursue a policy of opposition to whaling." And pursue it they did. From a past which included some of the bloodiest whaling traditions in history, the Australians lit out after the whaling nations with the shameless zeal that only the reformed can know. Along with the New Zealanders—whose whaling history, if anything, was even more sanguinary—the Aussies are now the acknowledged leaders in the battle to eliminate commercial whaling.

The whaling station at Albany fell into disrepair; its tanks deteriorated, and its wooden buildings began to crumble and rot. The great chains and winches that had clanked noisily as they hauled dead whales up the cement slipway silently rusted. Whales' bones discolored in the surf at Frenchman's Bay, and proud Albany, a center of Australian whaling for nearly two centuries, also began to deteriorate. Deprived of their noblest industry, the citizens of Albany searched for other ways to bolster their flagging economy. Whaling had been the ideal industry for this remote port; the humpbacks passed close to shore on their northward migrations, and not far to the south were the families of cachalots, following the instinctive urges that drove them from the poles to the Equator. With whaling gone, Albany turned to wheat and apples. A tuna fishery sprang up when the unemployed seafarers discovered that the great schools of bluefin tuna passed close to the shores of Albany on their way to their breeding grounds in the Great Australian Bight. But even this was to be denied to Albany; the government ruled that the tuna were immature when they were in Western Australian waters, and that they could only be caught by South Australian fishermen.

Was this town to vanish like the whales and whalers on whose blubber and blood it had been built? Not yet. Enter John Bell and the Jaycees Foundation of Australia. Bell had been a spotter pilot for the Cheynes Beach Whaling Company, and when everyone else had departed, he stayed on, trying to maintain the station by himself. It was an impossible job for one man, and he eventually got help from the Jaycees. They bought the whaling station, and with government and community support, renovated it, added new buildings and artifacts (including the dry-docked *Cheynes III,* the last of the whaleships), and turned it into "Whaleworld: The World's Largest Whaling Museum."

Time and change have caught up with Albany, and she moves toward the twenty-first century with the knowledge that the tradition of Australian whaling, so important to the development of the country, is preserved at Frenchman's Bay.

The ticket-of-leave men and the aboriginal oarsmen are gone; the Norwegians have left their descendants and their record-breaking carnage; and except for the preserved station at Albany, the shore stations and refitting facilities along the Australian coast have crumbled. At Cascade Bay on Norfolk Island there is only a rusting steam boiler perched above the remains of the slipway. But the right whales have begun to return. In a Japanese study, published in 1983, the scientists reported 75 right whales (and 30 sperm, 2 fin, 4 sei, and 2 minkes) during a three-week "sighting cruise" in an area of the Great Australian Bight, off Western and South Australia. This is probably more right whales than have been seen at any one time in Australian waters since Ben Boyd packed up and went to California.

New Zealand: 1890–1964

WHALING continued sporadically in New Zealand after the decline of the shore-whaling industry, mostly carried on by Maoris who took an occasional humpback in the Bay of Islands. They employed the old-fashioned methods, putting to sea in a longboat, harpooning the hapless whales, and trying them out on shore in the trypots that had been abandoned by their predecessors. By the 1870s, the customary fuel for lighting was petroleum-derived, and the market for whale products had fallen off sharply.

While the right whales had been hunted to the brink of extinction, there were still humpback whales spouting and swimming around the islands of New Zealand. Sperm whales were also hunted in this region at least until 1875, when Frank Bullen arrived

on the Solander Grounds in the fictional *Cachalot.* In Bullen's dubious book, he glorifies one of New Zealand's most colorful whaling captains, Paddy Gilroy, captain of the whaling barque *Chance.* (While Bullen does not identify his own ship, he is not reluctant to name Paddy Gilroy and *his* ship.) He describes Gilroy as "a queer little figure of a man—short, tubby, with scanty red hair and a brogue as thick as pea soup. Eccentric in most things, he was especially so in his dress, which he seemed to select on the principle of selecting the most unfitting things to wear."

Whatever had happened to the baleen whales had not happened to the New Zealand sperm whales. Bullen "realized how numerous those gigantic denizens of the sea really are. As far as the eye could reach, extending all round one-half of the horizon,

A rare photograph of New Zealand net whaling, showing a humpback swimming (from right to left) into the steel net in the Whangamumu Channel, Bay of Islands, around 1900.

the sea appeared to be alive with spouts—all sperm whales, all bulls of great size.'' The *Cachalot* took several sperm whales off New Zealand (including one that exploded "with a roar like the bursting of a dam," because it had decomposed when the crew was unable to process it during a storm), and from there headed home for New Bedford.

In 1890, an ex-New Bedford whaleman named H. F. "Bert" Cook began whaling at Whangamumu in the Bay of Islands. Because the Whangamumu Channel is only fifty yards wide at one point, Cook decided to string a net across the channel, snaring the humpbacks as they tried to swim past. At first the nets were made of rope, but when it was realized that no ropes could hold a struggling 50-ton whale, steel wire was used. The whales were not killed by the nets; in their struggles they became entangled, and the Maori whalemen harpooned them from waiting whaleboats. As practiced here, this was a fairly inefficient method of whaling, although three

hundred years earlier the Japanese had perfected net whaling to a remarkable degree. In his best year, Cook only managed to kill 19 whales. In 1910 the nets were abandoned in favor of a steam whale-catcher, *Hananui II,* and the annual bag rose to a high of 74 in 1927. As long as there were whales passing close to New Zealand's shores, there would be someone waiting to kill them.

The Norwegians, who had by this time started their prosperous Antarctic rorqual fishery, began to look elsewhere for more whales to kill. With their unfaltering sense of where the whales were, they fetched up on the shores of Australia and New Zealand. Humpbacks are usually considered poor whales to hunt, because their blubber is relatively thin and their baleen useless, but once the Norsemen went a-whaling, no cetacean was safe. In 1912, they sent the floating factory *Rakiura* with four catcher boats to the western South Pacific, and established the New Zealand Whaling Company. They killed humpbacks

The shore-whaling station at Whangaparaoa, Bay of Plenty. Workers strip the carcass of the whale (left) and boil down the blubber for oil.

in the Bay of Islands for a year or so, but there weren't enough whales to make a profit, so they covered their harpoon cannons and headed home.

At the narrow entrance to Tory Channel in Cook Strait—the same location that John Guard had chosen in which to become New Zealand's first whaler—Giuseppe Perano, an Italian immigrant, was to establish the whaling operation that was to be its last. Joe Perano, who is reputed to have improvised his whaling techniques, used fast motor launches to chase down the humpbacks, then shot them with a light harpoon gun that was mounted in the bows. This did not kill the whale but only stunned it so that the ingenious Peranos, *père et fils,* could insert a sharpened pipe, which was attached by a hose to a compressor, and pump air into the whale *while it was still alive,* to prevent it from sinking. (The Norwegians used the same system, but they humanely waited until the whale was dead before inflating it.) After the whale was inflated, the *coup de grace* was administered with an electrically detonated charge of gelignite on the end of a long lance.

During the heyday of Perano whaling, two of the sons of Joe Perano Senior were involved in a bitter fraternal rivalry. Joe Junior and Charlie often chased the same whales, shot harpoons at each other's boats, and rammed each other at sea. When Joe Senior died in 1951, another son, Gil, took over the operation, and ran it until 1964. The station at Te Awaiti (also known as Tarwithe and Tarwathie) was the longest-running whale show in New Zealand. The Perano family ran their station—with their barbarous methods—continuously from 1915 to 1964, although they had to change the object of their hunting when the humpback whale population collapsed in 1962. (This was not the fault of the Peranos, of course; the humpbacks that appeared off New Zealand's coasts wintered in the Antarctic, where they were harvested by the pelagic whalers. By 1964, when there were not enough humpbacks to support an industry, the International Whaling Commission declared them an endangered species.)

The primary product of the Peranos' enterprise was oil. Fluctuations in the market prompted them to investigate other uses for the whales as well, however, and they formed Whekenui By-Products Ltd. to experiment with animal feeds, leather and fertilizer. In 1950, they tried to market whale meat for human consumption. An enterprising fishmonger named V. A. Barnao, in Palmerston North, took space in the local newspapers, advertising

WHALE STEAK on sale today and tomorrow. The low-priced food of the future. Sold for the first time in the Southern Hemisphere. Direct from our own whalers— J.A. PERANO, LTD., TORY CHANNEL, PICTON. . . .

Try it, taste it. It's delicious. It's fresh. Tender, appetising, and economical. It has no fat, no bone, and therefore, no waste. Cook it like ordinary meat. A recipe will be supplied with every purchase. Take home a pound on Thursday. We guarantee that you will be back for more.

It was estimated that a good-sized humpback yielded more than 7 tons of whale steaks. The meat was cut into chunks and packed for shipment to Palmerston North to be sold to housewives. Even after the war's deprivations, New Zealand had a plentiful supply of beef and lamb, however, and whale meat did not catch on. The Peranos then tried to can it for sale abroad, and during the first year, they exported some four hundred tons of canned meat to England. Haste in preparing the next lot produced a disaster that spelled the immediate end of the whale-meat-canning industry: half the cans exploded on the way to England.

When the supply of humpbacks had run low, the Peranos decided to go into the sperm whaling business. They purchased the *Orca,* a 150-ton whale-catcher, and off they went. The sperm whales were too far offshore for the Peranos to tow them back to the station at Tory Channel, and after two years, the station closed down. It was the last gasp of whaling in New Zealand, an industry that had almost single-handedly been responsible for the founding of the country. For over a century and a half, whales had

Perano whalers chasing a humpback in Cook Strait, New Zealand. The chase boat *Narwhal* is curiously named, since the narwhal is only found in the Arctic.

been killed in New Zealand waters. Had it not been for the whales, the first settlers would not have come, and had it not been for the whalers, the story of the settlement of New Zealand would have been very different indeed.

Since the cessation of whaling in New Zealand, the Kiwis have become zealots on the subject of whale conservation. They have been in the forefront of the international battle to save the whales, at international forums such as the meetings of the International Whaling Commission, and on the numerous beaches of their own islands. Because whales and dolphins have demonstrated an ageless propensity to strand on the shores of New Zealand, a particularly fervent group dedicated to saving individual whales has also appeared. (One government study lists 798 strandings involving a total of 6,873 whales from 1840 to the present.) The New Zealand Department of Conservation has published a comprehensive book called "Marine Mammal Rescue," which details the mammals, methods and problems in saving whales, dolphins and seals.

Frank Robson, a dolphin-trainer at Marineland of Napier, has traveled the length and breadth of the two islands, trying (unsuccessfully for the most part) to rehabilitate beached cetaceans. In 1976 Robson wrote *Thinking Dolphins, Talking Whales*—a book primarily about his experiences as a trainer—and in 1984 he wrote *Strandings: Ways to Save Whales, a Humane Conservationist's Guide*. This is not the place to discuss the efficacy of returning stranded whales to the water, but it is a measure of the passion with which the inhabitants of New Zealand—the country that invented what is arguably the most insensitive method of whale-killing in the gory history of the industry—now approach whales. The country that was founded by whalers has completely renounced this heritage. With the zeal and fervor of reformed sinners, they have been in the forefront of the just and virtuous cause of whale conservation.

Canada: 1840–1950

NEW ENGLAND WHALERS of the eighteenth century found themselves chasing whales in Canadian waters long before there was a Canada. (The Union of Upper and Lower Canada was formed in 1839, and the British North America Act of 1867 established the Dominion of Canada.) In 1719, the Hudson's Bay Company outfitted a frigate and a sloop to explore the bay for whales, but the crews perished of scurvy on Marble Island, and the idea was abandoned. By 1740, whalers out of New England ports were chasing right whales and humpbacks around Newfoundland, and sperm whales offshore. The Gulf of St. Lawrence was also a magnet for whales and whalers; humpbacks and white whales were found in great profusion in the river's wide mouth.

Right whales were always killed when they were available; pound for pound, they yielded more oil and bone than any other species except the bowhead, and the whalers didn't have to suffer the hardships of the Arctic to hunt them. Eighteenth-century Massachusetts whalers invaded the Gulf of St. Lawrence and the Strait of Belle Isle in substantial numbers; Alexander Starbuck lists eight Cape Cod whalers sailing for that area in 1789. Nantucket whalers, who did things just a little differently, preferred the Grand Banks of Newfoundland, and several ships showed up in the Bay of Fundy between 1797 and 1820.

In 1840, the whalers had returned to Newfoundland, this time at the behest of the Newfoundland government, which offered an inducement of $200 to each of the first three vessels that landed ten tons of whale oil or fifteen tons of blubber. Once again, the whales of Newfoundland were under attack. Entrepreneurs in New Brunswick joined the festivities, and sent six of their own ships out of ports like Campobello, St. Stephen, and St. Andrews. Before the adoption of the grenade harpoon, the whalers could only kill the slow-swimming rights and humpbacks, but when they obtained the necessary artillery, they probably added fin whales to their inventory.

During the middle of the nineteenth century, American whalers found that there were plentiful bowheads in northern Hudson Bay, but the geography of that remote region precluded a concentrated fishery there. In order to be able to spend enough time on the whaling grounds, the whalers had to overwinter there, which, if they survived, would give them two whaling seasons with only one round trip. In order to protect themselves and their vessels from the rigors of an Arctic winter, the whalers would cut a berth in the ice, face the ship into the prevailing northerly winds, and cover the ship with a structure of boards, canvas and snow. By 1862, five New Bedford captains had selected Hudson Bay for their grounds, but not all of them spent the winter there. American whaling continued sporadically in Hudson Bay through the latter decades of the century, but was eventually supplanted by the steam whalers out of Scotland and northern England.

Wherever there were whales for the taking in the later nineteenth century, there were Norwegians taking them. Thanks to Svend Foyn, the patron saint of modern whaling, they had the technology, and they had an almost compulsive desire to employ their new-fangled armaments. They arrived in Newfoundland in 1893, and set up a whaling station at Snook's Arm in Notre Dame Bay. This enterprise was so successful that they soon opened another station, and by 1904 there were thirteen whaling stations in Newfoundland. The Newfoundland government became alarmed at the pace with which the Norwegians were killing off their whales, so in 1902 they passed a law that stations had to be a minimum of fifty miles apart. The Newfoundlanders also charged the Norwegians a license fee of $1,500 for each factory, which promptly put the Norwegians out of business. The Newfoundlanders filled the breach, and almost immediately found themselves beset by what Tønnessen and Johnsen described as "a whaling fever, a crazy wave of speculation unequalled in any area in the

history of whaling." Stations were set up all around Newfoundland; by 1904 there were fourteen there and thirteen on the coast of Labrador. Farley Mowat lived in Burgeo, Newfoundland, and while there, he interviewed an old man named "Uncle" Art Boggs, who remembered seeing the Norwegian whaling operation at Hermitage Bay:

Back about 1900 Norway fellows built a blubber factory eastward of Cape La Hume. They called it Balaena and, me son, it were some dirty place! They had two or three little steamers with harpoon guns, and they was never idle. Most days each of 'em would tow in a couple of sulphur-bottoms or finners and the shoremen would cut 'em up some quick. No trouble to smell that place ten miles away.

Too many whalers, not enough whales. The Newfoundland fishery crashed, and by 1905 stations were being abandoned and the catcher boats sold off. Because he held various patents on the production of guano and cattle feed from the carcasses of whales, Dr. Ludwig Rismüller managed to survive the collapse of the Newfoundland whaling industry. J. G. Millais, in his 1907 book about *Newfoundland and Its Untrodden Ways,* said of Rismüller that "he has done more for whaling and whale products than any other person." (Rismüller—and his inventions—would eventually find their way across Canada, and his processes would play an equally important role in the whaling of the Pacific Coast.) In 1905, whaling was considered an heroic endeavor; man against beast. In Millais' book, we get a painfully vivid picture of blue whaling out of the station at Burin Harbour:

At this moment [the whale has been shot] all eyes were riveted on a great commotion in the sea about 500 yards away. The next instant the whale appeared, rolling and fighting on the surface. It lashed the sea into white spume with its flippers and raised its head frequently right out of the water, opening its immense jaws. The leviathan of the deep was fighting hard with death, but the harpoon had penetrated its vitals, and its struggles only lasted about two minutes. Soon it grew weaker and weaker, until, casting forth a thin spout of red blood, it threw up its tail and sank in a mighty swirl.

Despite the bloody glory of the hunt, Newfoundland whaling was foundering. The price of oil was falling, and the stations were recording smaller and smaller catches. By 1914, the seven remaining companies killed 161 whales among them. The whalers headed up to the Gulf of St. Lawrence, where sealers had reported great numbers of whales. In 1911, the Norwegian-Canadian Whaling Company was set up on Sept-Îles, Quebec, but the station only functioned for a year. The Norwegians were back, and the Newfoundlanders were unhappy about it, fearing that the terribly efficient whalemen of Sandefjord would kill off all their whales. The Norwegians overcame the protests of their putative hosts, and by 1918 they had opened stations at Harbour Grace, Hawke's Harbour, and Beaverton. The whales taken included blues, fins, seis, humpbacks and an occasional sperm whale. In later years, no mention is made of the right whale, because it had been extirpated before the nineteenth century. There was also a fishery based on the unfortunate inclination of the gregarious pilot whales to allow themselves to be herded into shallow water, where they could be killed in large numbers.

ON THE CANADIAN west coast, the first whalers were the Indians of Vancouver Island. Their techniques spread south to the Olympic Peninsula, and north all the way to the Bering Sea. Right whales were taken in the Gulf of Alaska, the area known to nineteenth-century whalers as "the Northwest Coast," or simply "the Northwest." (A great mystery in the days when there was right whaling in the eastern North Pacific was the disappearance of the whales when they were not on their breeding grounds. In 1874, Charles Scammon wrote, "It has ever been a matter of mysterious conjecture with the most philosophical whalemen, where the northern Right Whales go to bring forth their young, and whither they migrate during the winter months." The mystery may never be solved, since there are hardly any right whales left in that area.) A French whaler, the *Gange,* discovered the whales off the Gulf of Alaska in 1835, and from that year onward, whalers picked off right whales wherever they encountered them. By 1849, when the right whale supply was running low, the whalers were en route to the rich grounds of the Bering Sea to harvest the last remaining stock of bowheads, and were also preoccupied with hunting the gray whales that migrated up and down the coast.

Prior to the publication of his *Whale Hunting with Gun and Camera* in 1916, Roy Chapman Andrews had visited whaling stations all around the world, from Korea to Alaska. He was fortunate to have seen the

The carcasses of four humpbacks await processing at the station at Kyuquot, Vancouver Island.

whales alive, and science benefited from his astute observations. Even in the days preceding the war, Andrews sensed that the industry was on a course toward disaster, and he wrote, "It is deeply to be regretted that the wholesale slaughter of the whales will inevitably result in their early commercial extinction, but meanwhile science is profiting by the golden opportunities given for the study of these strange and interesting animals."

In 1908, Andrews visited the stations at Sechart and Kyuquot on Vancouver Island. He was taken out on one of the catcher boats ("my first trip on a steam whaler"), where he eagerly watched and photographed the killing of a humpback, which was then towed back to the station:

The body was then hauled to the "carcass platform" at right angles to, and somewhat above the "flensing slip," the flesh was torn from the bones in two or three great masses by the aid of the winch, and the skeleton disarticulated. After the bones had been split and the flesh cut into chunks two or three feet square, they were boiled separately in great open vats which bordered the carcass platform on both sides. When the oil had been extracted, the bones were crushed by machinery making bone meal to be used as a fertilizer, and the flesh, artificially dried and sifted, was converted into a very fine guano. Even the blood, of which there were several tons, was carefully drained from the slip into a large tank, and boiled and dried for fertilizer. Finally, the water in which the blubber had been tried out was converted into glue.

By 1910, the Pacific Whaling Company had expanded substantially, and although there was still a rule stipulating one steamer per station, the company had added enough stations that they now operated ten catchers. Five of them were built in Norway in 1910, and after a dispute between the two principal owners of the company as to whether to name them after rivers in Scotland or rivers in Germany, an arbitrator suggested that they be named after colors, and the *Green, Black, White, Brown* and *Blue* arrived in Victoria in the spring of 1911. The company—now restructured as the Canadian North Pacific Fisheries—built the most ambitious whaling station in Canada, at Rose Harbour in the Queen Charlotte Islands. By the end of the summer of 1911, the ships of the CNPF had accounted for 1,806 whales, most of which were humpbacks. As with

right whales, humpbacks come close to shore to breed and deliver their calves, so the great majority of the whales killed were cows and calves. Commenting on this imbalance, a writer in a 1911 edition of *British Columbia Magazine* wrote that "the war on the whale has been truly turned into a massacre in the interests of commerce."

When the Norwegians learned that Canadian whaling was so successful that sometimes the hunting had to be suspended to allow for the processing of carcasses, they sent scouts to North America to investigate. They found the waters of Alaska far more promising than those of British Columbia, and accordingly, they initiated the "United States Whaling Company"—backed entirely by Norwegian capital. With the factory ship *Sommerstad* and three swift chasers (*Star I, II* and *III*), the Norwegians quickly established themselves as the dominant whalers in Alaskan waters. They built a station at Port Armstrong in 1911, and another at Akutan in the Aleutians in 1912. Until the discovery of large numbers of blue and fin whales, the enterprise was not particularly successful, but as with many other whaling ventures, the gigantic rorquals placed the operation in the black. The Tyee Company's only asset, the whaler *Sorensen,* was rammed by a harpooned blue whale and sunk, and since the company was unable to refinance, it folded. The Norwegians left Alaska to the Americans after that, since the problems of administering a station in the Aleutians—just about halfway around the world from Norway—proved to be insurmountable, even for the intrepid Norwegians.

Canadian whaling, like Yankee whaling of the previous century, was a curiously polyglot enterprise. Where the crews of the square-rigged whalers had been New England farmhands, Cape Verde Islanders, escaped slaves, Indians, Eskimos and Kanakas, the Canadian stations—such as the one at Rose Harbour—sported deckhands that were Chinese, Japanese, Native Indians and Norwegians. (The chaser boats, however, were crewed exclusively by Norwegians and Newfoundlanders, who had the necessary experience.) The imminent war slowed down international whaling in Canadian waters, since trade restrictions made it difficult for the whalers to sell their oil. When the war actually came, however, the rising price of whale oil kept the companies afloat until the

A right whale on the platform at the whaling station at Akutan in the Pribilof Islands.

Armistice, after which its use in margarine became widespread. (There was also a movement around this time to market whale meat as "sea beef," partly as a response to the deprivations brought about by the war, but as beef and pork again became available, whale meat was unsalable.) A lack of whales in the waters of British Columbia caused the owners of the station at Sechart to dismantle it in 1917, and whaling in the Canadian Pacific tapered off. Rose Harbour was closed down, as was Akutan, the latter turned into a strategic base for the Americans after Pearl Harbor. Pike (1954) estimated that some 7,000 humpbacks were killed in British Columbia waters between 1919 and 1929.

A group that called itself the Western Whaling Company contracted to buy and revive the Rose Harbour station in 1947, but when the Royal Canadian Air Force seaplane base at Coal Harbour be-

came available, they altered their venue accordingly. The Coal Harbour station was opened in 1948, and operated for twenty years, taking primarily fin whales. The hangars proved to be ideal for the processing of whale carcasses; there were flensing decks between the two hangars, and inside was housed the "reduction equipment," which reduced the carcass to products. For the most part, the products consisted of meat meal, but in 1953, an attempt was made to utilize fresh meat for animal food. It was cleaned and ground, packaged in fifty-pound paper bags, and stored for shipment. Since Canadians, like the British and the Americans, could not be persuaded to like whale meat, most of the meat went into the manufacture of pet food. After the owners made their money and the workers were paid, dogs and cats were the principal beneficiaries of the whaling industry.

Interlude: The White Whale

THE SUBTITLE of *Moby-Dick* is not, as many people believe, "The White Whale," but simply "The Whale." Melville's vindictive monster is not really white, but described as having "a peculiar snow-white wrinkled forehead and a high pyramidical white hump ... the rest of his body was so streaked and spotted and marbled with the same shrouded hue that, in the end, he had gained the distinctive appellation of the White Whale." In his chapter called "The Whiteness of the Whale," Melville writes that while whiteness sometimes "refiningly enhances beauty, as if imparting some special virtue of its own," he asks if it is "not so much a color as the visible absence of color, and at the same time the concrete of all colors; is it for these reasons that there is such a dumb blankness, full of meaning,

Beluga (*Delphinapterus leucas*)

During a visit to the St. Lawrence River in 1909, Roy Chapman Andrews participated in a beluga hunt, where the animals were shot by hunters from canoes.

in a wide landscape of snows—a colorless, all-color of atheism from which we shrink?" Although Ahab knows that he is not all white, he calls out to Captain Boomer of the *Samuel Enderby,* "Hast seen the White Whale?" Moby Dick is a malicious killer, a remover of legs and arms, a destroyer of ships and men, the quintessence of evil. Unlike its fictional cousin, the real white whale is a small, smiling, puddinglike creature, so docile and inoffensive that it has become a regular inhabitant of oceanarium exhibits.

On his visit to various whaling sites in Canada in 1908, Roy Chapman Andrews participated in a hunt for the white whale, or beluga, sometimes spelled "belukha."* This small whale belongs to the order *Monodontidae* ("one tooth"), along with the only other member of the order, the narwhal. Although belugas and narwhals occur elsewhere—Greenland and the Soviet Arctic for instance—they are most closely associated with Canada. Like the bowhead, these ani-

*Both words are derived from the Russian *belii,* which means "white." Some cetologists prefer "belukha" in order to differentiate the whale from the sturgeon from which the finest caviar is obtained.

mals are creatures of the Arctic ice, and except for strays like the beluga that was found off New Jersey in 1978, they restrict themselves to the high northern latitudes. The narwhal and the beluga are fairly small, and rarely exceed 16 feet in length. (This figure does not take into account the tusk of the male narwhal, which may increase the overall length of the animal by 7 feet.)

Both of these small Arctic whales have been hunted by Canadian Eskimos for centuries. They ate the meat, used the oil for cooking and lighting, and made thread from the long sinews of the back. Of all the whales, only the beluga has a thick skin that can be successfully tanned, and of all the cetaceans not officially classified as dolphins, the beluga was the first one to be maintained in captivity. Belugas are now commonly displayed in aquariums, and *Delphinapterus* is the first species of *whale* ever to give birth in captivity.

Back in 1909, however, the beluga was just another in the long list of whales that man was methodically killing off. Andrews journeyed up to the village of Tadoussac, where the Saguenay flows into the St. Lawrence River, in order to join a "porpoise hunter" in pursuit of the *marsouin blanc.* From a canoe, the hunters stalked a herd of belugas, and when they were within range, they began firing at them with shotguns. After shooting a whale, the hunters harpooned it so that it would not sink out of sight, and when it had expired, they dragged the carcass onto the beach: "We beached [the canoe] in a sandy cove where the gray rock wall rose in a jagged mass, making a perfect background for the white body, its purity intensified by the bright red streaks of blood which dripped from the bullet holes." The whale was skinned, and the hide, worth about seven dollars, was brought back along with the oil and the bones.

"Porpoise leather" is extremely durable and flexible. Because adult belugas—like all whales—have no hair or epidermal glands, their skin has no pores, and therefore the leather has no grain. Around the middle of the nineteenth century, a Monsieur C. Têtu of Rivière Ouelle, Quebec, patented a new process for tanning it, and the price soared from $40 per skin to $150. Because the animal was so much larger than its bovine counterparts, many more items could be fabricated from a single skin. (A single piece sixty feet long and eighteen inches wide could be cut from one hide.) Porpoise leather was used for the manufacture of machinery belts, boots, mail-bags, and especially boot-laces. Most of the hides were salted and shipped across the Atlantic to Dundee or Glasgow, where they were tanned. (The skin of the narwhal

was also made into leather, and was particularly desirable in France, where it was fashioned into gloves.) The oil from these chubby little whales was also valuable for commerce. A large specimen could yield 80–100 gallons of fine oil, which was used primarily for lubrication and soap-making. The head contained a particularly fine oil which was sold as "porpoise-jaw oil," a lubricant for watches and other delicate machinery. (A similar product was obtained from bottle-nosed dolphins and pilot whales.) White-whale oil burned with a particularly bright and consistent flame, so it was desirable for lighthouses.

Belugas have been hunted for centuries by the Canadian Eskimos, but the arrival of the Europeans signaled an increase in hunting pressure, and of course a corresponding drop in the white whale populations throughout Canada. Because they are almost obsessively gregarious animals, belugas are susceptible to drive fisheries, where they are herded into shallow water, and then killed. Between 1868 and 1911, more than 20,000 belugas were killed by Scottish and American whalers in the Lancaster Sound and Davis Strait regions.

The Inuit of the North Slope of Alaska also hunt the beluga, which they know as *sissuak.* During the spring migration the little whales pass hunting villages such as Wainwright, where they are hunted from kayaks or umiaks, but instead of harpoons the modern Eskimos use rifles. The thin blubber layer of the beluga, so eagerly eaten as *muktuk,* is not suf-

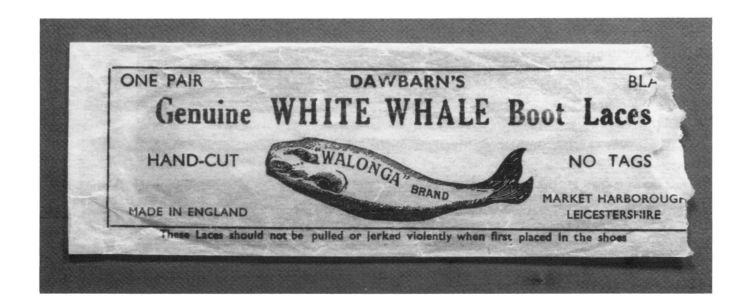

ficient to keep the animal afloat when it is dead, so before it sinks, the hunters have to snag it with a hook. When large numbers of small cetaceans become trapped in a closing lead, the Greenland Inuit call it a *savssat,* and the Alaskan Eskimos refer to the same event as *imay guraat.* Belugas occasionally feed on salmon, and they will chase them upriver, an event that renders them particularly susceptible to entrapment by Eskimo hunters. In *Hunters of the Northern Ice,* Richard Nelson described a *sissuak* hunt that took place "about twenty years ago" (the book was published in 1969) in the Kuk River off Wainwright where some 300 belugas were killed when the Eskimos trapped them in the river and kept them from escaping by buzzing across the outlet of the river in motorboats.

On one celebrated occasion, a *savssat* resulted in a rescue, not a slaughter. It was December 1984, and a great many *belukhas* (reports varied from 1,000 to 3,000) found themselves trapped for two months in the closing ice of Senyavin Strait, on the southern tip of the Chukchi Peninsula in the Bering Sea. They had been chasing fish when an east wind kicked up and blocked their escape route with a twelve-foot-thick wall of packed ice. Their plight was reported to Moscow, and while the residents of the nearby village of Yandrakinot tried unsuccessfully to feed the trapped whales with fish, Soviet military helicopters hovered overhead to survey the scene. The open sea was too far away for the belugas to negotiate the distance under the ice with a single breath. The icebreaker *Moskva* was summoned, and it plowed a channel through the ice which should have freed the whales, but they refused to enter the new channel. *Isvestia* (quoted in the *New York Times*) reported that the whales whistled, squealed and snorted, but they refused to come out. Then one Soviet observer recalled that dolphins liked music, so "music began to pour from the top deck: popular, martial, classical. The classical proved to be most to the taste of the belugas. The herd slowly began to follow the ship." As the icy air rang with Tchaikovsky and Prokofiev, the whales slowly moved toward freedom.* By late

February, the whales were free. Three years later, Soviet icebreakers (without the music) would again come to the rescue of trapped whales, but they would be Alaskan whales, not Siberian.

The range of the *marsouin blanc* is enormous. Five discrete stocks are recognized, and not one has been safe from the predation of man, despite the remoteness of some of these habitats. On the northern shore of western Canada, the Mackenzie River debouches into the Beaufort Sea, and this delta is the summer residence of the stock of some 7,000 belugas that winter in the Bering Sea. Off the coast of western Greenland are a large number of belugas that summer in Lancaster Sound, but the stock to the south, the so-called Cumberland Sound Stock, has been drastically depleted by hunting. The Davis Strait stock has been reduced from an initial estimated population of more than 5,000 to a struggling 600. Hudson Strait is the winter range of no fewer than three separate stocks of belugas, which summer at different locations in Hudson Bay.

Jacques Cartier reported seeing white whales in 1535, as he sailed up the St. Lawrence, and by the beginning of the seventeenth century, French colonists were killing them on both shores of that wide river. The whales were trapped in weirs, pursued in boats, stabbed with lances, and shot with shotguns, because fishermen believed that they were a threat to their industry. In the 1930s, the Department of Fisheries of Quebec paid a $15 bounty for each set of beluga tail flukes. Between 1932 and 1938, 2,233 bounties were paid. It would not be until 1944 that Vladim Vladykov would publish the results of his studies, which would show that the belugas were not interested in the cod, salmon and herring that made up the bulk of the commercial fish stocks, and fed primarily on squid, capelin and sand lance, species that do not appeal to people. During the time when belugas were taken for oil, leather and meat, and hunted to eliminate competition with the fishermen, the population of white whales in the St. Lawrence dropped from 5,000 to 500.

THE BELUGA is generally considered to be the first cetacean maintained in captivity. The first whale or dolphin exhibited in North America was probably a stranded bottlenose dolphin (it may also have been a harbor porpoise; the nomenclature then—as it is

*We don't really know which music was played for the belugas, but in an essay in *Outside* magazine, David Quammen wrote, "I loved the image of [Beethoven's] symphonic 'Ode to Joy' booming out over the Bering Sea while a thousand belugas each came through the channel, spouted once to the ship in thanks, and then arched and dove, disappearing."

now—was imprecise), which was displayed briefly at the Aquarial Gardens in Boston in 1861. The attraction of marine mammals was so great, however, that in that year and the next, six belugas were captured in the St. Lawrence River in Canada and shipped to New York in boxes lined with seaweed. One of the expeditions to the St. Lawrence was led by none other than P. T. Barnum, not only to collect the whales but also to collect the publicity.*

His first whales were transported to New York in a railway car and exhibited in a brick and cement tank in the basement of the museum, located in downtown Manhattan at Ann Street and Broadway. "I did not know how to feed and take care of the monsters," he wrote, "and moreover, they were in fresh water, and this, with the bad air of the basement, may have hastened their death, which occurred a few days after their arrival, but not before thousands of people had seen them." Not surprisingly, the white whales were an outstandingly successful exhibit, and Barnum had to have more:

Of this whole enterprise, I confess I was very proud that I had originated it and brought it to such a successful conclusion. It was a very great sensation, and it added thousands of dollars to my treasury. The whales, however, soon died—their sudden and immense popularity was too much for them—and I then despatched agents to the coast of Labrador, and not many weeks thereafter I had two more live whales disporting themselves in my monster aquarium.

His newest whales were exhibited on the second floor of the American Museum in a tank with plate-glass sides and saltwater pumped in from New York Bay. Now that he had fresh saltwater

*In his autobiography, Barnum explained the techniques he used to publicize his newest exhibits:

Elated as I was at the result of this novel enterprise, I had no idea of hiding my light under a bushel, and I immediately wrote a full account of the expedition, its intention, and its success, for publication in the Quebec and Montreal newspapers. I also prepared a large number of brief notices which I left at every station on the line, instructing telegraph operators to "take off" all "whaling messages" that passed over the wires to New York, and to inform their fellow townsmen at what hour the whales would pass through each place. The results of these arrangements may be imagined; at every station crowds of people came to the cars to see the whales which were travelling by land to Barnum's Museum, and those who did not see the monsters with their own eyes, at least saw some one who had seen them, and I thus secured a tremendous advertisement, seven hundred miles long, for the American Museum.

A diver feeds the belugas at the New York Aquarium at Coney Island. These friendly, docile, and loquacious animals are among the most popular of all aquarium exhibits.

in his aquarium ("which," he tells us, "I was the first to introduce into the country"), Barnum dispatched a fishing smack to Bermuda to collect tropical fish of "brilliant colors and unique forms." To round out his aquatic exhibits, Barnum bought the Aquarial Gardens in Boston, and brought the entire collection—which included several brook trout of four pounds or more—to New York. In his (1878) report on the beluga, Henry Lee wrote that there were "two swimming in the great tank at Mr. Barnum's Museum, New York, when that was burned in 1865."

In 1877, a single animal was captured in Labrador by a fisherman named Zach Coup, and in a seaweed-lined wooden box, shipped to Montreal, then to New York by train, where it was kept in the aquarium reservoir at Coney Island. The Labrador–Montreal–New York legs of the journey took fourteen days. On September 15, 1877, the crated creature was shipped across the Atlantic for exhibit at the Royal Aquarium at Westminster. When the whale arrived at Southampton eleven days later, it was transferred to London in a railroad car. The entire trip took twenty-five days.

The following year, another four specimens made the journey to England in seaweed-filled boxes, but only three survived the crossing. One was destined for the Pomona Gardens, Manchester; the second for Blackpool; and the third for Westminster. Based on these successes, the New York Aquarium (then located at the southern tip of Manhattan at the Battery) imported two more belugas that had been captured in Rivière-du-Loup on the St. Lawrence. As recorded in the Aquarium's guide for 1897, the whales were

placed in the large pool on the morning of June 5, 1897. The larger of them, a female, which was of a cream color and about ten feet in length, was injured in transportation and lived only five days. The smaller one, which lived until July 25, 1897, a male, was of a light lead color, and measured nine feet in length, this whale was moulting when it was received at the Aquarium, soon after it was placed in the pool large fragments of skin were found in the water.

The second whale died of strangulation, having choked on an eel that was evidently too large for it to swallow.

In later years, collecting and exhibiting the little white whales would become a small industry. In 1961, a team from the New York Aquarium, led by Dr. Carleton Ray, traveled to the Kvichak River in Alaska to collect belugas, which then became the first ones successfully exhibited at any aquarium. (One of these whales, named Alex, lived for over twenty years in captivity, first at the New York Aquarium at Coney Island, and then at the Mystic Marinelife Aquarium in Connecticut.) A year after the capture of Alex, another male was brought to Coney Island, and named Blanchon. Before he died in 1982, Blanchon was to sire two calves, the first ever conceived and born in captivity.

To date, several beluga calves have been born in captivity, but none has survived. In 1972, a calf was born to Blanchon and Frances, a nine-year-old female that had been captured in 1967 on the western shore of Hudson Bay. At the New York Aquarium, the calf swam headlong into a wall of the tank within minutes of its birth, and died immediately. The most celebrated of all beluga births took place at the Vancouver Aquarium on July 13, 1977. A female in an unsuspected state of pregnancy was collected on June 29 from the Churchill River in Manitoba, and delivered a calf two weeks later. (The gestation period of a beluga is fourteen months.) The calf—named *Tuaq,* an Eskimo word that means "the only one"—lived for sixteen weeks before succumbing to a massive bacterial infection. In 1981, another calf was born at Coney Island, but it never nursed, and died within weeks.

It is easy to see why the beluga is such a popular exhibit in aquariums. Here one of the white whales confronts a visitor through the glass at the New York Aquarium at Coney Island.

In July 1984, the New York Aquarium and Mystic Marinelife Aquarium in Connecticut mounted an expedition to collect belugas in Churchill, Manitoba. Canadian authorities require that Eskimos be utilized in this "roundup," primarily because the natives have a traditional understanding of beluga behavior. (In the past, the majority of beluga meat was used to feed sled dogs, which have been rendered obsolete by the snowmobile. "It is the snowmobile that has saved more belugas than anything else," said one of the natives. "You can't burn blubber in a gas tank.") The whales were rounded up with motorboats, and when the individuals were selected—they wanted healthy juveniles, not too young and not too old—a "jumper" leapt into the water and lassoed them. The captive whales were then placed in a holding tank, where they were examined by a veterinarian to make sure that they were healthy enough for a ride in a chartered 737. The expedition collected five whales, three of which were installed at Coney Island and two sent to Mystic. Because of their startling white color, their smooth, plump appearance, their frequent vocalizations—they are among the noisiest cetaceans—and of course, the fact that they are *whales,* belugas are among the most popular of all aquarium exhibits. Still, the success rate of breeding them in captivity remains at zero. In 1988, a female died at Sea World in San Diego while giving birth.

Despite the occasional captures, dead whales are more valuable to the Canadians of the Northwest Territories than live ones, and because the "natives" can still take as many whales as they want, the beluga fisheries continue on a small, subsistence scale. In 1949, the Inuit, Cree and Métis aboriginals purchased licenses to hunt belugas; the whales were turned into mincemeat and shipped to the Prairie Provinces to be fed to minks. In the 1960s, the Manitoba government developed a "sport fishery" for belugas, where big-game hunters could shoot these helpless animals from a boat, but public outrage at "shooting-fish-in-a-barrel" soon closed down this bizarre enterprise.

Because commercial hunting in northern Canada has ended and the native hunt is small, the threats to belugas consist largely of technological intrusions into their habitat. Power stations heat up the water, and the rivers in which they feed are being dammed. Oil companies are erecting artificial islands in the Mackenzie River delta, one of the calving grounds of the white whales. A gas pipeline has been proposed for Lancaster Sound. In the St. Lawrence, whale carcasses have been examined and the tissues found to have abnormally high mercury and DDT residues. With the exception of the St. Lawrence stock, however, beluga populations appear to be on the increase. Despite their early encouragement of the white whale hunt, and their enigmatic record in the International Whaling Commission, Canadians are now sensitive to the preservation of their wildlife, and the beluga continues to flourish in its northern habitat. The white whales, long symbolic of the Canadians' symbiotic interaction with nature, may prove that it is possible for men and whales to co-exist peacefully.

TEN

ANTARCTIC FORTUNES

Terra Australis Incognita

ANTARCTICA is arguably the most remote region of the planet. It is certainly farther from "civilization" than any other major part of the world. The closest land mass to the Antarctic continent is South America, but only the tip, the barren cape known as the Horn, approaches Antarctica. The gap between them is the most formidable passage in the history of sailing. It is therefore not a little surprising to discover that the greatest battles between the whaling nations—not to mention the greatest war against an animal ever waged by mankind—took place in this frozen, uninhabited wasteland at the bottom of the world.

Even the finding of the Antarctic was singular. Most other discoveries came about because explorers bumped into land masses or islands the existence of which they might have suspected. In the case of *Terra Australis,* however, explorers knew it was there—it had to be, according to the prevailing geographical knowledge, to balance the land masses of the Northern Hemisphere—so they bravely went searching for it, only to find that it wasn't where or what they thought it was.

There are two continents with parts of their land masses in the Southern Hemisphere, Africa and South America, and one that exists entirely south of the Equator, Australia. Since there is so much land in the Northern Hemisphere, early geographers assumed that the spherical Earth had to be balanced by a corresponding weight of land in the south, to keep it from wobbling uncontrollably. Rounding the southernmost extensions of South America and Africa, the early explorers discovered only that these continents were not attached to the hypothetical southern land mass. In 1488 the Portuguese navigator Bartolomeu Dias rounded the bottom of Africa, and a decade later he was followed by Vasco da Gama. When Ferdinand Magellan sailed from the South Atlantic through the straits that now bear his name and into the Pacific in 1520, he proved that South America was not attached at its southern extremity to anything else. Later, the British ship *Desire,* under the command of John Davis, came upon the Falkland Islands, and in 1599, the Dutchman Dirk Gerritsz probably spotted the South Shetlands.

In the first decade of the seventeenth century, the Dutch explorer Willem Jansz, sailing from the East Indies, landed on the west coast of the Cape York

The Antarctic continent and its surrounding features. The island groups identified are those mentioned in the text, and the Roman numerals I–VI refer to the IWC (International Whaling Commission) statistical whaling areas, defined on their northern boundaries by 40°S.

Peninsula, and in 1642, Abel Tasman landed on the island that he named Van Diemen's Land. In 1739, the French navigator Bouvet de Lozier thought he had discovered *Terres Inconnues,* but in fact he had come upon the most isolated island on earth: the island that would later be known as Bouvetøya is more than a thousand miles away from any other land. Thirty years later, Yves-Joseph de Kerguelen-Trémarec was also searching for the southern Eden when he came upon a group of lonely islands in the southern Indian Ocean. He was unable to land because of fog, but he returned to France claiming that he had discovered a new continent, which he grandly proclaimed *La France Australe,* or "South France." His monumental error resulted in his court martial, but the islands he found ensured his immortality, since they were named for him.

Australia would not be circumnavigated until 1802, by Matthew Flinders, but the redoubtable James Cook is believed to have been the first navigator to cross the Antarctic Circle, as he took the H.M.S. *Resolution* farther south than any ship had ever gone on his second voyage in 1774. Even though Cook circumnavigated the Antarctic continent, he never actually saw it, because of the ice and fog that accompanied him on his historic voyage. The discovery of *Terra Australis* would be one of the few discoveries denied to the greatest navigator of the eighteenth century; on two occasions he was only a day's sailing from the southern land mass, but he never laid eyes on it.

In January of 1775, Cook discovered (and named for his sovereign) the island of South Georgia, and although this island would figure significantly in the history of southern whaling, it meant precious little to Cook. He wrote that it was "a savage and horrible country," where "not a tree was to be seen, nor even a shrub big enough to make a tooth-pick." Tooth-picks notwithstanding, Cook recorded the presence of whales and seals, and his journals were responsible for the subsequent invasion of the South by Europeans, hell-bent on colonization and also the destruction of the indigenous—and unique—wildlife of this grand and isolated place.

It was a student of Cook's accomplishments, the Russian navigator Faddei Faddeevich Bellingshausen (also known as Thaddeus von Bellingshausen), sailing in the service of Tsar Alexander I, who made the next assault on the hidden continent. With the two ships *Vostok* and *Mirnyi,* Bellingshausen sailed south in 1819, and he too circumnavigated the Antarctic continent, also without seeing it. (Later, the Soviets would claim that Bellingshausen had indeed been the first to see the continent, but his journals do not indicate that he saw anything but ice, and he did not claim to have sighted land.)

The seals first brought the hunters to the isolated islands in the Southern Ocean. On the South African, South American and Australian southern coasts there existed vast undisturbed populations of various pinniped species of the genus *Arctocephalus,* collectively known as "fur seals." The classification of these animals (about which one author wrote, "There can scarcely have been a group of large mammals . . . whose taxonomy has been more involved") does not concern us here—as it did not concern the sealers—but their soft, dense fur does.

Even more than on the mainlands, the fur seals hauled out on the island groups: the Falklands, South Shetlands, South Orkneys, South Sandwich, Tristan da Cunha, the Crozets, Kerguelens, Prince Edward, Heard—and the cluster of islands south of New Zealand: Macquarie, Campbell, Chatham, Auckland, Bounty and Antipodes. Wherever these hapless seals congregated to breed, the sealers came to kill them. Fur seal bulls were known as "wigs," and the females "clapmatches." They were hit on the head with clubs, and then stabbed with lances until they bled to death. They were then skinned on the spot, since it was much easier to skin a freshly killed seal than one that had been left to dry out. The skins were salted and packed in layers known as "books." There were two primary applications for sealskins: they were either used for leather to make gloves, boots and shoes, or the fur was removed and employed in the manufacture of felt.

Many of the skins were destined for the "China Trade," although European markets also absorbed great numbers. The numbers are staggering. The first vessel outfitted specifically for sealing was the 1,000-ton *States,* owned by a Bostonian named Haley. In 1775 the *States* collected thirteen thousand sealskins from the Falklands, and sold them for fifty cents apiece in New York (they were resold for five dollars apiece in China). (Thirteen thousand skins at $5 apiece is $65,000, a veritable fortune in the eighteenth century.)

In addition to the fur seals, the islands were also home to another kind of pinniped, the elephant seal, largest of all the seals. These giants were hunted for their oil. They were fat and ugly, almost totally devoid of hair, and the males had a large, inflatable proboscis that accounted for their name and enabled the bulls to broadcast a snarling gurgle that sounded much more menacing than it actually was. Even though the noise made by the elephant seals was not particularly threatening, the sealers couldn't walk up to these monsters—the "beachmaster" bulls can grow to twenty feet long and weigh four tons—and hit them on the head. Early on, the bulls were killed with lances and left to bleed, while the cows and calves were clubbed. (Later, when the new technology was available, they would be shot.) The fat was stripped from the carcasses and tried-out, much the way whale oil would be rendered down later. The oil of elephant seals was used for lighting and lubrication, and it was also an important element in tanning leather to make it supple and waterproof. (How interesting to note that the oil of an already waterproof animal was removed, then employed to render the skin of another animal waterproof so that men could wear it.) It was the sealers who first came to islands like South Georgia. What was to become the most celebrated of all whaling stations on this island was *Grytviken,* which means "Caldron Bay," so named for the trypots of the sealers which the first whalers encountered there.

It is not easy to determine who first sighted the Antarctic mainland, since there is the possibility that some sealers actually saw it but kept it a secret to protect their interests. In 1819 the *Williams,* a British merchantman under Captain William Smith, was trying to round Cape Horn when she was blown to the southwest, and Smith spotted land through the sheeting snowstorm. His claim was not believed by the Admiralty, and after returning to Montevideo, Smith set out again to look for this land. With the *Williams* now under the command of navigator Edward Bransfield, they sighted the mainland, and probably landed at the north tip of Graham Land. Bransfield did not claim the place; instead he landed on the South Shetland Islands and planted the Union Jack there. In 1823, James Weddell sailed farther south than any man before him, and discovered, among other things, a sea and a seal (*Leptonychotes weddelli*) which carry his name.

The first sealers are recorded from the Falklands in 1766, when Bougainville sent a cargo of skins to France. At South Georgia, sealing began in 1786, when Captain Delano of the *Lord Hawkesbury* sailed for England with a load of skins from the Falklands and South Georgia. American sealers in the *Nancy* and the *Polly* left from Connecticut in 1792, and returned with full holds two years later. Between 1793 and 1820, sealers from Europe, America and Russia were crawling over the southern islands, slaughtering as many seals as they could, with not even a passing thought given to the future. It is estimated that as many as 3.5 million sealskins were collected between 1793 and 1807. Fortunes were made, doubled, and redoubled. By 1822 James Weddell had estimated that at least 1.2 million skins had been taken from South Georgia, and the species that lived there, the Antarctic fur seal, was practically extinct. The South Shetlands were discovered in 1819; four years later over 300,000 sealskins had been collected, and the "industry" was over. Within a thirty-year period, every one of the islands with seal rookeries had been decimated; the Chinese market fell, and southern sealing was, for all but the most enterprising sealers, over.

Seals are particularly easy animals to slaughter in large numbers because they tend to congregate on beaches during their breeding seasons, and all the sealers had to do was walk up to these innocent creatures and bash them on the head.

IN 1832 Captain John Biscoe in the Enderby ship *Tula* sailed around Antarctica for four months, confirming the existence of the continent. (Biscoe claimed the continent for England on the basis of a landing, but it seems that he actually set foot on Anvers Island, which is separated from the mainland by the Gerlache Strait.) In 1833–34, two more Enderby whalers, the *Magnet* and the *Eliza Scott,* Captains Kemp and Balleny, discovered more islands and probably saw the Antarctic mainland, but did not land on it. For the next decade, there was a race to discover new lands in the frozen South, and the place names bestowed upon various parts of the Antarctic continent indicate the fervor with which this was carried out. In the French corvettes *Astrolabe* and *Zélée,* Jules Sébastien César Dumont D'Urville penetrated the ice in 1837 and landed on a granite outcrop (thus indicating that he had reached *land* as opposed to ice), which he promptly named Terre Adélie after his wife. (A species of penguin was later named after the same woman.) In 1839 Captain James Clark Ross set sail from England in the *Erebus,* leading the expedition that also included the *Terror,* under the command of Francis Crozier. He discovered the Ross Ice Shelf (which he named the Victoria Barrier for his Queen), the Ross Sea, the Ross seal, the mountain he named Mount Terror, and the active volcano he named Mount Erebus.

Ross's charge was to contribute to the study of terrestrial magnetism, discover what new lands there were for discovering, and correct the erroneous charts. He returned to England in 1843 with tales of numerous black whales and ''hunch-backs,'' which was good news for the whalers, since it coincided with the collapse of the whale fishery in the north. The sperm whale fishery, which had flourished for almost a hundred years, was gasping like a beached whale. The number of ships leaving New Bedford and Nantucket dropped from four hundred to seventy-two between 1850 and 1872. During this period, of course, petroleum had been discovered in Pennsylvania. The demand for whalebone for corsets was insatiable, however, and since this material did not come from the toothed sperm whales, the whal-

ers began to look elsewhere for the right whales that could supply it to them. Once again, the whales saved the whalers, who repaid the favor by murdering them.

In 1873, searching for new grounds, the Germans sent Captain Eduard Dallmann in the steam whaler *Grönland.* The ship was equipped only to chase and catch the slower whales, *i.e.,* the right whales and the humpbacks, and when they found themselves among the swift, powerful rorquals, they were helplessly frustrated. While Yankee and British whalers were lowering the longboats and taking after the whales with hand-held harpoons, Norwegian whalers were blasting away at whales with exploding grenade harpoons.

Again in 1892, the British sent a whaling fleet from Dundee, consisting of four old-fashioned ships, the *Balaena, Diana, Active* and *Polar Star,* sailing to the Weddell Sea. Surrounded only by fast-moving, high-spouting blue and fin whales, the British were helpless. At the same time, however, a Norwegian expedition under the command of Carl Anton Larsen was also prowling the waters of the Antarctic. Although the *Jason* would also return empty, Larsen's vision of the future of Antarctic whaling would change the industry forever.

The British Head for the Antarctic

THE BRITISH and the Norwegians competed with each other for the various whales of the North Atlantic, but a rumbling was heard throughout the industry. Various expeditions had ventured to the polar south to investigate reports of enormous populations of whales in Antarctic waters.

South Georgia is a crescent-shaped island 105 miles long, and from 1½ to 19 miles wide, lying in isolated, mountainous splendor in the Southern Ocean. It is located midway between the 50th and 60th parallels, a little to the south of Cape Horn, and a little to the north of the tip of the Antarctic Peninsula, both of

which seem to point their icy fingers toward it as if to say ''here will be the focus of Southern Ocean industry.'' Its rocky coasts consist of numerous fjords and inlets, and many glaciers inch slowly down to the sea from the high, permanently snow-covered mountains. Runoff from the mountain snowfields provides ample fresh water, and two of these rivulets have been officially designated as rivers. When Carl Larsen visited South Georgia in 1903 aboard the *Antarctica,* he recognized that the island incorporated all the necessary elements for shore-whaling stations: its coasts are free from ice all year round; it has safe harbors, elevated land sites for buildings, a shelving beach, and most important, abundant fresh water.

It was as clear to Larsen as it was not to anyone else that the only way to conduct successful whaling activities in the South was to operate out of southern ports, thus eliminating the crippling costs of fuel required to get the whalers from Europe to the Antarctic, an eight-thousand-mile journey. Larsen returned to South Georgia by way of Norway in November 1904 with two sailing ships and a steam catcher, and proceeded to build and manage Grytviken, the first shore station in the Antarctic. Larsen's original catcher boat was the *Fortuna,* a hundred feet long and twenty feet in beam, and the first whale taken by this marriage of Argentine capital and Norwegian whaling expertise was, of course, a humpback.

In 1905, another Norwegian, A. A. Andresen, chose to try whaling out of the Strait of Magellan, and built a land station near Punta Arenas. The whales of the Straits proved to be scarce, the weather was terrible, and whaling was abandoned. Later that same year, another Norwegian expedition, commanded by Alex Lange in the floating factory *Admiralen,* cruised the Falkland Islands, and then the South Shetlands, where they killed blue whales and humpbacks. In the early years of Antarctic whaling, humpbacks were the favored target, because they were slow swimmers and congregated in enormous groups. In 1910–11, of 6,529 whales taken at South Georgia, 6,197 were humpbacks. (Whaling operations were only practicable during the Antarctic spring and summer, which run from October to April of the following year, hence the reference to an Antarctic season as including two calendar years.)

Because most of the islands, including South Georgia, belonged to the British, those who would kill whales and process them at these stations required a license to do so. Accompanying the Norwegian-Argentine franchise were ships from Chile and Argentina, and of course, the British themselves. Within ten years of Larsen's pioneering move, there were a dozen "floating factories" operating in South Georgia, and another dozen in the South Shetlands and the South Orkneys. An attempt was made to establish a shore station on the South Sandwich Islands, but conditions made it impracticable, and it was abandoned.

Note the distinction between "floating factories" and "factory ships." The former were converted cargo ships that had the apparatus on board to process whales that were brought to them, but the actual flensing took place alongside the ship, on a raftlike platform. The "factory ships," on the other hand, were often specially built vessels that could roam the Antarctic and rendezvous with the catcher boats wherever they found the whales. The freedom of the factory ships from the umbilicus of the shore was to become the major factor in the marked change—and increased efficiency—in whaling techniques. Because they were closest to the shore, the hapless humpbacks were killed off first, but the grenade-enhanced gunships were now able to catch and kill the blue and fin whales as well, and they did so with a vengeance that would not abate until these whales were almost exterminated.

The carcasses of the newly killed whales were brought to ships that were moored in the harbors and flensed alongside. The methods employed were not unlike those used by the southern whalers' predecessors, the sperm whalers who worked in the open sea; the whale was peeled in a circular fashion, rather like an orange. The strips of blubber were then hoisted aboard the floating factory, there to be deposited in the cookers, which were on board. The remainder of the carcass, which was known as the *skrott,* was simply discarded and left to rot in the harbor. (Later on, companies would utilize the entire carcass, but in the early years, when the number of whales seemed infinite, they used the best parts, and threw the remainder away. In some instances, the whalers took only the back blubber, and discarded an incredible 60 percent of the remaining blubber.) There were also shore stations built on South Georgia, the South Orkneys and the South Shetlands, which had the decided advantage of having much more room in which the men could work than the factory ships.

The main feature of the shore station was the flensing deck, or *plan,* a wooden ramp up which the carcass was winched for processing. There were facilities for the processing of blubber, meat, oil and bone, each of which required somewhat different techniques. Among the requirements for the establishment of a shore station were a suitable anchorage for the catchers and a plentiful supply of fresh water

On her first voyage to the Antarctic in 1911, the floating factory *Horatio,* shown here at Leith Harbor, South Georgia, caught fire in the English Channel. She was repaired and sailed again, only to burn and sink five years later.

for the generation of steam. It usually took less than an hour to reduce a whale to its component parts. In the 1904–05 season, the first of its operation, the station at South Georgia took 149 humpbacks, 11 blues and 16 sei whales. Ten years later (after reaching a peak year in 1910–11 of 6,197 humpbacks), the whalers had hit their stride with the rorquals, and took 940 blues, 1,716 fins and 512 humpbacks. These numbers may at first appear high, but they were nothing compared to the slaughter that would follow the introduction of the floating factory in 1925.

While the whalers were tied to the shore, however, they were subject to the restrictions imposed upon them by the putative owners of that land, in this case the British, through what was known as the Falkland Islands Dependencies. The British restricted the number of leases available and also the number of catchers that could be employed. When the British firm of Christian Salvesen & Co. requested permission to conduct shore whaling from South Georgia in 1908, the Colonial Office inexplicably refused their

request. Salvesen's "New Whaling Company" was forced to build a station in the less productive West Falklands, and in January 1909 it recorded the first kill of a whale by British whalers south of the Antarctic convergence. Overcoming the recalcitrance of the Colonial Office, Salvesen established its own station at Leith Harbour in 1909, but was restricted to two catchers. To circumvent this restriction, Salvesen simply requested another lease for Allardyce Harbour, and received permission for another two catchers. (The station at Allardyce was never built.) In 1911, Irvin & Johnson, a firm with yards in Aberdeen, Peterhead and North Shields, built a base on South Georgia which became known as the Southern Whaling and Sealing Company. At this time, the British were restricting the number of stations because they were genuinely alarmed about the possible destruction of the stocks; they declared the right whale protected (they were then so rare that hardly any were seen in Antarctic waters), and the whalers could not take nursing mothers with calves. Also, lease-holders had to utilize the entire carcass of the whale; no more leaving the skrotts to decompose in the harbors.

IT IS a common assumption that the earth has an infinite variety of goods and services to offer us, its favored inhabitants. Consider the matter of fuel, for example. For the first fires, people burned wood. Then the oil in the blubber of whales was discovered, and some plants, such as rape, cotton, flax and various palms, were found to contain usable oils. When wood became scarce, seams of coal were mined for fuel. Kerosene, also known as "coal oil" or "paraffin oil," was used for lighting throughout America and Europe. By the middle of the nineteenth century, the Industrial Revolution required a cheap source of lu-

bricants and illuminating oils. The first oil well in Pennsylvania did not represent the first industrial use of petroleum. Oil and gas from natural seepages had been known and utilized for thousands of years, from such disparate locations as China (where oil was encountered during the drilling of brine wells), Java, Cuba, Mexico and Peru, to Pennsylvania, where Colonel Drake's original well was drilled in the vicinity of a known surface seepage. We are running out of wood, coal and oil, and we have certainly run out of whales. We may not run out of plutonium for a while, but the question is not whether we will run out of fissionable material, but rather, whether we will run out of time.

By the turn of the twentieth century, it was obvious that petroleum distillates had replaced whale oil

Seven fin whales alongside a factory ship in the Antarctic.

for lubrication and lighting, and Dame Fashion had obviated the boned corset and the hoop skirt. Why then were all these whales being killed?

The market for whale oil underwent a major expansion around 1900. In 1903, a German chemist named Wilhelm Normann invented a process whereby animal oils could be converted to solid fats through a process known as "hydrogenation." Hardened whale oil could be used to produce hard soap and also margarine, which was becoming popular as an inexpensive substitute for butter. Even though whale oil was suitable for the manufacture of soap, its smell made it unpopular. Lever Brothers, the leading soap-makers in England, tried to convince consumers otherwise, but the dairy interests mounted a massive public-relations campaign in favor of soap made from tallow, and the public was bombarded with such unsavory terms as "cadaver fats," "half-rotten whales," and "chemically-changed fish oil." Paradoxically, the substance that was good enough for people to eat was not good enough for them to wash with. Because of its use in the manufacture of margarine, whale oil was becoming increasingly important to European commerce and industry, and therefore, more whales were being hunted. Lever Brothers bought up Testrup, a rival patent to Normann's, and also purchased a half-interest in the Norwegian hardening firm De Nordiske Fabriker, known as De-No-Fa.

By the time war was looming over Europe, whale oil had lost much of its unpopularity, and it was seen as a raw material in its own right rather than a substitute for better things. Finally, the factor that led to an exponential increase in whaling efforts was the need for the glycerin that is a by-product of the hydrolysis of whale oil. Glycerin is a component in the manufacture of nitroglycerin, and nitroglycerin is a component in the manufacture of dynamite.

When only the blubber was processed—as opposed to the bones as well—something on the order of 50 percent of the oil was wasted. Therefore, the British injunction to the whalers to utilize the entire carcass was not only in the interests of hygiene (the rotting carcasses were befouling the harbors), but it was also financially sound. Several Norwegian companies were formed expressly for the purpose of collecting and processing the skrotts.

Whale oil was the major product of the whaling industry, and it was used in the manufacture of margarine and cooking fats. Sperm oil, which comes only from the sperm whale, is a higher-quality oil that was used for smokeless candles in the nineteenth century, and later for cosmetics and as a superior lubricant, since it remains a surface film, whereas other oils tend to drain away. Whales also yielded what the whalers called "guano," which was not bird droppings, but rather a bone meal that was the by-product of the boiling-down of the meat and bone of the whale and was bagged and used as stock food and fertilizer. "Gluewater" (the liquid remaining in the boilers after the oil had been tapped) was sometimes centrifuged for its oil. This and *grax* (the gunk that remained in the bottom of a boiler after the boiling had been completed) were often added to the guano to increase its protein content. Very much a secondary product—and often not even that—were the teeth of sperm whales. Pelagic whalers might while away the time carving these peglike ivories into scrimshaw, but at the shore stations, there was little time—and less of a market—for carved teeth. More often than not, the tooth-studded lower jaws of the cachalots were discarded with the rest of the carcass.

At the outbreak of World War I, more than two-thirds of all whaling was carried out in the Falkland Islands Dependencies, which meant that the Allies controlled the great proportion of the sale of whale oil. Norway, a neutral country in the war, sold 34 percent of her oil to Germany-Austria, but the British quickly closed this loophole by refusing to sell coal to Norway if Norway continued to trade with the Central Powers. In desperation, Germany offered to pay as much as £300 a ton for whale oil, contrasted with the going price of £25 that the Allies were paying. In 1916, Britain temporarily canceled Norwegian licenses in the Antarctic to prevent the sale of this "contraband of war" to the Germans.

Although restrictions had been imposed in 1912 to control the number of whales killed and the disposition of their carcasses, by 1914 all restrictions were lifted in the interest of obtaining as much whale oil—and therefore as much glycerin—as possible. The gunners received a bonus for every whale they killed, and they were at liberty to fire at any and every whale they saw. During the wartime season of 1915–16, the total number of whales killed at South Georgia was 11,792. Even when there was no factory in sight to process the carcass, the men sometimes left one whale floating while they took off after another. The wastage was appalling. World War I, long regarded as one of the greatest cumulative tragedies in human history, was also a monumental disaster for whales, who gave their lives so that humans might die. Between 1904 and 1917, 175,250 whales were killed at South Georgia.

Fluctuations in the price of whale oil, the rivalry between the British and the Norwegians, and the rise in margarine production after the war led to a particularly complex relationship between the whalers and the buyers of oil. Lever Brothers bought the entire world production of whale oil in 1919, and in an example of what British whaling historian Gordon Jackson calls "vertical integration," they also acquired the Southern Whaling Company. Thus the soap-manufacturers not only controlled the market, they were also able to kill as many whales as were required to fill their needs. After the war, when the demand for glycerin had caused a four-fold rise in the price of whale oil, the regulations for full-carcass utilization were again imposed. Now that explosives were no longer critical, the attention of the whale-oil brokers could be turned to the expanding markets for margarine. The hostilities also saw the suspension of whatever research on other uses of whale products had been begun, but this was resumed almost immediately. The British levied a tax on all oil taken at stations leased from them, the money to be used to finance research expeditions to the South. Thus was R.M.S. *Discovery* reactivated.

This wooden-hulled three-masted barque had been built in 1901 for Robert Falcon Scott's historic assault on the South Pole. On the *Discovery* expedition, Scott, Ernest Shackleton and Edward Wilson sledged to latitude 82°16′S, the farthest south any man had ever been, but they could go no farther and turned back on December 30, 1902. After spending the entire year of 1903 in the ice, Scott returned to England in February of 1904. He embarked on another expedition in 1910 but was beaten to the pole by Roald Amundsen of Norway, who arrived there on September 8, 1911. Scott, having sailed from England in the *Terra Nova,* would reach the pole on January 17, 1912, unaware that Amundsen had beaten him until he saw the Norwegian flag snapping in the wind. ("The worst has happened. The Norwegians are first at the Pole. . . . All dreams must go.") Scott and his four-

man party (Wilson, Evans, Oates and Bowers) perished during their attempt to return to their ship in March of 1912.

In 1925 the *Discovery* was recommissioned and sent south once again, this time as a research vessel. The commissioning agency was the Interdepartmental Committee on Research and Development in the Dependencies of the Falkland Islands, otherwise known as the "Discovery Committee." The committee had met as early as 1918, and Alister Hardy, one of its early members, asked, ". . . is it not good to remember that the planning of such a quest of peace and science was contemplated and undertaken by a nation still struggling with the great war?" Composed of distinguished scientists and civil servants, the committee was dedicated to oceanographic research in the Antarctic, and the old *Discovery,* which Hardy had described as "a mere skeleton, reminding one of the dug-up remains of some ancient viking galleon," was to be its flagship.

In the spring of 1924, under the leadership of the zoologist Stanley Kemp, the *Discovery* sailed for the Southern Ocean. On board was perhaps the most impressive collection of cetologists ever assembled (although the science of cetology was in its infancy, and these men would only later become recognized as being the pioneers of the field), including N. A. Mackintosh, J. F. G. Wheeler, L. Harrison Matthews and Alister Hardy. (On subsequent "Discovery" voyages—the old *Discovery* was replaced in 1930 by the oil-burning steamship *Discovery II*—practically every British oceanographer, marine biologist, hydrographer and cetologist would be listed on the manifests at one time or another.) In 1924 the committee had set up the first biological research station in the Antarctic, at King Edward's Cove, opposite the Grytviken station on South Georgia.

As the British scientists were preparing to evaluate and correlate whaling activities in the Southern Ocean, the Norwegians were looking for more whales to kill. In 1923, they sent the factory ship *Sir James Clark Ross* to investigate the possibility of whaling in the Ross Sea (the ship was named for the man who discovered the sea because the Norwegians intended to send her there), and with the indefatigable Carl Larsen in command, they encountered huge whales in great profusion. (The voyage was not a success, although subsequent ones would be.) In 1925, however, another Norwegian innovation was to have an even greater effect on whaling: the *Lancing* left San-defjord endowed with a stern slipway, and therefore the ability to process whales anywhere they were caught. In order to remain competitive, the British had no choice but to redesign and refit their entire pelagic fleet. (One of the preslipway floating factories, the *Southern Queen,* had gone down in 1924.) The *Southern Empress,* a rebuilt petroleum tanker, was commissioned in 1928 and marked the beginning of the ascendancy of the British Antarctic fleet. This year also saw the entry of the Hector Whaling Company into the whaling derby. Organized by an Englishman named Rupert Trouton, Hector Whaling was unique in that its directors were drawn from Scandinavian banks, which created a somewhat confusing amalgamation of British and Norwegian interests. The tremendous investments in the southern fleet at this time put a strain on even the considerable resources of Lever Brothers, and in 1929 it merged with the Margarine Union to form Unilever.

By 1930–31, the Norwegian and British fleets had been converted to promethean floating industries. Attended by a small flotilla of catcher boats, every operative tanker was over 10,000 tons, and each was equipped with a stern slipway. Their decks were marked with the hatches of huge "digesters," into which the whale meat and blubber were dropped, with high-pressure cookers for the blubber and rotary cookers for the meat and bone. At this time, whaling was an attractive profession—although it obviously lacked the romance of earlier days—and because the crews of these seagoing slaughterhouses often exceeded five hundred per vessel, there was room for plenty of young Englishmen (and Irishmen, Scots, Welshmen and Shetland Islanders) to sign on for a voyage to the exotic Antarctic. There is a tradition in English literature of romantic travel writing, so a large body of work has emerged from this period of whaling history. Even though the whales were being killed off at an alarming rate—the 1930–31 season would see the greatest slaughter of blue whales in history—young would-be Richard Halliburtons described their adventures on board the various factories of the southern fleet. From their collected works, we are able to assemble a picture of life aboard a British whaleship during the heyday of the Antarctic fishery.

Aboard the ill-fated *Southern Queen,* J. S. Hodgson set out for the Antarctic in 1923. (He was the "south"

half of the team of Morley and Hodgson, who wrote *Whaling North and South.*) Although the ship was British, the captain and crew were almost all Norwegian. Almost everyone on whaling voyages complains of the smell, and Hodgson was no exception. Of the shore station at Saint Olaf's Harbor in South Georgia, he wrote: "The first impression of a whaling-station is received violently through the nose, and I admit that I have never experienced anything so overpowering." Unlike his co-author, Hodgson was unmoved by the size or majesty of the dead whales being hauled on the flensing deck. "I cannot say," he wrote, "that any sense of pity for the whale is of long duration. Instead, one is more concerned with the men who carry on the hunting in wild uncharted seas, braving perils hourly in weather that would be the death of the average townsman. . . . The cold is ferocious, biting to the very bone; the gallant little chasers are frequently caked with ice from top to bottom, every rope and bolt, while the accommodation below scarcely permits of breathing-space." Hodgson found the food very Norwegian and very boring, consisting of salt pork and whale meat, with no fresh fruit or vegetables and plenty of the tinned fish dumplings that are "beloved of the Scandinavian." (Hodgson reported that the plentiful meat of the quarry was prepared as "whale steak, whale sausages, minced whale, whale soup, whale potato pie, fried whale, boiled whale, baked whale, salted whale, and whale in many other forms, which I, not being a cook of adequate caliber, cannot describe.")

This was just before the introduction of the stern slipway, so flensing was done alongside the ship. With heavy hawsers securing the whale, a flat-bottomed scow was lowered, and the flensers worked on the whales while standing on its slippery surface in the water. As they stripped the blubber from the carcass, it was hauled aboard by windlass, and sliced up to fit into the cookers. Again Hodgson comments on the ambience: "The smell and filth above and below deck are abominable. . . . Fat and oil, thick messy stuff is everywhere; it is impossible to avoid it, and it is not at all pleasant to wade in." The blubber was tried-out in the boilers; the oil in the tongue was extracted under steam pressure, and the rest of the carcass, including the head, was reduced to pieces that could be fit into the boilers. From the start of the flensing to the cleaning of the decks—assuming there was not another carcass

standing by—it took only three-quarters of an hour to process a whale.

When not involved in the processing of whales, the men would collect fresh water (by digging a channel and letting the ice melt into funnel-shaped sacks, which were hosed into the water-boat), and they would wander about on Melchior Island in the South Shetlands, collecting penguin eggs.

While aboard the whale-catcher *Southern Maid,* Hodgson ruminated on the intelligence of the whale, suggesting that it was probably not particularly smart, or else it would not allow itself to be captured so easily. Furthermore, "Its great size . . . renders it immune from most of the dangers that beset other creatures of the sea, and thereby possibly lulls, in the course of time, the acute sense of danger that is the chief protection of other animals." The large whales have few natural enemies; in the Antarctic only packs of killer whales can threaten individual rorquals, and since this sort of confrontation does not take place very often, it is quite possible that alone among wild animals, whales might have expected to live out their lives in an unprecedented state of tranquillity. They never learned to avoid the killer boats, partially because the killing was so efficient that a harpooned whale rarely survived to communicate the nature of the danger to its fellows (if indeed whales are capable of such communications), and also because the whole business had lasted less than a single cetacean generation, hardly enough time to pass along the experience. The whales had lost the battle before they had a chance to learn what was happening to them.

THE PERIOD between the wars was a critical one for the whaling industry and even more important for the whales: as catches increased, the whaling nations became more aware of the need for some sort of international regulation of the industry. Much of the concern for the preservation of whales had to do with the preservation of the industry, and therefore, much of the talk about saving whales was only talk. The whaling companies had too much capital tied up in their businesses to accept any sort of restrictive quotas that might impinge on their profits.

Opposite: In the Southern Ocean, the moment that the grenade harpoon strikes the whale has been forever frozen in this remarkable photograph.

For the decade 1930–40, various meetings were held to discuss the possibilities of restrictions, but as Gordon Jackson has put it, "There is, in fact, little point in going through the details of the annual restrictive agreements for the simple reason that they did no good." In more prosperous times, concerned men might have been able to function more generously, but with the Western world sunk into a massive economic depression, it was not a good time for altruism. All the whaling companies were in trouble; De-No-Fa had lost £792,000 in 1931, and Unilever had lost £114,000. The Norwegian whaling companies had to mortgage their fleets, and did not sail at all in 1932–33. The price of whale oil was set at £13 a ton, and by the next season, it had fallen to £10. Most of the British companies were in trouble. To make matters worse, the bilateral monopoly that the Norwegians and the British had held on Antarctic whaling was beginning to crumble; to fill their needs for whale oil, other nations were entering the whaling business. Panama and Denmark joined in as minor players, and even the United States tried its hand at Antarctic whaling, sending the converted tanker *Frango* south in the 1930–31 season. But when Japan and Germany dispatched fleets to the Antarctic, they dramatically altered the balance of commercial whaling. Strained relations between Norway and Germany (culminating in the invasion of 1940) meant that Norway took the brunt of the pressure, and on the whole, Britain survived the whaling wars far better than the land and sea struggles that were to follow. In addition, more trouble for the whalers was in store: synthetic detergents were being developed which might replace whale-oil soaps.

The factory ship *Frango,* which was sold in 1930 by the Danes to an American company for the only modern, pelagic American whaling expeditions to the Antarctic. The voyage was a success, but the owners couldn't sell the oil because of low prices, and the Americans never went south again.

Norwegian Floating Factories

CARL ANTON LARSEN was born in Tjølling, Norway, in 1860, the son of a ship's captain. He went to sea almost as soon as he could walk, and as the center of whaling shifted from the north to the south, Larsen was ideally trained and dispositioned to escort the industry on its antipodean proclivities. He had successfully hunted fin and bottlenose whales in the Arctic, and when Christen Christensen was looking for a leader of his first Antarctic expedition in 1892, Larsen was a perfect choice. He skippered the *Jason* for five years, making highly successful sealing voyages, and returning to Norway with enticing tales of the herds of blue and fin whales that he saw but could not catch.

By the age of thirty, Larsen was justifiably famous as a captain and a whaleman. While in the employ of Christen Christensen, Sandefjord's first major works-owner, he had been to Spitsbergen, where he pioneered the use of on-board cookers on floating factories and the transportation of oil in fixed tanks instead of barrels. He had also become familiar with working in icy conditions, experience that was to serve him well in the Antarctic.

Larsen reported that "on our way there blue whales frolicked in countless shoals, as well as humpbacks, but there was no sign of the characteristic blowing of the right whale." Because they had been hunting for the right whale, they were unequipped to take the fast-moving blues and finners, and they decided to fill their holds with sealskins so as not to return home empty-handed.

The *Jason* returned to Sandefjord after a nine-month voyage (six of the nine months were spent in traveling back and forth), a failure. The following year she was sent back again, this time with sealing as her primary mission. She sighted a couple of right whales, and managed to shoot one, but again, seal-skins were her only cargo. Christensen's company could not survive this setback, and he was forced to sell his ships.

By this time, Larsen was becoming one of the most experienced of Antarctic skippers, even though he had managed to kill only one whale. In 1892 he was sent by eighty-four-year-old Svend Foyn back to the Antarctic, aboard the *Antarctica,* but again the results in terms of whaling were dismal. The *Antarctica* went south again in '94, and finally located the right whales 350 miles south of New Zealand, but this time the equipment failed, and they killed only a single calf. In 1903, Larsen sailed on a Swedish expedition led by Otto Nordenskjöld, an explorer and lecturer in geology who was preparing to send an expedition to the South to study the meteorological and magnetic conditions. Nordenskjöld bought the Norwegian sealer *Antarctic* for his flagship, and with Larsen as captain, the expedition sighted the South Shetlands on January 10, 1902. After scouting the Antarctic islands (and discovering the ideal site for a whaling station at Grytviken on South Georgia), their vessel was trapped in the ice at Hope Bay and sunk in the Weddell Sea. The men were forced to overwinter in one of the world's most inhospitable regions, spending the winter in a stone hut on Snow Hill Island, eating penguins. They were rescued by the Argentine ship *Uruguay* and taken to Buenos Aires, where a banquet was given in their honor. At this dinner, Larsen gave an inspired speech in what the Norwegian whaling historians Tønnessen and Johnsen call his "highly original English":

I tank youse vary mooch and dees is all vary nice and youse vary kind to mes, bot I ask youse ven I am here vy don't youse take dese vales at your doors, dems vary big vales and I seen dem in houndreds and tousands.

Larsen raised the money to establish a whaling station on South Georgia Island, and with the Compañía Argentina de Pesca ("Argentine Fishing Company"), Antarctic whaling had begun.

The first "commercial" whale killed in the Antarctic was shot by Adolf Amadeus Andresen, another Sandefjord man. Andresen had settled in southern Chile after a career as a seaman, and when he spied the herds of whales that passed through the waters of Tierra del Fuego, he returned to Norway where he learned the art of shooting whales with a cannon. He returned to Punta Arenas with a cannon mounted on the bows of a tugboat, and on New Year's Eve 1903, he shot a humpback whale. Within two years, the enterprising A. A. Andresen had formed a whaling company called the Sociedad Balleneras de Magellanes. After his eight-month sabbatical on the ice, C. A. Larsen returned to Buenos Aires and raised the money for what was to become the most important of all the early Antarctic whaling concerns, the Compañía Argentina de Pesca.

By 1903, the North Atlantic whales had been so effectively fished out that Norway declared a ban on all whaling in Norwegian waters, to take effect after the next season. In addition, the world's markets had been depressed by a great flow of linseed oil, so there was hardly a viable market for whale oil. The Nor-

wegians had been infected with whaling fever, however, and the absence of whales in their own waters would not keep the harpoons sheathed for long. When Larsen returned to Norway in 1904, trying to interest subscribers in the Compañía Argentina de Pesca, he found that he was unable to raise any interest in his own country, but with the money that had been raised in Argentina, he procured three ships, the sailers *Louise* and *Rolf,* and a new steam whaler christened *Fortuna.* These three vessels brought a complement of sixty Norwegians to South Georgia, along with three prefabricated wooden houses, which became the first structures at the Grytviken whaling station. Under Larsen's direction, these hard-working Norsemen labored almost around the clock for a month to erect the houses, build a slipway, a factory with twelve blubber cookers, and the other accoutrements needed for a whaling station. (In 1950, R. B. Robertson, traveling as ship's surgeon aboard a British factory ship, would describe South Georgia as "the most sordid, unsanitary habitation of white men to be found the world over, and the most nauseating example of what commercial greed can do at the expense of human dignity. I think that, if Captain Cook were to see it today, he would probably burst into tears.")

On November 16, 1904, the *Fortuna* arrived in

In 1905 the *Admiralen* became the first steam whaler to operate in the Antarctic. She is shown docked in Seattle in 1912.

Grytviken, and on December 22 the first whale—a humpback—was shot. The humpbacks frequented the bays of South Georgia, but when this inshore population was exhausted, the whalers moved farther offshore, where the whale of choice was the blue, since it yielded the most oil and meat per unit of catching effort. But since fin whales are more numerous than blues, and humpbacks are found closer to shore, the early history of Antarctic whaling revolved mostly around these two species.

South Georgia had been discovered in 1675 by the English explorer Anthony de la Roche, and again a hundred years later by Captain Cook, who had formally occupied it and named it for his sovereign. Shortly after Cook's discoveries were published, sealers arrived at South Georgia to harvest the abundant elephant and fur seals. What made this island particularly interesting to sealers and then whalers was that its shores are ice-free all year round. Although the island was recognized as British, it was officially named a dependency in the letters patent of 1887 establishing the Falkland Islands Dependencies, which included the Falklands, the South Shetlands, and South Georgia. Since the British had not set an official foot on the island since 1775, it was not unreasonable for Larsen to think that it was unoccupied and unclaimed. When a British expedition under the leadership of Ernest Swinhoe arrived at South Georgia and found that there was a whaling station there, first a protest, then complex negotiations ensued, eventually resulting in a twenty-one-year lease for the Compañía, which was signed on January 1, 1906. As soon as the ink was dry on the lease, other whaling interests, affected by the restrictive legislation and dwindling whale stocks of the north, turned their eyes to the south. By 1907, two more whaling companies were on the way to South Georgia, one from Sandefjord and one from Tønsberg.

The Norwegians quickly adapted to their environment—they were, after all, a people not unfamiliar with harsh weather conditions—and in some ways, adapted the environment to themselves. Larsen introduced reindeer to the island, which proliferated, and rabbits and cattle, which did not. Ships from Norway brought pigs and sheep which grazed on the tussock grass in the summer and were slaughtered for food in the fall. The nonindigenous mammal—besides man—that had the most pronounced effect on the island was *Rattus norvegicus,* the brown rat. Probably passengers on the early sealers, the rats invaded the island and flourished. At the whaling stations they gorged themselves on offal, while away from this source of sustenance, they fed on the eggs of ground-nesting birds.

By 1908, there were seventeen buildings on South Georgia, and over 150 men worked there. But every autumn, thousands of Vestfold men would travel south on the whaleships to harvest and process the whales. (And every spring, they would return home to Norway for summer, making it possible for some of the whalemen to miss winter for years at a time.) During the season, the ships would tow in so many whales that they couldn't be processed immediately, and there are records of as many as forty carcasses lying in the harbor at one time. The station resounded with the cackle of chickens and the quacking of ducks, along with the sound of wheezing and clanking engines. It was a lonely, difficult life, one that seemed made to order for the stoic Norwegians. Many of the men died in circumstances connected with whaling, and one estimate holds that between 1904 and 1922, some two hundred men were buried in the frozen ground of South Georgia or lost at sea. A typhus epidemic hit the island in 1912, and nine men died.

Others would come to the Antarctic to hunt the whales, but none adapted so well to their surroundings. The men of Vestfold molded the environment to suit them and turned South Georgia and the Southern Ocean into a bleak but bountiful version of a Norwegian fjord.

WHALING was conducted in the traditional fashion, where the catcher boats chased the whales, shot them with grenade harpoons, and then towed them back to the harbor for processing. At first, the processing was done aboard the floating factories, where the blubber was peeled in a circular fashion, just as it was in the old days of square-rigged sperm whaling. Later, when the processing took place on shore, the whale was stripped in a longitudinal fashion, the way a banana is peeled. The blubberless carcass was left to rot in the harbor. The stench of hundreds of tons of rotting meat must have been close to intolerable. Eventually, the British passed regulations that required the factories to process the entire whale, and many of the old floating factories, inadequate to the task, ceased operations.

The old dangers of square-rigged whaling were generally absent from the Antarctic, but because of the weather, whaling voyages were far from easy or pleasant. The Antarctic summer is not a tropical one, and sudden storms and howling gales are not unusual. Writing of a whaling voyage aboard the *Sir James Clark Ross* in 1923, Allan Villiers described the weather en route from Tasmania to the Ross Sea: "The second day out the wind came and the sea rose. The southwest gale shrieked through the sparse rigging of the old steamer and drove the great foamy seas upon her wooden-sheathed decks, while the little whalers in tow were tossed lightly about, lurching, pitching, heaving, and rolling like open boats in a storm. . . . We slowed down a little but the wind and sea continued to rise, so that soon the predicament was fast becoming unbearable." (Since this was only the second day out of Hobart, the crew, many of whom were Aussies like Villiers, were seriously unprepared, and had to avail themselves, "regardless of cost," of foul-weather gear from the ship's slop chest.) Later in the same voyage, Villiers describes the weather on December 20, the middle of summer: "Next day with the temperature at minus eight degrees Centigrade, their decks covered with ice and snow, and their riggings festooned with rime, the little fleet of six vessels entered the long-sought open waters of the Ross Sea."

Occasionally catcher boats were lost, but there is one celebrated instance where an entire factory ship went down. The floating factory *Fridtjof Nansen* was searching for the entrance to Cumberland Bay in November 1906 when she struck an underwater reef and broke into three parts. Nine men were lost, and forty-nine survivors were picked out of the freezing water by catcher boats and brought back to Grytviken.

The catcher boats were the mainstay of the fishery. They were small (up to 150 feet in length), steam-driven, and maneuverable enough to chase down the fast-moving rorquals. Whales were spotted from a crow's nest atop the steel foremast, and the cry of *hvalblast* indicated a whale's spout. The gunner (who was more often than not the master as well) steered the ship until it was close to the whale, then raced down the open catwalk to the harpoon cannon for the killing shot, giving control of the ship to the

mate. The dead whale was brought alongside, inflated with compressed air to keep it afloat, and marked with some sort of marker to identify it and enable the whalers to locate it again. (The first markers were flags, like the waifs of old, but they were replaced by lights, then radar reflectors, and finally, radio transmitters.)

Shore-whaling stations had the advantage of providing much more room for the processing of the enormous carcasses. Each station had a flensing deck with a boarded slipway, up which the whales would be winched. All around the slipway were the "factories" for the processing of oil, meat and bone. The various whale products were boiled down in enormous pressure cookers, the oil stored in casks and later in iron drums. For the first decade of whaling out of South Georgia, 1,738 blue whales were killed, 4,776 fin whales, and 21,894 humpbacks. (The number of humpbacks estimated to be alive today *throughout the world* is 5,000.) Most of these whales were killed inside the harbors; Tønnessen and Johnsen wrote that the incredible number of whales taken by the various stations on South Georgia "surpassed anything ever seen in the history of whaling." There were so many whales to be caught that the whalers took only the thickest blubber from the back and the belly, and discarded the rest of the carcass, allowing it to drift away into the harbor. The waste—of blubber and of whales—was colossal; there are few instances in mankind's long history of greedy exploitation that demonstrate such wanton, senseless destruction of a natural resource. Regardless of the consequences, the Norwegian whaling companies prospered, and in 1909, some of them were able to pay dividends of 120 percent to their investors.

With this kind of money to be made, the British figured they might as well participate in the bounty, so Christian Salvesen, of Leith (born Norwegian, of course), arrived in the Antarctic in 1908. Salvesen & Co. was already the largest whaling company in the world, with interests in Iceland, the Faeroes, the Falklands and South Africa, but it was still the Norwegians who dominated the industry. Writing in 1911, the Norwegian zoologist J. A. Mörch described the state of Norwegian whaling:

The situation to-day, then, is that, after a short run of six years, whaling in the Southern Hemisphere has attained a commercial importance entirely overshadowing that of the industry in our northern latitudes, which is now more

The Norwegian whaling
station at Leith Harbor,
South Georgia,
around 1914.

than forty years old. As an example, it may be mentioned that last season, from the island of South Georgia alone, fourteen whaling steamers brought 106,800 barrels of oil, which is more than the world's total production of whale-oil three years ago!

They expanded their range until they were spread out all over the Southern Ocean, and in 1912 there were four floating factories operating off the lonely South Sandwich and South Orkney islands, much closer to the pack ice than South Georgia. Ice-covered volcanic specks in the southern polar sea, these islands are even less hospitable to people than South Georgia, but just as attractive to whales, so the resourceful Norwegians devised a way of working up whales without benefit of land. A gunner named Petter Sørlle invented the stern slipway, which enabled floating factories to winch the entire whale aboard, thus becoming a completely self-contained processing plant with quarters for the whalers. Although Sørlle did not develop his invention until 1925, it was, like the harpoon gun of Svend Foyn, a Norwegian breakthrough that was to change the very nature of whaling. During the first phase of Antarctic whaling, the whales had to be caught within towing distance of a land station, but with the invention of the stern slipway, the whalers were freed from any land attachment and could roam any and all of the world's oceans. The pack ice, which had been the last refuge for the whales, no longer provided sanctuary. (The stern slipway made it possible to develop gargantuan, completely self-supporting factory ships, which would, in later years, roam the world harvesting the last of the rorquals in the Antarctic, and huge numbers of sperm whales in the remote reaches of the North Pacific.)

The Norwegians also established a whaling station on Kerguelen Island (also known, appropriately, as "Desolation Land"), another inhospitable volcanic rockpile in the middle of nowhere. A shore station was built there in 1908 for the taking and processing of whales and elephant seals, but the latter were more plentiful than the former, and although 420 humpbacks were taken there from 1908 to 1911, the station was considered a failure and was closed down.

Whaling continued through World War I because the price of whale oil soared during that period. The Norwegians had begun to comb the waters of South America and Mexico during 1912 and 1913, but the whales either weren't there or they evaded the whalers, and by 1920 the Norwegians had shut down their Latin American operations. In southern Africa, however, the Norwegians were hearing rumors of plentiful whales off both coasts.

In 1911, Norwegian whalers had reached the limits of their expansion; in addition to Antarctic and

Until 1925, all whaling guns were muzzle-loaders like this one, shown aboard a Norwegian whaler.

South African waters, they were now to be found near Australia, New Zealand and Alaska. The Norwegian consul in Sydney—who, like his South African counterpart, seemed to be primarily in the business of seeking out new whaling grounds for his compatriots—reported back to Christiania that there were whales aplenty off Australia, and soon the Norwegians were there with their cannons. This time, it was not Sandefjord that was represented, but the little town of Larvik. They did relatively poorly in Australian waters until Christmas Eve 1908, when the crew of one of the Larvik ships hauled in the largest lump of ambergris ever found, a 1,003-pound "boulder" that fetched £23,000 in London, and saved the floundering whaling company.

Norwegian whalers discovered that herds of humpbacks migrated up both coasts of the island continent. They established Western Australian shore stations at Albany and Point Cloates, and even named another promising territory Norwegian Bay after themselves. They sent a floating factory to Jervis Bay in New South Wales, and thence across the Tasman Sea to New Zealand. The Australians and the New Zealanders were not happy with the Norwegians' picking off *their* humpbacks, so they protested loudly and persistently, eventually driving the Nor-

wegians out. The last vestige of Norwegian whaling was in Norwegian Bay, where they found only female humpbacks with calves. The manager of the station wrote, "We could often go right over to them and drop the harpoon in their backs. It's unfortunate that cows with young should be killed, but there's nothing that can be done about it." The Norwegians regarded the slaughter solely as an economic imperative, as was expressed as recently as 1982 by Tønnessen and Johnsen: "the calf was helpless without its mother and soon died, either of starvation or an easy prey to sharks and killer whales. Whalers were not inclined to sentimentality when they had the prospect of extracting 50 to 60 barrels of oil, worth £300, from a large female."

Although whale oil was important for lighting and lubrication prior to the latter portion of the nineteenth century, it was not particularly useful for the manufacture of foodstuffs. The so-called cattle fats (butter and milk) and lard (pig fat) filled the world need for edible fats, supplemented by olive oil. Other oils used in the manufacture of food were coconut, palm, palm kernel and groundnut, and to a much lesser extent, cottonseed and linseed oil. When margarine was developed in France in 1869, its production quickly consumed much of the world's animal fats. (Margarine is made from animal fats mixed with vegetable oils and milk.) A firm, solid animal fat is required to give margarine its consistency, and whale oil, which is a liquid, could not be used. But when it was discovered in 1905 that whale oil could be hydrogenated and thus solidified and its unpleasant smell and taste removed, an entirely new market was opened. Whale oil could now be used in food-preparation, and also in the manufacture of soap. (It was not until 1929, however, that hydrogenated whale oil with a lower melting point was developed, which made it genuinely palatable.)

Just as the whalers were experiencing their greatest successes, along came World War I to throw a spanner into the works. Norway dominated Antarctic whaling, but countries like England, Japan and the United States were coming in for an increasingly larger share of the pie. Norway's major hydrogenation plant was controlled by the British firm of Lever Brothers, so Norwegian whale oil was not going to find its way to Germany. (Some of it did, and there are stories of various Norwegians "arranging" to have their transport ships seized by the German navy.) One cargo of oil that never got anywhere was that of the floating factory *Horatio*, which caught fire on March 11, 1916, and was towed out and sunk off Leith Harbor. The ship and 11,000 barrels of oil were lost.

The Norwegians were pressured by Britain to refrain from selling any oil to Germany—despite Germany's willingness to pay enormously inflated prices—a situation that might have compromised her neutrality. By threatening to withhold coal from Norway, Britain succeeded in keeping whale oil out of Germany. Since Britain was then the only buyer for Norwegian whale oil, she could dictate the price, and the price plummeted in 1916. "Norway was forced to produce cheap explosives for Britain," said

The Salvesen floating factory *Horatio,* with 11,000 barrels of oil aboard, was destroyed by fire on March 11, 1916.

the Norwegians, who resented, among other things, the low price they were getting for their oil. Six months after the war ended in 1918, the restrictions were lifted, and Norway was free to pursue the whales and sell the oil to whomever she pleased.

The British, however, had imposed regulations on the processing of the carcasses, including requirements for complete utilization and for a limited season on whaling (September 16 to May 31). With sanctions eliminated, the 1919–20 season turned out to be the greatest bonanza in the history of Norwegian whaling thus far. Lever Brothers, in England, purchased the entire world production, and the various whaling companies were able to declare shareholder dividends of anywhere from 80 to 240 percent. In the light of these enormous profits, the British government (through the Falkland Islands Dependencies) decided that the whalers should subsidize whatever research was necessary to study and preserve the whales and the industry. For the years 1922 to 1931, the whalers prospered as never before, and the scientific community—for the first time—became an integral part of the equation.* On the debit side of the ledger, during the same period, more whales were killed than ever before in history.

When Norway was required to sell all its oil to Britain, it found itself in the paradoxical position of being the world's foremost whaling nation, and at the same time having a shortage of fats. The Norwegians therefore had to violate their own 1904 ban on Finnmark whaling in order to provide their own country with meat and lubricating oils. Instead of whaling off the North Cape coast, however, they established stations up and down the coast of Norway. This local fishery, begun in 1916, was to become the mainstay of Norwegian whaling when the originators of Antarctic whaling were finally forced to retire. But for now, the Antarctic beckoned.

THE ROSS SEA is larger in square miles than France. Not only had pelagic whaling never taken place there, it was not even clear who—if anyone— had jurisdiction over the waters. Britain controlled the islands of her "dependencies" in the Southern

Ocean, but did that also mean that she could license whaling in the Ross Sea? There were rumors of enormous numbers of whales in this vast body of icy water. The Ross Sea Whaling Company purchased the *Custodian,* an old steamer which had originally been christened *Mahronda.* When the company bought the ship in 1923 and converted her to a factory ship, they named her *Sir James Clark Ross* (after the discoverer of the sea that bears his name), and planned to take her for the first whaling voyage ever to that unknown sea. She was outfitted with cookers, pressure boilers, capacity for 58,000 barrels of oil, and accommodations for a crew of 170. At 8,223 gross tons, she was the largest whaling vessel in history. She departed from Sandefjord and arrived in Hobart, Tasmania, in November 1923. There she picked up coal and water, and an aspiring Australian journalist named Allan Villiers, who had signed on as a laborer for twenty dollars a month and who would document the voyage in *Whaling in the Frozen South.* Also aboard was sixty-four-year-old Carl Anton Larsen, the father of Antarctic whaling.

In Villiers's chronicle, we get a vividly drawn picture of life aboard a Norwegian whaler.* He was aboard the factory ship, which towed five catcher boats, named *Star I, II, III, IV* and *V.* Everything was conducted under the watchful eye of Captain Larsen, who, "despite his threescore years or more . . . mounted to the lofty crow's nest with the agility of a boy, and remained there for three hours in the piercing wind, perched on the edge of the barrel, gazing at the ice with a knowing eye, alternately puffing on a big cigar and conning the ship." Obviously taken with the Norwegian character, Villiers describes the other crew members as "reliant, resourceful, ready for anything, masters of all they surveyed." (Later on, however, he remarks that the Norwegians are very matter-of-fact. "Things happen, and they meet them—that appears to be their philosophy of life summed up in a few words.") Of the horrible

---

*It was during this period that the British organized the *Discovery* expeditions, supported almost entirely by revenues raised from leases on Dependencies whaling stations. The science that resulted is discussed at greater length in the section on British whaling in the Antarctic.

*We also get a good reading on the whaleman's attitude toward whales at that time: "If they kill whales," he wrote, "well, others kill elephants in Africa for 'sport'. . . . The whale gets a poor run for his money nowadays, one admits; but he is a necessary commercial adjunct to the making of lard and a good soap. (His oil doesn't go into the inferior brands.) I am not greatly concerned about the fears of the blue whale's extinction. . . . The very immensity of the industry is the whales' best guarantee against extinction. For it naturally follows that, as soon as the whales begin to thin out at all they will be left alone."

The Norwegian factory ship *Sir James Clark Ross* in the Antarctic in 1924 with several whale carcasses alongside.

stench of the first blue whale killed in the Ross Sea, he wrote, "The smell was everywhere . . . it was in our food, in our coffee, in our clothes. We were steeped in it. . . . However, we all became thoroughly accustomed to whale odor by the end of the week, and ate the meat a week later."

The maiden voyage of the *Ross* was a qualified failure. She took very few whales in the season of 1923–24, and those that were killed by the catchers could not be processed at sea. The ship was fitted out to anchor in a harbor, not in the open sea. (Only the introduction of the stern slipway in 1925 would solve this problem.) The 100-ton blue whales were far too heavy for the tackle of the *Ross,* and at-sea flensing had to be abandoned. The ship needed to find a harbor, and they needed to find one before the seven whales they had already lashed alongside began to decompose. With the bloated carcasses in tow, the crew celebrated the arrival of 1924 at midnight "in broad bright daylight," anchored in Discovery Inlet, the only protected body of water they

could find in the Ross Sea. Even though New Year's Eve occurred in midsummer in the Antarctic, "The steam from the windlass froze on our faces, in the corner of our eyes, on our beards, our eye-brows and on our clothes until we were caked with ice, while the boiling water from the exhaust ran upon the deck and quickly became solid ice."

Once the *Ross* was safely anchored, processing of the carcasses began. Villiers called it a "strange wild scene. Steam gushes up from countless boiler pipes, clothing every rope, rail and wire in the ship with a heavy coating of ice and rime; blood-bespattered, blubbery men with razor-edged knives hack at the thick blubber, while a musical sound comes from the blacksmith's shop under the foremast where the bent harpoons are straightened and repaired." Comparing the flensing process of the *Ross* to the old sperm whaling days, Villiers writes: "As many as four days were required a few years ago to try out one small whale for sixty or seventy barrels of oil—the *Ross* was capable of flensing and trying out fifteen great blue whales for one thousand five hundred barrels of oil in one day."

It was cold and nasty work, but the crewmen on a Norwegian whaler were treated well. Gone were the rat- and roach-infested quarters; gone were the maggoty meat and putrid water; and in the Antarctic, at least, gone were the lazy days of sailing under a hot tropical sun. The men lived in tight but clean quarters—known as the "penguin rookery"—equipped with electric lights and steam heat. The sounds of wind and creaking rigging were replaced by the hiss and clank of engines. The romance of whaling under sail was replaced by the drudgery of industry, but there were no people better suited for this cold, unromantic life than the taciturn Norsemen. Because they were now working on what was literally a factory at sea, there was a greater division of labor than the old whaleships had known: the captain ruled, as always, with his subordinate staff of ship's officers, but now there were firemen, coalers, engineers, winchmen, boiler attendants, carpenters, gunners, the purser and stewards, and a doctor. The mainstay of the crew—and of the industry—were the hardy souls who butchered, stripped and processed the carcasses on decks that were slick with frozen blood.

When the blubber had been stripped from the carcass of the whale, it was dropped through holes in the deck into open cookers, ten-foot-high cylindrical vats that were heated by steam. Because the meat and bones were impregnated with oil, pressure cookers were used to extract it. (The use of pressure

During Antarctic whaling, men and equipment were often covered with ice. If left on deck for any time, whale carcasses would freeze harder than steel.

cookers was pioneered by Marcus Bull, the same man who ran the Norwegian station in Iceland in 1904.) When the cooking was done, the contents of the cookers were centrifuged to separate the oil from the blubber, leaving the *grax,* which was dried and bagged to be used for livestock feed or fertilizer. Practically the whole whale was reduced to oil; nothing was wasted but the whale itself.

At 5:30 A.M., the crew arose for the day's work. After putting on practically every article of clothing they possessed, they repaired to the galley for coffee and a smoke before commencing work at 6:00. To provide the necessary calories for a brisk introduction to the Antarctic morning, the whalermen drank coffee heavily loaded with sugar, and ate inch-thick slabs of brown bread slathered with margarine. (On some ships the custom was to fill one's mouth with sugar, then drink the coffee through it.) After two hours of work, the crew returned to the mess rooms for breakfast, which often consisted of fried whale beef and onions, with more brown bread and margarine. "Whale beef has a delightful aroma to a hungry man," wrote Villiers, "and is splendid food in a cold climate. It tastes somewhat like a greasily prepared steak, and is very tender, especially when hung for a few days." The bill of fare included whale beef, fish, potatoes, pea soup, and other meats and vegetables. It was not a particularly exotic menu, and most of the items on it were rich in calories, but the men needed healthy fare and they got it. They broke for an hour's lunch at noon, took a brown-bread-and-margarine break at 3:30, and except for the blubber crews—who had to work until all the blubber was flensed lest it freeze harder than steel—worked a twelve-hour day. There was precious little time between the evening meal and the morning call, and everyone was usually in bed by 9:30.

Life aboard the catcher boats was a smaller version of life on the factory ship, only these 100-ton steamers were much more susceptible to the rough seas, and were regularly tossed about like corks. Villiers wrote that one of the Tasmanians who volunteered for duty aboard one of the *Stars* became so sick that "to his intense sorrow . . . he was never able to work, or to sleep, or to eat, on the whole voyage!" The steamers were equipped with wireless sets that kept them in touch with the mother ship, and they could bunker enough coal to remain at sea

for two weeks. Since the visit of the *Ross* was the first to that sea since its eponymous discoverer's in 1841, many of the hunting expeditions of the catcher boats were actually voyages of exploration. Much of the natural history of the whales and other wildlife of the Antarctic was described for the first time on these sorties. For instance, the first recorded attack by killer whales on a blue whale was described by the crew of *Star I.* (After the orcas had killed the rorqual and fed on its tongue, the opportunistic whalers snagged the carcass and towed it to the floating factory for processing.)

One of the wonders of the Ross Sea—in fact, one of the true wonders of the world—is the great barrier that defines the leading edge of its ice shelf. On November 12, 1840, James Clark Ross inadvertently discovered a sea of ice that fills the interior of the great wedge-shaped chunk hacked out of the Antarctic continent. Ross named it the "Victoria Barrier" for his monarch, but it has since become known as the Ross Ice Shelf. From the sea, the barrier presents an impenetrable aspect, an unbroken perpendicular cliff of ice taller than the spars of the ships, beyond which rises a forbidding range of granitic, icy mountains.

The face of the ice barrier that Ross discovered in 1841 is not a barrier to entry into the Ross Sea. When the pack ice begins to close in, there is an entry at the mouth of the sea, somewhere between Cape Adare in the west and a point somewhere in the vicinity of the Edward VII Peninsula to the east. Because of the variable, shifting nature of the pack ice, geographical boundaries in the Antarctic are often unstable, and can vary from one year to the next. Thus Villiers could write, "no one knows what lies to the east" {of the mouth of the Ross Sea} when the whaleship *Ross* plied the ice barrier searching for an opening. Beyond this barricade is the Ross Sea itself (and beyond that, the ice shelf), which was a vast body of open water, reputedly full of whales.

The crew of the *Ross* encountered three kinds of whales: blues, fins and killers. The killers were of no interest to the whalers—except when they fed on the carcasses that floated alongside—but the blues and fins represented the greatest bonanza in whaling history. Huge, defenseless creatures, these rorquals were like ripe, icy plums, waiting to be plucked. And although the crew of the *Ross* tried, they met with only

In 1925, the *C. A. Larsen* sailed for the Antarctic with a huge—and hugely impractical—slipway in the bows. Once the Norwegians figured out how to cut a hole in the stern without interfering with the steering, whale carcasses were winched up through a great maw in the stern.

limited success, partly because the season of 1923–24 was particularly cold, and partly because they had not yet mastered the technology for open-water whaling in the southern ice. "The whales are as hard as wood," Larsen wrote. "It is deplorable that nothing can be accomplished with this tremendously valuable equipment. . . . If we only had a floating factory to hoist the whale on deck, we certainly need not have despaired."

By late February 1924, the absence of whales in the Ross Sea meant only that they had begun their northward migration. It was fall in the Antarctic, and the weather, which had been terrible, began to deteriorate. Blizzards raged, snow and sleetstorms

tore ships from their anchors, and in some instances the whale-catchers had to steam at full speed into the teeth of the storm just to maintain their positions. The ice began to close them in by early March, and trailing her fleet of whale-catchers as a mother goose her goslings, the *Ross* headed for New Zealand. She had collected only 17,500 barrels of oil—the ship's capacity was 58,000—from 10 fin and 211 blue whales, but still the voyage was considered a success. One of the blues measured 106 feet and was probably the largest whale ever caught.

The exploratory nature of the *Ross* expedition made it possible for whalers to visit the Antarctic for decades to come. Larsen successfully completed the first ice-whaling voyage in the Antarctic, but in November 1924, on board the *Ross* en route to the ice, he took ill and died of angina pectoris. He had expressed a wish that his body be embalmed, taken on the whaling voyage, and then brought back to Sandefjord, which was done. For the season 1924–25, the *Sir James Clark Ross* killed 408 blues and 19 finners, worth some thirty-two thousand barrels of oil.

Carl Anton Larsen died before the success of his explorations could be appreciated. By 1925 another Norwegian ship was commissioned, named after him, and endowed with two more innovations. She was oil-fired, and equipped with a slipway in the bows, so that the whales could be hauled up and processed on deck. This proved to be too cumbersome, however, since the port had to be laboriously shut before the ship could move. That same year, Petter Sørlle's invention of the stern slipway was finally brought into action. The "floating factory" which had been in use before was merely a larger, industrialized version of the old Yankee whaler, where the carcass was flensed alongside a ship, usually in a protected harbor, since the flensers could not stand on a wet, slippery carcass in the swell of the open sea, and certainly not in an Antarctic gale. Sørlle's contribution to whaling technology was the invention of the *stern* slipway, which consisted of a great maw cut in the stern of the ship, with an inclined ramp up which the dead whale could be winched. Although it sounds fairly simple to chop a hole in the stern of a ship—simpler than chopping one in the bow—the problems encountered had to do with the huge opening interfering with the rudder and the steering mechanism.

The *Lancing* left Sandefjord in June 1925, heading south, but before she arrived at the Antarctic, she stopped off the Congo coast to try the new equipment. The winches were not powerful enough to haul up a full-grown blue whale, the humpbacks stuck on the ramp, and there was a problem fastening a heavy cable around the tail stock of a whale in rough weather. The winches would be improved; "runners" would be installed on the inclined deck to ease the whale up; and the *hval kla* ("whale claw") would be introduced, a self-descriptive device that grabbed the tail of the whale and eliminated the inefficient and dangerous method of trying to throw a loop of cable around the flukes. The crew of the *Lancing* took 294 humpbacks in West African waters, and flensed every one on deck. They then headed for the Antarctic, to inaugurate a new epoch in which whales could be caught wherever they swam and processed on the spot. Like Foyn's *Spes et Fides, Lancing* was a benchmark in Norwegian—and therefore, worldwide—whaling history.

As efficiency increased, so too did the number of whales killed. The 1925–26 season witnessed the death of 531 whales; for 1926–27, another 1,117 whales died; and the numbers kept on climbing. In the prologue to the 1931 version of his book (written after the 1930–31 season) Allan Villiers wrote, "The oil, worth about one hundred and twenty-five dollars a ton is used for making soap, margarine, lard, and such prosaic things. . . . This season—1930–31—it was estimated that whales would bring into Norway seventy million dollars. Whaling is now one of Norway's leading industries."

The industry, as usual, was unaware of the consequences of its success. Of the 6,111 whales killed between 1923 and 1930, only 270 were not blues. Freed from the shackles of the British licensing system by the stern-slipway factory ship, the Norsemen could roam the Southern Ocean at will, with no restrictions on their catching but the ones they imposed on themselves—and they were not much given to controls. In fact, they raised their catches by increasing the number of whaleships and the number of areas in which they hunted; there seemed to be enough whales for everyone in Sandefjord. But there was still the problem of whaling in and around the Falkland Islands Dependencies; the British controlled these waters and still required licenses. So the Norwegians decided to apply the licensing system to their own industry, as a means of strengthening their position in negotiations with the British, and also, to a much lesser extent, because some people were beginning to worry about the stocks of whales. The British threatened to withdraw all their licenses unless the Norwegians ceased the uncontrolled pelagic killing. The two countries finally reached an agree-

The *Lancing,* the first whaling ship with a stern slipway, was launched in 1925.

The *Kosmos,* built in Ireland for the Norwegians in 1928, was the first floating factory built especially for the purpose of whaling. Previously, all other factory ships had been converted tankers. She is shown here at Wellington, New Zealand, in October 1929.

ment in 1928, whereby all British licenses would be renewed, and pelagic whaling would be conducted in the same manner as shore-based whaling.

The Norwegians continued to dominate ice whaling, although by 1930 the British were running them a close second. Business was so good in Norway that for the first time, a ship was built especially as a factory ship. Prior to 1928, every floating factory had been converted from a freighter or even a passenger liner. (The White Star liner *Suevic* was transformed into the floating factory *Skyttern* in 1929.) Commissioned by the Kosmos Company of Sandefjord and constructed in the Irish yards of Workman Clark, *Kosmos* was the largest tanker ever built up to that time. She had a gross displacement of 17,801 tons, and the capacity to store 120,000 barrels of oil in her capacious tanks. There were twenty-four boilers

below decks, and the enormous vessel could stay at sea for five months with her 21,200 tons of fuel oil. *Kosmos* was the first whaleship to include an airplane, but the experiment was a grim failure. Early in the 1929–30 season, the float-equipped *Gypsy Moth* took off with Leif Lier at the controls and the ship's doctor as passenger. The plane disappeared into the gray skies and was never seen again.*

As Norway and Britain jockeyed for whaling su-

---

*At about this time, the Norwegians also developed techniques for electrically killing whales. The problem was getting the electricity into the whale, and electric wires embedded in the forerunners (the lines attaching the whale to the ship) kept breaking. When the technology was perfected around 1935, it was discovered that while more effective than the exploding harpoon, electric whaling was also more expensive, and the idea was abandoned. It was later taken up by the Germans, who further refined it, but since their whaling industry was short-lived, they didn't have the opportunity to electrocute whales consistently.

premacy, the Norwegians developed the infamous "blue whale unit" (BWU) as a measurement device, and also, for the first time, introduced the idea of quotas. They needed some sort of benchmark that would enable them to report and compare catches. To maintain the high price of oil, the Norwegian Whaling Association and the British firm of H. K. Salvesen agreed to a formula whereby the whale quota would equal the barrel quota divided by 110, the average number of barrels yielded by a blue whale.* The whalers assigned relative values to the other species that they caught, as follows: One blue whale was the equivalent of two fins, two and a half humpbacks, or six sei whales. The catch statistics for early Norwegian whaling were set in BWUs, although at first there were no quotas at all. As J. L. McHugh wrote in his history of the International Whaling Commission, "It should not be necessary to explain why the BWU is illogical as a management unit"; it placed a totally unbalanced emphasis

on a single species—approximately as much effort was needed to catch, kill and process a blue whale as a fin, but you got twice the credit—so in the pure name of greed, the early whalers, and later the IWC, by their quotas effectively sentenced the blue whale to extinction.

Once the Antarctic had been firmly established as the world's premier whaling ground, whaling nations—now eager to share in the bounty—began to increase in number and in range. Although not all of them followed through, countries all over the world began to investigate entering the business. The ships of Argentina, Denmark, Germany and the United States joined the British and the Norwegians in the search for whales. By 1930, there were 38 ships with stern slipways, and a total of 184 catcher boats working the Antarctic. From the 1927–28 season to 1930–31, the pelagic catch in the Antarctic almost tripled, from a total of 13,775 whales to an almost inconceivable 40,201. Of this number, 28,325 were blues. For comparison, when C. A. Larsen found the blue whales of the Ross Sea in 1923, he managed to kill 211 in all. (Blue whale hunting was suspended forever after the 1965 season, when the whalers could only find 20 of the great rorquals; they killed them all.)

*Even though the old wooden barrels had not been used for years, the 40-gallon barrel remained the unit of measure for whale oil, six barrels making a ton. The average blue whale yielded between 80 and 140 barrels, although there is a record of a whale that was good for 305 barrels (50 tons). A fat fin whale might yield 30 to 50 barrels, or 5–8 tons of oil. After World War II, with the increase in processing efficiency, the per-whale yield increased to between 116 and 135 barrels per whale.

During the 1931–32 Antarctic season, the Norwegians did no Antarctic whaling. The fleet is shown here in the harbor at Sandefjord.

The whalecatcher *Petrel,* built in Oslo in 1928, sunk at her moorings after the whalers abandoned Grytviken. She was raised by the British Antarctic Survey, in hopes of turning the 115-foot ship into part of a museum on South Georgia.

After the boom season of 1930–31, when more ships killed more whales than in any single year in history up to that time,* the oil market was literally and figuratively flooded. Along with the glut of whale oil and the dearth of whales, the stock-market crash just about finished the Norwegian industry. The large buyers of whale oil (such as Unilever in England) were overstocked and offering greatly reduced prices

*In the Antarctic, the totals were as follows: 29,410 blue whales, 576 humpbacks, 10,017 fin whales and 145 sei whales, for a grand total of 40,148. This record stood for only seven years. In the 1938–39 season, the whalers, now joined in the hunt by Germany and Japan, killed 45,010 whales.

for oil. The whalers decided to lay up for the season of 1931–32, not going whaling at all. This, according to Tønnessen and Johnsen, was "a black day in the history of Norwegian whaling." But it was a bright day indeed for the British whaling industry, which sent five floating factories to the Antarctic, and accounted for 94 percent of the whales killed that season.

IT WAS about this time that the first international meetings were held to discuss the state of the world's whale stocks. In Paris in April 1930 the League of Nations called for a meeting of experts from France, Germany, Great Britain, Portugal, Norway and the United States. They debated various proposals, and met again in Geneva in 1931, where they adopted the previous year's report. This "Geneva Convention" was the basis for all subsequent international agreements, and included a ban on right whaling, a ban on shooting lactating females or calves, and a proviso that the convention would come into power when signed by eight nations, two of which had to be Norway and Great Britain. Britain, however, was only willing to sign a bilateral agreement with Norway—which negotiations took two more years—primarily to control the oil market between them, and not to conserve whale stocks. That this did not work was a function of several factors, including the breaking of Norwegian ranks (one of the whaling companies struck a deal with Unilever), the collapse of the price of whale oil, the start of Japanese whaling in the Antarctic, and Germany's increased pressure on Norway to allow it to enter the whaling business. Though Norway controlled the waves, Britannia controlled the marketplace.

As a second world war threatened to pit England against Germany, the British were determined to keep Norwegian whale oil from reaching Germany at all costs, but Norway, attempting to remain neutral, insisted upon its right to engage in normal trade. Whale oil was still important for the manufacture of margarine, but other, higher priorities intervened, and many of the floating factories were converted to tankers or troop-carriers, and the catchers to patrol boats. (Germany, already at war, submitted a proposal to Norway and Britain that their whaleships would be unmolested as long as she could count on receiving the lion's share of oil.) Norway had been a neutral country during World War I and tried this time to remain on the sidelines by negotiating with both Britain and Germany, but the British would only allow Norway to sell fish to the Germans, not whale oil. Norway's impartiality was destined to be short-lived, since the Germans needed ports even more than they needed Norwegian oil. On April 9, 1940, Norway was invaded. The Allies rushed to the aid of Norway, but as the situation in France began to deteriorate, the Allied troops were withdrawn, and until liberation in 1945, Norway was occupied by German troops. During the war, Norwegian whaling went on in a greatly reduced fashion, administered by the exile government in England. (King Haakon had left Norway on June 7, 1940, and remained in England for five years.) On January 15, 1941, the German raider *Pinguin* captured three Norwegian factory ships and eleven catcher boats in the Antarctic, with a total haul of 23,626 tons of oil. After delivering her prizes to Bordeaux, the raider was sunk by a British cruiser.

Germany Goes Whaling

GERMANY has had a long but sporadic association with whales and whaling. As early as the sixteenth century, whalers from Bremen, Hamburg and Schleswig-Holstein were taking Greenland whales in Spitsbergen waters. The British fishery had been stifled by the Muscovy Company's monopoly by around 1630, and although the Dutch dominated the field, other nations also joined in, including Germany. According to Elizabeth Ingalls, the journal of the German Friderich Marten's 1671 voyage is "one of the classics of whaling literature," and was contemporaneously translated into English, Dutch, French and Italian. In his "Comparative View" of the various nations involved in the Arctic fishery, Scoresby wrote, "Among the ports of Germany, that of *Hamburgh* occupies the most respectable place in the annals of the whale-fishery." From 1670 to 1719, the Hamburgers sent out a total of 2,289 voyages, and brought back the products of 9,976 whales. There was a substantial German participation in the South Seas fishery during the nineteenth century, enough at least to warrant a caricature of German whalers by Herman Melville, the self-appointed critic of all whalers who were not fortunate enough to be Americans. In the chapter of *Moby-Dick* where the *Pequod* meets the *Virgin,* the latter becomes the *Jungfrau,* and although there is some confusion about the actual nationality of the crew (Melville seems unable—or unwilling—to differentiate between Dutch

and Germans), whoever they are, they are objects of derision.* Before World War I, the Germans had made several attempts to enter the whaling business: in Iceland in 1903, in Chile in 1907, and in their territory of Southwest Africa in 1912.

To reduce Germany's dependence on foreign whale-oil imports and also to encourage domestic dairy production, Hitler declared war on the margarine trust on March 23, 1933, and established a "fat monopoly" which would control all imports, marketing and production of fats. The eating of margarine was characterized as being unpatriotic, and German butter production was subsidized by the government. This was known as the German "fat plan," and among its other results, it led to the building of a German whaling fleet.

During the period 1930–37, the Germans' consumption of whale oil was the highest of any nation in the world. It was only natural that they would want to eliminate the middleman and obtain the oil themselves. Carl Kircheiss, who had had whaling experience in Argentina, Alaska and the Antarctic, was the advocate of a German whaling industry, and by

*In a paper devoted to the defense of various foreign whalers ridiculed by Melville, de Jong admits that he has "doubts regarding the ability of some German whalemen," and quotes the 1845 journal of the Bremen whaler *Alexander Barclay* in which two boats are lowered after sperm whales, but break off the chase when they encounter a fin whale. This, of course, is the story that Melville tells about the "Dutch" whalemen of the *Jungfrau,* so it is possible that he was familiar with this tale.

1933 he had managed to assemble a consortium to buy a tanker that was refitted and christened *Jan Wellem*. The first factory ship whose technical machinery was entirely powered by electricity, *Jan Wellem* was accompanied by eight 1,700-horsepower catcher boats (named *Treff I* through *VIII*), and headed for the Weddell Sea in September 1936.

Walter Rau (1874–1940) was Germany's predominant twentieth-century whaler. He headed a concern that produced margarine, vegetable oils and animal fats, and it was therefore natural that he would want to involve himself in whale oil as well. In 1935 he commissioned a 14,869-ton floating factory that he named for himself, and eight catchers, *Rau I–VIII*. Norwegian managers, engineers and gunners were signed aboard at highly inflated wages. The Germans intended to expand their fleet further, and under the direction of Hjalmar Schacht, the German Economics Minister, they built the *Unitas*.

The *Walter Rau* was started in 1935, but not completed until 1937, because German shipyards were busy with other projects. At the same time, the *Terje Viken* was constructed, at a gross weight of 20,369 tons, the largest factory ship built up to that time. Because the Germans were inexperienced at whaling, they had to hire Norwegians, a situation that caused a great deal of resentment in Norway; not only was Norwegian whaling suffering the entry of other nations into the business, but Norwegian gunners, engineers and managers were defecting to the competition.

Unilever, which had huge factories in Germany, was still intent on total domination of the oil market, and it tried to corner the sales of whale oil to Germany. World War II had not yet started, but it was apparent to some observers that Unilever was placing sales before loyalty. Some Norwegians also appeared to be more interested in their own financial well-being than the well-being of their country, and continued to negotiate with the Nazis and Unilever. This "three-cornered transaction" went as follows, according to Tønnessen and Johnsen: "The whaling companies sold their oil, the German shipbuilding yards obtained contracts, and the German state obtained the whale oil it needed to carry out its fat plan, and this it managed to do without dipping into its scant reserves of foreign currency, which had to be reserved for raw materials essential to a war economy. Indirectly, Norwegian whale oil was assisting Germany's rearmament." The Germans had not much of a whaling history, and they realized that they could not possibly capture or process whales without Norwegian crews. (When they finally set out for the southern ice in the *Walter Rau*, the *Jan Wellem*, and the *Terje Viken*, the Norwegians aboard these ships were considered traitors.)

In January of 1939, the Germans attempted to purchase the entire holdings of the Sales Pool (a consortium of British and Norwegian whaling companies designed to control the price of whale oil), but the potential sellers refused to lower their price to conform to the German demands. The Germans threatened to expand their whaling interests to such an extent that they would put Norway out of business, and make them withdraw from the London Agreement, the first convention designed to regulate whaling. Because the Germans were unwilling to meet the price set by the Sales Pool, the oil was sold to Britain. Thus the Germans failed to secure 80,000 tons of whale oil, which would have enabled them to produce 160 million kilograms of margarine. Little Norway had outmaneuvered the Third Reich, and although the issue was only whale oil, it was one of a number of reasons for the German invasion that followed in the spring of 1940.

After Germany invaded Norway, all trade was suspended, but the invaders failed to capture some 55,000 tons of whale oil en route from the Antarctic, which subsequently found its way to Britain. Rather than outfit proper whaling expeditions, the Germans sent raiders to the Antarctic to seize Norwegian whaleships. On January 15, 1941, the *Pinguin* captured three factory ships and eleven catcher boats, with a total haul of 23,626 tons of oil.

As was the case with the "war to end war," the whales were not spared by World War II. Even as the combatants trained their weapons on each other, they continued to kill whales for their oil. Both the Axis powers sent expeditions south in 1940–41 (the Japanese operated the shore station at Grytviken from 1940 to 1942), although for the duration of the war the number of whales killed dropped sharply. (Norwegian whalers were busy hunting sperm whales off the coast of Peru to produce the valuable oil for the American armaments industry, and Azorean whalers, supplying the same need, reached heights of success that they had not achieved before or since.

The Japanese Arrive

WITH THE WHALES in short supply in her own coastal waters, the Japanese decided to join the rest of the world's whalers in the Antarctic hunt. Manned mostly by Taiji men, an ex-Norwegian factory ship named the *Tonan Maru* headed south in 1934.

The Japanese did not start using factory ships until the 1930s because they could operate from the Bonin Islands in the south and the Kurils in the north, which were so close to the whaling grounds that there was no need for floating factories. (Toyo Gyogyo K.K., subsequently Toyo Hogei K.K., planned to begin pelagic whaling in the Bering Sea in 1929, but could not find a suitable ship.) After World War II, the Soviets annexed the Kurils, and operated from the five Japanese land stations that had been established before 1913.

The Japanese purchased the Norwegian factory ship *Antarctic* in 1934, and renamed her *Tonan Maru,* which can be roughly translated as "Aspiration Toward the South." It was the first time that a factory ship had been sold to a foreign power without a stipulation that the crews and matériel had to be Norwegian. According to Tønnessen and Johnsen, "A chapter in the history of whaling had begun which even before the outbreak of the Second World War threatened to put other whaling nations out of business, and after the war actually succeeded in doing so."

Given the long and bloody history of whaling, it is difficult to determine which nation has the worst record. Making that determination not only requires an analysis of the historical imperatives, the economic and sociological climate of the times, and the very nature of the people doing the actual whaling, but it also cries out for an answer to the fundamental question of whether or not whales ought to be killed at all. If they should, for one reason or another, then the nation that kills them best should be acclaimed. If, on the other hand, a case can be made for their not being killed, then the nation that kills the most is the worst offender.

Among those nations that have been most successful at whaling—particularly insofar as numbers of whales killed is concerned—have been the Basques of the sixteenth century, who wiped out the northern right whale in European waters; the Dutch and British whalers of the eighteenth-century Greenland and Spitsbergen fisheries, who eliminated the bowhead in the eastern Arctic; Australians and New Zealanders who killed almost every breeding right whale that ventured into their waters; and the Yankee sperm whalers, who plied the Seven Seas in search of the mighty cachalot. Still, the history of whaling has few parallels to the rapacity of the Japanese whalers in the Antarctic. Where other nations, such as Norway and England, killed whales by the thousands in the Antarctic, at least they paid lip service to the plight of the whales or the future of the industry. The Japanese simply sailed south, caught as many whales as they could, and then peddled the oil and meat. When the first steps were taken to study conservation measures that might be necessary to preserve the whales, the Japanese refused to participate.

In 1935–36, their second season in the Antarctic, Japanese whalers produced 44,145 barrels of oil and large quantities of meat. (During the twentieth century, the Japanese were the only industrialized nation that ate whale meat. Unlike the other whaling countries, the Japanese sent refrigerator vessels to accompany the factory ships, so that the meat could be frozen and transported back to Japan. Not only were the Japanese killing the whales, they were simultaneously creating a market for the meat. South African whalers prior to 1967 used to grind up the meat and bone for fertilizer, but when the Japanese announced their interest in purchasing whale meat, South African whaling received an added stimulus. By 1988, the Japanese were buying the meat of the whales that the Icelanders claimed they were killing for research—but that is getting too far ahead of the story.)

On the crest of a rising oil market, the Japanese decided to construct their own ships rather than buy outmoded Norwegian vessels, and toward that end, they purchased the plans for the *Sir James Clark Ross* from the British shipyard that had built her. In 157 days (as contrasted with the eighteen months that the British would have taken), the *Nisshin Maru* was completed, along with eight 267-ton catcher boats. In 1936–37 the Japanese killed 1,116 whales, producing 91,368 barrels of oil, which were purchased by the Germans. This connection was only one of many that contributed to the Tokyo-Berlin Axis, but it was a significant one. The whales were contributing to Japanese and German preparations for war.

During the next season, the Japanese whaling companies of Taiyo Hogei and Nishon Hogei sent four expeditions to the Antarctic, each with a factory ship and an accompanying flotilla of catcher boats (including the *Seki Maru,* the world's first diesel-powered catcher), and returned to Japan with 388,683 barrels of oil. For this staggering amount, 5,582 whales were killed.

Tokyo continued to increase its whaling capacity; from zero in 1934, it had by 1938 captured 11.6 percent of the global whale-oil market, and seemed determined to increase its share. Until Japan was forced to direct its attention and its ships elsewhere in 1941, it had managed to kill 32,840 whales in seven seasons. More new factory ships were on the drawing boards when the war intervened.

Because she was still a neutral country in 1940, Japan could lease the Grytviken station on South Georgia from the British. Japanese whalers operated the station until April 9, 1940, when Germany invaded Norway. Since the season had ended by that time, the Japanese catchers were on their way home, and upon their arrival, most of the crews were inducted into the navy.

From 1941 to 1945, Japanese whaling was severely curtailed. It was rumored that some of the floating factories used their stern slipways to launch the miniature submarines that participated in the attack on Pearl Harbor, but by the end of the war, all the factory ships had been destroyed. Japan's whaling vessels and personnel were commandeered by the navy, and many of both were casualties of war. Fifty-one of the seventy-eight catchers operational in 1941 were destroyed by 1945. During the war, however, because they still needed meat and oils for domestic and military purposes, the Japanese continued to work the old Japan Grounds. During the years 1942–44, the offshore whalers took a total of 3,122 whales, mostly humpbacks and Bryde's whales in the spring, and sperm whales in the winter.

For the 1943 and 1944 seasons, the Ocean Fishing Company at Chichi Jima in the Bonin Islands refitted other ships, and catches soared in an attempt to fill the needs of an isolated island nation at war. While 1942 saw only 68 whales captured in the Bonins, the average for the next two seasons was 269. Iwo Jima is one of the Bonin Islands, and when the Americans finally took it on March 16, 1945, whaling came to a halt. It was not long, however, before the Japanese petitioned their conquerors for permission to reopen the whaling stations in the Bonins, and by November 1945, they were back in business.

Interlude: The Exhibition of Whales

THE EXHIBITION of whale carcasses probably began with the first whales that washed ashore. In medieval Europe—before anyone realized that there was a florin or a sou to be made from it—the curious probably came to see the gigantic carcasses that occasionally beached. People have always flocked to see dead whales because of their astonishing size, and it was only a matter of time before entrepreneurs realized that the carcasses or skeletons would be of more than passing interest to landlocked spectators or those who had not had the opportunity to see a real whale.

For reasons that became more and more obvious with the passage of time, it was more efficacious to exhibit the skeleton than the carcass, as in the case of the 95-foot blue whale that had washed ashore in Ostend, Holland, in 1827. (Until 1831, Belgium was part of the Netherlands.) For the next seven years, the "Ostend Whale" made the rounds of England, France and Holland. It was one of the most popular attractions of the day, and numerous descriptions and illustrations of it have survived. A French lithograph of 1828, for example, is entitled "The Ostend Whale Visited by the Elephant and the Giraffe," and shows the whale on its side, surrounded by scores of orderly, top-hatted gentlemen and the other large mammals mentioned in the title. Henry William Dewhurst's 1834 *Natural History of the Order Cetacea* includes a detailed discussion of the anatomy of the Ostend whale, and a complete history of its discovery, itinerary and destiny. The whale was originally found floating in the sea, and towed to Ostend. There it was reduced to its skeletal components, and its journey began. At the time, the taxonomy of the great whales was not clearly understood, and there was some debate about the species, but the problem was neatly solved by the Baron Cuvier in Paris, who pro-

NOW ON EXHIBITION
—AT—
FULTON SLIP,
EAST RIVER,

A MONSTER WHALE!

This Whale was caught off Provincetown Harbor, near Cape Cod. There are four kinds of Whales: the Sperm Whale, the Right Whale, the Hump-back Whale and the Fin-back Whale. This one is of the Hump-back species,

65 feet long, and 45 feet around the body at the hump, and weighs 70 tons.

The carcass will produce 40 to 50 barrels of oil. Its mouth measures 17 feet from the tip of the nose to the spout hole. The carcass is worth $500 for oil and bone. This whale has been dead 7 days to-day (Friday, March 27). He was bought by S. S. Swift & Co., of Provincetown, for $600, and was towed by one of Boston's biggest tugs to New York, which took four days and nights, and cost $450 for towage, and was landed in New York, on Tuesday. He was floated on the Dry Dock, foot of Stanton street, on Wednesday morning.

When captured 20 barrels of herring were taken out of him. He will be on exhibition from three to eight days longer, according to the weather.

This is the Largest Whale ever Exhibited in the U.S.

This Whale was struck by a bomb lance. A bomb lance is filled with dynamite, which explodes when it strikes the blubber, killing the Whale.

These gentlemen have expended over $1600 before taking in a cent. They gave New York the preference in exhibiting this monster of the deep, over any other city.

Exhibited by a 44-year old Whaler.
S. M. V. COUNTRY.

ILLUSTRATIONS OF THE WHALE, 10 CENTS EACH.

J. DICKSON & BRO., STEAM JOB PRINTERS, 24 Beekman St., N. Y.

LA BALEINE D'OSTENDE.

Visitée par l'Éléphant, la Giraffe, & les Osages.

"The Ostend Whale" (1827), visited by a variety of observers, including an elephant and a giraffe.

nounced it a *Balaenóptera Rórqual.* (At a length of 95 feet, it had to have been a blue whale; no other animal in the world has ever gotten to be that large.) "To whatever species the individual specimen in question belongs," wrote Dewhurst, "it is doubtless the largest animal that has ever been captured, and I do not hesitate to say that the skeleton is the most perfect in Europe."

The skeleton was prepared in a long wooden house, and when it was ready for transportation, it was accompanied by a *pavilion* that could be set up and dismantled on the spot. Because the whale had been "captured" when Ostend was part of Holland, there were those who believed it should belong to that nation. Monsieur Herman Kessels, the man who arranged for its grand tour, was afraid that the "King of Holland" (Prince William of Orange-Nassau) would claim it and present it to the University of Leyden, so he had it shipped across the Atlantic to America. Of the end of its wanderings, Dewhurst

wrote, "I understand the proprietors have embarked with this stupendous skeleton for the United States, where they plan to exhibit it." They may have done so, but documentation of the exhibition seems to have ceased after this 1834 citation, and the skeleton somehow wound up in the Natural History Museum in Leningrad.

In 1838, "under the distinguished and permanent Patronage of the Universities of Oxford and Cambridge," the skeleton of a blue whale which had been found off Plymouth was trailed through England in a series of carriages. From the broadside accompanying the exhibition of the "Stupendous Royal British Whale":

Heads of Families and Schools are respectfully invited to avail themselves of the present opportunity of impressing upon the young mind—"upon the tender thought"—a just sense of the boundless power of the Creative Hand which the study of nature is at all times capable of bestowing, for here, while standing in the body of the "biggest born'' hugest of all living creatures, it might be truly said we "look through Nature up to nature's God."*

In the early days of Yankee whaling, the whales were processed at sea, so there was little opportunity for landlubbers to see the victims or the process, and later the only American whaling stations were along the West Coast. In 1880, a fin whale was killed off Provincetown, Massachusetts, and towed to New York by tugboat, where it was placed on exhibition in a dry dock near the Fulton Ferry slip. No attempt was made to preserve the carcass, and when it began to spoil, the oil was tried-out for commercial utilization.

A whale had washed ashore at the Swedish city of Malmö in 1866, and was exhibited in Stockholm with its mouth propped open so wide that spectators could wander in and out. Subsequently, a cast was made of this whale, and it was exhibited alongside its skeleton in the Natural History Museum at Göteborg.

*The descriptions of this and the above skeleton are reproduced in Elizabeth Ingalls's catalogue of the whaling prints in the Francis B. Lothrop collection, now housed at the Peabody Museum of Salem, Massachusetts.

Also in 1866, whaling captain William Cash, of Nantucket, received the following letter:

Dear Sir:

When I was in Nantucket recently, I called to see your Whale's Jaw. It was a stunner, and I was sorry I could not see the man who captured it. I hoped you will carefully read the enclosed circular. Perhaps you will then feel that if the jaw was properly placed in my Museum, and its history and your name legibly inscribed on it, more of your friends (as well as the great public) would see it, than they would on your own premises.

Perhaps, also, these considerations would induce you to hand your name down to a grateful posterity by being identified as the *Donor* of this Jaw to the Free Museum in New York.

However, if you don't see it in that light, will you please inform me whether you will sell it to be placed in my Museum, and if so for what price.

Yours truly,
P. T. Barnum

Captain Cash was not swayed by Barnum's appeal to posterity, and the jaw remained in Nantucket, where it is now in the Whaling Museum.

Whaling museums, such as those in Nantucket and New Bedford, are usually concerned with the

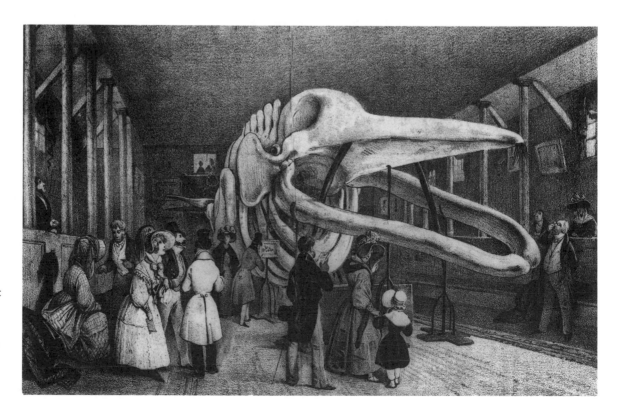

Inside its specially built pavilion, the skeleton of "The Ostend Whale" (a blue whale), drew appreciative crowds in Europe from 1827 to 1834.

The half-scale model of the *Lagoda* under construction in the Bourne Building of the New Bedford Whaling Museum; July 1918.

whaleship *Lagoda,* the centerpiece of the museum's displays. This model—the largest ship model in the world—was dedicated in 1916, and housed in a building that was built especially for it. The Bourne Building was named for Jonathan Bourne (1811–89), a New Bedford whaling merchant who had an interest in some twenty-four whaleships, one of which was the *Lagoda.* (The name comes from a mistake; she was supposed to have been named for Lake *Ladoga* in Russia, but the internal consonants became transposed and were never corrected.) The original *Lagoda* was a bark 108 feet long; the model measures 54 feet 9 inches on the waterline, but from the tip of the flying jib-boom to the tip of the spanker boom, the model is 82.5 feet long.

Also on display in the New Bedford Whaling Museum is one of the most remarkable paintings ever made, a 1,275-foot-long work of art by Benjamin Russell and Caleb P. Purrington. It is a "panorama," a type of moving picture that was popular in the early nineteenth century in England and America. A theatrical scenery painter named John Rowson Smith is said to have invented the form when he painted Napoleon's burning of Moscow in 1812. The exhibition was accompanied by church bells, cannon shots and pyrotechnics—evidently not unlike Tchaikovsky's commemoration of the same event, the *1812 Overture.*

exhibition of artifacts of whaling history, and are replete with harpoons, scrimshaw, and whaling prints. But since whaling history was so often dependent upon the natural history of the whales, the two subjects lend themselves to integration. At the whaling museum at Taiji, in Japan, for example, in addition to the whaleboats, harpoons and other whaling paraphernalia, there are whale skeletons and numerous displays on the biology of whales and dolphins. New Bedford exhibits a skeleton of a humpback, as well as a recently painted 100-foot-long mural showing Moby Dick. The whales in this painting are half-size, to complement the half-size model of the

The whaling museum at Taiji, Japan. The symbol of the museum is a right whale, a species that has been nearly extinct in Japanese waters for hundreds of years.

The Russell and Purrington panorama was painted in 1847–48 on sheets of cotton canvas eight and a half feet long, sewn together so they could be unrolled across a theater stage, and presented with a synchronized spoken narrative. It begins as the whaler *Kutusoff* leaves New Bedford, and then takes us to the Azores, across the South Atlantic, thence to South America, Hawaii and the Northwest Coast of North America, to Tahiti, around the Horn to Rio, and then home. Along the way, we see whales being hunted, whaleboats being stove by angry whales, techniques of cutting-in and trying-out, and a marvelous travelogue of places that landlubbers were not likely to see. The details of the ships and whaling are accurate because Benjamin Russell had actually sailed on the *Kutusoff* in 1841 and was able to communicate them to Purrington, a house-painter and decorator who never went to sea.

The New Bedford Whaling Museum has another painting dear to the hearts of whaling historians, Charles S. Raleigh's *Panorama of a Whaling Voyage in the Ship Niger,* painted from 1878 to 1880. Even though it is called a "panorama," Raleigh's work is a mere 197 feet long, and is not continuous, but rather a series of separate panels designed to hang round the walls of an exhibition hall. (It was last shown in its entirety in 1904, in the Masonic Building of New Bedford.) Like the Russell and Purrington panorama, this one shows what it was like to

sail aboard a whaler, and contains some of the most thrilling and informative scenes of nineteenth-century sperm whaling. Returning whalemen—if they did not immediately ship out again—were likely to remain in port cities, so these panoramas brought the romance and danger of the whaler's life to inland cities which the whalers might not ordinarily visit.

IN MUSEUMS such as Mystic Seaport and New Bedford, where the history of whaling is discussed, it is often considered instructive to show the process of whaling. There are any number of recent films that show the Japanese or the Norwegians killing whales, but they show the mechanized whaling of the twentieth century, not the traditional square-riggers in pursuit of the sperm whale. In their audio-visual presentations, however, both museums make use of an extraordinary film, made in 1922, which shows actual sperm whalers in action. The story in *Down to the Sea in Ships* concerns Patience (Marguerite Courtot), the daughter of the stern old Quaker whaleship owner (William Walcott), who would marry her childhood sweetheart (Raymond McKee), except that he is not a whaleman, a preference her father insists upon. (Also in the movie, playing the granddaughter of the shipowner, is seventeen-year-old Clara Bow, who disguises herself as a boy and stows away, causing all sorts of complications when she removes her stovepipe hat and her long hair tumbles out.) Our

The venerable *Charles W. Morgan,* built in New Bedford in 1841, was still a working whaler when this photograph was taken in 1920.

young man is shanghaied aboard the whaleship, and through the convoluted plot devices so beloved by early directors (this film was "personally directed" by Elmer Clifton), he overcomes a mutiny, gets promoted to boatsteerer, harpoons a sperm whale, and brings the ship home to New Bedford just in time to crash through the window of the Quaker meeting house to prevent Patience from marrying his archnemesis, Samuel Siggs, who had been responsible for the shanghaiing in the first place and had planned to steal the ship to sell it "to the goldfields."

As silly as the movie seems now, with its villains grinning lasciviously, its stalwart heroes triumphing through their eye makeup, and Clara Bow making anybody think she was a boy, *Down to the Sea in Ships* is probably the best whaling movie ever made.* Un-

*The film—whose original title was supposed to have been *Brawn of the Brine*—was an enormous success when it was first shown. A reviewer in the Boston *Globe* said that it was "Probably one of the most beautiful photoplays ever made," and it was rated among the ten best pictures of 1922. It played one New York theater for three months, and fifty-five Chicago movie houses in a single week.

like every film that followed it, this one contained genuine Yankee sperm whaling scenes, from the outfitting of the ship at the New Bedford wharf to sailing through rough weather (although in the concluding storm scenes, buckets of water are thrown to simulate rough seas crashing on the decks). Most important, the film showed the entire process of whaling, from the lowering of the boats to the harpooning, the Nantucket sleigh ride, the lancing, the tow, the cutting-in (complete with hungry sharks below the cutting stage), the bailing of the case, and finally, the trying-out, with the fires burning into the night. No wonder the museums have chosen to show the whaling parts of this film; it allows people to understand nineteenth-century sperm whaling in a way that no static exhibit ever could.

Assuming that only a dedicated naval historian would notice the differences between them, Hollywood employed a variety of ships in the film. The venerable *Charles W. Morgan,* which had made her last whaling voyage in 1921, was used for the dockside scenes in New Bedford.* For the sailing scenes, the studio hired the whaleship *Wanderer* (which was to run aground in a storm on Cuttyhunk Island only two years later), and when it came to the actual whaling, the cameramen were aboard the schooner *Gaspé* on a whaling voyage to the West Indies. (A special credit is given to A. G. Penrod and Paul H. Allen, "who, in small boats, stood by their cameras at the risk of their lives to photograph the fighting whales.")

In Vestfold, Norway, the birthplace of the father of modern whaling, the museum displays a model of *Spes et Fides,* Svend Foyn's first whale-catcher, various harpoons and lances, and the obligatory skeletons, to show the actual size of the creatures that men could dispatch by using their ingenuity and craft.

In British Columbia in June of 1935, the Pacific Whaling Company decided to tour a 55-foot, 66-ton fin whale that had been captured off southern California. They placed the embalmed whale on a railroad flatcar and sent it around the United States and Canada. It cost fifteen cents for an adult, and ten cents for a child to see "A Mystery of This Age," and a "Playmate of Dinosaurs and Mastodons, Last of a Race of Towering Giants." According to *The Whale Journal,* a combination newspaper/guide book issued by the Pacific Whaling Exhibition Company, the "Mammoth Sea Exhibit Draws Huge Crowds in Every City," which cities included Chicago, New York, Boston, Denver, Louisville and Tulsa. (In case a giant leviathan of the deep was not your cup of tea, the exhibit also included a flea circus, a family of penguins, a desiccated octopus, and a whaling captain named Whale Oil Dave, who "Might Have Stepped Out of the Pages of a Jack London Book, But He's Real, Live and Virile.") In an editorial, the company thanks "the newspapers throughout the country. From the leading metropolitan dailies to the remotest country weekly paper, editors have seen fit to give their heartiest support to the exhibition. . . . The Pacific Whaling Company realizes that its suc-

cess to a great extent has been the result of the support given by the newspapers and is appreciative of it."

Early in the twentieth century, the American Museum of Natural History in New York erected a full-size model of a blue whale. The original plan, according to Roy Chapman Andrews, who worked on it, was to cover it with paper, but "it couldn't be kept from buckling and sinking in between the ribs." With James L. Clark (who was later to become assistant director of the museum), Andrews finished it with wire netting and papier-mâché. The internal framework was wood, steel wire and iron pipe. (The blue whale model in the British Museum of Natural History was made of plaster of paris with "ribs" of wood like a ship's.) The New York version hung in the Hall of Mammals like a suspended dirigible until 1965, when the museum decided it was time to upgrade its whale exhibit. (It was no doubt aroused to do this by the appearance, a couple of years earlier, of a life-size model at the Smithsonian Institution in Washington.) After several rejected ideas (a beached whale carcass; a whale somehow shown in an ice field), it was decided to hang the whale from the ceiling of the Hall of Ocean Life, one of the most commodious exhibit halls in any museum in the world.* It would have to be: the model was going to be shown in the round, and was going to be 94 feet long.

Hung on a structure of steel I-beams and crafted of polyurethane foam with a fiberglass skin, the model was assembled in place and painted in an approximation of the blue whale's color scheme.† In 1968 the exhibit was unveiled to rave reviews. It was the largest whale model in existence (longer than the one in the British Museum of Natural History by six feet, and two feet longer than the Smithsonian's). It is an awesome exhibit, suspended from a single point in the vaulted ceiling of the great hall. While the

---

*The *Charles W. Morgan* was built in 1841 in New Bedford, and during a career that spanned eighty years, she made thirty-seven whaling voyages, and earned almost $1.5 million for her owners. From 1922 to 1935, she resided at the South Dartmouth estate of Colonel Edward Green, but when he died and left no money to maintain her, a group of businessmen brought her to Mystic Seaport in Connecticut. There she was completely repaired and refitted, and sat high and dry until 1973, when with great fanfare she was refloated. The *Morgan,* now the jewel of Mystic Seaport's extensive collection, is the only square-rigger remaining from the glory days of whaling.

*Prior to the installation of the blue whale model, the Hall of Ocean Life—which was officially opened in May 1933—contained skeletons of a fin whale, a gray whale, and a right whale, as well as a cast of a baby sperm whale that had been injured by a boat's propeller on the Brooklyn waterfront (after it died, it had been brought in the flesh to the museum).

†In an article in *Curator,* Richard Van Gelder, then the curator of mammals at the museum and the man putatively in charge of the whale project, admits that he had never seen a blue whale, and had no idea of what color it was supposed to be. It ended up being battleship gray, which is not particularly close to the slate-blue coloration that is responsible for the whale's common name.

Like a motionless dirigible, the early model of a blue whale hangs on wires from the ceiling of the Hall of Mammals in the American Museum of Natural History in New York. It was made of papier-mâché stretched over an iron framework.

true size of this, the largest animal that has ever lived, can be appreciated from this model, it is still a model, and it is very much out of its natural element. (Although the accompanying labels give the weight of a real blue whale, they do not tell the museum visitor that the *model* weighs a not insignificant ten tons.)

EVEN AFTER aquariums had successfully displayed captive dolphins, and museums had built full-size models of giant whales, real whales still held a fascination for the public, even if they were long dead and pumped full of formaldehyde. There was indeed something mystical about seeing a creature that was 60 or 70 feet long. People could understand an 8-foot dolphin, but its size was nothing compared to an animal longer than a railroad car.

As recently as 1954, an embalmed whale was the subject of an exhibition in Europe and America. Harpooned by a Dane named Leif Søgaard off the Norwegian island of Haroy, the 70-ton female finback made a tour of 165 European cities and then crossed the Atlantic on a freighter. To prevent—or more accurately, postpone—decomposition, the whale was injected with eight thousand quarts of

formaldehyde. Søgaard had planned to exhibit "Mrs. Harøy" for a few more years, but when the exhibit failed to charm the blasé New Yorkers, he had the carcass moved to Coney Island. There it began to decompose, and two days before the removal deadline imposed by the Department of Health, the whale mysteriously caught fire and burned.

In a 1954 issue of *Norsk Hvalfangst-Tidende,* the Norwegian Whaling Gazette, is the story of another "whale on show." This animal (a 65-foot fin whale) was harpooned off Cape Cod, embalmed, and placed aboard a small freighter. Under the auspices of Captain Oakes Anderson, it toured the United States by water, "through New York State then over to Ohio, and thence on both sides of the Mississippi and its adjacent rivers and canals." The enterprise was a success, "despite the fact that it stanks [*sic*] frightfully from the whale." Anderson apparently had to pay off various municipal officials to allow him to exhibit his malodorous whale, but he continued to tour. Finally his partners withdrew, and he was left alone with the carcass. "He was unable to sell it or give it away, and he dared not allow it to drift out to sea as he was afraid it would interfere with maritime traffic. Anderson therefore had no option but

Ninety-four feet long and weighing more than ten tons, the new blue whale model dominates the Hall of Ocean Life at the American Museum of Natural History in New York.

to continue travelling round and showing the whale." The story ends with Captain Anderson alone with his whale, and the possibility that the skeleton now resides in a museum near Albany.

Probably the most unusual "exhibition" of a whale ever recorded—if indeed it is not an old whaler's tale—is the whale in the iceberg. According to a story by C. F. Holder that appeared in *St. Nicholas Magazine* in 1884, a ship named *Laughing Polly* (the name alone makes the account suspect) is sailing in the South Shetlands when the lookout spies what he takes to be a ship in the distance. "Your ship is an iceberg," the captain tells him. "A pretty sailor-man you are not to tell an iceberg from a whaler." They steer directly toward the berg, and discover that the iceberg, which towers three hundred feet in the air, contains the body of a "rorqual nearly one hundred feet in length." The captain explains that the whale was not entombed at sea, but washed ashore on some ice-sheet, and ice and snow formed over it for many years until it broke away and became the imprisoning berg. As further proof of this tale, the author cites a "Captain Pendleton," who "saw a whale two hundred and eighty feet from the surface of the water in an ice-cliff eight hundred feet high." Since the

"explanation" is less plausible than the event itself, we must conclude that Mr. Holder had visited P. T. Barnum's circus once too often, and let his obviously fertile imagination procreate a wonderfully improbable event. Since whales on display are themselves wonderfully improbable events already, a whale in an iceberg should not surprise us all that much.

When Gigi, the juvenile gray whale, was captured and placed on exhibit at Sea World in 1971, she was the first—and thus far the only—large living whale ever intentionally exhibited to the public. In recent years, however, other cetaceans have become the subjects of exhibitions, almost always by accident. Occasionally, these accidents occur because whales strand on various beaches, and the public flocks to see the unfortunate creatures thrashing in the shallows. Although there have been instances where pilot whales and various smaller dolphins have been rescued and returned to sea, the larger beached whales almost always die.

In April of 1981, a juvenile sperm whale arrived on the beach at Coney Island, within the city limits of New York, a locale not ordinarily associated with living whales. The animal, which was about 25 feet long and thought to be a male, was christened

"Mrs. Harøy," a fin whale that had been harpooned off Norway and toured throughout Europe and America in 1954.

One of the strangest stories about whales is the one that describes a whale trapped in an iceberg. In the 1884 *St. Nicholas Magazine,* the story was told by Charles F. Holder, and illustrated by George R. Halm.

"Physty" (a diminutive of his generic name *Physeter*), and towed offshore. He showed up the next morning on a beach at Fire Island, some forty miles from the site of the original stranding. There he was towed to an empty boat basin, where assorted Good Samaritans ministered unto him by feeding him squid and antibiotics, and testing his exhalations for signs of the disease that had debilitated him. (It was determined that he had no fewer than four strains of pneumonia.) For a week various people swam with him, petted him, sang to him, and analyzed everything he did, from the rate of his breathing to the color of his eyes. (A sperm whale's eyes are brown.) It appeared that Physty was becoming weaker and weaker, and a marine-mammal veterinarian was scheduled to arrive to perform the necropsy. Perhaps because of the squid, perhaps because of the Chloromycetin, perhaps because of the rest he had received while remaining in the boat basin, Physty, who had been swimming on his side in the eight-foot-deep water, righted himself, and began to swim strongly. On the eighth day of his incarceration, the nets that were used to close off the boat basin were cut, and the young whale was herded out to sea by his rescuers in inflatable boats.

The presence of a whale—and a sperm whale at that—in the waters of New York was big news. Network television covered the event from the day Physty beached himself in the shadow of the roller coaster at Coney Island, and by the time he was released millions of people had seen his wrinkled hide and listened to his labored exhalations. Not only was it the first time a large living whale had been "rescued,"* it was the first time many people had ever seen a living whale. Because he was confined to such a small space, it was easy to film his behavior, almost as if he were in captivity. More often than not, however, whales do not perform in locations that are so convenient. (The first film ever made of free-swimming sperm whales was shot during the summer of 1983 in the Indian Ocean off Sri Lanka.)

In October 1985, a humpback whale evidently took a wrong turn around San Francisco, and instead of going to Hawaii, or cruising around the Farallon Islands, this one—quickly dubbed "Humphrey," although its gender was never determined—headed east. He swam into San Francisco Bay, passing Richmond (where two decades earlier he would have been harpooned, Richmond having been the site of America's last whaling station), and then progressed up the Sacramento River.

*Although Physty was last seen diving deeply some five miles from the boat basin, it is not clear that he was actually saved. He may have gotten sick again, and died at sea. Although he had almost a hundred miles of Long Island to strand on after his release, he was not seen again.

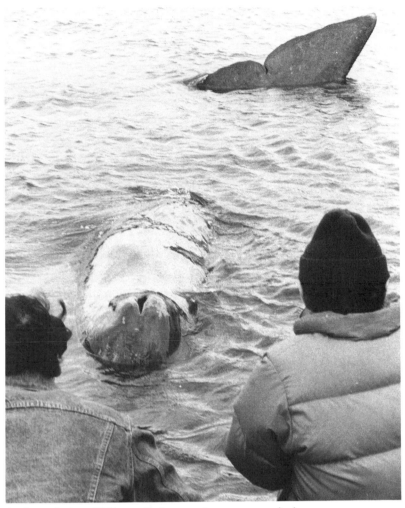

As he exhales, "Physty," the captive sperm whale, shows his off-center blowhole, and some twenty feet away, his tail flukes. On the right is the author.

After eight days in captivity, "Physty" is herded to freedom at Fire Island, New York. Huge crowds had been attracted to the scene by the extensive media coverage.

"Humphrey" the wayward humpback—identified by the pattern on the underside of his flukes— reappeared in San Francisco Bay in 1990, and managed to strand himself on a mudbank. He was released and headed back out to sea, but Humphrey-watchers feel that they have not seen the last of him.

A whale up the river is news. Humphrey made the national news programs, as did almost everybody who had an opinion as to why he was behaving in such an unusual manner, or how to get him to turn around. Scientists played killer whale sounds to frighten him; spectators played flutes and tambourines to entice him. The Coast Guard tried to herd him with power boats; helicopters chuddering overhead were supposed to frighten him into a 180-degree turn. Psychics sent Humphrey telepathic messages. Despite the combined efforts of the military, the scientists, the environmentalists and the media, Humphrey would not be deterred from his self-appointed rounds. For twenty-five days he meandered up the river, and finally, at the Rio Vista Bridge, some seventy miles upriver, Humphrey made the about-face that everyone wanted. (He was assisted in his decision by a barricading flotilla of vessels and a cacophony of noise-making devices called *oikomi,* which the Japanese use to herd dolphins.) On November 4, he swam under the Golden Gate Bridge and headed for the open sea.*

*Through the comparison of photographs of the pattern on the underside of the flukes, Humphrey was identified in the summer of 1986, swimming with other whales off the Farallon Islands, some thirty-five miles *west* of San Francisco. He continued, however, to make a habit of visiting the shallow waters around San Francisco, appearing again in the fall of 1988 and 1989 in both Drakes Bay and Bodega Bay. In October 1990, he stranded on a mudbank in San Francisco Bay, and with a massive group effort—and the usual attendant publicity—he was freed again to continue his anomalous wayfaring.

In a discussion of the Humphrey phenomenon, Patricia Warhol, the executive director of the American Cetacean Society, wrote, "Surely no whale— possibly excepting the one alleged to have swallowed Jonah, or Melville's mythical Moby Dick—ever received so much publicity, or inspired so much interest as the humpback that came to be known as Humphrey." By October of 1988, however, the media frenzy that accompanied Humphrey's wanderings would become a comparatively minor item, relegated to the back pages of the whale publicity chronicles.

That month, three gray whales became trapped in the ice off Point Barrow, Alaska. For three weeks the world watched as Eskimos, scientists and oil companies joined forces to try to rescue them. It seemed hopeless, because the ice was too thick, and the helicopter-towed rescue barge became mired in the ice almost two hundred miles from the whales. One of the whales eventually disappeared, probably because it panicked and tried to swim under the ice. On the twentieth day, two Soviet icebreakers came to the rescue, slashing through the thick ice to open a path for the whales to swim to freedom. "Operation Breakthrough" was a stunning international collaboration, but that was not the heart of the matter. The most remarkable aspect of this rescue effort was that it was shown from beginning to end, all around the world, on television.

When the gray whales got themselves trapped in Alaska, the media pounced on the event like a cat on a mouse. They spread the whales all over the front pages and newscasts of the entire world. Why? These were not members of an endangered species; we were not even responsible for their entrapment. They were merely victims of their own inexperience; they had strayed too far off course. How did it become our job to save them? Why was it considered a worthwhile investment to spend over a million dollars to save two wild animals? It was "the kitten in the tree" syndrome, only now the kittens were enormous whales, firmly ensconced as the darlings of the media. More than any other creatures, whales had become symbols of man's insensitivity to nature; benign animals that asked nothing more than to be left alone, and for their leviathan serenity, were slaughtered by the millions.

Alaskan Eskimos of the North Slope Borough regularly kill a small number of bowhead whales every year for (hotly contested) reasons of tradition and nutrition. It was, in fact, an Eskimo whaler who had first found the trapped gray whales, and his intention was to "put them out of their misery" and butcher them. He knew that they couldn't possibly escape on their own. When the news was leaked to the Lower Forty-Eight, the media circus commenced. At first, the networks were content to film the whales' snouts poking through the ice and to report on their impending demise, but when conservationists got hold of the story, the emphasis changed from simply watching them die to doing something about it. The oil companies, whose reputation was badly tarnished by their massive intrusion into this icy wilderness in the name of profit, were only too eager to help. Partly to save the whales, but more to present themselves in an environmentally favorable light, they marshaled their not inconsiderable forces, and began what would become a full-scale, high-technology assault on the ice. A "hoverbarge" was dispatched from Prudhoe Bay, some two hundred miles from the ice-trapped whales, with the intention of plowing a path through the pressure ridges that cut the whales off from the freedom of the open sea. When it became obvious that this $3 million craft could not possibly get to the whales, the rescuers resorted to more primitive means. They began to chop holes in the ice in the direction of the open sea—then some five miles away—which the whales were supposed to use to breathe their way to freedom. It was backbreaking, grueling work, and the prospects were dim at best, especially as it became obvious that the

The early efforts of the Eskimos consisted of cutting holes in the ice so the whales could breathe, and pushing the newly cut chunks under the edge with long poles.

Two Soviet icebreakers, *Admiral Makarov* and *Vladimir Arsenev,* arrive on the scene. All other efforts having failed, the icebreakers would smash a path to freedom for the whales.

whales were seriously debilitated, and probably could not last much longer.

By now, everyone was involved, up to and including the President of the United States, who phoned his support to the would-be rescuers. In the Anchorage *Daily News,* columnist Suzan Nightingale wrote, "On the front page of this newspaper, below the story about the whales, was a report that 5 million American children may suffer from chronic hunger. The Associated Press reported that 2 million people are on the edge of starvation in the Sudan. . . . Yet it is the whales, barnacled and bloody, that haunt, that capture our imagination and our prayers—and no doubt our dollars if we thought they would help." (She pointed out that there was no call from President Reagan when seven Eskimos were lost on the ice the previous June.) There is no question that our collective sympathies were with these unfortunate whales, but it is not at all clear why we went to such great lengths to save them.

Without the efforts of the rescuers, the whales would have expired naturally, as thousands of their brethren had done over the centuries. (Not far from where this extravaganza was being conducted, a single bowhead, a whale much better adapted to life in the ice, had become trapped and died.) Because we have elevated the cetaceans to creatures of mythic proportions, we saw in their plight a mirror of our own, and at the same time, we grasped an opportunity to expiate our past sins against them. Moreover, we could not resist a grandiose gesture that could not go unnoticed by the nations of the world that persist in their desire to kill whales for profit. Diplomatic initiatives to curtail whaling by the Japanese, for example, had proven almost fruitless. What better way to make the point than to show them how much we cared about whales?

So many people had become involved that it was impossible to abandon the unfortunate whales to their fate. The whole world was watching every step of the process, and none of the participants wanted to be the one to take the first step away from the problem. Even though the 1988 American presidential election was less than two weeks away, the whales had managed to grab top billing in the world's newspapers and television programs. Hourly updates were flashed around the world as the whales' fate became dimmer and their breathing more labored.

While the Americans do not have much in the way of icebreaking expertise, the Soviets do. They dispatched two icebreakers to the scene, and the reporters learned of the closing gap between the ships and the whales. On October 26, flying the stars and stripes and the hammer and sickle, the *Admiral Makarov* and *Vladimir Arsenev* plowed through the last of the frozen barriers, and the whales were free to leave.

In the end, with the Soviet icebreakers effecting a dramatic last-minute rescue to cheers heard around the world, the whales were saved, and we slept better on the night of October 28. Was it worth a million dollars? Of course it was. Not only were the animals saved (a point almost lost in the excitement surrounding the event), but we could all rejoice in the realization that groups that had traditionally been adversaries—the government and the Eskimos, the environmentalists and the oil companies, the Soviets and the Americans—could form a meaningful alliance when the stakes were high enough.

None of this could have occurred without television. It brought the gasping whales into our living rooms in an unprecedented manner. In the past, we had gotten to know the whales through their majestic and endangered appearance in films and documentaries, but for the first time, we were watching a live event that focused all our emotions on three endangered animals. This was not preservation in the abstract, where we were required to comprehend numbers of whales being killed or the possible extinction of a species, but *individuals* that were in trouble. They had even been given names, which brought us closer to them. They were not merely large, imperiled creatures, but *Putu, Siku,* and *Kanik* (or "Bonnet," "Crossbeak," and "Bone," depending upon whether the Eskimos or the biologists were doing the naming), and our hearts went out to them.

That the two rescued whales were freed was almost a footnote to the event. They were not outfitted with radio tags, ostensibly because it would have stressed them further, but more likely because the expense of tracking them on the remainder of their six-thousand-mile migration would have been prodigious. More significantly, in their weakened condition they were prime targets for the sharks and killer whales that patrolled their migration routes. Once we knew that they were free, it was enough, and we could relax our vigil. The event ended—for the people, if not for the whales—when the path was cleared to the sea. On the nightly news we had been witnesses to (and participants in) a great and glorious orgy of self-congratulation. We had done our part for the whales, and as they swam serenely down to the warm, saline lagoons of Baja California, we could return to our daily whaleless lives, knowing that they were safe. And if they weren't, well, that was nature taking its course.

In a larger sense, it doesn't really matter if the two whales lived or died. What was important was that the world had become aware of the plight of the whales—all whales, that is, not just Putu, Siku and Kanik—and for the expenditure of a mere million dollars, everyone involved reaped the rich rewards of a positive publicity barrage: the Eskimos (who had been getting a bad rap for their killing of the bowhead, a truly endangered species); the oil companies (who needed some positive publicity anyway); the government (always the villain); and even the surprise heroes of the drama, the Soviets, whose attempts at *glasnost* were substantially enhanced. And the rest of the world, snug in their living rooms and satiated with this twentieth-century homologue for Androcles and the Lion, could convince themselves that at least one of the world's problems—however small—was solved.

ELEVEN

THE BEGINNING OF THE END

The Regulation of Whaling

THE IDEA that whaling should be controlled is a relatively recent one. The early whalers, more or less independent of rules and restrictions, had recklessly and carelessly killed whatever species were available, and when one species seemed to be running low, they either looked for a new whale to replace the diminished one, or found a new area in which to hunt the original one. Only when it appeared that a particular whale was too scarce did it occur to anyone to apply some sort of protective measures, a paradigmatic case of locking the barn after the horse has been stolen.

The first whales to be hunted on a large scale were the rights, and wherever they had the misfortune to breed in protected waters otherwise desired by settlers—Australia, New Zealand, South Africa, Cape Cod—the whales were slaughtered. The slow-swimming humpbacks, another inshore-breeding species, were also hunted to the brink of extinction by whalers who wanted their plentiful oil. In the 1930s, when it was painfully obvious that there were hardly any right whales left, the whaling nations placed a ban on killing them. Humpbacks are now as rare as the right whales because it took another

thirty years before the whalers could bring themselves to stop the killing. For the other species of "great" whales, the story has been the same. The idea that steps might be taken *before* the precipice of extinction was reached may have occurred to some of the more enlightened whalers, but they seem not to have been able to convince their colleagues. The history of whale conservation—perhaps one of the saddest oxymorons of our time—has been characterized by the phrase "too little, too late."

In 1929 the Norwegians drafted the first domestic whaling legislation. The Norwegian Whaling Act was written to regulate whaling in the North Atlantic, because the Norwegians had decimated the rorqual stocks around their own country as well as the Faeroes, the Hebrides, the Shetlands and Ireland. This act forbade the capture of right whales, females and calves of all species, and blue whales less than 60 feet in length.

Using his own ideas about the common property of mankind and some of the precepts included in the Norwegian Whaling Act, an Argentine scholar named José Léon Suarez submittted a memorandum to the League of Nations in 1925 which resulted in the first International Convention for the Regulation of Whaling. Like its Norwegian predecessor, this convention protected right whales and females with calves, and because it was applied to all the world's oceans, it also protected the California gray whale. It also provided for the licensing of whaling vessels and the collection of statistics for catches. Suarez was worried about the extinction of the whales, and of course he was right. In a 1956 discussion of the regulation of whaling, J. T. Ruud, a Norwegian cetologist and whaling historian—and a longtime member of the Norwegian delegation to the International Whaling Commission—accused him of "overstating [his] case as men of zeal often do." The whaling nations were reluctant to accept what they perceived as unnecessary restrictions—especially those that interfered with freedom of the seas—and although the convention was actually signed by eight countries, it was not ratified by England until 1934, and it was boycotted by Japan, the Soviet Union, and Germany.

As the world was gearing up for a war in which millions of people would die, the same nations that would soon be belligerents were trying—in their traditionally ineffectual fashion—to wind down their war on the whales, which had been going on uninterruptedly for almost a thousand years. Perhaps there was something about an incipient war that reminded the prospective warriors that wanton killing might be wrong, but perhaps not. It was only some twenty-one years earlier that the armistice had been concluded on the "war to end war."

On May 24, 1937, a global conference on whaling was convened in London. Attending were delegates from Argentina, Australia, Ireland, Germany, Britain, Norway, South Africa and the United States, with Canada and Portugal sending observers. (By this time, whaling had become a multinational business; when the Argentine-registered tanker *Ulysses* set off from Norway in 1937 for the coast of Australia, the capital for the expedition had come from American, British, Danish and Norwegian sources.) An agreement was signed in London on June 8, but it protected no whales. In fact, after two weeks of negotiations, the whalers managed to agree to take 11,519 *more* baleen whales than they had caught in the previous season. The 1937–38 season saw the arrival in the Antarctic of Japanese and German floating factories with their attendant catcher boats. These two countries accounted for 84 percent of the production increase; much of this oil would be used to fuel the conflagration that was imminent.

A second London convention followed a year later, and this time there was open hostility between the British and the Norwegians. No new agreements were reached, and the international fleet of catcher boats set sail in 1938. Norway was joined again in the South by the fleets and factories of Britain, Japan and Germany. They killed 14,922 blue whales, 2,079 humpbacks, and 28,009 fin whales; a total of 45,010 whales, an all-time record for a single season. (The lopsided figures were in part because the Japanese ignored the 89-day catching limit and fished for 125 days.) From an analysis of the catch statistics, it was becoming clear that both the blue and humpback stocks were being overfished, and that it would only be a matter of time before the same thing happened to the finners. No animal species on earth could possibly suffer such monumental carnage and survive.

The meetings of 1937–38 were as much political as they were biological. Diplomats and cetologists attended in equal numbers, and often lobbied for totally opposite objectives. The biologists, led by Remington Kellogg of the United States, were interested in preserving the whale stocks, while the politicians were not so much concerned with preservation as they were with containment of the Japanese and Germans. For the Norwegians, politics and whaling were virtually synonymous, since the industry was one of Norway's most important, and they could hardly afford to subscribe to policies that would threaten their domestic economy.

On June 24, 1938, the "London Protocols" were signed, which included a total ban on the catching of humpbacks south of 40° south latitude until 1939; no baleen whaling in the so-called "Area I" (a sanctuary that had been suggested by Kellogg as part of his recommendation that the Antarctic be divided up into areas for management reasons); no factory-ship whaling except in the Antarctic; and to placate the Japanese—who had surprised everyone by coming to the meeting—a reduction in minimum allowable lengths for blue whales, fins and sperm whales. The presence and acquiescence of the Japanese were good news for the whaling community as a whole, but bad news for the Norwegians. For the first time, it was now evident that a country could engage in large-scale Antarctic whaling operations without Norwegian personnel or matériel. The Japanese were industriously building their own whaling fleet during this period, and they were operating without restrictions.

Even though Europe was on the brink of war, the nations persisted in holding conferences to discuss the allocation of whale stocks and the sale of whale oil. The latter was of great importance, since a war would mean less traffic and commerce between the various European nations. Now oblivious to world opinion—especially on something as minor as whaling—Japan sent her fleets to the South and began catching five weeks before the season was supposed to open, killing the humpbacks and undersized whales that had been expressly forbidden. Germany, on the other hand, adhered to the protocols, but suffered a disastrous season. Germany had acquired the Rhineland, Austria and Czechoslovakia, but could not acquire Norway's whale oil, since it would not meet the price, and the oil was sold to Unilever. Meanwhile, the whaling situation had become so complicated with agreements, protocols, recommendations and supplementary protocols, that no one knew who had ratified what.

Another meeting was called, for London in July 1939, with only the whaling nations (Germany, Britain, Japan, Norway and the United States) participating, and with Canada, Ireland, New Zealand and South Africa sending observers. It is difficult to imagine these countries—four of which would soon be adversaries in the greatest war in history—sitting down at a conference table to discuss size limits for humpback whales, but until actual hostilities broke out between them, they did just that.

Japan continued whaling in the South during the 1939–40 and the 1940–41 seasons, and the Germans decided it was easier to seize tankers than to kill and process the whales themselves in the remote Antarctic. Hitler believed that his navy could be better employed in the Northern Hemisphere, so only raiders were dispatched to the south.

Even as the war was being fought, the whaling nations were convening to coordinate the reconstruction of their fleets. In June 1943, a British-Norwegian Joint Committee met to plan for the future. It was at this conference that the plans were laid for the building of new factory ships, to be ready as soon as the war was officially over. Remington Kellogg had suggested in 1944 that at the conclusion of hostilities, the whaling nations ought to meet to establish some sort of guidelines for the future regulation of the industry. With Kellogg in the chair, the first meeting of the International Whaling Conference was held in Washington, D.C., in November 1945. There was much discussion as to whether or not the whaling commission should be a part or adjunct of the newly formed United Nations, but the idea was never accepted, and when it finally convened in 1949, the International Whaling Commission was a completely autonomous body. The history of the IWC is intricately intertwined with the history of whaling—in fact, with the exception of aberrant "pirate" whaling, it has *been* the history of whaling since 1949.

BY THE TIME the war ended, Japanese whaling was in ruins. Her factory ships and catchers had been mobilized for nonwhaling purposes, and by the end of the war, most of them were lost or damaged.

The Germans tried to rejoin the ranks of the whaling fraternity after the war, but their economy was in tatters, and they could not devote the requisite capital to the building of a factory ship. (Under the 1945 Potsdam Agreements, Germany was forbidden from building any ship over fifteen hundred tons, but the Germans probably could have refitted a passenger vessel.)

At the 1946 International Whaling Convention in Washington, guidelines were drawn up for an international organization whose expressed purpose was to "conserve whale stocks and thus make possible the orderly development of the whaling industry." This convention was based on the 1937 London Agreement and the protocols to that agreement signed in London in 1938 and in November 1945, and it led directly to the establishment of the International Whaling Commission in 1949. The signatories to the 1949 agreement were Australia, Canada, Denmark, France, Iceland, Mexico, the Netherlands, New Zealand, Norway, Panama, South Africa, Sweden, Great Britain, the United States and the Soviet Union. Japan, which had been reintroduced to whaling after the war in order to provide her people with meat, did not join the IWC until the next year of its existence. Bernard Stonehouse wrote:

The Whaling Commission faced the impossible task of controlling a powerful, profitable, highly capitalized,

There are few paintings glorifying mechanized whaling. This one by David Cobb shows a British catcher boat in the Antarctic, pursuing an unidentifiable whale.

fiercely competitive, multi-national industry—one which had no intention of accepting controls other than on its own terms. Though the terms of reference of the Commission recognized that, under proper management, whales could be harvested rather than quarried, the Commission itself had no power to enforce this view. Though individual nations varied in their approach, collectively, whalers saw no alternative to the rapid, efficient exploitation which had proved so successful for the industry in the past. Though the Commission had powers to vary whaling procedure, amendments which tended to restrict whaling were seldom agreed by all the delegates, and the demurral of one was usually sufficient for the proposal to be dropped by all. So conservation measures which might have maintained the industry in perpetuity, or have postponed its decline, fell by the wayside.

Article III of the convention stated that "The Contracting governments agree to establish an International Whaling Commission . . . to be composed of one member from each Contracting Government. Each member shall have one vote and may be accompanied by one or more experts and advisers." Thus

was the IWC born. Its first meeting depended upon the ratification of the convention by six of the signatory nations, and on May 30, 1949, the commission convened in London.

Birgir Bergensen (chairman of Norway's State Whaling Board) was elected the first chairman, with Remington Kellogg as vice-chairman. By this time, the Antarctic was the world's major whaling ground, with over 70 percent of the total number of whales killed coming from there. The opening paragraph of the convention of 1946 (as appended to the First Annual Report of the IWC) reads as follows:

The Governments whose duly authorized representatives have subscribed hereto,

Recognizing the interest of the nations of the world in safeguarding for future generations the great natural resources represented by the whale stocks;

Considering that the history of whaling has been overfishing of one area after another and of one species of whale after another to such a degree that it is essential to protect all species of whales from further over-fishing;

Recognizing that whale stocks are susceptible of natural increases if whaling is properly regulated, and that the increases in the size of whale stocks will permit increases in the number of whales which may be captured without endangering these natural resources;

Recognizing that it is in the common interest to achieve the optimum level of whale stocks as rapidly as possible without causing widespread economic and nutritional distress;

Recognizing that in the course of achieving these objectives, whaling operations should be confined to those species best able to sustain exploitation in order to give an interval for recovery of certain species of whales now depleted in numbers;

Desiring to establish a system of international regulations for the whale fisheries to insure proper and effective conservation and development of whale stocks on the basis of the principles embodied in the International Agreement for the Regulation of Whaling, signed in London on 8th June, 1937, and the protocols to that Agreement signed in London on 24th June, 1938, and 26th November, 1945; and

Having decided to conclude a convention to provide for the proper conservation of whale stocks and thus make possible the orderly development of the whaling industry;

Have agreed as follows. . . .

The IWC and its member nations then did precisely the opposite of what they had pledged to do. In his study of the role and history of the IWC, J. L. McHugh, a former United States commissioner, and chairman in 1971, wrote, "From the time of the first meeting of the Commission . . . almost all major actions or failures to act were governed by short-range economic considerations rather than by the requirements of conservation."*

Each of the IWC's signatories (or "contracting governments," as they are known in the reports of the meetings) has a single vote in the Technical Committee. (The Scientific Committee, which serves in an advisory capacity, is an unofficial body, and can only make recommendations which the delegates are

*McHugh wrote these words for a paper presented at a symposium in June 1971. At that time, he was critical of the IWC, but by 1975, his faith had been restored. In a popular magazine he wrote that "Only a couple of people understand the whaling issue in all its complicated details," and that "Practical people recognize that whaling is under reasonable control." He was wrong.

not bound to accept.) A three-quarters majority must pass any resolution, but because of some nations' reluctance to accept the will of the majority when the convention was being drawn up, there is a built-in device that potentially renders any resolution non-binding. Article V.3 of the convention (discussing the adoption of amendments to the *Schedule*) reads as follows:

Each of such amendments shall become effective with respect to the Contracting Government ninety days following notification of the amendment by the Commission to each of the Contracting Governments, except that a) if any Government presents the Commission objection to any amendment prior to the expiration of the ninety-day period, the amendment shall not become effective with respect to any of the Governments for an additional ninety days. . . .

In other words, if a contracting government does not wish to abide by a schedule amendment, it has ninety days in which to file an objection. When that objection is filed, the amendment does not bind the filing government. Furthermore, as soon as one country files an objection, the other governments have another ninety days to do so. In practice, this meant that as soon as one nation objected to a quota or other restriction, every other nation would follow suit, since they would not want to be bound by restrictions not applicable to their rivals. The inability of the IWC to enforce its rules—or, for that matter, to have them last from one meeting to the next—demonstrates its fundamental inadequacy, and in later years would permit some governments to make a mockery of its resolutions. Including such loopholes, however, was the only way to get the pelagic-whaling nations to join the IWC; if they had believed that they would *really* be restricted by arbitrary regulations on their industries, they would have sooner joined the SPCA.

The IWC also imposed upon itself a limit to its authority regarding the number of any member nation's factory ships. The same Article V that introduced the concept of the veto also contains this language: "These amendments to the Schedule . . . shall not involve restrictions on the number or nationality of factory ships or land stations, nor allocate specific quotas to any factory or ship [and] shall take into consideration the interests of the consumers of whale products and the whaling industry." No wonder the IWC was seen as a "whalers' club"! The rules were carefully crafted to impose no constraints on the members, except those they might choose to impose on themselves, and then they could reject them if they found them too restrictive.

Remington Kellogg, one of the framers of the original agreements and one of the whales' most ardent supporters, wrote (in a 1940 article in *National Geographic*): "In spite of these agreements [the post-IWC protocols] there has been no marked reduction in the total number killed. If the exploitation of the whale stock continues on the present scale, the time will come in the very near future when whales will become very much less numerous on the 'grounds,' the price of whale oil will rise, and consequently whaling operations will be intensified." The International Whaling Commission, which had been designed to achieve some lofty goals, achieved the very opposite of what it was supposed to do. The numbers of whales fell precipitously, and because of its pernicious ineffectiveness, the commission that was supposed to regulate whaling for the preservation of the industry, actually superintended the near elimination of the whales and the total elimination of the industry.

ONE OF the problems besetting the IWC was that of whaling nations that did not join. Argentina, Chile and Peru had signed the 1946 convention, but did not ratify it. They were carrying on whaling operations, but were not bound by the IWC's regulations. In 1952, Chile, Peru and Ecuador met in Santiago, and signed their own treaty, regulating "all" whaling in the South Pacific. They also established their own commission, which set somewhat more liberal regulations than the IWC; for example, each nation got to set its own quotas. In practice, the South Pacific Commission existed only on paper, and regulated nothing at all. Argentina joined the dues-paying, voting ranks of the IWC in 1959, but Chile and Peru did not join until 1979.* (Ecuador, an original

signatory of the South Pacific Treaty, never entered whaling commerce, and never joined the IWC.)

UNLIKE terrestrial mammals, whales are invisible to human observers for most of their lives, and it is only when they surface to breathe that they can be seen—providing there is someone to see them. The bowhead and the gray whale are in a different category. They can actually be counted, one by one, as they pass close to shore on their annual migrations.*

Vessels at sea can also count whales, but with every seagoing survey, there is always the problem of determining if the whale you see today is the same one you saw yesterday—or last week. That conundrum led to a program of whale-marking, in which special tags were fired into the blubber of whales, which tags would be examined if and when the whale was killed and processed. You could count whales, but they had to be killed first.

Whale marks also enabled researchers to identify migration patterns of certain species. The whalers obviously recorded the number of whales they killed and how long it took to kill that number. (Tabulation of the actual number of whales killed was the only certainty in this complex equation.) This led to the inclusion of the "Catch per Unit of Effort" (CPUE) as a factor in determining whale numbers. If it takes so many days to find so many whales in one season, and more time to find the same number the following season, it stands to reason that the number of whales has decreased.

If and when the population of a given species could be determined—and there were those who argued that it never could, and therefore we ought to err on the side of humanity and stop killing whales altogether—the scientists then had to figure out how many could be taken from the population without

*The whaling operations of Chile and Peru were actually satellite stations for the Japanese industry. The land crews were overseen by Japanese, and most of the whale products were shipped to Japan. In the 1980s, the Peruvians would prove to be among the most uncooperative of all the whaling nations, and would file one of the objections to the 1982 moratorium, even though the Peruvian whaling industry was so minimal as to be insignificant.

*The place chosen by researchers to count bowheads is Point Barrow, on the North Slope of Alaska. It is a hostile, ice-choked, frozen wasteland, not particularly conducive to field research. Researchers were often forced to take cover from blizzards or gales, and they therefore missed many of the whales they were supposed to be counting. Over the years, however, the population estimates have increased, not because the number of bowheads has increased, but because the counting techniques have become more sophisticated. In addition to shore spotting and airplane surveys, researchers have developed techniques that enable them to count whales by listening to and triangulating their phonations under water.

decreasing it. A population has a normal growth rate, based on the fecundity of the animals, the age and size at sexual maturity (an important factor if individuals are not to be killed before they have had an opportunity to reproduce), normal attrition rate, and many other elements that the population dynamicists use in their complicated formulas. From these calculations, there is supposed to emerge a quantity known as the "maximum sustainable yield of a given animal population." Ray Gambell, a whale biologist (and now secretary of the IWC) defined the concept thus:

In an ideal, unfished population the number of new recruits exactly balances the number of whales dying naturally, to produce a stable situation, limited by food supplies and other natural factors. As the stock is reduced by whaling the rate of recruitment increases and the natural mortality decreases. The resulting surplus of recruits over animals lost through natural deaths represents a yield which can be harvested indefinitely without causing any change in the total stock size. Paradoxically, a certain depletion of a previously unexploited stock increases the sustainable yield. At some particular stock size, generally about half the unfished populations, the surplus available reaches a peak known as the maximum sustainable yield (MSY).

Somehow, whale biologists who worked on the populations of the hunted whales managed to convince themselves that it would benefit the population if a number of whales were killed off. Gambell also wrote that with fewer whales in a given population, there is more food to go around, and they therefore grow larger and breed earlier and more frequently. By this convoluted reasoning, the truly endangered species, such as the right and the humpback, ought to have recovered by now, but as far as we know, their populations are approximately at the same pitiful level as they were when hunting them was banned. Fortunately for the remaining whales, not everyone agreed with Gambell or the other proponents of MSY.

IN 1945–46 three British and six Norwegian fleets sailed for the Antarctic. By the following year, the Netherlands, the USSR and South Africa joined the fray, and General Douglas MacArthur arranged for the Japanese to participate as well, by providing the

ships and matériel for their reentry into whaling. In that season, and in many to follow, the whalers were "authorized" to take 16,000 BWUs. (The "Blue Whale Unit" was the insidious device that equated 1 blue whale with 2 fin whales, 2½ humpbacks, and 6 sei whales, thus concentrating the whaler's grenades on the most productive species, the blue.) With such intensive hunting, no creature could survive. Valiantly, the giant blue whales struggled against their inevitable fate. The "high point" of blue whaling was the 1930–31 season, when 29,410 blues were killed, but for the next thirty-five years, the whalers took a total of 189,710 blue whales, an *average* of 5,420 blue whales per year. (During the war years 1942–44, only 523 blues were killed.) Even more fin whales (543,141) were slaughtered during the same period. Of course the blue whale population crashed, then the fin whales, and finally the sei whales. Nigel Bonner characterizes the history of postwar whaling as "an increasing fleet chasing a decreasing stock of whales."

Before World War II, there were no controls whatever on Antarctic whaling. It was conducted by any country, with any equipment, and on any species of whales the hunters felt inclined or able to kill. Although records were kept of the numbers of whales of various species that were killed, no one seemed unduly concerned about the decline in whale populations, and certainly there was no one in authority who opined that the numbers might be too high. The history of postwar commercial whaling in the Antarctic is equally grim.

As soon as the war ended, the whaling nations turned to the South, to continue their massive assault on the whales in the Antarctic. England and Norway, the first rivals for the plunder of the Southern Hemisphere, continued whaling up to 1963 and 1968 respectively; the Netherlands operated from 1947 to 1964. From the late 1960s onward, only Japan and the USSR continued to kill whales in the icy waters of the Southern Hemisphere. (When the moratorium on commercial whaling was passed in 1982, the last of the intrepid Antarctic whalers were fishing on the lowly minke whale—at a maximum length of 30 feet, previously considered not worth chasing.)

In order to understand what transpired on the fishing grounds of the Antarctic, it is necessary to examine the status of whale populations, before and after exploitation. After carefully analyzing the available data (and remaining fully aware of the difficulties involved in estimating populations of animals that spend most of their lives underwater), population dynamicist K. Radway Allen has estimated the Southern Hemisphere humpback population at some 3,000 animals, 2 percent of the original population. (Even more difficult than estimating current populations is estimating pre-exploitation populations.) Similar estimates are available for blue whales (11,000 animals left; 5 percent of the original population of some 200,000); fin whales (103,000 animals left, 21 percent of the original 490,000); and 37,000 sei whales, 19 percent of the original 191,000. Of course, in estimating numbers of killed you do not simply subtract 11,000 from 200,000 and conclude that there were 189,000 blue whales killed; if you analyze the number of whales killed every year, you realize that the figures are considerably higher. The actual number of blue whales killed from 1920 to 1966—the year they were declared "protected"—is 307,638. The remaining percentage of the population represents the estimated number of blue whales alive today, factoring in "recruitment," which covers all those whales born during the period under question, as well as natural mortality, and any other elements that affect populations, *except* the intrusions of mankind. (It is the very difficulty of estimating any whale populations at all that has been the root cause of some of the major disagreements within the IWC. Various scientists have devised various "models" for estimating populations, but as might be imagined, the success of a particular model depends to a great extent on whose ox is being gored—or in this case, whose whales are being estimated.)*

While the number of whales currently swimming around in the southern polar seas is an unknown quantity, the number of whales killed is a matter of record. In the Antarctic, the numbers are as follows:

*In recent years, the study of animal population dynamics has been assigned by some scientists to that category of mathematics known as "chaos." Because of the simultaneous interdependence and unpredictability of random factors (*e.g.*, age at sexual maturity, attacks by predators, climatic variations, disease), it is conceivable that the growth rate of a particular population of whales can *never* be known or predicted. In his 1987 book *Chaos,* James Gleick wrote, "Biologists' mathematical models tended to be caricatures of reality, as did the models of economists, demographers, psychologists, and urban planners, when those soft sciences tried to bring rigor to their study of systems changing over time."

Aboard the factory ships, the blubber was peeled from the whale—in this case a blue—and cut into smaller pieces for boiling down.

Number of Whales Killed in the Antarctic

SEASON	BLUE	FIN	SEI	HUMPBACK	SPERM
1919–20	1,874	3,213	71	261	8
1920–21	2,617	5,491	36	260	31
1921–22	4,416	2,492	103	9	3
1922–23	5,683	3,677	10	517	23
1923–24	3,732	3,035	193	233	66
1924–25	5,703	4,366	1	359	59
1925–26	4,697	8,916	195	364	37
1926–27	6,545	5,102	776	189	39
1927–28	8,334	4,459	883	23	72
1928–29	12,847	6,690	808	59	62
1929–30	17,898	11,614	216	853	73
1930–31	29,410	10,017	145	576	51
1931–32	6,488	2,871	16	184	13
1932–33	18,891	5,168	2	159	107
1933–34	17,347	7,200	0	872	666
1934–35	16,500	12,500	266	1,965	577
1935–36	17,731	9,697	2	3,162	399
1936–37	14,304	14,381	490	4,477	926
1937–38	14,923	28,009	161	2,079	867
1938–39	14,081	20,784	22	883	2,585
1939–40	11,480	18,694	81	2	1,938
1940–41	4,943	7,831	110	2,675	804
1941–42	59	1,189	52	16	109
1942–43	125	776	73	0	24
1943–44	339	1,158	197	4	101
1944–45	1,042	1,666	78	60	45
1945–46	3,606	9,185	85	238	273
1946–47	9,192	14,547	393	29	1,431
1947–48	6,908	21,141	621	26	2,622
1948–49	7,625	19,123	578	31	4,078
1949–50	6,182	20,060	1,284	2,143	2,727
1950–51	7,048	19,456	886	1,638	4,968
1951–52	5,130	22,527	530	1,556	5,485
1952–53	3,870	22,867	621	963	2,332
1953–54	2,697	27,659	1,029	605	2,879
1954–55	2,176	28,624	569	495	5,790
1955–56	1,614	27,958	560	1,432	6,794
1956–57	1,512	27,757	1,692	679	4,429
1957–58	1,690	27,473	3,309	396	6,535
1958–59	1,192	27,128	2,421	2,394	5,652
1959–60	1,239	27,575	4,309	1,338	4,227

Number of Whales Killed in the Antarctic (Continued)

SEASON	BLUE	FIN	SEI	HUMPBACK	SPERM
1960–61	1,744	28,761	5,102	718	4,800
1961–62	1,118	27,099	5,196	309	4,829
1962–63	947	18,668	5,503	270	4,771
1963–64	112	14,422	8,695	2	6,711
1964–65	20	7,811	20,380	0	4,352
1965–66	1	2,536	17,587	1	4,555
1966–67	4	2,893	12,368	0	4,960
1967–68	0	2,155	10,357	0	2,568
1968–69	0	3,020	5,776	0	2,682
1969–70	0	3,002	5,857	0	3,090
1970–71	0	2,888	6,151	0	2,745

The above figures (taken from McHugh, 1974) tell the story of Antarctic whaling more eloquently than any words. We can track the successive collapse of the blue whale, fin whale and sei whale populations (the humpbacks had already been decimated on their breeding grounds off Australia, New Zealand and southern Africa), and see the belated moment when the IWC decided to protect the blue whale. We can watch as the whalers begin to take an interest in the sperm whale again, bearing in mind that extensive whaling was going on throughout the world's oceans at the same time that the catcher boats were prowling the southern ice pack. While the number of sperm whales slaughtered annually in the Antarctic in the 1960s was small compared to the ceaseless massacre of Antarctic fin whales, in the 1960s, Soviet and Japanese whalers in the North Pacific were killing sperm whales in unprecedented numbers: the *average* number of sperm whales killed per annum for the years 1960 to 1970 was 20,738.

British Whaling

IN 1945, the whalers shipped out once again to the Antarctic. Among those who headed south were the British, who had worked the Antarctic since the discovery of the feeding grounds of the great rorquals at the beginning of the century. They geared up again after World War II, and for the 1945–46 season, sent the *Southern Venturer,* a new factory ship, accompanied by a fleet of new catcher boats. Based on the success of this venture, they built another factory ship, the *Southern Harvester;* with a German prize of war, the *Empire Venturer* (ex-*Terje Viken*), and the *Balaena,* the British had assembled a truly formidable fleet.

One outcome of the war was to have disastrous effects on the whales. Until the 1940s, whale-spotting was not very different from what it had been in Captain Ahab's time—that is, a man in a lookout scanned the horizon for whales, and upon spotting them, shouted his language's equivalent of "Thar she blows!" During the war, however, the Allies had developed a device for detecting submarines, which they referred to by the acronym of the organization that developed it: ASDIC (Anti-Submarine Detection Investigation Committee). This device, which was the underwater equivalent of radar, enabled the whalers to "lock on" to a submerged whale so that once spotted, it had very little chance of escape, unless the gunner missed it repeatedly.* Radar was also used in whaling, but only to find dead whales. Whereas in the past the catchers had marked their dead whales with a flag (called a "waif"), which they looked for after the killing had stopped, they were now able to implant the carcass with a metal reflecting device that could be picked up by the ship's radar, thus making it much easier to find floating carcasses in fog or rough seas.

Other war-related techniques would be applied to modern whaling, but after the failure of a plane to return to the *Kosmos* in 1929, aircraft were not utilized again for whale-spotting until the British *Balaena* expedition of 1946–47. The *Balaena* was equipped with two high-winged single-engine "Walrus" seaplanes, but since the whales were so numerous in those early years after the wartime hiatus, the planes were employed mostly for reporting of ice conditions.

John Grierson, whose *Air Whaler* is a detailed account of the men and planes of the *Balaena* in the Antarctic in 1946–47, wrote, "If the whales could be seen from above (and, after all, submarines had been seen from aeroplanes very successfully during the war, and on some occasions whales had even been shot at in mistake for submarines), then it should not be difficult to direct the whale boats towards them by means of wireless or visual signals." Flight Commodore Grierson and his crews did in fact spot whales more or less successfully, even though low clouds, snowstorms, high winds, and poor visibility made regular flights impossible. (From November 3, 1946, to March 16, 1947, they were able to make only

*Although it was impossible to prove, some whalemen thought that the whales could hear the asdic, and even though it enabled the catchers to locate the whales before they spotted them from the crow's nest, more would be frightened than would be caught. Some believed that asdic jammed the whales' own sonar system, and because they could not identify the source of their confusion, they took off in a straight line away from the sound-emitting boat. A South African whalerman told me that once asdic had been introduced, he felt that all the sport was taken out of whaling, since "the whale never had a chance."

twenty-six flights.) Whales could be spotted from the air and their positions radioed to the catcher boats; ice conditions likewise; and another "dividend" emerged: the pilots reported on the whereabouts and success of the other factory ships in the area, since the *Balaena* was warned to stay away from areas where the pilots observed no activity on the flensing decks of competing Norwegian whaleships. The British considered the experiment a qualified success but chose not to repeat it. Spotter airplanes were later employed in the fisheries of South Africa and Western Australia, and by 1953–54, the Norwegians and the Japanese factory ships were using spotter helicopters in the Antarctic (as was Onassis's *Olympic Challenger*), but "air whaling" never became an important part of whaling history.

For the most part, Grierson's account is a straightforward one, detailing the daily activities of the pilots and crews of the *Balaena*. Perhaps carried away with the success of his venture and the hearty camaraderie of his "Battle of Britain" veterans, Grierson proposed that the future of whaling lay in air-power, especially if the Americans—"the most progressive nation on Earth"—were to participate in the process. He speculated on the possibilities of shooting whales from the air with rocket harpoons, and even employing helicopters for this purpose. He imagined a science-fiction whaling enterprise, consisting of "a factory ship, with its automatic flensers and labour-saving gadgets, the depot or supply ship, acting as oil-tanker and refrigerating ship, equipped with a hangar and swinging-out platforms . . . on which her half-dozen helicopters could aspire and alight." Fortunately, his visions did not materialize, nor did his ringing prognostication for the future: "A new chapter in the history of civil aviation and of the British Merchant Navy was written by the aircrew of the *Balaena*. That will surely be followed by the evolution of an entirely new technique of air-whaling, a development based on our data, which will revolutionise this old-established industry."

The Norwegians, always in the avant-garde of any whaling enterprise, joined in the fray even faster than the British, and as soon as the ink was dry on the peace treaties, they sent forty-four catchers to the South. (At this time, Norwegian whaling received a substantial stimulus in the massive subsidies offered to the whaling companies by the government.) In

November of 1946, however, the International Convention for the Regulation of Whaling convened in London as the first step in the organization of what had heretofore been defined by the "catch-as-catch-can" philosophy of whaling. (In the previous year, the whaling nations had agreed to limit their pelagic season from December 8 to April 8, and to restrict their total catches to 16,000 blue whale units.) By 1947–48 there were fifteen factory ships from all the whaling nations operating in the Antarctic, and from 1950 to 1960, the average was twenty.

Britain was short of meat after the war, and the British were killing an enormous number of whales. Attempts were made to interest the British in the consumption of whale meat, but they were unsuccessful. All they could do with the protein-rich meat was grind it up for meal, or squeeze the juices out of it to flavor stews and soups. In 1949, the government tried again to interest the British in whale meat. It published recipes and sang the praises of this heretofore untapped source of protein. The postwar Britons resisted as if it were another Battle of Britain, and chose bubble and squeak over blubber and flukes. As Gordon Jackson diplomatically phrased it, "oriental methods of cooking and flavoring were more suited to whale meat than were traditional British cooking methods."

Aboard British ships, whalemen had no such reservations. Terence Wise sailed on the *Balaena* from 1957 to 1960, and in *To Catch a Whale,* he described the crew's preferences: "Whale meat, once regarded with horror in this country, is a true delicacy, especially to men who would otherwise have no fresh meat. Pieces weighing about twenty pounds are cut off and hung to dry on the lower rigging. After about three weeks it will have formed a hard black skin like leather which is cut off, leaving a meat very similar to veal and containing as much as 85 per cent pure protein. It does tend to be rather insipid owing to the complete lack of fat and our cooks usually inserted a roll of pork fat to moisten the meat."

The remainder of the whaleman's diet on these four-month voyages consisted almost exclusively of Norwegian food, since the cook and most of the crew were Norwegians, and the stores had been taken on in Husvik. They had kippers, fish pies, fish soup, fish stews, and various other piscene creations that the Norsemen found pleasing and the Englishmen found almost unbearable, as well as the standard seaman's fare of porridges and puddings. (The whalemen called the porridge *burgoo,* a word that can be traced back to the eighteenth-century prison hulks, and they also ate a stew they called *lobscouse,* which name derived from an old Yankee whalers' dish.)

British whaling was modern whaling. The mother ship was in constant radio contact with the catcher boats, and radar was used to detect icebergs in the dark, distant waters of the Antarctic. Earlier expeditions had employed airplanes for whale-spotting, but now helicopters were standard issue. The catcher boats were sleek, fast hunters, ranging from 350 to 500 tons, 150 to 200 feet in length and with a speed of 15 to 18 knots. Terence Wise called them "speed boats with guns." When a whale was captured, it was brought alongside, and then hauled up through the stern slipway by the "grab," and processed on the flensing deck. Reducing a warm, 80-ton animal to small pieces was a hellish job in what passed for decent weather in the Antarctic, but it was unimaginably worse in a sleet storm.

Life aboard one of the British factory ships was hard, but it retained some of the romance of old-time whaling—to the general public in England or Norway, if not to the whalemen trying to keep their footing on a slippery deck awash with hot blood and sloshing ice water. The men worked around the clock, seven days a week, often in impossible weather conditions. Sleep was possible only during slack periods in hunting. "When a whale is caught," wrote Terence Wise, "the men work in below zero temperatures, covered in a spray and at times up to their knees in sea, their fingers bleeding from unfelt injuries." Wise signed on as a winch-operator, so he did not actually participate in the flensing operations, but he observed them with a wry and articulate detachment:

Occasionally incidents occurred to break the monotony. There will be a sudden crunch and ripping sound as meat parts from bone too quickly, rushing across the deck before the winchman can avast heaving, sweeping a man off his feet to land in the blood. Or the guts cutter slices too close and punctures an overfilled intestine with a pop, sending its contents spluttering into the air. There are curses from the men, who turn to run, knowing it is too late. Semidigested food or faeces splatter down on them, to the glee of those out of range. The smell clings.

FLEET AIR ARM
AMPHIBIAN WALRUS

WHALE SPOTTING PLANE
KEEPS CONSTANT TOUCH
WITH SHIP

"FLOATING
WHALE FACTORY"

500 TON
CATCHER

500 TON
CATCHER

WHALES ABOUT
TO BE HAULED UP
THROUGH SLIP-WAY

In this illustration prepared for publication in *The Sphere,* a British magazine, the factory ship *Balaena* is shown in the Antarctic, with its spotter planes aloft.

On these voyages, the *Balaena* took sperm whales first, and while most of the oil was casked for trade, the men managed to requisition enough of it for their own purposes. Tradition held that it could cure baldness and arthritis, loosen any stuck nut or bolt, or make a fine sun-tan lotion. Deeper into the Antarctic, they began to catch fin whales for the oil, which was considered the primary product of British whaling. They also produced meat meal aboard the factory ship, as well as meat which was frozen and transferred to a refrigerator ship that followed the floating factory. Every ship working in the Antarctic would communicate its weekly catch to the Bureau of Whaling Statistics at Sandefjord, and when the quota of BWUs had been reached, the Bureau would signal the end of the season.

Toward the conclusion of the voyage—around late March or early April—the fresh foods were long gone, the weather was turning from merely bad to truly awful, and the men were exhausted and anxious to return to the dryness and warmth of home. Even if home was northern Norway, it was a tropical paradise compared to the roaring winds, whistling blizzards, freezing waters and miserable working conditions of the Antarctic. What attracted men to this life? Wise concludes his memoir of a whaling voyage with these words:

Wet, frozen, miserable, my hands dead and my head splitting, I often prayed for an end to this purgatory, for just five minutes in the warm mess with a mug of coffee, and wondered why the hell I had ever come. But when I had thawed out I knew why. I came because I wanted to: because of the companionship of men; because it is a way of life unfettered by the false complications of shore life; because with a heaving deck and the wild song of sea and wind there came a strange joy. The sheer rage and beauty of the elements—and your survival in spite of them—brought a peace that went deeper than physical exhaustion.

Ship's doctor aboard *Southern Harvester* on her maiden voyage in 1946–47 was Dr. Harry Lillic. He was so appalled by the cruelty involved in the exploding harpoons—he witnessed a single fin whale that was shot with five harpoons and took nine hours to die—that he began to lobby energetically for alternative methods of dispatching whales. First he considered poisons "such as curare or hydrogen cyanide . . . fired into the muscle of the whales in a dart from a light anti-tank gun or by rocket propulsion from a weapon of the bazooka class," or compressed gas, but eventually he hit upon electrocution "by a harpoon transmitting an electric current from a generator on the catching vessel, the current passing by an insulated copper cable incorporated into the foregoer rope trailing from the harpoon as it fired." In *The Path Through Penguin City*, Lillie's account of his whaling experiences (some of which is written as a dialogue between penguins), he wrote, "But could the men in the industry be callous enough to want the torturing of the whales to continue as the result of the old status being maintained? Certainly not; looking back on my days with those gunners in the Antarctic, I was convinced they would be glad indeed that they were at last to see the end of the era of vicious cruelty in whaling."

Although he could not interest Salvesen in his revolutionary ideas, he did convince Sir Vyvyan Board, a director of United Whalers Ltd. (owners of the *Balaena*), that more humane and efficient whaling could come from the use of electricity. In Norway in 1948, a United Whalers catcher was outfitted with an electrical harpoon fired from a "spigot gun," described by Dr. Lillie as "a flying gun barrel of high stress alloy steel fitted with a harpoon head that once more had no explosive in it." When whales were harpooned electrically, the amount of current was critical: too little and the whale would continue to breathe, filling up its lungs with water and sinking; too much and the flesh would be charred. In 1952, a Salvesen catcher, the *Setter V,* was outfitted with an electric harpoon gun, and tested in the North Atlantic. Lillie's book was published in 1955, when the idea of electrocuting whales still held promise. The dust-jacket copy reads (in part): "Dr. Lillie witnessed the death agony of these creatures many times, and as a result he devoted much thought to finding a less callous way of conducting the industry—a quest that was eventually taken up by one of the principal companies. After years of struggling with innumerable difficulties, his efforts are leading to the replacement of the exploding harpoon by that of the more humane electrical one." Of course, no such humane transition ever took place; the technology was inadequate (the fabricators could not effectively integrate the electrical cable and the forerunner), and although

The Salvesen factory ship *Southern Venturer* in the Antarctic in the 1950s. Notice the helicopter pad above the mouth of the stern slipway.

Grytviken, the South Georgia whaling station that had been operating continuously for fifty-eight seasons, was shut down by the British in 1962, then leased to the Japanese until 1964, after which it was closed forever. This photograph was taken in January 1990.

38 whales were killed in 1954, the system was considered flawed, and it was discontinued. (It would be reintroduced by the Japanese in 1956, but because electrocution stopped the circulation of the whale's blood and thus affected the freshness of the meat, they reverted to the tried and true exploding harpoon.)

A whaling chemist named Christopher Ash shipped out aboard the *Balaena* in 1951, and wrote up his adventures in *Whaler's Eye.* This was a busy and productive period for the British Antarctic fleet; five factory ships—*Balaena, Empire Victory, Empire Venturer, Southern Harvester* and *Southern Venturer*—cruised the ice in search of whales, and each had a number of catchers in attendance. For the 1951–52 season there were 19 floating factories, supported by 263 catchers. (At this time also, the the whaling navies of Norway, the Netherlands and Japan, as well as whalers owned by Aristotle Onassis, were competing in the whaling olympics.) The *Balaena* was also accompanied by the refrigerator ship *Samuel Enderby,* which froze the meat on deck by exposing it to the cold, and then took the frozen blocks to Immingham or Hull.

It had been only fifty-seven years since C. A. Larsen had returned from the Antarctic with tales of "houndreds and tousands of whales"; thirty-five years since the *Lancing* had first employed the stern slipway. The hunting of the larger rorquals was coming to an end. The period from 1950 to 1960 saw the destruction of the last of the blue and fin whales, and in the next decade, the demise of the Southern Hemisphere sei whales. Sei whales are oil-poor (whalers used to refer to them as "oilcloth whales" because of the thinness of their blubber), but a 40-ton animal has plenty of meat, and it was the meat that the Japanese wanted.

In 1961, Salvesen & Co. sold the *Southern Venturer* to the Japanese. Leith Harbour, the oldest British station in the Antarctic, was closed. Prices for oil continued to fall. By 1963, Salvesen had sold the *Southern Harvester* to the Japanese as well, thus concluding three and a half centuries of British whaling. The industry, like the manufacturers of whalebone corsets or buggy whips, simply found itself redundant. Cities like Hull and Whitby had risen on a foundation of bone and oil; London itself had been redesigned around the docks of the Greenlandmen. Where in 1790 there had been curved little streets and alleys, by 1810 there were the great docks of the Thames: the West India Dock was opened in 1802 on the Isle of Dogs, and in 1805, the London Dock opened in Wapping. The following year, the East India Dock was inaugurated, and in 1807, the Greenland Dock (where whale blubber was rendered in the midst of the city) was combined with the Howland Wet Dock in Rotherhithe. When the whaling industry declined, the docks were restructured. Where once whalemen told tales of voyages to the ice, flats have arisen. The Isle of Dogs is now one of interior London's most fashionable addresses.

Like her ex-colonials, the New Zealanders, the Australians and the Americans, the British switched from whaling to antiwhaling with celerity. Any International Whaling Commission resolution that even hinted at whale-killing for any reason was met with an impassioned protest from the United Kingdom's commissioner. At the 1987 meetings in Bournemouth, the British Minister of Agriculture, Fisheries and Food, John Selwyn Gummer, gave the welcoming address. Gummer declared himself and his countrymen once and for all on the side of the angels:

The vital decision reached by the majority vote in 1982 to introduce a moratorium on commercial whaling pending a comprehensive assessment of whale stocks is now very close to becoming a world-wide reality. All member nations have either halted or intend to halt their commercial whaling operations. We must now ensure that these widely welcomed decisions are not allowed to become mere empty words. It would be a tragedy if, under the guise of scientific study or subsistence hunting, commercial whaling were reintroduced. . . . The world will not forgive us if promises to protect the whale are betrayed by subterfuge.

Postwar Norway

THE WAR was a disaster for the whaling fleet: all the British and Japanese factory ships were torpedoed and sunk, and nine of Norway's vessels (including the original *Lancing* and *Kosmos*) were sent to the bottom. Because there was a worldwide shortage of meat, the whaling nations neglected to enforce any of the regulations that had been so laboriously crafted before 1940. Norwegians and Japanese fishermen killed whales wherever they could to feed their families. Because the American war machine required sperm oil as a lubricant for fine machinery, the United States, too, encouraged whaling wherever possible. During the war, however, the Southern Ocean was too remote—and the chances of being captured there too great—and the North Atlantic was the scene of devastating submarine warfare. This left the coast of South America available for whaling, and the Norwegians sent the factory ship *Thorshammer* to work the coasts of Chile and Peru. After Pearl Harbor, the Pacific became less safe, but the Americans' need for sperm oil was critical, and they continued to cultivate Norwegian sperm whaling. During this period, little or no attention was paid to size limits, and most of the whales taken seem to have been juveniles. "Necessity knows no law," wrote Tønnessen and Johnsen; in the name of democracy it was all right to kill the babies.

By the end of 1943, the German raiders had been put out of action, so the Norwegians campaigned again to be allowed to put to sea in pursuit of whales.

They sent the *Thorshammer* to the Antarctic from January to April of 1944, and the *Sir James Clark Ross* for the proper 1944–45 season. (This was not the original *Ross* [ex-*Mahronda*, etc.], but a newer version which had been built in 1930.) During the war, the Norwegian Whaling Committee was constantly active, and since so many factory ships and catcher boats belonging to other nations had been destroyed, Norway was prepared to go back into business as soon as the war was over.

In 1945, Norway had the only operating factory ships. Two of the German factory ships were discovered serving as floating fuel oil depots, and the reparations terms of the Potsdam Agreement gave one of them, the *Walter Rau,* to Norway, which promptly rechristened her *Kosmos IV.* (The other German factory ship, *Wikinger,* was given to the Soviet Union, and renamed *Slava.*) After the war, the price of whale oil rose to £100 a ton, and stayed up there until 1952. Once again, whaling was becoming an attractive industry, and the Norwegians were eager to partake of the bounty. Unfortunately, the Norwegians, who had led the world in the development of whaling technology, were now left with antiquated machinery and hopelessly outdated factory ships. (Norway had built a new factory ship, the *Kosmos V,* but the government could not grant her a concession because of international regulations governing the introduction of new ships into an existing fleet, and this modern whaler never sailed. She functioned as an ordinary tanker up until 1966, when she was sold to South Africa and used as a fish-meal factory.) Norway was losing her dominance of the whaling industry, and the reasons for this were complex and numerous. Norwegian whaling historians have suggested that the Norwegians knew the world whale quotas were much too high and would eventually result in the destruction of the whale stocks, and they therefore invested in the shipping business. This interpretation not only assigns to the Norwegians a clairvoyance that they could not possibly have had, it also gives a traditional whaling nation a sensitivity to the plight of the whales that not a single one of them has ever demonstrated. The primary reason for the erosion of the Norwegian industry was the appearance of the countries that were destined to become the superpowers of pelagic whaling, Japan and the Soviet Union.

Tønnessen and Johnsen wrote, "Americans, Argentinians, Australians, Austrians, Brazilians, Canadians, Chileans, Danes, Dutch, Finns, Germans, Italians, Japanese, Russians, Swedes, all had whaling plans, and practically everyone was thinking in terms of pelagic catching in the Antarctic." (Of these, only the Japanese, the Russians, and the Dutch outfitted expeditions to the Antarctic, but among them they managed to put the Norwegians out of business.) In response to the perceived threat of oceans filled with competing whaleships, the Norwegians developed the "Norwegian Crew Law," which forbade Norwegian nationals from working for foreign whaling companies. Since few other countries had the Norwegians' experience or expertise, competitors would be handicapped from the start, and the Norwegians felt that they could not regain their predominance if they helped everyone else to surpass them. This plan was based on the assumption that neither Japan nor Germany would be allowed to go back into the whaling business, however, and the assumption was wrong. Not only did the Japanese resurrect their whaling industry, but with the acquisition of the prize-of-war factory ship *Wikinger* (now *Slava*) by the Soviet Union, a new whaling nation entered the lists.

With the support of the Americans—and over the strenuous opposition of the Norwegians—the Japanese reentered the whaling business in 1946. Although the Germans were free to build a fleet after 1951, they chose not to, probably because of the stiff competition then being offered by the Norwegians, the British, the Japanese, the Soviets and the renegade *Olympic Challenger* owned by Aristotle Onassis.

From the 1945 season until 1953, the pelagic whalers took 16,000 blue whale units every year in the Antarctic. During these years, the industry busied itself with dividing up the BWUs, and to make best use of their men, matériel and money, the Norwegians combined their whaling companies into a single, state-subsidized organization. Although they sent their fleets elsewhere (they appeared in Western Australia at Shark Bay and Point Cloates, and in Queensland at Tangalooma), the main thrust of the whaling industry was still the Antarctic. It was becoming evident, however, that there were just not enough whales to justify the massive attack on their numbers. Since the whalers concentrated only on profits, a lower number of whales caught meant only one thing: they would have to step up their efforts.

Because of the conflicts over Antarctic quotas, the fabric of the IWC was beginning to unravel. Norway and the Netherlands both felt that the quota system was inequitable and was preventing them from free and unobstructed whaling. At the 1959 meeting in The Hague, both nations resigned from the IWC, and Japan, worried that non-IWC whalers would take a disproportionate share of the whales, also resigned. Less than ten years after its first meeting, the IWC had fallen apart. Three of the major powers had resigned and were planning to assign themselves quotas for Antarctic whales. The only whaling nations left in the fold were the Soviet Union and England.

Prior to this meeting, the question of public awareness of the slaughter of the whales had not been raised; the whalers went about their business, which consisted primarily of supplying whale oil to a needy world. With the dissension in the ranks, however, the machinery of the IWC became internationally newsworthy. Perhaps embarrassed by the bad press they were receiving, the commissioners voted to close ranks and bar the press from reporting on their exploits. The Chairman's Report contained the following language: "... the verbatim reports of the Commission meetings should be regarded as papers for transmission to the Contracting Governments not for general public distribution and quotations should not be permitted in a public press or in trade journals. . . ."*

Again for the 1960–61 season no quotas were set, and because the whale-killing threatened to get completely out of control, the commission appointed the "Committee of Three" to evaluate the stocks of Antarctic rorquals and make recommendations as to how to manage them. The committee consisted of Douglas Chapman, of the United States, Sidney Holt, of the United Nations Food and Agriculture Organization (FAO), and K. Radway Allen, of Australia.

*When the workings of the IWC became part of the environmental consciousness of the early 1970s this sensitivity to public opinion would eventually result in the press being barred from all but the opening ceremonies of the plenary session. All the public could find out about the disposition of the world's whales was what the commission chose to tell them. This was happening at the same time as the Watergate scandals, and freedom of the press was one of the battle cries of the time. As a result, a groundswell of public outrage arose when it became apparent that IWC member nations had taken it upon themselves to apportion whale stocks that were not theirs to apportion.

These men, all respected population dynamicists, carefully analyzed the available data, and concluded that the world's blue whale population—whatever it was—could not withstand any more hunting, and ought to be protected. The actual wording (in part) of the recommendations, surprisingly strong for such a document, is as follows: "As further suggested by the Scientific Sub-Committee, the agreement from four independent sources leaves no doubt that the stocks have been over-exploited and a programme of conservation should be initiated if the industry is to be maintained on a continuing basis."

As usual, what benefited the whalers had the opposite effect on the whales. With uncontrolled whaling taking place in the Antarctic from 1959 to 1962, the slaughter reached staggering proportions. In those four seasons, a total of 110,563 fin whales were killed. The 1960–61 season witnessed the death of 28,761 fin whales, the largest number of whales of a single species killed since the season of 1929–30, when 29,410 blues had been taken. That was the last season of successful blue whaling, and the population never recovered. The fin whale would soon follow on that inexorable path to annihilation. Not surprisingly, when the whalers headed south for the next season, they could only find 18,668 finners.

Despite the reduction in kills, the whalers kept up their bloody business; there were still whales to catch and money to be made from their deaths. But it was no longer the Norwegians who did the killing. The privately run companies of Norway and Britain could not compete with the government-subsidized Japanese and Soviet whaling fleets, and as other countries gave up the gun, these countries picked up the weaponry. The Dutch sold the *Willem Barendsz I* to the Japanese; the British sold the *Balaena* and the refrigerator ship *Enderby;* and finally, the Norwegians sold off their *Kosmos III* and five whale-catchers. Norway scrapped two more factories in 1961, and was struggling to keep her whaling business afloat.

The Soviets announced a five-year plan for whaling, and despite the declining stocks of whales, they sent three huge expeditions to the Antarctic in 1959–60. The Japanese had successfully lobbied the IWC for a new BWU allocation arrangement, whereby each whale-catcher was assigned a quota of 63 units, so as the Japanese bought the factory ships of other countries, they also picked up additional BWUs. The

Japanese, who did not employ Norwegian crews, were improving on the Norse technology. They were using a flat-headed harpoon, which was more effective than the old Svend Foyn design, and they added diesel power to their catchers. The Norwegians were being squeezed out of the business they had founded by Japan and the Soviet Union, two juggernauts that would dominate pelagic whaling until the business ended altogether.

The Japanese were involved in an aspect of pelagic whaling which had heretofore been unexplored: they used the meat for human consumption. They were therefore not dependent upon the highly variable market for whale oil, and could continue to kill whales with a guarantee that the products would be consumed immediately. Of course they also tried-out the whales for their oil, and this "double production" of meat and oil also meant that the Japanese were able to make approximately twice as much as other nations on the same number of whales killed. The Japanese hunger for whale meat was almost insatiable; they also contracted to buy the meat from other countries' ships to bring back to Tokyo in huge refrigerator ships that accompanied the floating factories. But it was the Soviets, building the factories *Sovietskaya Ukrania, Sovietskaya Rossiya* (sister ships of 33,000 gross tons), and *Dal'nii Vostok* (16,974 gross tons), that presented the greatest threat to Norwegian whaling.

The question of true quotas for individual nations—as opposed to a catch-as-catch-can BWU system—had been proposed as early as 1946, but it had always seemed too complicated: if each nation had its own proportion of the world's whales, wouldn't other countries want to join the party, and if so, how could the whaling nations be convinced to give up their share?

Tradition has played an important part in the whaling industry, and when the International Whaling Commission was formed in 1949, it was hard to imagine that new countries might want to join its ranks. Whaling was an expensive business, after all, and one that required expertise that came from years of experience. With the ponderous and threatening arrival of the USSR on the whaling grounds, the question of national quotas was raised again. Instead of the whalers' sharing a BWU allocation, they would divide up the catch according to a plan proposed by the Norwegians. The Soviets would get 20 percent of the total, Japan 33 percent, Norway 32 percent, the UK 9 percent, and the Dutch 6 percent. The whalers could not come to an agreement on these allocations, however, and by the time the meeting was about to begin in London in 1959, the Netherlands and Norway were prepared to resign rather than accept what they considered highly prejudicial quotas. New Zealand delivered a stinging criticism of the whaling nations' intractability ("We regret that the Commission has not yet found the courage to grasp the nettle of taking the action which is required in this connection. . . ."), and Remington Kellogg pleaded with them to hold on for another year. Nothing availed, and by the conclusion of the meeting, the IWC was torn apart. "Henceforth," wrote Tønnessen and Johnsen, "IWC meetings became get-togethers of pelagic nations, with the others as mere supernumeraries. While the Commission retained its right to fix the total quota, it was in reality the pelagic nations which decided how big it was to be." (There was not total anarchy on the whaling grounds, however, because the whaling nations eventually agreed to voluntarily accept quotas.)

The 1963 meeting in London was probably the most critical in the IWC's history. By this time, the report of the Committee of Three had been read and digested, and it was apparent that the whale stocks were at a dangerously low level. Finally—mercifully—the blue whale was granted protection throughout most of the Antarctic, and humpbacking was also prohibited. The blue whale unit, however, survived, and under the old system the whalers managed to find and kill 18,668 fin whales and 5,503 seis. At this rate, the whaling industry was well on the way to eliminating itself along with the source of its profits.

The 1964 IWC meeting was held, ironically, in Sandefjord. The Netherlands had dropped out of whaling, so the final act of this drama was to be played out by Norway, Japan and the USSR—the last of the pelagic whalers. The Euro/Asiatic nations, now the major whaling powers, campaigned to have their quotas raised, while Norway tried to wrest something out of the business before it ended. The quotas were drastically reduced at this and subsequent meetings, but by then it was almost too late. With smaller quotas, the great whaling armada was becoming superfluous, and several of the factory ships were converted to other functions. In 1966, the *Sir James Clark Ross* sailed for the last time, from Sandefjord to Taiwan, where she was broken up. Other whaleships ended up in the breaker's yard, but Norway still had enough men and matériel to sustain her industry for a short time.

By the 1967–68 season, the quota had been drastically reduced, to 3,200 BWUs for the entire Antarctic fleet. The whalers believed that their problems were solved, but then they were dealt another blow by the IWC's Scientific Committee, which announced that its earlier estimates of "sustainable yields" had been wrong, and recommended a further reduction in the quota. Norway's withdrawal from the field compensated for the reduction; the Norwegian whalers kept their quotas with them, and although they planned to reenter pelagic whaling, they never did. At the 1969 IWC meeting, the quota was set at 2,700 BWUs, and only Japan and the Soviet Union tried to find enough whales to fill it. They couldn't, and ended up with 2,469 units.

Japanese Whaling

WITH THE Japanese surrender on August 14, 1945, General Douglas MacArthur, Supreme Allied Commander, decreed that the Japanese ought to be encouraged to commence whaling again in order to provide much-needed meat for the vanquished and starving people. (This arrangement was not as altruistic as it appears on its face; while the Japanese were to get the meat, the Americans were to get the whale oil.) All the Japanese had available were two tankers of 11,000 gross tons apiece, and these were quickly converted to factory ships, *Hashidate Maru** and *Nisshin Maru*. (Originally, the Japanese were supposed to have spent only the 1946–47 season in the Antarctic, but somehow, this "one season" stretched into two, then three, four, five, and eventually, to forty more.)

From 1946 to 1951, the Japanese Antarctic fleet took 3,119 blue whales, 5,292 fins, 76 humpbacks, and 584 sperm whales. The attack on the sei whales had not begun. In 1951, after six postwar years of unregulated whaling, Japan became a member of the IWC.

In that year, the Japanese increased their fleet by the addition of the revamped 19,209-ton *Tonan Maru*. This was followed by the addition of another *Nisshin Maru*, built from scratch, and the only factory ship that the Japanese constructed after the war; all the others were acquired from other nations. The *Olympic Challenger* was purchased from Aristotle Onassis's outlaw whaling company in 1957, and the South African *Abraham Larsen* (ex-*Empire Victory*) became another *Nisshin Maru* in that same year.

Seiji Ohsumi, Japan's foremost sperm whale biologist, has written, "The North Pacific has been recognized as one of the world's major whaling grounds for sperm whales since the 19th century." In addition to their Antarctic activities, therefore, Japan's whalers also worked their own front yard, the Aleutian area of the North Pacific. According to Nishiwaki's 1967 study, most of the North Pacific, from the Bering Sea to the Equator, contains sperm whales, but the large bulls "migrate to the northward, clockwise for feeding." Although we know very little about the migratory habits of the sperm whale, it stands to reason that whalers, whether nineteenth-century Yankees or twentieth-century Japanese, would seek out the largest ones they could find, and male sperm whales are about a third again as large as females.

---

*In 1946, a young U.S. Army lieutenant named David Mc-Cracken was assigned to accompany the first Antarctic voyage of the *Hashidate Maru*, and in 1948 he published his (somewhat chauvinistic) observations in a book entitled *Four Months on a Jap Whaler*.

In his 1965 *The Stocks of Whales,* N. A. Mackintosh wrote, "It is hard to see any way at present of making even a wild estimate on the magnitude of the world population of sperm whales." By this time, however, it was necessary for the whalers to proclaim that they had some understanding of the population dynamics of the animals they were killing, so they began to count them. Whale-counting is even more complicated than predicting migration patterns—especially for animals that spend most of their lives swimming below the surface of the ocean out of sight of those who would count them—but in 1966, Nishiwaki estimated that there were some 150,000 male and female sperm whales migrating through the North Pacific. Within three or four years, as the controversy became more heated, the numbers went up proportionately. By 1971, Ohsumi was employing complicated mathematical formulas which factored in pregnancy rates, age at sexual maturity, and other poorly understood elements, and had estimated that there were 167,000 males and 124,000 females in the North Pacific.*

The first Japanese factory ship to work the North Pacific was the *Kaiko Maru* in 1946, followed by the *Baikal Maru,* which was sent out to sea with a flotilla of catcher boats in 1952 after working around the Bonin Islands. A second fleet was added in 1954, and a third in 1962. From 1962 to 1975, the Japanese operated three fleets in the North Pacific in competition only with the Soviets.

The Japanese literature is (perhaps deliberately) vague on the uses made of sperm whales. Tønnessen and Johnsen have written, "Even though sperm whale meat is used to some extent for human consumption in Japan, it is the least sought after. For this reason most of the sperm whale is reduced to oil." And what is the oil used for? Soviet cetologist A. A. Berzin writes:

The fatty substances obtained in sperm whale processing are unsuitable for human consumption because of the high content of unsaponifiable substances; they are being used as technical oils. . . . The fatty acids are used in the soap industry and the unsaponifiable substances in manufacturing detergents; the high molecular aliphatic alcohols in the leather and rubber industries; in the manufacture of cosmetics; in the degreasing [of] wool; and flotation of ores; the stock after fat extraction is used for preparation of gelatin. . . . Spermaceti oil is used as lubricants for fine mechanisms. . . . Solid spermaceti is used as carriers in manufacturing many medical and cosmetic products, mainly face creams and ointments, and for the production of lithographic ink. The therapeutic properties of spermaceti have been known for a long time; for instance, it is very good for the treatment of burns. . . . *The meat of sperm whales is inedible because it contains adipocere, but it is rich in proteins and is therefore valuable for the production of feed meal.* [My italics.] . . . Boiled sperm whale flesh can be used for feeding fur-bearing animals and in the preparation of dry protein. The liver of whales, particularly of the sperm, is the most valuable raw material for the vitamin industry. . . . The liver of one sperm whale contains as much carotene as 50 tons of carrots.

Ever since they began the massive hunt of sperm whales, the Japanese have insisted that they were taking the whales for human consumption. Sperm whale meat, like dolphin meat, is unappetizingly purplish-black in color because of its high myoglobin content, and it is said to have a most unpleasant taste. The eating habits of the Japanese are different from those of many Westerners, however (think of their liking for raw fish), and while they would probably have preferred to eat the meat of the baleen whales, they did indeed dine on the meat of the sperm whale.*

(By 1988, Taiyo Fisheries and Nippon Suisan Kaisha, the two major producers of stewed whale meat, had stopped processing it. According to a Japanese news release of April 6, 1988, "Instead, the companies have tried to placate their customers by offering substitutes—barbecued mutton and stewed horse meat—prepared in the same sweet-spicy, soy-based sauce that made canned whale meat such a delicacy for Japanese taste buds for most of a century." In the same release, Fumio Imanaga, presi-

---

*It was precisely these "models" that would cause so much dissension in the future. Those who would reduce the number of whales that could be killed argued that the Japanese estimates were too high and that they were deliberately misinterpreting the data; the Japanese, who had an obvious vested interest in high numbers, argued that their estimates were correct and even conservative.

*When I asked Seiji Ohsumi what was done with the meat, he wrote that "although sperm whale meat is not as delicious as the baleen whale meat, it is eaten by many Japanese people." He lists the methods of its preparation: steak, cooked, salted-dry, bacon, and *matsuura-zuke* (the thinly sliced nasal cartilage, which is soaked in sake). Someone else liked the meat of the sperm whale, or so we are told by Thomas Beale in his 1839 book. He quotes Cuvier: ". . . the Greenlanders are remarkably fond of its flesh, which they consider a delicate viand, when it is dried in smoke."

dent of the whaling company Nippon Suisan, is quoted as saying, "In the heyday of whale-meat consumption in Japan, almost 20 percent of our total canned-food sales came from stewed whale. During the years of postwar food shortages whale meat was a valued source of animal protein. To most Japanese who lived through those years, meat was synonymous with whale meat. Talk to any Japanese over 35. They'll tell you they will always remember the taste of whale meat stew with nostalgia." Perhaps it was the sperm whale meat that was stewed.)

Whatever became of the meat, it was the whale's oil that was important economically. In 1967, as the balance was shifting from the Antarctic (where they were simply running out of whales), to the North Pacific (which was an area that hadn't been regulated before), so too was the proportion of oil to other whale products: in 1962, sperm whales represented 57 percent of Japan's total catch; by 1975 they made up 93 percent of the total.

Even as the numbers of available whales dwindled, Japan (along with the Soviet Union) continued whaling in the Antarctic, as well as the North Pacific. The IWC set the quota for the 1968–69 season at 3,200 BWUs, to be divided between Japan and the USSR. On the whaling grounds, this was accomplished in the following manner: the whalers killed 2,893 fin whales and 12,368 sei whales. (To get the BWU total, divide the number of fin whales by 2—1,446—and add to it 12,368 divided by 6: 2,061. 2,061 + 1,446 = 3,507. The discrepancy was due to Norway's decision to retire from Antarctic whaling that year, which left her share of the quota unassigned.) Norway, for almost a century the leader of the whaling industry, had been elbowed out by Japan and the Soviet Union, and the products of her industry were now being used for pet food.

With Norwegian whalers *hors de combat* (or seeking employment in South Africa or Australia), the field was wide open for the Japanese and the Soviets. For the next ten years (1968–78), they killed hundreds of thousands of fin and sei whales in the Antarctic (humpbacks were fully protected all around the world by that time, as were blue whales), and an ever-escalating number of sperm whales in the North Pacific.

The total number of sperm whales killed by the Japanese from 1951 (the year Japan joined the IWC)

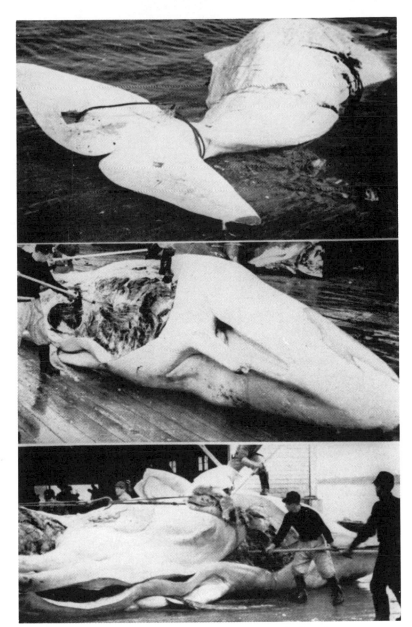

Moby Dick was fictional, but white sperm whales do exist. This one was captured by Japanese whalers in the North Pacific on April 19, 1957.

to 1976 was 124,458. (During the same period, Soviet whalers in the North Pacific killed 102,314, for a grand total of 226,772.) In Ohsumi's paper, from which the above figures were taken, he gives 60,842 as the number of sperm whales killed in the North Pacific for the period 1800–1909. The average per year for 1800–1909 is 558, while the average for 1951–76 is 9,880. A more eloquent testimony to the efficacy of modern whaling—and its catastrophic effect on whales—would be hard to find.

(Among the whaling statistics for 1957 was a record of a 35-foot-long male sperm whale that was

Aboard a Japanese whaler south of Tokyo, a Bryde's whale is gutted at sea, prior to towing back to the shore station.

completely white. Although he did not get to see it before it was flensed, and therefore could not observe its eye color, Seiji Ohsumi concluded that it was indeed an albino. "If it had not been killed in young generation," he wrote, "it would have reigned over the sea like the ancestor Moby Dick.")

It was during the period of intensified Japanese whaling that the antiwhaling movement was escalating throughout the rest of the world, and as part of the protest, a demonstration was arranged to coincide with the visit of Emperor Hirohito to Washington on October 2, 1975. As the first Japanese emperor to ever set foot on the soil of the continental United States alighted from his limousine at the South Portico of the White House to be greeted by President Ford, an airplane buzzed overhead, trailing a banner that read, "Emperor Hirohito Please Save the Whales." It would appear that the emperor did not have much influence with the whalers, however, and despite the protests—or perhaps because of them— the Japanese campaigned for increased quotas.

Since the mid-1970s, world opinion has been solidly opposed to Japanese whaling. In response to the petitions, editorials, demonstrations, protests, magazine articles and international condemnation, the Japanese dug in. They chose to interpret the antiwhaling attitudes as racially motivated—another instance of Europeans attempting to impose their customs on vulnerable Orientals. At first, the whal-

ing controversy seemed like a poker game, with each side holding cards that it dared the other side to play. The United States (the purported leader of the anti-Japanese movement) even went so far as to pass legislation (the Pelly Amendment and the Packwood-Magnuson Amendment) specifically designed to use against the Japanese. The Japanese threatened to pull out of the IWC and go whaling under their own rules. It was not the first time such threats would be expressed, nor would it be the last.

Nineteen seventy-six was another interesting year for the Japanese whaling industry. Although the quotas for most whale species were curtailed at the IWC meeting held in Canberra, Japan surprised the world by employing a tactic that would enable her to continue whaling without concern for IWC restrictions: she issued herself a scientific permit. The quota for Southern Hemisphere Bryde's whales for the 1976–77 season was zero. Despite this, the Japanese whalers managed to kill 225 of them, and except for a loud public outcry, there was nothing that anybody could do about it. The IWC has no enforcement capabilities and depends upon the willingness of the member nations to comply with its resolutions, but in this instance, the Japanese discovered a loophole large enough to drive a factory ship through.

Written into Article VIII of the International Convention for the Regulation of Whaling is this seemingly innocuous paragraph:

Notwithstanding anything contained in this Convention, any Contracting Government may grant to any of its nationals a special permit authorising that national to kill, take, and treat whales for purposes of scientific research subject to such other conditions as the Contracting Government thinks fit, and the killing, taking, and treating of whales in accordance with the provisions of this article shall be exempt from the operation of this Convention.

Obviously, this language was written into the convention to allow contracting governments to perform scientific experiments without falling under restrictions imposed on commercial whalers. In other words, if a country's scientists believed that they could find a cure for cancer by using whale oil, they shouldn't have to qualify as whalers to collect material for their experiments. (Prior to the passage of the Marine Mammal Protection Act in 1972, which, among other things, shut down the last American whaling station, United States whaling companies had regularly awarded themselves scientific permits for the taking of gray whales and sperm whales off the California coast, and they did indeed conduct research on the whales. For a study published in 1971, American cetologists Rice and Wolman examined 316 gray whales that were collected by catcher boats off the coast of central California.) It was nowhere written that the government had to tell anyone what they had in mind if and when they issued themselves a scientific permit, however, and when the Japanese awarded their whalers the right to harvest 240 Bryde's whales in the Southern Ocean, they were bound by no restrictions to identify the nature of the science that was the ostensible purpose of the hunt. In fact, their scientists wrote reports about the Bryde's whales, and almost two thousand tons of whale meat went right into the freezers of the whaling company and eventually into Japanese stomachs. By the following year, the IWC believed it had closed this loophole—by recommending that future applications be subject to scrutiny by the Scientific Committee—but as we shall see, it was not closed, only lightly papered over. In 1987 it would blossom into such an explosive issue that the very existence of the IWC would be threatened by it.

The moratorium that would encourage the whaling nations to seek devious ways to stay in business was still several years in the future, and the killing of whales was still a legal—although an increasingly unpopular—way to earn a living. And still in the forefront of the industry, sailing off in every direction in search of more whales to kill, were the Japanese.

They took another 114 Bryde's whales in the Southern Hemisphere in October and November 1977, and produced 750 tons of meat and 176 tons of oil. By this time, the Southern Hemisphere fin whale population had been so thoroughly decimated that the quota, which had been 1,450 in 1973 and 220 in 1975, was reduced to zero, and the stock was declared "Protected," placing it in the same category as the blue, right, gray and humpback whales.* The only large whales left to hunt were the seis and the sperm whales, and as the quotas for these animals were reduced, the 30-foot minkes were looking better and better to the whalers.

By this time, it was becoming apparent to everyone—except perhaps the Japanese—that the days of commercial whaling were numbered. The sounds of protest could be heard around the world, and only the terminally stubborn could maintain ignorance of the direction in which whaling was heading. Of course the IWC continued to establish quotas for various species, but these quotas continued to fall as more nations became aware of—and concerned about—the plight of the whales. Antiwhaling nations joined the IWC, and even more important, conservationists influenced their governments to campaign against whale-killing.

The Japanese and the Soviets continued to take whichever species were allowed to them under IWC regulations. As of 1980, the blue, right and humpback whales were fully protected, so they killed the fin, sei, Bryde's, minke and sperm whales. The quotas—and therefore the catches—for these species are as follows (see next page):

---

*The IWC classifies whales into three categories, as follows:

Sustained Management Stock (SMS): A stock of whales which is considered stable enough to apply a quota. The classifications are calculated on the basis of Maximum Sustainable Yield (MSY), the number of whales that can, according to the Scientific Committee, be removed from the population without adversely affecting the total population.

Initial Management Stock (IMS): A stock more than 20 per cent above the MSY stock level. Whaling may be permitted on these stocks according to the advice of the Scientific Committee.

Protection Stock (P): A stock below 10 per cent of MSY. No commercial whaling is permitted on these stocks.

SPECIES	1975–76	1976–77	1977–78	1978–79	1979–80
Fin	565	344	459	470	604
Sei	2,230	1,995	855	84	100
Bryde's	1,363	1,000	524	454	743
Minke	9,360	11,924	8,465	9,173	12,006
Sperm	19,040	12,676	13,037	9,360	2,203
TOTALS	32,558	27,939	23,520	19,541	15,656

(The above figures, taken from the IWC *Schedules,* are for all areas, and include quotas for male and female sperm whales, which were allocated separately.)

Note particularly the decline in sperm whale quotas. The quota for 1980–81 was set at 1,623, and for 1981–82, a zero quota was set for the Southern Hemisphere and the North Atlantic, with the North Pacific quota deferred until the next year. At the 1982 IWC meeting, the ten-year moratorium on all commercial whaling was passed, so the question of a North Pacific quota became moot. While there were to be no further quotas set for sperm whales, the moratorium was supposed to include a three-year phase-out period, so quotas for minke whales were set for the 1981–82 season "not to exceed" 8,102 whales, and commercial whaling could continue until the 1985–86 season, at which time it would end.

At least that's what the framers of the moratorium thought would happen—but after the euphoria of this accomplishment had subsided, it was painfully clear that more whale blood was going to be spilled. First, as permitted under the IWC's regulations, Japan, the USSR, Peru and Norway filed objections to the moratorium. That meant it was not binding on them, which somewhat diminished its effectiveness,

Bryde's whale on the flensing deck at the whaling station at Taiji, Japan, 1981. Notice the three ridges on the rostrum, which identify the species, and the white-fringed baleen.

since they represented most of the whaling carried out at the time. Because they did not file objections, Brazil, Iceland and South Korea appeared to be agreeing to suspend their operations. (Of these three countries, only Iceland had what might be called an autonomous whaling operation, since those of Peru, Brazil and South Korea were under the control of the Japanese.) There was still the question of minke whale quotas for the premoratorium period, and later, the thornier question of what—if anything—could be done about whaling nations that simply chose to ignore the moratorium.

At the 1982 IWC meeting, a quota for Southern Hemisphere minke whales was set at 7,072 whales. (An additional quota of 1,690 minkes was given to Norway for the North Atlantic, but our concern here is Japan.) It was believed at the time that giving substantial quotas to the Japanese would ameliorate their professed difficulties in phasing out their whaling industry. In fact, the Japanese seem to have spent that three-year period designing mischievous strategies, subterfuges and protestations of misunderstanding, so that they would not actually have to stop whaling. And up to 1988, they did not miss a season.

From 1982 to 1986, the Japanese continued to hunt sperm whales in the North Pacific and in the Antarctic. (They also began to speak about "research whaling," but these comments were not taken seriously until 1986.) The Southern Hemisphere minke whale quota was set at 6,655 in 1983, and was further reduced to 4,224 at the 1984 meeting in Buenos Aires. (There was also a North Pacific quota for minke whales, but that was taken by the South Koreans.) As usual, the Japanese professed to be shocked and surprised by the actions of the anti-whaling nations, and after the vote on minke whales, Japanese Commissioner, Kunio Yonezawa abruptly left the meeting. In an interview given during the Buenos Aires conference, Shigeru Hasui, managing director of Nippon Kyodo Hogei, was quoted as saying, "There are 40 member nations in IWC and only eight are involved in whaling and about half of the 40 joined in the last few years with the intention of voting against whaling, so it is easy to achieve a majority. So we think that we cannot bring serious discussion into the IWC as our viewpoint is totally ignored." When asked if the IWC had a future, Hasui replied, "In spite of the fact that the IWC has

so much data available it still seeks to impose a total ban on commercial whaling, so we believe it is no longer an arena we should participate in." Despite these thinly veiled threats to leave the commission, Japan has reluctantly remained a part of the international body that was working so hard to put her out of the whaling business.

To the Japanese consumer, whales were an almost inexhaustible source of good things, from food to medicines and lubricating oils.

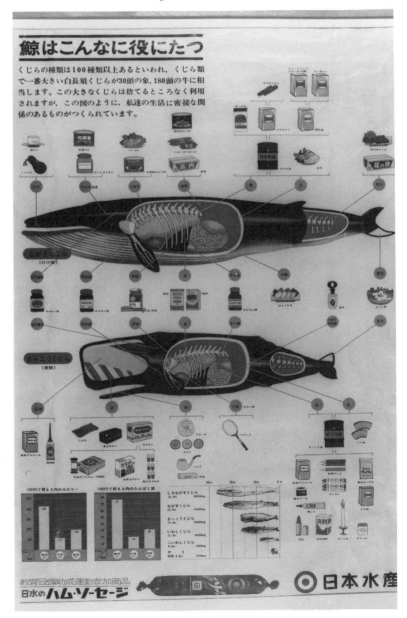

The Soviet Juggernaut

FADDEI FADDEEVICH BELLINGSHAUSEN was supposedly the first person to sight the Antarctic continent. Sent on a voyage of exploration by Tsar Alexander I, he sailed in the *Vostok,* a 600-ton corvette. He was accompanied by the *Mirnyi,* under Admiral Mikhail Lazarev, who had served for four years in the British navy. After meeting with Sir Joseph Banks, who had sailed with Cook some fifty years before, and acquiring charts and other navigational aids, they set sail from Portsmouth on September 5, 1819. They circumnavigated the Antarctic continent, sighted the South Shetlands and discovered the South Sandwich Islands. Bellingshausen (for whom an Antarctic sea was named) described various unique birds that he saw, including the penguins, of course, and on New Year's Day 1820, he wrote in his journal: "We saw whales playing about in the water, rising perpendicularly about one-third of their whole length, and then diving again, showing their horizontal tails." Upon their return in 1821, after a voyage that lasted just over two years, the expedition was scarcely acknowledged. It was an-

The Soviet factory ship *Yuri Dolgorukiy*

In heavy seas, catcher boats often sailed with their lee rails awash. This is No. 11, the Soviet catcher *Olg*.

other ten years before the results of Bellingshausen's journeys were published, and then in an edition of only six hundred copies. It appeared that the Russians were not particularly interested in another continent where the predominant features were ice and snow, and they did not return to the Antarctic for 137 years.

In 1946 the Soviets sent the factory ship *Slava* (ex-*Wikinger*, the German prize-of-war) to the South, commanded by Captain V. I. Voronin, but with Norwegian harpooners and flensers. In their first season, Soviet whalers took a total of 368 whales, almost half of which were blues. In 1955, Soviet whaling historians Zenkovich and Arsen'ev wrote, "Foreigners forecast failure, but their forecast failed." The Soviets learned the business well, and by 1948 they were ready to conduct all phases of the Antarctic fishery on their own. During the 1948–49 season, with no Norwegians aboard, the *Slava* took 1,107 whales, and by 1953–54, they had killed more than 3,000. During this period, the waters of the Antarctic were visited by factory ships flying the flags of Great Britain, Japan, the Netherlands, Argentina and Norway, and the stocks of rorquals suffered correspondingly. By this time, blue whales were severely reduced in numbers, and the primary object of the

southern fishery was the fin whale. In the 1953–54 season, the combined fleets took 2,697 blues and 27,659 finners.

When it was recognized that the North Pacific was as important an area for sperm whales as the Antarctic was for rorquals, the whalers adjusted accordingly. Until 1954, the Soviets operated only the flotilla of the *Aleut,* in the vicinity of the Kamchatka Peninsula and the Commander Islands, but as the other whaling nations also had access to these grounds, the whales were quickly fished out, and the whaling changed from an inshore operation to a purely pelagic one. The hunting area was extended throughout the North Pacific, all along the arc of the Aleutians to the Gulf of Alaska. As the quotas were increased, the Soviets added men and ships to their fleets; in 1956, they announced their five-year plan (1956–60) for whaling, which included the building of five factory ships. By the late 1960s, they were operating the *Aleut,* the *Sovietskaya Ukrania* (built in 1959), the *Yuri Dolgorukiy* (1960), the *Sovietska Rossiya* (1961), the *Vladivostok* (1962), and the *Dal'nii Vostok* (1963), all gigantic factory ships with diesel catcher boats doing the hunting. During the years 1956–64, the Soviets built sixty-seven new catcher boats, averaging 843 gross tons, their 3,600-horsepower engines capable of powering them at more than 19 knots. It was obvious that the Soviet Union was planning to become a major factor in the business of pelagic whaling. For this design, they benefited enormously from the support of the state; the other whaling countries like Britain, the Netherlands and Norway were trying to compete as privately run companies, and Japan was an enigma. (To this day, it is not known to what extent the Japanese whaling industry was subsidized by the government.) There seemed to be no way of stopping the Soviet juggernaut; it appeared that this latecomer to pelagic whaling was going to dominate it so completely that there would be no whales left for anyone else. By 1968, only the Soviet Union and Japan would be sending whaling ships to the Antarctic.

At the 1959 International Whaling Commission meeting, the Antarctic whaling nations were unable to arrive at national quotas for baleen whales. The Netherlands and Norway quit the commission, leaving it up to the individual governments to plan their own quotas. The Soviet Union refrained from participating in the discussions, but when the quotas had been worked out, it had ended up with 20 percent of the total. The same thing happened the following year, and the USSR was on the way to carving out a sizable portion of the Antarctic pie for herself.

When the Dutch and the Norwegians returned to the fold, it was clear that the dominant nations were going to be Japan and the USSR. Britain retired from whaling in 1963, and the Netherlands in '64. Only Norway was left to compete with the behemoths of the whaling industry, and the Norwegians could not contend with the socialized industries of Japan and the USSR. By 1967 Norway was gone, and the two North Pacific nations were left to argue over the number of whales they ought to be allowed to kill in the Antarctic.

By the time the field had been cleared, however, the whales of the Antarctic had been so reduced by the excesses of the competing nations that the whalers recognized they would have to look elsewhere. They decided to put their men and matériel to use in the North Pacific. (One of the problems with a reduction in quotas has always been the employment of the workers. Because they are different types of societies, Japan and the USSR have different approaches to this problem, but the solution is the same: don't lay off the whalemen.) When scientists realized that there weren't enough blue whales and humpbacks in the North Pacific to sustain an industry, they turned to the sperm whale. As of 1970, there were no quotas for this species, but by the following

A Soviet catcher boat, *Dezzkiy-45,* in the Antarctic.

The Soviet factory ship *Slava* (ex-*Wikinger*), acquired as a prize of war from Germany in 1945.

year, the whaling commission had set a limit of 10,481 for the Japanese and the Soviets, the only nations still in the pelagic-whaling business.

Other whalers continued to kill other whales. The Norwegians still hunted minke whales; the Canadians were killing fin whales out of Newfoundland stations; there were various Japanese-financed operations in South America; and the Australians were taking sperm whales off their west coast. Sperm whaling out of Durban was winding down, and "research whaling" was being conducted by the Americans in California on such a small scale as to make comparison with the whaling "flotillas" absurd. All these operations combined could not compare with the numbers of sperm whales being killed by the pelagic whalers.

In 1966, the Soviets brought up the *Slava,* the last Soviet factory ship to operate in the Antarctic. In 1964, pelagic whalers had taken 10,314 sperm whales in the North Pacific; by 1967, the figure was up to 15,469.

In 1966, the Soviet fleets took three times as many sperm whales as the Japanese (the actual count was 9,436 to 3,000), even though a large proportion of the whaling was taking place in Japanese waters. The Soviet cetologist B. A. Zenkovich has calculated that 86,000 sperm whales were taken in the fourteen-year period (1950–64) since the Soviets began sperm whaling. Soviet cetologists conducted intensive research on the whales they killed—obviously in the interest of continuing this highly profitable industry—and were more than a little surprised to discover that the whales were in trouble; they were much smaller and much younger than they had been in past seasons. A. A. Berzin, the Soviet scientist who wrote a comprehensive monograph on the sperm whale in 1972, said: "By the end of 1963 it had become clear that there was an urgent need of protective measures for sperm whales that come to subarctic latitudes for the summer. Absence of stringent international restrictions may prove fatal for the North Pacific sperm whales." Following this realization, the Soviets and the Japanese voted to *increase* the quotas for North Pacific sperm whales.

Mechanized sperm whaling was not very different from the old open-boat methods; it was just more

At a displacement of 33,154 gross tons, the 700-foot-long Soviet factory *Sovietskaya Rossiya* was the largest whaleship ever built.

efficient. The whales were spotted from a lookout, and then the catcher boat approached them, under minimum or no power so as not to frighten them. The gunners tried to shoot the whale on the left side, to get at the heart. When the whale was dead, it was brought alongside the catcher boat, and its body cavity was inflated with compressed air to keep it afloat. (Nineteenth-century whalers did not have the ability to pump dead sperm whales full of air, and evidently they didn't have to. Sperm whales are not supposed to sink, but the Soviets inflated them anyway, claiming that only the adults, with their thicker blubber layer, remained afloat after they were killed.)

The carcasses were delivered to the factory ships and then hauled up the slipway, where the blubber was stripped off, and the spermaceti ladled into kettles. The bones, meat and viscera were boiled together, and the teeth removed from the lower jawbone. In the nineteenth century, only the blubber, the spermaceti and the teeth were kept, but the modern Soviet whalers used every part of the whale except the smell. The skin was removed and tanned (apparently aboard the factory ship), and if it was not marred by parasite (or harpoon) holes, it was

cut into sheets that measured 70–120 by 50–80 centimeters (27–46 by 19–31 inches). A 52-foot whale yielded a hide that was 78 meters (255 feet) square, and weighed 1,030 kilograms (2,266 pounds, more than a ton). The thick whale leather was used to make shoe soles and heavy work gloves. The oils obtained from the boiling of the blubber, meat, and bones were used in the manufacture of soap and cosmetics, the greasing of wool, the floating of ores, and when the fats were removed, in the preparation of gelatin. Spermaceti oil was employed in the lubrication of fine machinery (including precision instruments for the space programs, missiles and submarines), and in the manufacture of face creams and ointments. Soviet citizens considered the meat of the sperm whale inedible, but it could be fed to fur-bearing animals, and in its dried state it was added to animal fodders. A whale-liver extract was also used in the manufacture of a preparation called Campolon MG, which the Soviets use to treat anemia. The pancreas yielded a substance used to make insulin, and the pituitary produced an adrenocorticotrophic substance for the treatment of arthritis and gout. A surgical sponge made from the collagen of the whale's flukes was used as a temporary replacement for donor skin in the treatment of burns. The tendons were used in the manufacture of glue.

Sperm whales are the only whales—in fact, they are the only animals on earth—that can produce the mysterious stuff known as ambergris. This crumbly, grayish-brown substance is sometimes found when a sperm whale is cut open, but it is only found in about three or four out of every hundred whales. It is usually encountered in smallish lumps in the whale's lower intestines, but sometimes great "boulders" are revealed when the whale is eviscerated.

The largest piece found by the Soviet whaling fleet weighed 595 pounds, and was extracted from a 50-foot male on the *Sovietskaya Rossiya* in 1967.

As described by the Soviet cetologists, sperm whales sounded like the panacea for all of mankind's ills. They provided food, medicine, leather, perfume, oil and numerous other products necessary for the good life in Petropavlovsk. Unfortunately, the whale supply was running low, and neither the Soviets nor any other whaling nation was willing to stop the killing. Perhaps they would have gotten the picture if the whales also laid golden eggs. Public opinion,

An adult bull sperm whale hauled up on the flensing deck of the *Olympic Challenger*. Notice the tooth-studded lower jaw, the absence of teeth in the upper, the configuration of the end of the whale's nose, and the profusion of scars.

rarely a factor in the Soviet scheme of things, would eventually put the Soviets out of the whaling business, but like every other whaling country, they would not go quietly, and before they muzzled their harpoon cannons, thousands more sperm whales would die.

And like their unfortunate predecessors who had been killed by intrepid harpooners all over the world, the twentieth-century victims of technological progress were killed from pole to pole. (Curiously, the nineteenth-century sperm whalers did not know of the concentrations of cachalots that were found off the Aleutians and Alaska; Townsend shows no kills there, and other historians do not mention the sperm whale grounds that were so heavily exploited by the Japanese and the Soviets. Later summaries, however, such as Gilmore's 1959 discussion of sperm whale strandings, identified the sperm whale grounds of Kamchatka and Kodiak.) Not only were the cachalots slaughtered in the North Pacific, but also in the Antarctic. After ignoring sperm whales for so long, the International Whaling Commission finally recognized their existence—or their way out of existence. The only whale that most people had ever heard of or imagined had finally achieved the ultimate recognition. The species could not have had a worse endorsement; the IWC's imprimatur was literally the kiss of death. In the annual conferences, whenever the subject of *Physeter macrocephalus* was raised, it was to determine how many of them might be killed.

IN THE mid-1960s, as the stocks of baleen whales fell to levels where the whalers found it uneconomical to search for them (in the whaler's parlance, the "catch per unit effort" was unsatisfactory), they noticed that there were still lots of whales around— they were just not the proper ones. The right whales were gone altogether, and blues, finners, seis and humpbacks had been reduced to such low levels that they were classified as protected or endangered. The economics and politics of whaling had reduced the killer fleets to those of Japan and the Soviet Union, two countries that were fully prepared to change their targets from baleen whales to sperm whales. Both nations needed the oil and fertilizer, and although the Soviets didn't eat the meat, their minks and sables did, and besides, if there was any left over, they could always sell it to the Japanese. For the Japanese, these previously untapped resources represented a vast new area to be plundered.

Like a trickle that eventually becomes a raging torrent, the sperm whale made its appearance in the *Annual Reports* of the IWC in marginal references. In a prepared statement to the IWC in 1965, amidst its concerns about the "depletion of baleen whale stocks," the USSR delegation "agreed . . . that it is necessary to reduce the catches of female sperm whales." (Male and female sperm whales would be treated almost as separate species, because of the variations in their range—the females remain separated from the males for most of the year, and inhabit different areas—and also because of the size differential. So that neither gender would be unduly taxed and thus become unavailable for breeding, the sexes were assigned separate quotas.)

Because it was becoming evident that sperm whales were going to replace baleen whales as the major objects of the fishery, a special session of the IWC was called for 1966. Among its conclusions: "a special group should be set up to undertake over-all stock assessments as soon as possible. To this end, complete effort statistics should be made available by each country to the International Whaling Commission." If sperm whales had been able to read, they would have departed for the planet Pluto. The mechanized whale navy was getting ready to train their warheads on the sperm whales, as soon as they conducted the research that they believed was necessary to justify the impending slaughter.

First they divided up the world into convenient sectors, so as to make it easier to monitor catches. It didn't matter that the whales did not respect these divisions, and freely wandered from one sector to another; nor did it matter that there was a strong possibility that the whales might migrate from one hemisphere to the other.

The Scientific Committee apportioned the Southern Hemisphere into nine divisions, and cut the North Pacific in half, under the (probably erroneous) assumption that there were two separate stocks of sperm whales in that area. It also decided that North Atlantic sperm whales constituted a single population, so for the benefit of the Norwegians, the Icelanders and the Canadians, that entire ocean was deemed a single "management area." In order

Until 1972, the Del Monte Company operated a shore station at Richmond, California, where they took humpbacks, grays and an occasional sperm whale. Their vessels consisted of converted fishing trawlers with a harpoon cannon mounted on the bows.

to estimate the number of whales that might be killed every year, the whalers had to have some idea of the population. Figuring out how many sperm whales were in the world's oceans was not an easy task, however, especially in the light of the animal's uncooperative habit of spending most of its life underwater. Undaunted by this minor impediment, the IWC researchers labored over their computers and spewed forth some numbers. Even though the estimates were couched in elaborately obtuse language and embellished with formulas incomprehensible to anyone but a population dynamicist, they were still only guesses. By 1983, the scientists estimated that there were some 111,400 male sperm whales and 162,600 females in the eastern North Pacific, and 61,000 males and 137,100 females in the western sector.*

For the year 1968, North Pacific sperm whalers took 12,740 males, and 3,617 females. The next year,

*These numbers totaled 472,100 animals, and combined with the estimated totals of Southern Hemisphere and North Atlantic sperm whales (in Gosho *et al.* 1984), the estimated world population is somewhere in the vicinity of 1,000,000 animals. Such numbers are useful in planning whaling operations, but when the International Decade for Cetacean Research (IDCR) report was presented at the IWC meeting in 1989, instead of the 600,000 animals supposed to be in the Antarctic, the researchers could only locate 3,059.

the figures were 11,239 and 3,605. In the IWC report for 1970, the Scientific Committee "agreed that it is desirable to slow down the decrease of male stock in view of apparent excessive catches . . ." and they recommended that "a further reduction in the catch of male sperm whales is desirable." The IWC therefore set the first quotas on sperm whales in 1970 for the 1971 season. They allocated 5,760 sperm whales to Japan, 7,716 to the USSR—and a surprising 75 to the United States, which was in the process of closing down the last of its whaling operations in California.* For the next three seasons, the commission set quotas of 6,000 males and 4,000 females for the North Pacific, but not once did the Soviet Union or Japan meet these quotas. At the same time, the two

*In 1970, when Kenneth Norris wanted to examine a sperm whale's head to try to identify the source of its sounds, he visited the whaling station at Richmond in San Francisco Bay. In *The Porpoise Watcher,* he describes the whaling station:

Down at the end of one such track was a gaunt building whose sign dimly proclaimed, "Del Monte Fishing Company." A single dirty bulb depended from a metal yardarm over the dirt street. From inside, through the grease-covered windows, came a hum of activity. A dump truck, comfortable in its rusting old age, stood slumped under a chute that pierced the building wall. From the chute came a mass of formless whale parts and oily fragments of blubber, sluiced into the recesses of the truck by a man standing in hip boots deep in the gurry.

nations were taking some 13,000 sperm whales in the Antarctic.

With savage intensity, the sperm whalers raised their catch figures, and the IWC, helpless against the powerful whaling nations, could only watch as the statistics soared to astronomical levels. From 1964 to 1974, 267,194 sperm whales were killed in the northern and southern oceans, an average of 24,270 per year.* With the passage of the United Nations resolution of 1972 on the cessation of whaling, the eyes of the world were on the IWC. Would this body conform to world opinion? Would they reduce the quotas of whales? When a moratorium was introduced to the IWC by the United States delegation at the 1972 meeting, the commission rejected it, and did so again in 1973. (The U.S. passed its own Marine Mammal Protection Act in 1972, which marked the end of American whaling.) The slaughter continued. In 1974, 21,217 sperm whales died.

CONSERVATION GROUPS by this time had targeted Japan and the Soviet Union as the villains of the piece, and they were beginning to apply pressure by collecting signatures on petitions to be presented to the respective embassies. United States congressmen, such as Alphonso Bell, of California, spoke out against the Japanese, saying: "The time has come for Japan and the Soviet Union to heed the international outcry and put an end to this rapacious industry." There were pressures that could be applied to the Japanese government, since whaling was known to be completely subsidized, and also because the United States did so much business with Japanese industry. To counter the attack, the Japanese hired public-relations consultants, published booklets about their whaling history and industry, and offered diplomatic responses to the charges being leveled at them.

The Soviets presented a different problem. They killed as many whales as the Japanese, but there didn't seem to be any way leverage could be brought to bear on them. There were no Soviet cars to refuse to buy, no radios, television sets or cameras to boycott. They did not deign to respond to charges against them. Votes in the IWC were clearly divided along whaling and antiwhaling lines.* When it appeared as if no one in authority was doing anything to stop the certain annihilation of the sperm whales, their saviors miraculously appeared. This unlikely cavalry consisted of the eco-guerrillas of Greenpeace, who had decided to resort to confrontational methods to stop the Soviet whale-killers.

GREENPEACE had managed to locate the factory ship *Dal'nii Vostok* in the North Pacific, some three hundred miles off the coast of California. The killer boats had been at work, and the Rainbow Warriors' first contact was with a dead whale—and an undersized one at that. They then approached the huge factory ship in their little rubber inflatables, and demanded (in Russian) that the whalers cease and desist. Greenpeace cameramen filmed the flensers high above them and the bloody rinse-water running out of the scuppers, but they were after bigger, more spectacular game: they wanted to put themselves between the whalers' harpoons and the whales.

When the catcher boat *Vlastny* set out after a pod of sperm whales, the inflatables followed. As soon as the whales were in range, the commandos positioned themselves so that the gunner would have to shoot directly over their heads in order to hit the whale. They were convinced that the harpooner would not fire for fear of hitting them, but they were wrong. The 250-pound cast-iron projectile whistled over their heads, and struck one of the hapless whales. Greenpeace's effort didn't stop the whaling, but by filming the event and making sure that the film was shown on television around the world, the group did make the world aware of the problem. For the first time, the media showed the cruelty of whaling. Until the age of television, whale-killing was something that only the whale-killers saw, but now it was being shown on the evening news, and a lot of people didn't like what they saw. A movement was gather-

---

*Also in 1972, the IWC called a special meeting to "carry out further analyses and to develop new population models for sperm whale stocks throughout the world." Scientists from the whaling nations (Australia, Canada, Japan, South Africa, United Kingdom, United States, Soviet Union) met in Vancouver, and produced a series of estimates for the then-exploited populations. In this report, the North Pacific stock was estimated at some 291,000 animals, and the "catchable population" in 1972 was somewhere between 107,000 and 133,000.

*In 1972, there were fifteen voting nations in the IWC. Of these, six were actively involved in whaling (Iceland, Japan, Norway, Panama, South Africa and the USSR). This bloc had the power to fend off any antiwhaling resolution that was introduced, since in order for such a resolution to pass, two-thirds of the membership had to vote for it.

ing momentum that would have a most remarkable effect on the whaling business: ordinary citizens were becoming involved in an issue that heretofore had been relegated to the meeting rooms of the IWC, and they would, in time, completely change commercial whaling.

In 1976, however, whaling was only different in the identity of the participants. In the North Atlantic, Icelandic, Norwegian and Canadian whalers were killing sperm whales; the Peruvians and Chileans were taking rorquals in the South Atlantic, and the pirate whaler *Sierra* was on the loose. Whaling on the high seas, with gigantic factory ships attended by fleets of catcher boats, was now the private domain of the Japanese and the Soviets. It was obvious that the elevated quotas and freewheeling catches were things of the past, and the numbers began to fall. A special meeting of the IWC was convened at Cronulla, Australia, in June 1977, to discuss the business of sperm whales.

The Scientific Committee recommended a quota of 763 sperm whales for the North Pacific, but in a move that made headlines around the world, the IWC emerged from the meeting with a quota of 6,444—nearly *ten times* the number recommended by its own scientists. Near chaos resulted; at the 1978 meeting, no revisions were made, and the recommendation of 763 remained the same as in 1977. This was not a number that the whalers were prepared to accept, of course, so they again ignored the Scientific Committee, and again assigned themselves a total of 6,344. Of this, the Soviets took 3,226.

Jean-Paul Fortom-Gouin appeared at the IWC as an adviser to the Panamanian delegation at the London meeting of 1978.* His delegation had planned to introduce a resolution for a moratorium on commercial whaling, but before the meeting actually began, the resolution was withdrawn and Fortom-Gouin recalled. It was rumored that the Japanese had applied pressure on the Panamanians by threatening to cancel a lucrative sugar purchase if they persisted in embarrassing Japanese whaling interests. The IWC's special publication on the sperm whale (published in 1980, but including the results of the

*It is not necessary for a delegate to maintain citizenship in the country he represents. Fortom-Gouin found it expedient to represent Panama in 1978, and in later years, he was to appear on other delegations, including the St. Lucian from 1983 to 1985, and the Antiguan in 1989.

two special meetings held in 1977 and 1978) contains a bewildering collection of mathematical formulae for the estimation of sperm whale stocks, and it also contains the voice of Jean-Paul Fortom-Gouin.

In an argument entitled "Reason for Recommending Zero Female Catch Limits for Sperm Whales," Fortom-Gouin (along with Sidney Holt) wrote, "Hunting has a negative effect on the nursery groups hunted," and "There is no indication that exploitation has any positive effect." It was evident that the scientists still had only the murkiest idea of how many sperm whales there were, and they had no idea at all how many they ought to allow the whalers to kill.

Although the Soviets took more whales, the Japanese were by far the most ardent advocates of higher quotas. The Japanese led the battle, and year after year the Soviet commissioners voted the straight whalers' line, virtually without comment. From 1978 to 1984, the Japanese commissioner was Kunio Yonezawa, an articulate and impassioned defender of whalers' rights. The Soviet delegates were almost always in agreement with the Japanese, but they were practically monosyllabic in their responses. Depending upon the vote, the Soviet commissioner either said "Yes" or "No." That was all. (It was the custom for countries to reserve the right to explain their votes, and more often than not, the position of a particular nation was elucidated at considerable length. During those years, the Japanese commissioner spoke in English, but the Soviets, if and when they had anything at all to say, spoke Russian first, and then had it translated.)

The Scientific Committee was so beset by conflicting methodologies of whale-counting that it was unable to produce any quotas for 1979. (In 1978, the Japanese had failed to approach their assigned quota of 3,800 male sperm whales in the North Pacific and 4,538 males and 1,370 females in the Southern Hemisphere.) Pressure was brought to bear within and without the IWC; by the 1979 meeting in Tokyo, of all places, factory-ship whaling was banned altogether (except for minke whaling), which amounted to an *ad hoc* moratorium on sperm whaling. There seemed to be no means, short of subverting the IWC's resolutions, for the whaling nations to continue to kill sperm whales. But the Soviets found a way.

A month after the meeting, they requested that a postal vote be taken on their request to take 1,508 male sperm whales. The proposal was defeated, with only three countries supporting it (Japan, the USSR and Peru), but they went whaling anyway. The *Sovietskaya Rossiya* took 201 whales, and the *Dal'nii Vostok* another 130, but they would later claim that they had misunderstood the resolution at the meeting in Tokyo, and thought the moratorium on sperm whaling was scheduled to begin in the 1980–81 season. Despite the questionable circumstances under which these whales were killed and their killing explained, they represented the last sperm whales caught by Soviet whalers.

Also in 1980, Soviet whalers harvested some 900 killer whales in the Antarctic, and when questioned, feigned ignorance of the classification of these animals. They claimed that their word for the species (*kosatka*) indicates that it is a dolphin (which it is), not a whale, and therefore not subject to IWC regulations. As a result of this "confusion," the killer whale was officially entered into the list of species whose hunting fell under IWC jurisdiction—at least according to the IWC. (The take of cetaceans for exhibition, however, was carefully and specifically excluded from the commission's authority.)

At the 1980 meeting at Brighton, England, a proposal for a blanket moratorium on sperm whaling was defeated, with the swing vote being cast by Canada. Sperm whale quotas set for the 1980–81 season were 400 for the Antarctic, and 890 for the North Pacific, with a "by-catch" of 11.5 percent, which meant that another 460 females would be killed because the take of cows was unavoidable with whales whose sex cannot easily be determined until the whale has been killed. (All these whales were allocated to the Japanese coastal sperm whale fishery; by this time, the Soviets had retired from sperm whaling.) At the same meeting, Southern Hemisphere minke whale quotas were set at 7,072. Slowly, the quotas were being lowered, although the pelagic whalers protested every reduction. (Sperm whale quotas for the previous season were 550 for the Southern Hemisphere, and minkes were 8,102.) Once again it was the Japanese who did the protesting, while the Soviets sat silently by, casting the *nyet* vote when necessary.

A surprising communiqué from Moscow arrived at IWC headquarters in Cambridge, England, in February of 1981, disavowing rumors that the Soviet Union was planning to retire from the whaling business. Commissioner Nikonorov wished the commission to know that the Soviet Union "as part of its general measures for the protection of nature," had ceased commercial whaling in the North Pacific in 1979, but "the fleet continues whaling in Antarctica . . . in limited numbers." At this time, the Soviets indicated that whaling was necessary for whale research; if somebody didn't kill the whales, they suggested, we wouldn't know anything about them. By 1981, however, the Soviet fleet had been reduced to one factory ship and five catcher boats—a far cry from the five factories and the eighty-odd catchers that had operated some ten years earlier.

The Dutch in the Antarctic

AFTER A HIATUS of a century and a half (their forays into the South Seas in pursuit of sperm whales in the nineteenth century had been largely unsuccessful), the Dutch decided to return to the whaling business. They planned to use whale oil as a substitute for the vegetable oils that they had lost as a result of the war in the Dutch East Indies (now Indonesia). Their return to whaling, however, was not to be easy. Because they felt threatened by new entries into whaling, the Norwegians had contrived

Launched in 1955, the Dutch floating factory *Willem Barendsz II* was 677 feet long and displaced 26,830 gross tons. (On the horizon at left is the original *Willem Barendsz,* only 504 feet in length.) The larger ship was the mainstay of Dutch Antarctic whaling until they quit in 1964.

the Norwegian Crew Law, which forbade their nationals from working for foreign whaling companies. In an attempt to prevent new countries from participating in what had heretofore been their arena, they also initiated domestic legislation that mandated against Norwegians' sailing on vessels which had not been involved in the whale fishery before the war. This plan was directed specifically against Japan and Germany, but the Soviets managed to circumvent the Norwegians when they acquired the German prize-of-war factory ship *Wikinger,* renamed her *Slava,* and thereby had a vessel that qualified for postwar whaling assistance. In spite of obstacles such as these, the Dutch were determined to enter the business, and no domestic Norwegian legislation was going to stop them.

At the 1946 meeting of the International Whaling Conference in Washington, the Norwegian Crew Law was a subject of much heated discussion. The chief delegate from the Netherlands, Fisheries Director D. J. van Dijk, excoriated the Norwegians for effectively excluding the Netherlands from pelagic whaling, and also for denying them the opportunity to replenish their depleted supply of necessary fats.

Although most of the plenary session was devoted to a discussion of this subject, it was not resolved, and by the end of the meeting, an "addendum" had been added to the Final Act, which stated the Dutch position for the record, even though it was rejected by the commission. (It was known that the British employed Norwegian crews, and suspected—but never proven—that the Soviets had asked for and received Norwegian assistance for the maiden voyage of the *Slava.*) The wording of this addendum is as follows:

The Conference recommends that in the interest of effective conservation and the development of whale stocks the Governments represented at the Conference refrain from taking any measures which might prevent any country adhering to the principles of the international whaling agreements from ratifying or entering into the international regulations for the preservation of whale stocks.

The resuscitated Dutch whaling industry was state-supported, and listed Prince Bernhard as its champion, much in the way that nineteenth-century Dutch whaling had been encouraged by King Willem I. The Dutch government guaranteed the purchase of the oil from Dutch expeditions, and since they also financed the building of new ships, they became the first of the state-run whaling operations. (Later, the Soviets and the Japanese would follow suit.)

In early 1946, the Netherlandsche Maatschappij voor Valvischaart N.V. purchased its first vessel, a tanker which was converted in the Amsterdam shipyards to a factory ship, and named *Willem Barendsz,* after the famous Arctic explorer. With eight catcher boats purchased from a Norwegian company that had been operating in Panama, the Dutch were ready to head for the South. There was still the problem of finding trained crews for the expedition in defiance of the Norwegian Crew Law. The first signs of cracks in the Crew Law were seen in the Netherlands, where independent Norwegian gunners immediately signed aboard the *Willem Barendsz,* because the inducements were so high. The Norwegian consul in Amsterdam was a director of the Dutch company, and in contravention of his country's instructions, immediately signed on some fifty Norwegians. (Barred from enlisting them in other countries, the Dutch also took to hiring Norwegian crews in Cape Town.) According to Tønnessen and Johnsen's (heavily biased) analysis of Dutch whaling, "It is hardly an exaggeration to say that the Norwegian gunners' evasion of the Norwegian law made Dutch whaling possible, and there was no nation destined to create so many difficulties for the IWC and regulation as the Netherlands."

The *Willem Barendsz* sailed from Amsterdam on October 27, 1946, with a heterogeneous crew aboard, but the catcher boats were manned almost entirely by Norwegians. (The Norwegian Crew Law applied to floating factories only, and not to catchers.) The Dutch were taking no chances with the most specialized of all whaling jobs, that of the man who actually shot the whale. In their attempt to resurrect their oil industry, the Dutch government fully supported the new whaling business, and in 1951 they entered into an eight-year contract with the whaling company. This agreement included the commissioning of a new factory ship and eight catcher boats, to

Opposite: Aboard the *Willem Barendsz* in the Antarctic. One can almost hear the whine and clank of the steam engines, feel the slippery gore underfoot, and smell the aroma of butchered whales.

be ready by the 1955–56 season, and the underwriting of all loans and interest payments.

The 623-foot *Willem Barendsz* slid down the ways in 1956 and immediately caused trouble in the industry. The Dutch protested the lowering of the 1958–59 quotas to 14,500 blue whale units, and no sooner had their objection been filed than the other whaling nations, not wanting to give the Dutch an unfair advantage, also lodged objections.

Very few signatory nations were concerned with whale-conservation, except insofar as it "made possible the orderly development of the whaling industry," and this "development" was destroying the very resource that sustained the industry. Prior to 1958, the quotas set by the IWC were based on the blue whale unit, and it was left to the individual whaling nations to compete for the whales on a free-for-all basis. The blue whale unit was a bad idea that had infected the IWC, and like a stubborn virus, could not be removed. In his 1974 essay on the management of whaling, Scott McVay wrote:

Why does the blue whale unit seem irrational today, and how does it work? One blue whale unit used to equal one blue whale, or two finbacks, or two and one-half humpbacks, or six sei whales; today only fin and sei whales are so tallied. First, by talking in "units" rather than "whales," you make it arithmetic, not biology. And bad arithmetic. Furthermore, such arithmetic removes the killing of whales from our concern for the viability of each species. The blue whale unit repudiates rational management, since what is not taken from one species can be taken from another, irrespective of what the latter can sustain. As if this were not enough, the blue whale unit quota has usually been set above scientific recommendations, thereby further reducing the remaining whale stocks.

In the early 1950s, whaling was a disorganized melee; the British commissioner R. G. R. Wall called it the "Whaling Olympic." The expeditions had sailed to the Antarctic, and on a predetermined opening day for the season all the catchers of every fleet began killing whales as fast as they could. At the end of the week, they radioed their accomplishments to the Bureau of International Whaling Statistics in Sandefjord, where a running tally was kept. The bureau then estimated the date on which the quota of BWUs would be reached, which kept the whalers competing until the last moment, since no fleet wanted to be caught short when the word came that the season was closed.

Whenever the IWC seemed to be on the brink of rational management procedures, one or another of the whaling nations would torpedo the relevant proposal. In 1953, the Scientific Committee recognized that the declining stocks of blue whales presaged trouble, and tried to delay the opening day of the season to January 15. When the Dutch threatened to file an objection, the proposal was dropped, since any nation's objection would inspire the objections of the other whaling nations, and would therefore render the proposal meaningless. The Scientific Committee in 1955 recognized that a catch limit by species would be advantageous, but the Norwegians opposed this, suggesting instead a reduction on the total number of whales caught. At the IWC's 1955 Annual Meeting (held in Moscow), the Scientific Committee recommended that the annual quota be reduced to 11,000 BWU, the equivalent of 22,000 fin whales.

The Dutch continued to oppose any reductions in quotas, and by 1958, they managed to engineer a return to the 15,000-BWU quota. The Norwegians tried in 1959 to remedy a rapidly deteriorating situation, but the Dutch were evidently determined to assert themselves despite world opinion—and despite the status of the whales—and they quit the IWC and announced that they would set their own quotas. Norway also felt compelled to resign when it became clear that the IWC was unable to affect the Netherlands' catch; Norway would not be bound by restrictive quotas that did not apply to other nations.

The commission was brought virtually to a state of helpless impotence by the withdrawal of Norway and the Netherlands. If the commission could not control its membership, how could it possibly affect nations that chose to ignore its regulations? In the Chairman's Report for 1960, the following statement appears: "Conscious of the importance of maintaining the Convention, the Commission showed a willingness to consider making some increase in the Antarctic permitted catch if thereby the loss of the three member countries which had given notice of withdrawal could be averted." The commission was willing to offer the Antarctic whaling countries higher quotas in order to keep them in, but even this enticement didn't work, and on July 1, 1959, ten years after the formation of the commission, it was open season on whales again. The Dutch said they would adhere to most of the IWC's regulations, except those on the number of whales that could be caught, and the Norwegians said they "would adhere to all the provisions of the International Whaling Convention except the Antarctic catch limit."

The whaling nations apportioned the whales to themselves as follows: Japan, 5,000 BWU; Norway, 5,800 BWU; and Britain, 2,500 BWU. The Netherlands declared that it would not take more than 1,200 BWU, and the USSR allotted itself 3,000 BWU, for a global total of 17,500 BWU, considerably higher than any quotas in past years, and considerably more than the whale populations could possibly tolerate. As a testimony to the artificiality of the quotas, it should be noted that regardless of the number of BWUs the whalers assigned to themselves, they couldn't find nearly enough blue whales to fulfill these quotas, and they continued to slaughter the smaller fin whales. The days of hunting the blue whale were over, but the blue whale unit, the device which had guaranteed its demise, lived on in infamy. In 1959–60, the season that the IWC stumbled so badly, only 1,192 blue whales were killed, but 27,128 fin whales died.*

The survival of the whalers was obviously considered far more important than the survival of the whale species, and it was equally apparent that the IWC was choosing to subscribe to the wording of the convention that referred to the "economic and nutritional distress" of the whaling nations, as opposed to protecting "all species of whales from further over-fishing."

BEFORE DETERMINING how to protect whales, either for the industry or for posterity, one has to have some idea of how many there are. Counting whales is a serious problem, one that would plague the IWC throughout its stormy existence. Since there were no absolutes, scientists differed on the methods that could be used to estimate populations, and often came up with widely divergent estimates. Moreover, scientists with a particular bias were more than likely to arrive at conclusions that supported their positions. Science is supposed to be an impersonal, predictable, replicable business, but science in the name of conservation—or even worse, in the name of commerce—is more than a little likely to be skewed. Thus scientists from antiwhaling nations managed to "prove" that there were fewer whales than the pro-whaling scientists thought there were, while scientists from whaling nations were usually able to demonstrate that there were enough whales of a given species to sustain whaling for a long time. Perhaps the most celebrated of the pro-whaling scientists was Professor E. J. Slijper of the Netherlands. The author of a widely read book on whales (*Walvissen*) and a ranking member of the Dutch delegation to the IWC throughout its most tumultuous years, Slijper categorically refused to accept estimates of populations that would indicate that whaling ought to be curtailed. He wrote that "The aim of the commission and its advisory biologists is not to prevent the elimination of whales, as many people might think. The latter goal is rather the aim of international conservationist organizations. . . . The real aim of the International Whaling Commission is to prevent the diminution of the present-day stock, to insure that this profitable source of oil, meat, and other valuable products will not be lost to our descendants."

In time for the June 1962 meeting, the Netherlands rejoined the IWC, and Norway, whose resignation had been based on the inability of the whaling nations to reach an agreement on Antarctic whaling, withdrew its resignation as of June 6. For the 1963–64 season, all the whaling nations were back in the fold and had their harpoon cannons primed. The agreement apportioned the catch between the five whaling countries as follows: Japan 33 percent, Norway 32 percent, USSR 20 percent, the United Kingdom 9 percent, and the Netherlands 6 percent.

The actual quota for 1963–64 was 10,000 BWU, but the whalers only managed to harvest 8,429, which indicated that the whalers had not taken the Committee of Three's report seriously enough. (The Committee of Three produced an IWC report in 1963 strongly suggesting that whaling be curtailed.) In the years that followed this imbroglio, even more whales were slaughtered in the Antarctic. In fact, the

---

*At approximately this time, the Japanese "discovered" a subspecies of blue whale, which they described as being smaller at sexual maturity than the blue whale, and for lack of a better name—for an animal that could reach a maximum length of 65 feet—they named it the *pygmy* blue whale. While cetologists were arguing as to whether or not *Balaenoptera musculus brevicauda* was a legitimate species, the Japanese began killing them. They killed 2,533 "pygmies" off the Kerguelen Islands during the four seasons from 1959 to 1963, but even if there was a distinct subspecies, not enough blue whales were left—of any size—to make killing them profitable.

whaling effort in the Antarctic reached its all-time high. By that time, of course, the blue whale stocks were so badly depleted that the whalers could hardly find any at all—they killed 718 in 1961–62, and 309 in 1962–63—but the number of fin whales taken reached a record 28,761 in 1961–62. As might have been predicted, within the next few years, they would have to start chasing the sei whale. According to the brilliant minds that had conceived the blue whale unit, a sei whale was only worth one-sixth as much as a blue whale, so with the blues and fins depleted, the hunters began methodically and systematically to eradicate the next-largest of the rorquals.

With an ever-diminishing share of the whales, the Dutch were muscled out of the business by the Soviets and the Japanese. In 1962 the *Willem Barendsz I* was sold to the Japanese (and became the *Nitto Maru*), and her successor, the *Willem Barendsz II*, after completing the 1963 whaling season, was sold to a South African concern and turned into a floating fish-processing factory. The ship was later seen in the North Pacific, flying the South Korean flag. With the sale of their fleet, the Dutch whalers became an extinct species. Their representatives have remained in the IWC, however, and like the commissioners of so many whaling countries that quit, they have diametrically reversed their philosophy on the killing of whales and become zealous preservationists.

The End of Commercial Whaling in Canada

CANADA was one of the original signatories of the 1946 International Convention for the Regulation of Whaling, and was present at the initial meeting of the International Whaling Commission in London in 1949. Among the resolutions passed by the fledgling IWC was one which permitted whaling nations to take small numbers of "endangered species" for research purposes. (This apparently harmless disposition would escalate into an international conflict that would almost destroy the IWC in the 1980s, but in 1950 it seemed like a good way to find out something about the biology of certain whale species.) A biologist named Gordon Pike was assigned the task of examining the carcasses of some Canadian whales, and from 1948 to 1968, he looked at gray whales, humpbacks and killer whales that were brought to the Pacific Biological Station at Nanaimo, British Columbia. Regardless of what happened to the companies that were established to hunt whales in Canadian waters, there were going to be carcasses hauled up on the flensing decks.

With the collapse of the pirate-whaling operations of Aristotle Onassis in 1954—discussed in the next section—several of the Norwegians who had been employed in this outlaw operation wound up in British Columbia. One of them was Arne Borgen, who had been a gunner aboard the *Olympic Challenger*. Borgen was hired to oversee the reconstruction of the Canadian whaling fleet at Coal Harbour, and he assembled Norwegian gunners from all over the world. He became captain of a fleet of five rebuilt chasers: the *Bouvet III, Nahmint, Polar 5, Globe VII* and *Lavalee.* The killer navy of the Western Whaling Company was afloat again. In 1957, they killed 635 whales; in 1958, 774; and in 1959, 869. (The 1959 catch included an 83-foot blue whale, 369 fin whales, 185 seis, 27 more blues, and 27 humpbacks.)

In 1961, the year the IWC scheduled its Annual Meeting for Vancouver, the Canadians reached an agreement with Japan's largest whaling concern, Taiyo Gyogyo K. K., to sell frozen whale meat to the Japanese market. The company was reorganized as Western Canada Whaling Company Limited, and four of its five catchers were renamed *Westwhale I* to *IV.* Two spanking new catcher boats from Japan were christened *Westwhale V* and *VI.* Although there were difficulties with language among the Norwegian and Japanese whalers, they had no problems with the harpoons, and the gunners from the two great whaling powers of the twentieth century produced a successful alliance. During the first season (1962) they managed to find and kill 713 whales, but the following year, they could only take 548. The Japanese-Canadian fleet continued to improve, but increased efficiency did not lead to increased profits, for the same reason as always: not enough whales. (By this time, the Soviet fleet was operating in the North Pacific, and it was believed that they were far more effective than the Canadians in reducing the whale populations.) In 1967, the Canadian fleet did not see a whale on fifteen of the first twenty-three days of the season. Coal Harbour did not reopen in 1968, and the *Westwhale* fleet was sold off.

BETWEEN the world wars, whaling was carried out from Newfoundland and Labrador stations, but in a reduced fashion. Opportunistically, the whalers took whatever whales they came across—blues, fins, seis, humpbacks, sperms—and in 1937, the year the world declared it fully protected, they killed what was probably the last right whale taken legally by a commercial whaler. Most of the whales taken were finners, but a look at the North Atlantic statistics suggests a lack of enthusiasm within the fishery. In 1924, for example, there were only two catcher boats working, and they took 12 blue whales, 144 finners, 16 humpbacks and 8 sperms. There was no whaling at all from 1931 to 1935, and again in 1938. In 1939, the North Atlantic stations took a total of 144 whales, and of these, 118 were finners.

After World War II, whaling was seen as a way to encourage employment and increase revenues—not to mention providing meat to a hungry populace. The station at Hawke's Harbour, Labrador, reopened in 1945, and Norwegian/Newfoundland consortiums conducted unrestricted whaling throughout the cold North Atlantic. (Farley Mowat, who eschews references, maintains that by 1951 the consortiums had "processed 3,721 finners together with several hundred 'other whales,' and had reaped an estimated return on their investments in excess of 900 per cent.") In 1963, a station was opened at Blandford, Nova Scotia, and although the Canadian flag flew over the stern of the catcher *Thorarinn,* the

crew and equipment were Norwegian. Fin and sei whales were killed in substantial numbers, and their meat and oil shipped to Japan. Two years later the Norwegians opened another station at Dildo, Newfoundland, and two years after that, another station was opened at Williamsport, a joint venture between the Newfoundland "Fisheries Products Limited" and the Japanese giant, Taiyo Fisheries. From 1964 to 1972, fin whales were being killed in Canadian waters, but in ever-decreasing numbers. The International Whaling Commission's Scientific Committee kept lowering the quotas, but despite this attempt to allow the whalers to conform to the realities of disappearing whale stocks, they were never able to meet the quotas. In 1972, the Canadian government "voluntarily" closed down the last of its commercial whaling operations. (The west coast stations had been shut since 1967.)

Throughout the stormy history of the IWC, Canada had been an active member, since she had a long and extensive participation in whaling. Following the United Nations "Stockholm Resolution" of 1972, which unanimously adopted a moratorium on whaling (one that was not to be followed by the IWC for another ten years), Canada unilaterally closed down its whaling operations, and in 1981, for reasons that were never satisfactorily explained, it withdrew from the IWC.

At the 1980 meeting at Brighton, Canada was among the nations designated as "Whale Murderers" by the environmentalists who protested outside the Metropole Hotel. Prime Minister Pierre Trudeau told Canada's House of Commons that Canada was intending to withdraw from the IWC: "We are not a whaling nation ourselves," he said. "We will still be able to express whatever arguments we can within the commission, but we will not be part of the decision by those countries which continue to be whaling nations." (In fact, sending observers to the IWC does not permit countries to "express whatever arguments they can"; observers play no part whatsoever in the business of the commission, and may not address the floor.) Some critics believed that the Canadian withdrawal was decided on because it appeared that the commission was going to impose regulations on the taking of small cetaceans (particularly belugas and narwhals), but whatever the reason, the Cetacean Protection Act became law in 1981 (the year before the IWC passed the moratorium), and Canada's small-whale fisheries were placed under provisional government control. Canadian Inuit may still kill belugas and narwhals, but no more large whales are being killed by Canadians.

IN THE 1950S some unusual whales were observed in the Atlantic off the coasts of Florida and Georgia. It was strange enough to see whales cavorting off these coasts where hardly any had been observed before, but it became stranger still when it was realized that these were right whales.* They then began to appear on the other side of Florida in the Gulf of Mexico, off Cape Cod, and by the mid-1970s they were observed off Nova Scotia. (The whales probably did not arrive at all these locations from somewhere else; they were probably there all the time, but no one had thought to look for them or identify them.) Right whales feed and calve in different locations, so the southern portion of this range was identified as a possible breeding ground (this determination was aided by the presence of calves), and the northern regions were suspected feeding grounds. (Observations of feeding whales helped lead to this conclusion.)

As mentioned earlier, whales do not pay much attention to national boundaries. They may swim from Georgia to the Bay of Fundy and back again every year, moving with their ponderous equanimity from the United States to Canada. The Gulf of Maine, where most of this population has been observed, is between the northeastern extremity of the United States and Nova Scotia. The adjacent Bay of Fundy, of course, is a Canadian phenomenon, its legendary tides rushing between the shores of New Brunswick and Nova Scotia. For purposes of this discussion, we will consider these right whales "Canadian," if only to find a convenient place to discuss their remarkable rediscovery.

A stock of whales that was considered extinct has miraculously reappeared. Most of the North Atlantic right whales had been killed off, to be sure—Reeves

*Studies of historical records since the unexpected appearance of right whales off the Georgia coast have revealed that the whales were not only known there in the past, they were hunted. Reeves and Mitchell (1983) have discovered that there was a brief "fishery" for right whales off Fernandina, Florida, after 1876, and that twenty-five to thirty right whales were taken between South Carolina and Georgia between 1875 and 1882.

and Mitchell (1983) report that 250 to 300 were taken between 1820 and 1899—but this still appears to be a remarkable comeback. In his analysis of the current sightings, Mead reports 795 ("individual whales rather than individual events") in Massachusetts, and 233-plus in Florida. He therefore concludes that

right whales seem to have a summertime concentration in the Bay of Fundy and adjacent waters and a broad wintertime concentration in the southern part of their range. There is a marked concentration of calves in Florida and adjacent waters, leading one to postulate that there may be a calving area nearby.

The right whale was the first cetacean species to be given worldwide protection. In 1937, before any international agreements were signed, the whaling nations recognized that there were too few of these great animals left, and made it illegal to kill a right whale, anywhere, any time. Whalers do not always obey the rules, even their own, and an occasional right whale was killed. In addition, animals would sometimes beach themselves and die, but by and large, these whales benefited from the absolute protection afforded them. In South Africa and Australia, where right whales were the first species hunted and the first species eliminated, there are reports of increased appearances by mothers and calves in inshore waters. They have not reappeared in numbers in Japanese or Soviet waters, however, nor have there been many reports of the species off Alaska. Isolated stragglers may show up in Hawaii or off California, but after causing conservationists' hearts to race, they blow their V-shaped spouts into the air and disappear forever like liquid shadows.

If there is a lesson here, it may be difficult to find, since we have to contrast the right whales' revival with the plummeting numbers recently assigned to blue whales. Blues were not protected for as long as the rights—they were being killed until 1968—but in twenty years, the blue whales have not recovered, and their numbers have now been estimated at a small fraction of what they were believed to be. All whales are different, and they have different nutritional and ecological requirements; they are not simply larger or smaller versions of the same oil and meat source. This was one of the lessons the whalers never learned, and it cost them their industry.

The Pirate Whaling
of Aristotle Onassis

ARISTOTLE ONASSIS, who was born in Smyrna (now Turkish Izmir) in 1906, held an Argentinian passport, but was essentially a citizen of the world, doing business in the United States, Europe, South America and the Middle East. During World War II, he and his friend Costa Grastos had experimented with whale-killing by recruiting United States Coast Guard observers who were flying observation blimps over the California coast to spot whales for them and dispatching hired fishing boats to kill the whales. Onassis had acquired a reputation as a ruthless, avaricious shipping magnate whose fortune was built on secret deals and intimidation of his rivals, but nowhere was his arrant disregard for other people's rules more evident than in his entry into whaling. In the 1940s there were few regulations concerning whaling, and although the business was only an adjunct to his oil-shipping enterprises, he contemplated killing whales for his greater profit— and his greater amusement.

In 1952, the *Olympic Challenger,* owned by a Greek with an Argentine passport, registered in Panama, and converted from a tanker to a whaling factory ship at the German yards at Kiel, sails through the Jutland canal that connects the Baltic and the North seas. Notice the helicopter on the afterdeck.

Peeling the blubber from the head of a sperm whale aboard the Onassis factory ship *Olympic Challenger* in the Ross Sea, 1951.

Onassis decided to enter the whaling business because he saw it as an arena in which a great deal of money could be made, as long as one didn't have to bother with rules and regulations. In the 1949–50 season, his activities greatly dismayed the International Whaling Commission member nations such as Norway, Japan and the Netherlands, because they realized that they would have to share the 16,000-BWU quota with another competitor. Their apprehensions were unfounded, since Onassis intended to play by his own rules and ignore the IWC completely.

He converted the *Herman F. Whiton,* a T-2 tanker, to a floating factory, which he christened *Olympic Challenger.* As with all his operations, this one was obfuscated by multiple holding companies, variegated registries, and colorful flags of convenience. The *Challenger* was financed by a corporation controlled by a Greek with an Argentine passport, affiliated with a dummy corporation in New York, registered in Panama, and run by something called the Olympic Whaling Company based in Montevideo, Uruguay. The ship's master was Lars Andersen, a Norwegian who had been convicted of collaborating with the Nazis, and whom Onassis had found in

Buenos Aires negotiating to manage Juan Perón's ill-starred whaling venture.*

Andersen became Onassis's expedition manager, and hired Wilhelm Reichert, another ex-Nazi, as captain. The *Challenger* was accompanied by seventeen catcher boats crewed by a total of 519 Germans, and the first helicopter ever used in pelagic whaling, which hovered over the whales like a bird of prey.

The maiden voyage of the *Olympic Challenger* was monstrously successful. Her Norwegian-trained German crews killed whales without the slightest regard for size, species or condition. They took endangered blue whales, female humpbacks with calves, and sperm whales so small that they had not developed teeth. His first season netted Onassis $4.2 million, and the *Olympic Challenger* continued to roam the seas as the scourge of organized whaling. The IWC could do nothing to stop or control this outlaw operation, and by the 1954 season, Onassis's business was flour-

*In 1951, Perón had commissioned a floating factory ship of 24,570 gross tons, to be the largest whaling ship in the world. He modestly named the ship after himself, but he was unable to arrange for financing, and although the ship was built—and probably secretly paid for by Onassis—she never sailed as a whaler, and lived out her career as a tanker.

ishing. His wife, Tina (the daughter of rival magnate Stavros Livanos), concerned about their standing in society, believed that the way to achieve social acceptance was to hobnob with American businessmen and socialites, so Onassis invited them aboard the *Challenger* to watch the sea turn red with the blood of slaughtered whales. He outfitted the lounge of his yacht *Christina* with barstools covered with the penis-skin of whales, with the teeth of sperm whales as footrests. One of Onassis's biographers wrote that "he was aroused by the spectacle of cruelty."

In September 1954, the *Olympic Challenger* and her flotilla of catcher boats were hunting off the west coast of South America. Onassis's whaleship flew the Panamanian flag, and because of the United States' close associations with Panama over the Canal, Reichert believed they were immune from harassment by other nations. The Peruvians had become incensed at the *Challenger*'s flagrant disregard of her sovereign rights, however, and threatened action if the *Challenger* continued to fish within her newly established two-hundred-mile limit. Of course Onassis was not to be intimidated by Peru, and he responded to its threats exactly as he had to the threats of the IWC: he laughed at them.

Unlike the IWC, however, Peru had a navy, and it seized the *Challenger* and four of the catcher boats. They were brought to the old whaling port of Paita and held there. It was assumed that the capture of the factory ship and her cargo would effectively close down Onassis's operations, and indeed it did, but he made more money after the fleet was seized than he would have if they had been able to continue whaling. He had taken out massive insurance policies to cover almost every contingency, including one

paying $30,000 per day for any interruption of whaling, as well as an incredible $15 million policy against seizure.

For six years, Onassis had operated completely outside the law, killing whales for fun and profit. The Norwegians were almost entirely responsible for shutting down his operation although it is difficult to identify their motives. Most likely they exposed his nefarious activities to reduce competition, but there is always the possibility that they were truly disturbed by his unscrupulous activities. Whatever the reason, in 1955 and 1956 in numbers of *Norsk Hvalfangst-Tidende* there were articles declaring that the "*Olympic Challenger* has not observed the provisions of the International Whaling Commission." The crew of the *Challenger* had tried to disassociate themselves from Onassis, but logbooks and affidavits obtained by the Norwegians clearly showed the connection. Through the publication in *Norsk Hvalfangst-Tidende* of various papers and photographs documenting the gross illegalities perpetrated by the *Challenger,* the Norwegians achieved what the International Whaling Commission could not: they drove Onassis out of the whaling business.

The Norwegians got a court order to seize sixty-three hundred tons of whale oil that had been illegally discharged in Hamburg, and shortly thereafter the *Challenger* herself was seized. The Japanese too had protested the illegal methods used by the renegade whalers, but just as international sanctions were to be applied, Onassis's partner Costa Grastos sold the entire fleet to the Japanese for $8.5 million. The name of the infamous factory ship *Olympic Challenger* was changed to *Kyokuyo Maru II,* and she continued in the service of the Japanese whaling fleet until 1970.

One of the Onassis fleet's powerful catcher boats, the *Olympic Leader.*

TWELVE

THE ANTI-WHALING MOVEMENT

"Save the Whales"

THERE WERE many diverse elements that contributed to what came to be known as the "Save the Whales" movement. Taken separately, none of them would have had the momentum to carry the entire conservation community toward a common goal, but *en suite* they had a carrying power that could not have been anticipated. Together, they would bring about the greatest single victory in the history of the environmental community, the elimination of commercial whaling.

Consolidating all its various species into a single symbol, we have elevated one animal to near-divine status. The people who accomplished this elevation did it unwittingly, not with the idea of creating a new mythology, but rather for purely practical reasons. In the new religion of environmental conservation, we have elected the whale as our flag-bearer, the symbol of everything that is wrong—or right—with our planet.

How did we get from deity to commodity and back to deity? Before television we relied on such primitive methods of communication as the magazine and the radio. Radio is not the medium most conducive to the study of cetology, so the earliest

records of the whale as a promotional entity can be found in magazines.

In January 1940, the *National Geographic* published an article by Remington Kellogg entitled "Whales, Giants of the Sea," which was accompanied by thirty-one paintings by Else Bostelmann of various whales, dolphins and porpoises. The subhead of the article reads, "Wonder Mammals, Biggest Creatures of All Time, Show Tender Affection for Young, But Can Maim or Swallow Hunters." Accompanying this article was a photograph of a bottle-nosed dolphin raising itself out of the water "like a dog taught to stand up and beg." The winsome and intelligent dolphin was about to make its debut, and man's perception of cetaceans would never be the same.

The first oceanarium in America had opened in St. Augustine, Florida, in 1938. It was called Marine Studios (later Marineland), and among its attractions were a small group of bottle-nosed dolphins. Marineland's first curator was Arthur McBride, and in one of the first of what would eventually become an avalanche of happy amalgamations of public relations and science, he wrote an article for *Natural History* magazine (January 1940), which was called

"Meet Mr. Porpoise." McBride was a scientist (he was the first man to deduce that dolphins used their acoustic senses for navigation), but he was also promoting the aquarium: "As we approach the giant tanks, we are astounded at the natural beauty of the place. . . . As we step into the lower corridor, soft blue lights lead us from porthole to porthole; and through these windows we gaze in awe at the fascinating, complex undersea world." The stars of this undersea world were the bottle-noses, called "porpoises" by McBride. As he wrote, "the first view of the large gray animals completely transforms previous concepts of them." Although McBride and his successors studied and observed the captive dolphins, they were also concerned with attracting visitors to the aquarium, and therefore in the popular literature, they emphasized the friendly qualities of the dolphin. Here is the opening paragraph of McBride's article:

Introducing the readers of NATURAL HISTORY to one of their most "human" deep-sea relatives. His astonishing habits, observed at Florida's Marine Studios, reveal an appealing and playful water mammal who remembers his friends and shows a strong propensity for jealousy and grief.

Marine Studios closed down shortly after the above article was published, but by the end of World War II it had reopened. By 1954, another Marineland had opened in Palos Verdes, California, and the race for tourist dollars was on. It quickly became apparent that there was money to be made in the aquarium business—which was transmogrified into the *oceanarium* business—and a company called Sea World began opening mammoth "theme parks" across the country, from San Diego to Orlando, from Ohio to Texas. Inevitably, the stars of these shows were the cetaceans, first the tractable bottle-noses and belugas, then the most powerful predators on earth, the killer whales. The first killer whale successfully maintained in captivity was Namu, exhibited at the Seattle Aquarium in 1964. Named for the town in British Columbia near which he was captured, Namu not only spawned a succession of major magazine articles (including one in *National Geographic* in 1966), but also a series of captive killers at Sea World all of which were named Shamu. (The name was ap-

plied indiscriminately to every whale, male or female, so that there would be continuity at the park, and so no one would realize that the captive whales occasionally died.) Because it was only peripherally in the business of ichthyological or cetological research, Sea World placed its emphasis strongly on circuslike performances, complete with funny costumes for the whales. The logo of Sea World is a cartoon killer whale.

In 1961, John Lilly had begun his experiments on the brains of bottle-nosed dolphins, and his research—which at first resulted in the death of his subjects—led to the popularization of the dolphin. The movie *Flipper* was released in 1963—with Lilly listed as "scientific adviser"—and the television show followed shortly thereafter. Dolphins, with their permanent smiles, cute little quacks and whistles, and happy willingness to perform, quickly became the darlings of the environmental movement. It mattered little that there was a tremendous difference between a sleek 8-foot bottle-nose, "smiling" and jumping through a hoop, and a 45-foot humpback with lumps all over its face and barnacles all over its flippers.

Feature films like *Flipper* led to a long-running television series of the same name, where the protagonist performed feats of intelligence not unlike Lassie (and in cahoots with a small boy, as might be expected), and finally to the 1967 novel by the Frenchman Robert Merle, *The Day of the Dolphin,* where the animals were trained to speak English and save the world from nuclear devastation. It was becoming harder and harder to separate the medium from the message. Everybody was falling in love with whales and dolphins, primarily because of the way that they were being depicted on television and in the movies: they were sensitive, intelligent creatures, whose only desire, it appeared, was to make our lives easier and more enjoyable.

But there is another side to the elevation of the whale as a media icon. At the same time that Flipper was warning us of danger, or Merle's dolphins were averting the destruction of the planet, tens of thousands of whales were being killed on the high seas. In 1966, Scott McVay wrote an article for *Scientific American* which he called "The Last of the Great Whales." It was the first time that the plight of the whales was brought to the attention of the general public. Two years later, McVay published "Can Le-

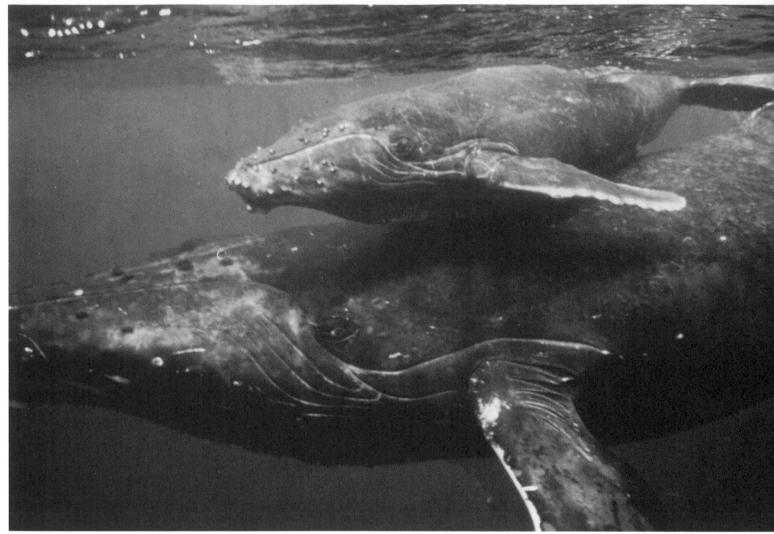

A humpback mother and her calf off the Hawaiian island of Maui. Jim Hudnall was among the first to dive with and photograph living whales.

viathan Long Endure So Wide a Chase?" in *Natural History.* Both articles revealed the extent of the killing that was being conducted under the aegis of the International Whaling Commission, and readers became outraged at the revelations.

No sooner were we made painfully aware of their decimation than we learned that the whales sang. In 1952, researchers had recorded the underwater vocalizations of humpback whales off Bermuda, but it was not until 1967 that Roger Payne, the man who would make humpbacks into recording stars, came to Bermuda with a primitive hydrophone. With his wife, Katy, he began to analyze these "phonations," and came to the remarkable conclusion that they were indeed *songs,* discrete phrases that were repeated over and over by individual whales. Payne recorded several of the songs and produced a record

that he called *Songs of the Humpback Whale.* They are eerie, haunting sounds, and it was altogether too easy to hear them as a cry for help. Not only were the whales on their way to extinction, they were singing their own dirge.*

From the liner notes for the Columbia record:

Whale songs have probably been heard, though seldom recognized as such, ever since man began to make voyages by sea. In the literature of whaling alone, there are many accounts of strange, ethereal sounds, reverberating faintly through a quiet ship at night, mystifying sailors in their bunks. . . .

*Later, the humpbacks would rise to even greater heights in their recording history: a record of their songs was inserted in the January 1979 issue of *National Geographic,* and 10.5 million copies were distributed, the largest number of a single record ever pressed.

(It was not the first time that seamen had noticed the musical inclinations of humpbacks. In 1856, Charles Nordhoff had written, "The humpback is in many regards a fish of very singular habits, differing in great measure from those of any other species of whale. . . . A whale would sometimes get under the boat . . . and there utter the most doleful sounds, interspersed with a gurgling sound such as a drowning man might make. The first time I heard these sounds it was almost incomprehensible to me that they could proceed from a whale.")

The Payne record sold remarkably well. People were fascinated by the idea of whales "singing," and besides, the songs have an eerie, other-worldly quality that is truly spellbinding. The year after the record was released, Payne and McVay published a paper in the journal *Science* entitled "Songs of Humpback Whales." Folksinger Judy Collins recorded "Farewell to Tarwathie," a New Zealand whalerman's song, in which she is accompanied only by the haunting sounds of humpback whales. Then the National Geographic Society published a book on animal behavior which included a chapter on the song of the whale.

Whales and dolphins are mammals with large, convoluted brains; they sing mysterious songs; and they have an aquatic intelligence that some feel is equal if not superior to our own. It is not surprising, then, that we chose them as the icons of the environmental movement; "Save the Whales" became the rallying cry for those who would protect the planet from the insidious depredations of mankind.

ANOTHER remarkable event that came out of this period (or perhaps caused it; sometimes it is hard to differentiate cause and effect) was the 1974 publication of a book called *Mind in the Waters.* Edited by Joan McIntyre, this collection of essays, poems, scientific discourses, photographs and drawings is "a basic compendium of information about whales and dolphins and a picture of the new understandings that seem to lie just beyond our present knowledge." It is simultaneously a celebration and a condemnation, for as it celebrates the whales and dolphins, *Mind in the Waters* also attacks the whalers: "The whale is a split in our consciousness," wrote McIntyre, "on the one hand viewed as product, as resource, as an article, an object to be carved up to satisfy the economic imperative; on the other, a view almost lost now, as the great leviathan, the guardian of the sea's unutterable mysteries."

Mind in the Waters became a sort of "whole whale catalogue," and Joan McIntyre was elevated to the status of high priestess of the "love the whale" movement. (When she heard of the Greenpeace efforts to interfere with Soviet whalers, she is reputed to have said, "I want to save the whales, but not *that* way.") She was the "founding mother" of the San Francisco–based Project Jonah in 1972, and represented that organization as an observer at the International Whaling Commission meetings from 1972 to 1975.*

Awareness of the plight of the whales coincided with the general rise of environmental awareness in the United States. Previously relegated to positions of quiet desperation, conservationist organizations suddenly found themselves leading the battles to save the redwoods, the Grand Canyon, the snail darter, the California condor . . . and the whales. McVay had sounded the alarm, and the environmental armies began to form. Organizations like the National Audubon Society, which had earlier been perceived as a cadre of "little old ladies in tennis shoes" whose main concerns were tufted titmice, suddenly acquired another symbol to accompany the snowy egret. In 1975, *Audubon* published a gloomy prognosis for the world's whales entitled "Vanishing Giants," in an issue devoted entirely to cetaceans. The magazine contained the first painted portraits of the great whales since Else Bostelmann's 1940 watercolors. As the "Save the Whales" movement gained momentum, it needed iconographic images to support it. Along with the illustrations, there appeared T-shirts, bumper stickers, lapel pins and posters. People took to the streets with petitions to be presented to the Soviet and Japanese embassies to show them that we cared about the whales they were killing. (By this time too, *Audubon* had published the first portfolio of underwater photographs of the living whale; Jim Hudnall was the first man to enter the water and

---

*McIntyre gave herself five years to achieve a moratorium on whaling, and fell short by only a couple of years. Frustrated by the failure of the movement, when her allotted five years were up, she moved to Hawaii. In a 1982 book called *The Delicate Art of Whale Watching,* she wrote, "My profession, so to speak, had been the politics of whale saving, and that profession had wearied me and turned me into a bitter person filled with doubt and anger."

photograph the humpbacks of Maalea Bay in Hawaii.) The time was ripe for the introduction of the most effective medium of all: television.

No single individual has been more responsible for the dissemination of information about the occupants of the sea than Captain Jacques-Yves Cousteau, the co-inventor (with Emile Gagnan) of the aqualung. Cousteau and his film crews have circumnavigated the globe in search of underwater subject matter. Not surprisingly, the topic of the opening episode of *The Undersea World of Jacques Cousteau* was sharks, but in November 1968, the first of his whale films was shown. There were underwater shots of finbacks and a sperm whale (the latter unfortunately lassoed to enable the divers to get close to it), and subsequent films were made of gray whales, humpbacks, right whales and various species of dolphins. From 1968 to 1976, *The Undersea World* brought whales (and such other mysterious denizens of the deep as squid, elephant seals, manatees and penguins) into the living rooms of the world.

In 1977 the film division of the National Geographic Society produced a general film called "The Great Whales." Written, produced and directed by Nicolas Noxon, it introduced the public-broadcasting audiences to whaling, using unsettling footage of whales being killed. Because they were available and accessible, the long-winged humpbacks (using footage by Jim Hudnall in Hawaii) were featured, as were the gray whales of Baja California—which were allowing themselves to be touched for the first time.

The airwaves were filled with images of whales. Now almost everybody knew what they looked like, and a great many people knew what they sounded like, too. Payne's humpback whale record has sold over half a million copies, making it by far the best-selling record of animal sounds in history. Paul Winter wrote a suite he called "Common Ground," which included cetacean counterpoint to his alto saxophone. But the best (or the worst) was still to come. The whale and the whaler were still disconnected images: whale portraits, bumper stickers, songs, numbers. The "Rainbow Warriors" of Greenpeace sailed into the North Pacific to do battle with the Soviet whalers—and they filmed themselves doing it.

The image of brave men in their tiny rubber boats as the gigantic killer ships towered menacingly over them was not easily dismissed or forgotten. Photographs were reproduced in magazines and newspapers, and flashed around the world on television. We not only knew that the nasty Soviets were killing whales, we saw pictures of them doing it. It was a masterful manipulation of the media, and Greenpeace was catapulted into the forefront of the whale-conservation movement.

Bumper stickers and T-shirts proliferated, emblazoned with the slogan "Save the Whales." Would-be whale-savers collected millions of signatures on petitions. Entire groups sprang up with only one purpose: to save the whales. The first of these was the American Cetacean Society, formed in Los Angeles in 1971. Then came the Whale Center in Oakland, and the Connecticut Cetacean Society in West Hartford. (Curiously, there was never an organization

Soviet defector Mikhail Baryshnikov models the antiwhaling (and anti-Soviet) T-shirt of the Animal Welfare Institute.

named Save the Whales, even though it was the rallying cry for an entire movement.) Now the major wildlife organizations joined the parade: World Wildlife Fund, National Wildlife Federation, Sierra Club, Animal Welfare Institute, Humane Society of the United States, National Audubon Society. In the early and mid-1970s, there were a multitude of articles and editorials about the rapacious Japanese or the heartless (and Communist) Soviet whalers slaughtering the hapless cetaceans. (In January 1975, to accompany an article by David O. Hill in *Audubon* magazine, I did ten paintings of the "great" whale species. In an editorial, the *New York Times* wrote that this issue "should help, through its text, to illuminate the role of these magnificent creatures and, through its illustrations, to arouse concern for their fate.")

While the conservation organizations were producing articles, holding rallies and collecting signatures, more radical elements were beginning to marshal their forces. This was the period of antiwar movement in the United States, and it was clear— at least to some people—that working within the system was not the way to get things done. The motley environmental cavalry was massing for the charge.

With the passage of the Marine Mammal Protection Act by Congress in 1972, the United States officially retired from the whaling business, and publicly dedicated itself to the conservation and protection of all marine mammals. The Act—hereafter the MMPA—is probably the most comprehensive legislation pertaining to marine mammals in the world. Section 101(a) reads as follows:

There shall be a moratorium on the taking and importation of marine mammals and marine mammal products, commencing the effective date of this Act, during which time no permit may be issued for the taking of any marine mammal and no marine mammal product may be imported into the United States. . . .

"Taking" is defined in the act as to "harass, hunt, capture, or kill, or attempt to harass, hunt, capture or kill any marine mammal." Quite simply, this meant that there was to be no more whaling in the United States and no more traffic in whale products, including whale oil, whale-meat pet food, scrim-

Christine Stevens, President of the Animal Welfare Institute and one of the moving forces behind the whale-preservation movement, collects signatures for a petition in Washington.

shaw—and also sealskin coats, walrus tusks, polar bear rugs and narwhal tusks. All displays of marine mammals in aquariums or oceanariums fell under the jurisdiction of the MMPA, and the Marine Mammal Commission was created (among other things) to

undertake a review and study of the activities of the United States pursuant to existing laws and international conventions relating to marine mammals, including, but not limited to, the International Convention for the Regulation of Whaling, the Whaling Convention Act of 1949, the Interim Convention on the Conservation of Fur Seals, and the Fur Seal Act of 1966. . . .

With the mechanism in place, the United States could now pursue its goals worldwide; it could join in the whale-conservation movement—as heralded by the Stockholm Resolution for a ten-year moratorium—with "clean hands."*

The United States position on whale conservation was further strengthened by the passage of two additional pieces of legislation, the Pelly and the Packwood-Magnuson amendments. The 1971 Pelly Amendment, which modified the 1967 Fisherman's Protective Act, reads as follows:

When the Secretary of Commerce determines that nationals of a foreign country, directly or indirectly, are conducting fishing operations in a manner or under circumstances which diminish the effectiveness of an international fishery conservation program, the Secretary of Commerce shall certify such fact to the President.

Upon certification, the President may decide whether to ban imports of fishery products from the offending country. (As used in the Pelly Amendment, the term "fishing operations" pertains to any resource of the sea, including marine mammals.) Pelly was first invoked in 1974, when Japan and the Soviet Union, having objected to the IWC quotas for Antarctic minke whales, set their own quotas. President Ford refused to order the embargo, however, believing that the offending nations would abide by future IWC quotas, and more significantly, that the embargo would harm American economic interests.

The Packwood-Magnuson Amendment (to the Fishery Conservation and Management Act of 1976) was designed to enhance even more the economic sanctions against those nations that diminished the effectiveness of the 1946 Whaling Convention. Under Packwood-Magnuson, "certification" refers specifically to "nationals of a foreign country . . . engaging in trade or taking which diminishes the International Convention for the Regulation of Whaling." Unlike the Pelly Amendment which was discretionary, Packwood-Magnuson entails a *mandatory* minimum reduction of 50 percent of the fishing

*The hands of the Americans were not as clean as some would have liked. At the moment of the passage of the MMPA, Alaskan Eskimos were killing—and would continue to kill—more of the seriously endangered bowhead whales than at any time since the steam whalers of the late nineteenth century almost wiped out the entire population.

allocations (of fin-fish, not whales) in the U.S. two-hundred-mile zone.

The United States had tried Antarctic whaling only once. In 1930, the American Whaling Company sent the *Frango* to the South, and although the expedition was a success as far as whale killing was concerned, the ship returned with a cargo of oil that could not be sold because of the depressed economic conditions at home, and the oil sat in barrels in a warehouse for five years before it was sold to European buyers. Even though the Americans had a long history of whaling, stretching back to the settlement of the country, they embraced the cause of whale-conservation with more enthusiasm than almost any other nation. With the closing of the last U.S. whaling station, at Richmond, California, in 1972 (with the unfortunate exception of the Eskimos' bowhead whaling in Alaska), the Americans were gearing up to join the battle to save the whales. It was not purely an American war, but since many of the battles took place on American soil—and even in the American courts and Congress—the "movement" became associated with American environmentalists.

It was a most peculiar coalition: the United States government (despite congressmen who were suborned by the Japanese and who fought any effort to restrict Japanese whaling operations); the conservative environmental community, and the guerrillas, to whom neither of the first two groups was acceptable. Nevertheless, their mission was the same—the elimination of commercial whaling—and while they often found themselves differing mightily on the strategy and tactics of what David Day (the author of the book of the same title) called "The Whale War," they awkwardly but doggedly worked together toward a common goal. Sometimes it was not altogether clear who the enemy was. The eco-commandos often saw the United States government as their adversary, especially when the government was supporting the Eskimos in their campaign for increased bowhead quotas. The government was, by definition, opposed to those who would break the law in pursuit of their goals, and the "legitimate" conservation organizations tried to hold the middle ground, supporting the government but occasionally condoning the ecotage tactics of the guerrillas. (Even the guerrillas were divided. Paul Watson, the commando who eventually took the *Sea Shepherd* to ram

Demonstrators carry signs in an attempt to influence delegates and passersby at the IWC meetings in Brighton, England, 1983.

and sink the pirate whaler *Sierra* in Oporto, Portugal, had been invited to leave Greenpeace because his methods were too violent.)

Throughout history, various species of whales had been killed for various reasons, but the sperm whale, whose meat was generally considered inedible to humans, was killed primarily for its oil. Sperm oil, which comes from the "case," a vast reservoir in the whale's nose, is one of the finest lubricants known because it retains its viscosity even under extremes of temperature and pressure. (The blubber of the sperm whale, like that of other whales, was also boiled down for oil, but the "head oil" was a much more valuable product.) In the mid-1970s a "solution" to the killing of sperm whales appeared to the conservationists, and it came, of all places, from the desert.

In the arid regions of the American Southwest grows an evergreen shrub known as jojoba (*Simmondsia chinensis*), whose encapsulated seeds contain a liquid wax that is almost indistinguishable from sperm oil. Jojoba oil, moreover, has none of the "fishy" odor of sperm oil, and it does not darken on sulfur-

ization. Since the oil of the jojoba could be used in the manufacture of candles, shampoos, face creams, waxes, and industrial lubricants, it appeared as if the killing of sperm whales was—or soon could be—over. Unfortunately, the jojoba (also known as goatbush, pignut, and coffeebush) is difficult to cultivate, and grows too slowly in the wild to be efficiently harvested. Despite the excitement of its "discovery" (a patent for the use of jojoba oil had been issued as early as 1936), and the hopes of the conservationists, the slaughter of the sperm whales on the high seas continued.

Perhaps the most significant event—albeit an inadvertent one—in the "Save the Whales" campaign was the admission of observers into the heretofore closed sessions of the International Whaling Commission. (To this day, the press is permitted to attend only the opening, ceremonial session of the IWC, and the only news that emerges from the daily meetings is that which either "leaks" out or is reported by delegates or observers after the day's events have concluded.) From 1970 onward, the number—and the variety—of "observers" increased dramati-

July 23, 1982, the day the moratorium was passed. Shown celebrating are the author; Tom Garrett, Deputy U.S. Commissioner; and Sir Peter Scott, President of the World Wildlife Fund and member of the British delegation.

cally. There were ten at the IWC's twentieth annual meeting in 1969 (four were representatives of governments with either an interest in whaling or its elimination—Italy, Peru, Portugal and Chile—and one was Charles Lindbergh, representing the Survival Service Commission of the International Union for the Conservation of Nature). By 1978 there were twenty-six observers (including those from five non-participating nations), and more significantly, there were several non-governmental observers, such as the representative from Greenpeace, who by this time had received official credentials to attend the meeting. In 1982, the year the moratorium was passed, there were *fifty-nine* additional people in the meeting room—not counting the observers from Ireland and Portugal, or those from internationally accredited organizations such as FAO (Food and Agricultural Organization of the United Nations) or IUCN (International Union for the Conservation of Nature). The presence of all these observers meant that the workings of the commission could no longer be hidden behind closed doors, and therefore, the often political actions of the delegations were available to public

scrutiny. The world wanted to know who was killing the whales, and who was allowing it to happen.

In addition to the observers at the IWC meeting, each member country could send its own nongovernmental observers who would participate as members of the delegation. Only the delegates themselves knew who or what their delegation's policy was, and while it can probably be safely assumed that no member of the Japanese or Soviet delegation was opposed to whaling, there were assuredly members of the American delegation who disagreed with the official government position. Side by side in the United States delegation's meetings, there were representatives from such diverse groups as the Department of the Interior, the Humane Society of the United States, the State Department, and the Alaska Eskimo Whaling Commission. Quite often these delegates had opposing constituencies to satisfy, but in the American town meeting tradition, they discussed, threatened, voted, argued, cajoled, wheedled and inveigled until something approximating a "position" was developed. Then they had to take this to the IWC, and try to convince other countries to vote their way.

Greenpeace

GREENPEACE began in 1969 as a protest movement against the detonation of a nuclear device of 1.2 megatons on Amchitka Island in the Aleutians. The threat of earthquakes, tidal waves, and nuclear fallout—not to mention the virtual destruction of an entire island—brought out the first of the eco-guerrillas. In the converted halibut-seiner *Phyllis Cormack*, a ragtag brigade of freaks, hippies, self-styled "ecologists" and hangers-on sailed north from Vancouver, heading for Amchitka, where they had the idea that anchoring in the blast zone would cause President Nixon to call off the test. In hindsight, it was lucky that they never made it, but that voyage was the beginning of what was to become one of the most powerful conservation organizations in the world. At that early moment, the strategy of Greenpeace was defined: it would use the media for all they were worth. Even the name "Greenpeace," according to Bob Hunter, first president and chronicler of the movement, "had a ring to it—it conjured images of Eden; it said ecology and antiwar in two syllables; it fit easily into a one-column headline; it had a track record; and it was identified with radical and militant action, albeit of a Gandhian order: flower children, civil rights, Ban the Bomb, conservation, Save the Redwoods, Wooden Ships, Woodstock, et cetera."

The next Greenpeace campaign—equally disorganized, calamity-prone, and bitterly fought—was in the South Pacific. Again it was a protest over nuclear testing, this time at Moruroa atoll, where the French, who owned the atoll, were planning to set off another nuclear device. The blast was detonated despite the presence of the *Vega* no more than fifteen miles from the fallout area, but perhaps even more important, the campaign involved David McTaggart (the *Vega* was his boat), who would play an increasingly important role in the affairs of Greenpeace.

Enter Paul Spong, a New Zealander with a degree in psychology from UCLA and an overwhelming interest in whales. He had worked for a while with the killer whales at the Vancouver Aquarium, and believed in the power of music to communicate with them.* Spong assembled a "Greenpeace Whale Show" in Vancouver to try to raise the money he required to get himself to Japan, in the belief that he could convince the Japanese that killing whales was wrong. In 1974 Spong finally arrived in Japan, and although he gave nineteen lectures in two months, he did not succeed in convincing the Japanese to suspend their whaling activities.

Upon his return from Japan, Spong took his wife, child, and whale show on the road in Canada, overtly to raise money, but covertly to locate someone who might assist him in his plan to confront the Soviet whaling fleet in the Pacific. In order to accomplish this, Greenpeace had to locate the Soviet whalers, and to locate them, somebody had to provide them with the coordinates.

Spong found the name of Åge Jonsgard, the grand old man of Norwegian cetology, and posing as a "detached scientist," he flew to Norway to discuss whale behavior. From Jonsgard, Spong extracted the name of Einar Vangstein of the Bureau of International Whaling Statistics in Sandefjord, and now posing as a researcher on sperm whales, he got Vangstein to tell him where he might find some to study. Vangstein directed him to the North Pacific, where the Soviet whalers had found sperms.

*In *Mind in the Waters,* Spong wrote a piece called "The Whale Show," which contains these observations:

We often play music to the whales, for we feel their interest in and perhaps appreciation of it. Sometimes, particularly on a still night, a pod or part of a pod, or perhaps just a single whale, will hover offshore for an hour or more, apparently tuning in to the music. Sometimes they seem to join in the celebration with the chorus of their voices and the dance of their bodies, visible to us from the bubbling phosphorescent wake they leave behind.

The *Phyllis Cormack,* now repainted and refitted (but still most unseaworthy), left Vancouver, faked a run to the north to throw off the Soviets (who, they were afraid, knew of their plans), and headed southwest. There was a Russian-speaking crew member aboard to monitor the broadcasts from the various Soviet and Polish fishing vessels in the area. On June 27, 1975—after fifty-eight days at sea and on the penultimate day of the IWC meeting in London—they found the Soviet whalers. (Paul Spong was not aboard the *Cormack;* he was in London proselytizing the press. The media plan was to confront the whalers while the IWC meeting was in progress, in order to garner the most coverage.) The factory ship *Dal'nii Vostok* and her flotilla of catcher boats were in the area of the Mendocino Trench, only three hundred miles off the coast of California.

With the United Nations flag, the Greenpeace flag, the British Columbia flag, the Canadian flag, the Oceanic Society flag, a Buddhist monastery flag and assorted other pennants snapping in the breeze, the *Phyllis Cormack* sallied forth, looking like the committee boat for a medieval yacht race. Two Zodiacs, small inflatable dinghies, were lowered for the first scrimmage with the Soviets. The David and Goliath parallel was unavoidable: *Dal'nii Vostok* was 750 feet long and as tall as a ten-story building; each of the rubber inflatables was fourteen feet long and powered by a fifty-horsepower outboard motor.

Their first contact was with a dead whale. Next to a floating radar reflector which enabled the whalers to find and collect their kill was the floating carcass of a sperm whale. At that time, there were size limits for sperm whales (the minimum was 30 feet), but this one was considerably smaller. Paul Watson (who would later achieve far greater heights in his war against the whalers) climbed aboard the undersized whale to give photographer Rex Wyler a sense of the actual size of the little whale: it was about 20 feet long.

When the *Cormack* had caught up with the *Vostok,* Russian-speaking crew member George Korotva delivered an ultimatum to the whalers: "We speak for the 53 members of the United Nations that voted in 1972 for a ten-year moratorium on all whaling. We ask you to stop killing whales at once, to leave this business, to convert your fleet to other uses. If you do not, we intend to do everything within our means

to prevent you." The Soviets, who first saw the Greenpeacers as some sort of nutty California excursion boat, saw no reason to fear this misguided troop of whale-lovers, and told them, according to Korotva, to "get fokked."

For three hours, the would-be whale-savers filmed the whale-killers, noting the rivers of blood that ran from the great ship's scuppers, and the incongruity of a woman in a bikini on the deck. It was not only to film the carnage that they had spent close to sixty days at sea, however. They were hoping for an opportunity to place their rubber boats (and themselves) between the harpoon gun and a whale, so that the gunner would have to choose between possibly hitting them and getting the whale.

By nightfall, with the light for filming all but gone, they got their chance. The catcher boat *Vlastny* took off after a fleeing pod of sperm whales, with the *Cormack* in hot pursuit. If the whales and their hunters had continued on their original course, the Greenpeacers would never have caught them (the *Vlastny* was approximately twice as fast as the *Cormack*), but in their panic, the whales turned and headed back toward the following fleet. The engine on one of the Zodiacs conked out as the 150-ton catcher boat bore down on the Greenpeacers. Watson tried to start it, failed, and the little rubber duckie was swept aside as the diesel-powered *Vlastny* pounded after the wheezing whales, her harpooner tracking their every move. Another Zodiac came to pick up the floundering heroes, and off they went again in hot pursuit of the Soviet killer boat.

When the Greenpeace crew were finally positioned between the harpoon and the whales, they believed they had accomplished what they had set out to do. Surely the harpooner would not endanger their lives by shooting the 250-pound cast-iron harpoon right at them. They bobbed in the darkening sea as the whales snorted and blew ahead of them. Then the harpooner fired.

The exploding harpoon was driven deep into the body of a whale ten yards beyond them. In a convulsion of blood and guts, the whale died. Another whale charged at the Greenpeacers, but abruptly changed course and headed for the *Vlastny.* With its powerful lower jaw clapping, this whale charged the harpoon boat and seemed to leap out of the water in an attempt to get to the gunner. When the whale

A Soviet whaler with a dead sperm whale off the bows confronted by the Greenpeace Zodiac in the North Pacific, 1976.

was close enough that the gunner had to point his cannon almost straight down, he shot it.

The Warriors of the Rainbow had achieved their goal, and they had recorded it all on film. Out of fuel, they headed back to San Francisco, and found that they had become heroes. Robert Hunter wrote:

With the single act of filming ourselves in front of the harpoons, we had entered the mass consciousness of modern America—something that none of the previous expeditions had achieved. It was Walter Cronkite himself who introduced our footage to the mass TV audience, footage that was then run on every single television channel in the U.S. and Canada, spilling over into Europe and even Japan. Weyler's photographs went out to every country in the world that had a wire service.

In 1976, the Greenpeace fleet sailed again in the North Pacific, this time with the converted minesweeper *James Bay* as their flagship. This time they encountered the Soviet whalers between California and Hawaii, and again, with their cameras whirring and clicking, they placed themselves between the whales and the whalers. The gunners did not fire, but retreated and moved off to the northwest, "perhaps frustrated by the men and women in the inflatable boats."

The day after the Soviet fleet had vanished over the horizon, the *James Bay* was visited by an unusually sociable school of sperm whales. Some of the more romantic Greenpeacers immediately concluded that it was the same school that was present the day before when they were driving off the whalers, but no one could really be sure. The whales blew and breached, cruising in convoy with the minesweeper. They surrounded the ship, raised their heads out of the water in what was variously interpreted as a salute or a gesture of gratitude, raised their flukes high into the air, and sounded. To Hunter, then Greenpeace's president, this was an even more significant event than the previous year's "kamikaze" mission:

In centuries to come, I was absolutely certain, people would look back on these recordings of ours—the films and tapes and notebooks, the charts and the readings—and say "Look, here, this is where the turning point occurred. It was not just that humans went out to save whales, but the whales came back to acknowledge the effort. It was the real beginning of the brotherhood between living creatures."

During the next whaling season, the *James Bay* found the factory ship *Vladivostok* some seven hundred miles off the California coast. The Rainbows

In 1977, Greenpeacers again confront the Soviet whaling fleet in the North Pacific. Notice the huge maw of the stern slipway in the *Dal'nii Vostok.*

again put themselves ahead of the catcher boats, but this time the gunners had no compunctions about firing over their heads. In the Zodiac, Patrick Moore turned to Mike Bailey and asked him to stop, fearful that one of the whales would surface under their rubber boat. Hunter wrote:

And then his right ear exploded. By the time he realized they'd shot, he realized also that they'd missed him. His first impression was that the whale had been hit ahead—there was an erupting of huge gray bodies and flukes thrashing in the air. The killer boat stopped. The Zodiac thankfully sighed to a halt. Then he realized that the harpoon had struck nothing but water. He wanted to feel jubilant, but more than that he wanted to vomit. He could feel a scream lodged like a fish bone in his throat.

As these crewmen returned to the *James Bay,* the exhausted whales were gunned down by the harpooners. More publicity followed this year's expedition, but no whales were saved.

It was not the purpose of the Greenpeace fleet to prevent individual whales from being harpooned. They realized that the oceans of the world were too vast, and their resources too puny to actively interfere with the massive hunt. They filmed the events,

but they were powerless to stop them. They recognized that they had to work through the press and the media. The images of these brave eco-guerrillas, risking their lives to save the whales, was one of the most compelling aspects in the propaganda war against the whalers.

Among the viewers of the television footage of the 1977 mission was the President of the United States. As a result of this film, Jimmy Carter threw his not inconsiderable influence behind the antiwhaling movement, and by the 1977 International Whaling Commission meeting in Canberra, the lines were drawn.*

It was "us" against "them," and it had been made abundantly clear who the bad guys were. The worldwide coalition of scientists, conservationists, politicians and guerrillas was a force unlike any other in the short, stormy history of environmental activism; a force whose elements were so diverse that they often didn't speak the same language. It was a motley

*Unfortunately, the lines did not extend into Carter's own administration. For his commissioner to the IWC he chose Richard Frank, a lawyer who was quite sympathetic to the Japanese position. When Frank's term of office was over (he continued to serve after the election of Ronald Reagan, who appointed his own commissioner), he was retained by the Japan Whaling Association as a legal adviser.

army that sometimes moved like a glacier, and sometimes at the speed of thought. In fits and starts, coughing and sputtering, behind the lines and on the barricades, it moved inexorably toward a single goal: the moratorium.

ONE OF the whaling bad guys in 1977 was Australia. Her participation in the whaling industry dated back to the founding of the country in 1788, but now there was only one station left, the Cheynes Beach Whaling Company, at Albany, on the lonely southwest coast of the continent.

September 1977. The self-proclaimed "Worldwide Anti-Whaling Movement," consisting of Greenpeacers and others, set out from Sydney in a ragged collection of trucks and station wagons, and drove the longest east-west coastline in the world, overheating and steaming their way across the Nullarbor Plain, and finally pulling into Albany. They were met by the underwriter of this exercise, Jean-Paul Fortom-Gouin, a Frenchman who lived in the Bahamas.

Since the Australian whaling operation was shore-based, there was no difficulty in finding it. There were, however, other problems. For instance, a group of bikers called "God's Garbage" showed up to heckle and harass the demonstrators. Then there were the sharks. No one had told them about the great white sharks that hung around just offshore waiting for a meal of whale-meat scraps. Suddenly the idea of going out in little rubber boats seemed considerably less attractive. And the media, always the major source of support for Greenpeace's efforts, appeared already to have been co-opted by the whalers. Before the Greenpeace brigade arrived, reporters had been there for a week, being shown the pleasures and importance of whaling.

Undaunted by the absence of a supportive press or by the presence of man-eating sharks, the Greenpeacers packed their Zodiacs with extra fuel—the Cheynes Beach whalers hunted a hundred miles offshore—and gave chase. Their first two efforts proved less than productive; both motors broke down, and the whalers killed 7 sperm whales offshore. The newspaper headline in the local paper read "Round I to Whalers." The environmentalists would lose every round, but they would win the fight. Twice harpoons were shot into whales as the Zodiacs bobbed ineffectually in front of the harpooners. One

of the Zodiacs was decoyed out to sea for ninety miles by a whaler who was under instructions to lead them away from the hunt. Winds and freezing rains whistled up from the Antarctic.

Robert Hunter ends his discussion of the attempts by Greenpeace to close down the Cheynes Beach station ("the last whaling station in the English-speaking world") with these words:

When we left Albany, we felt depressed, let down, and exhausted. It wasn't until months later that the federal government bowed to the pressure that had been generated by all the media coverage of the event, and ordered an inquiry into whaling in Australia, the first such inquiry ever called. Public-opinion polls had shown that feeling against whaling was running at something like seventy percent nationwide. We had not saved a single whale—yet, indirectly, we had precipitated a strong movement in that direction.

It is an exaggeration to suggest that the Greenpeace effort alone resulted in the Australian investigation into whaling.* (Project Jonah had been campaigning against whaling in Australia for several years before the Greenpeacers arrived.) It is true, however, that the coverage of whaling in the press brought the subject to the attention of the Australian public, and an inquiry was held. A government "Inquiry into Whales and Whaling" was scheduled to hold hearings in Albany and then in Melbourne, but the Albany hearings were canceled. On July 31, 1978, the day the hearings were to begin, the Cheynes Beach Whaling Company announced that "the directors believed that operations this year would result in a substantial loss and it was unlikely that there would be any profit in whaling in 1979," and that therefore the "board had decided whaling operations must end in the near future."

---

*Because it is Greenpeace's intention to put its members in the spotlight to gain recognition—and funds—it is often given sole credit for accomplishments that should be shared with other organizations or individuals. An example of this exaggeration appears in a generally well-written article about the organization in *Oceans* magazine, where the author wrote that ". . . Greenpeace pressured the IWC to vote for an indefinite moratorium on commercial whaling." In fact, there were many official and nongovernmental organizations involved in this lobbying, including the American Cetacean Society, the Whale Center, Friends of the Earth, the Humane Society of the United States, the Animal Welfare Institute, the Connecticut Cetacean Society, the Monitor Consortium, Project Jonah, the RSPCA, the Sierra Club, the World Wildlife Fund, and numerous others. Of all these organizations, Greenpeace was the one with the highest recognition factor.

. . .

GREENPEACE'S WAR was far from over. The Soviets and the Japanese were fighting their battles within the IWC, but on the open seas, the war against the whales still raged. Now Iceland was the focus. With her population of 240,000 hardy souls, Iceland could never claim a position as a major power, whaling or otherwise, but she did have a long history of whaling, and she was not going to give up the fishery without a fight. Although Iceland had been a member nation of the IWC since its first meeting, most whaling in Icelandic waters had been conducted by the ubiquitous Norwegians. (The Loftsson family, owners of the Icelandic whaling station at Hvalfjordur, is reputed to have enormous influence within Icelandic government circles.)

Despite the importance the Icelanders would later attach to whaling, it is not a particularly important part of their economy; in *Daughter of Fire*, an affirmative study of Iceland, Katharine Scherman writes, "Whaling is a very small part of Iceland's fish industry, but in recent years it has been attracting more disapproving attention than any of man's organized hunting." In the "Iceland" entry in the 1979 edition of the *Encyclopaedia Britannica*, whaling is not mentioned at all. In 1978, however, the latest of the ships named *Rainbow Warrior* was in Icelandic waters, disrupting what whaling there was. The funds for this effort had been raised by Alan Thornton from such unlikely bedfellows as the World Wildlife Fund, British comedian Spike Milligan, and the Beatles. At approximately this time, David McTaggart was assuming the leadership of Greenpeace International, which now had offices in France, the Netherlands, Germany and Denmark, in addition to its headquarters in Canada.

It was a combination of factors that prompted the Greenpeacers to target the Icelanders. They were the last whalers to hunt the fin whale—already hunted to commercial extinction in the Antarctic—and the Warriors of the Rainbow believed that they were threatened in the North Atlantic as well. Also, the Icelanders had acquired a reputation as cruel and insensitive "collectors" of whales, based on their roundup of killer whales for sale to oceanariums.

As soon as killer whale capture was banned in Canadian and American waters, those who would exhibit these magnificent creatures turned to Ice-land. Herring fishermen, eyeing great profits, began to fish for killer whales, and many were killed or injured in the process. Even more disgraceful, however, was the treatment given to the whales if and when they were captured: they were kept in tiny shallow pools where they were buffeted by icy winds every time they surfaced to breathe. The whales were severely frostbitten, their skin was cracked and bleeding, and they were starving. It was reported—but obviously not confirmed—that many orcas were released into the ocean in the middle of the night because they were not going to survive. The whales were being sold to the highest bidders, which were usually Canadian or American oceanariums, and the capture and sale were authorized by Thordur Asgiersson, who worked for the Icelandic Department of Fisheries and coincidentally happened to be Iceland's commissioner to the IWC. (In 1980 he was elected chairman, replacing Bollen of Australia.) An anti-Icelandic feeling ran high in the environmental community.

The first campaign against the Icelanders was a standoff; no harpoons were fired at the guerrillas, but they made the point that they were there to draw the world's attention to the whale-killing. By 1979, however, the Icelanders were sufficiently perturbed that they fired several grenade harpoons over the heads of the people in the Zodiacs, and then called out the marines. The *Rainbow Warrior* was seized by Icelandic gunboats in July 1979, and her inflatable boats—her only weapons in this war—were forcibly removed from her decks.

Because the moratorium was not scheduled to take effect until the 1985–86 season, there wasn't much that the antiwhalers could do until that year, but as soon as the Japanese announced their intention to begin "scientific research whaling," Greenpeace—and other rank-and-file conservationists—swung into gear. They first tried nonconfrontational methods: they took the Japanese government to court. (These methods had been successfully employed in the case of the dolphin slaughter, but they had failed when the conservationists tried to stop the Japanese from killing sperm whales by taking the Department of Commerce to court. The United States Supreme Court ruled in favor of the Japanese.) It was obvious that "research whaling" was a specious term used to describe commercial whaling by the Japanese, the

Icelanders, the Koreans and the Norwegians. Outraged at the failure of the IWC to act, the conservationists gathered and began again to make the world aware of the devious and dangerous practices of the whaling nations.

To the great consternation of the conservationists, the United States government entered into a bilateral pact with the Japanese, ignoring the restrictions of the IWC. Along with many other conservationist organizations, Greenpeace deplored the bilateral arrangement. David McTaggart was quoted as saying, "It is totally unacceptable that two member nations of the IWC fix their own catch limits without consulting the commission's Scientific Committee and other member nations." The conservationists sued the government. The lawsuit succeeded in Federal District Court and in the United States Court of Appeals, but at the Supreme Court level, it was ruled that the United States government could make a deal with the Japanese separately, thus avoiding certification under Packwood-Magnuson.

By April 1985, the Japanese had "conditionally" agreed to end commercial whaling by 1988, but no such restrictions were placed on "research" whaling, and it was to be this category of whaling—attempted in 1976 by the Japanese and roundly criticized at that time—that would bring the IWC almost to the brink of dissolution. (During the three years before the moratorium was scheduled to take effect, the Soviets and the Japanese continued to kill thousands of minke whales in the Antarctic.) Even though commercial whaling was all but over, it appeared that whales would still be killed by whalers. Only their *motives* would be different, a distinction that was probably lost on the whales.

When the Norwegians flouted the IWC ban on North Atlantic minke whaling in the spring of 1986, Greenpeace put to sea again. In the *Moby Dick,* a converted Dutch fishing boat, they left Hamburg for the coast of Norway. After twelve days of fruitless searching, they found a single Norwegian whaler, and using their now-standard method of circling the whaler in inflatables, they managed to stop the whale-killing for eight hours. Unfortunately, they also managed to get themselves arrested by the Norwegian coast guard, and were detained in the port of Vardø for six days. When they were released, they carefully steered clear of the twelve-mile coastal limit, and

found the minke whalers again. Under the threat of worldwide negative publicity—they couldn't deny that they were killing minkes in contravention of the moratorium if they were photographed doing so—the whalers scattered, leaving the pods of minkes behind, at least for the moment. Later that summer, however, after President Reagan decided not to impose sanctions on the Norwegians because, it was said, they had *intended* to comply with the moratorium, *Moby Dick* sailed again into the midst of the Norwegian fleet. She was captured and detained again, but the point was made: the Norwegians were still killing minke whales.

By the 1988 IWC meeting, held in Auckland, New Zealand, the subject of "research" whaling had been replaced by something called "small-type coastal whaling." Developed by the Japanese, this new concept was supposed to enable the poor villages of northern Japan to hunt minkes and some other whales in their immediate offshore waters, "as they had always done." This idea was apparently based on the success of the Alaskan Eskimos' aboriginal whaling, which seemed, despite great opposition, to pass the Technical Committee of the IWC year after year. If the Eskimos could hunt whales for subsistence, why couldn't the poor Japanese fishermen? Although they brought up the subject of small-type coastal whaling at the 1988 meetings, discussion was deferred until 1989, and the Japanese continued to "misunderstand" the moratorium. Early in 1989, they went back to the Antarctic to do some "research whaling" for minke whales.

After several years during which they had directed their efforts to other causes, the Greenpeacers were back on the high seas confronting the whalers. While various conservation organizations mounted protests and write-in campaigns, Greenpeace launched the boats. In February 1989, the Japanese factory ship *Nisshin Maru No. 3* was in the Antarctic looking for minke whales, and the Greenpeace vessel *Gondwana* was looking for the Japanese. As the *Gondwana* tried to insinuate herself between the whaleship and the whales, the Japanese attempted to grapple the Greenpeacers out of the way. This ungainly maneuver resulted in a collision between the two ships. As of the time of the collision, the whalers had killed 40 of a projected total of 300 minke whales that were to be taken for science.

Greenpeace coordinator Cindy Lowry was an important element in the rescue of the gray whales that had become trapped in the closing ice at Point Barrow, Alaska, in October 1988. Working with Campbell Plowden (who remained in Washington and arranged for the Soviet icebreakers that actually cut through the ice to free the whales), she was the coordinator of the rescue, boldly leaping over every bureaucratic obstacle to see that these hapless cetaceans might be freed. Although their mission is nothing less than the rescue of the planet, Greenpeace activists have a special fondness for whales, and wherever these animals are threatened, we are likely to find the Rainbow Warriors.*

*And we are likely to find them in most unlikely places, such as the Moscow Hit Parade. In the organization's eponymous magazine for July/August 1989, it was reported that the Greenpeace album "Rainbow Warriors" was the top-selling album in the Soviet Union. It was released on March 6, and contained numbers by American and British rock stars such as the Eurythmics, U2, and the Pretenders. By May 15, over one million copies of the record had been sold, with the proceeds earmarked for environmental work in the Soviet Union.

Pirate Whaling

ONCE THERE WAS a Japanese trawler named *Shunyo Maru.* She was transformed into the *Southern Fortune,* operating out of Curaçao. And *finally* (emphasis intentional), she became the *MV Tonna,* outfitted as a whaleship. She was registered as a fishing vessel flying the convenient flag of the Netherlands Antilles, despite the prominent harpoon cannon on her bows. (In fact, the *Tonna* belonged to Andrew M. Behr of South Africa, the owner of another pirate whaler, the *Sierra.*) Both ships were combined killer–factory vessels, which meant that they were highly efficient whalers that could capture the whales and process them at sea—avoiding identification of the true nature of their activities.

The *Tonna* had been operating successfully in the North Atlantic during the summer of 1978, and by mid-July, with her freezers filled with over four hundred tons of whale meat, she headed for the Canary Islands to offload. Some two hundred miles off Portugal, the skipper sighted a large fin whale and gave chase. The 50-ton whale was killed and brought alongside the 543-ton *Tonna.* As the crew labored to winch the whale up the *Tonna's* slipway, the heavily laden ship heeled over until her rails were underwater. Water poured into the ship through open portholes, and the crew took to the lifeboats as the dead weight of the whale began to pull the ship under, stern-first. In what must surely be one of the most misguided acts in the noble traditions of the sea, the captain, a Norwegian national named Kristhof Vesterheim, chose to go down with his ship, hanging on to the bridge with a bottle of beer clutched firmly in his hand. But while the tradition of going down with your ship had been parodied, the tradition of *Moby-Dick* had been fulfilled: the whale took the whaleship down with it.

The *Sierra* was a sister ship of the *Tonna* in all respects. She was a cloudily registered vessel that had apparently been built by the Dutch as a catcher boat in 1955 to accompany the factory ship *Willem Barendsz.* The Dutch whaling industry had shut down in 1964, and the catcher boat (then known simply as *AM. No. 4*) was sent back to the yards to be rebuilt. Her entire aftersection was removed and replaced with a stern slipway, and freezing equipment was added. In 1968 the combination catcher/processor set sail as the *Run,* flying the flag of the Bahamas. She killed some 1,676 whales along the western coast of Africa, mostly Bryde's whales, but also humpbacks and the rare southern right whales. Responding to a firestorm of public opinion, the government of the Bahamas withdrew its registration, and because she was the only asset of the company that owned her, the firm promptly declared bankruptcy. The *Run* was then registered as a fishing boat, owned by a dummy Liechtenstein corporation known as Beacon Sierra Ltd., and rechristened *Sierra*. Under Captain Arvid Nordengen, the *Sierra* (now flying the Somali flag) hunted up and down the Atlantic coast of Africa, putting in to Cape Town for repairs and supplies when necessary. Her crew consisted of men from various nations, most of whom were South African coloreds, but there were four who were listed as "Production Inspectors," and they were Japanese.

Sometime around 1973, Andrew Behr had sold the production of the *Sierra* to Taiyo Canada Ltd., the Canadian subsidiary of Taiyo Fisheries Co. of Japan. This was to consist of frozen whale meat harvested from the 400–500 whales it would be catching annually off the coast of Africa. Although the registry of the *Sierra* was a closely guarded secret, it was becoming clear that she was a piece of the puzzle that was Japanese whaling at this time. While she was claiming to support the International Whaling Commission and rigorously follow the rules, Japan was in fact subverting the resolutions by supporting illegal pirate whaling—and then claiming that she wasn't involved. By 1978 the issue was an acute embarrassment to the IWC, but less so to Japanese whaling interests, which were apparently willing to take any sort of risks in order to maintain a steady flow of whale oil and meat into Japan.

They had not reckoned on Paul Watson.

Already ousted from Greenpeace for advocating violence in the name of ecological protectionism (he was the Greenpeace *kamikaze* who had climbed aboard the dead sperm whale in the North Pacific as the Russians towered over him in the *Dal'nii Vostok*), Watson was the very model of an ecological commando. After parting with Greenpeace, he enlisted the financial and spiritual support of Cleveland Amory (founder of The Fund for Animals), and bought a 779-ton Yorkshire deep-water trawler for $120,000, which he cleaned up and named the *Sea Shepherd*. He refitted the ship with forty tons of rock ballast, reinforced her bow with eighteen tons of concrete, and headed for Newfoundland to confront the sealers. Later Watson took the *Sea Shepherd* to the North Atlantic to hunt down and sink the *Sierra*.

Having learned that the pirate whaler was oper-

ating off the coast of North Africa,* Watson took the *Sea Shepherd* across the Atlantic for a rendezvous at Oporto, in Portugal. On July 15, 1979, the two ships met at sea, and the *Sea Shepherd* chased the whaler into Oporto's port, Leixoes. There Captain Nordengen neatly fooled Watson by pretending to dock in the port. When the harbor pilots boarded the *Sea Shepherd* to guide her in, the *Sierra* took off. Portuguese harbor officials detained the *Sea Shepherd*, and Watson was afraid he would lose his opportunity to ram the pirate whaler. Faced with the option of breaking international law by running from harbor officials, who insisted that the *Sea Shepherd* remain in Leixoes until she could be properly cleared for Portugal, most of the crew chose to disembark. (As Watson later wrote, "Fourteen decided that what had been so noble and adventurous back in Boston, where it was all highly theoretical, had a different aspect at high noon here in Leixoes.") That left a crew of three to man the 206-foot, 779-ton ship. Escaping from the harbor, they found the *Sierra* anchored about a quarter of a mile offshore, and they headed straight for her.

"We hit," wrote Watson. "We hit just behind the harpoon gun's platform at the bow, and we kept on going. I was surprised at how lightly we felt the impact in the wheelhouse. But there was plenty of damage where the two ships had come together." The first blow was a warning, and then Watson came about and rammed the *Sierra* again, this time amidships. Despite a gaping gash in her side that was taking in water, the *Sierra* was able to make the harbor at Leixoes, while the *Sea Shepherd* attempted to make a run for England. She was intercepted by a Portuguese destroyer and brought back to Leixoes, passing the listing *Sierra* on the way: "Her crew, on the deck and roof of the bridge, yelled and screamed and cursed at us. We waved back cheerfully and made grand bows, as one does to acknowledge bravos for a fine performance. . . ."

Watson was released, although the Portuguese au-

---

*In his book, *Sea Shepherd,* Watson acknowledges that Craig Van Note of the Monitor Consortium (a conglomeration of conservationist organizations based in Washington) had "developed intelligence sources throughout the world," and was responsible for his locating the *Sierra*. Van Note is one of the most important people in the whale-preservation network, as a source of invaluable information and a catalyst for the entire conservation community, and as the writer of the "Save the Whales" ads for Christine Stevens's Animal Welfare Institute.

The pirate whaler *Sierra* suffered major damage when she was rammed by Paul Watson's *Sea Shepherd* off the coast of Portugal in July 1979.

thorities held his ship. He and the two crewmen, whose passports had been confiscated, escaped from Portugal and ended up in England. Watson took to the airwaves in America and generated an enormous amount of publicity for his actions on behalf of the whales. By the time Watson and his crew got back to Leixoes toward the end of 1979, most of the ship's removable objects had been plundered. Unable to repossess their ship, Watson and his crew decided to scuttle her.

In February of 1980, as Watson was being tried (and found guilty) in Canada for interfering with the seal hunt in Newfoundland, some unknown person or persons attached magnetic mines to the hull of the *Sierra* and sank her in the harbor of Lisbon. The *Sierra* had been repaired and outfitted for another season of whaling when she was sunk. The pirate whaler was later raised and scrapped. Shortly thereafter, the South African government impounded two more pirate whalers, and on April 27, two of Spain's five whaleships were blown up with limpet mines and sunk in the harbor of Marin near Vigo. (The Spanish whaling operation was at best a vague one, and more or less illegal.) To this day, the saboteurs have not been identified—all that is known is that they were a group of European activists—but along

with Paul Watson, they were largely responsible for the elimination of pirate whaling—at least in the Atlantic.

AN UNNATURALLY LARGE proportion of the problems of modern whaling have come from the Japanese hunger for whale meat. As long as they provided a ready market, "free-enterprise" outlaw whalers would continue to feed the system—and the Japanese. In Taiwan, for example, no fewer than four ex-Japanese vessels were converted to whale-catcher/processors. *Sea Bird, Sea Flower, Chi Hsin* and *Chu Feng* were crewed by Taiwanese, under the orders of experienced Japanese whalers, technicians and officers. They ranged the world's oceans, first routing the meat directly through Taiwan, and when this became too obvious, rerouting it through South Korea. As usual, the power behind this operation was the insatiable Taiyo Fisheries Company, this time hiding behind a Korean subsidiary. It was Greenpeace investigators who traced the convoluted path of the illegal whale meat from Taiwan through Korea and eventually to Japan, and when the United States threatened fishing sanctions against Taiwan and Japan, the Japanese closed down the Taiwanese operation. Attempts were made to sell a large stock-

The concrete-reinforced bow of the *Sea Shepherd* after ramming the pirate whaler *Sierra*.

pile of the meat to Japan through Hong Kong and the Philippines, but to date, it remains unclear whether the two thousand tons of meat has ever been sold or remains rotting on the docks.

As early as 1956, the Japanese were investing in Chilean whaling. Taiyo Gyogyo entered into negotiations with the Chilean company Pesquera del Sur for the purpose of conducting whaling from Coronel Bay. The first Japanese whaling enterprise in Chile was almost fully capitalized out of Tokyo, and the crews and ships were also provided by the Japanese. The Chilean part of the agreement was to provide the station and the equipment for the processing of the meat—all of which was to be shipped to Japan.

Another subsidiary of Taiyo opened up in Chile in 1977. Taito Seiko took over the stern trawler *Orient Maru No. 2,* and named her *Paulmy Star No. 3.* Now registered in Panama, the rebuilt whaler was sailed to Chile, whose government had just received a quota of 500 whales. (Chile had only joined the IWC in 1977, under pressure by the United States, which threatened Pelly Amendment certification, and with the concurrence of Japan, which wanted to continue to import whale meat.) The entire Chilean whaling industry consisted of the *Paulmy Star,* which exported 704 tons of whale meat in 1978, 320 tons in

1979, and 563 tons in 1980. At the end of the last year, the mutable *Paulmy Star* changed her name again, this time to *Juan IX,* and the colors of Panama were struck in favor of the Chilean flag. The new Chilean whaling industry, however, proved to be thoroughly inept at following IWC regulations, and by the 1982 meeting of the commission, the Chileans were in violation of almost every rule in the book. They had taken undersized whales and protected whales; they had caught them in protected waters; they had fished longer than they were supposed to; and they claimed to have processed the whales at a station that was closed. Sailing from Chome (near the historic port of Talcahuano) in 1984, the crew of the *Juan IX* managed to find and kill some 15 right whales, perhaps the most endangered species of large whale in the world.

Other illegal whaling operations—that is, those that ignored IWC regulations or claimed to do one thing while they were doing another—were taking place in Spain, where Taiyo financed the whaling operations of the Masso brothers. Spanish whalers hardly ever reported their catches, so little is known of the extent of their industry. Since the Spaniards do not eat whale meat, the meat was shipped to Japan. A ban had been effected on the import of whale

The Spanish whaler *Carrumiero* harassed by Greenpeace commandos off Cape Finisterre in August 1978.

meat from non-IWC nations, however, so to legitimize the transactions, Spain joined up in 1979.

As one subversive operation after another was exposed, the Japanese persisted in devising new ways to have whales killed by others so that the meat could be shipped to the Tokyo markets. The Philippines joined the IWC in 1981, abstained from the moratorium vote the following year, and by 1983 was in the commercial whaling business. An ex-Japanese vessel (the *Miwa Maru*) was converted into the catcher–factory ship *Faith,* and began to hunt down Bryde's whales, and reportedly, highly endangered humpbacks. Under heavy IWC pressure, Japan banned whale-meat imports from Manila, and after several years of trying to smuggle whale meat into Japan, the Philippine industry folded.

In August of 1981, Paul Watson took the *Sea Shepherd II* into the Bering Sea to protest—and stop, if possible—the killing of the 179 gray whales that the Soviets took every year, purportedly to feed Siberian Eskimos. ("Aboriginal whaling," the rubric under which the Alaskan Eskimos fought for a quota of bowheads, had been modified by the Soviets to enable them to hunt the whales from a catcher boat, the claim being that as long as it fed the Eskimos, the meat was being used for aboriginal subsistence.) Watson believed that the meat was not fed to aborigines at all, but rather to minks on Siberian fur

farms. Siberian natives are not accustomed to seeing foreign ships close to their shores, and they were understandably mystified at the presence of the *Sea Shepherd II.* Watson and his troops saw blue-eyed, blond women ("So much for the aboriginal justification for the hunt") chopping up hunks of whale meat and tossing them onto a conveyor belt. They saw a number of long, low buildings, obviously shelters for cages. They were, Watson wrote, "looking at a mink ranch! . . . The whales were simply a cheap source of fodder for a lucrative fur export business." The ecological warship was approached by Soviet helicopters and a destroyer, and threatened with seizure before escaping to the safety of international waters. Watson escaped the salt mines, but he led the way for the second stage of the Invasion of Siberia.

A week before the July 1983 IWC annual meeting was to convene in Brighton—not an accident of timing—the *Rainbow Warrior* landed an invasion force on a Siberian beach near the same village that Watson had briefly mystified two years earlier. Obviously the recipients of better intelligence this time (Greenpeace has never been very good at hiding their intentions), the Soviets pounced on the invading force. While the Save the Whales Reconnaissance Unit managed to outmaneuver the Soviet Siberian Defense Forces at sea, seven of the guerrillas were left on the beach. They were held in captivity for three days, but, probably to avert any more publicity, the Soviets decided to release them. A transfer was arranged, with the American delegation being led by Leo Rasmussen, the Mayor of Nome, Alaska. After solemnly giving the Soviets an "I Love Nome" button, Rasmussen took custody of the invaders, and they triumphantly returned to the United States. They had taken photographs of mink farms, but there was no specific evidence to demonstrate that gray whale meat was being consumed by the minks. The Soviet Union, thoroughly embarrassed by the peaceful "occupation" of its strategic territory (there are reputed to be submarine pens nearby), promised to release data on the aboriginal consumption of whale meat. Prior to 1955, Siberian Eskimos took an average of 20 whales a year for their own consumption. With the IWC variance, the number of whales leapt to almost ten times that, which suggests that more mustelids than Chukchis were consuming the whale meat.

The whaling moratorium was supposed to take effect in 1985–86. Long before that season, however, with their 1982 objection still in place, the Japanese contrived to continue taking sperm whales, a species that had already been declared protected, and which therefore had a zero quota. In 1981 they had requested and been granted a two-year quota for the species, which was supposed to be a phase-out of sperm whaling. After a confused season during which only seven whales were killed before the fleets were recalled, the Japanese lay low for 1983. Then in 1984,

Peruvian conservationist Felipe Benavides stands beside a dying 66-foot-long blue whale on the beach at Conchan, Peru. The whale had been illegally harpooned by whalers from the Japanese-owned station at Paita in February 1978.

they declared their intention to resume sperm whaling in the North Pacific. Instead of a phase-out, they
asked for a "phase-down," where they would continue to take some 400 whales per year until the
various whaling captains retired or died, conceivably
not before the year 2000. United States officials, reluctant to impose sanctions against the Japanese fishing industry for outlaw whaling, signed a bilateral
agreement with Japan, which condoned Japanese
whaling until 1988. A consortium of conservation
organizations filed suit against the Department of
Commerce for failing to certify the Japanese under
the Packwood-Magnuson Amendment, which called
for sanctions against any nation that diminished the
effectiveness of an international conservation agreement.

The Japanese whaling company Nippon Hogei
organized a Peruvian subsidiary in 1967, Compañía
Ballerna de Kinkai. (In 1977 this company became
known as Victoria del Mar, or Vicmar.) The company operated three whale-catchers which towed
their kills back to the station at Paita. Like Chile,
Peru joined the International Whaling Commission
in 1979 to avoid restrictions on the delivery of whale
meat from non-IWC countries to Japan. (Curiously,
in its pre-whaling days, Peru had been instrumental
in closing down the pirate whaling activities of Aristotle Onassis.) In subsequent investigations, neither
Peru nor Japan would admit to this operation, and
even when the Peruvian government attempted to
prosecute the illegal alien whaling operation, the killing continued.

Peru was one of the nations that filed an objection
to the moratorium, and Greenpeace decided to focus
attention on what it considered illegal Peruvian
whaling. (In the minds of the conservationists, the
situation was exacerbated by the fact that the Peruvian whaling company was owned by Taiyo Fisheries
of Japan.) They took the *Rainbow Warrior* into the
Peruvian harbor at Paita, and boarded the catcher
boat *Victoria 7*. Activists chained themselves to the
harpoon cannon, and one of them took to the crow's
nest. After some days of confusion, Peruvian marines came aboard and cut the chains. The protesters

were arrested and threatened with severe penalties
for piracy. Only the intervention of Felipe Benavides, a prominent Peruvian conservationist, saved
them from years in jail.* It would not be until 1986,
years after it had actually ceased whaling, that Peru
would withdraw its objection.

The conservationists did not restrict their activities to acts of protest or confrontation. Equally effective have been their disclosures of the illegal activities
of the pirate whalers. At almost every IWC meeting
in the past decade, Greenpeace has distributed a
pamphlet, usually illustrated with explicitly compro-
mising photographs, of illegal whaling operations
around the world. (The first of the "Outlaw Whalers" publications was written by Craig Van Note
and published in 1983 by the Whale Protection
Fund.) When they were not in a position to deploy
their troops to such places as Taiwan or the Philippines, they did manage to obtain photographs of the
pirate ships, incriminating labels on the whale meat,
and even the whalers at work. Through a network
of strategically placed agents, Greenpeace has been
able to document the insidious nature of pirate whaling, and thus bring these clandestine activities before
the public. When Campbell Plowden visited Hokkaido in 1979, he talked to an anonymous Japanese
whaleman who not only told him of the take of
Baird's beaked whales by minke whalers, but also
supplied him with photographs. (Baird's beaked
whales are not regulated by the IWC, but since they
actually get to be larger than minkes, most
conservation-minded countries believe they ought to
be.) In *Pirate Whaling 1980*, in a discussion of "the
unregulated minke hunters," photographs of the severed heads of Baird's beaked whales created a storm
of outrage, and although the effort has still not been
successful, the publication led to concerted efforts to
list the beaked whales in the *Schedule* of cetaceans
whose hunting can be regulated by the IWC.

*Benavides had been active for almost thirty years in his efforts
to drive foreign whalers from Peru's shores. In February 1978, near
the resort town of Conchan, a 65-foot female blue whale washed
ashore with massive, bleeding harpoon wounds, and died as Benavides watched.

Interlude: Looking at Whales

IN THIS ERA of whale consciousness, it is difficult to imagine a time when whales were not part of our lives. Unless we are Eskimos or out-of-work Japanese whalers, however, they do not figure prominently in our daily existence. They are with us nonetheless, looming off our shores and spouting in our collective awareness.

Men have maintained animal totems at least as far back as the cave paintings of Lascaux and Altamira. The Egyptians believed in a pantheon of animal deities, wherein gods took the form of the cat, the jackal, the baboon, the vulture, the ibis and the crocodile. At Knossos, the Cretans developed a cult around the bull, and in subsequent Greek mythology, we can mark the appearance of the swan, the eagle, the dolphin and even the three-headed dog. Incorporating the qualities of man and animal were the centaur (half man, half horse), and the minotaur (half man, half bull). Even the night skies were filled with animals: the Zodiac contains Ursus the bear, Taurus the bull, Canis Major the great dog, Aries the ram, Scorpio the scorpion, and Cancer the lowly crab. In the skies of the Southern Hemisphere is the constellation of Cetus, the whale.

Of course, animal totems were not restricted to Western civilization; Africans, Polynesians, Micronesians, North and South American Indians, Australian Aboriginals and the peoples of India have all demonstrated a need for supernatural beings in the form of animals.

With the rise of Christianity in the West, we began to adopt gods in the form of humans—in our own image, as it were—and animals began to appear symbolically, not as actual gods but as paradigms of Christian behavior. Medieval tracts such as the bestiaries of the twelfth and thirteenth centuries were focused on animals, most of them known to the authors, but some of them—the unicorn and the griffon, for example—known to nobody at all. The four evangelists, Mark, Luke, John and Matthew, are represented iconographically by a lion, a bull, an eagle and an angel, respectively, but it was the evangelists themselves who were the objects of veneration, not their animal surrogates.

Since man began killing whales, he has paradoxically immortalized them in various ways. Perhaps the most dramatic of these has been the painting of their portraits. Whales can be found in some very early rock paintings in Norway and also in the various totems of different cultures, from the Japanese to the Indians of the northwestern coast of North America.

Early anatomists studied whales because they were an important element in the mammalian kingdom. They were, of course, restricted to observations of dead animals, and their detailed drawings were not much better than the early illustrations of dead leviathans washed up on various beaches throughout Europe. The Dutch, and to a lesser extent the British, two nations who pioneered Arctic whaling, seemed to specialize in drawing whales, an activity that was obviously related to the inclination of whales to strand on their beaches. Whaling nations have to have access to the sea, and occasionally the whales saved them the trouble of launching their boats.

By the eighteenth century, as commercial whaling shifted into high gear, a tradition of whaling art had begun. Most frequently, the art depicted the ships that were employed in the whale fishery, often showing the exotic locations where whales were being killed. Thus, pictures of square-rigged ships surrounded by threatening icebergs proliferated, along with paintings and prints of tropical landscapes with

When William Morris Hunt (1824–79) painted *The Spouting Whale*, he left a great deal to the viewer's imagination.

towering volcanic peaks in the background. In these pictures, which were produced primarily during the eighteenth and nineteenth centuries, the only parts of the whale that could be seen were its spout, its broad back, or its flukes rising from the stormy seas—not a particularly effective method of portraying the whale, but then the animal was seen primarily as a source of blubber and bone, not as a living creature. The whale was appreciated more as an element of commerce than as a part of the animal kingdom. The schools of whales were regarded as natural—and limitless—resources, rather like the great stands of timber that were cut down for firewood, pulp and lumber. Just as the trees had no souls

or feelings, the whales were thought of as seagoing oil wells, to be harvested for commerce. No wonder that no one took the trouble to depict them as living, breathing creatures or as animals whose morphology and physiognomy were worth illustrating.

UNLIKE TREES—except for those that fell on lumberjacks—whales were regarded as dangerous, which led to another form of whale art: the whale as a menace.

As Yankee whalers achieved their global predominance, more and more instances occurred where whalers were upended, drowned, battered, or otherwise injured by vindictive whales. Never mind that these "aggressive" whales had been harpooned or were defending their young; never mind that there were very few documented instances of unprovoked attacks. The object of the fishery had the temerity to fight back, and thus interfered with commerce. In nineteenth-century America, the origin of much of this material, the whale took its place alongside the earthquake and the tornado as a natural disaster that impinged upon man's inalienable right to profit. An entire class of paintings and prints was created that showed the inherent dangers of whaling. Fragile whaleboats were upset, brave whalemen dumped into

the sea, and the whales spouted their last bloody breaths before they succumbed. It was man versus whale; heroic stuff, worthy of an aggrandizing art.

Not surprisingly, there are few illustrations glorifying the age of mechanized whaling. Factory-ship operations, where the whales were hunted down in diesel catcher boats and the carcasses hauled aboard four-hundred-foot-long ships for processing, did not lend themselves to picturesque illumination. Men ventured into the icy Antarctic, but little in the way of art resulted from these perilous journeys.

A change in the way whales were depicted ap-

The artist enters the whales' element. Portrait of a humpback family by Richard Ellis.

proached when the first oceanariums were opened just before World War II. Scientists were now able to study captive dolphins, and the intelligence and grace of these amiable creatures was revealed. But very few publications showed them in their natural surroundings.

Since the mid-1970s, however, a new art form has emerged: the depiction of the living whale and its relatives in the water. At first, these illustrations were employed primarily in "Save the Whales" campaigns, but they quickly evolved into a very specialized art form of their own. These were not the classic illustrations in which a whaleboat was shown in the jaws of an angry sperm whale, but rather the new illustrators showed the whale in its underwater habitat. The artist not only had to know what the various species looked like, but he also had to incorporate a highly specialized interpretation of dissolved light and shadow, which was different from any other sort of painting. Few painters used whales as their subjects before the introduction of scuba equipment and underwater photography; nobody could remain underwater long enough to know what it looked like down there.

The first awareness of living whales occurred at about the time that people became aroused about the slaughter of the whales on the high seas. Various conservation organizations—including several that had been formed specifically to protect the whales—began to distribute leaflets, broadsides and magazines which were intended to raise people's consciousness about the plight of the whales. But in order for people to want to preserve whales, the public had to know what they looked like, and to accomplish this, illustrators began to draw whales for these publications. The art of the whale-painter rose to its zenith at the same time as the grass-roots movement to preserve the whales escalated, from about 1975 to 1985.

By the 1980s, whale photography was a thriving art. All over the world (except where it was forbidden by statute), divers with underwater cameras were trying to capture the whale on film. Their work has appeared in books, magazines and films worldwide, and through them, we have begun to gain a sense of what the whale really looks like. In the December 1988 issue of *National Geographic* there is an article entitled "Whales: An Era of Discovery," in which Flip Nicklin's photographs illustrate everything from blue whales and fin whales to pilot whales and sperm whales, species that earlier were considered unphotographable.

FOR MANY, the perception of whales has been a function of direct observation, uncluttered by philosophical considerations or the subliminal meaning of whale songs. There are many locations where people can simply go out and *watch* whales. This form of whale observation is especially popular in the United States, partly because Americans have a love affair with whales, but also because America's coasts are particularly accommodating to various species.

From Seattle to San Diego on the West Coast, and from Maine to the Gulf of Mexico on the East, there are whales to be seen. Although they are totally cosmopolitan in distribution, killer whales are the prime attraction in the Pacific Northwest, especially around Puget Sound and the San Juan Islands. Humpbacks can be seen on both coasts, but they form the backbone of Massachusetts whale-watching. Fin whales and blues are occasionally spotted off California, especially in the southern portion of the state. (During the 1985 meeting of the American Cetacean Society, in Monterey, it was seen as an affirmation of purpose that blue whales appeared in Monterey Bay.) An entire industry has sprung up around watching gray whales off southern California as they migrate along the coast. (When they reach the lagoons of Baja, another whale-watching industry is waiting for them.)

The business of whale-watching is said to have begun in Massachusetts in 1975, when a commercial fisherman named Alvin Avellar took people out on his charter boat *Dolphin* solely for the purpose of watching whales. Since that time, Avellar has expanded his Provincetown fleet and business into a multimillion-dollar operation, and led the way for many other whale-watching activities. (In a 1989 discussion of the effects of whale-watching on whales, Douglas Beach and Mason Weinrich estimated that there were twenty-one companies in Massachusetts "that now rely on whale-watching for all or a substantial part of their income.") The humpbacks that feed on New England's Stellwagen Bank migrate to the Caribbean to breed and calve, and although there are fewer commercial opportunities to observe them on Silver Bank, there are people who travel thou-

In this incredible photograph, a humpback breaches directly in front of a group of excited whale-watchers off Maui, Hawaii.

sands of miles to watch the long-winged humpies in the warm Caribbean. (This is the same population that passes Bermuda on its way north or south, so there is yet another opportunity to catch a glimpse of these playful, endangered animals.)

Because Captain Avellar realized that he was not an expert on whales when he began his business—and because he recognized that his passengers wanted to know more about the animals they were watching—he entered into an association with a group of cetologists at the Center for Coastal Studies of Provincetown, in which the scientists would deliver brief lectures to the passengers in return for the unprecedented "platform of opportunity" provided by daily voyages among the whales. (The National Marine

Fisheries Service has established guidelines for whale-watching to prevent everybody from driving his boat among feeding or nursing whales. Only those with a government permit may participate.) From its modest beginnings, this program developed into one of the most sophisticated and important studies ever conducted on a population of great whales. Under the leadership of Dr. Charles "Stormy" Mayo, the scientists have studied feeding habits, migratory routes, parental associations, and even the effects of whale-watchers on the whales being watched. They have been able to track individual whales—to which they have given names—from birth to parenthood, and in some unfortunate cases, to death.

Humpbacks are also the featured attraction in Hawaiian whale-watching. They arrive from southeast Alaska (another location where they are studied) in the late fall, and congregate off the west coast of the island of Maui. (Interestingly, this location is right off the old whaling port of Lahaina.) At the time of a 1986 study by Whitney Tilt, there were perhaps a dozen companies in the Hawaiian Islands taking tourists out to watch the whales, with a gross income of some $3 million.

In 1981, Stephanie Kaza, then a research scientist at the University of New Hampshire, undertook to study the business of California whale-watching. She visited some forty sites and programs up and down the coast, and evaluated the ticket-sales figures, educational value, and other aspects of the various programs. Her results for 1981 were astonishing, and since then, all the numbers have increased exponentially. The total gross income for the programs was over $2 million, collected from a quarter-million individual whale-watchers. (In Tilt's 1986 survey, the gross income for 1983–84 was $2.6 million.) To the question of why whale-watching is so popular, she answers that it "meets the public's newfound love for marine mammals—especially whales—at a time when outdoor experiences are popular recreational pastimes."

In 1988, Scott Kraus, of the New England Aquarium (the man who rediscovered the New England right whale—from a whale-watching boat), attempted to determine "the value of the whale" from nonconsumptive uses (*e.g.*, whale-watching) as contrasted with consumptive uses (whaling). He concluded that whaling produced a far greater short-term income ($30–50 million from nonconsumptive uses; $154.2 million from commercial whaling), but

the real long-term value of whales is metaphorical. Whales have become icons that represent everything that is mysterious, wonderful, and life-giving in the oceans. We need a broader view of our interactions with the earth, and must convert the interest and concern for the welfare of whales to a similar concern and action about the ocean and its health. Whales are valuable, because they are the medium for that message.

Whale-watching programs are now available in Argentina, Australia, Canada and New Zealand—all countries with a past history of whaling. There are those who would introduce whale-watching to coun-

tries where whaling has recently ended or still goes on: Japan, Iceland, Norway. It may come to pass, but the problems are sociological as well as geographical. Tourists in Japan may not think it beneficial or pleasurable to watch the animal that might have been yesterday's lunch playing in its home; how many people in America visit feedlots to watch the cattle? The Japanese and the Icelanders have more or less eliminated the whales close to their shores, and there are probably very few people who would risk three or four days at sea in a small, uncomfortable boat to catch a glimpse of the back of a whale. There is no question that the proximity of the whales to American shores, at best an accident of evolution, has played an important part in the inspiration of the American people toward reverence for whales.*

The whale-watchers see their rolling backs or their towering spouts, but they have not seen the whale. There have been brave cameramen who have entered the whales' domain and brought back flickering images for our eager consumption, but to understand the whale, you must see it underwater, in what Loren Eiseley called "the blue light of eternity." In *The Delicate Art of Whale Watching*, Joan McIntyre wrote, "The reality of the whales is something else entirely; it is unimaginable and, for all I know, not perceptible by us. We do not go easily into their world, cannot even breathe its substance. If you really wish to see whales in their world, then you must strengthen and calm yourself enough to go into the water, alone, without any fancy gear and without the security of people around you; and then, then you might see whale and understand in your blood and marrow the power of whale and her beauty."

WHALES ARE infrequently treated as the subjects of major poems, although many major poets have figuratively touched on them in passing. In *Paradise Lost*, Milton speaks of Leviathan . . .

> Hugest of living creatures, in the deep
> Stretched like a promontory sleeps or swims,
> And seems a moving land; and at his gills
> Draws in, and at his breath spouts out a sea.

*In a 1989 publication, Tom Arnbom, a Swedish biologist, wrote that whale-watching has begun—somewhat tentatively—in Norway. Backed by a grant from the World Wildlife Fund, a Swedish conservation group has gone out on Norwegian whaleships to look for whales. Although they spotted sperm whales and minkes, they did not see many Norwegians on their trips.

This and other poetical allusions can be found in the introductory section of *Moby-Dick,* where Melville has collected "whatever random allusions to whales he could anyways find in any book whatsoever, sacred or profane."

In *Leaves of Grass,* Walt Whitman includes a poem entitled "A Song of Joys." Among the joys he celebrates are those of the engineer, the horseman, the soldier, the fisherman, the farmer and the whaleman:

O the whaleman's joys! I cruise my old cruise again!
I feel the ship's motions under me, I feel the Atlantic's breezes
*   fanning me,*
I hear the cry sent down from the mast-head, There—she
*   blows!*
Again I spring up the rigging to look with the rest—we descend
*   wild with excitement,*
I leap in the lower'd boat, we row out to our prey where he
*   lies,*
We approach stealthy and silent, I see the mountainous mass,
*   lethargic, basking,*
I see the harpooner standing up, I see the weapon dart from his
*   vigorous arm;*
O swift again far out in the ocean the wounded whale, settling,
*   running to windward, tows me,*
Again I see him rise to breathe, we row close again,
I see a lance driven through his side, press'd deep, turn'd in the
*   wound,*
Again we back off, I see him settle again, the life is leaving
*   him fast,*
As he rises he spouts blood, I see him swim in circles
narrower and narrower, swiftly cutting the water—I see him
*   die,*
He gives one convulsive leap in the center of the circle, and then
*   he falls flat and still in the bloody foam.*

When Whitman's paean to the joys of whaling was published in 1855, the killing of whales was perceived by most people as a noble and heroic exercise. By the 1980s, however, people had become substantially more ecologically sensitive, and no longer regarded whaling as a wholesome, joyful enterprise. It was probably inevitable that someone would write a proper narrative poem—a whale epic, if you will. An English poet, playwright and actor named Heathcote Williams wrote *Whale Nation,* a 751-line paean to the whale, which was—probably uniquely in the history of epic poetry—profusely illustrated. It was well received in Britain—Williams read it in its entirety on the BBC—and prominent literary figures reviewed it. Poet Laureate Ted Hughes called it "brilliantly cunning, dramatic and wonderfully moving, a steady accumulation of grandeur and dreadfulness," and in *The Observer,* the novelist and critic Anthony Burgess wrote, "What Mr. Williams is doing is not writing a poem so much as employing the lineation associated with poetry to drive home his own sense of the wonder of the whale."

Williams's long poem begins (and ends) with an introduction to the water planet: "From space, the planet is blue./ From space, the planet is the territory/ Not of humans, but of the whale." There follows an introduction to the biology and wonder of the whale, both general and specific ("Alien beings./ Their whole body: every bone, every membrane, every hollow,/ Part of an enormous ear,/ Twenty times as sensitive as man's"), and incorporates a doleful description of the useless uses to which man has put the whale:

> *. . . Though this particular lubricant*
> *May lead to all human cities clogged with rubble;*
> *Ending their existence like beached whales,*
> *Washed-up and rotting on the foreshores of civilisation,*
> *Whose foundations were built upon dead blubber.*

THIRTEEN

AFTER THE MORATORIUM

California's Love Affair with the Gray Whale

B Y THE TURN of the century, California whaling was effectively ended, primarily because the gray whales were in such short supply. Roy Chapman Andrews said, "The American fishery did not last long for continual slaughter on their breeding grounds soon so depleted the numbers of the gray whales that the hunt was no longer profitable, and the shore stations which had been established at various points along the coast finally ceased operations altogether. For over twenty years the species had been lost to science and naturalists believed it to be extinct." Andrews went to Ulsan (Korea), to investigate reports of a mysterious species of whale being hunted by Korean whalers and discovered that the whalers were killing *koku kujira,* the Japanese name for the gray whale. While it may have been scarce in California waters, it was evidently abundant enough on the other side of the Pacific to sustain a fishery.*

*During the military posturing that took place prior to World War I, the barren coasts of Baja, which had previously interested only gray whales, suddenly became strategically important. Because he believed that Germany needed a port in Mexico, and decided upon Magdalena Bay, Kaiser Wilhelm tried to *buy* the Baja Peninsula "for naval purposes" in 1902, and there were unsubstantiated rumors that the Japanese were planning to invade Mexico in 1908 in order to obtain a foothold in the West.

Japanese whalers have traditionally paid little heed to declining whale stocks, and the "Korean herd" of gray whales was no exception. From the establishment of the shore station at Ulsan in 1899 until the mid-1930s, some 1,500 gray whales were killed. In 1933, only two whales were taken, and the species was considered extinct in the Western Pacific. Norwegian pelagic whalers occasionally cruised off the Baja coast from 1914 to 1929, however, picking off an occasional gray whale, and there was even an American factory ship named the *California* that worked the coasts of Alta and Baja California.

By 1937, the whaling nations of the world had recognized that the gray whale was commercially if not biologically extinct, and the following year the International Agreement for the Regulation of Whaling (the precursor of the International Whaling Commission) was signed, forbidding the killing of gray whales. Neither Japan nor the Soviet Union were part of this agreement, and whalers of both nations continued to kill small numbers of gray whales when they encountered them. Killing of grays was prohibited except by aborigines and by governments who intended to use the products exclusively for consumption by aborigines.

When all hunting of gray whales ceased in 1938, the California population began an amazing comeback. Even though the whalers couldn't find any more whales to kill, it does not seem possible that the actual numbers had been brought close to zero. More likely, the remaining whales migrated farther offshore, or even rounded Cabo San Lucas, the tip of the Baja Peninsula, and found sanctuary in the Sea of Cortez. However they managed it, the surviving gray whales reproduced and proliferated.

Of all the great whales, grays are perhaps the easiest to tally. The earliest censuses were conducted from convenient locations on shore where people with binoculars counted the whales as they passed by. Dr. Carl Hubbs, America's premier ichthyologist, added the proper weight to the early counts, and on one expedition, to Baja California, he was accompanied by no less a personality than Errol Flynn. (Flynn's father was a professor of biology at the University of Belfast.) At Scammon's Lagoon, Hubbs and company took to the air in small planes, and also hovered over the whales in helicopters, a practice that was abandoned when it was discovered that the noise panicked the whales. (Both shore and aerial surveys had to be modified to account for those animals that passed by during the night or were underwater when the surveyors passed over.) Although we will never know the number of whales that remained after the two periods of whaling, estimates range from a few hundred to a couple of thousand. Whatever the actual figure, the numbers were sufficient for a comeback. (It is, perhaps, something in the nature of the gray whale that encouraged this renaissance. The right whale, hunted as intensively throughout the world, has not accomplished anything like the gray whale's return, and in fact is still considered an endangered species, even though there has been no commercial whaling on this species since 1937.)

As a young man, cardiologist Paul Dudley White (best known as President Dwight Eisenhower's heart consultant) had developed an interest in the hearts of whales, and around 1916, had published the first scientific description of a whale's heart. In 1956 he set out for Scammon's Lagoon to attempt to monitor the heartbeat of a gray whale. In a *National Geographic* article, White wrote, "Human hearts beat 50 to 90 times a minute. But the heart of a large whale pumps very slowly—perhaps fewer than 10 times a minute. No one knows exactly, for the pulse of the earth's most ponderous creature never has been taken satisfactorily." By today's standards, their equipment was primitive: they wanted to implant two electrodes into the back of a whale, and to do so were prepared to try a crossbow, a hand-thrown harpoon, or a lightweight shoulder gun. The whales were understandably skittish (one bashed a hole in one of the skiffs), and White and his colleagues failed. It would be another fifteen years before the pulse rate of a gray whale would be known, and the tests would be conducted on Gigi, a juvenile gray that was captured and held in captivity in San Diego. (Contrary to Dr. White's predictions, Gigi's heart beat 43 times per minute.)

In 1960 Raymond Gilmore estimated the total California population at 4,454 animals; when Dale Rice and Allen Wolman carefully analyzed all the available census material in 1971, they concluded that "the best estimate of the present population size of the California gray whale is approximately 11,000." In later years the estimate has risen, not only because the population has increased, but also because the methods of counting have improved. Stationed at Unimak Pass in the Aleutians (the first opening in the Alaska Peninsula, through which almost all the migrating gray whales pass), observers have counted the whales that pass by, compensated for those missed at night or because of poor weather conditions, and revised the total population estimates to 16,928 whales. Even though Scammon estimated the pre-exploitation population at 30,000 to 40,000 animals, his figures are now regarded as much too high, and the original population is now believed to have been approximately what it is today. Having survived two massive onslaughts, the resilient California gray whale has managed to return to its original numbers.

GIGI WAS the only large whale ever maintained in captivity. On March 11, 1971, a Sea World expedition to Scammon's Lagoon captured her and brought her back to San Diego in a specially designed sling rigged aboard the boat. She was 18 feet 2 inches long and weighed 4,300 pounds. She was put into a 55,000-gallon holding tank, where the handlers tried to feed her a mixture composed of whipping cream, cod-liver oil, yeast, ground squid, bonito, corn oil, vitamins and water. In her first two weeks in captivity, Gigi ate nothing and lost over 150 pounds. When the cream was eliminated from the mixture, however, the young whale began to feed (at first she was fed by inserting a hose into the corner of her mouth and pumping in the mixture), and soon she began to regain the weight she had lost.

In the next four months, she gained over a thousand pounds in weight and increased her length by almost two feet, so she had to be moved from her original tank to one that held over 100,000 gallons. From that moment onward, Gigi became the star attraction at Sea World. In addition to her place in Sea World's exhibition schedule, however (she was taught no tricks; she was just *there*), she was the subject of numerous scientific tests, since she was the first—and although no one knew it at the time, the last—large whale ever in a position to be examined clinically. Her respiration, metabolism and heartbeat were monitored; her blubber thickness measured; her blood was tested for coagulation; her chromosomes examined; her feeding patterns analyzed (after a while she began to eat frozen squid which she slurped up from the bottom of the tank); and the sounds she uttered were recorded and analyzed.*

After eight months at Sea World, Gigi had gained 4,200 pounds, and because she was now 24 feet long, she was transferred to a million-gallon tank. At her rate of gain (she was eating over a ton of squid every day, which resulted in a daily weight increase of 25 pounds), it was obvious that she would soon be too big even for this tank, and plans were developed for her release. It was decided to release her in March, in the hope that she would be able to join the rest of the gray whales as they passed by southern California on their way north.

On March 13, 1972, almost a year to the day after she had been captured in Scammon's Lagoon, Gigi was released into the Pacific five miles off San Diego. She had been equipped with a radio tag that would broadcast her whereabouts to receivers on shore, and she had been cryogenically branded to further assist in her future identification. (The radio pack was designed so that the bolts holding it to the blubber on her back would rust through in six months.) The radio signals were monitored until May, when they

ceased. Subsequently, there have been several confirmed sightings of Gigi, and by and large, the experiment in which "a baby whale was borrowed for science and returned to the sea" (the subtitle of the book by Eleanor Coerr and William Evans) is considered a qualified success. There were some who felt that the removal of a baby whale from its mother and its natural environment was an unnecessarily harsh expedient in the interests of science (especially since the science was often conducted in full view of admission-paying tourists), but since Gigi was returned to the wild and probably rejoined the herd, the venture cannot be regarded as a failure.

When the mystery writer Erle Stanley Gardner went to Baja in 1960, it was a largely undiscovered place, visited mostly by intrepid (or foolish) drivers of vehicles that could withstand the punishing terrain and the almost complete lack of facilities. (John Steinbeck had visited the Sea of Cortez with his friend Doc Ricketts in 1940, and wrote *The Log from the Sea of Cortez,* but they were mostly concerned about the life of the tide pools.) Shortly after his return, the prolific author of the Perry Mason novels wrote up his adventures in Baja in a book he called *Hunting the Desert Whale.* Through the lens of hindsight, Gardner's observations do not seem all that electrifying, but for 1960, before it had occurred to anyone that watching whales could become a veritable *industry,* it was a unique experience. Gardner and his small expedition camped at Scammon's Lagoon and observed the whales from small boats that they had towed all the way from Los Angeles. At that time, nobody really knew if the fabled "devilfish" of Scammon's time would endanger the little boats, and a lot of the book is devoted to the fears of the people about getting swatted by the whale's flukes or having their boats sunk. It would be another fifteen years before commercial vessels would enter the protected waters of the Baja lagoons, as whale-watching blossomed into a prosperous and lucrative industry.

Before long, hundreds, then thousands, would line the shores of southern California to watch the annual parade of the whales. At first it was a casual practice, where watchers simply stood at convenient vantage points and observed the whales as they swam by. Later, as the plight of the world's whales became known, more importance was attached to the viewing, even though these particular animals were not

*The entire issue of *Marine Fisheries Review* for April 1974 is devoted to the California gray whale, but most of the studies relate to Gigi. All the above-mentioned studies are included in this publication.

March 13, 1972. After a year in captivity at Sea World in San Diego, Gigi the juvenile gray whale was returned to the sea. She was positively identified in 1977, indicating that she had been successfully reintroduced to the wild.

considered endangered. They were whales, after all, and they were the closest ones we had.

In the winter of 1975–76, a most unusual phenomenon occurred in Laguna San Ignacio. Rather than cavort at a distance, some of the whales—often mothers with calves—began to approach the inflatable boats that contained the watchers. These "friendly whales" initiated contact with the boats, and even allowed people to touch them. Many over-enthusiastic observers saw in this activity the great breakthrough they had been waiting for: the whales obviously wanted to make friends with them. Since we were no longer killing them, the argument went, they had no reason to fear us. Quickly, this "curi-

ous" or "friendly" behavior became the *sine qua non* of the serious whale-watchers. Now mere observation was not enough; one hoped for interspecies contact, the experience of a lifetime. Hundreds of cetophiles flocked to Baja California in hopes of actually making contact with the "friendlies." Not all the whales were interested in such activities, but soon stories began to circulate about "the whales having forgiven us," and "a new era in human-cetacean interactions." A California newspaper trumpeted, "Gray Whales Losing Fear of Man, Evidence Indicates."

Unfortunately, mythology or mysticism clouded the whale-watchers' vision. Some of them forgot (or more likely, they never knew) that in Scammon's day

One of the "friendly" gray whales surfaces amidst the whale-watchers at San Ignacio Lagoon, Baja California.

these whales were known as "devilfish" because the females often attacked when their babies were threatened. In their overwhelming desire to make contact with the whales, the whale-watchers overlooked one of the fundamental precepts of mammalian behavior: the protective instinct of a mother for her young.

During the 1956 "Operation Heartbeat," one of the skiffs manned by Dr. White's crew was holed by an irate mother whale, and in April 1977 a similar incident occurred off Oxnard, California. A weekend sailor named Tom Bowers was in his twenty-seven-foot fiberglass boat when he encountered a pair of gray whales, obviously mother and calf. The whales sounded to starboard, and shortly thereafter, a single adult rammed the boat from the port side, lifting the stern three feet out of the water. Then the whale dove and whacked the stern with its tail, breaking a railing and hitting a crewman on the head, knocking him across the deck.

In late February of 1983, a small boat (known locally as a *ponga*) set out into Scammon's Lagoon with twelve tourists and an operator aboard. Although the Mexican government then prohibited boats from entering the lagoon from the Pacific, one man was authorized to take out tourists from shore. (Now the lagoon is closed to all tourism, to allow the whales

to breed in peace.) With several whales sighted in the distance, but none closer than fifty to seventy-five yards according to eyewitness reports, the captain cut the motor so the boat was drifting silently. Without warning, an adult whale rose up beneath the *ponga* and lifted it almost out of the water with its head. The little boat slid off the whale's rostrum, and at that moment one of the passengers, an elderly man, suffered a heart attack and died. As the whale and the boat subsided into the noisy, frothy confusion, the whale dove and struck the boat with its 12-foot flukes. In the turmoil, a second elderly man was cracked on the head, either by falling or by being hit with an oar. He was taken to shore and then flown to a California hospital, where he died from head injuries after two days of intensive care.

In the past, sperm whalers feared for their lives when they harpooned a whale from a flimsy boat, for the whales often splintered the boats in their frenzied struggles to escape the lance driven deep into their bodies. Whalemen were often seriously injured and some were killed when their cockleshell boats foundered or broke up under the thrashing flukes of a harpooned cachalot in its death throes. (There are very few instances of uninjured whales' attacking whaleboats, but there are some. Off the

Chilean coast in the 1830s, the sperm whale Mocha Dick developed the habit of attacking and sinking whaling *ships* as well as the boats that had been lowered to pursue him.)

At Scammon's Lagoon, however, the whale had not been harpooned. If it was protecting its young, none of the eyewitnesses saw any other whale in the vicinity, before, during or after the attack. (There is always the possibility that the attacking whale was protecting some other whales that were far away—or underwater—and so were not seen by the whale-watchers.) We do not know if the whale's actions were intentional or unintentional, aggressive or protective. While there are many things about the behavior of whales that we do not understand, we can probably assume that their actions are the result of some stimulus or intention, since very few creatures behave in an arbitrary or capricious manner. Only our ignorance or our inability to analyze their behavior would lead us to suggest the possibility of random or uncontrolled actions. Whatever it was that triggered the whale's actions, it was not the boat's motor, and there were no other whales visible.

When the first "friendly whale" initiated contact in 1976, no one knew that its approach was not an isolated, anomalous act. Although never common, these encounters did reoccur, with different whales and in different lagoons. (One such encounter took place off Vancouver Island in 1982.) The "attack" at Scammon's Lagoon might be nothing more than the panicked reaction of a single whale that was somehow disturbed and accidentally hit the boat. But what if it wasn't? What if this act presages others of a similar nature?

Because of their proximity to shore on the southward leg of their migration, gray whales have been the object of concentrated whale-watching, mostly in southern California. In January and February they pass San Francisco and Monterey, then Los Angeles, and finally San Diego, their last view of America before they enter Mexican waters and the sparsely populated Baja Peninsula. In the lagoons, they are observed from boats (an activity now carefully regulated by the Mexican government), which has resulted in an enormous number of people being exposed to whales—and vice versa.

Norwegian Postmortem

BECAUSE OF the fjords and the tendency of various whale species to come close to shore, particularly in northern Norway, the country has had a long tradition of small-whale hunting. Apparently, before the Norwegians killed the small whales, there was also a traditional fishery for basking sharks (*Cetorhinus maximus*). Curiously, this shark, one of the largest fishes in the world, can get to be larger than a small whale. Minke whales, which often enter the fjords to feed on fish, were hunted from about 1880 by fishermen in small boats which averaged about sixty tons. The Norwegians would eventually dominate whaling in the Northern and Southern Hemispheres, but the whaling carried on by fishermen—later to be

referred to by the International Whaling Commission as "small-type coastal whaling"—is different from the kind that involved trips to the forbidding Antarctic, exploding-grenade harpoons, and carcasses of whales being flensed on the decks of five-hundred-foot floating factories. This whaling was on a much smaller scale, and it provided an additional source of income for the fishermen. Small-whale hunting had begun around 1920, along the Møre coast of west-central Norway. It spread northward to the Lofoten Islands and Troms County, with its center at Vestfjorden. At the same time, there was a fishery for belugas around Spitsbergen. When the Norwegians quit whaling in 1967, it was assumed that that was the end of the story. Although they had pioneered technological whale-killing and dominated the industry for a century, it appeared that they were finally willing to let it go.

Then the Japanese introduced the concept of small-type coastal whaling at the IWC meeting in Auckland in 1988, and because the idea was not summarily dismissed, the Norwegians remembered that they too had a tradition of coastal whaling. They geared up for a presentation of their economic and sociological requirements, and by the IWC's fortieth annual meeting in 1989 (held in San Diego), they were pleading that their indigenous fishermen, like the Japanese, had a history of small-type whaling that went back a thousand years. They (like the Icelanders) quoted the "King's Mirror" (the thirteenth-century description of the various whales found in Icelandic waters), which demonstrated that their whaling history went back to the year 1200. The Norwegians also submitted a request for a scientific-research permit which would allow them to take a few fin whales and minkes in the North Atlantic.

While it would appear that the Norwegians haven't given up whaling altogether, another kind of oil has come to replace whale oil in their scheme of things, one that would have an even more profound effect on their economy.

In 1959 a huge gas field was discovered at Groningen in the Netherlands, suggesting that other fields might be found elsewhere in the North Sea. Prior to geological exploration, boundaries had to be drawn, and dotted lines were put on maps to indicate the offshore limits of Norway, Britain and Denmark. Petroleum geologists were not optimistic about the prospects for oil on the Norwegian continental shelf, and the early results supported their pessimism; the first holes came up dry—if you can have dry holes in the middle of the ocean.

Even though the area was unrelievedly hostile, with high seas, high winds and even higher expenses, the oil companies persevered—as oil companies will, given the potential rewards—and on December 23, 1969, the drilling rig *Ocean Viking* produced the first oil from the North Sea, at Ekofisk. (Place names are not of much use in the ocean, but the oil companies name the locations where drilling takes place.) In the 1970s, other international companies discovered more fields under the North Sea; the French firm Elf

found the gas field known as Frigg, and Mobil discovered Statfjord, the world's largest offshore oil field. Shell Oil found a gigantic gas field west of Bergen, which was named Troll.

By 1975, after four boom years, Norway was producing more oil than it could consume, and began exporting it. The oil was mostly transported by tankers bunkered at sea, but a pipeline was built from Ekofisk to Teesside, in Scotland, in 1975, and another to Emden, Germany, in 1977. Although foreign companies were responsible for the discovery of the oil, Norway has "Norwegianized" this important new sector of her economy, and Statoil is 100-percent government-owned. Before the 1985 fall in oil prices, oil accounted for 20 percent of Norway's gross national product, and 40 percent of her export earnings. The North Sea oil fields produced some 1.5 million barrels of oil a day. Having 35 percent of the known oil reserves in Western Europe, and an astonishing 50 percent of the natural gas, Norway can provide about one-quarter of the total European energy requirements.

Even though the figures on the Norwegian resource are almost incomprehensible (an estimated 12 billion barrels of oil and 65 trillion cubic feet of gas), there is still a finite amount of oil under the North Sea. That is not to say that the Norwegians have located all the oil fields, and they certainly haven't gotten all of the oil from the wells they have sunk, but they know they cannot continue to pump oil indefinitely. Unlike whales, oil fields are a nonrenewable resource. (Even more unlike whales, oil reserves cannot be seen. The water at Ekofisk is about two hundred feet deep, and the oil reserves are found in rocks another ten thousand feet below the sea bed.)

North of Finnmark, where the lines of longitude converge toward the Pole, the question of sovereignty arises out of the ice. The USSR has rightful claims to the oil and gas off her almost endless northern shoreline, from Murmansk eastward to the Bering Sea, and even Spitsbergen—which belongs to Norway—has oil potential which has been investigated by the Soviets. As of 1989, there was no agreement between Norway and the USSR on the line of demarcation in the Barents Sea.

The Russians might again pose a threat to Norwegian industry, but the real lesson to be learned from Norway's two adventures with oil can be found in the plaintive reflection of the Norwegian whaling historians Johann Tønnessen and Arne Odd Johnsen: "It is quite possible that today and well into the future the annual catch of 9,000 to 10,000 units would have been possible, and this would have supplied the world with 200,000 tons of fat, the main raw material for 300 million kg. of margarine, and 300,000 to 400,000 tons of meat to a hungry world."

The Norwegians and their accomplices heedlessly and irresponsibly destroyed most of the world's rorquals. (Some of the whaling, ironically, was done in the same area where the oil rigs now tower above the cold gray water.) It took some five hundred years for the whalers to decimate the right whales of the world, but that was because their breeding grounds were so spread out and hard to locate. The open-boat sperm whale fishery, begun in the early decades of the eighteenth century, lasted a little over a hundred years. (The second, mechanized phase of this fishery, where Australian, South African, Japanese and Soviet whalers cut down the survivors of the first phase, took another hundred years.) From the moment Svend Foyn of Vestfold shot his first blue whale off Norway, only seventy years elapsed before the whalers had demolished the world stock of these creatures. The greed of the whaling nations for short-term profits at the expense of the survival of the most magnificent animals on earth is an unforgivable crime against nature. Few humans will ever see the largest animal ever to have lived on earth powerfully rolling its broad back out of the water and raising its broad flukes into the air as it gracefully descends into the depths that once were its sanctuary.

The End of Whaling in Iceland

EARLY ICELANDERS did not hunt the minke because they believed that it was a "good" whale sent by God to protect them against the "bad" whale species. According to Icelandic whaling historians, minkes have been hunted for meat since 1914. Early in the fishery, small fishing boats with 38-mm. cannons were employed, but later on the boats and the armament became larger and more efficient. Icelanders ate the meat of these whales, utilizing the flukes, flippers, tongue, blubber and ventral grooves. Before controls were imposed in 1974, the fishery was completely unregulated. Icelandic authorities set catch limits and quotas for their own whalers, but it was not until 1977 that quotas for North Atlantic minkes were established by the IWC.

Along with the capelin, hake, cod and herring that make up the major proportion of Iceland's exports, fishermen also hunted the various species of large whales that inhabited or passed through the waters of Denmark Strait and the Norwegian Sea. These waters were familiar to Dutch and British whalers, who managed to eliminate the bowhead from the North Atlantic, even as far north as Spitsbergen, in the seventeenth and eighteenth centuries. In the early 1860s, two Americans, Thomas W. Roys (who in 1848 discovered the bowhead whales of the Bering Sea) and G. A. Lilliendahl, a fireworks manufacturer from New York, invented a primitive rocket harpoon that presaged the one perfected by the Norwegian Svend Foyn, and to test it out, they went a-whaling in the waters of Iceland. In 1865, they set up a shore station at Seydisfjördur and killed 49 whales, mostly blues. Although the method was successful, the company was affected by the slump in oil prices after the Civil War, and went bankrupt in 1867. The Norwegians continued whaling in the rich Icelandic waters until the Icelanders drove them out.

In response to the perceived Norwegian threat to their whales, the Icelandic parliament (*Althing*) declared a ban on whaling from 1915 onward. This ban continued until 1935, when the government issued a permit for a single station to be opened at Talknafjörd on the wild northwest corner of the island. When the first whaling station opened at Hvalfjörd (north of Reykjavik) in 1949, the crews were Norwegian, but they were there to train the Icelanders, and by the early 1950s, the Norwegians had left the field to their apt pupils. Iceland was one of the original signatories to the 1949 Convention for the Regulation of Whaling (the forerunner of the IWC), and was therefore involved in every decision from 1949 to the present that has affected the whaling industry.

Although Iceland boasts the longest continuous parliament in the world (its *Althing* has met annually since the year 903), it has a checkered history of occupation. It was an independent country from about 900 to 1262, when it allied itself politically with Norway. The Danes took over in 1380 and ruled until 1918, when the republic once again became independent. As a part of Denmark, Iceland was neutral during World War I, but during the second World War, she found herself occupied first by the British and then the Yanks because of her important strategic position in the North Atlantic. The last ties with the Danish crown were severed in 1944, and two years later, all combat troops were withdrawn, but permission was granted for the United States to maintain an air base at Keflavik. When Iceland joined the North Atlantic Treaty Organization in 1949, Keflavik became an important base in the NATO network.

From 1949 to 1985, Icelandic whalers from Hvalfjörd, operating well within the IWC's restrictions, took an annual average of 234 fin whales, 82 sperm whales, and 68 sei whales.* Fisherman/whalers from small villages also took minke whales, but until 1977 the minke was not considered important or large enough for its catch statistics to be recorded. From that year until the moratorium, Icelanders participated in the allocated take of North Atlantic minkes, along with Norway and Denmark. The discrete stocks of minkes were known as the East Greenland/Iceland Stock and the West Norway/Faeroe Islands Stock. (The IWC only determined how many whales from a given stock could be taken; the division of the spoils was up to the individual whaling nations.) When the moratorium was passed in Brighton in 1982, only four nations filed objections: Peru, the USSR, Norway and Japan. After a bitter battle in parliament, Iceland decided not to file an objection, so the world assumed—erroneously, as it turned out—that Iceland was going to retire its whaling ships and personnel. Those whaling nations that had filed objections obviously intended to continue whaling despite the moratorium. Although they eventually dropped their objections, Japan and Norway precipitated the major controversy of the late 1980s—the ruckus over "scientific-research whaling."

Because commercial whaling was officially over as of the 1985–86 season, those nations that wanted or needed whale meat had to find some way of collecting it legally. They hit first upon the scheme that had been employed by the Japanese in 1976 when they issued themselves a scientific permit to collect 240 Bryde's whales in the North Pacific. The resultant outcry was so shrill that the Japanese retired this strategy for a decade, preferring instead to work out various deals, particularly with the United States (the nation with the most effective anti-whaling legislation, but also with the strongest interest in the Japanese money machine), that would enable them to take a small number of whales in spite of the worldwide ban on whaling. This strategy failed too, so they reintroduced the "scientific whaling" argument, where they maintained that they had to kill a number of whales for research purposes, most of which had to do with the health or fecundity of a given population, or as some critics put it, "how many whales there were before they started killing them." The Japanese story is told elsewhere, but since Japan plays a significant role in the story of research whaling in Iceland, mention must be made of this unholy alliance.

The relationship among the major whaling nations has never been clear. It was easy enough to identify countries who had a viable whaling industry and would therefore be adversely affected by a moratorium which would put them out of business, such as Norway, Iceland, Japan and the USSR. There were,

*In 1956, a most peculiar episode in the long interaction of whales and men took place off Iceland. Fishermen decided that their livelihood was being threatened by the presence of large numbers of killer whales on the fishing grounds, and after trying to clear the nets of orcas themselves, the Icelanders called in the U.S. Air Force. The killers were dispersed with machine guns, rockets and depth charges.

however, other nations, such as Peru, Brazil, the Philippines, and South Korea, where the whaling industry was wholly or partially funded and manned by Japanese nationals, and while these whaling companies provided some employment for the local workers, very little of the product ended up in Brazil or Peru. Latin Americans have never developed much of a taste for whale meat, and the meat and oil from these South American and other Asian operations went directly to Japan. It was not at all clear, therefore, when the Icelanders introduced a "research whaling" proposal in 1985, whether they were acting independently or in concert with the Japanese. (Their claim that in order to fund their research they had to sell the meat to Japan raised a few eyebrows about their scientific credibility.)

At the 1985 IWC meeting, Iceland submitted the first of many "research proposals." For their science, they said they needed an "experimental catch" of 80 fin whales, 40 sei whales, and 80 minkes. (Also in their 1985 proposal was the suggestion that they might take a "limited experimental catch" of blue whales and humpbacks, but when the scientific community got word of this bizarre idea, it was quickly dropped.) Because Iceland had been content to maintain a position as a small nation with only a passing interest in whaling throughout the first decades of the IWC, her representatives (one of whom was chairman of the commission for 1979–81) kept a low profile during the early skirmishes of the "scientific whale wars," leaving the dirty work to that perennial whipping boy, Japan. For two years, the Scientific Committee debated the subject of scientific research whaling without coming to any conclusions. The longer the debate went on, however, the more nations decided to hop on the bandwagon, since it appeared likely that research whaling might indeed be a feasible idea.

At first it was only the Japanese who were proposing to kill whales for science, but then the Icelanders mounted an all-out campaign to take assorted whales for "research." Despite their articulate arguments, it was still obvious that this was nothing more than commercial whaling dressed up in fancy clothes. The Korean delegation, adept as always at obfuscation, also submitted a research proposal, but it was so poorly conceived and written that the Scientific Committee dismissed it out of hand. It is not

at all clear as to whether or not the Koreans continued whaling under their own permit, and if they did, what became of the meat. (It is not difficult to imagine that the Koreans might have sold the meat to the Japanese, just across the Korean Strait.)

The anti-whaling lobby was still not convinced that any of this so-called "science" was necessary; to them it looked very much like commercial whaling under another name. As opposed to the "benign" (also called "non-lethal") research that had been suggested years earlier as a means of studying whales without killing them, this seemed to be a throwback to the bad old days, where whales were killed for commerce, and then scientists were allowed to examine the carcasses. Why the sudden interest in examining dead whales when so many thousands could have been examined in the recent past? With the proposed sale of the meat to the Japanese, the odor of whaling wafted past the noses of the conservationist commissioners.

For the first year, the issue of "scientific permit whaling" was sent back to committee for reconsideration, and in 1986, the commission denied the applications of Japan, Iceland and Korea. Even though their requests were turned down, Iceland and Japan continued to kill whales for research. The Japanese were taking whales for their research program (maybe), but there was no question about the Icelanders: they were taking whales for the Japanese. The Icelandic program, which was originally estimated at 48 million Icelandic kroner, or approximately 1.2 million U.S. dollars, depended on the sale of the surplus whale meat to Japan. If they were able to sell the meat to Japan, they would realize some $30 million, a tidy profit for a "research program." If the Icelanders could not dispose of the 200 whales they were asking for, they would end up with more whale meat than their entire population could possibly consume.

In hopes of getting IWC approval, Iceland reduced its request from 200 to 120 whales. Even from 120 whales, the Icelanders would produce some 4,000 tons of meat, which is 8,000,000 pounds. If they didn't sell any or feed it to minks, that would work out to 33.3 pounds of whale meat for every man, woman and child in Iceland. At first, they were going to export 95 percent of the meat to Japan, but under pressure from the United States they reduced this figure to 49 percent, since they had to keep a "majority" of the meat in Iceland. This was still not good enough. In an address given in October 1986, Sir Peter Scott, ex-president of the World Wildlife Fund, said, "At this year's meeting, the International Whaling Commission passed a resolution that any whales caught for 'scientific purposes' should be disposed of primarily for local consumption. We have just learned that Iceland will be selling 49 percent of its catch to Japan for meat. This is a travesty of the concept of a catch 'for scientific purposes' and makes a mockery of the International Whaling Commission."

Despite an internal campaign designed to encourage Icelanders to eat more whale meat, the ssons and dottirs remained unconvinced, and the meat which was not fed to minks and foxes on fur farms rotted in the warehouses. (The Icelanders held the United States primarily responsible for their problems over whaling, and when the "Superpower Summit" was scheduled to take place in Reykjavik on October 9, 1986, many of the locals were inclined to boo President Reagan and to lobby for withheld support for the American airbase at Keflavik.)

In October, Greenpeace and the Humane Society of the United States staged a small demonstration outside the hotel in Washington where the Icelandic-American Chamber of Commerce was meeting. This was the first ripple in a wave of protest that would result in a massive boycott of Icelandic fish products. Within the month, those guerrillas who did not believe in economic sanctions or negotiations would strike a blow that would bring the Icelandic whalers to their knees, if not to their senses.

On November 9, 1986, a month after Presidents Reagan and Gorbachev had departed, two men of the Sea Shepherd Society took sledgehammers to the machinery and computers at the whaling station at Hvalfjörd. They then crept aboard two of Iceland's four whaleships as they lay at anchor in Reykjavik, opened the seacocks, and watched the ships sink to the bottom of the harbor. From his home base in Vancouver, Paul Watson told the media: "Iceland's whalers are criminals; they had to be brought to justice." He also threatened to sabotage Norway's whaling industry, but tightened security and lack of opportunity precluded such actions. Most other conservationists—including Greenpeace by this time—condemned Watson's guerrilla tactics, but everyone except the whalers agreed that diplomatic negotiations and boycotts weren't working. The two ships were refloated within ten days, and the Icelanders went back to their "research" whaling, where they planned to take 80 fin whales and 40 seis.

The Japanese continued to create a market for meat—legal or illegal—and by December 1986, they had imported 3,602 metric tons from Iceland. (Obviously, not all of this was from the 1986 harvest. There was a very strong possibility that they had simply stored their 1985 meat, relabeled it, and were now selling it to the Japanese as the product of their 1986 "research whaling.") In March 1987, the *Aoshima Maru,* a Japanese reefer, loaded hundreds of tons of whale meat in Iceland and prepared to sail to Japan. Unfortunately, the ship stopped at Hamburg, and because the Germans are signatories to the CITES (Convention for International Trade in Endangered Species) treaty which prohibits traffic in endangered species products, they seized the entire cargo on March 20.

The Icelanders and the Japanese submitted formal research proposals to the IWC at the 1987 meeting in Bournemouth. (So did the South Koreans, whose proposal was again considered unworthy of consideration, and later, the Norwegians.) The issue of scientific research whaling quickly became the major issue of the meeting. Much lobbying and name-calling took place, since one side felt (or claimed that they felt) that their scientific sovereignty was being threatened, while the other side felt that they were being forced into a position where, having successfully eliminated commercial whaling, they were being asked to condone it all over again, merely by giving it another name.

The forces of conservation formed a sort of united front, and using boycotts, economic pressure, political discussions and the inevitable propaganda, attacked the Icelanders. Even the Icelanders attacked the Icelanders. An organization called the "Icelandic Whale Friends Society" attached a pirate flag to the mast of one of the whalers in Reykjavik harbor, and a group of Icelandic biologists published an open letter to their government in which they said, ". . . we consider that Icelandic whaling is not justified under the present circumstances and it is wrong to associate it with science." Under increased pressure

When Swedish seaman Mats Forsberg visited the whaling station at Hvalfjörd in the summer of 1987, he was surprised to discover that some of the workers at the Icelandic station were Japanese.

brought about by Greenpeace and other environmental organizations, large importers of Icelandic fish products, such as Arthur Treacher's and Long John Silver's seafood restaurant chains, canceled their orders with the Icelandic suppliers. The fishing industry, Iceland's major source of export income, was dealt a crippling blow, and her intransigence over the whaling issue no longer seemed viable. Iceland still had one card to play, and she played it brilliantly. The United States, the source of Iceland's troubles over whales and fish, was Iceland's tenant at the air base at Keflavik.

A Harvard Law School–educated Icelandic lawyer named Gudmundur Eiriksson took the floor and delivered an articulate and impassioned plea for the sovereign right of Iceland to pursue its own science without interference from either the IWC or the United States. Implicit in his remarks was a threat to oust the U.S. forces from the NATO base at Keflavik if the United States persisted in hamstringing Icelandic research whaling. Although there were only 120 whales at stake, the discussions had pushed the

two countries to the brink of a major international incident. Would the United States cave in to the demands of little Iceland? Were 120 whales a fair trade for a strategic military base? Could tiny Iceland push the mighty United States government around? (Greenpeace investigators later obtained evidence that during the IWC meetings in Bournemouth in 1987, the United States commissioner was in regular contact with highly placed government officials, and instructed to be "constructively neutral" during the negotiations. This naturally enraged the anti-whaling forces, who expected the U.S. delegation to be in the forefront of the battle to thwart the devious "research whalers.")

The heretofore insignificant whaling issues were taken to the highest diplomatic levels: on September 9, 1987, a delegation of U.S. negotiators flew to Iceland to discuss the issues and crafted a bilateral agreement: Iceland could take 20 sei whales without U.S. sanctions; in return, Iceland was to submit her full research proposal to the IWC in 1988. Icelandic Foreign Minister Hannibalsson met with U.S. Secretary of State George Schultz on October 19 in Washington. Japan bought no more whale meat from Iceland (because they were promised fishing concessions if they refrained), and the North Atlantic seemed once again secure.

After the stormy 1987 IWC meeting at Bournemouth, the Icelandic *Althing* debated the pros and cons of scientific research whaling, trying to find a way to avoid certification under the Pelly Amendment that would embargo all fisheries products from the offending nation. By the spring of 1989, "research whaling" in Iceland had taken a most peculiar turn indeed. A strike of the scientists' union in Iceland effectively sidelined all scientists—obviously including those who would have been aboard the research whaleships—rendering the whole issue moot. Only a month before the IWC meeting in San Diego in June, the Icelanders had not decided if they could continue scientific whaling without any scientists, and the IWC could come to no binding conclusions either.

The environmental community, however, had no such reservations, and they initiated another boycott that had the Icelandic fish industry—and therefore, the entire Icelandic economy—reeling. Major buyers of Icelandic fish products, such as Wendy's and Long John Silver, canceled their contracts with Samband, the Icelandic fishermen's cooperative. Tengelmann, a giant West German supermarket chain, canceled $10 million worth of contracts. The Icelanders were ready to negotiate.

During the year that passed between IWC meetings, the United States and Iceland negotiators had evidently arrived at a compromise—obviously related to the NATO base at Keflavik—and when the issue of scientific research whaling was raised at the 1989 meetings at San Diego, a surprisingly restrained U.S. commissioner in the person of William Evans accepted the "generous offer" of the Icelanders to only take 68 fin whales and no sei whales. Iceland announced that it had no intentions to take any whales for scientific purposes in 1990, and no plans after that. When Japanese and Norwegian proposals came before the commission, they were met with disapproval and rancor, and voted down with a recommendation that the governments "reconsider" their proposals. As of 1989, it appeared that the Icelanders were finished with whaling.

The Bowhead Issue Continues

THE MOMENT at which the Alaskan Eskimos gave up their old ways and adopted modern whaling methods has been recorded. In his autobiography, Charlie Brower, the manager of the whaling station at Barrow, tells of the time he had been whaling with the Eskimos, "when the first whale anyone had seen in days broke directly in front of the *umiak*. There was only time to grab a handy whale gun and shoot before it pitched under the ice. . . . Whether or not my eleventh hour success with a bombgun made any deep impression on the Eskimos, the spring of 1888 marked the last season in which they kept to their old whaling customs. After that the younger crowd began more generally to adopt our whaling gear, tackles, guns, bombs and all."

The introduction of modern whaling gear would appear to be a boon to the Eskimos, but it would turn out to be one of the most troublesome and contentious issues in what became a ferocious battle between those who would save the whales and those who would save the Eskimos.

During the fifty years that followed the demise of steam whaling, the Eskimos did not require much saving, unless it was from the cold or from the innovations that were being steadily introduced to their "primitive" culture. They retained many of their original whaling techniques, since they had been developed over thousands of years and worked as well as or better than anything the Yankees had come up with. Eskimo hunters knew all about the bowhead whales, the weather, the ice. Skin boats were better for these waters than wood, so they continued to build and sail these graceful craft. Perhaps the most significant holdover, however, was the societal significance of the whale hunt. In the early days (pre-Roys, that is), a whale kill was a major event in the life of a village—in fact, it was *the* major event of the year—and the harpooner was greatly honored. After the kill, a whaling feast took place, and this too was integral to the life of the coastal Eskimo.

It is true that the whales were only bothered by the Eskimos as they migrated along the coast, and left alone when they reached their feeding grounds near Banks Island. But the Eskimo hunt, which historically had impinged but little on the total whale population, suddenly took a great leap forward, as yet another form of technology intruded on the otherwise isolated lives of the bowheads. Where the discovery of petroleum had affected them positively, sparing them from the oil-hungry industries that consumed their oil as unthinkingly as a whale consumes copepods, another intrusion of the petroleum industry would threaten the very sanctuary into which they took refuge from the whalers. The oil was seeping along the North Slope, and once again the bowheads were imperiled. It was Charlie Brower who discovered the oil seeps in the Sagavanirktok River delta at Prudhoe Bay.

The Eskimos had begun whaling to feed themselves; when the whalers arrived, this aboriginal whaling changed as more and more Eskimos were employed by the whalers, especially when the shore stations were set up. Eskimos who had no previous whaling experience drifted to the coastal villages and obtained jobs at the stations at Point Hope and Point Barrow. With the decline and disappearance of the whaling industry, the Eskimos returned to their aboriginal roots and for the next sixty years or so, they took about 15 whales a year, depending on conditions. Floyd Durham has done a study of the annual Eskimo catches at the three major whaling villages, Barrow, Point Hope and Wainwright, from 1852 to 1973. For the three villages, the totals (and the number of years for which data are available) were as follows:

Barrow (52 years): 371 whales (7 per year)
Point Hope (60 years): 241 whales (4 per year)
Wainwright (32 years): 48 whales (1.5 per year)

The total was 660 whales, and the combined average is 12.5 per year. Other villages also took whales, adding another 22 for the years 1961–73, for a combined total average of 14.5.

Before 1970, few Eskimos went whaling, because only a few could afford to lay out $500 for a weekly food bill for a crew of ten, not to mention $8,000 for a boat, guns, ammunition, tents, sleds and other gear. Then construction jobs on projects like the trans-Alaska pipeline became available to Eskimos, and there was a sharp increase in the number of young men who could afford the equipment to become whaling captains. By 1976 the number of crews had risen threefold. In that year, Barrow alone sent out thirty-six crews. Accordingly, the number of whales killed leapt upward.

In 1972, the Eskimos took 37 whales, but this number was not broken down further. In subsequent years, however, the totals were as follows:

YEAR	Killed and Recovered	Struck or Killed but Lost	TOTAL
1973	37	10	47
1974	20	31	51
1975	15	28	43
1976	48	43	91
1977	29	79	108
1978	12	6	18
1979	12	15	27
1980	16	18	34

It is obvious why the International Whaling Commission decided to curtail the Eskimo whalers after the 1976 and 1977 seasons: they were clearly on the way to eliminating the bowhead.

It was not until 1972 that the bowhead controversy came to the attention of the International Whaling Commission and immediately became an issue of international significance. Prior to that year, even though the IWC's mandate clearly included the bowhead, it was overlooked.*

In the twenty-third *Annual Report* of the IWC (1973), the following comment appears:

The [Scientific] Committee reviewed the scanty material on bowhead (Greenland right) whales in the Arctic. This included a paper by A. W. Mansfield (SC/24/17). It was agreed that the Committee ask the Commission to request Denmark, USA and USSR to obtain information on the aboriginal kill of bowhead, gray and other whales and report this to the Bureau [of International Whaling Statistics], if it is not now being done. The Committee also asks the Commission to urge the United States to take steps to reduce the waste due to lost whales of all species in its aboriginal fishery.

In the following year's *Report,* the committee "noted with pleasure the response of the countries concerned to last year's request for data on the aboriginal take of bowhead and other whales in the Arctic. The take of bowhead whales in the Arctic in 1972 was 37, all by United States aborigines." In 1975, the Scientific Committee "expressed its concern" about the lack of information on the stock and the increase in the catch, and in 1976 they requested more information from whalers' logbooks to try to determine the unexploited bowhead population. In 1977, the committee's tone was less conciliatory:

The Committee had available reports on studies of bowhead whales in Alaska. . . . They included new information on the number of whales killed, killed but lost, and struck but lost. There was evidence of increased effort. The initial size of the stock and its present condition are still unknown. The committee most strongly urges that this situation be rectified . . . and recommends that necessary steps be taken to limit the expansion of the fishery and to reduce the loss rate of struck whales (without increasing total take).

In 1978 the Scientific Committee "reviewed the new evidence available," and then wrote that

---

*In the 1946 *International Convention for the Regulation of Whaling,* the instrument that established the IWC, these words appeared: "Considering that the history of whaling has seen over-fishing of one area after another and of one species of whale after another to such a degree that it is essential to protect all species of whales from further over-fishing." The subject of "subsistence" or "aboriginal" whaling, however, would not be addressed until 1971, and would not be published until 1972.

"The best available scientific evidence indicates that the present stock size may be as high as 2,000 and as low as 600, 6–10% of an estimated initial stock." With the bowhead population in such bad shape, the committee finally took action. They wrote: "The Committee believes that on biological grounds exploitation of this species must cease. . . ." Following their recommendations, the commission "confirmed the Protection status of these stocks," and adopted a complete ban on bowhead whaling. The vote in the Plenary Session was 16 to 0, with the United States abstaining.

Conservationists applauded the IWC's decision, since it clearly seemed to support the American position as a leader in whale preservation. The Eskimos, however, didn't think very much of it. According to Jacob Adams, a Barrow whaling captain, "The Eskimos, stunned by the IWC moratorium which they saw as brought about by their own government's failures, responded initially with anger to this attack on their nutritional and cultural well-being." Upon learning of the decision, the Eskimos formed the Alaska Eskimo Whaling Commission (AEWC), and immediately petitioned the United States government to file an objection to the IWC's moratorium on bowhead whaling. The AEWC maintained that the IWC had no jurisdiction over them, and anyway, they knew a lot more about bowhead whales than some scientists from Australia or South Africa. There was the implicit threat that no matter what the IWC said, or for that matter, what the United States government said, the Eskimos were going to pursue their traditional and inalienable right to hunt the bowhead.

Public hearings were held in Washington. Every government agency that had anything to do with wildlife, Eskimos, or foreign policy got into the act. Press releases proliferated. ("Bowhead whale objection would doom all whales, conservationists warn; Carter to decide next week" read the headline on one dated October 14, 1977.) Every conservation organization developed a position and flooded the mails with printed interpretations of it. Newspapers wrote ringing editorials, mostly supporting the whales. For example, the *Washington Post* for October 1 had this to say: "Without serious evidence that a zero kill for one season would impose serious hardship on the natives, the issue shifts to the credibility

An Eskimo hunting party returns to camp towing a bowhead.

of the U.S. position on whaling. For years, we have portrayed ourselves as the world's conscience in whaling matters. For the United States suddenly to go soft when its own interests are involved—even when serious questions are raised about the legitimacy of those interests—is to invite a harsh suspicion of double standards. It is also to invite a return to the old ways of the whaling commission, when any nation could dissent with impunity and head out to the open sea for whales." The President of the United States had to draft a form letter to respond to the barrage of mail he was receiving on the subject of bowhead whales. In this letter, Jimmy Carter said, "Whales have become symbolic of our environmental problems as a whole."

To have accepted the IWC's recommendation would have meant the cessation of all Eskimo whaling, and a "betrayal" of the Eskimos themselves. To protest it, however, the United States would have to file an objection to the IWC resolution, and that had to be done within ninety days of the passage of that resolution. The State Department was not going to file this objection, but on October 21, District Court Judge John Sirica, responding to arguments from the AEWC, issued a temporary restraining order *requiring* the State Department to file an objection. On the day that the ninety-day objection period expired, Sirica's order was overturned, first by the Court of Appeals, and then by the Supreme Court. The United States government then sought a quota of 15 bowheads caught or 30 struck (whichever came first), but the IWC rejected this proposal, and at its special meeting in Tokyo, proposed a quota of 12 caught or 18 struck.

On the ice at Point Barrow in 1987, Eskimo whalers prepare to strip the blubber from the carcass of a bowhead whale. The tons of meat will be saved and eaten.

In the years that followed, as the techniques of counting became more sophisticated, the numbers of bowheads in the Arctic appeared to rise. It was not, of course, a true increase—as many of the advocates of Eskimo whaling would have wanted—but rather resulted from the introduction of new and better ways to find and count the bowheads as they passed the scientists' observation posts on the ice. Also introduced were additional methods for tracking and spotting whales; observers took to the air in small planes, and on shore, acousticians were counting bowheads by listening to them.

Even though the numbers continued to rise, the conservationists fought harder to stop what they considered a wasteful and dangerous practice. (The Eskimos, of course, maintained that they had known all along that the numbers were higher than the scientists said they were.) Biologists, population dynamicists, ethnologists, mathematicians and anthropologists joined the fray, and what had been the

least-known of the world's large whales (its only champion had been William Scoresby, whose book, however accurate, was published in 1820) almost overnight became the most studied species in history.

The battle was joined, but it was never altogether clear who was on what side. The elements of the controversy were always diverse, often too technical, and almost always contradictory. It was clear, for example, that the IWC's Scientific Committee believed that there were too few bowheads to allow any hunting at all. But what was to become of the Eskimos? Were they simply to be told to eat hamburgers and forget their traditions? (Bear in mind that the history of the United States with regard to aboriginal rights has not been a noble one. When Americans weren't taking the land from the Indians, they were shooting them or the buffalos on which the Indians lived, and when that didn't work, they tried to give them smallpox. Given this shameful performance, it was somewhat difficult to argue that the authorities ought to force the Eskimos, the last remaining aborigines, to give up their traditions because some bleeding hearts wanted to save the whales.) Lengthy studies were produced, detailing the Eskimos' nutritional, cultural and economic needs, most of which seemed to involve the bowhead whale. The Alaskan Eskimos were as closely studied as the whales.

In February 1979, the IWC convened a special meeting of experts in Seattle, "in recognition of the fact that in the preceding two years it had become increasingly involved with aboriginal (and in particular, bowhead) whaling." There were separate panels on Wildlife, Nutrition and Cultural Anthropology, and the results were published as an IWC Special Publication in 1982. In his introduction to this symposium, Ray Gambell, Secretary of the IWC, made these remarks:

The IWC has as its primary responsibility the conservation of the world's whale stocks and the orderly development of the whaling industry. The IWC also recognises that subsistence whaling may involve different considerations. It is against this background that the special pleas made by me and on behalf of the Eskimos have to be seen, and we ask that you as technical experts provide us with the necessary information to develop a suitable policy.

Did the IWC in fact "develop a suitable policy"? Under the very unusual circumstances in which it operated, the answer is a qualified yes. The Scientific Committee provided the guidance it was asked to provide, but it recognized that although it regularly recommended a zero quota on bowhead whales, "the Commission has consistently rejected this recommendation on grounds other than scientific ones."

SOME SCIENTISTS wanted to save the whales, and some wanted to save the whalers. The very remoteness of the whales' habitat made the issue even more problematical: nobody was quite sure how many whales there were left, or for that matter, how to find out. And on top of that, there was the continuing discussion about how many whales there *had been*. Counting whales in the high Arctic is difficult enough; trying to figure out how many there were before Thomas Roys arrived in 1848 was nearly impossible.

The near-impossibility of this task did not deter the intrepid scientists. Armed with such weapons as population models, esoteric estimating techniques such as the DeLury method, high-speed computers, airplanes and sophisticated listening devices, they estimated and argued. In 1977, the year in which 108 whales were struck for an all-time record, biologists had published their estimates of the total remaining bowhead population: 800 to 1,200. A year later, they had raised the figure to 2,264. In successive years, the figure would rise annually, until by 1988 it had reached 7,000.

A recent study suggests that there were five distinct stocks of bowheads prior to commercial exploitation. Howard Braham, the director of the Marine Mammal Laboratory in Seattle, estimates that the Spitsbergen stock consisted of some 25,000 animals; the Davis Strait–Baffin Bay stock was somewhere on the order of 11,000; perhaps 700 lived in Foxe Basin–Hudson Bay; 40,000 in the western Arctic (United States); and another 6,500 in the Okhotsk Sea. (The total for all these regions is 83,200, but it must be borne in mind that these are only rough guesses, projected backward. In addition, there is a considerable variable built into the estimates. For example, in his discussion of the numbers, Braham says that in 1848 "the Western Arctic stock once numbered 8,000 to 40,000. . . .") Although there is significant disagreement about the number of bowheads originally in the western Arctic, there is no question at all as to the number left from the Spitsbergen population: zero. An occasional bowhead is spotted in some of the other areas, but most of the world's remaining bowheads are found in the western Arctic.

At the same time the bowhead population was being so variously estimated, scientists were trying to determine what—if any—was a safe number that could be removed from that population (whatever it happened to be) so as not to reduce it over time. According to the 1979 *Report* of the Marine Mammal Commission, "The Commission's activities during 1978 and 1979 have been directed toward achieving the common goals of meeting the legitimate subsistence needs of Eskimos who hunt the bowhead whales and protecting the endangered bowhead population so as to allow its recovery, *if recovery is still possible* [my italics]." The details of this controversy are far too technical to review here, since the differences involve the interpretation of complex mathematical formulae which factor in such things as immature survival rate, a "fecundity" value, length at sexual maturity, and something called "survivorship." Suffice it to say that there were some who predicted the eventual eradication of the population, others who saw it stabilizing, and still others who thought that a minimal "harvest" would *increase* the population over time. And of course there were the Eskimos, who didn't believe a single word—or number—that the scientists produced.

Another element in this fractious equation is the subject of "struck-and-lost" whales. Because the Eskimos' hunting methods were fairly primitive—even with the darting gun and the bomb lance—and the conditions so unavailing for easy whaling with a clear shot, the Eskimo hunters quite often lost whales that had been harpooned—that is, an injured whale escaped under the ice. Thus the "struck-and-lost" whale figures prominently in the discussions, not only because it might die, but also because the hunters did not want to have counted against their quota those whales that escaped.

AS ALWAYS, oil plays an important part in the story of the Eskimos and the whales. On September 10, 1969, the State of Alaska accepted over a thousand bids to lease 179 tracts for oil-drilling on the North Slope, and shortly thereafter found itself richer by more than $1 billion. The oil fields were all in the vast almost empty area bordered by the Brooks Range on the south and the Beaufort Sea on the north. Included in this vast region of ice and tundra (incorporated as the North Slope Borough in 1972, it is larger than forty of the fifty states) are the villages of Barrow, Wainwright and Point Hope. Thus all the whaling villages that struggled to hunt and land bowhead whales are incorporated into the richest oil region in North America. At first the North Slope Borough levied taxes on the oil companies, but the Alaskan legislature voted that it could only raise $4 million per year. In 1971, the passage of the Alaska Native Claims Settlement Act made it possible for the pipeline project to continue, and the jobs provided by this enormous project precipitated a disastrous inflationary spiral. Among the beneficiaries of this economic bonanza were the Eskimos of the whaling villages, who suddenly found themselves making more money in a week than their fathers had earned in a year.* After long administrative and legislative delays, not to mention the problems of building a 789-mile-long, four-foot-diameter pipeline on and over some of the most difficult terrain in the world, the crude oil began to flow on June 20, 1977.

As if the Prudhoe Bay fields were not enough, even more oil was discovered offshore. In December 1979, the oil companies bid more than $1 billion for leasing rights to the eight-hundred-square-mile area off Prudhoe Bay in the Beaufort Sea. Now not only were the whalers involved with petroleum, the whales were too. The proposed drilling sites were in the Mackenzie River delta, off Banks Island in the Beaufort Sea, the whales' feeding grounds.

If and when the oil companies drill there, the destruction of the last habitat of the bowhead is a distinct possibility. Offshore drilling platforms are being built, and the noise of their construction is prodigious. (Remember how sensitive a bowhead's hearing is: it can detect the rattle of an oarlock half a mile away.) Airplanes, helicopters and boats regularly bruise the waters with the sound of their engines, and of course, there is always the possibility of an oil spill. (To date, there have been more than 23,000 oil spills of varying magnitude recorded from the Prudhoe Bay oil fields, including one of 200,000 gallons and another of 658,000 gallons.) The effects of an oil slick in the Beaufort Sea can only be guessed at, but it is a safe guess that it would not be good for the whales. (Whales, of course, breathe air, and would not be immediately affected by oil on their waters, but the effects on the food chain would be disastrous.)

In the middle of the controversy about how many whales there are, how many whales there were, and how many whales were being struck and lost, there was evidently an even larger issue: whether the oil-

---

*In *Going to Extremes,* Joe McGinniss writes (quoting a driller from Mobile, Alabama):
The oil companies used to hire a lot of Eskimos so they would not be accused of racism or of not giving jobs to Alaskans, and the Eskimos were making a thousand dollars a week and most of them hadn't seen a thousand dollars in their whole lives before and it was destroying them. . . . Whaling season was the worst. In spring and fall, they would just up and take off for Barrow or Point Hope and might not come back for a month; not until the season was over and the whale meat all gone. Whaling season was their big event of the year; the pipeline could wait. The oil had been there for thousands of years; let it sit; there were, after all, only a few weeks a year to get a whale.

drilling was going to destroy the habitat of the whales and thus render the whole controversy moot. Even though they recognize that the oil companies pose a serious threat to the whales, the Eskimos see no contradiction in working for the companies that may destroy their cultural nexus. Many of them are employed in Lower Forty-Eight–type jobs; they are plumbers, accountants, teachers, storekeepers—but inherent in their personae is the heart of the hunter. They see themselves as whalers, regardless of where the money to buy the boats comes from.

A valiant but ultimately doomed effort to resolve the problem was made by a California biologist named Ronn Storro-Patterson. His solution was to get the Eskimos to take unendangered gray whales instead of bowheads, thus eliminating all the conflicts. It was an imaginative solution, carefully thought out and presented, but the Eskimos refused to have anything to do with it. They claimed that the skin of the gray whale is covered with barnacles and therefore inedible; the gray whale is too skinny; it lives too far offshore for their little boats; it appears in the summer when they are otherwise occupied; it fights too hard when it is harpooned; and finally, their customs are traditionally designed around the bowhead.

At the 1978 IWC meeting, the United States, under Commissioner Richard Frank, tried to overthrow the Scientific Committee's recommendation of a zero quota on Arctic bowheads. After prolonged debate and backstage negotiating, the commission agreed to a 1979 quota of 18 whales or 27 strikes, whichever came first. Since the Eskimos had requested a quota of 45 whales (which, in fact, Frank had proposed), they were more than a little upset with the number they got, and they sued the government again. This time they argued that the IWC had not been established to control aboriginal whaling. Furthermore, wrote Jacob Adams, the Eskimos will "continue to engage in their own research on the bowhead; hunting methods and subsistence need limits will be established under AEWC management; those United States regulations implementing the IWC quota will be ignored; and the jurisdiction of the IWC over bowhead whaling by Alaskan Eskimos will be challenged in court." Their lawsuit was dismissed, but the threats persisted. There was no way to monitor the Eskimos' actual catches, and even if they exceeded them, there was no way to stop them. The United States was now at odds with the antiwhaling nations of the IWC, and also with the Eskimos, who were, after all, American citizens. Was there a position that could satisfy the Eskimos and the conservationists? The Scientific Committee, of course, was ostensibly apolitical, so it serenely continued to plump for a zero quota for bowhead whales. From the 1980 report:

The Committee reconfirms its recommendation at its Canberra, Cronulla, and Cambridge meetings that from a biological point of view the only safe course is for the kill of bowhead whales from the Bering Sea stock to be zero. It also believes that if present estimates of gross recruitment are accepted, then the population will decline, even in the absence of catches.

Among the studies submitted to the Scientific Committee was one by Howard Braham and Jeffery Breiwick, of the National Marine Mammal Laboratory, which suggested that the Bering Sea population of bowheads was in decline, had been so for some time, and would continue to decrease regardless of what the Eskimos did. According to their calculations, if high catches were allowed (what the authors called "the pessimistic parameter values"), the population would go extinct in forty-five years. "The moderate parameter values indicate a decline from 3,000 in 1970 to 2,026 in 100 years with zero catch beginning in 1981, while with 10 and 22 whales removed per year, the population declines to 1,424 and 638, respectively, in 100 years." The authors conclude that "both parties in this problem, the Alaskan Eskimos and the bowhead whale, are apparently in a no-win situation. A justified limited subsistence hunt unfortunately seems risky at this time if we want the bowhead population to recover."

Fortunately, the original estimates of the population were too low. This enabled the Eskimos to up their requests (although one conservationist grumbled that "this wasn't supposed to be a growth industry"), and even though its situation was regularly and systematically compromised, the United States managed to find an uneasy position at the IWC. America was both pro- and anti-whaling at the same time; it was one of the leaders in the battle for a total moratorium on all commercial whaling (passed in 1982), and at the same time, the acknowledged

Using tools similar to those of their ancestors, Eskimo whalers in Point Barrow strip the blubber from the carcass of a bowhead.

leader (albeit somewhat reluctantly) of the aboriginal-whaling movement.

At the 1980 meeting in Brighton, IWC Commissioner Frank asked for a continuation of the current quota, 18 bowheads landed or 22 struck. Again, the Scientific Committee had recommended that no bowhead whales at all be killed. "If the IWC approves a zero quota," said Frank, "we would have great trouble enforcing it." It was obvious that the antiwhaling bloc was vigorously opposed to the United States proposal. Australia claimed that even a catch of ten whales would "double the bowhead's rate of decline," and the Seychelles commissioner proposed a quota of 8 landed and 12 struck. When Frank intimated that the United States would file an objection to such a quota, it was defeated, and the issue was deferred to a time later in the meeting.

On Friday, July 25, at ten at night, another pro-

posal emerged: a three-year quota of 45 whales landed and 65 struck, no more than 17 to be taken in any one year. It was passed by a vote of 16 to 3, with 4 abstentions. The bowhead issue would not surface again at the IWC until 1983, but practically before the ink was dry on the agreement, the Eskimos of Kaktovik had violated it.

In earlier times, the village of Kaktovik played only a small role in Eskimo whaling history. It is located on tiny Barter Island, which supported an occasional whale hunt for subsistence, until the Air Force's DEW (Distant Early Warning) Line radar station arrived. With the money they earned from the construction of an airfield and the great listening devices pointed at Siberia, Kaktovik inhabitants suddenly found themselves rich enough to join their brethren in the whale hunts.

On September 14, 1980, after the National Marine

Fisheries Service (NMFS) had officially closed the hunt, Kaktovik hunters took a bowhead. The 1980 quota of 18 landed or 26 struck had already been reached, but despite this violation, NMFS officials dismissed the kill as the result of "poor communications." There was talk that the Eskimos had taken the whale to protest the quota, but this was dispelled when they caught two more in October. The problem was resolved by the signing of a cooperative agreement between the National Oceanic and Atmospheric Administration (NOAA)* and the AEWC, where the Eskimos were given authority to monitor their own hunt, and fine those captains who violated the regulations. In October 1982 the agreement was extended to apply into 1987; if NOAA and the AEWC cannot agree on a new quota, then last year's quota applies.

During the years 1981–83, the Department of the Interior, the Marine Mammal Commission, and numerous other agencies conducted studies that would, they hoped, shed light on this complex problem. The Eskimos too were applying their not-inconsiderable expertise, but they were also lunging forward into the 1980s, at least as far as whaling was concerned.

First they wanted to alter the IWC's definition of a "strike," because they felt that they were being unfairly penalized when a harpoon glanced off the back of a whale, or when the harpoon struck the whale but did not explode. Both of these eventualities had been considered strikes. Neither NOAA nor the IWC could be convinced by the Eskimos' arguments, however, and the old definition still applied. (In the IWC regulations, the term "strike" is defined as "to penetrate with a weapon used for whaling.") Obviously, a nondetonating harpoon was a strike, but a harpoon that just bounced off was a different problem.

By 1985, the two-year quota, which had been set in 1983, had expired. With the passage of the whaling moratorium, commercial whaling was officially over, but the whaling nations would continue to propose all sorts of innovative devices designed to allow them at least one more season. (In a surprise opening statement, the Soviet Union announced that it was going to end commercial whaling by 1987.) This

left Iceland and Japan with their "research" proposals, Norway with an attempt to redefine "small-type coastal whaling" so as to allow the fishermen/whalers of northern Norway to continue their minke hunting—and lastly it left the Eskimos.

To emphasize their points, the AEWC sent ten Eskimos to the July IWC meeting in Bournemouth, England. They were also represented by their legal counsel and by Senator Ted Stevens, of Alaska. (Any congressman who chooses to do so can become a member of the United States delegation.) At this time, the Bering Sea bowhead population was believed to consist of some 4,000 animals, so the Eskimos, bolstered by a favorable Interior Department study of their subsistence needs, raised their quota request to 35 strikes, from which they hoped to harvest 26 whales. This was a substantial increase over the 43 whales (with no more than 27 to be taken in a single year) that had been allocated for the *two* seasons of 1984 and 1985. The original proposal was defeated on the floor. Commissioner John Byrne, who had replaced Richard Frank in 1983 as the administrator of NOAA and the United States whaling commissioner, fought with the antiwhaling commissioners again, and a compromise emerged: the Eskimos would be given a three-year quota of 26 strikes for 1985, '86, and '87, with no more than 32 strikes in any one year. Naturally, the Eskimos intended to avail themselves of the full 32 for '85 and '86, and hope that the remaining figure of 26 would be raised by 1987.

By 1987, the bowheads were back in the news. The new United States commissioner, Anthony Calio, had made several trips to Alaska to confer with the Eskimos, and as the bloc quota was drawing to a close, it was clear that a new accommodation would have to be reached. In the meantime, the Eskimos had been improving their techniques, raising their efficiency to a new high of 69 percent, as contrasted with the dismal 33 percent of a decade before, where they were losing two whales for every one they beached.

For a change, the bowhead issue was overshadowed by a much more controversial one at the 1987 IWC meetings. Japan and Iceland (and to a lesser extent, South Korea) had offered more detailed proposals for scientific-research whaling. These were all defeated, but those countries decided to continue

*NOAA is the parent body of NMFS. The United States commissioner to the IWC has traditionally been the administrator of NOAA.

whaling anyway. Their actions threatened the existence of the IWC, since there wasn't much point in passing regulations and having member nations ignore them without even bothering to file objections simply because they didn't like them. Almost as an afterthought—there was a furor as the Icelanders threatened to walk out, or take their case to the World Court—the Eskimos got their 1987 quota increased to 32 whales.

A most peculiar situation had now developed with regard to the working definition of "aboriginal" whaling. While the Eskimos had entered the world of (relatively) high technology, and no longer lived in snow houses or traveled by dogsled (the former had been replaced by prefabricated houses, the latter by snowmobiles), they still insisted upon their "cultural" need to kill whales for traditional reasons. Despite critics who would have the Eskimos hunting whales with helicopters and sonar and blasting them with bow-mounted cannons, they still pursue whales in very much the same manner that they used a hundred years ago. And it is still cold, dangerous work.

It is the "struck-and-lost" problem that causes the most trouble, both to the Eskimos and to their critics. No other whaling enterprise has such a large built-in inefficiency factor, and to silence their critics on this subject—and also to improve their own efficiency—the Eskimos have gone outside normal channels. In fact, they have gone as far as Norway.

One of the problems with the old "black-powder" harpoon cannons has been their occasional reluctance to fire. When the powder got wet—no infrequent occurrence in the Arctic—the gun would not fire, and the whale would escape. Sometimes also, the gun would fire with only half a charge, which would not do too much harm to the whale, but would count as a strike against the whalers' quota.

The Norwegians had been under great pressure from the IWC to develop a more efficient way of killing minke whales. (Because explosive harpoons destroyed too much of the meat of the 30-foot minkes, they had been using the "cold harpoon," which used no explosives at all. Its great iron toggles pierced the flesh of the whale, and "hooked" it so it could be played like a 10-ton fish on a line, often for hours.) Cold harpoons were outlawed in 1986, and in response Norwegian scientists developed a much more powerful and efficient weapon using an explosive known as penthrite. Early experiments with penthrite harpoons injured many people, but development continued, and by 1987, the Norwegians, who were out of the business of commercial whaling, found themselves in the whaling-armaments business. They couldn't use their own invention, but the Eskimos, the last people in the world who were given an IWC whaling quota, certainly could.

So the Eskimos, who felt that increased efficiency would quiet their opponents, bought the new weapons from the Norwegians. They now are at nearly 90-percent efficiency, with virtually instantaneous kills. But the further the Eskimos move from their aboriginal techniques, the less need there seems to be to allow them to continue "subsistence" whaling. People who drive snowmobiles, who employ CB radios to signal the position of the whales, wear nylon parkas and moonboots to keep warm, and use tractors to haul the whales out of the water and onto the ice—and most important, whose income to allow all these improvements comes from the petroleum industry—no longer fit anybody's definition of aborigines, not even their own. And now that they have improved whaling ballistics to the point where they almost never lose a whale, how is it possible to acknowledge any of their whaling practices as aboriginal? Is it aboriginal only because the Eskimos (and more vocally, the Eskimos' lawyers) say it is? It is nowhere written that we must preserve a culture—or even some aspects of a culture—if the people in question choose to take themselves into the twentieth century. It is the height of anthropological arrogance to preserve "primitive" cultures like museum dioramas. All cultures, whether aboriginal or not, are part of the ever-diminishing global village. Progress is not reserved for city-dwellers only; it droppeth like the falling rain from heaven on everyone.

The USSR After
the Moratorium

ON JULY 23, 1982, the International Whaling Commission passed (by a vote of 27 for, 7 against, and 5 abstentions) an amendment to the *Schedule* that placed a total ban on commercial whaling.* The actual wording of the historic paragraph that put an end to a thousand years of whale-killing for profit is as follows:

Notwithstanding the other provisions of paragraph 10 [which provide for otherwise allowable commercial whaling], catch limits for the killing for commercial purposes of whales from all stocks for the 1986 coastal season and for the 1985–86 pelagic seasons and thereafter shall be zero. This provision will be kept under review, based upon the best scientific advice, and by 1990 at the latest the Commission will undertake a comprehensive assessment of the effects of this decision on whale stocks and consider modification of this provision and the establishment of other catch limits.

Note that "by 1990 at the latest" there was to be a "comprehensive assessment" to see if the moratorium was working, and that if in the years between its passage and 1990 the whales made a significant enough recovery, the commission might consider "the establishment of other catch limits." These provisions were largely overlooked during the euphoria that followed the passage of the moratorium; it appeared to the conservationists that they had finally won the whale

war. The cheering had barely subsided, however, when the first cracks began to appear.

Under IWC procedures, those member nations that wish to protest a decision made by the commission may file an objection within ninety days of the passage of the amendment embodying the decision. By November, Japan, Norway, Peru and the USSR had formally filed objections. The moratorium contained a three-year phase-out clause, ostensibly to allow the whaling nations to wind down their operations without undue economic pressure. Under the terms of the phase-out, whaling quotas were still going to be set for the 1983, '84, and '85 seasons, but nations with their objections still in place by 1986 would be considered in violation of the moratorium.

By the time of the 1983–84 season, the only large-scale whaling was taking place in the Antarctic, and this was on small-scale whales. Japan and the Soviet Union, still functioning under their objections to the moratorium, were sending fleets to the Antarctic to hunt minke whales. The conservationist bloc within the IWC, now swelled by the addition of several antiwhaling nations, continued to press for reduced quotas. That for Southern Hemisphere minke whales was reduced from year to year; it was 6,655 in 1983, and 4,224 in 1984. Only a whaling industry heavily underwritten by its government could afford to send its ships to the Antarctic, at great expense of fuel and salaries, for a couple of thousand 30-foot minkes. In 1985, USSR factory ships reported a catch of 3,027 minkes in the Antarctic, 1,086 over their quota. The United States certified the Soviets under the Pelly Amendment, costing them extensive fishing rights in United States waters. For this reason and probably many others, 1985 marked the beginning of the end of Soviet whaling.

Unlike Japan, Korea or Iceland, the Soviets saw

*By this time, the rolls of the IWC had swelled to thirty-seven nations, many of which had joined the commission just to vote against commercial whaling. Countries with an asterisk (*) were new to the commission in 1982. For the moratorium: Antigua(*), Argentina, Australia, Belize(*), Costa Rica, Denmark, Egypt(*), France, Germany(*), India, Kenya(*), Mexico, Monaco(*), the Netherlands, New Zealand, Oman, St. Lucia, St. Vincent, the Seychelles, Senegal(*), Spain, Sweden, the United Kingdom, the United States, Uruguay. Against: Brazil, Iceland, Japan, Korea, Norway, Peru, the USSR. Abstained: Chile, China, Philippines, South Africa, Switzerland. (Canada withdrew from the commission in 1981.)

no need to continue commercial whaling under the pseudonymous rubric of "research whaling." Except for the gray whales that are taken off Siberia every year—perhaps for the feeding of aborigines, perhaps for the feeding of minks—Soviet harpoon guns are silent. At the 1986 IWC meeting in Malmö, Sweden, the Soviets distributed an opening statement in which they announced their intention to cease all commercial whaling by 1987. Compared to the barrage of words and papers produced by the Japanese, the Soviets seem not only quiet, but almost serene.

In 1988, the Japanese submitted a proposal for a take of 370 minke whales for "ceremonial" purposes—another transparent subterfuge to reenter commercial whaling. In 1989, they proposed a new category of whaling: "small-type coastal whaling," for which they urgently needed an "interim" quota of 320 minkes to be taken in their coastal waters. In sharp contrast to the ludicrous attempts of the Japanese to override the moratorium, the Soviets, who had been the collaborators of the Japanese for so long, submitted a proposal for the revision of the Convention of 1946. In a rational and well-reasoned proposal submitted in 1988, they said:

The Soviet Government believes that it is appropriate to focus the Convention on the conservation and study of whales (rather than the regulation of whaling). . . . Such an extraordinary phenomenon of nature as whales deserves complex and comprehensive study which may be performed in the most effective and fruitful way only on the basis of international cooperation. . . . The USSR Government takes due account of concern expressed by Soviet public opinion, and appeals voiced by world opinion.

For years the Soviets practiced noncooperation and intransigence as elements of their national whaling policy. They voted against every proposal that would have lessened the clout of the whalers or reduced quotas. They have not, for reasons known only to them, withdrawn their objection to the moratorium even today, although it appears obvious that it is not because they intend to go whaling again.

Today's USSR is not the same country that stubbornly refused to acknowledge the existence of conservation; it is the Soviet Union that dispatched two icebreakers to rescue three gray whales trapped in the ice in Alaska. And it has completely reversed its policy on whales and whaling. While they represent only a small portion of the inhabitants of the planet that may benefit from *perestroika,* the whales are fortunate to have escaped the harpoons in the nick of time.

The End of Japanese Whaling

ON NOVEMBER 4, 1984, the Japanese North Pacific sperm whale fleet set sail, despite the fact that there had been no quota set for this species. Since Japan had not withdrawn its objection to the whaling moratorium of 1982, she was operating legally, but the conservationist community was up in arms. Once again, however, economics prevailed over ecology, and because of the delicate nature of Japan–United States trade relations, a "bilateral agreement" was struck. The Americans agreed not to impose economic sanctions if the Japanese would withdraw their objection to the moratorium by April 1, 1985. The American government apparently believed that if and when the Japanese withdrew their objection, they would no longer be in contravention of the treaty to which the U.S. was a signatory, and thus not susceptible to the sanctions of the Packwood-Magnuson Amendment. This concession to commerce so outraged the environmentalists that they brought suit against the Secretary of Commerce

Three Japanese catcher boats with their harpoon cannons covered. Note the sharply raked bows and the catwalk from the bridge to the gun.

and the Secretary of State, claiming that the imposition of Packwood-Magnuson was "nondiscretionary," and did not allow for any deals on the side.

Judge Charles R. Richey of the United States District Court ruled in favor of the twelve conservationist groups,* and the Federal Court of Appeals upheld his ruling. In June 1986, however, the United States Supreme Court reversed the lower court's ruling, and by a 5 to 4 majority, found that the bilateral agreement was legal. The Japanese were able to continue whaling, even though they had withdrawn their objection and were therefore bound by the moratorium. They took 200 sperm whales in each of the 1986 and 1987 seasons in the North Pacific, thus maintaining their fleet and their whalemen without a break.

Even though the conservationists lost their case, the Japanese had agreed to withdraw their objection, and thus were forced to concede that they would quit commercial whaling by 1988. The International Whaling Commission had classified North Pacific

*American Cetacean Society, Animal Protection Institute of America, Animal Welfare Institute, Center for Environmental Education, Connecticut Cetacean Society, Defenders of Wildlife, Friends of the Earth, The Fund for Animals, Greenpeace USA, The Humane Society of the United States, International Fund for Animal Welfare, The Whale Center.

sperm whales as a "protection stock," which meant that the catch limit for this species is automatically (and unambiguously) set at zero. It appeared as if the Japanese had been outmaneuvered, and even though they had managed to hang on for three more years, the end of their whaling history seemed imminent. Those who believed that Japanese whaling was coming to an end underestimated the dogged determination of the Japanese, and the importance of "science" in modern whaling.

In fairness to the Japanese, it should be noted that they consistently put their eggs in the "science" basket. They chose to accept the findings of the IWC's Scientific Committee, whose reports were quite often at variance with the political strategies of the antiwhaling nations. For example, there was no question that the bowhead whale, hunted by the Alaskan Eskimos, was the most endangered of all the large whale species. Since 1972, when the IWC first became involved in the bowhead controversy, there was *never* a season when the bowhead was not classified as "protected," and in 1977 the Scientific Committee recommended that all aboriginal bowhead whaling be banned. And yet the Americans, among the leaders of the antiwhaling movement, continued to campaign for quotas on bowheads. This incongruity was not lost on the Japanese, and off the record and on, they tried to compare their "subsistence" whaling with that of the Eskimos. During the heated discussions that preceded the 1982 passage of the moratorium, Commissioner Yonezawa said, "The Scientific Committee has shown that there is no justification for a total moratorium. . . . There are more than 300,000 minke whales in the Antarctic, and there are less than 4,000 bowheads. . . . How can you vote against whaling on a small portion [of the minke population] if you can vote yes on a bowhead hunt?"

The Japanese had tried whaling under the umbrella of scientific research in 1976, when they issued themselves a permit to take 240 Bryde's whales in the South Pacific. Although their approach was roundly condemned, the Japanese evidently did not feel the need to pursue this program, and for the next ten years, while they continued to argue that they were the only ones who believed in science, they were, because their commercial whaling was continuing, able to kill whales more or less legally. With the passage of the moratorium, however, they found themselves with their backs to the wall, and if there was any way at all that they could kill whales—for love, money, or science—they were going to do it.

The subject of research whaling came up at the IWC's 1985 meeting, and it was agreed to submit the discussions to a working group, which would report to the next meeting of the commission. In 1986 Japan hesitantly introduced a proposal for scientific-research whaling (similar to their notorious Bryde's whale proposal of 1976), but the commission voted to postpone discussion until 1987.

In September of that year, the American conservation groups that had filed the earlier lawsuits against the government petitioned to have the previous ruling overturned, claiming that Japan had misrepresented its intentions to suspend its whaling operations and in fact was preparing her fleet to sail south in direct violation of the bilateral agreement as well as the IWC moratorium on commercial whaling. The prestigious Washington law firm of Arnold and Porter was arguing the case for the conservationists—*pro bono,* of course—so the Japanese hired Richard Frank, the former United States whaling commissioner and administrator of NOAA, and his sidekick Eldon Greenberg, who had been NOAA's general counsel during Frank's tenure.

Although the Japanese had issued themselves a permit to take 825 minkes and 50 sperm whales every year for ten years, by the time they actually sailed they had reduced their research needs to 300 minkes. (One of the truly peculiar aspects of this controversy is the number of whales needed for "research." Opponents of the original Japanese plan claimed that even 825 whales was too small a sample to produce any meaningful results, so 300 would provide even less. The argument that Japan should therefore be allotted *more* whales to study was forwarded, but quickly retracted.) Because the IWC had rejected all four research proposals at its June meeting, the Japanese fleet was going to be acting in direct contravention of the IWC ruling, and was putting herself in a position where the United States would have to begin certification procedures under the Packwood-Magnuson and Pelly amendments. Even a postal vote, where the IWC member nations were polled to see if they approved of Japan's revised research program (they overwhelmingly didn't), failed to stay the determined Japanese whalers, and on December 20, the factory ship *Nisshin Maru No. 3* sailed for the Antarctic with her attendant fleet of four catcher boats.

And on February 9, 1988, after the Japanese whalers killed the first minke in the Antarctic, Secretary of Commerce C. William Verity sent a letter to President Reagan in which he said:

Under the Packwood-Magnuson Amendment to the Magnuson Fishery Conservation and Management and the Pelly Amendment to the Fishermen's Protective Act, when I determine that nationals of a foreign country are conducting fishing operations which diminish the effectiveness of an international fishery conservation program, I am required to certify that fact to you. By this letter, I am certifying that nationals of Japan are conducting whaling operations that diminish the effectiveness of the International Whaling Commission's (IWC's) conservation program.

Under the terms of the certification, the president had sixty days in which to inform Congress of the action he intended to take against Japan. On April 6, he cut off Japan's fishing privileges in American waters: "I am directing the Secretary of State under the Packwood-Magnuson Amendment to withhold 100 per cent of the fishing privileges that would oth-

Nisshin Maru No. 3, the last of the Japanese factory ships.

erwise be available to Japan in the U.S. Exclusive Economic Zone." This sounded drastic, but in fact it only eliminated 3,000 metric tons of sea snails and 5,000 tons of Pacific whiting. To the dismay of the conservationists, however, no trade sanctions were imposed.

Despite the Japanese insistence to the contrary, it is obvious that their pelagic whaling was not a "traditional" industry. While there had indeed been coastal whaling from the shore stations of Taiji, Wakayama, Wadaura, etc., it was not pursued with the fervor that accompanied large-scale factory-ship whaling, mostly because there weren't enough whales in Japan's inshore waters to warrant the initiation of a major industry. When modern techniques of whaling were introduced after the Russo-Japanese War, the Japanese began to pursue whales with unprecedented fervor, perhaps as a way of demonstrating to the world that they were indeed a modern nation with fully developed naval capabilities. Until after World War II, *kujira* was not a particularly important food in Japan. Why then have the Japanese continued to battle for their "right" to kill whales? In the face of mounting criticism, with the quotas dropping so drastically that even a full quota (of minke whales) would result in a massive economic loss, they have doggedly persisted, taking their battles to the IWC, the streets, and on two occasions, to the United States Supreme Court.*

There is an interesting contrast between the Norwegian whaling industry, which had been the first, and those of the Japanese and Soviets, which were the last. While the Norwegian government regarded the privately run industry as a primary source of tax revenues, exactly the opposite was true of Japan and the Soviet Union. For their own reasons, the Japanese and Soviet governments subsidized their whaling industries, and despite the reduction of quotas and the subsequent unprofitability of the business, these nations persevered. In their analysis of the economics of Soviet whaling, Tønnessen and Johnsen concluded that "for Kr.100 million the Russians could have bought what it cost them Kr.240 million to produce." They go on to write that "economic considerations . . . can therefore not have been the reason why a country with such ample natural re-

*It was not, of course, the "right to kill whales" that was placed before the Supreme Court, but rather the applicability of the Packwood-Magnuson and Pelly amendments, two Congressional resolutions that were enacted to respond to nations whose actions were in contravention of America's declared conservation policies.

The whaling shrine at Taiji: a full-sized right whale.

sources as theirs should have felt compelled to carry out their exceedingly expensive Antarctic whaling."

For the Japanese, too, whaling was an increasingly unprofitable industry, although the extent of Japanese government support of whaling has never been disclosed. They continued because they maintain (within and without the IWC) that whale meat constitutes an important part of their national protein consumption. In addition, Japan's heavy investment in Antarctic whaling made it increasingly difficult to scuttle its whaling fleet, and there was also the argument that so many Japanese were involved in whaling that to put them all out of work would result in an upheaval within a labor force in which people were simply not fired. Another factor was the Japanese perception of injustice: why was it that the Greenland and Alaskan "aborigines" were allowed to kill endangered whales while they were not? (At later meetings, the Japanese would make a futile attempt to redefine the term "aborigine" for the IWC, proposing a definition which they believed—or professed to believe—would make subsistence whaling applicable to them.) Lastly—and perhaps most importantly to the Japanese—there was a general aversion to being told what to eat or how to catch it. In the past, they showed a strong disinclination to conform to the demands of external agencies. In the 1930s, when they felt threatened by the perceived collusion of the Americans, the British, the Chinese and the Dutch to deprive them of oil and other natural resources (the "ABCD encirclement"), the Japanese went to war.

A 1988 letter to the editor of the *Yomiuri Daily* of Tokyo probably sums up the vast distance that still exists between the Japanese and those who would stop her whaling:

Reportedly the U.S. government is considering trade sanctions against Japan due to Japan's scientific whale hunt designed to determine the feasibility of future commercial whaling. . . .

First of all, we must get this straight: whales are born to be exploited. Unless we start with this consensus, our arguments will get nowhere.

Second, we should emphasize that minke whales are not on the endangered species list. Therefore, there can be nothing wrong with catching a reasonable number of them.

Third, we should repeat that no one has the right to dictate to others what they should or should not eat. No one but the barbarians who do not appreciate cultural relativism and subtlety would undertake such an absurdity. One senses a tinge of cultural arrogance lurking on the part of those who attempt to discredit whaling.

It now seems possible that thousands of whales had to die because the Japanese simply didn't like being told what to do. These arguments, beginning to emerge around 1970, would become increasingly strident by the 1980s and would eventually result in major confrontations between the whaling and the nonwhaling nations of the world.

In the early 1970s, conservation groups distributed anti-Japanese materials and collected signatures on petitions which were to be presented to the Japanese embassy to demonstrate how strongly Americans felt about the preservation of whales. They organized boycotts of Japanese products in an attempt to get the Japanese government to eliminate or cut back the whaling policies that Americans found so abhorrent. Across the Pacific, the response was predictable. A defensive and bitter anti-American reaction developed, with newspapers commenting acidly on the sentimental and misguided American notions about whales. There were suggestions that the antiwhaling movement was secretly being financed by American manufacturers who feared Japanese competition. The Japanese maintained that the Americans did not understand the complexities of their employment situation, and that eliminating whaling would create chaos within their country. And finally the Japanese did not believe—as the Americans so fervently and emotionally did—that the whales they were hunting were becoming extinct.

It is still difficult to identify the Japanese motivation for insisting on their right to kill whales. It is true that the conservationist nations of the International Whaling Commission "stacked" the commission to enable them to achieve their stunning 1982 victory, but it is equally true that being outmaneuvered—especially in the light of the 1972 United Nations resolution (in which 52 nations unanimously voted for an immediate moratorium on commercial whaling)—does not automatically call for the death of thousands of whales. (To counter the imbalance that they perceived by the introduction of antiwhaling nations, Japan brought Brazil into the IWC. Brazil's only connection with whaling was the wholly Japanese-owned stations at Costinha and Cabo Frio. Later this plan would backfire, when Brazilian conservationists led their country into the ranks of the anti-whaling nations.) The whales suffered because of the actions of countries whose policies did not coincide with those of the Japanese. "Saving face" was also suggested as a reason for Japan's recalcitrance, but again, this seems an oversimplified ex-

planation. If the Japanese had quit whaling altogether, surely it would have been possible to concoct a rationale for doing so that would have allowed them to exit the industry with dignity. It might also be argued that as Japan rose to her current position as the dominant power of the Pacific Rim, she felt more and more able to flex her economic muscles.

Perhaps the Japanese believe in living for the moment and letting future generations take care of themselves. After all, the world recognizes the possibility of a nuclear holocaust, but only Japan has experienced the horrors of an atomic bomb. Is there a connection between her phenomenal economic growth and her deliberate obfuscation of the principles of natural-resource conservation? Can a country with limited resources and an insatiable appetite for raw materials afford to preserve the resources of other nations? (Conversely, can the United States, a nation of 240 million people spread out over 3.5 million square miles, understand what it feels like to live on a chain of rocky islands of which only 13 percent of the land is arable?)

There is a critical difference between Western and Japanese utilization of resources. Americans live in a vast, rich country, with millions of acres committed to raising food (or sometimes, in accordance with a policy that must be totally incomprehensible to the Japanese, to purposely *not* raising food), and the luxury to devote an equal amount of space to the preservation of wilderness. Crammed into the rocky islands of Japan is a teeming throng, whose population is half that of the United States. Conservation is a luxury that the Japanese can ill afford if they expect to feed their 120 million people. Lack of space also means that the Japanese cannot economically raise cattle or pigs, since most of the feed that might be used to cultivate these animals has to be imported.

Therefore, the final Japanese argument for whaling has to do with food. As quotas decreased, Japanese interest in eating whale meat rose. Japan found that its whaling was more practical than that of the other pelagic nations, since it could utilize the meat as well as the oil. Pro-whaling propaganda flowed out of the Japan Whaling Association, with booklet after booklet listing Japanese whale-meat restaurants, recipes, and statistics demonstrating the Japanese love of this food. In one such publication, the following statement appears:

We hope that whaling will resume. There is a problem if the moratorium continues, because whales are a part of our environment and our life. Of course we could eat pork or beef, but I don't think we would have much zest for living, or could work hard without whale meat.

(Actually, the attitude of the Japanese consumer to whale meat is somewhat similar to the American's taste for lobster. Many Americans like lobster, especially in New England, and if the lobster was declared an endangered species—which in some areas it is—and people were forbidden to eat it, there would probably be cries of deprivation throughout Maine and Massachusetts. But because lobster is a luxury and an expensive food item, it is difficult to imagine Americans—even those whose ancestors had caught and eaten lobsters for centuries—claiming that they were being denied an inalienable right if lobsters were protected.)

From their earliest whaling days, the Japanese have defined whale meat however it suited them at the time. As early as the Nara Period (A.D. 710 to 784), the Buddhist emperors had forbidden the killing of four-legged animals and the eating of their meat, so the Japanese simply decided that the whale was a fish, and therefore outside the restrictions. By the fifteenth century, the restrictions had lapsed, and although it was far from the food of the common peasant, whale meat began to appear on the tables of the nobility. After the Japanese had perfected the art of net whaling and were taking more whales than they had been able to obtain in the past, they developed a taste for whale meat and accordingly began to design various methods of preparing it.

As a food item, whale meat is no different to the Japanese than what pork, beef or chicken is to Americans or Europeans. To the Japanese, foods from the sea are primarily considered as *foods,* and not as fish, mammals or crustaceans. It is probably not accidental that the booklets mentioned above never illustrate the whale; they only show pictures of meat-preparation, markets and shrines. (In all fairness, Western recipes for veal scallopini, turkey breast or filet of sole rarely include pictures of calves, turkeys or fish.) The Japanese simply cannot understand why everyone is making such a fuss about something that they want to eat. Masaharu Nishiwaki, one of Japan's leading cetologists, put the Japanese argument very succinctly when he wrote,

Domesticated animals, such as cattle, sheep, and pigs were at one time wild (many thousands of years ago). For their own good, human beings have become accustomed to eating, raising, and utilizing these animals. Even today man must rely on animal protein for the sake of his health and well being. Although we feel respectful gratitude and pity towards these animals, we, as human beings, have no other choice but to take their lives and consume them. Whales, from this point of view, are really no different from domesticated animals.*

Because of the Japanese predilection for calling things by names that will make them more acceptable, the introduction of "scientific-research whaling" in 1986, even though it was obvious that the program was nothing more than commercial whaling under another name, was a perfect solution to the problem, and one to which the Japanese cannot understand why anyone would object. It would appear that to the Japanese, calling a whale a fish—or a food item, or a bird, for that matter—changes its character, and it actually becomes what you call it.

Most of the Japanese arguments are correct. Japan is an island nation, and gets a large proportion of its protein from fish and shellfish. In other countries, people eat the meat of animals, such as ducks and deer, that they do not raise for slaughter. The whales being hunted are not on the brink of extinction. The Japanese do indeed eat the meat, and are not hunting the whales for lipstick, margarine or shoe polish. The IWC, they argue, was founded to protect whales *for* rather than *from* the whaling industry.

The moratorium was passed in June 1982. Since it was scheduled to take effect in the 1985–86 season, the Japanese and the Soviet pelagic-whaling fleets had three full seasons in which to hunt whales and then phase themselves out of whaling. The Japanese did no such thing. They continued to hunt whales, and instead of phasing out, they spent as much time—and probably as much money—as it would have taken them to find other jobs for their whalers, in-

---

*This penchant for remaining emotionally detached from the animals you kill to eat is not uniquely Japanese. In his discussion of British Antarctic whaling, Terence Wise wrote:

Although this whale was so fresh from the sea and life, with hot blood running from the wound in its back where the harpoon protruded, I felt absolutely no compassion for the creature. This may seem callous but I think the novelty and the knowledge that the carcass represented money took away most feelings. . . . Whaling is an industry that produces food for man by killing whales— just like slaughtering cattle or sheep—and the only complaints concerning the killing seem to stem not from the ethics but the method employed.

venting excuses and revising history to justify the continuation of their whaling industry.

First they announced that they did not intend to abide by the moratorium. Then, from 1982 to 1986, they took as many minke whales in the Antarctic as they could under the quotas that were awarded annually. When the United States threatened to certify the Japanese for obstructing the efficacy of the moratorium, they began negotiations that resulted in a peculiar bilateral agreement that allowed them—outside of any IWC restrictions—to take a quota of sperm whales in the North Pacific. This resulted in a lawsuit by conservation organizations, not against the Japanese (who would have been rather too difficult to sue in United States courts), but rather against the U.S. Department of Commerce, which had cut the deal. The conservationists lost their suit, but it was clear that the American conservation movement, which had toiled so hard for the passage of the moratorium, was not about to trade the lives of whales for imports of Hondas, Nikons or Panasonics.

In 1985, the Japanese brought up scientific-research whaling again, in association with the Koreans and the Icelanders. In fact, the Icelanders were the leaders in this movement, threatening to pull out of the IWC if the United States did not relent, and even to close down the NATO base at Keflavik if the U.S. persisted in its campaign to put the Icelanders out of business. (The Icelanders had not objected to the moratorium, so they found themselves in the peculiar position of having agreed to cease whaling, and then, three years later, as the moratorium was scheduled to take effect, trying to reopen their whaling business.) The Japanese tried the "scientific" approach for three years, from 1985 to 1988. Then at the 1988 IWC meeting, they took a completely new tack: they discovered that they had been conducting "small-type coastal whaling" for centuries, and shifted their attack to this new arena. Dropping the "scientific" approach, the Japanese delegation distributed the report of an international workshop which asked (in its preface), "If small-scale whaling by aboriginal societies is justifiably allowed to continue, due to the social, nutritional, religious and local-level economic importance of this resource harvesting activity, then why not small-type coastal whaling also?" (Obviously, the "social, nutritional, religious and local-level economic" considerations were derived directly from the Alaskan Eskimos'

bowhead whale requirements; if the Alaskan aborigines could have this variance, why not the Japanese?)

On July 1, 1986, the Japanese ambassador to the United Kingdom presented a note to the secretary of the IWC, in which the Japanese withdrew their objection to the moratorium. Despite this document—which contained language suggesting that the withdrawal would be withdrawn if the United States certified the Japanese for sanctions under the Packwood-Magnuson Amendment—the Japanese continued to lobby for scientific-research whaling, small-type coastal whaling, or any other type of whaling that would enable them to stay in business.

By 1989, the Japanese had run out of arguments. There was a worldwide ban on the killing of sperm whales; the moratorium on commercial whaling seemed to be firmly in place and not one request for "research whaling" had been accepted by the IWC's Scientific Committee—not from Japan, not from Iceland, not from Korea. Their elaborate proposal for a redefinition of "small-type coastal whaling" was rejected. The Joint Whaling Company (Nippon Kyodo Hogei) was dissolved, its directors retired, and its employees were laid off. The "large-type" coastal whalers, such as Nitto Hogei and Nihon Hogei, which sent ships offshore to hunt Bryde's whales, were no more. The shore stations at Wadaura, Taiji and Ayukawa were closed down and the machinery sold off. Now the only whaling done from Japanese ships today is "research whaling"—one vessel collects minkes in the Antarctic—and small-type whaling, where only beaked whales and pilot whales are killed.

From their humble, local beginnings as subsistence whalers who threw nets over whales and then dispatched them with swords, the Japanese grew to be the predominant industrial-whaling nation in the world. They utilized the oil, the meat, the bones, the blubber, the intestines, the flukes and even the belly-pleats. From the Russo-Japanese War in 1904, when they acquired the Russian whaleship *Mikhail*, to the mid-1960s, when they worked the coastal waters of Japan, the Antarctic, and the open North Pacific simultaneously, they were probably responsible for the death of more whales than any other nation in history. (The Norwegians matched them stride for stride until the mid-1960s when the Japanese killed tens of thousands of sperm whales in the North Pacific.) Japan is a nation with one foot in the past and the other in the future. Adhering to a rigid behavioral code in their homes and offices and behaving like buccaneers in the world's marketplaces, the Japanese manifest the inherent contradictions that have always characterized their culture to Westerners. This conflict between past and present was nowhere more evident than in their whaling history. "Traditional" values conflicted with "modern" requirements as the Japanese attempted to demonstrate that their whaling had been going on unchanged for centuries, while at the same time they refined modern weaponry to make the killing more efficient.

It was the environmental movement that brought an end to Japanese whaling, just as it had done in the other countries where governments succumbed to public pressure. (Of the countries that quit in recent years, only Norway ceased whaling for purely economic reasons. Even though Norway is a country of breathtaking views and supposedly crystalline waters, she is remarkably short of practicing environmentalists, especially where whales are concerned.) Americans, Englishmen, Australians, Frenchmen, Dutchmen and Greenpeacers all worked to put the Japanese out of the whaling business. From the passage of the moratorium in 1982 until their reluctant submission in 1989, the Japanese struggled for every whale, and even while the negotiations were going on, they continued the killing.

One of the most surprising aspects of the Japanese *volte-face* has been the emergence of a *Japanese* antiwhaling movement. If we are to judge from their press releases, antiwhaling Japanese have been around a relatively long time, but it was only in 1989 that their press releases were distributed to the delegates at the IWC meeting. (Strongly worded releases also came from the Japanese All-Seaman's Union, and the Japanese Whaling Association, but these were in favor of a continuation of whaling.) A group calling itself the Elsa Nature Conservancy has evidently been crusading for a cessation of whale-killing since the passage of the moratorium in 1982. At the San Diego meeting in 1989, this organization, under the directorship of Eiji Fujiwara, presented its material to the IWC. In his "opening statement," Fujiwara wrote,

The Japanese whaling industry is structurally a semi-government operation and to the world opinion which has tilted toward the ban on commercial whaling, the Fisheries Agency of the government and the whaling companies together stood against it. Moreover, they carried out propaganda and manipulated the public opinion so that there would be no voice against the national policy within the nation.

In another handout, Fujiwara attacked his government's position on small-type whaling:

We conclude from our research that the argument by the Japanese government is groundless in terms of the Ayukawa whaling because of the following:

1) The Ayukawa small-type whaling was started only in 1933 by the outsiders. Therefore, it is not a tradition.

2) Small-type coastal whaling is commercial whaling.

3) The financial contribution of whaling is insignificant in the town economy.

4) The habit of eating whale meat was established only recently.

5) The local consumption of whale meat is decreasing.

6) Very little cultural heritage of whaling exists.

7) The town government has acquired post-whaling plans.

Obviously, one conservation organization does not speak for the Japanese people, but the very appearance of such contrary views indicated a critical weakening of the Japanese government's heretofore unassailable position. This was the signal the environmentalists had been waiting for, although few of them recognized it for what it was. As with so many aspects of Japanese culture, the inner workings of the whaling industry have been successfully hidden from prying round-eyes. Thus, when the industry finally decided to cease and desist, it was done in such an inscrutable fashion that very few Westerners knew it had happened. Commercial whaling in Japan ended some time in 1988, not with the roar of a final harpoon cannon, but with a sigh, not unlike the exhalation of a whale.

The End of
Whaling for Profit

THERE MUST BE something in man that, upon seeing a whale offshore or at sea, induces an almost uncontrollable desire to kill it. Scott McVay has asked the questions that the whaling industry— and the world that let them kill its whales—should have asked itself:

What is it in our nature that propels us to continue a hunt initiated in earlier times? Are we like some lethal mechanical toy that will not wind down until the last bomb explodes in the last whale's side? What is it that makes so small a thing of eliminating in our lifetime the oceanic role of the largest creature that has ever lived on our planet? What is it that kills the goose that lays the golden egg? Is our own obituary scrawled in the fates of the bowhead and the right whale, the blue and the hump-back—all species that no longer contribute to the biological systems of which they were a part for millions of years? What is the true use of whales beyond bone, beef and blubber?

The history of whaling is marked by some significant dates, only a few of which we can pinpoint. The day that the first early man encountered a beached whale carcass is lost. The moment that the Basque lookouts spotted their first right whale will never be known, but we can identify 1596 as the year that Willem Barendsz discovered Spitsbergen. Dutchmen and Englishmen in high-pooped sailing vessels braved Arctic cold and ship-crushing ice to hunt the bowhead for its baleen "finnes," which were used in the manufacture of corset stays and busks for ladies of fashion. Halfway around the world, an enterprising Japanese named Kakuemon Taiji threw a wisteria-vine net over a whale, and launched his countrymen on a course of cetacean destruction that would continue uninterrupted for four hundred years. When the *Mayflower* arrived at Cape Cod on

November 21, 1620, the Pilgrims found themselves in the company of black right whales, and decided to remain rather than continue on to Virginia, their original destination. In 1712, Christopher Hussey may have been blown off the Nantucket shore in a storm, and may have killed the first sperm whale in New England waters. Even if the story is apocryphal, there is no doubt that the Nantucketers shortly thereafter began to roam the world in search of the mighty, square-headed cachalots, and developed an industry that would change the way the Western world was lit and lubricated. When the British shipped their first load of convicts to Botany Bay in 1788, they could not have known that the captains would find the waters of Australasia thick with whales. Quick to capitalize, the whalers rounded the Horn in 1789, and discovered the rich whaling grounds of the eastern Pacific. The Nantucket whaler *Maro* encountered more than the riches of Cipango in 1820 when the concentrations of sperm whales were found on the Japan Grounds. Captain Thomas Welcome Roys, who blew off his hand testing a rocket harpoon, sailed through the Bering Strait in 1848, and found these heretofore unexplored waters filled with fat bowheads. In 1855, another whaling captain sailed over the barrier bar at an isolated lagoon on the lonely peninsula that is Baja California, and another whale species was marked for slaughter. Just when it seemed that the world's whales were destined to provide their fat to lubricate the industrial revolution, Colonel Edwin Drake drilled the Western world's first oil well at Titusville, Pennsylvania. Did the discovery of petroleum save the whales?

Hardly. In fact, it provided the impetus for the whalers to mechanize and modernize their industry, and armed with the exploding grenades of Svend Foyn, they took out after the whales with a ven-

GRAND BALL GIVEN BY THE WHALES IN HONOR OF THE DISCOVERY OF THE OIL WELLS IN PENNSYLVANIA.

geance that was fueled by equal portions of greed, blood-lust, and technology. The great rorquals, long considered too fast and too powerful for the whalers in their open rowing boats, were now in firing range. They were harpooned, shot, exploded, poisoned and electrocuted in numbers that defy the imagination. Millions of tons of whales were reduced to their components, for the lights, machines, wars, fashions and tables of the world. Deep in the bone-chilling cold of the Antarctic, the great whales had remained unmolested since the morning of the world. In fifty years, the rapacious whalers found them and slaughtered them to near-extinction. They shot them under the lowering skies of the Ross Sea, and hauled them aboard factory ships with gaping maws that swallowed these 100-ton creatures and reduced them to oil and fertilizer in an hour.

When it appeared that the whalers would run out of whales if they kept up the carnage, they convened to figure out a way whereby they could preserve their industry before they ran out of whales. On May 30, 1949, representatives from fifteen nations met in London, and the International Whaling Commission was born. For the next forty years, this organization, which was supposed to preserve whales for the industry, sat and watched as the whales vanished and the industry deteriorated before their uncomprehending eyes. Compared to the millennium that it took the whalers to reduce the whale stocks to vestigial, scattered populations, the end came remarkably quickly. One by one, the whaling nations quit their deadly, costly, anachronistic business. In 1972, the United Nations passed a unanimous resolution calling for a complete cessation of worldwide whaling. That year, the United States passed its own Marine Mammal Protection Act, which protected all whales, dolphins and seals in American waters, and closed down the last of the American whaling stations. South Africa shut down Durban in 1975, and the Australians conducted an inquiry in 1978 which resulted in the elimination of Australian whaling. In 1982, only the Soviets and the Japanese were killing whales on the high seas.

On July 23, 1982, probably the most important date in the thousand-year history of whaling, the IWC voted for a moratorium on all commercial whaling. Killing whales for money was almost over. Many of the whaling countries protested, objected and litigated; they invented myriad subterfuges and excuses to continue their unnecessary and wasteful business. Faced with declining profits, declining whales, and a manifold increase in global criticism, however, the Soviets quit in 1987 and the Japanese in 1988.

We will not know for years whether the end of whaling came too late. The "great" whales were all decimated to the point where they may never recover. Right whales, humpbacks and bowheads have been reduced to sparse shadow populations throughout the world. We have no idea how many sperm whales there are. Even with worldwide protection, the rorqual species are struggling to survive. We may witness the death of the last blue whale in our lifetime.

When the IWC convened in Brighton in 1983, Peru had withdrawn her objection to the moratorium in exchange for a quota of 165 Bryde's whales which otherwise would not have been allocated. This set the stage for the 1984 meeting, which was, ostensibly, to be the last meeting of the IWC at which whaling quotas would be set. In 1985, the primary subjects would be the moratorium itself (already passed), and the relatively small numbers—but by no means small *issues*—of the whales to be taken by various aboriginal peoples for their own consumption. The days in which the delegates from the whaling nations sat around a table and parceled out the world's whales to their killer ships are over.

SINCE the moratorium has taken effect, whaling has diminished considerably, but whales are still being killed in Alaska, Japan, Norway and Iceland, and various dolphins (not under the jurisdiction of the IWC) are dying in tuna nets and on beaches around the world. Commercial whaling is over, and so the IWC, now deprived of its dedicated function, "to provide for the proper conservation of whale stocks and thus make possible the orderly development of the whaling industry," has no visible purpose, and because of lack of support, very little money. The meetings continue, and the discussions concern the comprehensive assessment* and the concept of "scientific-research whaling." At the 1989 meetings, an air of inconclusiveness could be felt. It is not clear any more what purpose (if any) the IWC is supposed to serve. Assuming that the whaling nations do not take over the forum and reestablish whaling for profit, the watchdog commission has outlived its usefulness. It began as an organization that encouraged the slaughter of the whales, passed through a stage where some of its member nations opposed others on basic whaling issues, and came out of the tunnel into an age of conservation.

Despite its Scientific Committee—members of which labored long and hard to produce a body of science that the commission usually ignored in the name of expediency—it was politics that fueled the IWC. And in most nations, politics is the bedfellow of finance. There was a lot of money to be made from whale-killing. Those who would see the IWC as an organization whose purpose it was to save whales for any other purpose than to be shot by whalers are guilty of an egregious misreading of the history of whaling. That humane killing, marine sanctuaries, and even a complete moratorium on whaling were discussed—and even more astonishingly, *passed*—is a reflection on the times, not on the humanity of the whalers. Every one of them, up to and including those who would later champion a cessation of commercial whaling, wanted more money, which translated into more whales killed. They fought among themselves for allocations and higher quotas, but in the early years of the commission, the cry of "Save the Whales" was only faintly heard.

*The "comprehensive assessment" included in the wording of the *Schedule* amendment that proclaimed the moratorium in 1982 is the last hope of the whalers. It states that "by 1990 at the latest the Commission will undertake a comprehensive assessment of the effects of this decision on whale stocks and consider modification of this provision and the establishment of other catch limits." If an assessment of whale stocks indicates enough of an increase by 1990, the IWC might consider repealing the moratorium and reestablishing whaling for profit.

And finally, it was not the IWC that failed; it was the member nations. The annual meetings only served as a forum for the whaling nations to argue for their right to kill whales for profit; the IWC made no rules that the contracting governments did not propose or support. The commission, after all, had no powers that had not been granted to it by the member nations, and its only employees were administrative. To blame the IWC for the death of whales is like blaming the League of Nations for World War II. Its failure lay in the inability of the whaling countries to recognize that the IWC could have served a positive function. Instead, they bickered over quotas, resigned when things didn't go their way, and generally behaved in a greedy, chauvinistic and uncooperative fashion—the way nations traditionally behave. Of course they didn't support the conservation of whales; they had more important things to worry about, such as money, power and national pride. The whales were pawns in this power struggle, and they died by the millions. Like foot soldiers in another kind of war, they died so that other men could assert themselves. It is probably the greatest miracle of all that any whales survived the protracted war declared upon them by the whale-killers, since there were periods when the whaling industry looked like nothing so much as an all-out, international effort to rid the world of whales.

In the early days of the whale fishery, very few people recognized the delicate nature of the relationship between men and whales. For the most part, men saw whales as products; a perpetual source of matériel for commerce, industry and fashion. Occasionally, however, a small voice was heard to wonder about this one-sided affair, in which one side gave everything while the other took. In 1804, Comte Bernard-Germain de la Cépède, a French anatomist and naturalist, published *Histoire Naturelle des Cétacés,* in which he wrote,

Man, attracted by the treasure that the victory over the whales might afford him, has troubled the peace of their immense solitary abodes, violated their refuges, sacrificed all those which the icy, unapproachable polar deserts could not screen from his blows; and the war he has made on them has been especially cruel because he has seen that it is large catches that make his commerce prosperous, his industry vital, his sailors numerous, his navigators daring, his pilots experienced, his navies strong and his power great.

Thus it is that these giants among giants have fallen beneath his arms; and because his genius is immortal and his science now imperishable, because he has been able to multiply without limit the imaginings of his mind, they will not cease to be the victims of his interest until they have ceased to exist. In vain do they flee before him; his art will transport him to the ends of the earth; they will find no sanctuary except in nothingness.

Afterword

When I began this book, whaling had not ended. The moratorium had been passed in 1982, and was scheduled to take effect in 1985–86, but various whaling countries kept trying to devise some subterfuge to ensure that their whalers could keep working. First four countries filed objections to the moratorium. Then it was "scientific-research whaling," and "small-type coastal whaling." When neither of these schemes passed, they went whaling anyway, claiming their sovereign right to do whatever they wanted, despite the International Whaling Commission, and despite the world view that whale-killing was anachronistic, cruel, and even barbaric.

During my research and writing, however, it appeared as if the end was almost at hand: when their machinations failed to gain support in the commission, the whalers shut down their stations and transferred their ships and men to other pursuits. I actually believed that I was seeing the end of whaling, and I wrote the book as if mankind's war on whales had a recognizable beginning, a middle and an end. Like any other war, however, this one was not over when the shooting stopped.

I did not reckon on the determination of some countries to continue what they had "always" done—even if they had been doing it only for a couple of decades. Yes, many of the whalers did retire their ships and close down their stations, but it may have been a publicity stunt to curry world approbation. When I was in Iceland in the summer of 1990, I saw four of the *Hvalur* whale-catchers tied up in the harbor at Reykjavik. Their cannons were gone, giving the sharply raked bows an odd incompleteness: these ships were *designed* to have a harpoon gun mounted on the bows. When I asked an Icelandic sailor what they were going to do with the ships now that whaling was over, he told me that they were

saving them; they believed they would soon go whaling again.

When the Soviets declared that their whaling industry would be shut down in 1987, I (and everyone else) believed them. The Soviets, after all, were not easily influenced by boycotts and grass-roots protests; if they said they were going to quit whaling, they were probably doing so for reasons of their own. When a Japanese spokesman told me that their whaling stations were closed down, their factory ships turned into tankers, and all their catcher boats converted, I believed him too. The Icelanders, despite their protests, had not even filed an objection to the moratorium when it was passed in 1982, so I assumed, perhaps too naively, that their interference with the conclusion of this thousand-year-old slaughter was just saber- (or rather harpoon-) rattling. I knew that the northern Norwegians and the Greenlanders would continue to take some whales for their own consumption, and I thought that they, like the Alaskan and Canadian Eskimos, ought to be able to hunt small numbers of whales for non-commercial purposes. I believed that the reduction of the number of whales killed, from the tens of thousands of two decades ago to the couple of hundred of today was, if not acceptable, then at least something the world could live with. As far as Eskimo "subsistence whaling" in the Alaskan arctic was concerned, I had tried to make my position known—I felt that the survival of an endangered species of whales took precedence over the "survival" of what I perceived to be a non-threatened culture—but I was hamstrung by government intrigues too arcane for me to comprehend, let alone to influence.

I had not reckoned on the sheer orneriness of the whalers, although as a historian I should have realized that nobody likes being told what to do, especially sovereign nations who feel that their economy—or traditions, or diet—is being threatened, or that they are the victims of unjust discrimination.

The Icelanders submitted yet another research proposal to the IWC's 1990 meeting at Noordwijk in the Netherlands. It was rejected by the Scientific Committee, but Iceland is a country in which calm appearances often bely rumblings below the surface, politically as well as geologically. The Icelanders enthusiastically joined Japan and Norway in an attempt to overthrow the moratorium on commercial whaling, arguing once again that they needed the jobs, the money, the meat, and the pride that accrue from killing whales. (Norway has never withdrawn its objection to the moratorium, so of all the whaling nations, it has the shortest route from non-whaling back to whaling.) Off the record, Iceland threatened to join a North Atlantic whaling cartel (with Norway, Denmark and Canada) if the IWC continued

to pursue the course that would completely eliminate industrial whaling. The Soviet Union, whose decision to terminate its whaling came as such an enormous surprise to the world, is making noises about its need for research whaling. Like the Japanese, the Soviets always performed the necessary research on the whales they killed; to suggest that they need a couple of hundred more statistics to add to their existing thousands is ludicrous. The Japanese hinted that they might simply quit the IWC if they were not allowed to resume whaling.

Future IWC meetings will demonstrate if the anti-whaling coalition is strong enough to withstand the pressure, or if the whaling nations can overthrow world opinion on the agonizingly interminable argument about humankind's "right" to slaughter whales. Rather than writing about the end of whaling, I may have produced only a long interim report. I seriously hope not.

Reykjavik harbor, August 1990. Three Icelandic catcher boats tied up at the dock with their harpoon cannons removed. Will they ever sail again?

Glossary of Whaling Terms

Accumulator: A series of cables and springs on a *catcher boat* that absorbed the shock of a struggling whale after it had been harpooned.

Ambergris: A crumbly, grayish-brown substance found only in the intestines of sperm whales.

Barrel: A unit of measurement equal to 31.5 gallons. "Barrels" were not actually used aboard whaleships; the oil was stored in *casks.*

Blanket Piece: The long piece of blubber stripped from the whale and hauled aboard the ship.

Boatheader: The officer in charge of a whaleboat; the man who actually steered the whaleboat.

Boatsteerer: In Yankee whaling, the harpooner who manned the first oar and changed places with the boatheader when the latter prepared to kill the whale.

Bomb Gun: A smooth-bored shoulder gun from which was fired a bomb lance.

Bone: The keratinous plates of baleen that hang from the upper jaw of certain whales; also known as "whalebone."

Bowhead Whale: *Balaena mysticetus.* Also known in various times and various fisheries as the Greenland whale, the polar whale, and the mysticetus.

Butt: A cask holding 126 gallons.

Cachalot: The sperm whale (*Physeter macrocephalus*); name used by the French but derived from the Basque language.

Capstan: A ship's device with spokes radiating horizontally from a central hub; used to winch up anchor cables, mooring lines or pieces of blubber during flensing.

Catcher Boat: First steam-powered, then diesel, the boats armed with harpoon cannons that killed the whales for processing at shore stations, aboard floating factories and factory ships.

Case: The membrane-enclosed reservoir of clear oil found only in the nose of the sperm whale.

Cask: The general name given to wooden barrels (of varying sizes) used to store oil, food, water, etc., aboard a whaleship.

Clean Ship: A ship that returns to port with no oil.

Cooker: A steel tank aboard factory ships used to cook the meat and blubber of whales; later, pressure cookers.

Cooper: A barrel-maker.

Cutting-in: The process of removing the blubber and whalebone from a whale carcass.

Cutting Stage: A platform of boards suspended from the starboard side of a whaler from which the carcass was cut-in and the blubber removed. Employed only in the sperm whale fishery.

Dart: To heave (or pitch, or toss) the harpoon. The word "throw" was never used.

Darting Gun: A small gun attached to the harpoon shaft that detonated when the iron struck the whale.

Draw: To pull out; as when the harpoon pulled out of the whale.

Drift Ice: Ice that moves with the current.

Drogue: A piece of wood fastened to a whale line to slow own the harpooned whale.

Duck: Linen or cotton cloth, lighter than canvas; used for outer clothing, especially trousers.

Duff (also Plum Duff): A mixture of flour, yeast, raisins and lard.

Factory Ship: A self-contained factory with facilities for hauling whales on deck and processing them aboard.

Fall: In British whaling, the act of lowering the boats after a whale.

Fast Boat: A boat attached by a line to a running whale.

Fast Whale: A whale that has been harpooned but not killed.

Fish: The whaleman's term for a whale.

Fishery: A collective term applied to the hunting of a particular species of whale, *e.g.,* "the Bowhead fishery," or a particular location, *e.g.,* "the Greenland fishery."

Flensing (also Flenching; Flinching; etc.): Stripping the blubber from the whale.

Floating Factory: The predecessor of the *factory ship;* whales were flensed alongside and processed aboard.

Floe: A sheet of sea ice.

Flue: The barb of a harpoon.

Flukes: The tail or caudal fin of a whale.

Flurry: The final struggle of a dying whale.

Foreganger: A line that connects the harpoon to the main whale line. It was spliced to a hand harpoon and fixed to a sliding ring in gun harpoons.

Gally: To frighten a whale during the approach.

Gam: A visit between whaleships at sea.

Gluewater: The liquid residue after cooking; used in the manufacture of glue. (Nor.)

Grax: The solid residue remaining after boiling blubber; used to manufacture fertilizer. (Nor.)

Green Hand (also Greenhorn; Greenie): A sailor on his first whaling voyage.

Grounds: An area where whales were known to congregate, *e.g.,* "the Japan Grounds," "the Western Island Grounds," etc.

Guano: Dried meat and bone meal; a product of modern processing used as a fertilizer. (Nor.)

Gunner: Aboard a *catcher boat,* the officer who manned the harpoon cannon and shot the whale.

Hardtack: A thick, square biscuit, baked hard to resist dampness.

Headbone: The whale's upper jaw, to which the baleen was attached.

Head Matter: The oil from the *case* and the *junk* of a sperm whale.

Horse Piece: A piece of blubber several inches wide and a few feet long; removed in the next step after cutting the blanket piece.

Hval-Kla (Whale-claw): The huge pincers used aboard *factory ships* to grab the carcass and drag it up the slipway. (Nor.)

Iron: The whaleman's name for the harpoon, and also the entire instrument, including the wooden shaft.

Junk: The spongy mass below the *case* in the sperm whale's head; an additional source of spermaceti oil.

Kanaka: Whaleman's term for Polynesians; from the Hawaiian for "native islander."

Kayak: An Eskimo word for a narrow skin boat for one (rarely two) hunters.

Kreng: The stripped carcass of the bowhead; used in the nineteenth-century British Greenland Fishery.

Krill: A Norwegian word meaning whale food, usually referring to the shrimplike crustacean *Euphausia superba.*

Lance: The instrument used for killing the whale after it had been harpooned.

Larboard: The port side of a vessel; used only on whaling ships after the eighteenth century.

Lay: The whaleman's share of the profits of a whaling voyage.

Lead: A lane of open water in the ice.

Life: The heart and lungs of a whale, where the lance was aimed.

Lobscouse: Beef and bread hash, sometimes with vegetables added.

Loose Whale: A whale that has been harpooned but to which no lines were attached.

Making-off: Chopping the blubber into pieces to pass through the bunghole of the casks. (Br.)

Mince: To slice the blubber before boiling.

Nantucket Sleigh Ride: The towing of a whaleboat by a running whale; probably a layman's term and seldom used in the fishery.

Nipped: To be trapped in the ice. (Br.)

Pitch-Pole: To throw the iron high so that it made a considerable arc before hitting the whale.

Plum-Pudding Voyage: A short New England whaling voyage, often in the North Atlantic.

Polar Whale: The bowhead, *Balaena mysticetus.*

Right Whale: *Balaena glacialis.* Also known in various times and in various fisheries as the black right whale, black whale, Biscayan right whale, and *Noordkaper.*

Ripsack: The gray whale, *Eschrichtius robustus.*

Rorqual: Any of the groove-throated whales of the genus *Balaenoptera.*

Salt Horse: Salted beef, stored in casks.

Salt Junk: Salted pork, stored in casks.

Scrimshaw: The whaleman's art of carving on sperm whale teeth, but also on other bones as well as walrus teeth, etc.

Shooks: Barrel staves.

Shore Station: A facility on land for the processing of whales.

Skrott: The flensed carcass of a whale. (Nor.)

Slop Chest: The ship's store, from which were dispensed clothing, tobacco, knives, etc.

Small: The narrowest part of the whale's caudal peduncle; just forward of the insertion of the flukes.

Sound: To dive deeply; often to escape the pain of the harpoon.

Spectioneer: In the British fishery, the chief harpooner who directed the flensing of the whale, from the Dutch *Specksnyder,* or "blubber-cutter."

Sperm Oil (also Spermaceti): The clear amber oil contained in the *case* of the sperm whale.

Stern Slipway: The opening and ramp in a factory ship that allowed a full-sized whale to be hauled aboard for processing.

Stove: Broken, smashed, holed; as a ship or boat.

Strike: To harpoon a whale; to make fast.

Sulfurbottom: The blue whale, *Balaenoptera musculus.*

Toggle Iron: A harpoon with a hinged head that rotated when in the whale's flesh to prevent it from drawing out.

Train Oil: See "Whale oil."

Try-out: To render the oil from the blubber.

Trypot: An iron caldron set over a fire in the brick fire box for the boiling of the oil.

Tryworks: The brick oven in which the pots were set for the trying-out of the oil.

Tun: A measure of volume; the equivalent of 252 gallons.

Umiak (also Oomiak): An Eskimo skin boat for eight or more men.

Whalecraft: The equipment used for fastening to and killing a whale, cutting-in, trying-out and stowing down the oil.

Whale Oil: The oil obtained from any whales except the sperm whale.

Windlass: A contrivance for hauling in lines under strain. Where the axle of a *capstan* is vertical, that of the windlass is horizontal.

Bibliography

ADAMS, J. 1979. The IWC and Bowhead Whaling: An Eskimo Perspective. *Orca* 1(1):11–12.

ADAMS, J. E. 1975. Primitive Whaling in the West Indies. *Sea Frontiers* 21(5):303–13.

ADAMSON, P. (n.d.) *The Great Whale to Snare: The Whaling Trade of Hull.* City of Kingston upon Hull Museums.

AGUILAR, A. 1981. The Black Right Whale, *Eubalaena glacialis,* in the Cantabrian Sea. *Rep. Intl. Whal. Commn.* 31:457–59.

———. 1985. A Review of Old Basque Whaling and its Effect on the Right Whales (*Eubalaena glacialis*) of the North Atlantic. *Rep. Intl. Whal. Commn.* (Special Issue) 10:191–99.

ALLEN, E. S. 1973. *Children of the Light: The Rise and Fall of New Bedford Whaling and the Death of the Arctic Fleet.* Little, Brown.

ALLEN, G. 1916. The Whalebone Whales of New England. *Mem. Boston Soc. Nat. Hist.* 8(2):109–322.

ALLEN, K. R. 1980. *Conservation and Management of Whales.* University of Washington Press.

ANCHER, E. A. 1976. *Mosman's Bay: The Romance of an Old Whaling Station.* Mosman Historical Society. Sydney.

ANDERSON, C. R. 1939. *Melville in the South Seas.* Columbia University Press.

ANDERSON, J. 1878. *Anatomical and Zoological Researches Comprising an Account of the Zoological Results of the Two Expeditions to Western Yunnan in 1868 and 1875, and a Monograph of the Two Cetacean Genera* Platanista *and* Orcaella. London.

ANDREWS, R. C. 1911. Shore-Whaling: A World Industry. *National Geographic* 22(5):411–42.

———. 1916. *Whale Hunting with Gun and Camera.* D. Appleton.

———. 1929. *Ends of the Earth.* G. P. Putnam's Sons.

ANON. 1860. A Summer in New Bedford. *Harper's New Monthly Magazine* 21(121):6–19.

ANON. 1908. The Production of Whalebone. *National Geographic* 29(12):883–85.

ANON. 1951. Dutch Whaling Operations. *Norsk Hvalfangst-Tidende* 40(4):202–3.

ANON. 1954. The Japanese Whaling Industry. *Norsk Hvalfangst-Tidende* 43(11):625–31.

ANON. 1954. Rotary Whale Harpoons. *Norsk Hvalfangst-Tidende* 43(11):650–51.

ANON. 1954. Whales on Show. *Norsk Hvalfangst-Tidende* 43(8):457–59.

ANON. 1955. "Olympic Challenger" has not observed the provisions of the International Whaling Convention. *Norsk Hvalfangst-Tidende* 44(11):645–61.

ANON. 1955. The Soviet Whaling Industry. *Norsk Hvalfangst-Tidende* 44(3):150–52.

ANON. 1955. Wounded Whale Attacks Catching Boat. *Norsk Hvalfangst-Tidende* 44(3):133–34.

ANON. 1956. "Olympic Challenger" has not observed the provisions of the International Whaling Convention. *Norsk Hvalfangst-Tidende* 45(1):1–16.

ANON. 1956. War Against Killer Whales in Iceland. *Norsk Hvalfangst-Tidende* 45(10):570, 573.

ANON. 1957. The Chilean/Japanese Whaling Station in Chile. *Norsk Hvalfangst-Tidende* 46(7):396–97.

ANON. 1957. Japanese Whaling from Chile. *Norsk Hvalfangst-Tidende* 46(1):12–13.

ANON. 1958. Factory Ship Equipment from West Germany to Russia. *Norsk Hvalfangst-Tidende* 47(9):458.

ANON. 1958. Good Season for the Union Whaling Company at Durban. *Norsk Hvalfangst-Tidende* 47(2):82.

ANON. 1958. The Russian Expansion. *Norsk Hvalfangst-Tidende* 47(10):507.

ANON. 1978. Hunting of the Gray Whale Could Be Revived. *New York Times* June 18, 1978:10.

ANON. 1985. Whaling in the Caribbean. *Center for Environmental Education Report* 3(2):6.

ANTHONY, H. E. 1933. Glimpses into the Hall of Ocean Life. *Natural History* 33(4):365–80.

ARAI, Y., AND S. SAKAI. 1952. Whale Meat in Nutrition. *Sci. Rep. Whales Res. Inst.* 7:51–67.

ARISTOTLE. *Historia Animalium.* Translated by D'Arcy Wentworth Thompson. Clarendon Press. 1910.

ARLOV, T. B. 1990. *Norwegian Sealing and Whaling in the 17th and 18th Century.* Paper presented at the 15th Annual Whaling Symposium, Kendall Whaling Museum, Sharon, Mass. Oct. 13–14, 1990.

ARNBOM, T. 1989. The New Whalewatchers. *WhaleNews* 39:1–2.

ARRIAN. 1983. History of Alexander and Indica. Loeb Classical Library. Harvard University Press. Cambridge.

ASHLEY, C. W. 1938. *The Yankee Whaler.* The Riverside Press (Houghton Mifflin).

AXELSON, E. 1980. Table Bay: The Gradual Shaping of a Sailors' Haven. *Oceans* 13(4):14–19.

BACH, J. 1982. *A Maritime History of Australia.* Pan Books.

BAILEY, A. M., AND R. W. HENDEE. 1926. Notes on the Mammals of Northwestern Alaska. *Jour. Mammal.* 7:9–28.

———, AND J. H. SORENSEN. 1962. Subantarctic Campbell Island. *Proc. Denver Mus. Nat. Hist.* 10:1–305.

BAKER, A. N. 1983. *Whales & Dolphins of New Zealand and Australia.* Victoria University Press.

BAKKEN, A. 1964. One Hundred Years of Norwegian Whaling. *Norsk Hvalfangst-Tidende* 53(11):122–37.

BALCOMB, K. 1991. What's It All About, Humphrey? *Whalewatcher* 24(4):3–5.

BANFIELD, A. W. F. 1974. *The Mammals of Canada.* University of Toronto Press.

BANNISTER, J. L. 1974. Whale Populations and Current Research off Western Australia. In W. E. Schevill, Ed., *The Whale Problem: A Status Report.* pp. 239–54. Harvard University Press.

———. 1986. Notes on Nineteenth Century Catches of Southern Right Whales (*Eubalaena australis*) off the Southern Coasts of Western Australia. *Rep. Intl. Whal. Commn.* (Special Issue) 10:255–67.

BARKHAM, S. H. 1984. The Basque Whaling Establishments in Labrador 1536–1632—A Summary. *Arctic* 37:515–19.

BARNES, R. H. 1980. Cetaceans and Cetacean Hunting: Lamalera, Indonesia. *World Wildlife Fund Project No. 1428.* Gland, Switzerland.

BARNUM, P. T. 1870. *Struggles and Triumphs, or, Forty Years' Recollections.* J. B. Burr & Co.

BARTHELMESS, K. 1987. Walfangtechnik vor 375 Jahren: Die Zeichnungen in Robert Fotherby's "Journal" von 1613 und ihr Einfluss auf die Druckgraphik. *Deutsches Schiffahrtsarchiv* 10:289–324.

———. 1989a. The Sperm Whales *Physeter macrocephalus* at Berckhey in 1598 and on the Springersplat in 1606— A Discovery in Early Iconography. *Lutra* 32(21):185–92.

———. 1989b. Walkinnlanden in Wanten: Maritime Motivkunde als historische Datierungshilfe (Whale Jawbones in the Shrouds: Maritime Iconography as a Datable Source for a Badly Documented Historical Practice). *Deutsches Schiffarchiv* 12:243–64.

———. 1990a. *Olympic Challenger: The Brief History of the Onassis Whaling Venture, 1950–56.* Paper presented at the 15th Annual Whaling Symposium, Kendall Whaling Museum, Sharon, Mass. Oct. 13–14, 1990.

———. 1990b. *Jaws: Uses of Baleen Whale Mandibles.* Paper presented at the 15th Annual Whaling Symposium, Kendall Whaling Museum, Sharon, Mass. Oct. 13–14, 1990.

BASBERG, B. L. 1990a. *Whaling or Shipping? Conflicts over the Use of the Norwegian Whaling Fleet During World War II.* Paper presented at the 15th Annual Whaling Symposium, Kendall Whaling Museum, Sharon, Mass. Oct. 13–14, 1990.

———. 1990b. *Report on the 1990 Norwegian Antarctic Expedition, Including the Husvik and Stromness Stations.* Paper presented at the 15th Annual Whaling Symposium, Kendall Whaling Museum, Sharon, Mass. Oct. 13–14, 1990.

BASS, G. 1972. *A History of Seafaring Based on Underwater Archaeology.* Thames and Hudson.

BEACH, D. W., AND M. T. WEINRICH. 1989. Watching the Whales. *Oceanus* 32(1):84–88.

BEAGLEHOLE, J. C. 1966. *The Exploration of the Pacific.* Stanford University Press.

BEALE, T. 1835. *A Few Observations on the Natural History of the Sperm Whale.* London.

BECKER, P. 1985. *The Pathfinders: The Saga of Exploration in Southern Africa.* Penguin.

BEDDARD, F. E. 1900. *A Book of Whales.* John Murray.

BENNETT, A. G. 1932. *Whaling in the Antarctic.* Henry Holt.

BERGENSEN, B., AND J. T. RUUD. 1941. Pelagic Whaling in the Antarctic. IX. The Season 1938–39. *Hvalradets Skrifter* 25:5–31.

———, J. LIE, AND J. T. RUUD. 1939. Pelagic Whaling in the Antarctic. VIII. The Season 1937–38. *Hvalradets Skrifter* 20:5–30.

BERNSTEIN, A. 1959. *Masterpieces of Women's Costume of the 18th and 19th Centuries.* Crown.

BERZIN, A. A. 1972. *The Sperm Whale.* Izdatgel'stvo "Pischevaya Promyshlennost" Moskva 1971. Translated from the Russian by Israel Program for Scientific Translations. Jerusalem.

———, AND N. V. DOROSHENKO. 1980. Right Whales of the Okhotsk Sea. *Sci. Com. Rept. Intl. Whal. Commn. SC/32/PS2.*

———. 1981. Distribution and Abundance of Right Whales (*Balaenidae*) in the North Pacific Ocean. *Intl. Whal. Commn. SC/33/PS11.*

BEST, P. B. 1970. Exploitation and Recovery of Right Whales *Eubalaena australis* off the Cape Province. *Div. Sea Fisheries Invest. Rept. S. Afr.* 80:1–20.

———. 1974. Status of the Whale Populations off the West Coast of South Africa, and Current Research. In W. E. Schevill, Ed., *The Whale Problem,* pp. 53–86. Harvard University Press.

———. 1982. The Status of Right Whales off South Africa. *Sci. Rep. Intl. Whal. Commn. SC/32/PS4.*

———, AND L. C. SURMON. 1974. Conservation and Utilisation of Whales off the Natal Coast. *Jour. South Afr. Wildl. Mgmt. Assoc.* 4(3):149–56.

———, AND G. J. B. ROSS. 1986. Catches of Right Whales from Shore-based Establishments in Southern Africa, 1792–1975. *Rep. Intl. Whal. Commn.* (Special Issue) 10:275–89.

BICKFORD, A., S. BLAIR, AND P. FREEMAN. 1988. *Ben Boyd National Park Bicentennial Project; Davidson Whaling Station; Boyd's Tower; Bittangabee Ruins.* NSW National Parks and Wildlife Service.

BIRKELAND, K. B. 1926. *The Whalers of Akutan: An Account of Modern Whaling in the Aleutian Islands.* Yale University Press.

BLACK, L. T. 1980. Early History. In L. Morgan, Ed., "The Aleutians." *Alaska Geographic* 7(3):82–105.

———. 1988. The Story of Russian America. In W. W. Fitzhugh and A. Crowell, Eds., *Crossroads of Continents,* pp. 70–82. Smithsonian Institution.

BLAINEY, G. 1974. *The Tyranny of Distance: How Distance Shaped Australia's History.* Macmillan.

BLAIR, S., A. BICKFORD, AND P. FREEMAN. 1987. Davidson's Whaling Station, Twofold Bay. *Heritage Australia* 6(3):13–16.

BOAS, F. 1930. *The Religion of the Kwakiutl Indians.* Columbia University Press.

———. 1955. *Primitive Art.* Dover.

BOCK, P. 1966. *A Study in International Regulation: The Case of Whaling.* Ph.D. Dissertation, New York University. University Microfilms.

BOCKSTOCE, J. R. 1977a. Eskimo Whaling in Alaska. *Alaska Magazine* 43(9):4–6.

———. 1977b. An Issue of Survival: Bowhead vs. Tradition. *Audubon* 79(5):142–45.

———. 1977c. *Steam Whaling in the Western Arctic.* Old Dartmouth Historical Society. New Bedford, Mass.

———. 1978a. The Arctic Whaling Disaster of 1897. *Alaska Geographic* 5(4):27–34.

———. 1978b. History of Commercial Whaling in Arctic Alaska. *Alaska Geographic* 5(4):17–25.

———. 1978c. A Preliminary Estimate of the Western Arctic Bowhead Whale (*Balaena mysticetus*) Population by the Pelagic Whaling Industry: 1848–1915. *Rep. No. MMC77/08 (PB 286–797) Nat. Tech. Info. Svc.* Springfield, Va.

———. 1980. Battle of the Bowheads. *Natural History* 89(5):52–61.

———. 1986. *Whales, Ice, & Men: The History of Whaling in the Western Arctic.* University of Washington Press.

———. 1990. Changing Images of the Northwest Passage. *National Geographic* 178(2):2–33.

———, AND D. B. BOTKIN. 1980. The Historical Status and Reduction of the Western Arctic Bowhead (*Balaena mysticetus*) Population by the Pelagic Whaling Industry: *Final Rept. to NMFS, Contract No. 03-78-M02-0212.* Washington, D.C.

BODFISH, H. H. 1936. *Chasing the Bowhead.* Harvard University Press.

BOERI, D. 1980. Oil on Troubled Alaskan Waters. *New York Times Magazine* Nov. 9, 1980:132–55.

———. 1983. *People of the Ice Whale.* E. P. Dutton.

BOGEN, H. S. I. 1954. Compañía Argentina de Pesca S.A. *Norsk Hvalfangst-Tidende* 43(10):553–88.

BONNER, W. N. 1982. *Seals and Man: A Study in Interactions.* University of Washington Press.

BOOTH, A. E. 1964. American Whalers in South African Waters. *S. Afr. Jour. Econ.* 32:278–82.

BOREAL INSTITUTE OF NORTHERN STUDIES. 1988. *Small-Type Coastal Whaling in Japan.* Boreal Institute for Northern Studies. Edmonton, Alberta.

BOWEN, S. L. 1974. Probable Extinction of the Korean Stock of the Gray Whale. *Jour. Mammal.* 55(1):208–9.

BRAHAM, H. W. 1982. Comments on the World Stocks of Bowhead Whales and Estimating Total Population Abundance in the Western Arctic. *Sci. Rep. Intl. Whal. Commn.* SC/34/PS13.

———. 1982. Uncontrolled Exploitation of White Whales and Narwhals. *Cetus* 4(2):6.

———. 1984a. The Bowhead Whale, *Balaena mysticetus. Marine Fisheries Review* 46(4):45–53.

———. 1984b. The Status of Endangered Whales: An Overview. *Marine Fisheries Review* 46(4):2–6.

———. 1989. Eskimos, Yankees and Bowheads. *Oceanus* 32(1):54–62.

———, AND J. M. BREIWICK. 1980. Projection of a Decline in the Western Arctic Population of Bowhead Whales. *Nat. Marine Mammal Lab.* Seattle.

———, AND B. KROGMAN. 1977. Population Biology of the Bowhead (*Balaena mysticetus*) and Beluga (*Delphinapterus leucas*) whale in the Bering, Chukchi, and Beaufort Seas. *Proc. Rep. U.S. Dept. Commerce, Northeast and Alaska Fish. Cntr.* Seattle.

———, B. KROGMAN, S. LEATHERWOOD, W. MARQUETTE, D. RUGH, M. TILLMAN, J. JOHNSON, AND G. CARROLL. 1979. Preliminary Report of the 1978 Spring Bowhead Research Program Results. *Rep. Intl. Whal. Commn.* 29:291–306.

———, B. KROGMAN, J. JOHNSON, W. MARQUETTE, D. RUGH, R. SONNTAG, T. BRAY, J. BRUEGGEMAN, M. DAHLHEIM, M. NERINI, S. SAVAGE, AND C. GOEBEL. 1980. Population Studies of the Bowhead Whale (*Balaena mysticetus*): Preliminary Results of the 1979 Spring Research Season. *Rep. Intl. Whal. Commn.* 30:391–404.

———, AND D. W. RICE. 1984. The Right Whale, *Balaena glacialis. Marine Fisheries Review* 46(4):38–44.

BREWINGTON, M. V., AND D. BREWINGTON. 1965. *Kendall Museum Paintings.* Kendall Whaling Museum. Sharon, Mass.

———. 1969. *Kendall Museum Prints.* Kendall Whaling Museum. Sharon, Mass.

BRITTEN, B. 1989. A Checkered Stewardship of Whales: The International Whaling Commission. *Whalewatcher* 23(3):14–17.

BROEZE, F. J. A. 1977. The Dutch Quest of Southern Whaling in the Nineteenth Century. In M. Nijhoff, *Economisch-En Sociaal-Historisch Jaarboek* 40:66–112.

BROWER, C. D. 1942. *Fifty Years Below Zero, A Lifetime of Adventure in the Far North.* Dodd, Mead.

BROWN, M. 1987. The Zeal of Disapproval. *Oceans* 20(3):36–41.

BROWNE, J. R. 1846. *Etchings of a Whaling Cruise, With Notes of a Sojourn on the Island of Zanzibar. To Which is Appended a Brief History of the Whale Fishery, Its Past and Present Condition.* Harper & Brothers. Reprinted 1968, Harvard University Press.

BROWNELL, R. L., AND C. CHUN. 1977. Probable Existence of the Korean Stock of the Gray Whale, *Eschrichtius robustus. Jour. Mammal.* 58(2):237–39.

BRUEMMER, F. 1969. The Sea Unicorn. *Audubon* 71(6): 58–63.

———. 1971. Whalers of the North. *The Beaver* (Winter 1971):44–55.

———. 1974. The Northernmost People (Greenland's Polar Eskimos). *Natural History* 83(2):24–33.

BRYANT, J. 1982. Trends in Melville Scholarship: Dissertations in the 1970s. *Melville Society Extracts* 50:12–13.

BRYDEN, M. M. 1978. Whales and whaling in Queensland waters. *Proc. Royal Soc. Qld.* 88:5–18.

BUDKER, P. 1959. *Whales and Whaling.* Macmillan.

BULLEN, F. 1899. *The Cruise of the "Cachalot": Round the World after Sperm Whales.* D. Appleton.

BURN-MURDOCH, W. G. 1917. *Modern Whaling & Bear-Hunting.* Seeley, Service & Co. Ltd.

BURTEL, M. 1828. *Art de Faire Les Corsets, Les Guêtres et Les Gauts.* Andot.

BURTON, R. 1971. *The Life and Death of Whales.* Universe Books.

BURTON, R. F. 1875. *Ultima Thule; or, A Summer in Iceland.* William P. Nimmo.

BUSBY, L. 1986. Whaling at the Crossroads. *Greenpeace Examiner* 11(3):16–19.

BUSCH, B. C. 1980. Elephants and Whales: New London and Desolation. *American Neptune* 40(2):117–26.

BUSCH, B. C. 1985. Cape Verdeans in the American Whaling and Sealing Industry, 1850–1900. *American Neptune* 45(2):104–16.

BYRNE, M. ST. C. 1926. *The Elizabethan Zoo.* (Selected from Philemon Holland's Translation of Pliny 1601 and Edward Topsell's "Historie of Foure-Footed Beastes" 1607 & his "Historie of Serpents" 1608.) Haslewood Books.

CALDWELL, D. K., AND M. C. CALDWELL. 1975. Dolphin and Small Whale Fisheries of the Caribbean and West Indies: Occurrence, History and Catch Statistics—with Special Reference to the Lesser Antillean Island of St. Vincent. *Jour. Fish. Bull. Canada* 32(7):1105–10.

———, W. F. RATHJEN, AND J. R. SULLIVAN. 1971. Cetaceans from the Lesser Antillean Island of St. Vincent. *Fish. Bull.* 69(2):303–12.

CAMERON, I. 1974. *Antarctica: The Last Continent.* Little, Brown.

CAPLIN, R. A. 1854. *Health and Beauty: or, Corsets and Clothing, Constructed in Accordance with the Physiological Laws of the Human Body.* Darton & Co.

CAREY, L. 1986. May the Moon Smile Upon the Hunters of the Sea (Lembata Whalers). *Ligabue* 5(9):102–24.

CARTER, N., AND A. THORNTON. 1985. *Pirate Whaling 1985 and a History of the Subversion of International Whaling Regulations.* Environmental Investigation Agency. London.

CHAPMAN, D. G. (WITH S. J. HOLT AND K. R. ALLEN). 1964. Special Committee of Three Scientists. Final Report. *Rep. Int. Whal. Commn.* 14:39–106.

CHAPMAN, F. P. 1977. Some Notes on Early Whaling in False Bay. *Bull. Simon's Town Hist. Soc.* 9(4):132–59.

CHITTLEBOROUGH, R. G. 1954. Aerial observations on whales in Australian waters. *Norsk Hvalfangst-Tidende* 43(10):198–200.

CHRISP, J. 1958. *South of Cape Horn: A Story of Antarctic Whaling.* Robert Hale.

CHRISTRUP, J. 1988. Weird Science: Killing Whales in Order to Save Them. *Greenpeace* 13(5):12–13.

CHURCH, A. C. 1938. *Whale Ships and Whaling.* Bonanza Books.

CLARK, C. W. 1991. Moving with the Heard. *Natural History* 3/91:38–42.

CLARK, K. 1977. *Animals and Men.* William Morrow.

CLARK, M. 1980. *A Short History of Australia.* New American Library.

CLARKE, M. R. 1979. The Head of the Sperm Whale. *Scientific American* 240(1):128–41.

CLARKE, R. 1952. Electric Whaling. *Nature* (London) 69(4308):859–60.

———. 1953. Sperm Whaling from Open Boats in the Azores. *Norsk Hvalfangst-Tidende* 42(7):373–85.

———. 1954. Open Boat Whaling in the Azores. *Discovery Reports* 26:281–354.

COCKRILL, W. R. 1955. *Antarctic Hazard.* Frederick Muller.

COERR, E., AND W. E. EVANS. 1980. *Gigi: A Baby Whale Borrowed for Science and Returned to the Sea.* G. P. Putnam's.

COLMER, M. 1979. *Whalebone to See-Through: A History of Body Packaging.* Johnson & Bacon.

COLWELL, M. 1969. *Whaling Around Australia.* Rigby Ltd.

COMPTON-BISHOP, Q. M. 1982. Sperm Whaling in the Azores. *Whalewatcher* 16(3):9–11.

CONWAY, W. M. 1906. *No Man's Land: A History of Spitsbergen from its Discovery in 1596 to the Beginning of Scientific Exploration of the Country.* Cambridge University Press.

COOK, J. A. 1926. *Pursuing the Whale.* Houghton Mifflin.

COOPER, J. F. 1823. *The Pilot.* New York.

CRAWFORD, J. C. 1880. *Recollections of Travel in Australia and New Zealand.* Trubner.

CRAWFORD, M. D. C., AND E. A. GUERNSEY. 1951. *The History of Corsets in Pictures.* Fairchild Publications.

CREDLAND, A. G. (n.d.) *The Diana of Hull.* City of Kingston upon Hull Museums and Art Galleries.

———. 1982. *Whales and Whaling.* City of Kingston upon Hull Museums, Shire Books.

CREMERS-VAN DER DOES, E. C. 1980. *The Agony of Fashion.* Blandford Press.

CROWTHER, W. E. L. H. 1943. A Surgeon as Whaleship Owner. *Medical Journal of Australia* 1(25):549–54.

CUMBAA, S. L. 1985. Archaeological Evidence of the 16th Century Basque Right Whale Fishery in Labrador. *Rep. Intl. Whal. Commn.* (Special Issue) 10:187–90.

CUSHING, D. H. 1988. *The Provident Sea.* Cambridge University Press.

DAKIN, W. J. 1938. *Whalemen Adventurers.* Angus & Robertson.

DALL, W. H. 1874. Catalogue of the Cetacea of the North Pacific Ocean. In C. M. Scammon, *The Marine Mammals of the Northwestern Coast of North America: Together with an Account of the American Whale Fishery.* Carmany and G. P. Putnam's.

DALL, W. H. 1899. How Long a Whale May Carry a Harpoon. *National Geographic* 10(4):136–37.

DAMPIER, W. 1702. *Dampier's Voyages.* 1906 edition edited by John Masefield. E. Grant Richards.

DARLING, J. D. 1988. Whales: An Era of Discovery. *National Geographic* 174(6):872–909.

DARWIN, C. 1860. *The Voyage of the Beagle.* 1962 Edition, Doubleday.

DAVIDSON, R. 1988. *Whalemen of Twofold Bay.* Privately printed, Eden, NSW.

DAVIS, E. Y. 1946. Man in Whale. *Natural History* 6:241.

DAVIS, L. J. 1986. *Onassis: Aristotle and Christina.* St. Martin's Press.

DAVIS, M. R., AND W. H. GILMAN. (EDS.) 1960. *The Letters of Herman Melville.* Yale University Press.

DAVIS, W. M. 1874. *Nimrod of the Sea, or, The American Whaleman.* Christopher Publishing House.

DAWBIN, W. H. 1954a. The Maori Went A-Whaling—and Became One of the World's Best Whalemen. *Pacific Discovery* 7(4):19–22.

———. 1954b. Maori Whaling. *Norsk Hvalfangst-Tidende* 43(8):433–45.

———. 1954c. Whales and Whaling in the Southern Ocean. In F. Simpson, Ed., *The Antarctic Today,* pp. 151–97. A. H. & A. W. Reed.

———. 1956. Whale Marking in South Pacific Waters. *Norsk Hvalfangst-Tidende* 43(8):433–45.

———. 1966. The Seasonal Migratory Cycle of Humpback Whales. In K. S. Norris, Ed., *Whales, Dolphins, and Porpoises,* pp. 145–70. University of California Press.

———. 1967. Whaling in New Zealand Waters. In *An Encyclopedia of New Zealand,* pp. 3–7. Government Printer, Wellington.

———. 1984. Whaling and Its Impact on the People of the South Pacific. In P. Stanbury and L. Bushell, Eds., *South Pacific Islands,* pp. 77–90. The Macleay Museum, University of Sydney.

———. 1986. Right Whales Caught in Waters Around South Eastern Australia and New Zealand During the Nineteenth and Early Twentieth Centuries. *Rep. Intl. Whal. Commn.* (Special Issue) 10:261–67.

DAY, A. G. 1970. *Melville's South Seas.* Hawthorn Books.

DAY, D. 1987. *The Whale War.* Routledge & Kegan Paul.

DEIMER, P. 1983. Sperm Whale Fishery off Madeira. *Int. Whal. Commn.* SC/35/Sp5.

———, J. GORDON, AND T. ARNBOM. 1988. Sperm Whales Killed in the Azores During 1987. *Int. Whal. Commn.* SC/40/Sp5.

DE JONG, C. 1976. A Whaleboat the First Museum Ship in South Africa? *Restorica* (Bulletin of the Simon van der Stel Foundation, Pretoria) 17(33):77–78.

———. 1978. *A Short History of Old Dutch Whaling.* University of South Africa.

———. 1983. The Hunt of the Greenland Whale: A Short History and Statistical Sources. *Rep. Int. Whal. Commn.* (Special Issue) 5:83–106.

———. 1986. Melville's Mockery of Foreign Whalers. *Deutsches Schiffartsarchiv* 9:217–26.

DE SMET, W. M. A. 1981. Evidence of Whaling in the North Sea and English Channel during the Middle Ages. In *Mammals in the Seas.* FAO Fisheries Series No. 5, Vol. III, pp. 301–9. Food and Agriculture Organization of the United Nations. Rome.

DEWHURST, W. H. 1835. *The Natural History of the Order Cetacea and the Oceanic Inhabitants of the Arctic Regions.* London.

DIAMOND, M. 1988. *The Seahorse and the Wanderer: Ben Boyd in Australia.* Melbourne University Press.

DIJKSMAN, R. 1986. Death on Jan Mayen: A Whaling Tragedy of 1634. *Polar Record* 23(143):196–201.

DINGHAM, R. 1978. Lessons from the History of Sealing and Whaling in Japanese-American Relations. In J. Schmidhauser and G. O. Totten, Eds., *The Whaling Issue in U.S.-Japan Relations,* pp. 17–27. Westview Press.

DOW, G. F. 1925. *Whale Ships and Whaling.* Marine Research Society. Salem, Mass.

DOYLE, A. C. 1893. The Glamour of the Arctic. *McClure's Magazine* 2:391–400.

———. 1897. Life on a Greenland Whaler. *The Strand Magazine* 13:16–25.

DRUCKER, P. 1951. The Northern and Central Nootkan Tribes. *Bull. Bureau of American Ethnology* 144.

DUDLEY, P. 1725. An Essay upon the Natural History of Whales, with Particular Account of the Ambergris found in the Sperma Ceti Whale. *Phil. Trans. Royal Soc. London* 33(387):256–59.

DUGUY, R., AND D. ROBINEAU. 1973. *Cétacés et Phoques des Côtes de France.* Annales de la Société des Sciences Naturelles de la Charente-Maritime.

DU PASQUIER, T. 1982. *Les Baleiniers Francais au XIXe Siècle 1814–1868.* Terre et Mer.

DURHAM, F. E. 1972a. Greenland or Bowhead Whale. In A. Seed, Ed., *Baleen Whales in Eastern North Pacific and Arctic Waters,* pp. 10–14. Pacific Search Press.

———. 1972b. History of Bowhead Whaling. In A. Seed, Ed., *Baleen Whales in Eastern North Pacific and Arctic Waters,* pp. 5–9. Pacific Search Press.

———. 1977. Subsistence Hunting by Natives of NW Greenland. In *Proc. (Abstracts) Second Conference on the Biology of Marine Mammals,* p. 62. San Diego.

———. 1979a. The Catch of Bowhead Whales (*Balaena mysticetus*) by Eskimos, with Emphasis on the Western Arctic. *Contrib. Sci. Nat. Hist. Mus. Los Angeles County* 314: 1–14.

———. 1979b. An Historical Perspective on Eskimo Whaling and the Bowhead Controversy. *Orca* 1(1):5–6.

D'URVILLE, J. D. 1841. *Voyage au Pole Sud et dans l'oceanie sur les corvettes l'Astrolabe et la Zélée.* Paris.

DUYCKINCK, E. A. 1851. Melville's *Moby-Dick;* or, *The Whale. New York Literary World* 9 (Nov. 22, 1851): 403–4.

EDWARDS, E. J., AND J. E. RATTRAY. 1956. *Whale Off: The Story of American Shore Whaling.* Coward-McCann.

ELKING, H. 1722. *A View of the Greenland Trade and Whale Fishery, with the National and Private Advantages Thereof.* London.

ELLIS, L. B. 1982. *History of New Bedford and its Vicinity: 1602–1892.* D. Mason & Co.

ELLIS, R. 1977. Of Men, Whales, and Captain Scammon. *National Parks and Conservation* 51(10):8–13.

———. 1980. *The Book of Whales.* Alfred A. Knopf.

———. 1981a. Physty: An Encounter with a Sperm Whale. *Whalewatcher* 15(3):17–20.

———. 1981b. The Whale That Visited New York. *Underwater Naturalist* 13(3):5–12.

———. 1985. A Sea Change for Leviathan. *Audubon* 87(6):62–79.

———. 1986. The Hagiography of the Whale. *Whalewatcher* 20(1):11–15.

———. 1987. Painting a "Leviathan" Mural. *The Artist's Magazine* 4(5):76–87.

———. 1988a. The Flying Whalers. *Oceans* 21(4):60.

———. 1988b. The Whalers of Lomblen. *Intrepid* 3:16.

———. 1989a. Moby-Dick Comes to Hollywood, 1930 Version. *Underwater Naturalist* 18(3):14–16.

———. 1989b. Whales Down Under. *Australian Geographic* 16:58–79.

———. 1989c. The Exhibition of Whales. *Whalewatcher* 23(4):11–14.

ELY, B.-E. S. 1849. *"There She Blows:" A Narrative of a Whaling Voyage, in the Indian and South Atlantic Oceans.* James K. Simon. 1971 edition, edited by Curtis Dahl, Wesleyan University Press.

ERNGAARD, E. 1972. *Greenland Then and Now.* Lademann Ltd.

ESCHRICHT, D. E., AND J. REINHARDT. 1866. On the Greenland Right-whale (*Balaena mysticetus,* Linn.), with especial reference to its geographic distribution and migrations in times past and present, and to its external and internal characteristics. In W. H. Flower, Ed., *Recent Memoirs of the Cetacea,* pp. 1–150. The Ray Society. Translated from *K. Videnskabernes Selskabs Skrifter* 5 (1861).

EVANS, P. 1986. *Ari: The Life and Times of Aristotle Onassis.* Summit Books.

EVERITT, R. D., AND B. D. KROGMAN. 1979. Sexual Behavior of Bowhead Whales Observed off the North Coast of Alaska. *Arctic* 32(3):277–80.

EWING, E. 1971. *Fashion in Underwear.* Batsford.

FISCHER, M. 1881. Cétacés du Sud-Ouest de la France. *Actes Soc. Linn. Bordeaux,* 4th series 5:5–219.

FISHER, R. H. (ED.) 1981. *The Voyage of Semen Dezhnev in 1648.* The Hakluyt Society.

FITZHUGH, W. W. 1988. Eskimos: Hunters of the Frozen Coasts. In W. W. Fitzhugh, and A. Crowell, Eds., *Crossroads of Continents: Cultures of Siberia and Alaska,* pp. 42–51. Smithsonian Institution.

FLAYDERMAN, E. N. 1972. *Scrimshaw and Scrimshanders, Whales and Whalemen.* N. Flayderman & Co.

FOOTE, D. C. 1975. Investigation of Small Whale Hunting in Norway. *Jour. Fish. Res. Bd. Canada* 32(7):1163–89.

FORTOM-GOUIN, J.-P., AND S. J. HOLT. 1980. Reasons for Recommending Zero Female Catch Limits for Sperm Whales. *Rep. Int. Whal. Commn. Sperm Whales* (Special Issue) 2:261–62.

FOWLER, O. S. 1846. *Tight-Lacing, Founded on Physiology and Phrenology: or the Evils, Inflicted on Mind and Body, by Compressing the Organs of Animal Life, thereby Retarding and Enfeebling the Vital Functions.* Privately published, New York.

FOX-DAVIES, A. C. 1909. *A Complete Guide to Heraldry.* Thomas Nelson.

FOY, S. 1982. *The World of Whales: The Story of Whales and Whaling at Albany, Western Australia.* Jaycees Community Foundation.

FRAKER, M. A. 1984. *Balaena mysticetus: Whales, Oil, and Whaling in the Arctic.* Sohio Alaska Petroleum Company and BP Alaska Exploration Inc.

———. 1989. A Rescue that Moved the World. *Oceanus* 32(1):96–102.

FRANCIS, D. 1984. *Arctic Chase: A History of Whaling in Canada's North.* Breakwater Books.

FRANK, S. M. 1985. "Vast Address and Boldness": The Rise and Fall of the American Whale Fishery. In G. S. Perry and H. Richmond, Eds., *The Spirit of Massachusetts: Our Maritime Heritage,* pp. 20–29. Massachusetts Department of Education. Boston.

———. 1986. *Herman Melville's Picture Gallery.* Edward M. Lefkowicz.

FRASER, F. C. 1937. Early Japanese Whaling. *Proc. Linn. Soc. London* 150th Session (1937–38):19–20.

———. 1970. An Early 17th Century Record of the Californian Grey Whale in Icelandic Waters. *Investigations on Cetacea* 2:13–20.

———. 1977. Royal Fishes: The Importance of the Dolphin. In R. J. Harrison, Ed., *Functional Anatomy of Marine Mammals,* pp. 1–44. Academic Press.

FREEMAN, M. B. 1976. *The Unicorn Tapestries.* The Metropolitan Museum of Art.

FRIZELL, J. 1981. The Pirate Whalers Versus the Environmentalists. *Oceans* 14(2):25–28.

FROST, S. (CHAIRMAN) 1978. *Whales and Whaling.* Australian Government Publishing Service.

FURUTA, M. 1984. Note on a Gray Whale Found in the Ise Bay on the Pacific Coast of Japan. *Sci. Rep. Whales Res. Inst.* 35:195–97.

GAMBELL, R. 1971. A Short History of Modern Whaling off Natal. *Mercurius* 14:37–44.

———. 1972. Sperm whales off Durban. *Discovery Reports* 35:199–358.

———. 1973. How Whales Survive (Sustainable Yields). In N. Calder, Ed., *Nature in the Round,* pp. 193–202. Weidenfeld & Nicolson.

GARCIARENA, D. 1988. The Effects of Whalewatching on Right Whales in Argentina. *Whalewatcher* 22(3):3–5.

GARDEN, D. S. 1977. *Albany: A Panorama of the Sound from 1827.* Thomas Nelson.

GARDNER, E. S. 1960. *Hunting the Desert Whale.* William Morrow.

GARNER, S. (ED.) 1986. *The Captain's Best Mate: The Journal of Mary Chipman Lawrence on the Whaler Addison, 1856–1860.* University Press of New England.

GASKIN, D. E. 1972. *Whales, Dolphins & Seals: with Special Reference to the New Zealand Region.* Heinemann Educational Books.

———, AND G. J. D. SMITH. 1977. The Small Whale Fishery of St. Lucia, W.I. *Rep. Intl. Whal. Commn.* 27:493.

GATES, D. J. 1963. Australian Whaling Since [the] War. *Norsk Hvalfangst-Tidende* 52(5):123–27.

GESNER, C. 1560. *Historia Animalium.* Zurich.

GILMORE, R. M. 1955. The Return of the Gray Whale. *Scientific American* 192(1):62–67.

———. 1959. On Mass Strandings of Sperm Whales. *Pacific Naturalist* 1(10):9–16.

———. 1960. A Census of the California Gray Whale. *U.S. Fish and Wildlife Service Special Scientific Report: Fisheries No. 342.*

———. 1961. *The Story of the Gray Whale.* Privately printed, San Diego.

———. 1969. Introduction and Annotations to Mocha Dick, or, The White Whale of the Pacific. *Oceans* 1(4): 65–80.

———. 1978. Right Whale. In D. Haley, Ed., *Marine Mammals of the Eastern North Pacific and Arctic Waters,* pp. 62–69. Pacific Search Press.

GLASS, K., AND K. ENGLUND. 1989. Why the Japanese are so Stubborn about Whaling. *Oceanus* 32(1):45–51.

GLEICK, J. 1987. *Chaos: The Making of a New Science.* Viking Penguin.

GLOCKNER, D. 1983. Determining the Sex of Humpback Whales (*Megaptera novaeangliae*) in Their Natural Environment. In R. Payne, Ed., *Communication and Behavior of Whales,* pp. 447–64. American Association for the Advancement of Science.

GOLDER, F. 1914. *Russian Expansion in the Pacific 1641–1850.* Arthur H. Clark Co.

———. 1925. *Bering's Voyages: An Account of the Efforts of the Russians to Determine the Relation of Asia and America.* American Geographical Society.

GOODE, G. B. 1884. *The Fisheries and Fishery Industries of the United States.* U.S. Government Printing Office. Washington, D.C.

GOODWIN, G. G. 1946. The End of the Great Northern Sea Cow. *Natural History* 55(2):56–61.

GOSHO, M. E., D. W. RICE, AND J. M. BREIWICK. 1984. The Sperm Whale, *Physeter macrocephalus. Marine Fisheries Review* 46(4):54–64.

GRADY, D. 1982. *The Perano Whalers of Cook Strait.* A. H. & A. W. Reed.

———. 1986. *Whalers and Sealers in New Zealand Waters.* Reed Methuen.

GRAVES, W. 1976. The Imperiled Giants. *National Geographic* 150(6):722–51.

GREEN, L. G. 1958. *South African Beachcomber.* Howard Timmins.

GREENLAND HOME RULE AUTHORITY. 1988. *Our Way of Whaling. Arfanniariaaserput.* Copenhagen.

GREENPEACE. 1980. *Outlaw Whalers.* San Francisco.

———. 1983. *Unregulated Whaling.* London.

———. 1984. *Outlaw Whalers: Special Report 1984.* London.

———. 1985. *Scientific Whalers? The History of Whaling under Special Permits.* London.

GRIERSON, J. 1949. *Air Whaler.* Sampson Low, Marston & Co., Ltd.

HACQUEBORD, L. 1984. A History of Early Dutch Whaling: A Study from the Ecological Angle. In *Arctic Whaling: Proceedings of the International Symposium,* pp. 135–48. University of Groningen.

———. 1987. A Historical-Archeological Investigation of a Seventeenth-Century Whaling Settlement on the West Coast of Spitsbergen in 79° North Latitude. *Norsk Polarinstitutt Rapportserie* 38:19–34.

———. 1988. Three Seventeenth Century Whaling Stations in Southeastern Svalbard: An Archaeological Missing Link. *Polar Record* 24(149):125–28.

HAKLUYT, R. 1598. *The Principal Navigations, Voyages, Traffiques and Discoveries of the English Nation.* London. 1972 edition, Penguin English Library.

HALEY, N. C. 1948. *Whale Hunt: The Narrative of a Voyage by Nelson Cole Haley, Harpooner in the Ship Charles W. Morgan 1849–1853.* Ives Washburn.

HALL, E. W. 1982. *Sperm Whaling from New Bedford.* Old Dartmouth Historical Society. New Bedford, Mass.

HALL, J. W. 1968. *Japan: From Prehistory to Modern Times.* Charles E. Tuttle Co.

HARDY, A. C. 1967. *Great Waters.* Harper & Row.

HARLOW, V. T. 1964. *The Founding of the Second British Empire, 1763–1793: New Continents and Changing Values.* Longmans Green.

HARMER, S. F. 1928. The History of Whaling. *Proc. Linn. Soc. London* 140:51–95.

———. 1931. Southern Whaling. *Proc. Linn. Soc. London* 142:85–163.

HARRISON, D. 1981. *The White Tribe of Africa.* Macmillan.

HARRISON, R. J. 1979. Whales and Whaling. In E. J. Slijper, *Whales,* pp. 391–431. Cornell University Press.

HASHIURA, Y. 1969. *Whaling at Taijiura: A Series of Scrolls.* Heibonsha.

HAVERSTICK, I., AND B. SHEPARD. 1965. *The Wreck of the Whaleship Essex.* Harcourt Brace & World.

HAWES, C. B. 1924. *Whaling.* Doubleday, Page.

HEADLAND, R. 1984. *The Island of South Georgia.* Cambridge University Press.

HEFFERNAN, T. H. 1981. *Stove by a Whale: Owen Chase and the* Essex. Wesleyan University Press.

HEGARTY, R. B. 1964. *Birth of a Whaleship.* New Bedford Free Public Library.

HEINZELMANN, W. 1980. *The Azores.* Published by the author, Basel.

HEIZER, R. F. 1943. Aconite Poison Whaling in Asia and America: An Aleutian Transfer to the New World. *American Ethnologist* 133:415–68.

HELMS, P., O. HERTZ, AND F. KAPEL. 1984. The Greenland Aboriginal Whale Hunt. *Report to the Standing Subcommittee on Aboriginal/Subsistence Whaling. Intl. Whal. Commn.* TC/36/AS/2.

HEMBREE, E. D. 1980. Biological Aspects of the Cetacean Fishery at Lamalera, Lembata. *World Wildlife Fund Project No. 1428.* Gland, Switzerland.

HENDERSON, D. A. (ED.) 1970. *Journal Aboard the Bark Ocean Bird on a Whaling Voyage to Scammon's Lagoon. Winter of 1858–1859.* Dawson's Book Shop.

———. 1972. *Men & Whales at Scammon's Lagoon.* Dawson's Book Shop.

———. 1984. Nineteenth Century Gray Whaling: Grounds, Catches and Kills, Practices and Depletion of the Whale Population. In M. L. Jones, S. L. Swartz, and S. Leatherwood, Eds., *The Gray Whale: Eschrichtius robustus,* pp. 159–86. Academic Press.

———. 1991. Gray Whales and Whalers on the China Coast in 1869. *Whalewatcher* 24(4):14–16.

HERRMANN, P. 1954. *Conquest by Man.* Harper & Brothers.

HERRON, M. 1976. A Not-Altogether Quixotic Face-off with Soviet Whale-Killers in the Pacific. *Smithsonian* 7(5):22–31.

HILDER, B. 1958. Whaling at Norfolk Island. *Walkabout* 24:10–13.

HILL, D. O. 1975. Vanishing Giants. *Audubon* 77(1):56–107.

HIRASAWA, Y. 1978. The Whaling Industry in Japan's Economy. In J. Schmidhauser and G. O. Totten, Eds., *The Whaling Issue in U.S.-Japan Relations,* pp. 82–114. Westview Press.

HIRATA, M. 1951. Experimental Investigation of Flattened Head Harpoon: An Attempt for Restraining Ricochet. *Sci. Rep. Whales Res. Inst.* 6:199–207.

HJORT, J. 1933. Whales and Whaling (Essays on Population). *Hvalradets Skrifter* 7:7–29.

———, J. LIE, AND J. T. RUUD. 1932. Norwegian Pelagic Whaling in the Antarctic. *Hvalradets Skrifter* 3:5–37.

———. 1933. Norwegian Pelagic Whaling in the Antarctic. The Season 1932–33. *Hvalradets Skrifter* 8:3–36.

———. 1934. Norwegian Pelagic Whaling in the Antarctic. The Season 1933–34. With a Note on the Limits of the Pack Ice in the Area Between 40°W and 110°E. *Hvalradets Skrifter* 9:5–43.

———. 1935. Norwegian Pelagic Whaling in the Antarctic. V. The Season 1934–35. *Hvalradets Skrifter* 12:5–52.

———. 1937. Pelagic Whaling in the Antarctic. VI. The Season 1935–36. *Hvalradets Skrifter* 14:5–30.

———. 1938. Pelagic Whaling in the Antarctic. VII. The Season 1936–37. *Hvalradets Skrifter* 18:5–31.

HOARE, M. 1982. *Norfolk Island: An Outline of Its History, 1774–1981.* University of Queensland Press.

HODGKINSON, R. 1975. *Eber Bunker of Liverpool.* Roebuck.

HOHMAN, E. P. 1928. *The American Whaleman.* Reissued 1972, Augustus M. Kelley.

HOLDER, C. F. 1884. Imprisoned in an Iceberg. *St. Nicholas Magazine* 12(2):143–45.

HOLLANDER, A. 1978. *Seeing Through Clothes.* Viking.

HOLT, S. J. 1977. International Cooperation to Protect the Whales. *Oceans* 10(4):62–64.

———. 1986. Loopholes for Leviathans. *BBC Wildlife* (June 1986):282–89.

HORRIDGE, G. A. 1982. *The Lashed-Lug Boats of the Eastern Archipelagoes, the Alcina MS and the Lomblen Whaling Boats.* No. 54, Marine Monographs and Reports, Trustees of the National Maritime Museum.

HOUSBY, T. 1971. *The Hand of God: Whaling in the Azores.* Abelard-Schuman.

HOWARTH, D. 1974. *Sovereign of the Seas: The Story of Britain and the Sea.* Atheneum.

HOYT, E. P. 1975. *Mutiny on the Globe.* Random House.

HUBBS, C. L., AND L. C. HUBBS. 1967. Gray Whale Censuses by Airplane in Mexico. *Calif. Fish and Game* 53:23–27.

HUDNALL, J. 1977. In the Company of Great Whales. *Audubon* 79(3):62–73.

HUEVELMANS, B. 1965. *In the Wake of Sea Serpents.* Hill & Wang.

HUGHES, R. 1986. *The Fatal Shore: The Epic of Australia's Founding.* Alfred A. Knopf.

HUMBLE, R. 1978. *The Explorers.* Time-Life Books.

HUNT, W. R. 1975. *Arctic Passage: The Turbulent History of the Land and People of the Arctic Sea.* Scribner's.

HUNTER, R. 1978. *To Save a Whale: The Voyages of Greenpeace.* Chronicle Books.

———. 1979. *Warriors of the Rainbow: A Chronicle of the Greenpeace Movement.* Holt, Rinehart & Winston.

HUSTON, J. 1980. *An Open Book.* Alfred A. Knopf.

HWANG, S. Y., AND M. D. MUN. 1984. *Ban-qu Dae: Rock Pictures in Ul-Ju.* Dongguk University Press.

ICHIHARA, T. 1966. The Pygmy Blue Whale, *Balaenoptera musculus brevicauda,* a New Species from the Antarctic. In K. S. Norris, Ed., *Whales, Dolphins, and Porpoises,* pp. 79–III. University of California Press.

IHIMAERA, W. 1987. *The Whale Rider.* Heinemann.

INGALLS, E. 1987. *Whaling Prints in the Francis B. Lothrop Collection.* Peabody Museum of Salem. Salem, Mass.

INGE, M. T. 1982. Melville in the Comic Books. *Melville Society Extracts* 50:9–10.

———. 1986. Melville in Popular Culture. In J. Bryant, Ed., *A Companion to Melville Studies,* pp. 695–739. Greenwood Press.

INSTITUTE OF CETACEAN RESEARCH. 1990. *Japanese Research on Antarctic Whale Resources.* Tokyo.

INTERNATIONAL WHALING COMMISSION. 1950–1990. *Annual Report.* IWC. Cambridge.

———. 1977. *Report of the Special Meeting of the Scientific Committee on Sei and Bryde's Whales.* IWC. Cambridge.

———. 1982. *Aboriginal/Subsistence Whaling (with Special Reference to the Alaska and Greenland Fisheries).* IWC Special Issue 4. Cambridge.

IVASHIN, M. V. 1982. Russian Hunting for Right Whales in the Sea of Okhotsk (XVIII–XIX Centuries). *Intl. Whal. Commn.* SC/34/PS21.

————. 1985. Whale Hunting and Science. *Science in the USSR* 93:92–95, 113–19.

IVERSEN, B. 1955. Whaling Activity in Iceland. *Norsk Hvalfangst-Tidende* 44(10):362–68.

IVERSEN, I. 1957. Donkergat in Saldanha Bay Again in Operation. *Norsk Hvalfangst-Tidende* 46(6):308–18.

JACKSON, G. 1978. *The British Whaling Trade.* Adam & Charles Black.

JACOBS, W. 1985. *The Birth of New Zealand.* Kowhai Publishing.

JAPAN WHALING ASSOCIATION. 1977. *Whaling Controversy: Japan's Position.* JWA. Tokyo.

————. 1980. *Living with Whales.* JWA. Tokyo.

————. 1981. *Man, Whales & The Sea.* JWA. Tokyo.

————. 1987. *Whale and Traditions of Diet.* JWA. Tokyo.

JENKINS, J. T. 1921. *A History of the Whale Fisheries.* Reissued 1971, Kennikat Press.

JOHNSON, J. H., AND A. A. WOLMAN. 1984. The Humpback Whale, *Megaptera novaeangliae. Marine Fisheries Review* 46(4):30–37.

JONAITIS, A. 1986. *The Art of the Northern Tlingit.* University of Washington Press.

JONES, A. G. E. 1986. *Ships Employed in the South Seas Trade 1775–1861.* Roebuck.

JONES, D. 1980. *The Whalers of Tangalooma.* The Nautical Association of Australia, Inc.

JONES, M. L., AND S. L. SWARTZ. 1984. Demography and Phenology of Gray Whales and Evaluation of Whale-Watching Activities in Laguna San Ignacio, Baja California Sur, Mexico. In M. L. Jones, S. L. Swartz, and S. Leatherwood, Eds., *The Gray Whale: Eschrichtius robustus,* pp. 309–74. Academic Press.

JONSGARD, A. 1955. Development of the Norwegian Small Whale Industry. *Norsk Hvalfangst-Tidende* 44(12):697–718.

————. 1964. A Right Whale (*Balaena* sp.) in All Probability a Greenland Right Whale (*Balaena mysticetus*) Observed in the Bering Sea. *Norsk Hvalfangst-Tidende* 53(11):311–13.

————. 1980. Bowhead Whales (*Balaena mysticetus*), Observed in Arctic Waters of the Eastern North Atlantic after the Second World War. *Sci. Com. Rep. Intl. Whal. Commn.* SC/32/PS23.

————, AND E. J. LONG. 1959. Norway's Small Whales. *Sea Frontiers* 5(3):168–74.

JONSSØN, J. 1965. Whales and Whaling in Icelandic Waters. *Norsk Hvalfangst-Tidende* 54(11):245–56.

JOSSELYN, J. 1672. *New England Rarities Discovered.* Reprinted 1972, Massachusetts Historical Society.

KAEPPLER, A. L. 1978. *"Artificial Curiosities": Being An Exposition of Native Manufactures Collected on the Three Pacific Voyages of Captain James Cook, R.N.* Bishop Museum Press.

KAPEL, F. O. 1975. Preliminary Notes on the Occurrence and Exploitation of Smaller Cetaceans in Greenland. *Jour. Fish. Res. Bd. Canada* 32:1079–82.

————. 1977. Catch of Belugas, Narwhals and Harbour Porpoises in Greenland, 1954–75, by Year, Month and Region. *Rep. Intl. Whal. Commn.* 27:507–22.

————. 1983. Whale Observations off West Greenland in June–September 1982. *Intl. Whal. Commn.* SC/35/03.

KAWASUMI, T. 1990. *John Manjiro (Manjiro Nakahama) and the American Whale Fishery: An Historical Approach.* Paper presented at the 15th Annual Whaling Symposium, Kendall Whaling Museum, Sharon, Mass. Oct. 13–14, 1990.

KELLOGG, R. 1940. Whales, Giants of the Sea. *National Geographic* 77(1):35–90.

KERR, M., AND C. KERR. 1980. *Australia's Early Whalemen.* Rigby.

KNAPK (GREENLAND HUNTERS' AND FISHERMEN'S COOPERATIVES). 1987. *Whaling in Greenland.* Nuuk.

KOHLER, C. 1928. *A History of Costume.* George Harrap and Company. 1963 edition, Dover.

KOSTER, J. 1979. The Whales' Best Friend: Confederate Captain Who Would Not Surrender. *Oceans* 12(3):3–7.

KRAUS, S. D. 1989. Whales for Profit. *Whalewatcher* 23(2):18–19.

————, AND J. H. PRESCOTT. 1982. The North Atlantic Right Whale (*Eubalaena glacialis*) in the Bay of Fundy, 1981, with Notes on Distribution, Abundance, Biology and Behavior. *Intl. Whal. Commn.* SC/34/PS14.

KIM, W.-Y. 1986. *The Art and Archaeology of Ancient Korea.* Taekwang Publishing.

KRISTOF, E. 1973. The Last U.S. Whale Hunters. *National Geographic* 143(3):346–53.

KRUPNICK, I. I. 1984. Gray Whales and the Aborigines of the Pacific Northwest: The History of Aboriginal Whaling. In M. L. Jones, S. L. Swartz, and S. Leatherwood, Eds., *The Gray Whale: Eschrichtius robustus,* pp. 103–20. Academic Press.

————. 1988. Economic Patterns in Northeastern Siberia. In W. W. Fitzhugh and A. Crowell, Eds., *Crossroads of Continents,* pp. 183–90. Smithsonian Institution.

KUGLER, R. C. 1976. The Historical Records of American Sperm Whaling: What They Tell Us and What They Don't. *FAO Scientific Consultation on Marine Mammals.* ACMRR/MM/SC/105.

————. 1980. The Whale Oil Trade, 1750–1775. *Publications of the Colonial Society of Massachusetts* 52:153–73.

————. 1983. Historical Survey of Foreign Whaling: North America. In *Arctic Whaling: Proceedings of the International Symposium,* pp. 149–57. University of Groningen.

————. 1986. Random Notes on the History of Right Whaling on the "Northwest Coast." *Rep. Intl. Whal. Commn.* (Special Issue) 10:17–18.

KUNZ, G. F. 1916. *Ivory and the Elephant.* Doubleday, Page.

LACEPEDE, B.-G. E. 1804. *Histoire Naturelle des Cétacés.* Chez Plassan.

LAKE, P. A. 1975. Harvesting: A Working Day of the Whale Catcher *W-17. Oceans* 8(3):40–43.

LAMPSON, H. H. 1929. "Whales and Whaling: Port Elizabeth's Priceless Skeletons." *Port Elizabeth Advertiser* Oct. 29, 1929.

LANTIS, M. 1938. The Alaska Whale Cult and its Affinities. *American Anthropologist,* n.s. 40:438–64.

LARSEN, H. E., AND F. G. RAINEY. 1948. Ipiutak and the Arctic Whale Hunting Culture. *Mem. Amer. Mus. Nat. Hist.* 42.

LARSON, K. 1978. Close Encounters (of the Whale Kind). *Sea Frontiers* 24(4):194–202.

LAWSON, W. 1949. *Blue Gum Clippers and Whale Ships of Tasmania.* D. & L. Books.

LAXALT, R. 1985. The Indomitable Basques. *National Geographic* 168(1):69–71.

LAYCOCK, G. 1988. Wilderness by the Barrel. *Audubon* 90(3):100–23.

LEAVITT, J. F. 1973. *The Charles W. Morgan.* Marine Historical Association. Mystic, Conn.

LEE, H. 1875. *The White Whale.* R. K. Burt.

LEHANE, B. 1981. *The Northwest Passage.* Time-Life Books.

LEY, W. 1948. *The Lungfish, the Dodo, & the Unicorn.* Viking Press.

————. 1968. *Dawn of Zoology.* Prentice-Hall.

LILLIE, H. R. 1955. *A Walk Through Penguin City.* Ernest Benn Limited.

LINDQUIST, L. 1972. Last American Whaling Operation Legislated Right out of Business. *National Fisherman* 52(10):20a–21a.

LIPTON, B. 1975. Whaling Days in New Jersey. *Newark Museum Quarterly* 26(2 & 3):1–172.

LOVERING, J. F., AND J. R. V. PRESCOTT. 1979. *Last of Lands: Antarctica.* Melbourne University Press.

LUBBOCK, B. 1937. *The Arctic Whalers.* Brown, Son & Ferguson.

LURIE, A. 1981. *The Language of Clothes.* Random House.

LYTLE, T. G. 1984. *Harpoons and Other Whalecraft.* Old Dartmouth Historical Society. New Bedford, Mass.

MACKAY, D. 1985. *In the Wake of Cook: Exploration, Science & Empire, 1780–1801.* St. Martin's Press.

MACKINTOSH, N. A. 1962. *The Stocks of Whales.* Fishing News (Books) Ltd.

MACLEOD, I. (ED.) 1979. *To the Greenland Whaling: Alexander Trotter's Journal of the Voyage of the* Enterprise *in 1856 from Fraserburgh & Lerwick.* The Thule Press.

MACY, O. 1835. *The History of Nantucket, Being a Compendious Account of the First Settlement of the Island by the English, Together with the Rise and Progress of the Whale Fishery; and Other Historical Facts Relative to Said Island and its Inhabitants.* Hilliard, Gray & Co.

MAHER, W. J., AND N. J. WILMOVSKY. 1963. Annual Catch of Bowhead Whales by Eskimos of Point Barrow. *Jour. Mammal.* 44(1):16–20.

MALLEY, R. C. 1983. *Graven by the Fishermen Themselves.* Mystic Seaport Museum.

MALLORY, G. K. 1977. Charles Melville Scammon. *Oceans* 10(4):40–44.

MANSFIELD, A. W. 1971. Occurrence of the Bowhead or Greenland Right Whale (*Balaena mysticetus*) in Canadian Arctic Waters. *Jour. Fish. Rev. Bd. Canada* 28:1873–75.

————, T. G. SMITH, AND B. BECK. 1975. The Narwhal, *Monodon monoceros,* in Eastern Canadian Waters. *Jour. Fish. Res. Bd. Canada* 32(7):1041–46.

MARINE FISHERIES REVIEW. 1974. *The California Gray Whale* 36(4):1–64.

MARINE MAMMAL COMMISSION. 1979. *Annual Report of the Marine Mammal Commission: A Report to Congress.* Marine Mammal Commission.

———. 1980. *Annual Report of the Marine Mammal Commission: A Report to Congress.* Marine Mammal Commission.

MARKHAM, C. R. 1881. On the whale fisheries of the Basque provinces of Spain. *Proc. Zool. Soc. London* 62: 969–76.

———. 1889. *A Life of John Davis, the Navigator, 1550–1605, Discoverer of Davis Straits.* George Philip & Son.

MARQUETTE, W. M. 1977. *The 1976 Catch of Bowhead Whales (Balaena mysticetus) by Alaskan Eskimos, with a Review of the Fishery, 1973–1976, and a Biological Summary of the Species.* Northwest & Alaska Fisheries Center Processed Report, NOAA/NMFS.

———. 1978. Bowhead Whale. In D. Haley, Ed., *Marine Mammals of Eastern North Pacific and Arctic Waters,* pp. 70–81. Pacific Search Press.

———. 1979. The 1979 Catch of Bowhead Whales (*Balaena mysticetus*) by Alaskan Eskimos. *Rep. Intl. Whal. Commn.* 29:281–89.

MARTIN, K. R. 1972. The Successful Whaling Voyage of the *Lucy Ann* of Wilmington, 1837–1839. *Delaware History* 15(2):85–103.

———. 1974. *Delaware Goes Whaling.* The Hagley Museum. Greenville, Del.

———. 1975. *Whalemen and Whaleships of Maine.* Marine Research Society. Bath, Maine.

———. 1979. Whalemen of Letters. *Oceans* 12(1):20–29.

MATSEN, B. 1986. The Aleutians: Black Current, Dark Land, Resilient Peoples. *Oceans* 19(1):39–43, 71.

MATTHEWS, L. H. 1938. The Sperm Whale, *Physeter catodon. Discovery Reports* 17:93–168.

———. 1968. *The Whale.* Simon and Schuster.

———. 1978. *Penguins, Whalers, and Sealers: A Voyage of Discovery.* Universe Books.

MAYNARD, F., AND A. DUMAS. 1858. *Les Baleiniers.* 1937 edition, Hillman-Curl.

MCCARTNEY, A. P. 1984. History of Native Whaling in the Arctic and Subarctic. In *Arctic Whaling: Proceedings of the International Symposium,* pp. 79–111. University of Groningen.

MCCLOSKEY, M. 1985. Whaling by Any Other Name: Report from Bournemouth. *Oceans* 18(5)65–66.

MCCRACKEN, D. R. 1948. *Four Months on a Jap Whaler.* National Travel Club.

MCGINNISS, J. 1980. *Going to Extremes.* Alfred A. Knopf.

MCHUGH, J. L. 1974. The role and history of the International Whaling Commission. In W. E. Schevill, Ed., *The Whale Problem,* pp. 305–35. Harvard University Press.

———. 1975. The Truth about Whaling. *Sea Frontiers* 21(6):371–73.

MCINTYRE, J. 1974. *Mind in the Waters.* Scribner's.

———. 1982. *The Delicate Art of Whale Watching.* Sierra Club Books.

MCLAUCHLAN, G. (ED.) 1985. *New Zealand.* Insight Guides, APA Productions. Hong Kong.

MCLAUGHLIN, W. R. D. 1962. *Call to the South: A Story of British Whaling in the Antarctic.* Harrap.

MCNAB, R. 1913. *The Old Whaling Days.* 1975 edition, Golden Press.

MCVAY, S. 1966. The Last of the Great Whales. *Scientific American* 215(2):13–21.

———. 1971. Can Leviathan Endure So Wide a Chase? *Natural History* 80(1):36–40, 68–72.

———. 1973. Stalking the Arctic Whale. *American Scientist* 61(1):23–37.

———. 1974. Reflections on the Management of Whaling. In W. E. Schevill, Ed., *The Whale Problem,* pp. 369–82. Harvard University Press.

MEAD, J. G. 1986. Twentieth-Century Records of Right Whales (*Eubalaena glacialis*) in the Northwestern Atlantic Ocean. *Rep. Intl. Whal. Commn.* (Special Issue) 10:109–19.

———, AND E. D. MITCHELL. 1984. Atlantic Gray Whales. In M. L. Jones, S. L. Swartz, and S. Leatherwood, Eds., *The Gray Whale: Eschrichtius robustus.* pp. 33–53. Academic Press.

MEAD, T. 1961. *Killers of Eden.* Angus & Robertson.

MELVILLE, H. 1847. *Omoo: A Narrative of Adventures in the South Seas.* New York.

———. 1849. *Mardi.* New York.

———. 1851. *Moby-Dick.* New York. 1967 Norton Critical Edition, edited by H. Hayford and H. Parker, W. W. Norton.

M'GONIGLE, R. M. 1980. The "Economizing" of Ecology: Why Big, Rare Whales Still Die. *Ecology Law Quarterly* 9(119):120–237. School of Law, University of California, Berkeley.

MIALL, B. (TRANS.) 1923. *Master Johann Dietz, Surgeon in the Army of the Great Elector and Barber to the Royal Court.* London.

MILAN, F. A. 1980. *On the Need of the Alaskan Eskimos to Harvest Bowhead Whales.* U.S. Dept. of Interior. Mimeo.

MILLAIS, J. G. 1907. *Newfoundland and its Untrodden Ways.* Longmans Green.

MILLER, P. A. 1979. *And the Whale Is Ours: Creative Writing of American Whalemen.* David R. Godine.

MILLER, T. 1975. *The World of the California Gray Whale.* Baja Trail Publications.

MITCHELL, E. D. 1973. The Status of the World's Whales. *Nature Canada* 2(4):9–25.

———. 1974. Trophic Relationships and Competition for Food in Northwest Atlantic Whales. *Proc. Can. Zool. Soc.* 1974:123–33.

———. 1975. *Porpoise, Dolphin and Small Whale Fisheries of the World: Status and Problems.* IUCN Monograph No. 3. Morges, Switzerland.

———. 1979. Comments on Magnitude of Early Catch of East Pacific Gray Whale (*Eschrichtius robustus*). *Rep. Intl. Whal. Commn.* 29, SC/30/41:307–14.

———. 1983. Potential of Logbook Data for Studying Aspects of Social Structure in the Sperm Whale, *Physeter macrocephalus*, with an Example—the Ship *Mariner* to the Pacific, 1836–1840. *Rep. Intl. Whal. Commn.* (Special Issue) 5:63–80.

———. 1986. Aspects of Pre–World War II German Electrical Whaling. *Rep. Intl. Whal. Commn.* (Special Issue) 7:115–40.

———, AND I. B. MCASKIE. 1974. Marine Mammals of British Columbia. *Bull. Fish. Res. Bd. Canada* 171:1–54.

———, AND R. R. REEVES. 1980. Factors Affecting Abundance of Bowhead Whales (*Balaena mysticetus*) in the Eastern Arctic of North America, 1915–1980. *Sci. Com. Rept. Intl. Whal. Commn.* SC/32/PS1.

———. 1981. Catch History and Cumulative Catch Estimates of Initial Population Size of Cetaceans in the Eastern Canadian Arctic. *Rep. Intl. Whal. Commn.* 31:645–82.

———. 1983. Catch History, Abundance, and Present Status of Northwest Atlantic Humpback Whales. *Rep. Intl. Whal. Commn.* (Special Issue) 5:153–212.

———, V. M. KOZICKI, AND R. R. REEVES. 1986. Sightings of Right Whales (*Eubalaena glacialis*) on the Scotia Shelf, 1966–1972. *Rep. Intl. Whal. Commn.* (Special Issue) 10:83–105.

MITCHELL, M. 1936. *Gone with the Wind.* Macmillan.

MIYAZAKI, I. 1955. Survey of Whaling Operations from Land Station in Japan in 1954. *Norsk Hvalfangst-Tidende* 44(4):189–200.

MIZROCH, S. A., D. W. RICE, AND J. M. BREIWICK. 1984a. The Blue Whale, *Balaenoptera musculus. Marine Fisheries Review* 46(4):15–19.

———. 1984b. The Fin Whale, *Balaenoptera physalus. Marine Fisheries Review* 46(4):20–24.

MIZUE, K. 1950. Factory Ship Whaling around Bonin Islands in 1948. *Sci. Rep. Whales Res. Inst.* 14:106–18.

MOOREHEAD, A. 1966. *The Fatal Impact: An Account of the Invasion of the South Pacific 1767–1840.* Hamish Hamilton.

MORCH, J. A. 1911. On the Natural History of the Whalebone Whales. *Proc. Zool. Soc. London* 92(157):661–70.

MOREBY, C. 1982. What whaling means to the Japanese. *New Scientist* 96(1335):661–63.

MORGAN, L. 1977. A New Look at Subsistence Whaling. *Alaska Geographic* 43(9):8–11.

———. 1978a. Early Native Whaling in Alaska. *Alaska Geographic* 5(4):45–49.

———. 1978b. Modern Eskimo Whaling. *Alaska Geographic* 5(4):135–43.

MORISON, S. E. 1962. *Whaler out of New Bedford.* (Introduction to a film based on the Purrington-Russell Panorama.) Old Dartmouth Historical Society. New Bedford, Mass.

———. 1971. *The European Discovery of America: The Northern Voyages A.D. 500–1600.* Oxford University Press.

MORLEY, F. V., AND J. S. HODGSON. 1926. *Whaling North and South.* The Century Co.

MORTON, H. 1982. *The Whale's Wake.* University of Hawaii Press.

MOSER, D. 1976. The Azores, Nine Islands in Search of a Future. *National Geographic* 149(2):261–88.

MOUNTFIELD, D. 1974. *A History of Polar Exploration.* Hamlyn.

MOWAT, F. 1984. *Sea of Slaughter.* Atlantic Monthly Press.

MUMFORD, L. 1929. *Herman Melville.* Harcourt, Brace & World.

MURPHY, R. C. 1922. South Georgia, an Outpost of the Antarctic. *National Geographic* 41(4):410–44.

———. 1933a. Floating Gold: The Romance of Ambergris. Part I. *Natural History* 33(2):117–30.

MURPHY, R. C. 1933b. Floating Gold: The Romance of Ambergris. Part II. *Natural History* 33(3):303–10.

———. 1947. *Logbook for Grace*. Macmillan.

———. 1967. *A Dead Whale or a Stove Boat*. Houghton Mifflin.

NAKASHIMA, L. 1977. Fall Whaling in Barrow. *Alaska Magazine* 43(9):97.

NELSON, R. K. 1969. *Hunters of the Northern Ice*. University of Chicago Press.

NERINI, M. 1984. A Review of Gray Whale Feeding Ecology. In M. L. Jones, S. L. Swartz, and S. Leatherwood, Eds., *The Gray Whale: Eschrichtius robustus*, pp. 423–50. Academic Press.

NICHOLS, G. 1975. *Eschrichtius robustus*. Oceans 8(3):60–65.

NICHOLS, T. L. 1983. California Shore Whaling: 1854 to 1900. Unpublished Master's Thesis, California State University, Northridge.

NICKERSON, R. 1978. *Lahaina: Royal Capital of Hawaii*. Hawaiian Service.

NICOL, C. W. 1980. *Down to the South Ocean*. Japan Whaling Association.

———. 1981. *Taiji: Winds of Change*. Japan Whaling Association.

———. 1987. *Harpoon*. G. P. Putnam's.

NIEUHOFF, J. 1673. *Embassy from the East-India Company of the United Provinces to the Grand Tartar Cham, Emperor of China, Deliver'd by Their Excellencies Peter de Goyer and Jacob de Keyzer, At His Imperial City of Peking. Wherein The Cities, Towns, Villages, Ports, Rivers, &c. In Their Passages from Canton to Peking, Are Ingeniously Describ'd*. London.

NIKONOROV, I. V., M. V. IVASHIN, V. G. MAKAYEV, AND I. PH. GOLOVOLEV. 1987. Soviet Whalemen at [the] Antarctic. *Rybnoe khozayistvo* 8:1–12.

NISHIWAKI, M. 1966. Distribution and Migration of Larger Cetaceans in the North Pacific as shown by Japanese Whaling Results. In K. S. Norris, Ed., *Whales, Dolphins, and Porpoises*, pp. 171–91. University of California Press.

———. 1967. Distribution and Migration of Marine Mammals in the North Pacific Area. *Bull. Ocean Res. Inst. Univ. Tokyo* 1:1–64.

———. 1969. Tusks of unicorn (*Monodon monoceros*) owned by Prince Takamatsu. *Jour. Mam. Soc. Japan* 4:159–62.

———. 1978. Failure of Past Regulations and the Future of Whaling. In J. Schmidhauser and G. O. Totten, Eds., *The Whaling Issue in U.S.-Japan Relations*, pp. 44–59. Westview Press.

———, AND T. KASUYA. 1970. Recent Record of Gray Whale in the Adjacent Waters of Japan and a Consideration of its Migration. *Sci. Rep. Whales Res. Inst.* 22:29–37.

NORDHOFF, C. 1856. *Whaling and Fishing*. Moore, Wilsatch, Keys & Co.

NORMAN, C. 1975. Plenty of Potential for Jojoba Oil. *Nature* (London) 265(5506):272–73.

NORRIS, K. 1973. *The Porpoise Watcher*. W. W. Norton.

———. 1978. Marine Mammals and Man. In H. P. Brokaw, Ed., *Wildlife and America*, pp. 320–38. U.S. Fish and Wildlife Service; U.S. Forest Service; National Oceanic and Atmospheric Administration.

O'BARRY, R. 1988. *Behind the Dolphin Smile*. Algonquin Books.

OHSUMI, S. 1958. A Descendant of Moby Dick, or, A White Sperm Whale. *Sci. Rep. Whales Res. Inst.* 13:207–209.

———. 1977. Bryde's Whales on the Pelagic Whaling Ground of the North Pacific. *Rep. Intl. Whal. Commn.* (Special Issue) 1, SC/SP 74/Doc. 23:140–49.

———. 1978. Provisional Report on the Bryde's Whales Caught under Special Permit in the Southern Hemisphere. *Rep. Intl. Whal. Commn.* 28:281–87.

———. 1979. Provisional Report of the Bryde's Whales Caught under Special Permit in the Southern Hemisphere in 1977/78 and a Research Programme for 1978/79. *Rep. Intl. Whal. Commn.* 29:267–73.

———. 1980. Catches of Sperm Whales by Modern Whaling in the North Pacific. *Rep. Intl. Whal. Commn.* (Special Issue) 2, SC/SP/1:11–16.

———. 1980. The Sperm Whale Catch by Japanese Coastal Whaling in the Sanriku Region. *Rep. Intl. Whal. Commn.* (Special Issue) 2, SC/SP78/7:161–68.

———, AND F. KASAMATSU. 1983. Right whale sightings in the waters south of Western Australia in summer, 1981/82. *Sci. Com. Rep. Intl. Whal. Commn.* SC/34/PS.

O'LEARY, B. 1977. Magic and Poison: The Whaling Technologies of Three Northern Cultures. Unpublished Manuscript. Kendall Whaling Museum Symposium, Sharon, Mass.

O'LEARY, B. 1984. Aboriginal Whaling from the Aleutian Islands to Washington State. In M. L. Jones, S. L. Swartz, and S. Leatherwood, Eds., *The Gray Whale: Eschrichtius robustus,* pp. 79–100. Academic Press.

OLMSTEAD, F. A. 1936. *Incidents of a Whaling Voyage.* Charles E. Tuttle, Rutland, Vt. Originally published 1841, Appleton.

OLSEN, O. 1913. On the external character and biology of Bryde's whale (*Balaenoptera edeni*), a new rorqual from the coast of South Africa. *Proc. Zool. Soc. London* 94:1073–90.

O'MAY, H. 1978. *Wooden Hookers of Hobart Town, Whalers out of Van Diemen's Land.* T. J. Hughes.

OMMANNEY, F. D. 1933. Whaling in the Dominion of New Zealand. *Discovery Reports* 7:239–52.

———. 1938. *South Latitude.* Longmans Green.

———. 1971. *Lost Leviathan.* Dodd, Mead.

OMURA, H. 1950. Whales in the Adjacent Waters of Japan. *Sci. Rep. Whales Res. Inst.* 4:27–113.

———. 1958. North Pacific Right Whale. *Sci. Rep. Whales Res. Inst.* 13:1–52.

———. 1959. Bryde's Whale from the Coast of Japan. *Sci. Rep. Whales Res. Inst.* 14:1–33.

———. 1962. Further Information on Bryde's Whales from the Coast of Japan. *Sci. Rep. Whales Res. Inst.* 16:7–18.

———. 1974. Possible Migration Route of the Gray Whale on the Coast of Japan. *Sci. Rep. Whales Res. Inst.* 26:1–14.

———. 1977. Review of the Occurrence of Bryde's Whale in the Northwest Pacific. *Rep. Intl. Whal. Commn.* (Special Issue) 1, SC/SP74/Doc25:88–91.

———. 1978. The Origin of the International Whaling Commission. In J. Schmidhauser and G. O. Totten, Eds., *The Whaling Issue in U.S.-Japan Relations,* pp. 28–34. Westview Press.

———. 1984. History of Gray Whales in Japan. In M. L. Jones, S. L. Swartz, and S. Leatherwood, Eds., *The Gray Whale: Eschrichtius robustus,* pp. 57–77. Academic Press.

———. 1988. Distribution and Migration of the Western Pacific Stock of the Gray Whale. *Sci. Rep. Whales Res. Inst.* 39:1–9.

———, AND S. OHSUMI. 1974. Research on Whale Biology of Japan with Special Reference to North Pacific Stocks. In W. E. Schevill, Ed., *The Whale Problem,* pp. 196–208. Harvard University Press.

PAGE, C. 1981. *Foundations of Fashion. The Symington Collection. Corseting from 1856 to the Present Day.* Leicestershire Museums.

PALMER, H. V. R. 1974. An Old Ship and a New Coat of Paint [Restoration of the *Charles W. Morgan*]. *Oceans* 7(4):66–67.

PARKER, A. 1957. "Larsen—Pioneered an Industry." *Natal Daily News* April 13, 1957.

PARKS, G. B. 1928. *Richard Hakluyt and the English Voyages.* Special Publication No. 10. American Geographical Society.

PARR, A. E. 1963. Concerning Whales and Museums. *Curator* 6(1):64–76.

PARRY, J. H. 1974. *The Discovery of the Sea.* Dial Press.

PATERSON, R., AND P. PATERSON. 1989. The Status of the Recovering Stock of Humpback Whales (*Megaptera novaeangliae*) in East Australian Waters. *Biological Conservation* 47(1989):33–48.

PAULDING, H. 1831. *Journal of a Cruise of the U.S. Schooner Dolphin in Pursuit of the Mutineers of the Whale Ship* Globe. G. and C. Carvill. 1970 edition, University of Hawaii Press.

PAYNE, K. B. 1991. A Change of Tune. *Natural History* 3/91:45–46.

PAYNE, R. 1970. *Songs of the Humpback Whale.* (Phonograph record.) Capitol Records, ST-620.

———. 1972. The Song of the Whale. In *The Marvels of Animal Behavior.* pp. 144–67. National Geographic Society.

———, AND E. DORSEY. 1983. Sexual Dimorphism and Aggressive Use of Callosities in Right Whales (*Eubalaena australis*). In R. Payne, Ed., *Communication and Behavior of Whales.* pp. 295–329. American Association for the Advancement of Science.

———, AND S. MCVAY. 1971. Songs of Humpback Whales. *Science* 173:585–97.

———, O. BRAZIER, E. M. DORSEY, J. S. PERKINS, V. J. ROWNTREE, AND A. TITUS. 1983. External Features in Southern Right Whales (*Eubalaena australis*) and Their Use in Identifying Individuals. In R. Payne, Ed., *Communication and Behavior of Whales.* pp. 371–445. American Association for the Advancement of Science.

PEARSON, M. 1985. Shore-based Whaling at Twofold Bay: One Hundred Years of Enterprise. *Jour. Royal Aust. Hist. Soc.* 71(1):3–27.

PEQUEGNAT, W. E. 1958. Whales, Plankton, and Man. *Scientific American* 198(1):84–90.

PERLMAN, E. S. 1977. Confrontation: Greenpeace Foundation Puts Itself on the Line. *Oceans* 10(4):58–61.

PETERSEN, R., E. LEMCHE, AND F. O. KAPEL. 1982. Subsistence Whaling in Greenland. *Intl. Whal. Commn.* TC/33/WG/S3.

PHILLIPPS, G. F., J. A. GRIEG, AND J. LOGAN. 1983. *The Founding of the Eden Killer Whale Museum with a Short History of Eden.* Privately published.

PIKE, G. C. 1954. Whaling on the Coast of British Columbia. *Norsk Hvalfangst-Tidende* 43(3):117–27.

———, AND I. B. MCASKIE. 1974. Marine Mammals of British Columbia. *Bull. Fish. Res. Bd. Canada* 171:1–54.

PINKERTON, K. J., AND R. GAMBELL. 1968. Aerial Observations of Sperm Whale Behavior. *Norsk Hvalfangst-Tidende* 57(6):127–38.

PIVORUNAS, A. 1979. The Feeding Mechanisms of Baleen Whales. *American Scientist* 67(4):432–40.

PLANCHE, J. R. 1876. *A Cyclopaedia of Costume or Dictionary of Dress.* Chatto & Windus.

PLOWDEN, C., AND Y. KUSUDA. 1987. *Small-Type Commercial Whaling in Japan.* Humane Society of the United States.

PLUTTE, W. 1984. The Whaling Imperative: Why Norway Whales. *Oceans* 17(2):24–26.

PORSILD, M. P. 1918. On "Savssats": A Crowding of Arctic Animals at Holes in the Sea Ice. *Geographic Review* 6:215–28.

PRICE, W. S. 1985. Whaling in the Caribbean: Historical Perspective and Update. *Rep. Intl. Whal. Commn.* 35:413–20.

PROULX, J.-P. 1986. *Whaling in the North Atlantic from Earliest Times to the Mid-19th Century.* Canadian Printing Service.

PURRINGTON, P. 1972. *4 Years A-whaling.* Barre Publishers.

QUAMMEN, D. 1985. Icebreaker: A Brief Rapprochement Between Whales and Russians. *Outside* 10(6):21–26.

RAINEY, F. G. 1940. Eskimo Method of Capturing Bowhead Whales. *Jour. Mammal.* 21(3):362.

RANDIER, J. 1966. *Men and Ships Around Cape Horn, 1616–1939.* David McKay.

RATHJEN, W. F., AND J. R. SULLIVAN. 1970. West Indies Whaling. *Sea Frontiers* 16(3):130–37.

RAY, C. G. 1962. Three Whales That Flew. *National Geographic* 121(3):346–59.

———, AND W. E. SCHEVILL. 1974. Feeding of a Captive Gray Whale. *Mar. Fish. Rev.* 36(4):31–38.

REEVES, R. R. 1976. Narwhals: Another Endangered Species. *Canadian Geographical Journal* 92(3):12–17.

———. 1977. Hunt for the Narwhal. *Oceans* 10(4):50–57.

———. 1979. Right Whale: Protected but Still in Trouble. *National Parks & Conservation* 53(2):10–15.

———. 1980. Spitsbergen Bowhead Stock: A Short Review. *Mar. Fish. Rev.* 42(9&10):65–69.

———. 1983. Bottlenose Whaling in the Arctic, Part I: The Scots. *The Beaver* 63(4):46–51.

———. 1984a. Bottlenose Whaling in the Arctic, Part II: The Norwegians. *The Beaver* 64(2):52–55.

———. 1984b. Modern Commercial Pelagic Whaling for Gray Whales. In M. L. Jones, S. L. Swartz, and S. Leatherwood, Eds., *The Gray Whale: Eschrichtius robustus,* pp. 187–200. Academic Press.

———, AND M. BARTO. 1985. Whaling in the Bay of Fundy. *Whalewatcher* 19(4):14–18.

———, AND E. D. MITCHELL. 1981. The whale behind the tusk. *Natural History* 90(8):50–57.

———. 1981. White Whale Hunting in Cumberland Sound. *The Beaver* (Winter 1981):42–49.

———. 1983. Yankee Whaling for Right Whales in the North Atlantic Ocean. *Whalewatcher* 17(4):3–8.

———. 1984. Catch History and Initial Population of White Whales (*Delphinapterus leucas*) in the River and Gulf of St. Lawrence, Eastern Canada. *Le Naturaliste Canadien* 111:63–121.

———. 1986a. The Long Island, New York, Right Whale Fishery: 1650–1924. *Rep. Intl. Whal. Commn.* (Special Issue) 10:201–20.

———. 1986b. American Pelagic Whaling for Right Whales in the North Atlantic. *Rep. Intl. Whal. Commn.* (Special Issue) 10:221–54.

———. 1987a. Catch History, Former Abundance, and Distribution of White Whales in Hudson Strait and Ungava Bay. *Le Naturaliste Canadien* 114(1):1–65.

———. 1987b. Hunting Whales in the St. Lawrence. *The Beaver* 67(4):35–50.

———. 1988. History of Whaling in and near North Carolina. *NOAA Technical Report NMFS 65.* U.S. Department of Commerce.

———, AND S. TRACY. 1980. Monodon monoceros. *Mammalian Species.* American Society of Mammalogists.

REEVES, R. R., J. G. MEAD, AND S. KATONA. 1978. The Right Whale (*Eubalaena glacialis*) in the Western North Atlantic. *Rep. Intl. Whal. Commn.* 28:303–12.

REILLY, S. B. 1984. Assessing Gray Whale Abundance: A Review. In M. L. Jones, S. L. Swartz, and S. Leatherwood, Eds., *The Gray Whale: Eschrichtius robustus*, pp. 203–23. Academic Press.

REISCHAUER, E. O. 1974. *Japan: The Story of a Nation*. Alfred A. Knopf.

REYNOLDS, J. N. 1932. *Mocha Dick, or The White Whale of the Pacific*. Scribner's.

RIBEIRO, A. 1983. *A Visual History of Costume: The Eighteenth Century*. Batsford.

RICE, D. W. 1974. Whales and Whale Research in the Eastern North Pacific. In W. E. Schevill, Ed., *The Whale Problem*, pp. 170–95. Harvard University Press.

————, AND A. A. WOLMAN. 1971. *The Life History and Ecology of the California Gray Whale (Eschrichtius robustus)*. Special Publication No. 3. American Society of Mammalogists.

————, AND H. W. BRAHAM. 1984. The Gray Whale, *Eschrichtius robustus. Marine Fisheries Review* 46(4):7–14.

RICHARDS, R. 1982. *Whaling and Sealing in the Chatham Islands*. Roebuck.

RICKARD, L. S. 1965. *The Whaling Trade in Old New Zealand*. Minerva.

RIENITS, R., AND T. RIENITS. 1968. *The Voyages of Captain Cook*. Hamlyn.

ROBERTSON, R. B. 1954. *Of Whales and Men*. Alfred A. Knopf.

ROBSON, F. 1976. *Thinking Dolphins, Talking Whales*. A. H. & A. W. Reed.

————. 1984. *Strandings: Ways to Save Whales, A Humane Conservationist's Guide*. Science Press.

ROBSON, L. 1985. *A Short History of Tasmania*. Oxford University Press.

ROSE, L. 1984. *Richard Siddons of Port Jackson*. Roebuck.

ROSE, T. 1989. *Freeing the Whales: How the Media Created the World's Greatest Non-Event*. Birch Lane Press.

ROSS, G. J. B. 1971. A Note on Early Whaling at the Cape of Good Hope. *Africana Notes and News* 19(7):300–2.

————. 1983. *Extracts on Whales and Whaling and Related Subjects from the Natal Pictorial Mercury 1904–1914*. Privately published.

ROSS, M. J. 1982. *Ross in the Antarctic: The Voyages of James Clark Ross in Her Majesty's Ships* Erebus *and* Terror, *1839–1843*. Caedmon of Whitby Press.

ROSS, W. G. 1979. The Annual Catch of Greenland (Bowhead) Whales in Waters North of Canada, 1719–1915. *Arctic* 32:91–121.

————. 1985. *Arctic Whalers, Icy Seas*. Irwin.

————, AND A. MACIVER. 1982. *Distribution of Kills of Bowhead Whales and Other Sea Mammals by Davis Strait Whalers, 1820–1910*. Arctic Pilot Program.

ROUSSELOT, J.-L., W. F. FITZHUGH, AND A. CROWELL. 1988. Maritime Economies of the North Pacific Rim. In W. W. Fitzhugh and A. Crowell, Eds., *Crossroads of Continents: Cultures of Siberia and Alaska*, pp. 151–72. Smithsonian Institution.

ROWLEY, J. C. 1982. *The Hull Whale Fishery*. Lockington Publishing Company.

RUGH, D. J. 1984. Census of Gray Whales at Unimak Pass, Alaska: November–December 1977–1979. In M. L. Jones, S. L. Swartz, and S. Leatherwood, Eds., *The Gray Whale: Eschrichtius robustus*, pp. 225–48. Academic Press.

RUHEN, O. 1966. *Harpoon in My Hand*. Minerva Limited.

RUUD, J. T. 1956. International Regulation of Whaling. *Norsk Hvalfangst-Tidende* 45(7):374–87.

SANDERSON, I. 1956. *Follow the Whale*. Little, Brown.

————. 1960. A-h-h, B-l-o-o-w-s! *American Heritage* 12:48–64.

SAYERS, H. 1984. Shore Whaling for Gray Whales along the Coast of the Californias. In M. L. Jones, S. L. Swartz, and S. Leatherwood, Eds., *The Gray Whale: Eschrichtius robustus*, pp. 121–58. Academic Press.

SCAMMON, C. M. 1874. *The Marine Mammals of the Northwestern Coast of North America: Together with an Account of the American Whale-Fishery*. Carmany, and G. P. Putnam's.

SCARFF, J. E. 1986. Historic and Present Distribution of the Right Whale (*Eubalaena glacialis*) in the Eastern North Pacific South of 50°N and East of 180°W. *Rep. Intl. Whal. Commn.* (Special Issue) 10:43–63.

SCHEFFER, V. B. 1976. Exploring the Lives of Whales. *National Geographic* 150(6):752–67.

SCHERMAN, K. 1976. *Daughter of Fire: A Portrait of Iceland*. Little, Brown.

SCHEVILL, W. E. (ED.) 1974. *The Whale Problem*. Harvard University Press.

SCHILDKRAUT, L. 1979. The Killerwhale in the Art and Myth of the Tlingit Indians. *Carnivore* 2(3):4–8.

SCHMEMANN, S. 1985. Russians Tell Saga of Whales Rescued by Icebreaker. *New York Times* March 12, 1985:C3.

SCHMITT, F. P. 1971. *Mark Well the Whale! Long Island Ships to Distant Seas.* Kennikat Press.

———. 1973. Whaling's Last Refrain? *Sea Frontiers* 19(5):306–12.

———. 1979. Vessels vs. Whales. *Sea Frontiers* 25(3): 140–44.

———, C. DE JONG, AND F. H. WINTER. 1980. *Thomas Welcome Roys: America's Pioneer of Modern Whaling.* University Press of Virginia.

SCHNALL, U. 1989. *North European Whaling in the Middle Ages.* Paper presented at the 14th Annual Whaling Symposium, Kendall Whaling Museum, Sharon, Mass. Oct. 14–15, 1989.

———. 1989. *Whales and Whaling as an Economic Factor in Medieval Iceland and Norway.* Paper presented at the 14th Annual Whaling Symposium, Kendall Whaling Museum, Sharon, Mass. Oct. 14–15, 1989.

SCOGIN, R. 1977. Sperm Whale Oil and the Jojoba Shrub. *Oceans* 10(4):65–66.

SCORESBY, W. 1820. *An Account of the Arctic Regions with a History and a Description of the Northern Whale-Fishery.* Archibald Constable, Edinburgh. 1969 edition, David & Charles.

———. 1851. *My Father: Bering Records of the Adventurous Life of the Late William Scoresby, Esq., of Whitby.* Longman, Brown, Green, and Longmans. 1978 reprint, Caedmon of Whitby Press.

SCOTT, W. 1821. *The Pirate.* 1876 edition, George Routledge & Sons.

SCUDDER, B. 1990. Ceasefire in the Whaling War. *Iceland Review* 27(4):39–41.

SEARLE, C. L. 1935. "When Whales were Hunted in Algoa Bay." *Eastern Province Herald* May 7, 1935.

SERGEANT, D. E. 1953. Whaling in Newfoundland and Labrador Waters. *Norsk Hvalfangst-Tidende* 42(12):687–95.

———, AND P. F. BRODIE. 1975. Identity, Abundance, and Present Status of Populations of White Whales, *Delphinapterus leucas,* in North America. *Jour. Fish. Res. Bd. Canada* 32(7):1047–54.

SHEPARD, O. 1930. *The Lore of the Unicorn.* Houghton Mifflin.

SHERMAN, S. C. 1965. *The Voice of the Whaleman.* Providence Public Library.

SHIMADA, B. M. 1947. *Japanese Whaling in the Bonin Island Area.* U.S. Department of the Interior. Fish and Wildlife Service Fishery Leaflet 248.

SHINDO, N. 1975. *History of Whales in the Inland Sea.* Junnosoke Oomura.

SIGURJÖNSSON, J. 1981. Icelandic Minke Whaling. *Intl. Whal. Commn.* SC/33/Mi9.

———. 1985. *Whale Research in 1986–1989: An Outline of Programme and Budget.* Hafrannsoknastonunin (Marine Research Institute). Reykjavik.

———. 1988. The Intensified Programme of Whale Research in Iceland. *Modern Iceland* 4:29–33.

———. 1989. To Icelanders, Whaling Is a Godsend. *Oceanus* 32(1):29–36.

SILALAH, I. S. 1980. Observation and Research on the Cetacean Fishery of Lembata, Indonesia. *World Wildlife Fund Project No. 1420.* Gland, Switzerland.

SIMPSON, M. 1986. *Whalesong: A Pictorial History of Whaling and Hawaii.* Beyond Words.

SIMPSON, M. B., AND S. W. SIMPSON. 1990. *Whaling on the North Carolina Coast.* Division of Archives and History. North Carolina Department of Cultural Resources. Raleigh.

SINCLAIR, K. 1985. *A History of New Zealand.* Penguin.

SLIJPER, E. J. 1962. *Whales.* Cornell University Press.

SMALL, G. L. 1968. *The Virtual Extinction of an Extraterritorial Pelagic Resource—The Blue Whale.* Ph.D. Dissertation, Columbia University.

———. 1971. *The Blue Whale.* Columbia University Press.

SMITH, C. E. 1922. *From the Deep of the Sea.* Adam & Charles Black.

SOMNER, G. 1984. *From 70 North to 70 South: A History of the Christian Salvesen Fleet.* Salvesen Ltd.

SPENCE, B. 1980. *Harpooned.* Crescent.

STACKPOLE, E. A. 1953. *The Sea-Hunters: The New England Whalemen During Two Centuries, 1635–1835.* Lippincott.

———. 1972. *Whales & Destiny: The Rivalry between America, France, and Britain for Control of the Southern Whale Fishery, 1785–1825.* University of Massachusetts Press.

STACKPOLE, R. A. 1969. *American Whaling in Hudson Bay, 1861–1919.* Mystic Historical Association. Mystic, Conn.

STAMP, T., AND C. STAMP. 1975. *William Scoresby: Arctic Scientist.* Caedmon of Whitby Press.

———. 1983. *Greenland Voyager.* Caedmon of Whitby Press.

STANTON, W. 1975. *The Great United States Exploring Expedition of 1838–1842.* University of California Press.

STARBUCK, A. 1878. *History of the American Whale Fishery From its Earliest Inception to the Year 1876.* Part IV, Report to the U.S. Commission on Fish and Fisheries, Washington. Reprinted 1964, Argosy-Antiquarian Ltd.

STARKS, E. C. 1922. A History of California Shore Whaling. *Fish. Bull. No. 6, State of California Fish and Game Commission.*

STEFFANSON, V. 1938. *The Three Voyages of Martin Frobisher.* Argonaut Press.

STEINBECK, J. 1951. *The Log From the Sea of Cortez.* Viking.

STEJNEGER, L. 1887. How the Great Northern Sea-cow Became Exterminated. *American Naturalist* 21(12):1047–54.

———. 1936. *Georg Wilhelm Steller: The Pioneer of Alaskan Natural History.* Harvard University Press.

STEVENS, C. 1974. Battle for the Whales. *Audubon* 49(4):307–9.

STEWART, H. 1979. *Looking at Indian Art of the Northwest Coast.* Douglas & McIntyre.

STONEHOUSE, B. 1972. *Animals of the Antarctic: The Ecology of the Far South.* Holt, Rinehart & Winston.

STORRAR, P. 1987. *Plettenburg Bay.* Struik.

STORRO-PATTERSON, R. 1977. Gray Whale Protection. *Oceans* 10(4):45–49.

———. 1980. The Hunt of the Gray Whale by Alaskan Eskimos: A Preliminary Review. *Sci. Rep. Intl. Whal. Commn.* SC/32/PS7.

SURMON, L. C., AND K. J. PINKERTON. 1961. Some Aspects of Offshore Whaling. *C.S.I.R. Symposium S-2. Marine Studies off the Natal Coast,* pp. 59–67.

———, AND M. F. OVENDEN. 1962. The Chemistry of Whale Products. *The South African Industrial Chemist* (April 1962):62–72.

SWARTZ, S. L., AND M. BURSK. 1979. The Gray Whales of Laguna San Ignacio: After Two Years. *Whalewatcher* 13(1):7–9.

SWIDERSKI, R. M. 1982. The Whale is Listening: Music and Performance in Arctic Whaling. *Whalewatcher* 16(3):12–13.

TAYLOR, H., AND J. BOSCH. 1979. Makah Whalers. *Carnivore* 2(3):10–15.

TERRY, W. M. 1950. *Japanese Whaling Industry Prior to 1946.* U.S. Department of the Interior. Fish and Wildlife Service Fishery Leaflet 371.

THOMPSON, G. M. 1975. *The Search for the Northwest Passage.* Macmillan.

THOMPSON, W. W. 1907. The Early Days of the Cape Sea-Fisheries. *African Monthly* 2:166–72, 610–16.

TIEDE, T., AND J. FINDLETON. 1986. *The Great Whale Rescue.* Pharos Books.

TILT, W. 1986. Whalewatching Comes of Age. *Whalewatcher* 20(1):19–22.

TILTON, G. F. 1929. *"Cap'n George Fred" Himself.* Doubleday.

TØNNESSEN, J. N., AND A. O. JOHNSEN. 1982. *The History of Modern Whaling.* C. Hurst & Co., and Australian National University Press.

TOTTEN, G. O. 1978. Nature of the Whaling Issue in U.S. and Japan. In J. Schmidhauser and G. O. Totten, Eds., *The Whaling Issue in U.S.–Japan Relations,* pp. 1–16. Westview Press.

TOWNSEND, C. H. 1886. Present Condition of the California Gray Whale Fishery. *Fish. Bull.* 6:346–50.

———. 1935. The Distribution of Certain Whales as Shown by Logbook Records of American Whaleships. *Zoologica* 29(1):1–50.

TROUP, J. A. 1987. *The Ice-Bound Whalers: The Story of the Dee and the Grenville Bay, 1836–37.* Orkney Press.

TRUE, F. W. 1904. The Whalebone Whales of the North Atlantic. *Smithsonian Contributions to Knowledge* 33.

TUCK, J. A., AND R. GRENIER. 1981. A 16th-Century Basque Whaling Station in Labrador. *Scientific American* 245(5):180–90.

———. 1985. 16th Century Basque Whalers in America. *National Geographic* 168(1):40–68.

UNION WHALING COMPANY, LTD. 1953–1971. *Reports and Accounts.* Union Whaling Company, Ltd., Durban.

VAN DEINSE, A. B., AND G. C. A. JUNGE. 1936. Recent and Older Finds of the California Gray Whale in the Atlantic. *Temminckia* 2:161–88.

VAN DOREN, C. 1917. *The Cambridge History of American Literature.* Macmillan.

VAN GELDER, R. G. 1970. Whale on My Back. *Curator* 13(2):95–119.

VAN NOTE, C. 1979. *Outlaw Whalers.* The Whale Protection Fund.

VAUGHAN, R. 1984. Historical Survey of the European Whaling Industry. In *Arctic Whaling: Proceedings of the International Symposium,* pp. 121–45. University of Groningen.

VAUGHAN, R. 1986. Bowhead Whaling in Davis Strait and Baffin Bay during the 18th and 19th Centuries. *Polar Record* 23(144):289–99.

VENABLES, B. 1969. *Baleia! Baleia! Whale Hunters of the Azores*. Alfred A. Knopf.

VERNE, J. 1870. *Twenty Thousand Leagues Under the Sea*. 1962 edition, Bantam.

VERNEY, P. 1979. *Homo Tyrannicus: A History of Man's War Against Animals*. Mills & Boon.

VERRILL, A. H. 1926. *The Real Story of the Whaler*. D. Appleton & Company.

VESILIND, P. J. 1983. Hunters of the Lost Spirit. *National Geographic* 163(2):150–96.

VIBE, C. 1950. The Marine Mammals and Marine Fauna in the Thule District (Northwest Greenland) with Observations on Ice Conditions 1939–41. *Meddeleser om Grønland* 150(6):1–115.

VILLIERS, A. J. 1925. *Whaling in the Frozen South: Being the Story of the 1923–24 Norwegian Whaling Expedition to the Antarctic*. Bobbs-Merrill.

———. 1958. *Give Me a Ship to Sail*. Hodder & Stoughton.

———. 1967. *Captain James Cook*. Scribners.

VINCENT, H. P. 1949. *The Trying-Out of Moby-Dick*. Houghton Mifflin.

VIOLA, H. J., AND C. MARGOLIS. (EDS.) 1985. *Magnificent Voyagers: The U.S. Exploring Expedition, 1838–1842*. Smithsonian Institution Press.

VLADYKOV, V.-D. 1944. Chasse, biologie, et valeur économique de Marsouin Blanc ou Béluga (*Delphinapterus leucas*) de fleuve et de golfe Saint-Laurent. *Etudes sur les Mammiferes Aquatiques* 15:1–194.

———. 1947. Nourriture du Marsouin Blanc ou Béluga (*Delphinapterus leucas*) de fleuve St. Laurent. *Etudes sur les Mammiferes Aquatiques* 19:1–160.

WALKER, L. W. 1949. Nursery of the Gray Whales. *Natural History* 58(6):248–56.

WALKER, T. W. 1971. The California Gray Whale Comes Back. *National Geographic* 139(3):394–415.

WANG, P. 1984. Distribution of the Gray Whale (*Eschrichtius gibbosus*) off the Coast of China. *Acta Theriologica Sinica* 4(1):21–26.

WARD, N. F. R. 1987. The Whalers of Bequia. *Oceanus* 30(4):89–93.

WARD, S. (ED.) 1990. *Who's Afraid of Compromise?* Institute of Cetacean Research. Tokyo.

WARHOL, P. 1986. Humphrey. *Whalewatcher* 20(2):13–15.

WATERMAN, T. T. 1920. *The Whaling Equipment of the Makah Indians*. University of Washington Publications in Anthropology.

WATKINS, W. A., AND W. E. SCHEVILL. 1976. Right Whale Feeding and Baleen Rattle. *Jour. Mammal.* 57:58–66.

WATSON, L. 1981. *Sea Guide to the Whales of the World*. Hutchinson.

WATSON, P., AND W. ROGERS. 1982. *Sea Shepherd: My Fight for Whales and Seals*. W. W. Norton.

WATTUM, C. 1953. The New Seafaring, Whaling, and Archaeological Section at the Vestfold Fylkesmuseum. *Norsk Hvalfangst-Tidende* 42(10):580–89.

WAUGH, N. 1954. *Corsets and Crinolines*. Theater Arts Books/Methuen.

WEAVER, R. 1919. The Centennial of Herman Melville. *The Nation* 109:146.

WEBB, R. L. 1982. Whale Hunters of the Northwest Coast. *Whalewatcher* 16(3):3–5.

———. 1988. *On the Northwest: Commercial Whaling in the Pacific Northwest. 1790–1967*. University of British Columbia Press.

WELLINGS, H. P. 1936. *Benjamin Boyd in Australia*. Bega.

WENDT, H. 1959. *Out of Noah's Ark*. Houghton Mifflin.

WERNICK, R. 1979. *The Vikings*. Time-Life Books.

WESTERKOV, K., AND K. PROBERT. 1981. *The Seas Around New Zealand*. A. H. & A. W. Reed.

WHIPPLE, A. B. C. 1954. *Yankee Whalers in the South Seas*. Doubleday.

WHITAKER, I. 1984. Whaling in Classical Iceland. *Polar Record* 22(134):249–61.

———. 1985. The King's Mirror (*Konungs skuggsjá*) and Northern Research. *Polar Record* 22(141):615–27.

———. 1986. North Atlantic Sea Creatures in the King's Mirror (*Konungs skuggsjá*). *Polar Record* 22(142):3–13.

WHITE, P. D., AND S. W. MATTHEWS. 1956. Hunting the Heartbeat of a Whale. *National Geographic* 110(1):49–64.

WHITE, T. H. 1954. *The Book of Beasts: Being a Translation from a Latin Bestiary of the Twelfth Century*. Jonathan Cape.

WHITING, E. M., AND H. B. HOUGH. 1953. *Whaling Wives*. Houghton Mifflin.

WHITMAN, W. 1855. *Leaves of Grass*. 1931 edition, Aventine Press.

WILKIE, D. 1929. Whaling Days in Tasmania: Hobart a Hundred Years Ago. *The Wentworth Magazine* (October 1929):4–6.

WILLIAMS, H. (ED.) 1964. *One Whaling Family.* Houghton Mifflin.

WILLIAMS, H. 1988. *Whale Nation.* Jonathan Cape.

WILSON, M. S., AND E. H. BUCK. 1979. Changes in Eskimo Whaling Methods. *Carnivore* 2(1):35–42.

WINN, L. K., AND H. E. WINN. 1985. *Wings in the Sea: The Humpback Whale.* University Press of New England.

WISE, T. 1970. *To Catch a Whale.* Geoffrey Bles.

WOLMAN, A. A. 1979. Current Status of the Gray Whale. *Rep. Intl. Whal. Commn.* 29:275–79.

WOOD, G. C. 1954. *In a Sperm Whale's Jaws.* Dartmouth College. Hanover, N.H.

WOOD, G. L. 1982. *The Guinness Book of Animal Facts and Feats.* Guinness Superlatives Ltd., Middlesex.

WOOLF, L. 1923. Herman Melville. *The Nation & The Athenaeum* 33:688.

WRAY, P. 1975. Nobody Needs to Kill Sperm Whales. *Cetacean Times* 1(3):32–34.

YAMAMOTO, Y., AND H. HIRUTA. 1978. Stranding of a Black Right Whale at Kumomi, Southwestern Coast of Izu Peninsula. *Sci. Rep. Whales Res. Inst.* 30:249–51.

YOSEI, Y. 1829. *Yogiotoru Eshi ("Whaling in Words and Pictures"). Investigations on Cetacea,* Vol. XIV (Supplementum), 1983.

YOUNG, G. 1978. Norway's Strategic Islands. *National Geographic* 154(2):267–83.

ZENKOVICH, B. A., AND V. A. ARSEN'EV. 1955. Short History of Whaling and Modern Conditions at USSR. In S. E. Kleinenberg and T. I. Makarova, Eds., *Whaling at USSR (Rybnoe khozayistvo),* pp. 5–29. Moscow.

Index

Illustration Credits

Frontispiece: New Bedford Whaling Museum   Endpapers: Kendall Whaling Museum

Part One: The Quarry

Part Two: Man Meets Whale

Part Three: The Later History of Early Whaling

Part Four: Inshore Whaling

Part Five: The Sperm Whale Fishery

Part Six: Right and Gray Whaling

Part Seven: The Heavy Artillery

Part Eight: Aboriginal Whaling

Part Nine: Whaling Outside the Antarctic

page 323: William H. Dawbin
326: Roy Chapman Andrews, Neg. no. 23591, Department of Library Services, American Museum of Natural History
328: Neg. no. 7511, Special Collections Division, University of Washington Libraries
329: Richard Ellis

page 330: Roy Chapman Andrews, Neg. no. 24365, Department of Library Services, American Museum of Natural History
331: Kendall Whaling Museum
333: Collection of Richard Ellis
334: Rick Miller, New York Zoological Society
335: Valerie Hodgson, New York Zoological Society

Part Ten: Antarctic Fortunes

343: Christian Salvesen & Co., Ltd., Edinburgh
344: Christian Salvesen & Co., Ltd., Edinburgh
348–49: Christian Salvesen & Co., Ltd., Edinburgh
350: Kendall Whaling Museum
352: Commander Christensen's Whaling Museum, Sandefjord
355: Commander Christensen's Whaling Museum, Sandefjord
356: Commander Christensen's Whaling Museum, Sandefjord
357: Commander Christensen's Whaling Museum, Sandefjord
359: Tasmanian Museum and Art Gallery
360: Tasmanian Museum and Art Gallery
362: *Illustrated London News*
363: Commander Christensen's Whaling Museum, Sandefjord
364: Commander Christensen's Whaling Museum, Sandefjord
365: Commander Christensen's Whaling Museum, Sandefjord

366: Bjørn Basberg
371: Kendall Whaling Museum
372: Kendall Whaling Museum
373: Kendall Whaling Museum
374: (top and bottom) New Bedford Whaling Museum
375: Richard Ellis
376: Kendall Whaling Museum
378: Neg. no. 31716, Department of Library Services, American Museum of Natural History
379: Neg. no. 337536, Department of Library Services, American Museum of Natural History
380: (top and bottom) Kendall Whaling Museum
381: (top right) *New York Daily News*
381: (bottom) Richard Ellis
382: Ken Balcomb, Center for Whale Research, Friday Harbor, Washington
383: Frank Baker, BP Exploration, Alaska
384: Frank Baker, BP Exploration, Alaska

Part Eleven: The Beginning of the End

389: Kendall Whaling Museum
393: The Making New Zealand Collection, Alexander Turnbull Library, Wellington
398: Kendall Whaling Museum
399: Christian Salvesen & Co., Ltd., Edinburgh
400: Dag Naevestad
407: Courtesy Seiji Ohsumi, Far Seas Research Institute
408: Richard Ellis
410: Richard Ellis
411: Kendall Whaling Museum
412: P. Golubovsky
413: Courtesy M. V. Ivashin

414: P. Golubovsky
415: Courtesy M. V. Ivashin
416: Courtesy M. V. Ivashin
417: Richard Statile, Courtesy Victor B. Scheffer
419: Kendall Whaling Museum
423: Kendall Whaling Museum
424–25: W. L. van Utrecht
431: Courtesy Barthelmess Whaling Archive, Cologne
432: Richard Statile, Courtesy Victor B. Scheffer
433: Courtesy Barthelmess Whaling Archive, Cologne

Part Twelve: The Anti-Whaling Movement

Part Thirteen: After the Moratorium

Afterword

A Note About the Author

One of America's most celebrated marine artists, Richard Ellis has been studying and painting whales for the past two decades. In pursuit of his subject matter, he has observed whales and whaling in Hawaii, Bermuda, the Azores, Newfoundland, Baja California, Alaska, Patagonia, Japan, the Galápagos, Norway, Iceland, the Faeroes, Australia, New Zealand, South Africa, and Indonesia. His paintings have been exhibited at various museums and galleries around the world. He has written and illustrated articles for numerous magazines, including *Audubon, Reader's Digest, National Geographic, Scientific American, Science Digest,* and *Skin Diver.* He is the author of *The Book of Sharks, The Book of Whales,* and *Dolphins and Porpoises.* He belongs to the Society for Marine Mammalogy, the Society of Vertebrate Paleontologists, and the Explorers Club. Mr. Ellis was a member of the American delegation to the International Whaling Commission from 1980 to 1990. He lives in New York City.

A Note on the Type

This book was set in a typeface called Garamond. Jean Jannon has been identified as the designer of this face, which is based on Garamond's original models but is much lighter and more open. The italic is taken from a font of Granjon, which appeared in the repertory of the Imprimerie Royale and was probably cut in the middle of the sixteenth century.

Composed by Creative Graphics, Inc.
Allentown, Pennsylvania

Printed and bound by Courier Book Companies, Westford, Massachusetts

Designed by Mia Vander Els

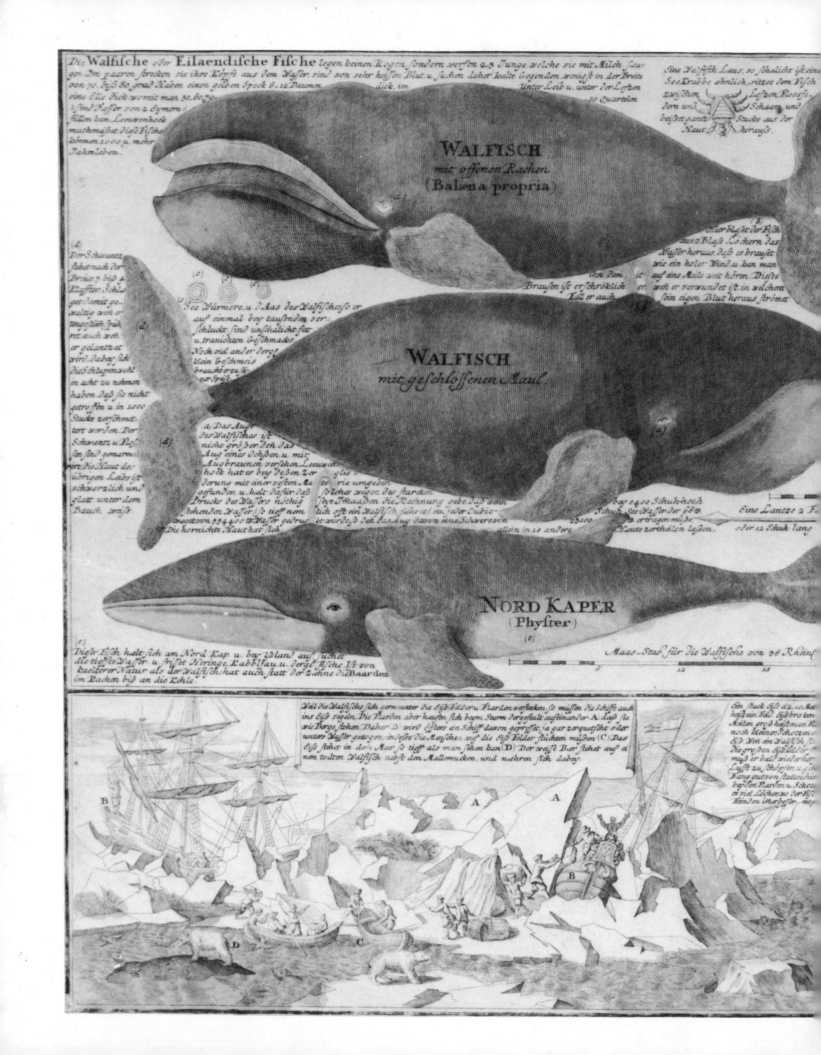